ENCYCLOPEDIA OF
AMERICAN
IMMIGRATION

Volume 2
Galvan v. Press—Pakistani immigrants

Edited by
Carl L. Bankston III
Tulane University

SALEM PRESS
Pasadena, California   Hackensack, New Jersey

Editor in Chief: Dawn P. Dawson

Editorial Director: Christina J. Moose *Research Supervisor:* Jeffry Jensen
Project and Development Editor: R. Kent Rasmussen *Photo Editor:* Cynthia Breslin Beres
Manuscript Editor: Tim Tiernan *Production Editor:* Andrea E. Miller
Indexer: R. Kent Rasmussen *Design and Graphics:* James Hutson
Acquisitions Editor: Mark Rehn *Layout:* William Zimmerman
Editorial Assistant: Brett S. Weisberg

Frontispiece: *Eastern European immigrants bound for the United States around the turn of the twentieth century.* (The Granger Collection, New York)

Cover photo: (The Granger Collection, New York)

Library of Congress Cataloging-in-Publication Data

Encyclopedia of American immigration / edited by Carl L. Bankston III.
    p. cm.
  Includes bibliographical references and index.
  ISBN 978-1-58765-599-9 (set : alk. paper) — ISBN 978-1-58765-600-2 (vol. 1 : alk. paper) —
ISBN 978-1-58765-601-9 (vol. 2 : alk. paper) — ISBN 978-1-58765-602-6 (vol. 3 : alk. paper) —
1. United States—Emigration and immigration—History. I. Bankston, Carl L. (Carl Leon), 1952-
  JV6450.E66 2010
  304.8'73003—dc22

2009054334

First Printing

PRINTED IN THE UNITED STATES OF AMERICA

CONTENTS

Contents

COMPLETE LIST OF CONTENTS

VOLUME 1

VOLUME 2

VOLUME 3

Contents li
Complete List of Contents liii

ENCYCLOPEDIA OF
AMERICAN
IMMIGRATION

G

GALVAN V. PRESS

THE CASE: U.S. Supreme Court decision concerning deportation

DATE: Decided on May 24, 1954

SIGNIFICANCE: In the context of the Cold War, the *Galvan* decision upheld the authority of the U.S. government to order the deportation of persons who had been members of the Communist Party, even if there was no good evidence that they had understood the party's advocacy of violent revolution.

The McCarran Internal Security Act of 1950 included a provision for deporting any alien who was a member of the Communist Party at any time after entering the United States. Juan Galvan, an alien born in Mexico, had lived in the United States for more than thirty years. In 1948, he admitted to the Immigration and Naturalization Service (INS) that from 1944 to 1946 he had been a member of the Communist Party, but at a later hearing in 1950, he denied having ever joined the party. After a witness claimed otherwise, the hearing officer concluded that he had been a party member and ordered his deportation for that reason. Galvan's petition for a writ of habeas corpus was rejected by both the District Court and the Court of Appeals for the Ninth Circuit.

By a 7-2 margin, the U.S. Supreme Court upheld both the statute and the deportation order. Speaking for the majority, Justice Felix Frankfurter discussed three main issues. First, the use of the word "member" in the statute did not just refer to persons who had joined the party fully conscious of its violent goals. Second, the INS had obtained sufficient evidence to reasonably conclude that Galvan had been a member of the party. Finally, based on the "broad power of Congress over the admission and deportation of aliens," Frankfurter wrote that there was no good reason to conclude that the statute violated constitutional principles of due process. Justice Hugo L. Black and William O. Douglas wrote strong dissenting opinions.

Thomas Tandy Lewis

FURTHER READING

Belknap, Michal. *The Supreme Court Under Earl Warren, 1953-1969.* Columbia: University of South Carolina Press, 2005.

Stevens, Richard. *Reason and History in Judicial Judgment: Felix Frankfurter and Due Process.* New Brunswick, N.J.: Transaction, 2008.

SEE ALSO: Citizenship; Congress, U.S.; Constitution, U.S.; Deportation; Due process protections; Frankfurter, Felix; Immigration law; McCarran Internal Security Act of 1950; Supreme Court, U.S.

GARMENT INDUSTRY

DEFINITION: Industry encompassing all aspects of clothing manufacturing

SIGNIFICANCE: Fueled by immigrant labor since the massive surge of Jewish and Italian immigrants to New York City during the decades surrounding the turn of the twentieth century, the American garment industry was long a major economic portal to recently arrived immigrants. It was especially important to Jews from the Russian Empire, Italians from the south of their native land, Chinese, Latin Americans, and Southeast Asians. The industry has provided immigrants with jobs, entries into their new culture, and business opportunities.

Before the massive migration of the early twentieth century, most wholesale garments were made in workshops owned by German Jews of earlier immigrations. The Jews who arrived during the early twentieth century already had a long history of garment work in their native countries, largely because Jews observed religious restrictions on certain materials in their clothes, so they preferred to make their own garments. The influx of poor Russian Jews to the United States happened to coincide with a surging American demand for factory-made clothes, and new production systems were emerging. Small contractors rented workshops within the New York tenements in which the immigrants lived. These contractors, most of whom were themselves Russian Jewish immigrants, had more success than large manufacturers in recruiting labor, as the workers whom they recruited were usually from their own Russian hometowns. Job opportunities for these immigrants were often limited by language difficulties and economic necessity, and the Russian contractors could push their laborers to greater efforts of productivity than large manufacturers. This tendency to use small workshops for small-scale contracting long remained a feature of the garment industry.

EARLY LABOR ORGANIZATION

In 1900, the International Ladies' Garment Workers' Union (ILGWU) was organized at a conference of New York City East Side delegates and representatives of the American Federation of Labor. Their goal was to improve the wages and working conditions of the city's thousand of garment workers, most of whom were young female immigrants. In 1909, the new union called a strike against the more than five hundred shirtwaist manufacturers in New York. Settlement of the strike in early 1910 significantly improved working conditions but did not attain the recognition of the union that the ILGWU had demanded. Nevertheless, membership in the local union had grown to ten thousand members, and many immigrants had achieved a new sense of dignity and confidence on the picket lines. The settlement did not, however, improve conditions at all garment-making facilities. In March, 1911, 146 mostly immigrant workers were killed in a fire at the Triangle Shirtwaist Factory. The tragedy did, however, have the beneficial effect of attracting public and government attention to the dangerous conditions in many garment workplaces.

Meanwhile, the New York garment industry remained robust. It expanded during the 1920's, but by the 1930's other cities in the United States were attracting sizable concentrations of garment manufacturers. By the 1940's, Boston, Philadelphia, Chicago, and Baltimore had become important

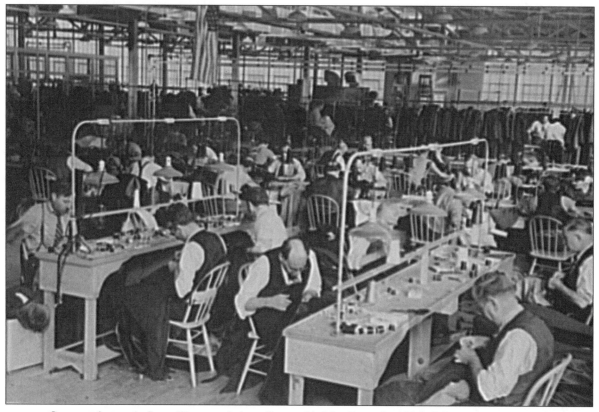

Garment factory in Jersey Homesteads (now Roosevelt), New Jersey, in 1936. (Library of Congress)

garment centers. In 1941, only 39 percent of all American clothing manufacturers were located in New York City. A decade later, the South and then the Far West became productive centers of industry growth. By then, the importation of foreign-made clothing was rapidly increasing in the United States. Initially, Japan and Hong Kong were the only important supplies of clothes to the United States. Eventually, however, virtually every country throughout the world with a developed garment industry found a share of the U.S. market. Due to higher labor and capital costs at home, U.S. manufacturers found it difficult to compete, and the industry shrank.

RENEWAL OF THE GARMENT INDUSTRY

Although Russian Jews and Italians had dominated the garment industry in New York since 1914, many immigrants wanted something better for their children and dissuaded them from pursing similar employment. Their withdrawal from the industry opened opportunities to other groups of immigrants, such as Puerto Ricans and Africans. Between 1930 and 1936, about 30 percent of gainfully employed Puerto Rican workers in the United States were either garment or hand-sewing workers. However, most of them worked at home until the 1940's and early 1950's, when they began to enter the garment workshops in great numbers.

Despite the differences in when they arrived, the reasons for their immigration, their prior experiences, and their different cultures, African and Puerto Rican women workers had experiences in the garment industry similar to those of their Jewish and Italian predecessors. The Puerto Rican and African women were generally relegated to the lowest-paid unskilled and semiskilled jobs in the industry. However, they earned even lower pay than their Jewish and Italian counterparts who had done the same jobs. The period during which African and Puerto Rican workers entered New York City's garment industry was an important factor in causing this disparity, as New York's garment industry was already on its way from being one of the highest-paid industries to becoming one of the lowest paid.

In 1969, New York City's economy had a sudden downturn and vacancy rates in industrial buildings soared. In the Lower Manhattan district bordering New York's Chinatown, rents dropped dramatically and many Chinese entrepreneurs started their own garment factories. As their Jewish and Italian predecessors had done, the Chinese organized ethnic business associations. However, they started from a stronger base, drawing on greater collective resources. Chinese owners from Hong Kong recruited other immigrants from Hong Kong, while new immigrants from mainland China tended to hire immigrants from the mainland.

The tremendous number of Asian and Latin American immigrants to the West Coast during the 1970's and 1980's created a boom in Los Angeles's garment trades. Immigrants from Southeast Asia, El Salvador, and Guatemala found opportunities for work in the city's garment workshops, and ethnic networking assured immigrant owners of a certain reservoir of trust and dependability. Garments made in Los Angeles took their place among those made in New York, and the rise of the garment industry allowed West Coast clothing designers who were once obscure to become nationally, and even internationally, known.

DECLINE OF THE GARMENT INDUSTRY

The North American Free Trade Agreement is a trilateral trade pact created by the leaders of Mexico, Canada, and the United States that went into effect in 1993. One of the most powerful and wide-reaching international treaties in the world, it reduced trade and investment barriers among the three North American nations through a gradual and methodical process. Its goal was to reduce tariffs among Mexico, Canada, and the United Sates over a period of years, making it easier to trade goods across national borders. *Maquiladoros*, or small Mexican factories, sprang up along the border on the Mexican side, and many jobs from the American garment industry were lost to these factories. Especially disturbing to the workers was the fact that their jobs were exported partly to take advantage of low wages and environmental standards.

Another blow to the garment industry was the World Trade Organization, which defines the rules of trade among nations at a near-global level. Created in early 1995, it had 153 nation members that account for more than 95 percent of the world's trade. The stated aim of the organization was to promote free trade and stimulate economic growth, but American labor unions condemned the labor-rights records of developing countries. They claimed that the more the World Trade Organization promoted globalization, the more labor rights would suffer. After China joined the World Trade Organization in 2001, it would eventually double its exports to the United States. China had a strong competitive edge in clothing manufacture because of its government's exploitation of the millions of rural Chinese who migrated to China's cities in search of work—much like Europeans had flocked to the United States a century earlier.

ILLEGAL IMMIGRATION AND THE GARMENT INDUSTRY

During the last decades of the twentieth century, more and more illegal immigrants were arriving in the United States by clandestinely crossing the U.S. border with Mexico. Mexican agricultural workers had long crossed the border to work in seasonal American farming industries, but most had returned home when their harvesting work was finished. In contrast, many workers from Mexico and Central American nations were entering the United States illegally in the hope of finding steady, permanent jobs that would permit them to stay. Many of these people found steady jobs in the Los Angeles garment industry.

The problem of illegal immigrants became a topic of public discussion, and attempts were made by the federal government to improve border security. However, many U.S. employers were becoming dependent on undocumented workers, who were willing to work for lower pay than American workers. In August of 2007, the U.S. Department of Homeland Security announced a controversial new immigration enforcement policy. It issued a "No-Match" regulation intended to help employees ensure that their workers are legal, and to help the government identify and crack down on employers who knowingly hire illegal immigrants. This new policy caused a great deal of consternation within Los Angeles's multibillion-dollar garment industry. Some manufacturers threatened to move their operations offshore.

In October of 2007, a U.S. district court judge issued a preliminary injunction that prevented the Department of Homeland Security from carrying out its new policy. The judge who ruled in the case of *AFL-CIO v. Chertoff* accepted the plaintiffs' argument that such a rule would cause thousands of employers to bear significant expenses and would likely lead to unfair terminations of many workers because of errors in the Social Security database that was to be used to identify undocumented immigrants.

In late 2008, when the United States was entering into a severe recession and Congress was debating the implementation of a massive economic stimulus package, the U.S. House of Representatives passed a bill with a provision to ensure that new jobs go to Americans and not to illegal immigrants.

Sheila Golburgh Johnson

FURTHER READING

Bacon, David. *Illegal People: How Globalization Creates Migration and Criminalizes Immigrants.* Boston: Beacon Books, 2008. Shows the human side of globalization, exposing the way it uproots people in Latin America and Asia, driving them to emigrate.

Gordon, Jennifer. *Suburban Sweatshops: The Fight for Immigrant Rights.* Cambridge, Mass.: Belknap Press, 2005. A record of the Workplace Project founded by the author in 1992 to help immigrant workers in the underground suburban economy of Long Island, New York. This book discusses new possibilities for labor organizing, community building, and participatory democracy.

Green, Nancy L. *Immigrants: Ready-to-Wear and Ready-to-Work—A Century of Industry and Immigrants in Paris and New York.* Durham, N.C.: Duke University Press, 1997. Compelling comparative study of the garment industries in France and the United States that analyzes the garment industry from the point of economic, social, cultural, political, and gender history.

Louie, Miriam Ching Yoon. *Sweatshop Warriors: Immigrant Women Workers Take on the Global Factory.* Cambridge, Mass.: South End Press, 2001. Examination of transnational sweatshops through the eyes of Korean, Chinese, and Mexican women forced to leave their homelands to take exploitative labor jobs in the world's sweatshops.

Woloch, Nancy, ed. *Early American Women: A Documentary History, 1700-1900.* Belmont, Calif.: Wadsworth, 1992. Collection of more than seventy-five primary sources, almost all written by women. Each chapter begins with a generic history.

SEE ALSO: Asian immigrants; Captive Thai workers; Chinese family associations; Family businesses; International Ladies' Garment Workers' Union; Jewish immigrants; New York City; Sweatshops; Triangle Shirtwaist fire; Women immigrants.

GARVEY, MARCUS

IDENTIFICATION: Jamaican immigrant, social activist, and journalist
BORN: August 17, 1887; St. Ann's Bay, Jamaica
DIED: June 10, 1940; London, England

SIGNIFICANCE: The first person of African descent to galvanize black people throughout the world with the idea of returning to Africa, Garvey founded the Universal Negro Improvement Association (UNIA), which sought to deliver African Americans from injustice, encourage racial self-improvement, and promote a back-to-Africa movement. He also started the Black Star Line shipping company to help promote black economic independence and to provide transportation back to Africa.

Born in the British Caribbean colony of Jamaica in 1887, Marcus Garvey was the son of sharecroppers. At the age of fourteen, he moved to Jamaica's capital city, Kingston, where he became a printer. There he learned the journalism trade, which would later enable him to set up newspapers that he would use to organize and address workers who were victims of racial injustice. He traveled throughout Central America, South America, and Europe and witnessed the living conditions of people of African descent around the world. Eventually, he returned home to Jamaica and started the UNIA, a racial uplift organization for all peoples of African descent.

Disappointed by the lack of support from the black community in Jamaica but determined to continue this path of liberating his people from oppression and inequality, he went to the United States, hoping to gain some financial support from the African American educator Booker T. Washington. Garvey arrived in the United States in 1916, after Washington had already died but nevertheless found an eager audience for his message that he had not found in Jamaica. In New York City's Harlem district, his black nationalist ideas were accepted, as he promoted the back-to-Africa movement and established the shipping company the Black Star Line.

As Garvey traveled throughout the United States, he witnessed the living conditions of African Americans and spoke and met with African American leaders. The economic disaster of World War I, racial discrimination, lynching, and the injustices faced by African Americans opened the door to a leader willing to speak up and support racial pride and economic independence. Over the next half dozen years, Garvey built the largest mass movement of black people in

Marcus Garvey. (Library of Congress)

the world, finding his strongest support in the Caribbean, Central America, and the United States. However, his Black Star Line fell short of success as a result of negligence and the need for financial resources. In 1922, J. Edgar Hoover of the federal government's Bureau of Investigation (forerunner of the Federal Bureau of Investigation) started investigating Garvey for financial fraud. In 1925, Garvey was sentenced to federal prison on mail-fraud charges. Two years later, he was deported to Jamaica, never to return to the United States. Eventually, he returned to England, where he died in 1940. By then, his UNIA was only a fraction of its former size.

Garvey was very influential at a time when there was a need for leadership for descendants of Africans. He was effective because he sought to improve the self-esteem and condition of black people all over the world. His published speeches and letters address issues of injustice and offer suggestions for the elevation of self-esteem based on racial pride and economic independence.

Diana Pardo

FURTHER READING

Cronon, Edmund David. *The Black Moses: The Story of Marcus Garvey and the Universal Negro Improvement Association.* Madison: University of Wisconsin Press, 1969.

Garvey, Marcus. *Selected Writings and Speeches of Marcus Garvey.* Edited by Bob Blaisdell. New York: Dover, 2004.

Grant, Colin. *Negro with a Hat: The Rise and Fall of Marcus Garvey.* New York: Oxford University Press, 2008.

Hill, Robert A., ed. *The Marcus Garvey and Universal Negro Improvement Association Papers.* 9 vols. Berkeley: University of Californa Press, 1983-1996.

SEE ALSO: African Americans and immigrants; Economic opportunities; Emigration; Liberia; Universal Negro Improvement Association; West Indian immigrants.

GAY AND LESBIAN IMMIGRANTS

SIGNIFICANCE: U.S. immigration law has historically excluded openly gay and lesbian individuals on various bases, ranging from classifications of them as morally or medically unfit to their perceived social and political threats to the desirable character of American society. This practice began to be challenged during the 1950's and was eliminated in 1990 by congressional repeal of a statutory provision barring entry to persons determined to be psychopathic personalities or sexual deviants.

The original regulatory purpose of U.S. immigration law was to deal with the management of easily recognized and defined ethnic, racial, and social groups, with existing provisions applied (with varying degrees of accuracy and success) to populations that did not fall within these categories. In the case of gay and lesbian immigrants, the underlying concept of homosexuality did not exist as such until the end of the nineteenth century. Prior to that time, U.S. immigration officials had to utilize certain sections of federal laws originally intended to address questions of public welfare and health concerns to bar homosexuals from immigrating.

STATUTORY BARS TO IMMIGRATION

The federal Page Law of 1875 provided for the exclusion of people who had been convicted of crimes involving "moral turpitude," was interpreted as including sodomy, while an 1885 statute barred persons who were judged incapable of taking care of themselves and would thus become "public charges" supported by the state. Homosexuals were considered by immigration officials to be both mentally and physically degenerate—a combination that would render them unable to function in society. This approach was applied to identified gay and lesbian people until 1917, when a ruling from the federal government's solicitor of labor invalidated its application to "moral perverts," unless actual proof of their lack of means of support existed.

The most problematic aspect of excluding persons of same-sex orientation was identifying them so that extant laws could be applied. While in many urban gay communities certain items of dress and certain social mannerisms and behaviors were used by homosexuals to signal their sexual orientation nonverbally, the fashions of these codes varied widely from country to country and were not known to most U.S. immigration personnel. Only those individuals who admitted their sexual histories after being legally admitted to the United States were subject to deportation. An example of this is the case of a young Greek immigrant who, in the course of an investigation on charges of breaking and entering in 1912, confessed that he had been sexually active with men in St. Louis, Missouri. He was deported to Argentina.

The Immigration Act of 1917 kept the older exclusionary bases of medical and moral grounds, adding new language referring to "constitutional psychopathic inferiority." This term reflected the intent of the discarded public charge category by preserving the idea that sexual inversion was the result of a permanent psychological defect, which, instead of forcing the state to support homosexual immigrants, would drive these immigrants to prey upon American youth. Between 1917 and American entry into World War II in 1941, roughly three dozen people per year were deported under this provision.

The expanded Immigration and Nationality Act of 1952 kept the older language of federal immigration laws, rephrasing it to cover people suffering from mental disorders or psychopathic personalities. Despite the absence of anything language in the law specifically targeting homosexuals, the Immigration and Naturalization Service (INS) interpreted its text as prohibiting the immigration of identifiable homosexuals, and it began deporting dozens of gay people each year. The morally suspect character of homosexuals was not forgotten, with a requirement that immigrants be of "good moral character" taken from an earlier immigration law and used to deny applications for citizenship to gay and lesbian foreigners.

CHALLENGES TO RESTRICTIVE LAWS

The 1950's and 1960's witnessed legal challenges to the exclusionary policy, notably the case of *Rosenberg v. Fleuti* (1963), which held that the term "psychopathic personality" was too vague for general application, a judgment that led to an amendment of the 1952 act through the explicit addition of the term "sexual deviation." The Canadian plaintiff in *Boutilier v. Immigration and Naturalization Service* (1967) presented psychiatric testimony attesting to his lack of pathology. He appealed his case to the U.S. Supreme Court but was nonetheless eventually deported.

Immigration law and policy were early targets of the American gay rights movement, which was sparked by the Stonewall riots in New York City in 1969 and assisted by an erosion of the legal, medical, and psychiatric beliefs used to support and rationalize existing legislation during the 1970's. The removal of homosexuality from the list of recognized mental illnesses by the American Psychiatric Association in 1974 led to a letter to the INS from the Public Health Service in 1979 stating that immigrants would no longer be examined for "psychopathic personalities" as grounds for exclusion. In 1976, the INS had issued a confusing announcement stating that while entry would not be denied to anyone who had been a "practicing sexual deviant," immigration officials would reserve the right to deny full citizenship to people convicted of homosexual acts. This policy persisted until 1980, when the INS instructed its personnel not to ask about applicants' sexual orientations. However, the INS continued to exclude immigrants who admitted to being homosexual. In 1983, that policy that was invalidated by the U.S. Supreme Court's ruling in *Hill v. Immigration and Naturalization Service*. In 1990, the section of the INS statutes mandating the exclusion of people determined to be sexual deviants or psychopathic personalities was repealed.

LATE TWENTIETH AND EARLY TWENTY-FIRST CENTURY ISSUES

Although sexual orientation stopped being used as a basis for immigrant exclusion during the 1990's, that decade witnessed the rise of new issues for lesbians and gay men applying for entry and citizenship. These issues centered on definitions of family, acquired immunodeficiency syndrome, and quests for political asylum. Immigrants applying for U.S. residency under family petitions were required to be legally recognized spouses, children, siblings, or parents of American citizens. The refusal of U.S. immigration law to recognize the validity of same-sex partnerships—even those recognized by other nations, such as Canada—bars both same-gender partners who have formally wed and individuals who have established relationships with American citizens and wish to join their partners in the United States.

The same-sex marriage issue was further complicated when the Defense of Marriage Act was signed into law on September 21, 1996. This controversial piece of legislation defined marriage in the United States as limited to the unions of a man and a woman. It thus explicitly relieved the federal government from recognizing same-sex marriages as valid relationships. In early 2000, Representative Jerrold Nadler of New York introduced in the House of Representatives a bill for a law to be called the Permanent Partners Immigration Act. That bill called for the addition of the term "permanent partner" to all sections of federal immigration laws relevant to married couples. The bill was referred to the House Judiciary Committee and subsequently to the Subcommittee on Immigration and Claims, which took no action. Later attempts to reintroduce the bill also failed. When it was introduced again in early 2007 as the Uniting American Families Act, it gained bipartisan support but was still not passed through 2009.

In 1987, U.S. senator Jesse Helms of North Carolina introduced an amendment to a law to prohibit the entry of immigrants testing positive for the human immunodeficiency virus (HIV), which can lead to the acquired immunodeficiency syndrome (AIDS). The amendment was justified as a public health measure, but it was been not uniformly applied and has been attacked by many American and international health organizations. Reforms in the Immigration Act of 1990 reforms gave the secretary of health and human services discretion to decide what diseases would be used as grounds for exclusion of immigrants, but in 1993 a second amendment was passed by Congress specifically excluding persons infected with HIV. The spread of AIDS beyond the gay and lesbian community has widened the impact of this portion of immigration law with uncertain results.

Granting political asylum to persons who can demonstrate legitimate and clear fears of persecution in their home nations has long been a part of U.S. immigration law. However, the application of this principle to gay and lesbian immigrants has re-

quired a shift in perspective. The concept of regarding homosexuals as members of a persecuted minority who should be classified as refugees and be eligible for asylum in the United States came into use only during the last decades of the twentieth century. An early, if unintentional, example of this was the influx of several thousand gay Cubans to the United States as part of the Mariel boatlift in 1980.

In 1994, a ruling from the Board of Immigration Appeals declared a Cuban gay man to be eligible for asylum, followed by a directive from Attorney General Janet Reno that immigration officials were to consider lesbians and gays under the rubric of a "social group" as stated in the existing regulations. This placed openly gay and lesbian people in a stronger position to request asylum than those who concealed their sexual orientations. The situation was further complicated with the introduction in 1997 of a one-year filing deadline, making any gays or lesbians who had arrived in the United States prior to April 1, 1997, ineligible to file for asylum.

LGBT ACTIVISM

The growth in federal agencies involved with lesbian, gay, bisexual, and transgender (LGBT) immigration has been matched by the rise of LGBT activist organizations dedicated to advocacy and reform. The oldest such organization is the New York-based Immigration Equality, which was founded in 1994 as the Lesbian and Gay Immigration Rights Task Force. Lambda Legal, the Human Rights Campaign, and the International Lesbian and Gay Association have also made immigrant rights a priority of their civil rights work. Chief among the strategies proposed has been the creation of a pool of same-sex couples facing challenges to their own immigration status to serve as lobbyists in an effort to get the American Families Act passed and signed into law.

Other goals have included expanding the number of law firms who agree to accept LGBT immigration cases on a pro bono basis, educating both immigration judges and asylum officers on the legal rights of LGBT immigrants and asylum applicants, and raising awareness in corporate America of the impact that excluding skilled personnel on the basis of sexual orientation has on the national labor pool.

The use of an immigrant's HIV status as the basis

for denial of admission to America has remained problematic into the twenty-first century, despite the development of drugs that have made AIDS a manageable condition. Immigrants wishing to obtain HIV waivers are required to provide documentation attesting that they have received counseling on AIDS and its manner of transmission and do not constitute a public health threat to the United States. Qualifying for the waiver is also essential for obtaining permanent residency, even when prospective immigrants already have employers willing to sponsor their applications for legal permanent residence.

Robert B. Ridinger

FURTHER READING

Andriote, John-Manuel. *Victory Deferred: How AIDS Changed Gay Life in America.* Chicago: University of Chicago Press, 1999. Excellent analysis of the devastating impact of acquired immunodeficiency syndrome in the United States during the 1980's and 1990's.

Badgett, M. V. Lee. *When Gay People Get Married: What Happens When Societies Legalize Same-Sex Marriage.* New York: New York University Press, 2009. Study of how same-sex marriages have influenced societies that also includes some discussion of immigration issues.

Canaday, Margaret. "Who Is a Homosexual? The Consolidation of Sexual Identities in Mid-Twentieth-Century American Immigration Law." *Law and Social Inquiry* 28, no. 2 (2003): 351-386. Interesting essay on the problem of defining homosexuality that provides insights in the difficulties that immigrants historically faced.

Eskridge, William N. "Immigration, Asylum, and Deportation Law and Policy." In *Encyclopedia of Lesbian, Gay, Bisexual and Transgender History in America,* edited by Marc Stein. New York: Charles Scribner's Sons, 2004. Broad discussion of the manifold legal issues surrounding gay immigrants.

Luibhéid, Eithne. "Sexuality, Migration, and the Shifting Line Between Legal and Illegal Status." *GLQ: A Journal of Gay and Lesbian Studies* 14, nos. 2-3 (2008): 289-313. Up-to-date exploration of legal problems that gay immigrants confront.

SEE ALSO: Acquired immunodeficiency syndrome; *Boutilier v. Immigration and Naturalization Service;* History of immigration after 1891; Immigration Act of 1917; Immigration Act of 1990; Immigration and Nationality Act of 1952; Mariel boatlift; Marriage; "Moral turpitude"; Stereotyping.

GEARY ACT OF 1892

THE LAW: Federal legislation designed to limit Chinese immigration to the United States
DATE: Became law on May 5, 1892

> **SIGNIFICANCE:** Enacted to reinforce and extend provisions of the Chinese Exclusion Act of 1882, the Geary Act prevented further immigration from China and required established Chinese residents of the United States to carry certificates of residence. The act grew out of an assumption that low-wage Chinese laborers were responsible for the economic downturn in the last quarter of the nineteenth century.

The Chinese Exclusion Act, passed in 1882, put a ten-year federal moratorium on the immigration of Chinese laborers, and increased restrictions on Chinese immigrants already living in the United States. When the act expired in 1892, a new bill was proposed by California Democratic congressman Thomas J. Geary. Geary's bill extended the immigration moratorium for ten additional years and required existing Chinese immigrants to obtain official certificates of residence from the Internal Revenue Service. Immigrants found without these certificates faced up to one year of hard labor followed by deportation. Bail was not permitted for immigrants arrested for being in the country illegally, and only a "credible white witness" could testify on behalf of an accused Chinese immigrant. The Geary Act was upheld by the U.S. Supreme Court in 1893, in *Fong Yue Ting v. United States.* In 1902, the act was extended indefinitely, but Congress eased restrictions during the 1920's and finally removed them in 1943.

Cynthia A. Bily

FURTHER READING

Ancheta, Angelo N. *Race, Rights, and the Asian American Experience.* Piscataway, N.J.: Rutgers University Press, 2006.

Kim, Hyung-chan. *Asian Americans and the Supreme Court: A Documentary History*. Westport, Conn.: Greenwood Press, 1992.

Motomura, Hiroshi. *Americans in Waiting: The Lost Story of Immigration and Citizenship in the United States*. New York: Oxford University Press, 2006.

SEE ALSO: Asian immigrants; Asiatic Exclusion League; Bayard-Zhang Treaty of 1888; Chinese Exclusion Act of 1882; Chinese immigrants; Congress, U.S.; Deportation; *Fong Yue Ting v. United States*; History of immigration after 1891; McCreary Amendment of 1893.

GENTLEMEN'S AGREEMENT

DATE: Signed on March 14, 1907

THE TREATY: Informal agreement between the governments of Japan and the United States that limited Japanese immigration to the United States to nonlaborers, laborers already settled in the United States, and members of their families

SIGNIFICANCE: In the wake of Japanese military victories over the Chinese and the Russians as well as following the turmoil of the San Francisco earthquake of 1906 and a resultant segregation order by the San Francisco Board of Education against Japanese and Korean schoolchildren, President Theodore Roosevelt's federal government negotiated a Gentlemen's Agreement with Japan that defused threats of war, ended the segregation order, and limited Japanese immigration.

After Japan's Meiji Restoration began in 1868, Japanese emigrants began to seek their fortunes in California. After the passage of the Chinese Exclusion Act of 1882, labor shortages drew increasing numbers of Japanese immigrants both to Hawaii (especially after its annexation in 1898 by the United States) and to California, especially the San Francisco Bay Area. Japanese victories in the Sino-Japanese War (1894-1895) and the Russo-Japanese War (1904-1905) established the previously closed country as a world power, even as California and other West Coast states began to extend antimiscegenation laws to bar marriages between whites and "Mongolians."

SAN FRANCISCO EARTHQUAKE AND AFTERMATH

Unlike the earlier Chinese immigrants who were mostly male and lived in or near the Grant Street Chinatown, Japanese Americans in San Francisco lived throughout the city. Before the 1906 earthquake, there were ninety-three Japanese children in twenty-three different elementary schools. Also, anti-Asian sentiment was being redirected from the Chinese to the Japanese by statements from San Francisco mayor Eugene Schmitz; a series of articles in the *San Francisco Chronicle* describing the "yellow peril"; and the Asiatic Exclusion League, which was organized by one hundred San Francisco unions in 1905 in order to extend the Chinese Exclusion Act to cover Japanese and Koreans, boycott Japanese workers and Japanese-owned businesses, and segregate Japanese and Korean students from public schools.

The San Francisco earthquake of April 18, 1906, destroyed municipal records that had inflamed fears concerning the incursion of the supposedly more aggressive, clever, and acquisitive Japanese. On October 11, 1906, as temporary and rehabilitated public schools were ready to reopen, the San Francisco Board of Education ordered the segregation of Japanese and Korean schoolchildren with the already segregated Chinese. Although the few Koreans complied with the order, Japanese parents objected strenuously. The Japanese government lodged a formal protest, claiming that the order violated the treaty of 1894. President Theodore Roosevelt, who had received a Nobel Peace Prize earlier in 1906 for helping to negotiate the treaty that ended the Russo-Japanese War, articulated his sincere "regard and respect for the people of Japan" in his December 3, 1906, state of the union address. Roosevelt subsequently called San Francisco government and board of education officials to Washington and facilitated the negotiation of what has since been termed the Gentlemen's Agreement of 1907.

LEGACY OF THE GENTLEMEN'S AGREEMENT

The Gentlemen's Agreement forced the rescinding of the board of education order. In return, the Japanese government agreed not to issue

President Theodore Roosevelt. (Library of Congress)

any new passports for Japanese citizens who sought to work in the United States. However, parents, children, and wives of Japanese laborers already in the United States could still immigrate to the United States. Also, critics of the agreement noted the loophole that Japanese laborers could still freely immigrate to the territory of Hawaii, and the "picture bride" industry subsequently developed, in which single male Japanese laborers in the United States could select a Japanese bride from the old country solely on the basis of mailed photographs. The provisions of the Gentlemen's Agreement allowed immigrant Japanese communities to develop complex family networks in a manner that the previous male-only Chinese communities never achieved. There were 90 Japanese-owned businesses in San Francisco in 1900 and 545 by 1909, despite the negative financial ramifications of the 1906 earthquake. According to the 1900 U.S. Census, there were 72,257 citizens of Japanese heritage living in the United States (42 percent in California); by 1920, there were 138,834 (70 percent in California). Continuing anti-immigration senti-

ment led to the Immigration Act of 1924, effectively halting all further Japanese immigration to the United States until the passage of the Immigration and Nationality Act of 1952.

Richard Sax

FURTHER READING

Chan, Sucheng. *Asian Americans: An Interpretive History.* Boston: Twayne, 1991. Comprehensive social and political history of four principal Asian immigrant cultures (Chinese, Japanese, Filipino, Korean) includes treatment of diplomatic and legal landmarks and struggles.

Daniels, Roger. *The Politics of Prejudice: The Anti-Japanese Movement in California and the Struggle for Japanese Exclusion.* Berkeley: University of California Press, 1999. Details issues of regionalism and racial politics in late nineteenth and early twentieth century California.

Esthus, Raymond A. *Theodore Roosevelt and Japan.* Seattle: University of Washington Press, 1967. Chronological history that describes how statesmanship kept the United States and Japan on diplomatic terms even as Japan waged war with the Russians, annexed Korea, and negotiated the informal Gentlemen's Agreement with the United States.

Kiyama, Henry, and Frederik Schodt. *The Four Immigrants Manga: A Japanese Experience in San Francisco, 1904-1924.* Berkeley, Calif.: Stone Bridge Press, 1999. Manga (graphic novel) treatment of four Japanese immigrants to San Francisco, humorously poking fun at the quirky and culturally obtuse behavior of their employers from the perspective of student-workers.

Neu, Charles E. *Troubled Encounter: The United States and Japan.* Malabar, Fla.: R. E. Krieger, 1979. Diplomatic study of Japanese-U.S. relations from beginning of the Meiji Restoration (1868) through the late twentieth century. Details how the Gentlemen's Agreement of 1907 was a precursor to more draconian immigration measures of 1924 that exacerbated relations between the two countries.

_____. *An Uncertain Friendship: Theodore Roosevelt and Japan, 1906-1909.* Cambridge, Mass.: Harvard University Press, 1967. Describes Roosevelt's complex relationship with the Japanese government during the latter years of his second term as well as the legacy leading into the diplomacy policies of the William Taft administration.

Takaki, Ronald. *Strangers from a Different Shore: A History of Asian-Americans.* Boston: Little, Brown, 1989. Historical study of Asian Americans with significant treatment of the settling of Japanese America and resultant ethnic stereotyping, prejudice, and state and federal legal issues.

SEE ALSO: Alien land laws; Amerasian children; Anti-Japanese movement; Asiatic Exclusion League; California; Immigration Act of 1924; Immigration and Nationality Act of 1952; Japanese immigrants; San Francisco; "Yellow peril" campaign.

GEORGIA

SIGNIFICANCE: Georgia was originally settled by immigrants from various parts of Europe. Later, slaves were brought in from Africa and the Caribbean. During the century following the Civil War, Georgia's population declined, but during the late twentieth century, Asian immigrants arrived in the state, followed by large numbers of Mexicans.

The original inhabitants of Georgia were several Native American tribes: the Apalache in the south, the Yamasee along the coast, and Cherokees and Creeks throughout the entire region. In 1526, Spain made its first attempt to plant a colony on the eastern seaboard; it is now believed that the Spanish settlement was not located in South Carolina, as had been thought, but on the Georgia mainland. However, many of the early Spanish settlers fell ill and died, and the survivors abandoned the colony, leaving few permanent traces of their presence behind. During the first half of the seventeenth century, the Spanish built forts and established missions in Georgia, but they were not able to maintain their ascendancy against the Brit-

ish, who soon laid claim to the Carolinas, Georgia, and part of Spanish Florida.

In 1731, the British crown granted a charter to a group of men led by General James Edward Oglethorpe, whose purpose was to establish a new colony called Georgia, in which there would be no slavery, no hard liquor, and no Roman Catholics. Oglethorpe offered land and supplies to poor laborers from England. Georgia was also a safe haven for those fleeing persecution by the Roman Catholic Church, among them German Lutherans and Moravians and French Huguenots. In 1733, forty-two Jews arrived in Savannah, most of them Sephardic Jews driven out of Portugal. In 1736, the colonists were joined by Scottish Highlanders, many of them Jacobites whose property had been confiscated after the rebellion of 1715. Lutherans from Salzburg, Germany, established the town of Ebenezer, upriver from Savannah, and Moravians also settled there, though they later moved north. Scots founded New Inverness (now Darien) on the Altamaha River.

Because of frequent attacks by the Spaniards and Indians, along with restrictions that made trade difficult and the establishment of large plantations impossible, most of the original colonists had left Georgia by 1743. However, after the original prohibition against slavery was rescinded in 1750, the colony attracted prosperous settlers, many of whom became planters and merchants.

PROFILE OF GEORGIA

Region	Southeast coast
Entered union	1788
Largest cities	Atlanta (capital), Augusta, Columbus, Savannah, Athens
Modern immigrant communities	Koreans, Asian Indians, Mexicans

Population	*Total*	*Percent of state*	*Percent of U.S.*	*U.S. rank*
All state residents	9,364,000	100.0	3.13	9
All foreign-born residents	860,000	9.2	2.29	9

Source: U.S. Census Bureau, *Statistical Abstract for 2006.*
Notes: The U.S. population in 2006 was 299,399,000, of whom 37,548,000 (12.5%) were foreign born. Rankings in last column reflect total numbers, not percentages.

During the next few years, large numbers of slaves were brought into Georgia from Africa and from the Caribbean. By the 1830's, however, the once wealthy planters were in economic trouble, in large part because their intensive cotton cultivation had ruined the soil. Many of them uprooted their households and moved west to Alabama and Mississippi, taking their slaves with them.

Meanwhile, after 1815, Irish colonists fleeing poverty and oppression had been coming to Georgia. Though at first their lack of education held them to menial jobs, they developed strong communities and became a political force. Savannah later became known for its annual Irish festival.

After the Civil War (1861-1865), the hard-pressed planters made their land available for sharecropping, but tenants could barely survive on what they made, and the whites who went to work in the new cotton mills fared no better. As one of the poorest states in the Union, Georgia attracted few immigrants. Only metropolitan Atlanta offered some opportunities, at least for whites; the rest of the state remained in the grips of poverty, which was only intensified during the Great Depression of the 1930's. After World War II, many black and some white Georgians fled to the North, where they could earn better wages as factory workers.

During the 1970's, immigrants from Korea and Vietnam began settling in Georgia, where many of them opened shops. Well-educated Asian Indians arrived to fill vacancies in medical and professional fields. During the 1980's, a new wave of Latin American immigrants flooded into Georgia. By 2006, according to the Migration Policy Institute, 32.2 percent of the foreign-born population of Georgia came from Mexico. About half of them were undocumented immigrants. Their lack of education forced them into low-paying jobs with no health benefits, and they had to rely on government welfare programs. They often faced resentment from native-born Americans, and they became easy targets for criminals.

Rosemary M. Canfield Reisman

FURTHER READING

Cobb, James C. *Georgia Odyssey.* 2d ed. Athens: University of Georgia Press, 2008.
Coleman, Kenneth, ed. *A History of Georgia.* 2d ed. Athens: University of Georgia Press, 1991.
Mohl, Raymond A. "Globalization, Latinization, and the *Nuevo* New South." In *Other Souths: Diversity and Difference in the U.S. South, Reconstruction to Present,* edited by Pippa Holloway. Athens: University of Georgia Press, 2008.
Murphy, Arthur D., Colleen Blanchard, and Jennifer A. Hill, eds. *Latino Workers in the Contemporary South.* Athens: University of Georgia Press, 2001.

SEE ALSO: African Americans and immigrants; Asian immigrants; Austrian immigrants; British immigrants; Crime; Florida; French immigrants; German immigrants; Irish immigrants; Jewish immigrants; Mexican immigrants; South Carolina.

GERMAN AMERICAN PRESS

DEFINITION: German-language newspapers catering to German immigrants

SIGNIFICANCE: As German immigrants reached the United States and began settling in the interior of the country, the German American press catered to their need for news and information, providing stories about their adopted homeland while keeping in touch with Germany. The German American press became one of the largest and most powerful ethnic presses in the country, aiding German politicians at both state and national levels.

Ethnic presses in the United States were a major force in American journalism during the nineteenth century, when mass European immigration was bringing millions of non-English speakers into the United States. The German-language press was one of the most influential of the ethnic presses. The first German newspaper in the British colonies was published by Benjamin Franklin in 1732. However, his *Philadelphische Zeitung* lasted only a few months, and other German language dailies had similarly short life spans. In 1735, John Peter Zenger was publishing the *New York Weekly*, a German American paper, when he was charged with libel. His trial expanded freedom of the press by making it more difficult for government officials to sue for libel.

Meanwhile, developments in Europe invigorated the German American press as political turmoil accelerated German emigration. The revolutions of 1848 and subsequent government crackdowns drove millions of central Europeans from the continent. As German émigrés arrived in North America, they found newspapers such as the *New York Staats-Zeitung*, a major daily established in 1834, already flourishing and ready to cater to German speakers hungry for news about their adopted homeland.

A GROWING PRESENCE

As new German immigrants settled throughout the United States, their daily newspapers followed. By the 1850's, Cincinnati alone had four German-language newspapers, and St. Louis had three. The most influential of these papers were St. Louis's *Anzeiger des Westens*, or *Western Informant* and the *Cincinnati Volksblatt*. Both papers supported the abolitionist movement and the Republican Party, which formed during the mid-1850's. In Illinois, the *Staats Zeitung* was the official Republican voice in the German community, and it gained prominence during the 1860 presidential campaign.

As the circulations of German-language papers topped one hundred thousand in cities such as Chicago and New York, German American politicians used the papers as campaigning tools. Carl Schurz, a German-born Republican who became a political reformer and secretary of the interior for President Rutherford B. Hayes, used his part ownership in the *St. Louis Westliche Post* to promote his own political career. German-language newspapers also closely followed the military exploits of German American generals, such as Franz Sigel. With their large readerships and captive audiences of German immigrants who were not yet familiar with English, the papers became a force in politics and were courted by politicians eager to communicate with their German constituents.

The German American press also aided in the rise of major newspaper magnates, who used ethnic newspapers to expand their overall readership. For example, Joseph Pulitzer published the St. Louis *Westliche Post* along with his *St. Louis Post-Dispatch*, providing a gateway as German immigrants adopted English and switched their loyalty to English-language newspapers.

DECLINE OF THE PRESS

European turmoil during the 1870's and 1880's drove more Germans to emigrate to North America, increasing demand for German-language papers. New York City alone had more than a half-dozen such papers, while many rural communities with German settlers had their own German papers. However, as German immigration waned, and second- and third-generation German Americans adopted English, the German papers saw their readerships decline. Rural papers were the first to shut down. During the early years of the twentieth century, mergers left most large cities with only one or two German-language dailies each.

American entry into World War I in 1917 proved to be the end of the German American press's influence in American politics. Much of the fall of the papers may be attributed to the German entrepreneur George Vierek, who established a pro-German newspaper called *The Fatherland* in August, 1914, at the time the war was starting in Europe. The circulation of the paper grew rapidly, as German Americans sought news about the course of the war. Vierek used his newspaper as a propaganda machine for the German government, receiving reports from the German Information Service. His paper defended the German government against charges of war crimes and brutality against civilians. It also attacked British influence in American foreign policy, taking particular aim at the Wilson administration when it tilted in favor of the Allies. Many German newspapers supported the candidacy of Charles Evans Hughes during the 1916 presidential election, believing that he was less likely than President Woodrow Wilson to lead the United States into the war against Germany. Their endorsements of Hughes would not be forgotten by Wilson after he won the November, 1916, presidential election and took the country into the war the following April.

In 1918, Wilson signed the Trading with the Enemy Act, which regulated all trade with Germany and its allies. Such trade included news reports passed on to the German-language press. Onerous regulations were imposed requiring costly record keeping by the newspapers as they were forced to record all their contacts with the German government.

Such regulations weakened the German language press, while growing distrust of the loyalty of German speakers led to the demise of half of the German newspapers during the early 1920's. The end of large-scale German immigration and the general economic turndown of the Great Depression reduced the circulation of the German newspapers, leaving only a few in the largest American cities such as New York. By the turn of the twenty-first century, fewer than two dozen German American newspapers were still publishing. These included Chicago's *Amerika Woch*, New York's *Staats Zeitung*, and the *Florida Journal*.

Douglas Clouatre

FURTHER READING

Fleming, Thomas. *The Illusion of Victory*. New York: Basic Books, 2003. Discusses how the Wilson administration used the national emergency to attack ethnic groups including Germans suspected of supporting their homeland during World War I.

Gross, Ruth. *Traveling Between Worlds*. College Station: Texas A&M Press, 2006. Study of German immigration into the United States that includes coverage of such institutions as churches and the press.

Heinrich-Tolzmann, Don. *The German American Experience*. Amherst, N.Y.: Humanity Books, 2000. Wide-ranging study of how Germans who emigrated to the United States became an integral part of their new country's cultural and political system.

Keller, Phyllis. *States of Belonging*. Cambridge, Mass.: Harvard University Press, 1979. Examines several German intellectuals, including publishers of German American newspapers and journals.

Miller, Sally, ed. *The Ethnic Press in the United States*. Westport, Conn.: Greenwood Press, 1987. Shows how immigrant presses were an important part of arrivals to United States, including the active German American press.

SEE ALSO: Austrian immigrants; European revolutions of 1848; German immigrants; History of immigration, 1783-1891; Italian American press; Pulitzer, Joseph; Spanish-language press; World War I.

GERMAN IMMIGRANTS

SIGNIFICANCE: The first non-English-speaking immigrant group to enter the United States in large numbers, Germans played major roles in American economic development, the abolitionist movement, U.S. military forces, and other spheres during the nineteenth century, and German immigrants continued to make important contributions to the United States during the twentieth century.

Most German immigration to the United States occurred during the nineteenth century, but Germans began arriving as early as 1608, when they helped English settlers found Jamestown, Virginia. Germans also played an important role in the Dutch creation of New Amsterdam, which later became New York City, during the early 1620's. Other early German immigrants helped to settle North and South Carolina. By the nineteenth century, German immigrants were advancing farther inland to states such as Nebraska, Ohio, Illinois, Missouri, Wisconsin, Kansas, Minnesota, and Texas.

EARLY IMMIGRATION, 1608-1749

Two forces were paramount in prompting early German immigration: heavy taxation and German laws of primogeniture, which permitted only the eldest sons in families to inherit their fathers' land. These forces, along with seemingly constant and disruptive German wars, gave many young Germans strong motivations for emigrating to a new country, where they could hope to own their land and prosper with minimal government hindrance.

The first American region in which large numbers of Germans settled was Pennsylvania. Germantown, near what is now Philadelphia, was the first of many permanent German settlements in the British colonies—many of which had the same name. After Germantown was founded in 1683, German immigration to Pennsylvania grew more rapidly. By the mid-eighteenth century, Pennsylvania's approximately 50,000 German immigrants made up about 40 percent of the colony's entire population. Amish and Mennonite religious communities and the creation of the perhaps inaptly named "Pennsylvania Dutch" established Pennsyl-

PROFILE OF GERMAN IMMIGRANTS

Country of origin	Germany
Primary language	German
Primary regions of U.S. settlement	Pennsylvania, New York, Missouri, Minnesota, Ohio, Illinois, Nebraska
Earliest significant arrivals	1608
Peak immigration periods	1840's-1920's, 1950's
Twenty-first century legal residents*	63,214 (7,901 per year)

*Immigrants who obtained legal permanent resident status in the United States.

Source: Department of Homeland Security, Yearbook of Immigration Statistics, 2008.

vania as a primary stronghold for German immigration. Pennsylvania was also becoming a base from which Germans migrated to other colonies, including what is now northern West Virginia, most of Maryland, parts of North Carolina, and the western regions of Virginia and South Carolina.

Taking their name from *Deutsche*, the German word for "German," the Pennsylvania Dutch were the primary builders of Philadelphia and many of its neighboring communities in what became a six-county region that would be known as "Pennsylvania Dutch Country." Pennsylvania's Amish communities have kept alive German culture through their rejection of modern technology, their continued wearing of early German farming attire, and their ability to speak both old and modern forms of German. German farmers, craftsmen, and indentured servants helped develop Pennsylvania.

LATE EIGHTEENTH CENTURY DEVELOPMENTS

During the late eighteenth century, the Industrial Revolution began transforming the economies of the many German states from agricultural to manufacturing bases, making it more difficult for farmers to prosper. The lure of apparently unlimited farmland in North America, coupled with news from successful immigrants to provide a powerful lure to emigrate. From the late eighteenth

century through much of the nineteenth century, millions of Germans went to the United States. Many of them were farmers who brought skills that contributed significantly to the agriculture of the Midwest, and many settled and helped build cities such as Milwaukee and Cincinnati.

The success of many early German immigrants in agriculture helped draw many German-born businessmen to the United States, where some of them built beer breweries that prospered alongside local agriculture. Some the best-known American breweries, such as Pabst, Anheuser-Busch, Schlitz, Blatz, and Miller, were started by Germans.

Because Philadelphia was at the center of American opposition to British colonial rule, it is not surprising that Germans played an important role in the American Revolution that led to the independence of the United States. By the late eighteenth century, many German immigrants had deep roots in North American and were eager to help fight for independence. However, Great Britain's use of German mercenaries against Americans helped give German Americans a bad name.

Known as Hessians because most of them were from the German state of Hesse, as many as 30,000 German mercenaries may have fought for Great Britain, and they may have constituted as many as one-third of all British combat troops in the Revolutionary War. These Germans fought ruthlessly against the Americans, but they paid a heavy price in casualties. Nearly one-quarter of them died from illnesses, and another quarter may have died in combat. It is not known exactly how many of the German troops remained in the United States after the war, but their number seems to have been high. Moreover, many Hessian mercenaries prospered after the war, thanks to the fact that the new U.S. government lacked the funds to send them back to Europe.

German immigrants who fought on the American side were also recognized for their valor and loyalty. Some held high commands. A particularly well-known German general in the war was Baron Friedrich Wilhelm von Steuben, who volunteered his services as a trained Prussian general to the American cause free of pay. Von Steuben was especially valuable in teaching discipline and drill to revolutionary soldiers, few of whom had any formal military training. The colonial troops were initially ridiculed by British troops for their inability to hold line and their eagerness to retreat. Von Steuben helped transform the untrained men into efficient soldiers. Steubenville, Ohio, was later named in his honor.

First Century of American Independence, 1783-1900

Through the half-century following the Revolutionary War, German immigration increased steadily. Many of the new arrivals settled in such major cities as New York and Philadelphia, but independence from Great Britain allowed the United States to open up the West to settlers, greatly expanding agricultural opportunities for Germans and other immigrants.

Although much of the prosperity that German immigrants enjoyed in North America was based on their success in agriculture, Germans played a leading role in opposing slavery, which provided most of the farm labor in southern U.S. states. Some of the German leaders in the American abolitionist movement were political refugees from the many failed revolutions of 1848 in Europe who came to the United States filled with liberal ideals.

After the U.S. Civil War began in 1861, German immigrants again played a prominent role in the fighting. Some Germans fought for the Confederacy during the war, but the overwhelming majority of Germans involved in the conflict fought on the Union side. Indeed, nearly one-quarter of all Union Army troops were German Americans, about 45 percent of whom had been born in Europe. Among the most outstanding German officers in the Union Army were Carl Schurz, Max Weber, Louis Blenker, and Franz Sigel. Many Germans who fought for the Union brought considerable military experience. A slave state that remained in the Union, Missouri had a large German population that supplied many soldiers to the Union cause. After the war ended in 1865, German immigration continued to rise at a rate faster than that of any other immigrant group into the early twentieth century.

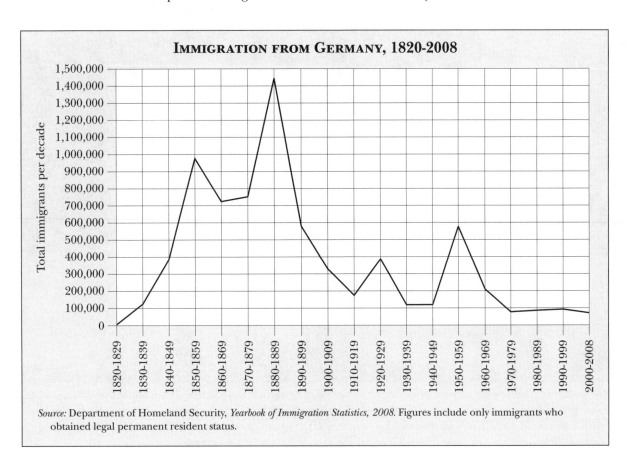

IMMIGRATION FROM GERMANY, 1820-2008

Source: Department of Homeland Security, *Yearbook of Immigration Statistics, 2008.* Figures include only immigrants who obtained legal permanent resident status.

TWENTIETH TO TWENTY-FIRST CENTURIES

German immigration to the United States continued to grow until 1914, when World War I began in Europe. The U.S. declaration of war against Germany in 1917 began the first period of anti-German sentiment since the Revolutionary War, when Great Britain used German soldiers against Americans. Anti-German fever during the war caused many Americans to vilify German Americans, especially those known still to speak German, and recently arrived German immigrants. Only a small number of German Americans openly supported Germany's position in the war. Many of them were imprisoned for sedition or attacked by mobs.

During the war, former U.S. president Theodore Roosevelt went as far as to say neutrality was not an option and dual loyalty could not exist.

Rising anti-German sentiment saw many German names disappear from the names of businesses, schools, and even public streets. Indeed, World War I helped accelerate the obliteration of German subcultures within the United States. Many German-language magazines and newspapers stopped publishing. German Americans avoided speaking German in public, and school systems stopped teaching German. Many German Americans anglicized their own surnames: "Mueller" became "Miller," "Schmidt" became "Smith," and "Franz" became "Franks." Fear of American hostility, not the war itself, did much to destroy visible traces of German culture in the United States.

American entry into World War II in 1941 renewed American animosity toward Germans. Anti-German and anti-Japanese campaigns began shortly after Japan launched its sneak attack on

German immigrants on the steerage deck of the immigrant ship Friedrich der Grosse. *When World War I began in August, 1914, the U.S. government seized the ship, which happened to be laid up in New York harbor. After the United States entered the war in 1917, the Navy used the ship, renamed USS* Huron, *to transport troops across the Atlantic. Over the next two years, the ship completed fifteen round-trip voyages.* (Library of Congress)

420

Pearl Harbor on December 7, 1941. The United States had still not fully recovered from anti-German animosity during World War I, and the new war against Germany's already reviled Nazi regime renewed American distrust of Germans. Using the Alien and Sedition Acts of 1798, the U.S. government legally detained more than ten thousand German Americans during the war. German businesses suffered vandalism and many Germans were attacked by American mobs. Meanwhile, the Holocaust in Europe led to another increase in German immigrants following the war. Most of these people were German Jews who had suffered greatly under the Nazi regime.

An ironic aspect of the war was the fact that the supreme Allied military commander and future president of the United States, Dwight D. Eisenhower was himself of German descent. Some of his ancestors had been members of the Pennsylvania Dutch communities. The war also brought to the United States the great German theoretic physicist Albert Einstein and German rocket expert Wernher von Braun, who would later help shape the American space program.

After memories of World War II receded and Eisenhower became a popular U.S. president, German heritage lost some of the negative stigma it had acquired over the previous decades. This development was aided by growing American distrust of the Soviet Union and the beginning of the Cold War. With an ominous new international threat looming, Americans were becoming less inclined to worry about differences among their own subcultures.

Despite early twentieth century anti-German movements, many traces of German culture have survived into the twenty-first century. These can be seen in product names such as Bayer, Heinz, Chrysler, Busch, and Budweiser, and in such now thoroughly American items of cuisine as hot dogs (frankfurters) and pretzels. In addition to foods and beers, German culture has provided the American educational system with the concept of kindergarten, which was regularly practiced in Germany following the increased immigration during the early nineteenth century. Other German contributions to American culture include two-day weekends, gymnasiums, Christmas trees, and theme parks.

Keith J. Bell

FURTHER READING

Brancaforte, Charlotte L., ed. *The German Forty-eighters in the United States.* New York: Peter Lang, 1990. Eighteen essays covering a wide range of topics, including a reappraisal that many of the immigrants were not radicals or revolutionaries.

Creighton, M. *The Colors of Courage: Gettysburg's Forgotten History: Immigrants, Women, and African Americans in the Civil War's Defining Battle.* New York: Basic Books, 2006. Depicts the forgotten heroism of Germans and other immigrant peoples in one of the bloodiest battles in American history.

Fogleman, Aaron Spencer. *Hopeful Journeys: German Immigration, Settlement, and Political Culture in Colonial America, 1717-1775.* Philadelphia: University of Pennsylvania Press, 1996. Details the everyday struggles of common German immigrants to the colonies during the eighteenth century and includes many individual stories.

Heinrich-Tolzmann Don. *The German American Experience.* Amherst, N.Y.: Humanity Books, 2000. Thought-provoking examination of how German immigrants have blended into American society.

Kamphoefner, Walter, and Wolfgang Helbich, eds. *Germans in the Civil War: The Letters They Wrote Home.* Translated by Susan Carter Vogel. Chapel Hill: University of North Carolina Press, 2006. Fascinating collection of documents presenting the firsthand views of German immigrants who fought in the U.S. Civil War.

Kennedy, David M. *The American People in World War II: Freedom from Fear, Part II.* New York: Oxford University Press, 1999. This book places immigration issues in the broad context of America at war and looks at American attitudes toward German immigrants.

Spalek, John, Adrienne Ash, and Sandra Hawrylchak. *Guide to Archival Materials of German-Speaking Emigrants to the U.S. After 1933.* Charlottesville: University of Virginia Press, 1978. Invaluable handbook for historical and genealogical research into German/Austrian immigration during the mid-twentieth century. Especially strong on Holocaust-related immigrants.

Tolzmann, Don Heinrich. *The German-American Experience.* New York: Humanity Books, 2000. Comprehensive study of German immigrants in the United States, with sections on politics and nativism, German rural and urban communities, and German-speaking communities.

Trumbauer, L. *German Immigration*. New York: Facts On File, 2004. Details personal stories of German immigrants to the United States and the key players in the formation of the country.

Wittke, Carl. *Refugees of Revolution: The German Forty-eighters in America*. Philadelphia: University of Pennsylvania, 1952. A classic work on the experience of the Forty-eighters in the United States. Heavy emphasis on biography.

SEE ALSO: Austrian immigrants; Civil War, U.S.; Einstein, Albert; German American press; History of immigration, 1620-1783; History of immigration, 1783-1891; History of immigration after 1891; Holocaust; Prisoners of war in the United States; Schurz, Carl; Strauss, Levi; World War I; World War II.

GLOBALIZATION

DEFINITION: Transformation occurring as movements of people, goods, and ideas among countries and regions increase greatly

SIGNIFICANCE: Many countries, including the United States, are undergoing serious demographic transformations as a result of changing global migration patterns. Immigrants bring with them customs, practices and behavior patterns different from those of the receiving countries. Branches of the original culture are recreated in host countries, particularly within urban ethnic enclaves. Although multiethnicity is common in large urban communities, it can be threatening to native-born citizens.

In many ways the nature of migration has changed. Individuals migrate among countries for more than economic reasons. The creation of global culture brought about by a revolution in mass communications has encouraged foreign influences through media. Globalization of communication technology has helped to influence migration. By creating linkages between receiving and sending countries, communication technology has provided means by which news and information is readily available almost everywhere. This developed has helped to foster increasing immigration into the United States. Information about job opportunities is readily spread; earlier immigrants help later immigrants with housing, employment, and networking opportunities. Successful transitions from one country to another encourage still more immigration that may continue even after the original reasons for immigrating are no longer present.

Acculturation occurs when the attitudes and behaviors of individuals from one culture are affected by contact with a different cultures. In order for acculturation to occur, a relative cultural equality must exist between the giving and receiving cultures. Acculturation differs from assimilation, which occurs when the cultural characteristics of a minority group become lost within a larger culture. The acculturation process affects a variety of behaviors, values, and beliefs. For individual immigrants, the amounts of time they have spent in their host countries and their ages when they immigrate have been shown to correlate with their likelihood of acculturation and are good indicators of an individual's level of acculturation in the absence of more detailed information. Three dimensions of acculturation have been defined: assimilation, biculturalism, and observance of traditionality. Biculturalism is the ability to live in both worlds, with denial of neither. Observance of traditionality is the rejection of the dominant culture.

Sandra C. Hayes

FURTHER READING

Aneesh, A. *Virtual Migration: The Programming of Globalization*. Durham, N.C.: Duke University Press, 2006.

Bacon, David. *Illegal People: How Globalization Creates Migration and Criminalizes Immigrants*. Boston: Beacon Books, 2008.

Reimers, David M. *Other Immigrants: The Global Origins of the American People*. New York: New York University Press, 2005.

Spiro, Peter J. *Beyond Citizenship: American Identity After Globalization*. New York: Oxford University Press, 2008.

SEE ALSO: "Brain drain"; Chain migration; Drug trafficking; Economic consequences of immigration; Ethnic enclaves; Foreign exchange students; Garment industry; Health care; "Immigrant"; Mexican immigrants.

GODFATHER TRILOGY

IDENTIFICATION: Francis Ford Coppola's films based on Mario Puzo's 1969 novel *The Godfather*, about the family of a Sicilian immigrant who builds a criminal empire in New York that one of his sons inherits

DATES: Released in 1972, 1974, and 1990

SIGNIFICANCE: The winner of nine Academy Awards and dozens of critical and film-industry awards, and with *The Godfather* (1972) and *The Godfather: Part II* (1974) voted among the ten best American films ever, the trilogy occupies an iconic place in American cinema and culture. Viewed by hundreds of millions in and outside the United States, its portrayal of Sicilian immigrants, New York's Little Italy, and the organized crime underworld vie in many viewers' minds with historical truth.

In a 1963 testimony to the Congressional Hearing on Organized Crime, Joe Valachi, a "soldier" in the Genovese crime family, was the first mobster to publicly acknowledge the existence and power of the Mafia. His testimony, broadcast on radio and television and published in newspapers, was devastating for the mob, already reeling from the 1957 Apalachin exposure when New York State police had accidentally uncovered a meeting of several Mafia bosses from all over the United States. However, while the Italian crime syndicate stretching across the United States was no longer invisible to the public, few Americans gave it a second thought. Together with Mario Puzo's novel, the *Godfather* blockbusters changed that.

The Godfather (1972) opens in 1945. A decision not to enter the narcotics trade brings Vito Corleone, Italian Mafia family boss, onto a violent collision course with other New York crime families. Peace ensues only after a series of assassinations, instigated by his youngest son, Michael, who takes over the "business" after his father's death and removes the crime family to Las Vegas. The plot of *The Godfather: Part II* (1974) is complex and ambitious (the film runs two hundred minutes). Now a billionaire reaping the benefits of legalized gambling in Las Vegas, during the late 1950's Michael Corleone expands his criminal base, buys political clout, and successfully fends off a federal indictment, while competing against an aging Jewish boss from Miami (modeled after Meyer Lansky). Running in parallel is the story of his father who, as a boy, arrived at Ellis Island from Sicily in 1901, only to rise as a crime lord ("Don") in Little Italy. The much weaker *Godfather: Part III* (1990) picks up the story in 1979 and essentially reprises the plot of the first film, with the aging Michael passing the reins to the crime empire amid a new wave of machinations and assassinations.

The films are steeped in the Italian immigrant experience in the United States. Italian dialogue

Marlon Brando (right) as Don Corleone, with his son, played by Al Pacino. (Museum of Modern Art, Film Stills Archive)

(with subtitles) is ubiquitous, in *Godfather: Part II* amounting to almost half of the film. Scenes of baptism, first communion, wedding, family dinners, and other aspects of Italian Roman Catholic religion and culture are painstakingly recreated. Street life during the early decades of New York, the annual Feast of San Gennaro, and other traditions combine with extensive footage from rural and small-town life in Sicily to enrich the film's gangster plot and give it an authentic feel of the immigrant experience, not to mention a criminal underworld twist to the American Dream of "rags to riches."

Peter Swirski

FURTHER READING

Jones, Jenny M. *The Annotated Godfather: The Complete Screenplay.* New York: Black Dog & Leventhal, 2007.

Messenger, Christian K. *The Godfather and American Culture: How the Corleones Became "Our Gang."* Albany: State University of New York Press, 2002.

Puzo, Mario. *The Godfather.* New York: New American Library, 1978.

SEE ALSO: Anglo-conformity; Crime; Criminal immigrants; Drug trafficking; Ellis Island; Films; Italian immigrants; Labor unions; Literature; Little Italies; New York City.

GOLDEN VENTURE GROUNDING

THE EVENT: After a freighter named the *Golden Venture* grounded off Queens, New York, 276 undocumented Chinese passengers were taken into custody by federal authorities

DATE: June 6, 1993

LOCATION: Rockaway Peninsula, Queens, New York

SIGNIFICANCE: The *Golden Venture* incident raised public awareness of the fact that dur-

A police rescue boat attempts to remove the last passengers from the Golden Venture *as men who have already been rescued watch in the foreground.* (AP/Wide World Photos)

ing the 1990's thousands of Chinese immigrants were entering the United States without legal documentation. Federal authorizes prosecuted the *Golden Venture* crew and parties responsible for the smuggling attempt and detained the would-be immigrants.

When the *Golden Venture* grounded, some passengers dove off the ship into the sea. During the rescue procedure ten people drowned or died of hypothermia and six others escaped. Those surviving were sent to detention centers, where 90 percent of them applied for political asylum. Public opinion on how to treat these survivors ranged from humanitarian appeals for full exoneration to calls for their immediate deportation.

The fates of individual survivors varied. The juveniles were transferred to court custody; some were given political asylum in the United States or South America, but many were deported. In February, 1997, President Bill Clinton awarded humanitarian paroles to the fifty-three remaining detainees, but this gesture did not alter their legal status.

After they were freed, they were left to pursue their own destinies in America. More than half of those who had been deported are believed to have later returned to the United States.

During the several years that the detainees were incarcerated in York County prison, some of them created more than ten thousand intricate paper sculptures that were later exhibited throughout the United States.

Cynthia J. W. Svoboda

FURTHER READING

Chin, Ko-Lin. *Smuggled Chinese: Clandestine Immigration to the United States.* Philadelphia: Temple University Press, 1999.

Kwong, Peter. *Forbidden Workers: Illegal Chinese Immigrants and American Labor.* New York: New Press, 1997.

SEE ALSO: Border Patrol, U.S.; Chinese immigrants; Citizenship; Deportation; Due process protections; Illegal immigration; Immigration and Naturalization Service, U.S.; Immigration law; New York State; Smuggling of immigrants; Transportation of immigrants.

GOLDMAN, EMMA

IDENTIFICATION: Lithuanian-born American anarchist and feminist

BORN: June 27, 1869; Kovno, Lithuania, Russian Empire (now Kaunas, Lithuania)

DIED: May 14, 1940; Toronto, Ontario, Canada

SIGNIFICANCE: A forceful voice for the nascent anarchist movement in the United States, Goldman founded the magazine *Mother Earth* and crisscrossed the United States lecturing about anarchy and supporting anarchists, immigrant and labor groups, women, and others oppressed by the government and institutionalized capitalism.

In 1885, Emma Goldman, having rejected her brutal father, the prospect of domestic life, and state-sanctioned oppression of radicals and Jews, emigrated from Russia to the United States. In the immigrant communities of New York, she experienced sweatshop life, worker oppression, and an unhappy marriage. Inspired by the persecution of eight anarchists involved in the Haymarket riot of 1886, Goldman joined the American anarchist movement that in its early stages attracted European, Russian, and Jewish immigrants.

Notoriety attended Goldman's advocacy of birth control, the poor, and antimilitarism. She engaged in public demonstrations and hunger strikes. Jailed on several occasions, she worked tirelessly for others accused of challenging the government, the law, and social norms. With Alexander Berkman, she conspired to murder company manager Henry Clay Frick during the Homestead, Pennsylvania, standoff between Carnegie Steel and the Amalgamated Association of Iron and Steel Workers in 1892. In 1901, she was blamed—but not convicted—for inciting Leon Czolgosz to assassinate President William McKinley. In 1906, she began publishing *Mother Earth*, a magazine promoting anarchy.

Although Goldman's own philosophy of anar-

Emma Goldman riding a public streetcar in 1917. (Library of Congress)

chy shifted over time, her enduring tenet was individual freedom of expression. Despite numerous struggles in America, Goldman embraced the country's essential belief in the individual. She was deported in 1919 for her antiwar efforts, but President Franklin D. Roosevelt allowed her return in 1934. She died in 1940 and was buried in Chicago.

Jennie MacDonald Lewis

FURTHER READING

Chalberg, John C. *Emma Goldman: American Individualist.* Edited by Mark C. Carnes. 2d ed. New York: Pearson Longman, 2008.

Goldman, Emma. *Red Emma Speaks: An Emma Goldman Reader.* Edited by Alix Kates Shulman. 3d ed. Amherst, N.Y.: Prometheus-Humanity Books, 1996.

SEE ALSO: Birth control movement; Deportation; Former Soviet Union immigrants; Immigration Act of 1903; Jewish immigrants; Labor unions; Red Scare; Sacco and Vanzetti trial; "Undesirable aliens"; Women's movements.

GOMPERS, SAMUEL

IDENTIFICATION: English-born American labor activist
BORN: January 27, 1850; London, England
DIED: December 13, 1924; San Antonio, Texas

SIGNIFICANCE: Undeniably one of the leading figures in labor history, Gompers was already an ardent unionist prior to leaving London for New York City in 1863. The giant union he cofounded in 1881, the American Federation of Labor, was based on the pragmatic principles he had learned in England.

At a young age, Samuel Gompers was immersed in working-class culture, toiling as an apprentice

Samuel Gompers and his wife, Sophia, in 1908. (Library of Congress)

shoemaker and cigar maker in London. Upon his arrival in the United States, he rose quickly through the ranks of union leadership and became an American citizen in 1872. His decision to immigrate was based on a desire for higher wages and freedom from European anti-Semitism, as he had been born a Jew. In 1881, he cofounded what became the American Federation of Labor (AFL) and, except for one year, served as president until his death. He rose to the rank of first vice president of the Cigar Makers' International Union in 1896.

Gompers displayed his British cultural origin by repudiating the class hatred that plagued continental unions. The beliefs he had embraced in England—for example, that union policy should be practical and nationalistic—served him well in the United States. By accepting only skilled labor, he guaranteed substantial bargaining clout. However, he strongly supported immigration restrictions because he felt that immigrants bidded down the price of labor, a view many saw as hypocritical. Also, his policies were of little use to unskilled laborers, who were excluded from the AFL.

Thomas W. Buchanan

FURTHER READING

Gompers, Samuel. *Seventy Years of Life and Labor.* 1925. Reprint. Ithaca, N.Y.: ILR Press, 1984.

Sloane, Arthur A. *Hoffa.* Cambridge, Mass.: MIT Press, 1991.

SEE ALSO: British immigrants; Davis, James John; Industrial Workers of the World; Jewish immigrants; Labor unions.

GONZÁLEZ CASE

THE EVENT: Asylum petition and legal custody battle of a young boy who dramatically escaped drowning during his mother's attempt to reach the United States on a small boat ignited a political feud

DATE: November 25, 1999-June 28, 2000

SIGNIFICANCE: What may have been the world's most closely watched custody battle became a cause célèbre that reached the U.S. Supreme Court, strained U.S.-Cuba relations, and had future political repercussions.

On Thanksgiving Day in 1999, a five-year-old Cuban boy named Elián González was found clinging to a rubber inner tube floating off the coast of South Florida. Five days earlier, the boy had left Cárdenas, Cuba, on a seventeen-foot boat with his mother and twelve others hoping to reach the United States. When the vessel sank during a storm, Elián and a young couple were the only survivors.

After the U.S. Coast Guard turned Elián over to the Immigration and Naturalization Service (INS), INS agents paroled Elián to the family of his great-uncle Lázaro González, who were living in Miami's Little Havana district. Meanwhile, Cuban president Fidel Castro charged that the boy had been "kidnaped" and demanded that he be returned to his father in Cárdenas. Castro threatened that if Elián were not returned to Cuba within seventy-two hours, he would cancel the U.S.-Cuba negotiations on migration that were scheduled to be held in Havana. Massive Cuban protest rallies were staged daily in front of the U.S. Interests Section in Havana.

U.S. President Bill Clinton's administration rejected Castro's ultimatum and declared that a Florida family court would rule on Elián's custody. However, that plan was reversed on December 9, when Deputy U.S. Attorney General Eric Holder stated that Elián's fate would be settled by the INS itself. The U.S.-Cuba migration talks were then held on December 13, as originally scheduled.

Six days afterward, the U.S. government ended a six-day hostage standoff in a Louisiana jail by secretly negotiating with Cuba to settle the deportation demands of six criminals who had arrived in Florida during the 1980 Mariel boatlift. The return of Elián was speculated to be part of the deal. Two weeks later, INS commissioner Doris Meissner rejected a political asylum petition filed on Elián's behalf and Attorney General Janet Reno upheld the right of Elián's father to have custody. The great-uncle of Elián who had received temporary custody of Elián in state court then challenged the INS ruling in federal court.

On April 12, 2000, Reno ordered the Florida relatives to surrender Elián. The family defied her and obtained an injunction keeping the boy in America. Ten days later, Reno authorized a predawn raid by 151 heavily armed federal agents who battered in the door of Elián's relatives' home and seized him. The boy was then reunited in Washing-

Havana taxi passing a public poster calling for Elián González's return to his homeland in early 2000. (AP/Wide World Photos)

ton, D.C., with his father, who had arrived in the capital city two weeks earlier.

On June 1, the Eleventh U.S. Circuit Court of Appeals ruled that the INS had acted properly in denying Elián asylum but ordered that the boy remain in the United States pending the appeal of his great-uncle's case. Three weeks later, the court reaffirmed its decision, which was challenged by the Miami family in the U.S. Supreme Court on June 26. Two days later, the Court declined to intervene, and Elián and his father immediately returned home to a hero's welcome in Cuba.

The Clinton administration's handling of the González case greatly angered the large and strongly anti-Castro Cuban American community in Florida. When Clinton's vice president, Al Gore, ran for president in November, 2000, Florida's Cuban Americans voted heavily against him. Their votes may have cost Gore the presidency. He lost narrowly, and the election hinged on Florida. Two years later, Reno ran for governor of Florida and lost in the primary.

In 2003, Elián's father, whom Castro had decorated as a national hero, won a seat in Cuba's National Assembly after running unopposed. Elián frequently appeared at political rallies with Castro, whom he called a friend and "father." A museum was dedicated to Elián in his hometown and he is portrayed on a statue in front of the U.S. Interests Section in Havana. In 2008, Elián joined Cuba's Young Communist Union.

Antonio Rafael de la Cova

FURTHER READING

De los Angeles Torres, Maria. *In the Land of Mirrors: Cuban Exile Politics in the United States.* Ann Arbor: University of Michigan Press, 1999.

Diaz, Guarione M. *The Cuban American Experience: Issues, Perceptions, and Realities.* St. Louis, Mo.: Reedy Press, 2007.

Fernandez, Alfredo A. *Adrift: The Cuban Raft People.* Houston, Tex.: Arte Público Press, 2000.

SEE ALSO: Cuban immigrants; Due process protections; Families; Florida; Immigration and Naturalization Service, U.S.; Little Havana; Mariel boatlift; Miami; Presidential elections; Supreme Court, U.S.; Washington, D.C.

GOSPEL SOCIETY

IDENTIFICATION: Christian-based support organization for Japanese immigrants
DATE: 1877-1906
LOCATION: San Francisco, California
ALSO KNOWN AS: Fukuinkai

> **SIGNIFICANCE:** Founded in San Francisco by Japanese Christian students, the Gospel Society was the first immigrant association established by Japanese in the United States. The organization played an integral part in helping many new Japanese immigrants adjust to life in America while pursuing their studies. It was also instrumental in shaping the development of Japanese Protestant Christianity.

At the end of the nineteenth century, many Japanese immigrants arrived in the San Francisco area after being told that it was possible to work and study in the area. The Gospel Society was formed by recent converts to Methodism and Congregationalism to assist these often penniless students. The first meeting place was an austere, windowless room in the basement of the Chinese Methodist Episcopal Mission in the city's Chinatown. Every Saturday night, thirty-five members assembled for Bible study and debate. For a fee of thirty-five cents per month, the society provided community support, room and board, and help with job searching. Over the years, a variety of splinter groups emerged, including a group that formed the First Japanese Presbyterian Church of San Francisco. In 1886, the group moved out of the Chinese Mission basement with the newly established Japanese Methodist Episcopal Mission. Despite the success of the Japanese Mission, the Gospel Society remained an

autonomous student residence until the great San Francisco earthquake of 1906.

Joy M. Gambill

FURTHER READING

Ichioka, Yuji. *The Issei: The World of the First Generation Japanese Immigrants, 1885-1924.* New York: Free Press, 1988.

Yoshida, Ryo. "Japanese Immigrants and Their Christian Communities in North America: A Case Study of the Fukuinkai, 1877-1896." *Japanese Journal of Religious Studies* 34, no. 1 (2007): 229-244.

SEE ALSO: California; Issei; Japanese American Citizens League; Japanese immigrants; Missionaries; Religions of immigrants; San Francisco.

GRAHAM V. RICHARDSON

THE CASE: U.S. Supreme Court decision on rights of resident noncitizens
DATE: Decided on June 14, 1971

> **SIGNIFICANCE:** The *Richardson* decision was the first in a series of rulings that struck down discriminatory state laws denying public benefits to noncitizens.

Carmen Richardson, a legally admitted resident alien, had been living in Arizona since 1956. When she became totally disabled in 1964, she applied for welfare benefits that were administered by the state with federal subsidy. Her application was denied because of an Arizona statute requiring a person either to be a citizen or to have resided in the country for fifteen years. After the district court decided in Richardson's favor, the state's commissioner of public welfare, John Graham, appealed the case to the Supreme Court. Until that time, the Court had usually upheld laws that discriminated against noncitizens.

The Supreme Court unanimously ruled that the Arizona law was unconstitutional and that Richardson was entitled to benefits. Writing the opinion for the Court, Justice Harry A. Blackmun made four major points. First, from the perspective of equal protection, alienage, like race, is a suspect classification, because aliens are a discrete and politically weak minority. As a result, all governmental discrimination based on alienage must be justified by the standard of strict scrutiny, requiring a compelling governmental interest. Second, the Arizona law was contradictory to the federal Social Security Act of 1935, and that federal law overrides state law. Third, immigrants admitted into the country had the "right to enter and abide in any state," with the same rights for public assistance as citizens. Finally, Congress possessed plenary power to establish regulations concerning the admission of immigrants into the country, and it had already put restrictions on the admissibility of paupers. The opinion left unanswered the extent to which Congress might have more discretion in distinguishing between the privileges of aliens and citizens.

Thomas Tandy Lewis

FURTHER READING

Greenhouse, Linda. *Becoming Justice Blackmun: Harry Blackmun's Supreme Court Journey.* New York: Henry Holt, 2005.

O'Brien, David M. *Constitutional Law and Politics.* 7th ed. New York: W. W. Norton, 2008.

SEE ALSO: *Bernal v. Fainter*; Citizenship; Congress, U.S.; Constitution, U.S.; Due process protections; *Foley v. Connelie*; Immigration law; *Plyler v. Doe*; Supreme Court, U.S.

GREAT DEPRESSION

THE EVENT: Severe worldwide economic downturn that intensified anti-immigrant nativism within the United States

DATE: 1929-1941

> **SIGNIFICANCE:** Immigration was a thorny issue during the Depression. Legislation was already in place barring certain ethnic groups from entering the United States, and immigration remained restricted during the era owing to economic factors. Many refugees fleeing Nazi persecution were denied entrance to the United States because of ethnic quotas.

Beginning in the 1880's, nativists, who favored the interests of native-born Americans over those of immigrants, succeeded in securing legislation that restricted immigration. The first legislation directed against a specific ethnic group, the Chinese Exclusion Act of 1882, prohibited the entry of Chinese laborers into the United States, and it was not until 1943 that the act was repealed. With the passage of the Immigration Act of 1891 and the opening of Ellis Island the following year, the federal government assumed full control over immigration, and the United States continued its restrictive immigration and naturalization policy. The Immigration Act of 1917 banned immigration from most Asian countries and introduced a literacy test for all immigrants over the age of sixteen. The Immigration Acts of 1921 and 1924 significantly limited immigration from southern and eastern Europe by assigning a quota for each nationality based on past U.S. Census data. In 1929, the year of the stock market crash that precipitated the Depression, the national origins system established by the Immigration Act of 1924 went into effect. Canadians and Latin Americans were exempt from the quota system.

MEXICAN REPATRIATION

Because the Immigration Act of 1924 specifically excluded Asian immigration, the United States turned to Mexico as its primary source of cheap labor during the late 1920's. With its proximity to the United States, Mexico supplied thousands of both legal and undocumented workers to labor on farms and ranches and in construction and mining in the Midwest and Southwest. These immigrants joined Mexican Americans, some of whom were descendants of Mexicans who had entered the United States following the Mexican War of 1846-1848. At the time of the Depression, several hundred thousand people of Mexican ancestry were living in the United States.

Rampant job losses caused by the Depression generated anti-Mexican sentiment, which had grown following World War I and had since redoubled with the massive number of Mexicans who immigrated during the mid-1920's. As the Depression deepened, government authorities determined that the expense would be less to return Mexicans to Mexico than to keep them on the welfare program.

With the cooperation of the Mexican government, the United States repatriated about one-half million Mexicans between 1929 and 1935. Some of the people sent back to Mexico were actually U.S.

More Oklahomans reach Calif. via the cotton fields of Ariz.

Dust Bowl conditions in the Plains states of the Midwest sent many poor American farmers on the road to find agricultural work in the Far West. The resulting influx of migrant American workers severely limited the number of jobs available for foreign workers. (Library of Congress)

citizens with long-established residences and others who were tricked or forced to go. Indicative of their historical pattern of immigration and deportation, Mexicans were welcomed back to the United States a decade later, when they were invited to fill the gaps in the American workforce as the United States mobilized for World War II.

ROOSEVELT ADMINISTRATION

After Franklin D. Roosevelt became president in 1933, he made no significant changes in the immigration policy he inherited from his predecessor, Herbert Hoover. In the midst of anti-immigration popular sentiment, Roosevelt supported the immigration quotas established by the Immigration Acts of 1921 and 1924 but, lacking Hoover's nativist

zeal, succeeded in drastically lowering the number of deportations. By providing relief through the New Deal, Roosevelt decreased the annual number of deportees from nearly 20,000 in 1933 to fewer than 9,000 in 1934 and maintained that number until the 1940's.

As the Depression wore on, immigration into the United States declined significantly. The average annual number of immigrants for 1931-1940 was 6,900—a mere trickle compared to the 1.2 million total for the year 1914 alone. Despite the decrease in immigration, however, public sentiment against immigrants, particularly Filipinos, continued to increase. The massive number of Filipino immigrants who arrived during the 1920's, the targets of violent attacks by U.S. citizens, continued to vex immigration restrictionists. Proclaimed by federal courts as American nationals following the Spanish-American War in 1898, when the Philippines became a U.S. colony, Filipinos entered the United States without restriction. The Tydings-McDuffie Act of 1934 provided for Philippine independence in ten years (but actually delayed until 1946) and also conferred alien status on Filipinos residing in the United States. The legislation created an annual quota of fifty immigrants per year.

During World War II, thousands of Jewish refugees fled Nazi persecution, and a number of them were refused asylum in the United States because of its restrictionist immigration policy. At the time, the United States made no distinction between immigrants and refugees; thus, both groups were subject to immigration quotas. During the early years of his administration, Roosevelt, though aware of Adolf Hitler's inhumane regime, made no effort to liberalize immigration laws, though some of his close advisers urged him to do so. Moreover, the annual German immigration quota was not being filled; according to Roosevelt's critics, the thousands of unfilled quota spaces could have been allocated to German Jewish refugees. The United States did not pursue a rescue policy for Jewish victims until 1944.

Mary G. Hurd

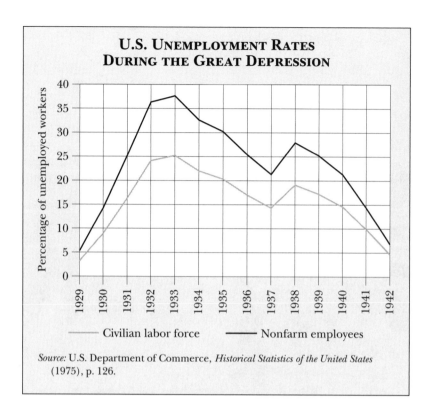

U.S. Unemployment Rates During the Great Depression

Source: U.S. Department of Commerce, *Historical Statistics of the United States* (1975), p. 126.

FURTHER READING

Chomsky, Aviva. *"They Take Our Jobs!" and Twenty Other Myths About Immigration.* Boston: Beacon Press, 2007. In debunking the most common misconceptions about immigration, Chomsky provides informative discussions on history, law, and racism.

Daniels, Roger. *Coming to America: A History of Immigration and Ethnicity in American Life.* 2d ed. New York: HarperPerennial, 2002. Daniels examines individual racial groups entering the United States, their patterns of immigration, and the reactions of U.S. citizens to these groups.

Krikorian, Mark. *The New Case Against Immigration: Both Legal and Illegal.* New York: Sentinel, 2008. Krikorian argues that since economic, societal, and even technological changes in the United States hinder the assimilation of immigrants, the United States should permanently reduce immigration.

Mills, Nicolaus, ed. *Arguing Immigration: The Debate over the Changing Face of America.* New York: Simon & Schuster, 2007. Contains a wide variety of opinions on immigration from the standpoints of politics, economics, and race and ethnicity.

Rauchway, Eric. *The Great Depression and the New Deal: A Very Short Introduction.* New York: Oxford University Press, 2008. Analyzes Roosevelt's New Deal policies to combat the Great Depression.

SEE ALSO: Anti-Filipino violence; Anti-Semitism; Asian immigrants; Bracero program; Emigration; Filipino Repatriation Act of 1935; German immigrants; Holocaust; Immigration Act of 1917; Immigration Act of 1924; Mexican deportations of 1931; Push-pull factors.

GREAT IRISH FAMINE

THE EVENT: Devastating potato blight that caused mass starvation
DATE: 1845-1852
LOCATION: Ireland

SIGNIFICANCE: One of the single-most influential events in U.S. immigration history, Ireland's great potato famine induced a massive wave of Irish emigration to Great Britain, Canada, and the United States, where Irish immigrants quickly became the nation's second-largest ethnic group. Most of the immigrants settled in the large urban centers of New York, Boston, Philadelphia, and San Francisco.

The hsitory of Irish immigration to the United States goes back well before the nineteenth century, but the Great Irish Famine that began during the late 1840's brought the greatest number of Irish immigrants to America. Before the famine began, Ireland was already a desperately poor country. The only European country controlled by another country, it had been ruled by Great Britain for many centuries. Ireland had virtually no significant manufacturing sector. Most Irish were farmers who worked tiny plots of land, paying stiff rents to British landlords and living in primitive mud and stone huts.

By 1844, Ireland's population had swelled to 8.4 million, most of whom had lives built around potatoes. In 1845, the Phytophthora fungus, believed to have arrived from America, infected Ireland's potato crops and quickly spread throughout the country. Great Britain's response was minimal, but as the fungus ravaged the crops every year, successive British governments determined that providing aid to the Irish would only create greater dependency. By 1851, British neglect had contributed to the deaths of 1.1 million people who perished from starvation or from famine-related diseases. Meanwhile, another 1.5 million Irish people were immigrating to North America and England.

ARRIVAL IN AMERICA

Most refugees from Ireland's famine arrived in the United States nearly destitute. They settled in cities, where they had few skills needed in the industralizing urban economies. About 650,000 Irish immigrants arrived in New York alone. Because of their outdated clothing and distinctive accents, they were easily identified and made victims of various unscrupulous schemes. Landlords promising comfortable rooms left them in overcrowded, vermin-infested tenements. Others, promising railroad and boat passage to other parts of the nation, sold them phony tickets.

The immigrants took whatever unskilled jobs they could find, working on the docks, pushing carts, or digging canals and laboring on the railroads. Their lives were so harsh that their mortality rates remained high. For example, 60 percent of children born to Irish immigrants in Boston died before the age of six. Adult immigrants lived an average of only six years after their arrival in the United States. When these immigrants arrived, they were a comparatively docile and law-abiding population. However, many of them turned to crime out of boredom, desperation, and anger. Young Irish immigrants in New York City formed criminal gangs, and the area known as Five Points became a cauldron of all manner of criminal activity.

IRISH STEREOTYPES

Invidious stereotypes of the Irish were quickly imported from Britain. Cartoons on both sides of the Atlantic depicted the Irish as brutish, simian, bellicose, and always drunk. With employment opportunities limited, the Irish turned to crime and drink, which only exacerbated the public perception of them as troublemakers and public scourges. As suspicions increased, a common sentiment was expressed in the "No Irish Need Apply" signs that limited their economic and social opportunities.

In an overwhelmingly Protestant country, the Roman Catholic Irish were further reviled. During the 1850's, such prejudice was institutionalized in the creation of the Know-Nothing Party, a nativist political group that sought to curb immigration and the spread of Roman Catholicism. The party's largest victory came in 1854, when it elected candidates to every state office in Massachusetts.

With the outbreak of the U.S. Civil War, many Irish immigrants served valiantly in both armies; however, because of their tenuous social position, many Irish were targets for military conscription. Resentment of such practices erupted in 1863 in the New York draft riots, when Irish created a major civil disruption over having to fight in a war to free slaves whom they regarded as competition for the few jobs the Irish could secure.

The Irish also imported some of their secret societies that were established to undermine British rule in their homeland. One of these was the Molly Maguires, who were active in the coalfields of Pennsylvania during the 1870's. They were alleged to have used coercion and intimidation against owners and other miners; historians, however, disagree on the extent of their criminality.

ASSIMILATION

Fearing discrimination and abuse, the Irish banded together in their parishes and led major efforts to build churches, parochial schools, and major private universities where they and their children felt comfortable. Catholicism, a minor religion before the arrival of the Irish, grew to become the largest single denomination by the early twentieth century, and much of that growth and visibility was due to the devotion of the Irish.

Systematically marginalized by a hostile culture, the Irish quickly realized that citizenship and their vote were among their most powerful weapons. The Irish understood the efficacy of ward politics, starting small and local and eventually taking over city halls and state governments. The Irish were also eager to take civil service jobs that offered relative security. There were certainly abuses, the most egregious being the Tammany Hall corruption in New York, but the Irish soon dominated Massachusetts politics, the apogee of which came with the election of John F. Kennedy to the presidency in 1960 and the creation of the closest thing to a political dynasty in the United States. In the twenty-first century, the Irish can be found in all professions and are among the most successful ethnic groups in America.

David W. Madden

As this 1880 cover of Harper's Weekly *shows, the problem of insufficient food continued to afflict Ireland well after the great potato blight.* (Library of Congress)

FURTHER READING

Gribben, Arthur, ed. *The Great Famine and the Irish Diaspora in America.* Amherst: University of Massachusetts Press, 1999. A collection of twelve essays commemorating the 150th anniversary of the famine that considers life in Ireland, historical perceptions of the events, and the creation of the Irish American identity.

Laxton, Edward. *The Famine Ships: The Irish Exodus to America.* New York: Henry Holt, 1996. A careful, detailed history of the often unseaworthy "coffin ships" that transported destitute Irish to Canada and America.

Miller, Kerby. *Emigrants and Exiles: Ireland and the Irish Exodus to North America.* New York: Oxford University Press, 1985. The most authoritative study of Irish immigration to Canada and America and the ways in which the displaced transplanted their culture to the New World.

Miller, Kerby, and Paul Wagner. *Out of Ireland: The Story of Irish Emigration to America.* Washington, D.C.: Elliott & Clark, 1994. A photoessay companion to the 1995 PBS documentary of the same name that considers not only the famine but also the entire experience of Irish immigration to America.

Woodham-Smith, Cecil. *The Great Hunger: Ireland, 1845-1849.* London: Penguin Books, 1991. One of the most authoritative histories of the causes and results of the famine, considering its political, economic, and social consequences.

SEE ALSO: Anti-Catholicism; California gold rush; Canada vs. United States as immigrant destinations; Fenian movement; History of immigration, 1783-1891; Irish immigrants; Molly Maguires; Natural disasters as push-pull factors; New York City; Push-pull factors.

GREEK IMMIGRANTS

SIGNIFICANCE: Although Greeks have accounted for a relatively small percentage of the total immigrants to the United States, they have formed strong ethnic communities that have kept alive their language, traditions, and religion. Persons of Greek ancestry account for 0.4 percent of the current population of the United States.

Significant numbers of Greeks did not begin immigrating to the United States until the 1880's. However, the first Greek immigrants arrived during the 1820's, when the Greek war of independence from the Ottoman Empire left Greece with a large foreign debt, and the lack of industrialization forced inhabitants to look elsewhere for employment.

After the Turks captured Constantinople in 1453, Greece became part of the Ottoman Empire.

PROFILE OF GREEK IMMIGRANTS

Country of origin	Greece
Primary language	Greek
Primary regions of U.S. settlement	East Coast states, Midwest
Earliest significant arrivals	1824
Peak immigration periods	1900-1917, 1970's
Twenty-first century legal residents*	7,429 (929 per year)

*Immigrants who obtained legal permanent resident status in the United States.
Source: Department of Homeland Security, *Yearbook of Immigration Statistics, 2008.*

Inspired by the late eighteenth century revolutions in North America and western Europe, as well as their own sense of Greek nationalism, a group of Greek loyalists planned a rebellion against the Ottoman state. They gained the support of numerous countries, including Great Britain, France, and Russia. Greece became an independent nation after signing the Treaty of Adrianople in 1832.

IMMIGRATION BEGINS

Following the end of its war of independence, Greece faced a number of internal economic challenges. The country was slow to industrialize through the nineteenth century. As late as 1879, more than 80 percent of its people still lived in rural communities. Currants were Greece's chief export product, and their price declined so much that many Greek farmers went bankrupt and were unable to pay their taxes. This poor economic climate prompted many Greeks to emigrate.

With the encouragement of the Greek government, young men began leaving the country during the late nineteenth century in the hope of gaining employment in the United States. Large-scale Greek immigration to the United States began in 1880, with the largest numbers immigrating during the early twentieth century. Between 1900 and 1920, more than 350,000 Greeks immigrated to the United States. About 95 percent of the immigrants who came between 1899 and 1910 were men. In

Emigrants boarding small boats in Patras, Greece, on their way to the steamship that will take them to America in 1910. (Library of Congress)

keeping with Greek tradition, these men often worked to secure dowries for their sisters back home. In 1905 alone, Greek immigrants remitted more than four million dollars to their families in Greece. Most did not intend to stay in the United States.

GREEKS IN THE UNITED STATES

Upon arriving in the United States, most Greek immigrants found jobs in various industries. In New England, for example, they worked in textile mills. A particularly large Greek community formed in Lowell, Massachusetts, where many Greek men worked in the mill. In Utah and Colorado, Greeks found work in copper and coal mines. In California they worked in railroad gangs. Many were victimized by *padrones*, labor brokers who recruited immigrants for jobs in exchange for the immigrants' wages.

Around the turn of the twentieth century, Greek immigrants began going into business for themselves. They opened shoeshine parlors, candy shops, and, most notably, restaurants. Their first restaurants served native cuisine to fellow Greeks.

In Chicago, some moved into the lunch business, working from street carts that sold inexpensive fare to factory workers. After the Chicago city council banned the sale of food on city streets, the immigrants turned to opening permanent establishments. Using mainly family members for labor and requiring little start-up money, the restaurant business was the first stable economic base for Greeks in America. By 1919, one of every three restaurants in Chicago was operated by a Greek.

A major unifying force for the Greek community in America was the church. The first Greek Orthodox Church in the United States, the Holy Trinity of New Orleans, was founded in 1864. By 1918, nearly 130 Orthodox churches had been founded across the country. Local community organizations called *kinotis* raised the necessary funds to establish the churches. Many Greeks sought the close-knit communities they had in their home country, and the churches provided the immigrants with forums in which to share their common beliefs. During the early twenty-first century, Greek Orthodox churches have continued to serve as cultural and social centers for many Greek communities within the United States.

LATE TWENTIETH CENTURY IMMIGRATION

Prior to 1965, the United States had established quotas restricting immigration from certain countries and ethnic groups. The quotas favored immigrants from northern and western European countries. The Immigration Act of 1924 had imposed harsh restrictions on non-western European immigrant groups. Under that law, only one hundred Greeks per year were allowed entry into the United States.

In 1965, the Democratic-controlled U.S. Congress passed the Immigration and Nationality Act. Whereas previous immigration acts had imposed quotas by country, the 1965 act established hemispheric quotas, and distributed visas based on job skills and family reunification. Many Greek Americans used the new law to bring members of their families to the United States. Between 1960 and 1980, more than 170,000 Greeks immigrated to the United States, many with family reunification visas.

During the first decade of the twenty-first century, approximately 1.4 million persons of Greek ancestry were living in the United States. They resided in all fifty states, with the greatest numbers living in large cities such as Chicago, New York City, and Detroit. Many Greek immigrants have assimilated into American culture, but have remained strongly connected to Greek traditions, religion, and ethnicity.

Bethany E. Pierce

FURTHER READING

Contopoulos, Michael. *The Greek Community of New York City: Early Years to 1910.* New Rochelle, N.Y.: Aristide D. Caratzas, 1992. History of one of the largest concentrations of Greek immigrants in any American city.

Moskos, Charles. *Greek Americans: Struggle and Success.* 2d ed. New Brunswick, N.J.: Transaction Publishers, 1989. Scholarly study of Greeks in America through the 1980's.

Orfanos, Spyros D., ed. *Reading Greek America: Studies in the Experience of Greeks in the United States.* New York: Pella, 2002. Collection of essays examining a variety of issues surrounding Greek immigrants.

Saloutos, Theodore. *The Greeks in the United States.* Rev. ed. New York: Greekworks.com, 2007. Comprehensive study of Greek immigrants. Includes an introduction by Charles Moskos, and historiographical essay by Alexander Kitroeff.

Scourby, Alice. *The Greek Americans.* Boston: Twayne, 1984. Broad study of Greek Americans with background information on Greek history, several chapters on immigrants, and a chapter on changes in Greek American family structures.

SEE ALSO: Congress, U.S.; Economic opportunities; History of immigration after 1891; Huffington, Arianna; Immigration Act of 1921; Immigra-

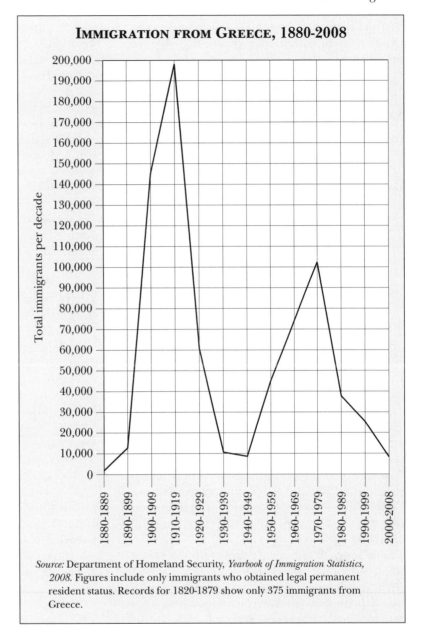

IMMIGRATION FROM GREECE, 1880-2008

Source: Department of Homeland Security, *Yearbook of Immigration Statistics, 2008.* Figures include only immigrants who obtained legal permanent resident status. Records for 1820-1879 show only 375 immigrants from Greece.

tion and Nationality Act of 1965; Italian immigrants; Quota systems; Turkish immigrants; Yugoslav state immigrants.

GREEN CARD

IDENTIFICATION: Film, written by Peter Weir, about a French immigrant to the United States who enters into a marriage of convenience

DATE: Released in 1990

SIGNIFICANCE: *Green Card* tells the story of an American woman and a French immigrant living in New York City who enter into a marriage of convenience for different reasons. Complications develop when Immigration and Naturalization Service agents seek evidence that their marriage has been undertaken solely to enable the immigrant husband to obtain his green card.

Green Card opens by introducing a young American woman named Brontë (Andie MacDowell) who cannot obtain a lease on an upscale New York apartment unless she is married. At the same time, a French waiter named Georges (Gérard Depardieu) who needs a green card to work in the United States and become a citizen seeks an American wife so he can get that card. After a mutual friend brings Georges and Brontë together, the couple get married and then say goodbye to each other immediately after the ceremony.

The amicably estranged couple's troubles begin when two Immigration and Naturalization Service (INS) inspectors randomly, it is presumed, investigate them to determine whether they have satisfied the immigration laws concerning the green card and their lawful permanent residence. Audiences unaware of federal immigration regulations might see these government agents as intruders. However, the film makes it clear that the INS is obligated to investigate green card petitioners to deter fraudulent behavior.

As nearly a year passes by, both characters go through changes in their lives as they come together to learn more about each other's habits and behaviors so they can make the INS inspectors think they have entered their marriage in good faith. Each of them must provide, as the law states,

general and specific supporting evidence that Georges's obtaining of his green card has not been fraudulent, and they must have a common residence. The rest of the film shows them trying to learn about each other. As they grow closer, they behave more deceitfully toward their friends and relatives. Georges knows, and the audience learns, that his ability to obtain permanent resident status can be lost if they are found out—and the law allows for his immediate removal from the United States and the possibility of his being permanently banned. Eventually, the government deports Georges. However, love wins out as the film ends, as Brontë prepares to go to France to join her husband, who is waiting for her.

James F. O'Neil

FURTHER READING

Bray, Ilona M. *Fiancé and Marriage Visas: A Couple's Guide to U.S. Immigration.* 5th ed. Berkeley, Calif.: Nolo, 2008.

Gania, Edwin T. *U.S. Immigration Step by Step.* 3d ed. Naperville, Ill.: Sphinx; Sourcebooks, 2006.

Motomura, Hiroshi. *Americans in Waiting: The Lost Story of Immigration and Citizenship in the United States.* New York: Oxford University Press, 2006.

Wernick, Allan. *U.S. Immigration and Citizenship: Your Complete Guide.* 4th ed. Cincinnati: Emmis Books, 2004.

SEE ALSO: Citizenship and Immigration Services, U.S.; Deportation; Films; French immigrants; Green cards; Immigration law; Intermarriage; Marriage; "Marriages of convenience"; Resident aliens; Yugoslav state immigrants.

GREEN CARDS

DEFINITION: Identification cards issued by the federal government to aliens who qualify for permanent resident status and therefore have the right to live and work in the United States for indefinite periods

SIGNIFICANCE: Immigrants without green cards have no legal right to reside permanently or to work in the United States. In addition to facing possible criminal charges and deportation by the federal government, undocumented aliens who attempt to work in the country are vulnerable to abuse from their employers and other unscrupulous persons because they cannot seek redress from the U.S. legal system.

Every alien who resides in the United States must be registered with the U.S. government, and those who wish to reside permanently are legally required to obtain green cards. Not every alien who applies for a green card receives one. The U.S. Congress decided that a highly skilled immigrant workforce is needed to sustain the nation's economic progress and gave priority status to immigrants with exceptional talents, such as acclaimed actors, musicians, and painters. Immigrants with advanced academic degrees also receive priority.

Immigrants who qualify as priority workers are not required to go through the complicated and time-consuming procedure of obtaining labor certification to obtain their green cards. Formal certification procedures require prospective employers of applicants to demonstrate that no Americans or already established permanent residents are ready, willing, and able to take the jobs offered to the new immigrants at the wages that prevail. Labor certification is designed to guarantee that the employment of new immigrants will not adversely affect the wages and working conditions of workers who are already resident in the areas in which the jobs are performed.

Green Card Fraud

U.S. Citizenship and Immigration Services imposes requirements for immigrants not applied to U.S. citizens because immigrants lack the protections of American citizenship. Aliens over the age of eighteen who are permanent residents must at all times carry valid green cards or risk being found guilty of a misdemeanor. Immigrants who leave the United States for periods of more than six months risk losing their green cards on the principle that long absences from the country may betray lack of interest in residing in the United States. Immigrants can also lose their green cards by failing to report changes of address or for committing crimes.

Immigrants can obtain green cards by marrying American citizens or permanent residents. One of the best-known provisions of immigration law, this principle has often led to abuses. During the early 1980's, the Immigration and Naturalization Service reported that as many as one-half of all petitions for green cards based on marriages were fraudulent, as they were entered into solely for the purpose of obtaining green cards. In 1986, Congress responded to these concerns by passing the Immigration Marriage Fraud Amendments to eliminate as many "paper marriages," or "marriages of convenience," as possible. American citizens and permanent residents who conspire with would-be immigrants to evade immigration laws by means of fraudulent marriages can be charged with federal crimes. Permanent residents convicted of this crime can be deported. Both permanent residents and U.S. citizens convicted of the crime can serve jail time, be fined, or both. Immigrants who are proven guilty of fraud permanently lose all chance of ever living legally in the United States.

When applications for new or renewed permanent resident cards are denied, applicants are sent letters detailing the reasons. Immigrants cannot appeal negative decisions. They can, however, submit motions to have their denials reconsidered when new facts can be presented or their denials can be shown to have been based on incorrect applications of law or immigration policy.

Obtaining Green Cards

A primary goal of U.S. immigration law is to help keep immigrant families together. Consequently,

---

Why Green?

Despite their popular name, "green cards" have not always been green. Officially known as Alien Registration Receipt Cards, they were first introduced during the 1940's, when the federal government issued them on green plastic. During the 1960's and 1970's, however, the government issued the cards on blue stock. During the 1980's, the cards became white stock, and during the 1990's they were pink.

Through all these color changes, the cards have always included their owners' photographs, federal registration numbers, dates of birth, and ports of entry into the United States. The cards are generally issued for periods of ten years, but they can be renewed indefinitely.

immediate relatives of American citizens are guaranteed green cards. Immigrants who overstay their visas or work without authorization can still qualify for green cards if they are the minor children of legal residents or the parents of adult American citizens. Classes of immigrants who cannot qualify for green cards after they are in the United States include stowaways, aliens who have failed to follow deportation orders, or those who have failed to appear at scheduled removal proceedings or asylum interviews.

The federal Immigration Act of 1990 permitted a total of 675,000 immigrants to obtain green cards each year, and each individual country can send up to 25,620 immigrants to the United States. Demand for visas in some countries, notably Mexico and the Philippines, typically greatly exceeds supply, requiring applicants from those countries to wait for years to obtain immigration documents from the United States.

Each year, the U.S. State Department conducts a free Diversity Visa lottery that is also known as the "green card lottery" to distribute applications randomly for 50,000 green cards. Winners of the lottery are given the opportunity to apply for visas but no guarantees that they will receive them. Lottery entrants must be from eligible countries—which

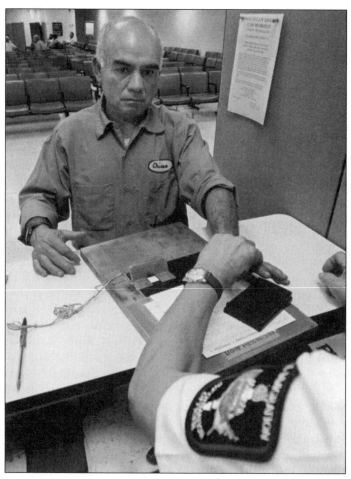

Salvadoran immigrant being fingerprinted by a Los Angeles Immigration and Naturalization Service officer while renewing his green card in 1999. (AP/Wide World Photos)

vary from year to year—and have at least twelve years of education or two years of skilled work experience. The lotteries have become the targets of scam artists who claim that they can increase would-be immigrants' chances of winning the lottery for a price.

Caryn E. Neumann

FURTHER READING

Anosike, Benji O. *How to Obtain Your U.S. Immigration Visa for a Temporary Stay: The Non-Immigrant Visa Kit.* Newark, N.J.: Do-It-Yourself Legal Publishers, 2003. Detailed, practical manual explaining almost every imaginable procedure in obtaining documentation to immigrate legally.

Bray, Ilona M. *Fiancé and Marriage Visas: A Cou-ple's Guide to U.S. Immigration.* 5th ed. Berkeley, Calif.: Nolo, 2008. How-to book that provides a good, easy-to-follow guide to immigration policies on marriage issues, including the awarding of green cards.

Cortes, Luis, Jr. *A Simple Guide to U.S. Immigration and Citizenship.* New York: Atria Books, 2008. Useful and up-to-date manual for immigrants working to become U.S. citizens.

Farrell, Mary H. J. "For Immigrants Trying to Obtain the Coveted Green Card, Marriage May Be a Treacherous Strategy." *People Weekly,* February 25, 1991, 93-96. Interesting article on legitimate and fraudulent marriages entered into for the purpose of obtaining green cards.

Lewis, Loida Nicolas. *How to Get a Green Card: Legal*

Ways to Stay in the U.S.A. 6th ed. Berkeley, Calif.: Nolo, 2005. Practical handbook offering step-by-step guidance on obtaining green cards.

SEE ALSO: Deportation; Due process protections; Employment; Families; Illegal immigration; Immigration and Naturalization Service, U.S.; Immigration law; "Marriages of convenience"; Passports; Permanent resident status; Resident aliens.

GRESHAM-YANG TREATY OF 1894

THE LAW: U.S.-Chinese agreement that suspended immigration of Chinese laborers to the United States for ten years but allowed conditional readmission of immigrants who were visiting China
DATE: Signed on December 7, 1894
ALSO KNOWN AS: Sino-American Treaty of 1894

SIGNIFICANCE: The Gresham-Yang Treaty did away with the terms of the Scott Act of 1888 and placed exclusion and registration laws passed since 1882 on a proper treaty basis. Proposed renewal of the treaty caused China to call for a boycott of American goods and the U.S. Congress to extend exclusion indefinitely.

The Scott Act of 1888 excluded virtually all Chinese from entering the United States, including those who had traveled from the United States to visit China. It was superseded in 1894 by the Gresham-Yang Treaty, which stipulated total prohibition of immigration of Chinese workers into the United States for the next ten years, with the promise that immigrants who were visiting China could be readmitted. Readmission was allowed only if returning Chinese immigrants had family living in America or property or debts owed to them of at least one thousand dollars. The treaty exempted Chinese officials, students, and merchants.

In 1904, China refused to renew the Gresham-Yang Treaty and asked to negotiate a less harsh agreement. Chinese merchants called for a boycott of American goods. Unrest over the mistreatment of Chinese immigrants in America changed the political landscape in China by fueling political participation of the Chinese populace. The administrations of U.S. presidents William McKinley and Theodore Roosevelt showed little concern over China's repeated protests and warnings. When China denounced the Gresham-Yang Treaty in 1904, the U.S. Congress extended exclusion indefinitely.

Alvin K. Benson

FURTHER READING
Cassel, Susie Lan, ed. *The Chinese in America: A History from Gold Mountain to the New Millennium.* Walnut Creek, Calif.: AltaMira Press, 2002.
Lee, Erika. *At America's Gates: Immigration During the Exclusion Era, 1882-1943.* Chapel Hill: University of North Carolina Press, 2007.

SEE ALSO: Alien Contract Labor Law of 1885; Anti-Chinese movement; Burlingame Treaty of 1868; Chinese Exclusion Act of 1882; *Chinese Exclusion Cases*; Chinese immigrants; Contract labor system; Geary Act of 1892; McCreary Amendment of 1893; Taiwanese immigrants.

GROVE, ANDREW

IDENTIFICATION: Hungarian-born chief executive officer of Intel
BORN: September 2, 1936; Budapest, Hungary

SIGNIFICANCE: The third person hired by the cofounders of the Intel Corporation, the Hungarian-born Grove rose relatively quickly to the company's top management position.

Born in Hungary's capital city, Budapest, András Gróf grew up in the town of Bácsalmás near the border with present-day Serbia. His early childhood was darkened by the virulent anti-Semitism of Nazi Germany, then the "liberation" by the Soviet Union that quickly turned into an oppressive regime. When he was four, he contracted scarlet fever and lost most of his hearing.

After Hungary's failed uprising against the Soviet Union in 1956, the twenty-year-old Gróf fled to the United States, where he Americanized his surname to Grove. He earned a doctorate in chemical engineering from the University of California in

Berkeley in 1963 and was subsequently hired at Fairchild Semiconductor by Robert Norton Noyce, whom he followed to the microchip maker Intel. Grove often collided with Noyce's personnel policy, which he considered excessively liberal, and he eventually took over the day-to-day managerial functions, driving his employees hard but winning their respect because he drove himself just as hard. From 1987 to 1998, he served as Intel's chief executive officer, and from 1979 to 1997 he served as president. After nominally retiring from Intel, he continued to advise the company and remained a respected figure throughout Silicon Valley.

Leigh Husband Kimmel

FURTHER READING

Jackson, Tim. *Inside Intel: Andy Grove and the Rise of the World's Most Powerful Chip Company.* New York: Dutton, 1997.

Tedlow, Richard S. *Andy Grove: The Life and Times of an American.* New York: Portfolio, 2006.

Yu, Albert. *Creating the Digital Future: The Secrets of Consistent Innovation at Intel.* New York: Free Press, 1998.

SEE ALSO: Hungarian immigrants; Jewish immigrants; *A Nation of Immigrants*; Pulitzer, Joseph; Railroads; Religion as a push-pull factor; Tesla, Nikola.

GUATEMALAN IMMIGRANTS

SIGNIFICANCE: Civil war, natural disasters, and economic hardships combined to cause Guatemalan immigration to the United States to begin a rise during the 1960's that has continued to grow into the twenty-first century. Guatemalans have become the second-largest Central American immigrant community after Salvadorans.

Before 1930, the U.S. Census did not break down Central American immigration by countries, but in any case, overall immigration from that region was small. According to the U.S. Census, only 423 Guatemalans were formally admitted into the United States during the 1930's. The number of Guatemalan immigrants remained low until the 1960's, when a significant increase began to occur. The

PROFILE OF GUATEMALAN IMMIGRANTS	
Country of origin	Guatemala
Primary language	Spanish
Primary regions of U.S. settlement	California, Texas, Illinois, New York, Florida, Washington, D.C.
Earliest significant arrivals	Early twentieth century
Peak immigration period	1980's-2008
Twenty-first century legal residents*	138,021 (17,253 per year)

*Immigrants who obtained legal permanent resident status in the United States.

Source: Department of Homeland Security, *Yearbook of Immigration Statistics, 2008.*

majority of Guatemalan immigrants have arrived in the United States since the mid-1980's.

During the 1980's, the number of Guatemalans granted legal permanent resident status reached almost 60,000, continuing a growth pattern that started during the 1960's. The numbers of immigrants have continued to rise, with 145,111 Guatemalans granted legal permanent resident status between 2000 and 2008. The 2000 U.S. Census listed the total number of Guatemalan immigrants living in the United States as 480,665. Of that number, 111,375 were naturalized U.S. citizens and 369,290 were listed as "not a U.S. citizen." However, these numbers tell only a part of the story, as the majority of Guatemalan immigrants are undocumented aliens. The number of actual Guatemalan immigrants in the United States in 2008 was estimated to be as high as 1.3 million people.

PUSH-PULL FACTORS

Factors that have contributed to Guatemalan immigration into the United States have included Central American civil unrest, natural disasters, and economic problems. A thirty-six-year civil war began in Guatemala in 1960, when the right-wing military rose up against the increasingly liberal government. The war left thousands dead and drove tens of thousands to flee to Mexico and the United States. During the 1980's, Guatemala's indigenous communities endured the worst of the war's violence, as they were suspected by the military of aiding the rebel forces. Because the U.S. government backed the right-wing Guatemalan leaders, it denied personal petitions for political asylum from Guatemalans during that period. The refusal to grant protected status prompted some religious groups in the United States to form the Sanctuary movement, an activist movement that aided undocumented immigrants from Guatemala and El Salvador.

A series of natural disasters in Guatemala left thousands of families without homes, land, or work, driving many of them to emigrate. In 1976, an earthquake destroyed much of Guatemala City and its environs, leaving 26,000 dead, 76,000 injured, and thousands more homeless. In 2005, Hurricane Stan caused torrential rain and mudslides that killed as many as 2,000 people in Guatemala and devastated entire villages.

A low standard of living, poor health care, and unfair land distribution have all contributed to Guatemalan immigration to the United States. Guatemala has the highest infant and child mortality rate, the lowest life expectancy, and the worst malnutrition problem in Central America. During the early twenty-first century, more than 60 percent of Guatemala's people were living in poverty. The majority of the adult working population were engaged in migrant farm labor for the coffee, sugar, and cotton plantations.

For Guatemalans attempting to emigrate to the United States, the journey north is difficult, dangerous, and expensive. Fees for guides facilitating illegal entry into the United States can be as high as fifteen hundred U.S. dollars. Rape, robbery, injury, and death are some of the dangers in migrating north.

TRANSNATIONAL GUATEMALAN IMMIGRANT COMMUNITIES

The largest Guatemalan immigrant community in the United States is in Los Angeles; it is estimated at more than 100,000 people. Other large Guatemalan immigrant communities have arisen in Houston, Chicago, New York City, Washington, D.C., southern Florida, San Francisco, Miami, New Orleans, and the Phoenix-Tucson area in Arizona. These communities tend to be transnational; as their members work to create new lives for themselves in the United States, they continued to maintain ties with their home communities. Many Guatemalan immigrants send financial remittances to relatives in their Guatemalan hometowns that constitute a substantial portion of the latters' incomes. In 2005, immigrants sent more than $3 billion to relatives in Guatemala.

A special problem arising from Guatemalan immigration has been the spread of gang culture from the United States to Guatemala. Beginning during the 1990's the U.S. government began targeting undocumented immigrants in the penal system for deportation. Many of these deportees have been in the United States so long that they have no memory of having lived in Guatemala. After they return to their original homeland, they tend to continue their criminal activities.

Elizabeth Ellen Cramer

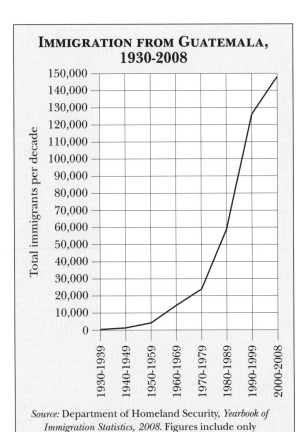

IMMIGRATION FROM GUATEMALA, 1930-2008

Source: Department of Homeland Security, *Yearbook of Immigration Statistics, 2008.* Figures include only immigrants who obtained legal permanent resident status.

FURTHER READING

Bacon, David. *Communities Without Borders: Images and Voices from the World of Migration.* Ithaca, N.Y.: ILR Press, 2006. Through candid photos and oral histories, this book tells the story of transnational communities made up of Guatemalan and Mexican migrants and of their struggles for better working conditions, improved health care, and the retention of their cultures.

Fink, Leon, and Alvis E. Dunn. *The Maya of Morganton: Work and Community in the Nuevo New South.* Chapel Hill: University of North Carolina Press, 2003. Study of how indigenous Guatemalan Mayans have battled unfair labor practices in the poultry plants of their new home in North Carolina.

Foxen, Patricia. *In Search of Providence: Transnational Mayan Identities.* Nashville, Tenn.: Vanderbilt University Press, 2007. Tells the story of a community of the K'iche Mayan Indians—members of the largest indigenous group in Guatemala—who have settled in Providence, Rhode Island.

Hamilton, Nora. *Seeking Community in a Global City: Guatemalans and Salvadorans in Los Angeles.* Philadelphia: Temple University Press, 2001. Drawing on her twenty years of work with the Central American community in Los Angeles, Hamilton tells of the immigrants' experiences with war and poverty in their homelands and of the creation of their new home in the United States.

Stolen, Kristi Anne. *Guatemalans in the Aftermath of Violence: The Refugees' Return.* Philadelphia: University of Pennsylvania Press, 2007. Looks at Guatemalan immigration patterns in the aftermath of the Civil War.

SEE ALSO: El Rescate; History of immigration after 1891; Honduran immigrants; Immigration lawyers; Latin American immigrants; Push-pull factors; Refugees; Salvadoran immigrants; Sanctuary movement.

GUEST-WORKER PROGRAMS

DEFINITION: Government-sponsored programs permitting the temporary importation of workers in specific occupations

SIGNIFICANCE: Guest-worker programs in the United States, such as the mid-century bracero program, have often met with controversy due to variable labor conditions and their perceived effect on American wages and job availability.

Guest-worker programs import laborers from other countries into the United States for temporary employment. Early variants of such programs included indentured servitude during the colonial period, when European immigrant workers agreed to fixed terms of labor in exchange for transportation and other costs. The recruiting of Chinese railroad workers and other forms of contract labor during the mid-nineteenth century were also forms of indentured servitude; they were eventually outlawed by the Foran Act of 1885. Another form of indentured servitude was the nineteenth century Italian *padrone* system, which was facilitated by labor contractors with transatlantic ties. These early forms of indentured servitude did not always require that the laborers return to their home countries at the end of their terms of service, but many indentured laborers did.

The best-known guest-worker arrangement in the United States was the bracero program, which imported millions of Mexican agricultural laborers between 1942 and 1964. The imposition of this program required the repeal of the Foran Act, but growers' associations successfully convinced the U.S. Congress that manpower shortages during World War II required new sources of farm labor. The program ended in 1964 amid increased scrutiny by labor regulators and in face of competition from the widespread mechanization of agricultural work.

During the early twenty-first century, President George W. Bush's proposal to expand guest-worker programs met with significant criticism across the political spectrum. As late as 2009, the United States continued to maintain limited guest-worker programs for agricultural, low-skilled, and skilled labor, through the issuance of "H" type temporary work visas.

Sarah Bridger

FURTHER READING
Bustamante, Jorge, Clark Reynolds, and Raul Hinojosa Ojeda. *U.S.-Mexico Relations: Labor Market Interdependence.* Stanford, Calif.: Stanford University Press, 1992.
Griffith, David. *American Guestworkers: Jamaicans and Mexicans in the U.S. Labor Market.* University Park: Pennsylvania State University Press, 2006.
Jordan, Don. *White Cargo: The Forgotten History of Britain's White Slaves in America.* New York: New York University Press, 2008.
Ngai, Mae M. *Impossible Subjects: Illegal Aliens and the Making of Modern America.* Princeton, N.J.: Princeton University Press, 2004.

SEE ALSO: Alien Contract Labor Law of 1885; Bracero program; Contract labor system; Economic consequences of immigration; Employment; Farm and migrant workers; Federation for American Immigration Reform; Indentured servitude; Mexican immigrants.

Meyer Guggenheim. (The Granger Collection, New York)

GUGGENHEIM, MEYER

IDENTIFICATION: Swiss-born American industrialist
BORN: February 1, 1828; Lengnau, Switzerland
DIED: March 15, 1905; Palm Beach, Florida

SIGNIFICANCE: Originally an impoverished Jewish peddler from Switzerland, Guggenheim built a worldwide mining conglomerate after immigrating to the United States.

Born during the early nineteenth century in a Jewish ghetto in the Aargau canton of Switzerland, Meyer Guggenheim worked as a traveling peddler in Switzerland and Germany. In 1848, Guggenheim immigrated to the United States at the age of twenty and settled in Philadelphia. In 1854, he married Barbara Meyers, whom he had met on the Atlantic voyage; they would have ten children.

Guggenheim's remarkable rise in the world of industry bore several marks of his immigrant background. His success as a peddler of stove polish and instant coffee to Pennsylvania Dutch miners and farmers was helped by his native command of German. After acquiring capital through his grocery store, lye factory, and railroad speculation, Guggenheim relied on Swiss relatives to supply imported laces and embroideries at great profit. Free from the restrictions he faced as a Jew in Europe, Guggenheim tenaciously built an American business dynasty. He groomed his seven sons to advance his enterprises, sending them to schools in Zurich and Paris. Upon their return, he formed M. Guggenheim's Sons in 1877, giving each son an equal share in the partnership.

Guggenheim acquired silver mines and smelting operations in Colorado, expanding into Monterrey, Mexico, in 1890. By the turn of the century, M. Guggenheim's Sons dominated the American Smelting and Refining Trust and mining interests worldwide. Soon the Guggenheims relocated to mansions in New York City. Meyer Guggenheim died in 1905. The philanthropy that his descendants pursued during the twentieth century reflected Guggenheim's cosmopolitan perspective and determination to make a permanent legacy in his adopted country.

Howard Bromberg

FURTHER READING

Davis, John H. *The Guggenheims (1848-1988): An American Epic.* New York: Shapolsky, 1988.

Unger, Irwin, and Debi Unger. *The Guggenheims: A Family History.* New York: HarperCollins, 2005.

SEE ALSO: Anti-Semitism; Family businesses; Jewish immigrants; Marriage; New York City; Pennsylvania; Philadelphia; Swiss immigrants.

H

HAITIAN BOAT PEOPLE

THE EVENT: Attempts by Haitian asylum seekers to reach the United States on small boats
DATE: Late 1970's to early twenty-first century
LOCATION: Waters off the coast of South Florida

> **SIGNIFICANCE:** Defining the Haitian boat people as economic rather than political refugees allowed the United States to refuse asylum to thousands of Haitians and raised serious questions about human rights standards and treatment of refugees in the United States.

Large-scale Haitian immigration to the United States began during the 1970's when Haitians, attempting to escape Jean-Claude "Baby Doc" Duvalier's dictatorship, sailed for the United States. Before 1977, about 7,000 boat people had arrived in the United States; by 1979, 8,300 more had arrived. U.S. policy decided that Haitians were not political refugees but economic immigrants, seeking jobs and better living conditions, making them ineligible for asylum. Thus, no Haitians were given refugee status, and every Haitian landing in the United States was subject to immediate deportation. The 1980 Mariel boatlift, in which 125,000 Cubans and 40,000 to 80,000 Haitians tried to immigrate to the United States, caused President Jimmy Carter to reevaluate U.S.-Haitian policies. He created a class of immigrant, the "Cuban/Haitian entrant (status pending)," allowing Haitians who had entered up to October 10, 1980, to apply for asylum. Any Haitian entering after that date was faced with incarceration and deportation.

In 1981, President Ronald Reagan reinforced the policy and began interdiction of Haitian boats. For the next ten years, U.S. Coast Guard ships returned any seized boat carrying Haitian refugees to Port-au-Prince, Haiti. Interviews were supposed to be conducted on board, and anyone with a legitimate request was to be granted asylum. However, during that period, only twenty-eight applications for asylum were granted out of approximately twenty-five thousand. Many reported never having actually been interviewed at all.

In 1991, the numbers of asylum seekers dropped when Jean-Bertrand Aristide, the first democratically elected president of Haiti, took office. How-

Haitian sailboat loaded with 155 people awaiting a U.S. Coast Guard cutter to pick them up off the coast of Miami, Florida, in June, 1994. (AP/Wide World Photos)

ever, within months a violent military coup ousted Aristide, leading to the murders of fifteen hundred Aristide supporters and precipitating a new immigration crisis. By 1992, tens of thousands of Haitians attempted to sail to the United States for political asylum. However, President George H. W. Bush claimed that because there were no human rights violations going on in Haiti, the United States could not recognize Haitian refugees as political asylum seekers. In 1992, thirty-seven thousand Haitians were repatriated or incarcerated in holding facilities such as Guantanamo Bay, Cuba.

Human rights groups condemned the American refusal to accept Haitian refugees even after the fall of Aristide. Citing numerous murders of repatriated Haitians, violations of Haitians' civil rights, and imprisonment and harassment upon repatriation, these groups tried to change the status of the Haitian boat people to political refugees. Human rights groups asserted that the United States was in violation of the 1951 Convention and subsequent 1967 Protocol Relating to the Status of Refugees, and President Bush was found to be in violation of the Refugee Act of 1980. However, by defining Haitians as economic relief seekers and not refugees, the United States was allowed to maintain its repatriation policy.

Taking office in 1993, President Bill Clinton had opposed Bush's repatriation/interdiction policy and promised that he would be generous toward Haitian refugees. Coast Guard personnel remarked that seven hundred new boats were built by Haitians awaiting Clinton's presidency. However, in a reversal of opinion, Clinton reinstated Bush's policy.

In 1993, the U.S. Supreme Court agreed that only those refugees who actually make it to U.S. soil on their own could be considered for refugee status and that anyone interdicted would be repatriated. This controversial policy, along with continued interdiction at sea, remains in effect in the early twenty-first century.

Leslie Neilan

FURTHER READING

Gaines, Jena, and Stuart Anderson, eds. *Haitian Immigration.* Broomal, Pa.: Mason Crest, 2003.

Garrison, Lynn. *Voodoo Politics: The Clinton/Gore Destruction of Haiti.* Los Angeles: Leprechaun Press, 2000.

Haines, David W., ed. *Refugees in America in the 1990's: A Reference Handbook.* Westport, Conn.: Greenwood Press, 1996.

SEE ALSO: Bureau of Immigration, U.S.; Coast Guard, U.S.; Commission on Immigration Reform, U.S.; Cuban immigrants; Dominican immigrants; Florida; Haitian immigrants; Infectious diseases; Mariel boatlift; Refugees; Transportation of immigrants.

HAITIAN IMMIGRANTS

SIGNIFICANCE: Although Haitians are citizens of the second-oldest republic in the Western Hemisphere, an island nation located only seven hundred miles from the United States, they have experienced unique difficulties in finding acceptance as immigrants and have become one of the most abused groups of immigrants in modern American history. Black-skinned, French- and Creole-speaking, and generally very poor, Haitians have been slow to assimilate into American society.

A comparatively small Caribbean nation whose people are virtually all descendants of African slaves, Haiti occupies the western third of the island of Hispaniola, which it shares with the Dominican Republic. Immediately to its west is the larger island of Cuba, and the much smaller island of Puerto Rico lies to the east of Hispaniola. After a 1697 treaty between France and Spain split the island into French and Spanish colonies, France began developing its western portion as the colony of Saint-Domingue. Saint-Domingue proved a deadly home to European settlers, but over the course of the next century, African slave labor made it a prosperous sugar- and coffee-producing colony. During the 1790's, the black workers on whose backs the colony's prosperity was built rose up in revolt. After a decade of bloody wars, the slaves ousted the French and established the independent nation of Haiti in 1804.

Over the next two centuries, Haiti never gained full political stability and became one of the poorest nations in the world. Nevertheless, its population continued to grow. By the twentieth century, its limited arable land could not easily feed all its people, and emigration to other countries became an increasingly attractive option for many Haitians.

TWENTIETH CENTURY PRESSURES

During the early twentieth century, many rural Haitians began moving to the cities, causing such overcrowding that many city residents sought better living conditions abroad. Some went east, overland to the adjacent Dominican Republic, and some went to French-speaking African countries and to French Canada. Many others emigrated to the nearby United States. Mostly from Haiti's small middle and upper classes, these emigrants were generally well educated—some had attended schools in France—and most found new homes and good jobs abroad.

During the 1950's and 1960's, Haitian emigration increased after President Francois "Papa Doc" Duvalier declared himself ruler for life and deprived his citizens of privileges and rights they had enjoyed under earlier regimes. The best-educated Haitians—doctors, lawyers, teachers, and engineers—who opposed Duvalier were special targets of his animosity. They left the country in large numbers, creating a serious "brain drain" that the country could ill afford. Indeed, so many qualified doctors left between 1957 and 1963 that only three of the 264 graduates of Haiti's lone medical school remained in Haiti.

From 1957 until his death in 1971, Duvalier continued his repressive regime. As the country's economy deteriorated, more Haitians fled to America, where the sympathetic U.S. government welcomed them. During only three decades, the United States issued more than one million entry visas to Haitians. Many were given to semiskilled workers who ostensibly wanted only to visit relatives already in the United States. However, many of these people overstayed their allotted time limits with the intention of gaining permanent residence status.

By the 1960's, immigrants to the United States were coming not only from Haiti's cities but also from its villages and small towns. After arriving, these immigrants tended not to venture far from where they first set foot in America. As a result, they congregated in South Florida, where large Haitian communities arose in Miami and other South Florida cities. As the numbers of French- and Creole-speaking Haitians increased, the welcoming attitudes of the U.S. government and the American public cooled. However, after Lyndon B. Johnson became president in 1963, he focused on domestic issues and the expanding Vietnam War and regarded Haitian immigration as little more than a minor annoyance.

LATE TWENTIETH CENTURY BOAT PEOPLE

The less welcoming attitude of Americans did not, however, reduce Haitian interest in coming to the United States. Poverty, political repression, and crime were making life in Haiti increasingly difficult. Impediments placed in the way of emigrants by both the Haitian and U.S. governments simply forced the emigrants to become more inventive. During the 1970's, Haitians began trying to reach the United States on small, often unseaworthy boats, risking drowning at sea. During the 1980's, the exodus of Haitians by boat was so great that many people were using almost any craft that would float to reach South Florida. The distance they had to travel was several times greater than that required by Cubans sailing small boats to Florida.

The Haitians using small boats to emigrate were generally from the poorest classes—those who could not afford airfares or government exit visas. Because they arrived in the United States with no kind of documentation that would allow them to enter legally, they tried to enter surreptitiously.

PROFILE OF HAITIAN IMMIGRANTS

Country of origin	Haiti
Primary language	French
Primary regions of U.S. settlement	South Florida, East Coast
Earliest significant arrivals	Early 1950's
Peak immigration periods	1980's-2008
Twenty-first century legal residents*	166,890 (20,861 per year)

*Immigrants who obtained legal permanent resident status in the United States.
Source: Department of Homeland Security, *Yearbook of Immigration Statistics, 2008.*

Those who successfully entered the United States then had to live underground until they could legitimize their presence. The U.S. Immigration and Naturalization Service estimated that about 55,000 Haitian boat people safely reached the United States after 1980, but it also admitted as many as another 45,000 may have escaped detection. The number of would-be immigrants who perished at sea can only be conjectured. About 85 percent of the boat people settled in Miami.

Most of the Haitian immigrants who came during the 1980's were related to Haitians already living in the United States when they arrived. These immigrants were generally literate with some job skills and were consequently able to contribute to their new communities. However, as the total number of these exotic black immigrants increased, a backlash against them developed in the United States. As with many earlier immigrant groups in America, the Haitians were accused of placing new burdens on America's already overburdened welfare systems and of taking jobs from American citizens.

During 1981 alone, nearly 1,000 Haitian boat people arrived in South Florida every month. Some came indirectly, after first passing through the Bahamas. The U.S. government tried to reduce the flow of illegal immigrants through an agreement with the Haitian government that allowed it to interdict Haitian boats before they neared the Florida coast and return Haitian immigrants to Haiti.

HAITIANS IN THE UNITED STATES

Haitians are culturally distinct from other West Indians, most of whom speak Spanish or English. French is the official language of Haiti, but many rural Haitians speak only Haitian Creole, which isolates them linguistically. After Haitians settle in the United States, they tend not to identify with other nonwhite immigrant groups or even with African Americans.

Most Haitians are devout Christians, both Roman Catholics and Protestants, whose Christian religious rituals typically incorporate special island features. A large majority of recently arrived Haitians in South Florida attend weekly services at churches, which—like their island counterparts—play more than a spiritual role by helping the sick and the poor. Haitians have great respect for reli-

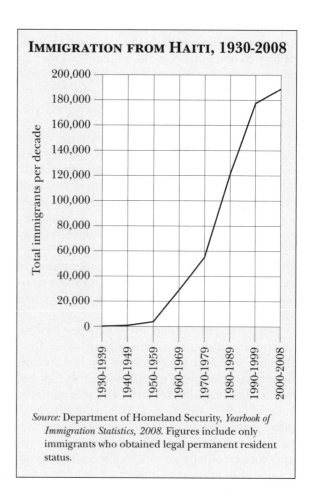

IMMIGRATION FROM HAITI, 1930-2008

Source: Department of Homeland Security, *Yearbook of Immigration Statistics, 2008.* Figures include only immigrants who obtained legal permanent resident status.

gion and members of the clergy. This respect was evident when Haiti made a former priest, Jean-Bertrand Aristide, its first democratically elected president in 1991, after the Duvaliers were ousted from power.

Black, non-English speaking, and culturally exotic, Haitian immigrants have experienced innumerable instances of prejudice and discrimination in the United States. Most are of African descent, so historically they faced the same discriminatory Jim Crow laws and racist attitudes as black Americans. However, even after strong civil rights laws and softening American attitudes toward racial minorities began making life in America more equitable for nonwhite peoples, Haitian faced new forms of discrimination. The slowness with which they have assimilated is doubtless partly due to their own reluctance to abandon Haitian customs and the insistence of many of them on continuing to speak Haitian Creole, at least among themselves. Their retention of voodoo rituals and other traditional religious and medical practices, as well as their frequent return visits to Haiti, have all helped brand them as "different."

During the 1970's and 1980's, a new negative stereotype was attached to the Haitian immigrants: They were accused of being disease carriers. Initially, tuberculosis was said to be endemic among the Haitian population. An even worse condemnation came later, when Haitians were officially "identified" as acquired immunodeficiency syndrome (AIDS) carriers. This designation was later removed by the U.S. Centers for Disease Control and Prevention, but the U.S. Food and Drug Administration refused to accept blood donations from all persons of Haitian descent during the late 1980's.

During the 1980's, about 800,000 people of Haitian descent were living in the United States. They included naturalized citizens; legal immigrants; nonimmigrants, such as students, temporary workers, tourists, Haitian government personnel, and employees of international organizations; undocumented aliens; persons on transitional status; and refugees requesting political asylum. Those seeking refugee status came by the thousands during the four years of military rule in Haiti, from 1991 to 1994, following the exile of "Baby Doc" Duvalier. The situation in Haiti being so horrendous, many were granted refugee status and resettled in areas all around the nation.

TWENTY-FIRST CENTURY TRENDS

In 2004, nearly 450,000 foreign-born Haitians were living in the United States. Florida and New York were home to most, followed by Massachusetts, New Jersey, Connecticut, Maryland, Washington, D.C., Pennsylvania, Georgia, Illinois (particularly Chicago), and California. Miami, Florida, had an ethnic enclave called "Little Haiti." New York City had Haitian enclaves in East Flatbush, Brooklyn, Elmont, and Long Island. Queens is also a favored location for those Haitians with the means to purchase single-family homes, the preferred type of residence. Boston also has a Haitian enclave.

In these and other areas, Haitians have set up many businesses that cater to the special needs of their fellow countrymen. Along with barbershops and car services, they operate restaurants specializing in Haitian cuisine. Haitians able to support

themselves and their families in America tend not to forget their allegiance to their homeland and relatives they have left behind. They are estimated to remit as much as 600 million dollars a year to relatives in Haiti. These remittances have become an important part of the Haitian national economy.

Jane L. Ball

FURTHER READING

Foner, Nancy, ed. *American Arrivals: Anthropology Engages the New Immigration.* Oxford, England: James Currey, 2004. Discusses health care, education, and issues of cultural values and practices among immigrants, including Haitians, and how they adapt to American society.

Gaines, Jena, and Stuart Anderson, eds. *Haitian Immigration.* Broomal, Pa.: Mason Crest, 2003. Overview of Haitian immigration since the 1960's, the conditions in Haiti causing emigration, and adjustments and problems faced. Written for readers aged twelve and older.

Schiller, Nina, and Georges Fouron. *Georges Woke Up Laughing: Long-Distance Nationalism and the Search for Home.* Durham, N.C.: Duke University Press, 2001. Recounts the Haitian immigrant experience in America, the daily struggles for survival for both the immigrants and those left behind. Combines history, autobiography—coauthor Fouron is a Haitian immigrant—and ethnography.

Shaw-Taylor, Yoku, and Steven Tuch, eds. *The Other African Americans: Contemporary African and Caribbean Immigrants in the United States.* Lanham, Md.: Rowman & Littlefield, 2007. Comparative study of Haitian, Jamaican, Dominican, and African immigrants in the United States.

Shell-Weiss, Melanie. *Coming to Miami: A Social History.* Gainesville: University Press of Florida, 2009. History of immigration to Miami since 1880 that examines the struggles of Haitians, Cubans, and other Latin American peoples to achieve citizenship and labor rights in the United States.

Stepick, Alex, and Nancy Foner. *Pride Against Prejudice: Haitians in the United States.* Boston: Allyn & Bacon, 1998. Describes the struggles of Haitian immigrants, the causes and consequences of their immigration, and how family, community, and culture help them maintain their pride while coping with prejudice and economics.

Zéphir, Flore. *Haitian Immigrants in Black America: A Sociological and Sociolinguistic Portrait*. Westport, Conn.: Greenwood Press, 1996. Provides multiple perspectives on Haitian immigration experiences, based on hundreds of interviews with Haitian immigrants, especially as they reveal how they cope with America's system of racial classification and how they view themselves as a distinct ethnic group.

SEE ALSO: Acquired immunodeficiency syndrome; Danticat, Edwidge; Dominican immigrants; Florida; Haitian boat people; *Immigration and Naturalization Service v. St. Cyr*; Miami; Quota systems; Religions of immigrants; *Sale v. Haitian Centers Council*; Settlement patterns.

HAMBURG-AMERIKA LINE

IDENTIFICATION: Transatlantic passenger shipping company
DATE: Established in 1847
LOCATION: Based in Hamburg, Germany
ALSO KNOWN AS: Hamburg Amerikanische Packetfahrt Actien Gesellschaft (HAPAG); Hamburg-Amerika Linie; Hamburg-America Line, Hamburg-American Line

SIGNIFICANCE: From 1881 until 1914, the Hamburg-Amerika Line was the largest shipping line in existence. It transported hundreds of thousands of emigrants from Germany, Scandinavia, and eastern Europe to the United States, Canada, Latin America, and other destinations around the world.

The German city of Hamburg lies on the Elbe River, a navigable waterway that empties into the North Sea. Also accessible by railroad from the east and south, Hamburg became the most important emigration port in continental Europe during the last decades of the nineteenth century, outstripping its rival German port, Bremen, during the 1890's. Hamburg became the point of embarkation not only for German and Scandinavian emigrants, but also for Russian and Polish Jews, many of whom were fleeing persecutions that had started in czarist Russia in 1881.

By 1914, when World War I interrupted shipping, the Hamburg-Amerika Line had a fleet of 175 active steamships, several of which could carry one thousand passengers each. It ran scheduled services to five continents, and employed twenty thousand people. Its steamships crossed the North Atlantic in a little over one week. Most immigrants to the United States traveled by the lowest-cost class, which was known as "steerage." Such passengers were accommodated between decks in closely packed bunks. However, despite their crowding, they were relatively comfortable, and the shipping line provided them with three meals a day. The cost of a typical adult steerage ticket was equivalent to about twenty U.S. dollars—a price that decreased slightly as the demand rose. Children's fares were the adult fares. Ships arriving in New York docked at company piers in Hoboken, New Jersey, from which passengers were ferried to the immigrant processing stations—Castle Garden between 1855 and 1891 and Ellis Island afterward.

Under the directorship of Albert Ballin, the son of a German-Jewish mercantile family, the shipping company expanded its reach into eastern Europe during the 1890's, sending agents to recruit passengers, sell them rail and steamship tickets, and connect them with temporary lodging at the embarkation port. Ballin's agents set up health inspection checkpoints at the frontiers of the German state and arranged "disinfection" routines for emigrants prior to their eventual embarkation. This latter procedure was done because passengers found to be carrying contagious diseases could be turned back at U.S. ports of immigration, leaving the shipping company to pay for return to Europe.

As the flow of emigrants needing accommodation began to overwhelm the capacity of Hamburg's hotels and hostels, Ballin arranged for the construction of an emigrant village, the *Auswandererhallen* (emigrant halls), to be built on Veddel Island in the Elbe, on the outskirts of Hamburg. Able to accommodate as many as five thousand people at one time, the village provided dormitories, kosher and nonkosher dining halls, shops, a bandstand, and houses of worship, including a synagogue. It also had facilities for quarantine and further health inspections. When sailing day arrived, the passengers loaded their belongings onto tenders, which transported them down the Elbe to Cuxhaven, the city's deep-water outport, where giant transatlantic ships awaited their boarding.

German emigrants boarding a ship at the port of Hamburg. (NARA)

Between 1850 and 1938, approximately 5 million people emigrated from Europe aboard Hamburg-Amerika Line ships. During World War II, Germany's Nazi government expunged Albert Ballin's name and contributions from the historical record. The emigrant village he had built was demolished in 1962. During the 1970's, the Hamburg-Amerika Line merged with the Norddeutscher Lloyd of Bremen to establish the modern Hapag-Lloyd shipping company. Hapag's detailed passenger records, covering the period 1850-1934, have survived and are housed in the Hamburg State Archive, and Ballin's reputation has been restored. Twenty-first century American tourists may visit BallinStadt, a re-creation of the *Auswanderer* village on Veddel Island and a center for family history research.

Karen Manners Smith

FURTHER READING

Baines, Dudley. *Emigration from Europe, 1815-1930.* New York: Cambridge University Press, 1995.

Fry, Henry. *The History of North Atlantic Steam Navigation.* London: Sampson Low, Marston, 1896.

Groppe, Hans-Hermann, and Ursula Wöst. *Via Hamburg to the World: From the Emigrants' Halls to BallinStadt.* Translated by Paul Bewicke and Mary Tyler. Hamburg, Germany: Ellert and Richter Verlag, 2007.

Page, Thomas W. "The Transportation of Immigrants and Reception Arrangements in the Nineteenth Century." *Journal of Political Economy* 19, no. 9 (1911): 732-749.

SEE ALSO: Austrian immigrants; Ellis Island; European immigrants; German immigrants; Hungarian immigrants; Infectious diseases; Jewish immigrants; Pacific Mail Steamship Company; Polish immigrants; Russian and Soviet immigrants; Transportation of immigrants; World War I.

HAMPTON V. MOW SUN WONG

THE CASE: U.S. Supreme Court decision on the rights of aliens

DATE: Decided on June 1, 1976

> **SIGNIFICANCE:** The *Hampton* decision took an expansive view of noncitizens' right to public employment and severely restricted the extent to which the federal government and federal agencies might refuse to employ noncitizens.

Mow Sun Wong was an alien immigrant residing lawfully and permanently in the United States. When he applied for a position with the U.S. Civil Service Commission, his application was rejected solely because of the agency's policy of employing only American citizens. Many federal agencies maintained the same policy. In a class-action suit, Wong and four other resident aliens accused the agencies of unconstitutional discrimination. The Supreme Court had previously struck down such discrimination when practiced by state governments. Although the district court upheld the federal agencies' policy, the court of appeals reversed and held that the policy of excluding all aliens without a special justification violated the principle of equal justice under the law, which had been established as a component of the due process commanded by the Fifth Amendment.

By a 5-4 vote, the Supreme Court agreed with the court of appeals. Writing for the majority, Justice John Paul Stevens presented a long, nuanced discussion of the issues. Although endorsing the idea that the "overriding national interests may [often] provide a justification for a citizenship requirement in the federal service," Stevens repudiated the notion that "any agent of the national government may arbitrarily subject all resident aliens to different substantive rules from those applied to citizens." Whenever the national government deprives a person of "an aspect of liberty," it must explicitly refer to that interest and show that

the deprivation directly promotes that interest. Distinguishing between mandating a rule and passively accepting it, moreover, Stevens observed that Congress had allowed but never commanded the Civil Service Commission to refuse to employ aliens legally residing in the country.

Thomas Tandy Lewis

FURTHER READING

O'Brien, David M. *Constitutional Law and Politics.* 7th ed. New York: W. W. Norton, 2008.

Schwartz, Bernard, ed. *The Burger Court: Counter-Revolution or Confirmation?* New York: Oxford University Press, 1998.

SEE ALSO: Chinese immigrants; Citizenship; Congress, U.S.; Constitution, U.S.; Due process protections; Immigration law; Supreme Court, U.S.

HANSEN EFFECT

DEFINITION: Groundbreaking theory in European American immigration studies

> **SIGNIFICANCE:** In 1938, shortly before he died, social historian Marcus Lee Hansen revolutionized the understanding of the assimilation of immigrant generations into American life by suggesting that assimilation and ethnic identity within the so-called melting pot of America were far more complex than had been assumed.

At the turn of the twentieth century, immigrant studies within American academia were restricted by a lack of perspective and hard data. The great era of European immigration had not quite ended and historians generally considered the influx of poorly educated, lower-class Europeans into East Coast cities more as a pressing social problem than as a historical phenomenon. Establishment historians drew upon an Anglo-Saxon model to define America, arguing that Anglo-Saxon—that is, northern and western European—families had initially settled the New World, expressed by the New England town system. That tradition—specifically Protestant religious structures, patriarchal communities, and competitive economic markets—created the industrial order, the political dynamic of a constitutional government, and the economic class system that had come to define America.

Scholars paid little attention to immigrants from southern and eastern Europe. When historian Frederick Jackson Turner revolutionized the concept of American history during the late nineteenth century by shifting the focus from New England to the frontier, a new impetus was given to studying the impact of immigrants in shaping the American character. Turner argued that in confronting the frontier, immigrants necessarily shed their European customs and forged a kind of American identity.

At issue then was the process of assimilation itself. One of Turner's history students at Harvard University was Marcus Lee Hansen (1892-1938), a Wisconsinite of northern European descent from the rural Midwest. Hansen came to appreciate the complexity of the question of immigration studies. For more than four years during the early 1930's, he gathered data in Europe and the Plains states and came to theorize that the melting pot model was inadequate to explain the experience of American immigrants because ethnic identity was not entirely surrendered to the collective identity. In a historical society pamphlet titled *The Problem of the Third Generation Immigrant* (1938), Hansen formulated his thesis: That the third generation, the grandchildren, wished to recover the ethnicity of their grandparents.

According to Hansen's thesis, the first generation, as foreign born, inevitably maintained the language and customs of their Old World identity. Their children sought to assimilate into the American identity and deliberately distanced themselves from the customs and language of the Old World. However, the grandchildren sought to recover the original ethnic identity. What the son wanted to forget, the argument went, the grandson wished to remember. Hansen proposed that assimilation and ethnic identity could actually be part of the same process, that the third generation could adapt to their New World environments without sacrificing ethnic identity. Ethnicity was then a generational process, with each generation struggling with the implications of its cultural heritage. Thus assimilation was best studied within, rather than across, generations.

Because Hansen died of renal failure while still in his forties, he was never able to examine the experience of nonwhite immigrants and the special problems posed by Native Americans. However, his theory, as a challenge to the melting pot, gained interest. This was particularly true after World War II, when America's international reputation suffered during the prolonged Cold War, the Korea and Vietnam conflicts, civil rights unrest, and a series of national political scandals. Within that heated environment, Hansen's thesis was embraced as an early, albeit indirect, proponent of multiculturalism and the celebration of diversity.

Joseph Dewey

FURTHER READING

Bayor, Ronald H. *Race and Ethnicity in America: A Concise History*. New York: Columbia University Press, 2003.

Daniels, Roger. *Coming to America: A History of Immigration and Ethnicity in American Life*. New York: Harper, 2002.

Hansen, Marcus Lee. *The Problem of the Third Generation Immigrant*. Rock Island, Ill.: Augustana Historical Society, 1938.

Takaki, Roger. *Debating Diversity: Clashing Perspectives on Race and Ethnicity in America*. New York: Oxford University Press, 2002.

Zlner, Mette. *Re-imagining the Nation: Debates on Immigrants, Identities and Memories*. New York: Peter Lang, 2000.

SEE ALSO: Anglo-conformity; Assimilation theories; Cultural pluralism; European immigrants; Families; History of immigration after 1891; Identificational assimilation; Melting pot theory; Migrant superordination; Push-pull factors.

HAWAII

SIGNIFICANCE: Hawaii is one of only four U.S. states in which residents of European ancestry do not form a majority, and it is home to large Asian immigrant communities, including Japanese, Chinese, Filipino, and Koreans. Many of Hawaii's native-born citizens are descendants of Chinese, Filipino, and Japanese immigrants who came during the nineteenth and early twentieth centuries to work the islands' sugar cane plantations, and immigration from Asia has continued into the twenty-first century.

Hawaii was originally settled by Polynesian islanders. Western traders first arrived during the late eighteenth century, bringing with them Chinese sailors, who began settling in Hawaii in 1789. These early Asian settlers, who were virtually all male, intermarried with Hawaiian women and assimilated into Hawaiian culture. Intermarriage between Chinese immigrants and native Hawaiians was common well into the nineteenth century.

In 1887, American and European businessmen in Hawaii forced King Kal kaua I to abdicate his power by signing a constitution that gave voting rights exclusively to wealthy Americans, Europeans, and the few native Hawaiians who had achieved significant wealth. The new constitution disenfranchised the islands' many Asian immigrants. Kal kaua's sister, Queen Liliuokalani, was deposed when she attempted to regain sovereignty for Hawaiians. In 1900, the United States annexed Hawaii as a U.S. territory.

SUGAR CANE INDUSTRY

During the late nineteenth and early twentieth century, white plantation owners imported numerous workers from Asia. Initially, most of these workers were from China and Japan. The first labor recruits came from China in 1850; by 1887, 26,000 Chinese were working on Hawaii's sugar cane plantations, but about 38 percent of them eventually returned to China. Between 1868 and 1924, 200,000 Japanese workers came to Hawaii; eventually, about 55 percent of them returned to Japan. During this same period, 7,300 Korean workers came to Hawaii; 16 percent eventually returned home. Asians were not, however, the only labor immigrants. Almost 13,000 Portuguese workers had also been imported by 1899, and 5,000 Puerto Ricans by

Japanese sugar plantation workers in Hawaii around 1890. (Hawaii State Archives)

1901. Meanwhile, the white plantation owners established a hierarchical system that kept workers divided by ethnic groups to make it difficult for them to organize.

Recruitment campaigns in the Philippines brought the first Filipinos to Hawaii in 1906. Called "Hawayanos," these first Filipino immigrants were Tagalog-speaking sugar cane workers. Like the earlier Asian immigrant workers, Filipinos came to Hawaii to earn money to take home. The numbers of Filipino workers immigrating to Hawaii increased dramatically over the next fifteen years, from 150 in 1907 to approximately 3,000 per year between 1911 and 1920. By the 1930's, Filipino workers outnumbered Japanese in the sugar plantations, even though 7,300 of them were repatriated to the Philippines during the Great Depression.

Sugar cane plantation owners preferred Filipino workers because they worked for the lowest wages. Moreover, as Filipinos were technically considered U.S. nationals because the United States administered the Philippines, they were not restricted by federal laws that barred importation of workers from other Asian countries. The Filipino workers could also be used as levers in labor disputes again Japanese plantation workers.

Filipino immigrants to Hawaii were typically rural and poorly educated, and were often unaware of their legal rights. The harsh conditions they endured on the sugar plantations were unexpected, and linguistic differences between different Filipino groups and from the Japanese and Chinese plantation workers meant that communication among immigrant workers was difficult. However, after Hawaii became a U.S. territory in 1900, immigrant workers enjoyed more rights and were no longer effectively indentured. Consequently, labor costs rose, and workers began to unionize.

Pablo Manlapit, who came to Hawaii as a laborer in 1909, became the first Filipino lawyer in the United States during the 1920's. He helped organize the Filipino Labor Union in Hawaii and advocated for the rights of Filipino workers. He also worked with the Japanese Federation of Labor

PROFILE OF HAWAII

Region	South Pacific Ocean
Entered union	1959
Largest cities	Honolulu (capital), Hilo, Kailua
Modern immigrant communities	Chinese, Japanese, Filipinos

Population	Total	Percent of state	Percent of U.S.	U.S. rank
All state residents	1,285,000	100.0	0.43	42
All foreign-born residents	210,000	16.3	0.56	26

Source: U.S. Census Bureau, *Statistical Abstract for 2006.*
Notes: The U.S. population in 2006 was 299,399,000, of whom 37,548,000 (12.5%) were foreign born. Rankings in last column reflect total numbers, not percentages.

(later the Hawaiian Federation of Labor) during a sugar workers' strike in 1920. His work as a labor agitator led to his being deported to the mainland United States in 1924. He returned to Hawaii in 1933 and continued to agitate, but his deportation to the Philippines two years later ended his career in the Hawaiian labor movement.

Hawaii's rich multicultural mix of immigrant workers led to the creation of a Hawaiian form of Creole English, sometimes called "Hawaiian Pidgin." It combined native Hawaiian, English, Japanese, Chinese, Ilocano, Tagalog, and Portuguese vocabulary, allowing plantation workers of all ethnic backgrounds to communicate with one another. Hawaiian Creole was still being spoken during the early twenty-first century.

JAPANESE AMERICANS AND WORLD WAR II

The United States entered World War II at the end of 1941, immediately after Japan launched a sneak attack on the great Pearl Harbor naval base in Hawaii. By that time, roughly one-third of Hawaii's population, about 150,000 people, were Japanese or of Japanese descent. In contrast to the Japanese residents of the western states of the United States, almost all of whom were interned throughout the war, only about 1 percent of Hawaii's Japanese residents were interned. The federal government declared martial law in Hawaii after the Pearl Harbor attack, but attempting to intern one-third of the islands' population would have been a logistical nightmare and caused an economic disaster.

Nevertheless, Hawaii hosted two internment camps: Sand Island, in Honolulu Harbor, and Honouliuli, on the southwestern shore of Oahu. Some Japanese immigrants in Hawaii were sent to internment camps on the mainland.

Postwar Immigration

During the 1990's, an influx of nearly 50,000 new immigrants brought Hawaii's total foreign-born population to 212,000, accounting for about 48 percent of the state's overall population increase. Between 1985 and 2000, approximately 4,800 immigrants from newly independent Micronesia and the Marshall Islands moved to Hawaii. This led the Hawaiian government to sue the federal government for inadequately reporting the impact on Hawaii of unrestricted immigration from these territories to Congress.

Melissa A. Barton

Further Reading

Ch'oe, Yong-ho, ed. *From the Land of Hibiscus: Koreans in Hawai'i, 1903-1950.* Honolulu: University of Hawaii Press, 2007. Collection of scholarly essays on Korean immigration to Hawaii and immigrant culture.

Duus, Masayo Umezawa. *The Japanese Conspiracy: The Oahu Sugar Strike of 1920.* Translated by Beth Cory, adapted by Peter Duus. Berkeley: University of California Press, 1999. Narrative account of the 1920 sugar strike by Japanese and Filipino workers originally written for Japanese readers.

Kerkvliet, Melinda Tria. *Pablo Manlapit: A Filipino Labor Leader in Hawai'i.* Honolulu: University of Hawaii Press, 2002. Historical account of one of Hawaii's most controversial labor leaders, who fought for the rights of sugar cane workers before World War II.

Odo, Franklin. *No Sword to Bury: Japanese Americans in Hawai'i During World War II.* Philadelphia: Temple University Press, 2004. Tells the story of Japanese American college students barred from serving in World War II and of their immigrant community.

Patterson, Wayne. *The Korean Frontier in America: Immigration to Hawaii, 1896-1910.* Honolulu: University of Hawaii Press, 1988. Useful survey of the earliest years of Korean immigration to Hawaii.

Young, Nancy Foon. *The Chinese in Hawaii: An Annotated Bibliography.* Honolulu: University of Hawaii Press, 1973. Comprehensive bibliography of material on Chinese Americans in Hawaii up to the date of its publication.

See also: Anti-Japanese movement; Chinese immigrants; Filipino immigrants; *Imingaisha*; Immigration Convention of 1886; Japanese immigrants; Korean immigrants; Portuguese immigrants; Puerto Rican immigrants; World War II.

Hayakawa, S. I.

Identification: Japanese Canadian immigrant, college president, and U.S. senator
Born: July 18, 1906; Vancouver, British Columbia, Canada
Died: February 27, 1992; Greenbrae, California

Significance: A notable scholar of semantics, Hayakawa also had a political career. He represented California in the U.S. Senate, where he launched a movement to establish English as the official language of the United States by introducing the English Language Amendment in 1981.

Born in Vancouver in 1906, Hayakawa was the son of a Japanese immigrant to Canada. After completing high school in Winnipeg, he continued his education at the University of Manitoba and McGill University in Montreal, earning a master of arts degree in English in 1928. In 1935, he completed his doctorate in English and American literature at the University of Wisconsin.

Hayakawa taught English at the University of Wisconsin from 1936 to 1939 and at the Illinois Institute of Technology from 1939 to 1947. As a Canadian immigrant, he was not subject to internment during World War II. Because of wartime restrictions, Hayakawa had to wait until 1954 to become a U.S. citizen.

In 1955, Hayakawa became a professor of English at San Francisco State College (now known as San Francisco State University). He was promoted to college president in 1968. Hayakawa was elected to the U.S. Senate as a Republican in 1976. He introduced the first English Language Amendment in 1981. After leaving the Senate in 1983, he

S. I. Hayakawa (right) with President Richard M. Nixon in 1969, when Hayakawa was president of San Francisco State College. (Time & Life Pictures/Getty Images)

founded U.S. English, an organization that promoted English as the official language of the United States. Hayakawa died in 1992.

John David Rausch, Jr.

FURTHER READING

Baron, Dennis. *The English-Only Question: An Official Language for Americans?* New Haven, Conn.: Yale University Press, 1990.

Gallegos, Bee, ed. *English: Our Official Language?* New York: H. W. Wilson, 1994.

Tse, Lucy. *"Why Don't They Learn English?" Separating Fact from Fallacy in the U.S. Language Debate.* New York: Teachers College Press, 2001.

SEE ALSO: Asian immigrants; Bilingual education; Canadian immigrants; Education; English as a second language; English-only and official English movements; Higher education; Japanese immigrants; World War II.

HEAD MONEY CASES

THE CASE: U.S. Supreme Court decision on immigration law
DATE: Decided on December 8, 1884

> **SIGNIFICANCE:** The *Head Money Cases* expanded the powers of Congress to control immigration, to use taxation in regulating commerce, and to repeal treaties with foreign countries.

Before the 1880's, individual U.S. states exercised the primary role in the admission of immigrants. In the Immigration Act of 1882, Congress moved to assume greater control over immigration policy. In order to obtain funds to compensate the states for the burden of financing needy immigrants, Congress approved a federal head tax of fifty cents on every immigrant. Owners of passenger ships challenged the constitutionality of the tax on the grounds that the tax was not applied uniformly throughout the United States, that the law was not passed to provide for common defense or general welfare, and that the tax conflicted with foreign treaties previously approved by the Senate.

The U.S. Supreme Court unanimously rejected each of the three arguments against the head tax. Speaking for the Court, Justice Samuel F. Miller explained, in the first place, that a fee was uniform because it "operates precisely alike in every port of the United States where such passengers can be landed." Second, the head tax was not to be considered as an exercise of the taxing power, but rather it was a "mere incident of the regulation of commerce," designed to mitigate "the evils inherent in the business of bringing foreigners to the United States." Finally, because the U.S. Constitution recognized treaties and federal statutes to be of equal authority, Congress had almost an unlimited discretion to modify or disregard treaties.

Thomas Tandy Lewis

FURTHER READING

Fairman, Charles. *Mr. Justice Miller and the Supreme Court, 1862-1890*. Clark, N.J.: Lawbook Exchange, 2003.

LeMay, Michael, and Elliott Robert Barkan, eds. *U.S. Immigration and Naturalization Laws and Issues: A Documentary History*. Westport, Conn.: Greenwood Press, 1999.

SEE ALSO: Citizenship; Congress, U.S.; Constitution, U.S.; Due process protections; History of immigration after 1891; Immigration law; Supreme Court, U.S.

HEALTH CARE

DEFINITION: Professional medical and mental health services

SIGNIFICANCE: The access of recently arrived immigrants to health care in the United States has often been limited by cultural and language barriers, lack of information, and economic disparities. Thus, alternative medicines and traditional healers have become important parts of immigrant health care. Immi-

grants' struggle for health care has continued into the twenty-first century, with ongoing efforts to incorporate immigrants and refugees into the American health care system.

Concern about the possible threats to public health that might be brought into the United States by new immigrants has long been a concern of U.S. immigration law. The Immigration Act of 1891 required medical inspections of immigrants before they left their home countries and immediately after their arrival in the United States. Subsequent immigration acts during the 1890's and the early twentieth century barred diseased immigrants from the United States and expanded the categories of excludable immigrants.

Although the actual number of people who were deported for medical conditions around the turn of the twentieth century was quite small, memoirs and oral histories from that era reflect immigrants' fear of medical inspection processes and physicians at American ports. In Ellis Island, through which about 70 percent of immigrants entered the United States during that time period, U.S. Public Health Service officers examined new immigrants. With hundreds of newcomers arriving daily at the reception center, detailed and thorough examinations were often impossible, and physicians relied on various clues to weed out immigrants with physical or mental defects. Immigrants found to be suffering from contagious and dangerous diseases who could not earn their livings due to their physical or mental conditions were detained for more thorough inspections and afterward often deported to their home countries, unless they recovered. Developments in medical technology, such as X rays for tuberculosis and Wasserman tests for syphilis, aided inspections of immigrants between 1882 and the mid-1920's.

THE AMERICAN HEALTH CARE SYSTEM

Immigrants from the Old World found the American health care system cold, distant, and frightening. Their cultural identities were often threatened by American hospitals and reform-minded individuals, who introduced them to new means of treatment and care but did not consider cultural confusions the immigrants might have experienced. Immigrants and their families did not want to commit themselves to hospitals because they were worried about possible long separations and even possible deaths through hospitalization.

Immigrants also received health care at dispensaries, alms houses, and private charities, which served diverse groups of people. Immigrant hospitals and medical facilities were built to provide health care with attention to immigrants' cultural and medical needs. Reform-minded individuals and communities also partook in the establishment of various medical facilities for immigrants, in which Western medical practices and traditional cures were often combined. Immigrants also looked for alternative means of care and treatment from traditional healers within their own ethnic communities. One such example was ethnic pharmacies, where they could find more familiar and accessible treatments for their ills.

IMMIGRANT HEATH CARE PROBLEMS

As late as the early twenty-first century, many immigrants were still experiencing the same kinds of health care problems that immigrants had experienced a century earlier. Their suspicions of American health care providers and hospitals have not gone away. In particular, immigrants with no prior exposure to Western medical facilities are likely to fear encounters with the American health care system. Moreover, various immigrant groups have experienced inequalities in receiving health care. They lack information regarding where and how to get appropriate health care in their new home. Language and cultural barriers prevent them from seeking health care services and increase their distrust of American hospitals and other medical institutions. Although hospitals are required to provide interpretation and translation services for non-English-speaking immigrants, they are not always equipped to fulfill such needs. The geographical inaccessibility of medical facilities has also prevented economically disadvantaged newcomers from getting proper care.

Another important problem for immigrants has been the lack of health insurance, which is partly attributable to their lower levels of education and poverty rates. Lack of health insurance has posed special problems for immigrant workers, who are typically more likely to get injured at work and to get injured more seriously than their native-born counterparts. This has been particularly true for Hispanic immigrant laborers, many of whom perform demanding physical work. When they are injured at work, they typically hesitate to take time off for medical treatment for fear of losing their jobs. Undocumented immigrant workers are even more reluctant to seek medical treatment, fearing exposure of their illegal immigration statue and possible deportation. Even insured immigrants and their families have less access to health care than insured native-born American citizens for nonfinancial reasons such as unfamiliarity with the American health care system.

MENTAL HEALTH CARE

Because of the stresses that many immigrants encounter in adjusting to life in the United States, their psychological well-being has become an important social and policy issue. Traumatic experiences in home countries, cultural and language barriers, and discrimination can all combine to aggravate the mental health problems of immigrants. While mental health care has been increasingly utilized in the United States, many immigrants are still unwilling to use such services because of their cultural norms and beliefs. In many Asian countries, for example, stigmas attached to mental illness inhibit people from seeking medical help.

Many immigrants are also handicapped by not having information about the availability of mental health care services. Moreover, the scarcity of mental health care providers who understand the cultural norms and languages of immigrant groups has prevented many immigrants from receiving proper care. Research has shown that immigrants often manifest their mental health problems in ways different from those of native-born Americans. For example, Asian immigrants are more likely than Americans to manifest mental distress through somatic symptoms. Medical health care providers who do not understand ethnic-specific symptoms of mental illness may not be able to offer timely medical interventions.

The mental health of Southeast Asians who have taken refuge in the United States since the 1960's has drawn special attention from health professionals and social workers. For example, Hmong refugees from the war-torn country of Laos are known to have suffered from posttraumatic stress disorder even before their arrival in the United States. However, due to their cultural and language differences and the lack of American medical professionals familiar with Hmong culture and language, these immigrants have generally not received proper treatment and care.

The languages of some immigrant cultures do not have words for mental illness, but this does not mean that the people themselves are immune from mental distress. Thus, Southeast Asian refugees frequently use traditional healers and therapies. When administered in conjunction with Western medical practices, such measures are of great benefit to mentally stressed immigrants. American health care professionals have consequently become increasingly aware of the importance of understanding cultural and ethnic differences and finding ways to provide better care for immigrants and refugees.

CULTURAL NEGOTIATIONS IN HEALTH CARE

Understanding cultural differences of immigrants is crucial to providing appropriate health care services. As was the case during the early twentieth century, immigrant hospitals and medical facilities in major American cities have continued to serve not only members of their own ethnic groups but also those of other immigrant groups. Immigrants are also active in cultural negotiations. In general, they have received less health care than native-born Americans, but they have tried hard to improve their conditions. In addition to visiting American hospitals for medical care, they have also utilized traditional and ethnic care systems within their immigrant communities, often receiving good results by using both systems. Increasingly, American health professionals have accepted alternative drugs and therapy systems brought to the United States by immigrants. They have shown greater respect for various measures adopted by immigrants to treat their minds and bodies and been willing to work with non-Western medical practitioners. Growing numbers of ethnic medical professionals who understand cultural and ethnic differences of immigrant patients have been making available better health care services for immigrants.

WELFARE POLICIES AND IMMIGRATION

Policy issues regarding heath care of immigrants have interested many Americans. Again, as was the case during the early twentieth century, concerns that immigrants may bring diseases into the country and drain taxpayer dollars to pay for their care have persisted into the twenty-first century. The federal Personal Responsibility and Work Opportunity Reconciliation Act and the Illegal Immigration Reform and Immigrant Responsibility Act of 1996 both restricted Medicaid eligibility of immigrants, except in emergencies, during their first five years of residence in the United States.

California's Proposition 187, which eliminated all public services except emergency health care for undocumented immigrants, helped start nationwide debates on health care and immigrants. Despite government efforts to restrict health care for undocumented immigrants, there have been continuing efforts to provide immigrants with health care, regardless of their legal status. State- and community-based programs, such as free clinics and nonprofit institutions, have served immigrants, both documented and undocumented. Educational efforts to inform immigrants of available resources have been launched as well.

Immigrants and refugees in the United States have often been misunderstood and unfairly stigmatized as potential health menaces. During the early twentieth century, Jewish immigrants from eastern Europe were blamed for spreading trachoma, the eye disease that eventually led to blindness. Italian immigrants were associated with polio epidemics. In late nineteenth century San Francisco, Chinese immigrants were accused of bringing bubonic plague. During the 1930's, Mexicans in Los Angeles were expelled for tuberculosis. During the 1970's tuberculosis reemerged as the immigrant disease in many American urban centers. During the 1980's and 1990's, Haitian immigrants were widely associated with acquired immunodeficiency syndrome (AIDS). As a consequence, a large number of Haitians in the United States lost their jobs, housing services, and other opportunities due to their perceived association with the disease.

In addition to being stereotyped without concrete evidence, immigrants and refugees—in particular, those who are undocumented—have been blamed for draining health care resources of the United States. However, their cultural values and ethics have made positive contributions to American society as well. Various efforts to promote cultural understanding and knowledge of the immigrant population have been going on in spite of numerous problems that have threatened the health care access of immigrants in the United States.

Ji-Hye Shin

FURTHER READING

Conway, Lorie. *Forgotten Ellis Island: The Extraordinary Story of America's Immigrant Hospital.* New York: Collins, 2007. History of the Ellis Island Hospital with photographs and vignettes from the early twentieth century.

Fadiman, Anne. *The Spirit Catches You and You Fall Down: A Hmong Child, Her American Doctors, and the Collision of Two Cultures.* New York: Farrar, Straus and Giroux, 1997. Accounts of a Hmong refugee family and various parties involved in providing care and treatment for Hmong refugees in America.

Hoy, Suellen. *Chasing Dirt: The American Pursuit of Cleanliness.* New York: Oxford University Press, 1996. History of American attitudes toward cleanliness that includes Americanization efforts toward immigrants and minority groups.

Kraut, Alan M. *Silent Travelers: Germs, Genes, and the "Immigrant Menace."* Baltimore: Johns Hopkins University Press, 1995. Synthesis of immigration history and the history of medicine that provides an overview to public health, diseases, and health care of immigrants during the nineteenth and twentieth centuries.

Kretsedemas, Philip, and Ana Aparicio, eds. *Immigrants, Welfare Reform, and the Poverty of Policy.* Westport, Conn.: Praeger, 2004. Analysis of how welfare policy is implemented and experienced at the local level by immigrants and minorities.

Markel, Howard. *When Germs Travel: Six Major Epidemics That Have Invaded America and the Fears They Have Unleashed.* New York: Vintage, 2004. Study that examines six epidemics—tuberculosis, bubonic plague, trachoma, typhus, cholera, and AIDS—to explore American public health efforts in relation to immigration.

SEE ALSO: Acquired immunodeficiency syndrome; Disaster recovery work; Ellis Island; Illegal Immigration Reform and Immigrant Responsibility Act of 1996; Immigrant aid organizations; Immigration Act of 1891; Infectious diseases; Intelligence testing; Proposition 187; Welfare and social services.

HELSINKI WATCH

IDENTIFICATION: Nongovernmental human rights organization

DATE: Founded in 1978; absorbed into Human Rights Watch in 1988

SIGNIFICANCE: Helsinki Watch was a U.S.-based group made up of private citizens devoted to monitoring compliance with the Helsinki Final Act, an international agreement signed in 1975 by thirty-five countries pledging to respect basic human and civil rights. The organization focused on human rights abuses in the Soviet Union, Eastern European nations, and the United States, documenting violations of the Helsinki Final Act in lengthy research reports and frequent press releases.

Helsinki Watch was conceived as an organization focused primarily on Eastern European human rights activists, working both to influence government policy and to keep the repression of dissidents under an international spotlight. Helsinki Watch, and in particular its executive director, Jeri Laber, sought to garner public support and attention for the plight of repressed or imprisoned individuals by issuing press releases, writing op-ed pieces, and speaking out publicly. Over time, Helsinki Watch became well known for the quality and comprehensiveness of its research reports, which were relied upon by policymakers, diplomats, and others interested in Helsinki compliance. Finally, Helsinki Watch sought to influence diplomats through direct contact, making itself a permanent, visible presence at international meetings.

Helsinki Watch and its staff worked with ethnic interest groups focused on Eastern Europe as well as organizations concerned about the plight of Soviet Jews. Dissidents who had emigrated from the Soviet Union and Eastern Europe often worked closely with Helsinki Watch, offering firsthand accounts of human rights violations to the organization's researchers. Helsinki Watch pursued a range of objectives, including advocating for those who wished to emigrate from the Soviet Union and Eastern Europe, in particular for reasons of religious freedom or family reunification. In 1988, Helsinki Watch, along with committees devoted to monitoring human rights abuses elsewhere in the world, became part of a larger organization, Human Rights Watch, which is devoted to human rights internationally.

Sarah B. Snyder

FURTHER READING
Laber, Jeri. *The Courage of Strangers: Coming of Age with the Human Rights Movement.* New York: PublicAffairs, 2002.
Neier, Aryeh. *Taking Liberties: Four Decades in the Struggle for Rights.* New York: PublicAffairs, 2003.

SEE ALSO: El Rescate; Jewish immigrants; New York City; Russian and Soviet immigrants; West Indian immigrants.

HENDERSON V. MAYOR OF THE CITY OF NEW YORK

THE CASE: U.S. Supreme Court decision on federal power over immigration
DATE: Decided on October 1, 1875

SIGNIFICANCE: Based on Congress's exclusive authority to regulate international commerce, which included the landing of passengers, the *Henderson* decision had the effect of striking down all state laws regulating immigration.

The attempt of states to impose various kinds of taxes on immigrants and other passengers entering the United States was a controversial issue for many decades during the nineteenth century. In several decisions, including *Cooley v. Board of Wardens of the Port of Philadelphia* (1852), the Supreme Court held that the commerce clause prohibited the states from passing laws that placed a burden on Congress's power to maintain national uniformity in regulating international commerce. As the number of immigrants increased in the post–Civil War years, many Americans were concerned about an alleged "flood of pauperism emigrating from

Europe." The states of New York and Louisiana required ships to post a bond on each entering passenger in order to indemnify the states for the costs associated with immigrants needing financial assistance. The two states argued that the bonds were not a regulation of commerce but rather a legitimate exercise of their "police power."

The U.S. Supreme Court unanimously ruled that the required bonds violated the U.S. Constitution because they interfered excessively with foreign commerce. Writing the opinion for the Court, Justice Samuel F. Miller explained that whenever a state statute "invades the domain of legislation which belongs exclusively to the Congress," such a statute is unconstitutional and therefore void. Although Miller acknowledged that the payment of bonds was somewhat related to the police power of the states, he nevertheless found that charging such a requirement made it impossible for Congress to maintain one uniform system of rules for the landing of passengers and immigrants in all ports throughout the United States. As a result of the *Henderson* decision, all the immigration legislation of the seaboard states was held to be unconstitutional. In response, the states abolished their immigration commissions, and private philanthropic organizations assumed most of the burden of assisting needy immigrants. The decision encouraged the federal government to pass sweeping new immigration laws in 1882.

Thomas Tandy Lewis

FURTHER READING
Fairman, Charles. *Mr. Justice Miller and the Supreme Court, 1862-1890.* Clark, N.J.: Lawbook Exchange, 2003.
LeMay, Michael, and Elliott Robert Barkan, eds. *U.S. Immigration and Naturalization Laws and Issues: A Documentary History.* Westport, Conn.: Greenwood Press, 1999.

SEE ALSO: Citizenship; Congress, U.S.; Constitution, U.S.; Due process protections; History of immigration, 1783-1891; Immigration law; *New York v. Miln*; *Passenger Cases*; Supreme Court, U.S.

HIGHER EDUCATION

DEFINITION: College-level, graduate school, and professional-school level education

SIGNIFICANCE: International scholars and students have made great contributions to the United States—economically, in helping to advance science and technology, and in increasing international understanding. However, as global competition for highly educated and skilled people has increased, fewer international scholars are choosing to come to the United States. This development could handicap the United States in future global competition, especially in the fields of science and technology. At the same time, making access to U.S. universities easier for foreign students threatens to create problems for domestic students and create security problems.

Since the 1940's, the United States has led the world in attracting international scholars and students to its institutions of higher learning. Definitions vary, but international students are persons who are not American citizens or permanent residents, who have temporary visas, and who are enrolled full-time at American universities, either to pursue a degree or to attend at least one semester as exchange students. International scholars are persons who are not American citizens or permanent residents, who have temporary visas, and who are engaged full-time in research or teaching programs at American institutions.

NUMBERS AND TRENDS

Data on international students and scholars are reported in the annual "Open Doors" report of the Institute of International Education (IIE). The IIE has conducted the annual census of international students and scholars in the United States since its founding in 1919. Since 1954, it has published "Open Doors" reports, which are based on surveys sent to more than two thousand accredited U.S. institutions.

From 1954-1955 through 2007-2008, the number of international students in the United States increased more than 1,800 percent—from 34,323 to 623,805. The latter number represents a 7 percent increase over the figure for 2006-2007. In 2008, international students represented about 3.5 percent of all college students in the United States. Their numbers have increased during every academic year, except those between 2002-2003 and 2005-2006, when their numbers dropped by about 4 percent. This drop was largely due to stricter visa restrictions and increased scrutiny of foreign students and scholars put in place in the United States following the September 11, 2001, terrorist attacks. In 2006-2007 and in 2007-2008, enrollments rebounded. Since 2001-2002, Asian countries have sent more students to the United States than any other region of the world, with India sending the most. In 2007-2008, fully 61 percent of all international students came from Asia, with India, Japan, China, and South Korea accounting for approximately 40 percent of the total.

According to United Nations Educational, Scientific, and Cultural Organization (UNESCO) reports, the United States ranked first in the world in attracting international students in 2008, when it hosted 20 percent of international students. The top ten U.S. states, which accounted for slightly more than 60 percent of all international students in the United States in 2007-2008, are, in descending order, California, New York, Texas, Massachusetts, Florida, Illinois, Pennsylvania, Michigan, Ohio, and Indiana.

In 2007-2008, 48.8 percent of international students in the United States were at the graduate level. According to the IIE, these international students represent 12 percent of all graduate students in the United States. In the fields of science and engineering, the international student percentage goes up to 30 percent, and for doctorates awarded in science and engineering it increases to 43 percent.

About 50 percent of recent international graduate students in the United States come from the nations of India, China, and South Korea. The drop-off in applications and admissions of international students to graduate school in the United States following the September 11, 2001, attacks was greater than that for all international students. However, the Council of Graduate Schools (CGS) found that a rebound in enrollments began in 2005-2006, with an increase of 1 percent, followed by a 7 percent increase in 2006-2007, and a 3 percent increase in 2007-2008. Enrollments still lagged slightly behind the figures from before the decline.

DOCTORAL STUDENTS

International students who earn doctoral degrees have a special importance; they often remain in the United States after they complete their formal studies and make crucial contributions to research and science. The Survey of Earned Doctorates by the National Opinion Research Center (NORC) estimates that in 2007, 16,947 international students received doctorates in the United States, representing 38.1 percent of all doctorates awarded in the country. The increase in foreign doctorates has been steady and substantial, as in 1977 foreign students received only 4,854 doctorates, representing 15.5 percent of all doctorates.

The proportion of international students earning American doctoral degrees ranged from a low of 13 percent in education to a high of 68 percent in engineering. International students also received 53 percent of all American doctorates awarded in the physical sciences. Students from Asia have earned about 68 percent of doctorates awarded to international students in the United States since the 1990's, with China leading all other nations.

INTERNATIONAL SCHOLARS

The "Open Doors" report on international scholars reported that 106,123 foreign scholars were teaching and doing research in the United States in 2007-2008, an increase of 8 percent over 2006-2007 and of 70.2 percent over 1996-1997. Of these scholars, 65.6 percent were men, a decrease of 8.6 percent since 1996-1997. The vast majority, 71.0 percent, were primarily involved in research. Another 12.0 percent were in teaching, 9.7 percent in research and teaching equally, and 6.9 percent in other work.

The biological and biomedical sciences had more international scholars than any other fields. Health sciences (17.7 percent), engineering (12.8 percent), and physical sciences (12.1 percent)

President John F. Kennedy at the White House with students from Nigeria, Pakistan, Iran, Colombia, Morocco, and other countries who came to the United States to study at American colleges and universities in 1961. (AP/Wide World Photos)

ranked second, third, and fourth; U.S. social sciences and history were a distant fifth at 4.1 percent. In 2007-2008, the 23,799 scholars from China constituted 22.4 percent of all international scholars in the United States, more than any other nation. India was a distant second at 9.4 percent. Overall that year, 41.1 percent of international scholars were from China, India, and South Korea. Harvard was by wide margin the number one destination with 3,712 international scholars, Stanford University being second with 2,824. Seven of the top ten destination universities were in California.

STAY RATES

International scholars, students, and graduates who have remained in the United States have contributed greatly to research labs, universities, and other high-tech institutions. However, there is virtually no information on stay rates for international undergraduate degree recipients or for scholars who arrive here with doctorates. The annual Oak Ridge Institute for Science and Education report, "Stay Rates of Foreign Doctorate Recipients," covers doctorates in science (including economics and social sciences) and engineering. The most recent report was issued in 2007, including data through 2005.

Stay rates are looked at in terms of one, two, five, and ten years. The 2007 report found the two-year stay rate was 40 percent in 1989; it increased to 71 percent in 1992, declined after the 2001 terrorist attacks, and rebounded to 66 percent by 2005. The five-year stay rate for those getting doctorates in 2000 was an all-time high of 68 percent, and the ten-year stay rate in 2005 was 62 percent. Five-year stay rates from 2000 to 2005 for the four countries with the most doctorate recipients were as follows: China (92 percent), India (85 percent), Taiwan (50 percent), and South Korea (42 percent). Five-year stay rates also varied by degree field, with computer and electrical engineering highest at 76 percent, and physical sciences, computer science, and life sciences all running close seconds at 73 percent. The lowest stay rate was economics (44 percent). This report is optimistic about the chances of current foreign doctoral students remaining in the United States, pointing out the recent rebound in stay rates, the high long-term stay rates, and a similar turnaround in recent graduates who say they wish to stay.

MOST POPULAR FIELDS OF STUDY AMONG INTERNATIONAL STUDENTS, 2007-2008	
Field	*Percent*
1 Business and management	19.6
2 Engineering	17.0
3 Physical and life sciences	9.3
4 Social sciences	8.7
5 Mathematics and computer sciences	8.2
6 Fine and applied arts	5.6
7 Health professions	5.1
8 Intensive English language	4.6
9 Education	3.1
10 Humanities	3.1
Other	15.7

Source: UNESCO

NORC's Survey of Earned Doctorates asks international graduates whether they plan to stay in the United States. Past research indicates most of the recipients who state they plan to stay actually do so. The percentage of foreign doctoral recipients planning to stay had reached an all-time high of 71.7 percent in 2001, declined after the terrorist attacks, and rebounded in 2005, with the percentage saying they planned to stay at 74.7 percent in 2006. That year's doctoral recipients from China (89.8 percent) were most likely to say they intended to stay, followed closely by Bulgaria (88.9 percent), India (88.1 percent), and Iran (88.0 percent). The lowest percentage was Chile (30.1 percent), with South American countries having generally lower percentages. The 2006 survey found that graduates in chemistry (90 percent), biological/biomedical sciences (88 percent), and electrical engineering (87 percent) were most likely to say they planned to stay, while graduates in education (43 percent), social sciences (60 percent), and humanities (62 percent) were least likely.

CONTRIBUTIONS

NAFSA: Association of International Educators conservatively estimated that foreign students and their dependents contributed approximately $15.5 billion to the U.S. economy during the 2007-2008 academic year. The figures for the previous two academic years were only slightly lower.

Several recent studies have found that in terms of scientific publications, citations, and patents, international students and scholars have made exceptional contributions to the United States, proportionately greater than those made by U.S.-born scientists. In many fields of science and engineering, foreign students make up the majority of doctorate recipients. Foreign scholars and graduates fill important positions in universities, high-tech industries and research establishments.

International students and scholars enrich American campuses and businesses by adding diversity and providing American students and scholars with greater understanding and knowledge of foreign cultures and governments. Even after international scholars leave, many of them continue to collaborate with scholars in the United States. Many return to their home countries to become respected scientists and leaders, bringing with them positive attitudes toward the United States and fostering mutual understanding, respect, and cooperation.

ISSUES AND PROBLEMS

For many years, the high quality of educational and research opportunities in the United States has resulted in a brain drain of talented students and scholars from other nations. Due to increasing global competition for these people from both developing and developed nations, this trend has slowed and appeared to be reversing in 2009. Two reports from the Ewing Marion Kauffman Foundation from that year found that fewer foreign students expressed a desire to remain permanently in the United States than in the past, and that more perceived the United States to be declining as a land of opportunity. Greatly improved opportunities in many developing countries, particularly those of India and China, may well influence stay rates of graduates and scholars.

Developed nations have also increased their efforts to retain and attract international students and scholars. In particular the forty-six European Higher Education Area (EHEA) countries have initiated the Bologna Process to make academic standards and quality assurance standards of its nations more comparable and compatible, resulting in greater mobility among nations and increased collaboration.

The majority opinion, particularly in academia and research institutes, is that having fewer international scholars and students studying and working in the United States would be detrimental to the scientific and technological innovation crucial to the success of the U.S. economy. There is a counter opinion, mostly articulated by the Center for Immigration Studies, that having too many foreign-born scholars and students in the United States is counterproductive. They contend that NAFSA greatly exaggerates the economic contribution of foreign students and that the United States is damaging its long-term competitiveness by displaying a preference for foreign over domestic students.

Critics have further argued that U.S. scholars, researchers, and students are denied opportunities and discouraged from choosing careers in science and engineering because of foreign-born competitors. The negative impact is argued to be particularly great on minority students. They also propose that student visas are an ideal way for terrorists to enter and stay in the United States and that foreign scholars might take part in espionage for their governments and businesses. While the decline in the U.S. economy that began in 2008 has resulted in some U.S. firms reducing their hiring of foreign scholars and students due to fear of political backlash, the federal government and U.S. universities have continued to work to increase their number.

Jerome L. Neapolitan

FURTHER READING

Committee on Policy Implications of International Graduate Students and Postdoctoral Scholars in the United States, Board on Higher Education and Workforce, National Research Council. *Policy Implications of International Graduate Students and Postdoctoral Scholars in the United States.* Washington, D.C.: National Academy Press, 2005. This book explores the impact of international students and scholars on the United States, particularly educational institutions.

Gürüz, Kemal. *Higher Education and International Student Mobility in the Global Knowledge Economy.* Albany: State University of New York Press, 2008. Examines how the international mobility of students has changed over time.

Institute of International Education. *Higher Education on the Move: New Developments in Global Mobility.* Leetsdale, Pa.: IIE Books, 2009. Collection of eight articles, each by a different author, exploring recent changes in higher education, the world economy, and governmental changes.

_____. *Open Doors 2008: Report on International Educational Exchange.* Leetsdale, Pa.: IIE Books, 2009. Annual report that provides a statistical analysis of international students and scholars at U.S. academic institutions. Much of the data and analysis are available at the Open Doors Web site (http://opendoors.iienetwork.org).

Wadhwa, Vivek, Anna Lee, Richard Freeman, and Alex Salkeyer. *Losing the World's Best and Brightest.* Kansas City, Mo.: Kauffman Foundation, 2009. Report arguing that the United States may be on the verge of experiencing a reverse brain drain.

SEE ALSO: "Brain drain"; Chinese Student Protection Act of 1992; Economic consequences of immigration; Education; Foreign exchange students; Hayakawa, S. I.; Homeland Security, Department of; Multiculturalism; Science.

HISTORY OF IMMIGRATION, 1620-1783

SIGNIFICANCE: Immigration from Europe and Africa to America during the seventeenth and eighteenth centuries created the population that existed at the time the United States came into existence. The groups that made up this original population contributed greatly to the events and traditions that would shape the nation throughout its history.

The colonies that became the United States were founded as British outposts, and most of the European immigrants to those colonies were from Great Britain. However, the early British settlers came as distinct groups to different geographic areas. In addition, early American immigrants included people from other places in northern Europe, as well as involuntary immigrants from Africa.

EARLY ENGLISH IMMIGRATION TO NEW ENGLAND, 1620-1642

Jamestown, in Virginia, was founded in 1607 and is generally regarded as the first permanent English settlement in North America. However, the 1620 establishment of Plymouth Bay Colony in Massachusetts by the religious immigrants known as the Pilgrims may be regarded as the beginning of large-scale migration from Europe to the territory that would eventually become the United States. The Pilgrims came from English dissenters against the Church of England, known as Separatists, who believed that they should separate themselves from the state Church entirely. In order to follow their separate faith without persecution from English authorities, communities of Separatists went into exile in Holland. However, it was difficult for the English religious refugees to find any work other than in the hardest and lowest-paying occupations, and their economic situations were often precarious. Also, the intensely religious exiles were suspicious of Dutch culture, and they worried about their children losing their English customs. Their leaders managed to get England's King James I to agree to allow them to resettle in America, and they obtained support from financial speculators in the London Virginia Company in return for granting the company a large portion of the crops to be produced in the New World.

On September 16, 1620, the *Mayflower* sailed from Plymouth, England, with 102 emigrants, forty-one of whom were Separatists. Two months later, they arrived at Cape Cod in modern Massachusetts. After tense encounters with Native Americans, they resettled at Plymouth Bay in December. They had a difficult struggle to establish themselves, but eventually, with new arrivals, the colony at Plymouth became one of the bases of the new American population.

An even greater contribution to the American population, in sheer numbers, began with the Puritans, who believed in purifying the established church, a decade after the voyage of the *Mayflower.* In 1630, seventeen ships left England for America. The most famous of these was the *Arabella*, on which the Puritan leader John Winthrop sailed. Mainly stemming from the area of East Anglia in England, the Puritans left during a time when Archbishop William Laud was attempting to eliminate Puritan influences from the Church of England and King Charles I was attempting to rule without calling Parliament into session. The decade of the 1630's, leading up to the English Civil War (1642-1651), was a time of economic depres-

The Mayflower. (R. S. Peale and J. A. Hill)

sion, as well as a period in which the Puritans were out of favor in the English church and state.

The years 1630 to 1640 are known as the Great Migration. The largely Puritan immigrants from England settled in New England, north of the settlement at Plymouth Bay, in a stretch of land known as the Massachusetts Bay Colony. The major centers of the new colony were the eastern coastal Massachusetts towns of Boston and Salem. During the Great Migration, an estimated two hundred ships reportedly carrying approximately 20,000 people arrived in Massachusetts. Although migration to New England dropped dramatically after the Great Migration, the descendants of the people who entered Massachusetts in those years settled much of the northeastern region of the United States and later spread westward throughout the country.

ENGLISH SETTLEMENT IN VIRGINIA, 1642-1675

In the South, the tiny Virginia colony that had barely maintained its existence during the years that Massachusetts became a center of European settlement began to expand rapidly just as the Great Migration ended in the North. In 1642, only 8,000 colonists lived in Virginia. At the beginning of that year, Sir William Berkeley became governor of Virginia, a post he would hold until 1676. Berkeley began a campaign to draw some of England's

elite to Virginia. This campaign was assisted by the rise of the Puritans to power and the execution of King Charles I in 1649. Many of the future leaders that Virginia provided to the United States and to the Confederacy were descendants of these aristocratic immigrants.

The largest portion of Virginia's early immigration, though, came from the humblest section of the English population. About three-quarters of the new arrivals in Virginia during the middle to late seventeenth century came as indentured servants, people bound to serve masters without wages for specified periods of time for the price of their passage. The early immigration patterns of Virginia, then, made it a highly unequal society from the very beginning. By 1660, Virginia had a population of about 30,000 people. Neighboring Maryland, also populated largely by indentured servants, held about 4,000 in that year.

QUAKER IMMIGRATION, 1675-1725

The Society of Friends, popularly known as the Quakers, is a Christian religious group that emphasizes the inward experience of faith and the equality of people. It was founded during the mid-seventeenth century, and the Quakers' rejection of social hierarchy led to their persecution in England. Soon after the denomination was established, Quaker immigrants were arriving in America. In 1675, large-scale migration began when the first ship of Quaker passengers reached Salem in West Jersey. Other ships followed, docking in Delaware Bay.

The number of Quakers arriving in the Delaware Valley was so great that by 1750 they made up the third-largest religious denomination in the American colonies. Their growth had been assisted by Quaker leader William Penn's efforts to create a Quaker region in America to which members of the faith in England would be encouraged to relocate. In 1681, he managed to obtain a charter from King Charles II for 45,000 square miles, which the king dubbed Pennsylvania. In 1682, Penn arrived in his colony on the ship *Welcome.* Under his leadership, Pennsylvania drew not only Quaker immigrants but also members of other persecuted religious groups attracted by the policy of religious toleration.

SCOTTISH, SCOTCH-IRISH, AND ENGLISH IMMIGRATION, 1715-1775

People from the north of England, Scotland, and northern Ireland made up much of the migration to the western frontier regions of the early American colonies, especially to the rugged mountainous areas. The northern Irish migrants were mainly Scotch-Irish, descendants of people from Scotland who had moved to Ireland in earlier centuries. Most of the Irish in America before the nineteenth century were actually Scotch-Irish.

Northern Irish migration peaked between the 1750's and the early 1770's, with an estimated 14,200 people from northern Ireland reaching America from 1750 to 1759, 21,200 from 1760 to 1769, and 13,200 in the half-decade leading up to the American Revolution. Most of the Scots migration took place from 1760 to 1775, when about 25,000 new arrivals came to the colonies. The counties of North England, bordering Scotland, experienced a series of crop failures that were especially severe in 1727, 1740, and 1770. Each of these crop failures resulted in famine that sent successive waves of immigrants to America. Together, the Scottish, Scotch-Irish, and North English immigrants probably made up 90 percent of the settlers in the back country of America. Arriving after the lands along the eastern coast had been taken, these hardy individuals made up the original American frontier folk.

DUTCH, SWEDISH, AND GERMAN IMMIGRATION, 1630-1783

The most significant groups of European immigrants to the colonies of North America before the revolution came from the northern lands of Holland, Germany, and Sweden. The Dutch attempted to found their first colony during the late 1620's, when Dutch trading interests established the col-

Late nineteenth century depiction of Peter Minuit negotiating with Algonquian Indians to purchase the island of Manhattan in 1626. (Francis R. Niglutsch)

ony of New Netherland, with New Amsterdam as its capital. During the mid-seventeenth century, officials in Holland began actively encouraging migration to their colony, so that the population of New Netherland grew from about 2,000 people in 1648 to about 10,000 in 1660. Only about half of these were actually Dutch, though, and the rest consisted mainly of Belgians. In 1664, the British seized New Netherland and changed its name to New York. People with Dutch names and ancestry continued to make up a small but important part of the New York population, particularly among the elite of the area.

Swedes arrived on the northeastern coast in 1637 and founded a colony on Delaware Bay in 1638. Peter Minuit, a former director-general of the Dutch colony of New Netherland who had been born in the German state of Westphalia, led this initial Swedish settlement. New Sweden included areas of the modern states of New Jersey, Maryland, Pennsylvania, and Delaware along the Delaware River. Tensions with New Netherland led to a Dutch takeover of New Sweden in 1654, but the Dutch continued to recognize the colony as a self-governing settlement of Swedes. In 1681, following the British takeover of all the northeastern lands, William Penn received a charter for Pennsylvania, ending the distinctly Swedish identity of the region.

By the time the United States won its independence, Germans made up the largest national origin group in the country, aside from the groups stemming from the British Isles. In the year 1683, Dutch and German people in religious minorities purchased land in Pennsylvania, north of Philadelphia, and founded Germantown. One of the largest migration waves from the lands of Germany began when Protestants from the Palatine area of Germany fled political disorder and economic hardship in their homeland in 1709. After making their way to Holland and then England, about 2,100 Palatine Germans reached America in 1710, settling mainly in New York.

During the early eighteenth century, other German colonists settled in Virginia, the Carolinas, and Massachusetts. Pennsylvania, though, became the main center of German settlement, in part because the Quaker tradition of the state offered religious tolerance to German Lutherans, Mennonites, Amish, and other religious movements.

Probably about half the Germans who arrived in Pennsylvania between 1725 and the American Revolution came as redemptioners, who paid for their passage by working for a certain number of years. In all, an estimated 84,500 Germans reached the thirteen American colonies between 1700 and 1775. After the revolution, an estimated 5,000 German mercenary soldiers, mostly from the state of Hesse, who had been fighting for the British and been taken prisoner by the Americans, remained in the new country.

AFRICAN INVOLUNTARY IMMIGRATION, 1640-1783

African immigration to North America dates back to the time of the first European arrivals. During the entire period of American colonial history, involuntary immigrants arrived as slaves from Africa, mainly West Africa. Between 1700 and 1775, an estimated 278,400 Africans reached the original thirteen colonies that became the United States.

Slave importation to the coastal states of the South grew rapidly during the late seventeenth century and the first half of the eighteenth century because of the growth of the tobacco and rice economies. Imports of slaves to tobacco-growing Virginia reached 7,000 per decade for the 1670's through the 1720's and then nearly doubled to 13,500 per decade until the 1750's. South Carolina, where rice had become an important crop, began importing slaves at about the same level as Virginia during the early eighteenth century and then increased to more than 20,000 during the 1720's. While slave importation began to slow in Virginia during the later eighteenth century, it continued at about 17,000 per decade in South Carolina from the 1750's to the 1790's. By the time of the first U.S. Census in 1790, as a result of involuntary immigration and the increase of native-born slaves, people of African ancestry made up one-fifth of the American population.

Carl L. Bankston III

FURTHER READING

Fischer, David Hackett. *Albion's Seed: Four British Folkways in America.* New York: Oxford University Press, 1989. Intended to trace the cultural contributions of different segments of British society to America, this book is also one of the best general works on the places of origin and settlement of people from Britain in America during the colonial period.

Fogleman, Aaron Spencer. *Hopeful Journeys: German Immigration, Settlement, and Political Culture in Colonial America, 1717-1775*. Philadelphia: University of Pennsylvania Press, 1996. Excellent account of colonial German migration that divides its attention between the lands left behind in Europe, explaining why the Germans left, and the new world they found in America. It also contains informative tables on colonial immigration in general, as well as German immigration in particular.

Moore, Susan Hardman. *Pilgrims: New World Settlers and the Call of Home*. New Haven, Conn.: Yale University Press, 2007. Through looking at the life histories of the approximately one-third of English immigrants to America from 1640 to 1660 who returned to England, this book looks at motives for both migration and return.

Weaver, John C. *The Great Land Rush and the Making of the Modern World, 1650-1900*. Montreal: McGill-Queen's University Press, 2003. General work on how European colonization of other lands transformed world economy and society.

See also: British immigrants; Canadian immigrants; Constitution, U.S.; German immigrants; History of immigration, 1783-1891; History of immigration after 1891; Massachusetts; Pilgrim and Puritan immigrants; Slave trade; Virginia.

HISTORY OF IMMIGRATION, 1783-1891

SIGNIFICANCE: The first century of American independence saw great population growth, particularly from the new immigration of Germans and Irish, as the federal government gradually developed a coherent national immigration policy.

During the nineteenth century, the U.S. government began collecting statistical information on immigration and took its first steps toward formulating a national immigration policy. Although immigration did not attain the levels it would reach toward the end of that century, economic opportunities in the new nation and problems in other countries attracted many immigrants who settled new regions and helped build the country's infrastructure.

EVOLUTION OF FEDERAL IMMIGRATION POLICY

Until the first quarter of the nineteenth century, the new federal government was content to leave control over immigration policy to the individual states. The first major federal law to deal specifically with immigration—and not naturalization—was the Steerage Act of 1819. This statute gave the federal government information on immigration by requiring that all vessels reaching American shores deliver passenger lists to customs officials, who were required to send copies to the U.S. State Department, which, in turn, submitted the lists to Congress. The Steerage Act also limited the numbers of passengers on arriving and departing ships.

Congress did not move to impose federal controls over entry into the country until the second half of the nineteenth century. Several of the earliest federal immigration laws were directed against Chinese immigrants, who had begun arriving in the United States in significant numbers during the 1850's. These Asian immigrants came to be seen as undesirable because their culture differed from that of the predominantly white majority population and because of the competition they offered other workers. An 1862 federal law prohibited the transportation of Chinese "coolies," or manual laborers, by American ships. Twenty years later, that anti-Chinese law was followed by the Chinese Exclusion Act of 1882. The latter law suspended all immigration of Chinese laborers for ten years, barred Chinese immigrants from naturalizing as American citizens, and established provisions for their deportation. The principle of excluding Chinese immigrants was later indefinitely extended and not repealed until 1943.

Meanwhile, the first attempt to centralize control of immigration in general in the hands of the federal government came in 1864 with a law that authorized the president to appoint an immigration commissioner under the secretary of state. That law established provisions for contracts in which immigrants could be bound to use their wages to pay off the cost of their transportation to the United States. That law was repealed in 1868.

In 1875, the U.S. Supreme Court ruled that state laws regulating immigration were unconstitutional because they were inconsistent with the exclusive power of the U.S. Congress to regulate foreign commerce. In March of that same year, Congress passed a law prohibiting the entry of classes of undesirable immigrants. Congress also made it illegal to transport Asian workers to the United States without their free consent, forbade contracts to supply Chinese "coolies," and gave customs officials the duty of inspecting immigrants. This was followed by the Immigration Act of 1882, which set up state boards under the U.S. secretary of the Treasury as a way of controlling immigration. This law also added new categories of excluded undesirable immigrants and set a tax on new arrivals in the United States. The creation of the Office of the Superintendent of Immigration in the Department of the Treasury in 1891 and the designation of New York Harbor's Ellis Island as the location for the first national immigrant reception center in 1890 began the modern, federally controlled period in American immigration history.

EARLY NINETEENTH CENTURY IMMIGRANTS

The earliest decades of the new nation saw relatively little new immigration. During the 1780's, while the nation was governed under the Articles of Confederation, the loosely joined states went through difficult economic times, and the future of the independent country seemed too insecure to encourage new immigration. However, even as the nation began settling into a more stable form after adoption of the U.S. Constitution in 1789, immigration was still well below the levels it would later reach. Europe's Napoleonic Wars, which lasted until 1815, and the War of 1812 between Great Britain and the United States made it difficult for emigrants to leave Europe. During the three-decade period between 1789—when the United States adopted its new Constitution and form of government—and 1820, fewer than 500,000 new immigrants arrived in the United States.

During that same period, the same political conditions that made leaving European more difficult also motivated some Europeans to emigrate. For example, during the 1790's, English radicals and Irish opposed to English rule fled their homelands to America. The Revolution in France brought new French arrivals at the end of the eighteenth century. Other French-speaking immigrants fled slave uprisings in Haiti and other West Indies colonies around the same time. These French-speaking newcomers settled mainly in coastal cities, notably in Charleston, New York, Baltimore, and Philadelphia, as well as in New Orleans, which became part of the United States in 1803 as a result of the Louisiana Purchase.

The most numerous non-English-speaking immigrants in the United States at the time of independence were Germans. Germans also constituted one of the significant immigrant groups at the opening of the nineteenth century. Many of those Germans came from what is now the southwestern part of Germany, which was then a poor area. Bad German harvests in 1816-1817 set in motion a flood of emigration out of that region. Although many of the emigrants moved east, to Russia, about 20,000 people from southwestern Germany came to America to escape famine.

IMMIGRATION AFTER THE STEERAGE ACT

The year 1820 is the first year for which detailed immigration statistics for the United States are available, thanks to the Steerage Act of the previous year. During 1820, 8,385 immigrants arrived in the United States. Most, 43 percent, came from Ireland. The second-largest group, 29 percent, came from Great Britain. Hence, almost three-quarters of all immigrants who arrived in the United States during that year came from the British Isles alone. The next-largest groups came from the German states, France, and Canada. During the 1820's, French immigrants moved ahead of Germans as the second-largest group after people from the British Isles. The second half of that decade also saw a steep rise in overall immigration, with the numbers of arrivals rising from slightly fewer than 8,000 in 1824 to more than 22,500 in 1829.

People from Ireland, who already constituted the greatest single immigrant group during the 1820's, were drawn to the United States by both continuing poverty in their original homeland and the growing demand for labor in America. For example, New York State's Erie Canal, which was under construction from 1818 to 1825, drew heavily on immigrant Irish labor. That project began a long history of Irish immigrant labor helping to build the American transportation infrastructure. The rapid commercial success of the Erie Canal

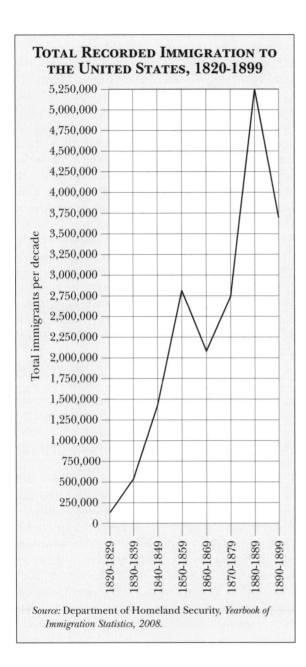

TOTAL RECORDED IMMIGRATION TO THE UNITED STATES, 1820-1899

Source: Department of Homeland Security, *Yearbook of Immigration Statistics, 2008.*

arrivals jumped suddenly from 22,633 in 1831 to 60,482 in 1832 and continued at levels roughly equal to that of 1832 through the rest of the decade.

The 1840's saw yet another surge in the tide from Europe, with 1,713,251 newcomers reaching U.S. shores from 1841 to 1850. This figure was almost triple that of the 1830's and twelve times that of the 1820's. Once again, the most important sources of new immigrants were Ireland (780,719 people) and Germany (434,626). Next highest was the United Kingdom, with 267,044 immigrants. This wave of the 1840's occurred mostly toward the end of the decade, with overall numbers rising from 78,615 in 1844 to 114,371 the following year, and reaching 297,024 in 1849.

At the approach of the mid-nineteenth century, some immigrants were drawn by the availability of land in the vast reaches of North America. Economic development also offered opportunities beyond agriculture for newcomers. Industrialization created jobs in mills and as manual laborers in cities. The expansion of railroads was another major force attracting immigrant labor. In 1830, the United States had a total of only 23 miles of railroad tracks. Only one decade later, this figure had grown to 2,818 miles. It rose to 9,021 miles in 1850 and 30,626 miles in 1860. Immigrants from Ireland played a particularly significant role in laying new railroad tracks.

Economic hardships and political disorders in the sending countries also helped stimulate emigration to the United States. The most significant event was the Great Irish Famine of 1845-1851, which was caused by a devastating potato blight. Irish were already the most numerous immigrants, and the famine drove even more of them to leave their homeland in the hope of finding relief in North America. In the various German states—which would not be united under a single government until 1871—a wave of failed revolutions in 1848 created a flood of political refugees who swelled the ranks of German Americans.

IMMIGRANT POPULATION AT MIDCENTURY

By the middle of the nineteenth century, first-generation immigrants made up one-tenth of the total population of the United States. The 1850 U.S. Census showed that the United States—including Minnesota, New Mexico, Oregon, and

stimulated the building of more canals in other parts of the country, increasing the need for immigrant labor.

The rate of immigration quadrupled during the 1830's, from a total of 143,439 arrivals between 1821 and 1830 to 599,125 between 1831 and 1840. New immigrants came from a wide variety of European countries, but most of the 1830's expansion was driven by a dramatic growth in arrivals from Ireland (207,381) and Germany (152,454). New

Utah, which were not yet states—was home to 2,240,581 foreign-born people. This figure constituted 10 percent of the total U.S. population, including persons held in slavery. Among the states and territories, New York had the largest immigrant population at midcentury, with 655,224 foreign born, who constituted more than 21 percent of the state's total population. Fifty-five percent of New York's immigrant residents were Irish; Germans constituted another 17 percent, and immigrants from England, Scotland, and Wales made up an additional 17 percent. The vast majority of all these immigrants were concentrated in the New York City area.

New York State had the largest number of immigrants in 1850, but it also had the largest total population, and there were other states with higher proportions of immigrants. The highest percentages of immigrants lived in the state of Wisconsin (36 percent of the white population) and the territory of Minnesota (33 percent). Other states with high proportions of immigrants included California (24 percent) and Louisiana. The latter was a slave state in which 26 percent of white residents and 13 percent of all residents were foreign born in 1850.

Wisconsin was home to a large number of German-speaking immigrants, who made up about one-third of all the state's immigrants. Some of these Germans, especially those from the southern German state of Bavaria, had settled in Milwaukee. Aside from the Bavarians, Wisconsin's Germans tended to be farmers who settled in rural areas. Minnesota was about to draw large numbers of immigrants from Scandinavia in the years after the U.S. Civil War. However, in 1850, a majority of the foreign-born residents of the territory came from Canada, with smaller proportions of Irish (18 percent of immigrants) and Germans (12 percent).

California's large immigrant population in 1850 consisted mainly of people from Mexico. In the 1850 U.S. Census, Mexicans made up about 36 percent of the state's foreign born. This was a heritage of California's historic connection with Mexico. Other California immigrants came mainly from Ireland (15 percent of foreign born) and Germany (10 percent). California also had smaller percentages of immigrants from all over the world. Many immigrants were drawn to the state by the discovery of gold in 1849, but most people who flocked there at the beginning of the gold rush came from other parts of the United States. However, the state's gold rush was about to stimulate a great wave of international immigration that would increase California's foreign-born residents to 39 percent of the total population in 1860.

Louisiana held the largest concentration of immigrants in the South in 1850. New Orleans, as the largest port in the South and the second largest in the nation after New York, was a natural place of entry for people from other countries. As elsewhere, the Irish made up the largest immigrant group in Louisiana. An estimated 26,580 Louisianans, or nearly 38 percent of immigrants, were Irish-born in 1850. The Irish who arrived after 1830 were most often poor peasants who settled in the area known as the City of Lafayette, which was later incorporated into New Orleans and is still identified as the Irish Channel, and provided much of the labor for digging the city's system of canals.

Many of the immigrants in both Louisiana and neighboring Texas in 1850 were Germans, who had entered the United States through New Orleans. Of the one in ten Texans who were foreign born at midcentury, over two-thirds came from Germany. These German Texans settled chiefly in the southeastern part of the state.

Most of the southern slave-holding states had low rates of immigration during the first half of the nineteenth century. The slave economy did not hold out the opportunities of the other, industrializing parts of the country. However, Maryland, one of the northernmost southern slave states, was home to an estimated 59,500 immigrants in 1850. This was the largest number of foreign-born people in any southern state except Louisiana, and it accounted for nearly 12 percent of Maryland's entire free population. As in Louisiana, Maryland's early foreign-born population was primarily the consequence of mid-nineteenth century immigration from Germany and Ireland, since Germans made up the majority (55 percent) of immigrants in the border state in 1850 and the Irish made up one-third. These immigrants were heavily concentrated in the port city of Baltimore, where Germans had begun to arrive during the eighteenth century. Irish immigration was stimulated by the potato famine of the 1840's and supported by railroad work on the Baltimore-based B&O Railroad. Southwest Baltimore, in particular, became an Irish community during the nineteenth century. The B&O Railroad also opened piers for immigration at Locust Point in 1868, making Baltimore a primary point of entry for immigrants to the United States.

LATE NINTEENTH CENTURY

Immigration continued to climb through much of the third quarter of the century, with people from Germany and Ireland making up most of the

new arrivals. For the first time, though, immigrants from China, pushed by political and economic problems in the home country and by opportunities created by the California gold rush and jobs on a railroad that was expanding across the country, began to enter the United States in significant numbers. From 1841 to 1850, only thirty-five newcomers to the United States came from China. During the 1850's, this figure shot up to 41,397. The

Editorial cartoon from a late nineteenth century California newspaper expressing the fear that the United States would be overwhelmed by foreign immigrants—particularly the Irish and Chinese immigrants caricatured in the cartoon. (Library of Congress)

numbers of Chinese immigrants reached 64,301 between 1861 to 1870 and then almost doubled to 123,201 between 1871 and 1880. Chinese immigration began to drop following the Chinese Exclusion Act of 1882, decreasing to 61,711 between 1881 and 1890 and continuing to drop in the following decades.

As the nation faced and entered Civil War, overall immigration dipped, reaching low points of fewer than 92,000 immigrants in both 1861 and 1862. Even during the war, however, immigration began to rise again. Immigrants served on both sides during the war, but far more served in the Union army than the Confederate because the North had a much greater immigrant population. The image of the Irish, who had long been subject to suspicion and prejudice in the United States, suffered when poor immigrant workers from Ireland were the most active and violent participants in riots that broke out in cities such as New York and Boston in July, 1863, in reaction to the military draft.

The Civil War was enormously destructive, but it also helped to stimulate the national economy and to push the nation toward more industrialization. In 1869, the railroad tracks connecting the East and West Coasts were finally completed, helping to create a single nation-wide economy. The mining of coal, the primary fuel of the late nineteenth century, drew more workers, as total output of coal in the United States grew from 8.4 million short tons in 1850 to 40 million in 1870. Pennsylvania and Ohio, important areas for coal mining, increased their immigrant communities, notably attracting people from Wales, an area of the United Kingdom with a long mining tradition. By 1870, Ohio had 12,939 inhabitants born in Wales and Pennsylvania had 27,633, so that these two states were home to over half the nation's Welsh immigrants.

The railroads encouraged settlement of the farmlands of the Midwest and made possible the shipment of crops to the spreading cities. Scandinavians were among the immigrant groups that arrived to plow the newly accessible lands. Minnesota held 35,940 people born in Norway, or close to one-third of America's Norwegian immigrants by 1870. Minnesota was also home to the second-largest population of Swedes in America, with 20,987. Another midwestern state, Illinois, had attracted 29,979 Swedes by 1870. Another 10,796 Swedes had settled in Iowa, adjoining Illinois on the north-

west and just south of Minnesota. About two-thirds of America's Swedish-born population could be found in Illinois, Minnesota, and Iowa.

As the nation entered the 1880's, it entered into a remarkable period of economic expansion that would make the United States into one of the world's greatest industrial powers by the time of World War I (1914-1918). It also began a dramatic rise in immigration as part of this economic expansion. Numbers of immigrants increased from 2,812,191 in the decade 1871 to 1880 to 5,246,613 from 1881 to 1890, in spite of the exclusion of Chinese immigrants following 1882. Sources of immigration also began to shift, from the northern and western European countries to southern and eastern European countries, so that immigration from Italy grew from 11,725 during the 1860's to 307,309 during the 1880's and immigration from Russian and Poland grew from 4,539 to 265,088. The United States was beginning the great immigration wave of the end of the nineteenth and the beginning of the twentieth centuries.

Carl L. Bankston III

FURTHER READING

Brancaforte, Charlotte L., ed. *The German Forty-eighters in the United States.* New York: Peter Lang, 1990. Eighteen essays covering a wide range of topics, including a reappraisal that many of the immigrants were not radicals or revolutionaries.

Gleeson, David T. *The Irish in the South, 1815-1877.* Chapel Hill: University of North Carolina Press, 2001. One of the few modern studies of southern immigrants.

Laxton, Edward. *The Famine Ships: The Irish Exodus to America.* New York: Henry Holt, 1998. Drawing on research in Ireland and compilations of stories passed down to descendants of Irish immigrants in America, the author tells the histories of Irish immigrants during the years of the great potato famine.

Mahin, Dean B. *The Blessed Place of Freedom: Europeans in Civil War America.* Washington, D.C.: Potomac Books, 2003. Comprehensive examination of the views of European immigrants and visitors on America during the U.S. Civil War and of their participation on both sides in the fighting.

Silverman, Jason H., and Susan R. Silverman. *Immigration in the American South, 1864-1895.* Lewiston, N.Y.: Edwin Mellen Press, 2006. Account of southern efforts to market the region to prospective immigrants.

Van Vugt, William E. *Britain to America: Mid-Nineteenth Century Immigrants to America.* Champaign: University of Illinois Press, 1999. Offers a portrait of immigration from the islands of Great Britain to the United States from 1820 to 1860.

Weaver, John C. *The Great Land Rush and the Making of the Modern World, 1650-1900.* Montreal: McGill-Queen's University Press, 2003. General work on how European colonization of other lands transformed the world economy and society.

See also: California gold rush; Canals; Chinese Exclusion Act of 1882; German immigrants; Great Irish Famine; History of immigration, 1620-1783; Immigration Act of 1882; Irish immigrants; Know-Nothing Party; Philadelphia anti-Irish riots; Railroads.

History of immigration after 1891

Significance: The period from the end of the nineteenth century to the early twenty-first saw the federal government taking control over immigration policy. It also saw the two greatest immigration waves in the nation's history, as well as a period of highly restrictive immigration laws during the decades between those two waves.

During the century following the first U.S. Census in 1790, the population of the United States grew by nearly 60 million people, from just under 4 million to almost 63 million. During the next century, between 1890 and 1990, the population grew by close to 186 million, adding about three times as many people in the second century as in the first. By 2007, the nation had added another 45 million in just seventeen years. A large part of the country's population growth, throughout its history, had occurred through immigration.

Era of Federally Controlled Immigration

Until the end of the nineteenth century, immigration to the United States was under the loose control of the individual states. In 1875, the U.S. Supreme Court ruled that state laws regulating immigration were unconstitutional because they were inconsistent with the exclusive power of the U.S. Congress to regulate foreign commerce. This recognition of the exclusive power of Congress over immigration opened the way to immigration policy and therefore to the establishment of procedures and locations for federal control of immigration. The construction of the Ellis Island federal immigration facility during 1891 symbolized the beginning of the modern period in American immigration history.

The Office of the Superintendent of Immigration, originally in the Department of the Treasury, took charge of immigration issues in that same year, 1891. This became the Bureau of Immigration in 1895. The bureau was transferred to the Department of Commerce and Labor in 1903 and became the Bureau of Immigration and Naturalization in 1906. This was moved to the Department of Labor in 1913 and split into the Bureau of Immigration and the Bureau of Naturalization. In 1933, these bureaus were joined as the Immigration and Naturalization Service (INS), which President Franklin D. Roosevelt moved to the Department of Justice in 1940. In 2003, President George W. Bush established the Department of Homeland Security and reorganized the INS as the U.S. Citizenship and Immigration Services (USCIS) under the authority of this new department.

First Modern Immigration Wave

The growth of the American population through immigration was primarily a result of the growth of the American economy, which provided new opportunities. That economy had been growing rapidly throughout the first half of the nineteenth century. The U.S. Civil War caused disruption, but it also stimulated production in the North, and it ultimately created a more politically and economically unified nation. The completion of the transcontinental railroad in 1869 meant not only that people could travel relatively quickly from the East Coast to the West Coast but also that goods from one part of the country could be shipped and sold to other parts of the country. This completion of the transportation infrastructure spurred rapid industrialization in the decades following the Civil War. By 1890, the United States had outstripped the leading industrial nations of Europe to become the world's foremost producer of manufactured goods. The quickly developing industrial economy required workers, and the availability of jobs drew immigrants to American shores in unprecedented numbers.

As a result of the flow of new workers into the country, the nation's new industrial working class rapidly became disproportionately foreign born. The Dillingham Commission, set up by Congress in 1907 to study the perceived immigration problem, looked at twenty-one industries and found that 58 percent of the workers in these industries were immigrants. The commission found that immigrants were particularly significant in construction work, railroads, textiles, coal mining, and meatpacking.

Transportation systems had linked the United States, and they also made it easier to reach North America from Europe. Train systems in Europe by the late nineteenth century enabled Europeans to reach their own coastal cities. The replacement of sailing ships by steamships cut travel time over the ocean from one to three months during the 1850's to ten days by the 1870's.

During the first decade of the period of federal control of immigration, 1891 to 1900, 350,000 newcomers reached the United States. In the decade after, from 1901 to 1910, this number more than doubled to 800,000 new arrivals. Although the absolute number of foreign-born people was greater at the end of the twentieth century, immigrants made up a larger proportion of the American population during the late nineteenth and early twentieth centuries, when 15 percent of Americans were immigrants. Because of continuing immigration, moreover, by 1910 another 15 percent of native-born Americans were children of two immigrant parents and 7 percent of native-born Americans had at least one immigrant parent, so that immigrants and children of immigrants made up more than one-third of the U.S. population.

The large immigrant population of the United States came from places that had sent few people in earlier years. America's population at its beginning consisted mainly of people from northern and western Europe and people of African heritage, and newcomers in the first century of the nation's existence continued to come primarily from northern and western Europe. As recently as 1882, 87 percent of immigrants came from the northern and western European countries. By the end of the century, though, economic hardship in southern Europe and political oppression combined with poverty in eastern Europe, together with the improved transportation, led to a geographic shift.

By 1907, 81 percent of immigrants to the United States came from southern and eastern Europe. According to the statistics of the Dillingham Commission, of the 1,285,349 foreign-born people who arrived in the United States in 1907, 285,943 (22 percent) came from the Russian Empire and 338,452 (26 per-

Ship carrying European immigrants to Ellis Island, c. 1905. (The Granger Collection, New York)

cent) came from the Austro-Hungarian Empire. Eastern European Jews, fleeing persecution in the two empires, made up many of these arrivals. Italy alone sent 285,731 people (22 percent of total U.S. immigrants) during that year, most of them coming from impoverished southern Italy.

The southwestern part of the United States had been part of Mexico until the middle of the nineteenth century, and many Spanish-speaking people of the same ethnic backgrounds as Mexicans lived in that part of the country. However, the United States had been attempting to anglicize the Spanish-speaking parts of the country since it took possession of this area. After the Mexican Revolution began in 1910, refugees from south of the Rio Grande began to move northward. Between 1910 and 1920, more than 890,000 legal Mexican immigrants arrived in the United States.

Increasing numbers of immigrants arriving from countries that were alien to many native-born Americans and to English-speaking officials raised concerns in the public and among policy makers. Many of those reaching American shores settled in low-income sections of the growing cities in the traditionally rural nation. Perceptions of immigration as a social problem led to a string of new laws, resulting, by the 1920's, in highly restrictive immigration policies.

LEGISLATIVE RESPONSES TO THE FIRST WAVE

At the beginning of the federal period in American immigration history, Congress passed the Immigration Act of 1891, which enabled federal inspectors to examine people on arrival and to reject entry to those who were diseased, morally objectionable, or whose fares had been paid by others. The year after that, Congress renewed the Chinese Exclusion Act of 1882, which had banned new Chinese immigration and Chinese eligibility for citizenship. Thus, federal legislative responses to immigration from the beginning were guided by the idea of keeping out undesirable immigrants and by the idea that some national origin groups were less desirable than others. The Immigration Act of 1903 not only consolidated earlier legislation, it also barred those who were politically objectionable, such as anarchists. Extending this line of action, a new immigration act in 1907 added more categories of people to the list of those to be excluded, and it restricted immigration from Japan.

The Immigration Act of 1917 expanded exclusions still more by identifying illiterates, people entering for immoral purposes, alcoholics, and vagrants as classes that would not be allowed into the country.

Following World War I, Congress enacted laws that would reduce immigration dramatically for three decades. The Immigration Act of 1921, also known as the Emergency Immigration Act, attempted to reduce southern and eastern European immigration by limiting the number of immigrants from any country to 3 percent of the number of people from that country living in the United States in 1910. In 1924, a new immigration act carried the quota concept further by limiting immigrants from any country to 2 percent of the number from that country living in the United States in 1890.

Restrictive legislation brought a drop in immigration. The Great Depression of the 1930's helped to maintain low immigration, since massive unemployment meant that the United States had fewer jobs to offer. Foreign-born people obtaining legal permanent residence status in the United States decreased from a high of 8,202,388 in the peak years 1909-1919 to 699,375 in 1930-1939.

LEGISLATIVE CHANGES

Immigration continued to be low during the World War II years, but there were some indications of a loosening of American immigration law. The United States and China, then under the Chinese Nationalist government, were allies against Japan, and this alliance encouraged American lawmakers to pass the Immigration Act of 1943, which repealed the Chinese Exclusion Act of 1882 and allowed Chinese to become naturalized citizens, although only 105 Chinese were actually allowed to immigrate each year. Worker shortages in the United States due to the war led the U.S. government to establish the bracero program in 1942 to bring in Mexican agricultural laborers.

The Immigration and Nationality Act of 1952, also known as the McCarran-Walter Act, retained the national origin criterion of 1924. It set an overall ceiling for immigrants and within that ceiling gave each country a cap equal to 1 percent of the individuals of that national origin living in the United States in 1920. The new immigration law, enacted at the height of the Cold War, placed new ideological restrictions on immigration, denying admission to foreign communists. The McCarran-Walter Act also added a series of preferences to the national origins system. The preference system became the basis of a major shift in American immigration policy in 1965.

The Hart-Celler Act, also known as the Immigration and Nationality Act of 1965, revised the McCarran-Walter Act and turned U.S. immigration policy in a new direction. Acting in the spirit of recent civil rights legislation, Congress removed the national origins quota system and instead emphasized the preference system. Family reunification became the primary basis for admission to the United States, followed by preferences for people with valuable skills.

The Immigration and Nationality Act of 1965 went into effect in 1968, and its liberal provisions made possible another great wave of immigration at the end of the twentieth century. Along with those classified as immigrants, the United States also received large numbers of refugees, leading to the passage of the Refugee Act of 1980 to accommodate this additional group of arrivals. By the end of the twentieth century, new concerns over immigration, especially growing undocumented immigration, led the nation to attempt to control the flow across the borders.

In an effort to respond to undocumented immigration, Congress enacted the Immigration Reform and Control Act of 1986, which granted amnesty to immigrants who had entered illegally before 1982 but made it a crime to hire undocumented immigrants. Ten years later, the Illegal Immigration Reform and Immigrant Responsibility Act of 1996 made it easier to deport undesirable immigrants, and it increased the size and activities of the U.S. Border Patrol.

Hmong refugees learning about life in the United States in a cultural orientation class in a Thailand refugee camp in 2004. A great change in U.S. immigration patterns that began during the late twentieth century was a huge increase in the numbers of Asians coming to the United States. (Getty Images)

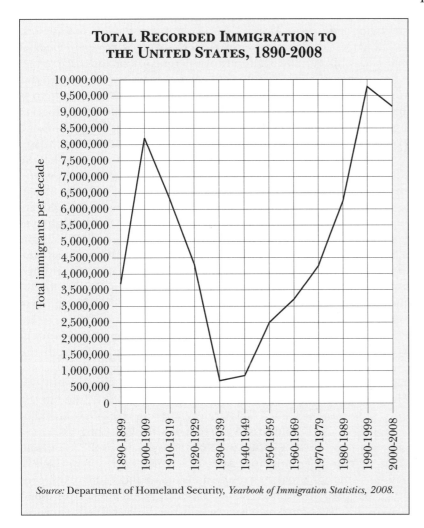

TOTAL RECORDED IMMIGRATION TO THE UNITED STATES, 1890-2008

Source: Department of Homeland Security, *Yearbook of Immigration Statistics, 2008.*

immigration wave came mainly from Latin America and Asia. From 1820 to 1970, 79.5 percent of immigrants had arrived from countries in Europe, 7.7 percent from countries in the Americas other than Canada, and only 2.9 percent from Asia. During the period 1971 to 1979, only 18.4 percent of immigrants to the United States were from Europe, while 41 percent came from countries in the Americas and 34.1 percent came from Asia. Latin Americans and Asians continued to make up most of this wave of immigration. As a result, only 13 percent of foreign-born people living in the United States in 2007 had come from Europe, while 27 percent had been born in Asia and 54 percent had been born in Latin America. Mexicans had become by far America's largest immigrant group, constituting 31 percent of all immigrants in the United States in 2007.

The heavy immigration from Mexico was a consequence of economic problems in that country, as well as a result of opportunities and relatively liberal immigration policies in the United States. More than 70 percent of Mexico's export revenues came from oil at the beginning of the 1980's. As the price of oil declined beginning about 1982, Mexico had less revenue coming in, provoking a debt crisis, and the country's already existing problems of poverty became worse. Legal immigration from Mexico began to move upward rapidly, from a little over 621,000 in the decade 1970-1979 to over one million during the 1980's.

The Immigration Reform and Control Act of 1986 encouraged some undocumented Mexicans in the United States to remain by offering amnesty, and it encouraged others to move into the United States on a long-term basis by intensifying control of the border, making it more difficult to move

SECOND MODERN IMMIGRATION WAVE

The 1965 change in immigration policy helped produce the greatest immigration wave in U.S. history in terms of sheer numbers of immigrants reaching American shores. After decreasing since the 1920's, the foreign-born population of the United States suddenly began to grow during the 1970's, increasing from 9,619,000 (4.7 percent of the total population) in 1970 to 14,080,000 (6.2 percent) in 1980, reaching 19,767,000 in 1990 (7.9 percent), and then 31,108,000 (11.1 percent) in 2000. By 2007, the foreign-born population had reached an estimated 38,060,000, or 12.6 percent of all people in the United States.

The places of origin of America's immigrants also changed. While earlier immigrants had come primarily from Europe, those in the post-1965

back and forth. The longer-term orientation led many workers to move further north, away from the border. In 1994, a second economic shock hit Mexico, with the devaluation of the peso, which caused dramatic inflation and a decline in living standards. In response to the economic problems, legal migration grew even more during the 1990's, with more than 2.75 million Mexicans entering the United States. From 2000 to 2005, the United States received an average of 200,000 legal permanent residents from Mexico every year.

Illegal immigration also grew at a rapid pace, with the largest number of illegal immigrants arriving from Mexico. Undocumented immigration into the United States rose from an estimated 130,000 undocumented immigrants each year during the 1970's to an estimated 300,000 per year during the 1980's, and their numbers continued to go up. By January, 2007, the estimated undocumented immigrant population of the United States was 11,780,000. A majority (59 percent) were from Mexico, and 11 percent were from the Central American nations of El Salvador, Guatemala, and Honduras, having arrived by way of Mexico.

REFUGEES

The United States classifies "refugees," or people admitted to the United States because of conflict, natural disaster, or persecution in their homelands, separately from "immigrants," people admitted to legal residence in the country. Refugees have, however, been a significant part of the immigration wave that began during the late twentieth century. U.S. refugee policies began before the 1965 change in immigration law. In 1948, Congress enacted the Displaced Persons Act to admit people who had been uprooted during World War II. The beginning of the Cold War gave added motivation to the American refugee program, and the Refugee Relief Act of 1953 granted admission to people fleeing countries that had fallen under communist domination. The Soviet occupation of Hungary in 1956 resulted in new refugees, and the Refugee Escape Act of 1957 explicitly defined refugees as people fleeing communism. In theory, though, refugees were to be counted under the per-country ceiling established by the McCarran-Walter Act, and the added numbers were charged against future ceilings or admitted under special presidential paroles.

America's anticommunist refugee program expanded after Fidel Castro took power in Cuba at the beginning of 1959 and Cubans opposed to Castro, who soon declared himself a communist, began to flee their island nation. President John F. Kennedy's administration established a program of assistance for Cubans, and this program was institutionalized by the Migration and Refugee Assistance Act of 1962. The first wave from Cuba left the island nation between 1959 and 1962. A second wave followed from 1965 to 1974, when the Cuban and U.S. governments agreed to arrange flights between the two countries for Cubans who wished to leave. The Cuban refugee flow slowed substantially after the halting of the flights. In 1980, though, the Cuban government faced internal unrest. This led to a third wave of Cuban refugees. Hoping to ease public unrest on the island, the Cuban government decided to open the port city of Mariel to unrestricted emigration. Vessels from Mariel brought more than 125,000 refugees from Cuba to the United States over a six-month period.

Following the end of the Vietnam War in 1975, Southeast Asian refugees began to resettle in the United States. Largely in response to movement of Southeast Asian refugees, the U.S. Congress passed the Refugee Act of 1980, which was the most comprehensive piece of refugee legislation in U.S. history. As a result, hundreds of thousands of refugees from Vietnam, Cambodia, and Laos were resettled in North America during the early 1980's. In 1980, more than 170,000 people from these three countries entered the United States. The flow of refugees continued so that by the year 2007, the United States was home to an estimated 1.5 million people who described their ethnic background as Vietnamese, close to 220,000 people who described themselves as Cambodian, 200,000 people who identified as Laotian, and more than 200,000 who identified as Hmong, a minority group from Laos.

Carl L. Bankston III

FURTHER READING

Alexander, June G. *Daily Life in Immigrant America, 1870-1920*. Westport, Conn.: Greenwood Press, 2007. Detailed study of the diverse immigrants who arrived in the United States during one of the nation's great immigrant waves. It approaches the topic through thematic chapters that look not only at daily lives but also distribution and settlement patterns, temporary and permanent residency, and individual and family migrations.

Martínez, Rubén. *The New Americans*. New York: New Press, 2004. Written as a companion book to a PBS television miniseries, this presents five portraits of new immigrants to the United States.

Shanks, Cheryl. *Immigration and the Politics of American Sovereignty, 1880-1990*. Ann Arbor: University of Michigan Press, 2001. An exploration of how political trends and issues in the United States have shaped American immigration policy over time.

Suro, Roberto. *Strangers Among Us: How Latino Immigration Is Transforming America*. New York: Alfred A. Knopf, 1998. Readable portrait of late twentieth century Latino immigrant life with discussions of how the nation has been changing as a result of large-scale Latino immigration.

Waters, Mary C., and Reed Ueda, eds. *The New Americans: A Guide to Immigration Since 1965*. Cambridge, Mass.: Harvard University Press, 2007. Collection of descriptive essays on the various immigrant groups that have made up the post-1965 immigration wave and on the key topics concerning this wave.

SEE ALSO: Asian immigrants; Dillingham Commission; Ellis Island; History of immigration, 1620-1783; History of immigration, 1783-1891; Immigration Act of 1917; Immigration Act of 1924; Immigration and Nationality Act of 1952; Immigration and Nationality Act of 1965; Immigration waves; Refugees; World War II.

HMONG IMMIGRANTS

SIGNIFICANCE: The Hmong are one of the most recent Asian immigrant groups to come to the United States. Their main home is in the northern mountain regions of Laos. The Hmong and other Laotian immigrants were helped by the passage of the Indochina Migration and Refugee Assistance Act of 1975 in their efforts to relocate after the Vietnam War ended.

PROFILE OF HMONG IMMIGRANTS

Countries of origin	Laos and Vietnam
Primary language	Hmong
Primary regions of U.S. settlement	California, Michigan, Minnesota, Wisconsin
Earliest significant arrivals	Mid-1970's
Peak immigration period	1970's-1980's
Twenty-first century legal residents*	30,000 (estimated; 3,750 per year)

*Immigrants who obtained legal permanent resident status in the United States.
Source: U.S. Census Bureau.

The Hmong people have no significant history of immigration to the United States before 1970. By the year 2000, Hmong immigrants numbered around 170,000 according to U.S. Census data. When they began migrating to the United States, they were encouraged by various settlement agencies to disperse throughout the country. However, because of their kinship patterns and collectivist nature, they instead tended to congregate within communities where other Hmong lived. Consequently, 89 percent of these immigrants settled in California, Wisconsin, Minnesota, and Michigan.

AMERICAN INVOLVEMENT WITH THE HMONG

During the Vietnam War, Hmong villagers worked alongside the U.S. Central Intelligence Agency (CIA) in their fight against the North Vietnamese in what has been called a "secret war" in Laos. Their assistance on what was supposed to be neutral territory resulted in problems for Hmong veterans on several different levels. After the South Vietnam capital of Saigon fell to North Vietnamese forces and the war ended, Laos was taken over by Pathet Lao communist forces, and the Hmong were targeted for reprisals because of their support of U.S. involvement in Southeast Asia. At risk of severe retaliation from the Lao government, Hmong and other Laotian exiles escaped to Thailand, where they were placed in refugee camps. Upon resettlement to the United States, the Hmong immigrants achieved refugee status largely because of their war efforts on behalf of the Americans as well as their need to escape the communist regime in Laos.

IMMIGRATION AFTER 1975

In response to the plight of Indochinese communities such as the Hmong after the Vietnam War, the U.S. Congress enacted legislation to enable Southeast Asian refugees to come to the United States. Many immigrants from that region were well educated and possessed valuable job skills. In contrast, however, a large part of the Hmong immigrants were poorly educated and were unskilled workers, as most had been farmers in their home country, and other aspects of the Hmong economy were not highly advanced. These factors, among others, influenced group assimilation processes even though American officials and citizens were initially supportive of Hmong migration.

Between 1981 and 1986, only a few thousand Hmong refugees came to the United States. Admis-

sions picked up between 1987 and 1994, when more than 50,000 Hmong entered the country. From 2004 until 2006, pressure from human rights groups contributed to the resettlement to the United States of an additional 15,000 Hmong immigrants from a refugee camp in Thailand. Afterward, immigration from northern Laos to the United States slowed.

HMONG IN THE UNITED STATES

Hmong communities in the United States have stabilized. U.S. government estimates indicate that between 170,000 and 186,000 Hmong were living in the United States by 2008. However, estimates from nongovernment sources have suggested that there may actually be between 250,000 and 300,000. About 60,000 Hmong reside in the state of Minnesota, with about 30,000 in the Minneapolis-St. Paul area alone. The first Hmong refugees came from a subsistence and agrarian background, but later waves of immigrants came with some knowl-

Shaman conducting a traditional good-luck ritual for members of a Hmong family preparing to leave a Thai refugee camp for the United States in 2004. (Getty Images)

edge of technology and Western culture. Overall, the American Hmong population was young and highly urban by the year 2009. In fact, the Minneapolis-St. Paul area has the largest Hmong urban population in the world. The majority of Hmong Minnesotans have already become second- or third-generation American-born citizens.

With a relatively short history in the United States, the Hmong still struggle with cultural identity issues. The initial culture shock that occurred during their first wave of immigration resulted in a slower assimilation rate than was anticipated, even though some younger Hmong Americans adapted relatively quickly. The Hmong have not abandoned their collectivist family structures and this has helped them achieve a level of economic stability. Like those of Vietnamese immigrants, Hmong families often pool resources and incomes in order to buy homes, businesses, and cars.

In Minnesota, Hmong residents generate more than $100 million in revenues annually and entrepreneurs have successfully revitalized the University Avenue area of St. Paul. Even though the first wave of Hmong immigrants was not as prepared to cope with the technologically advanced capitalistic society of the United States, over the years they have become upwardly mobile, a situation that indicates a positive future.

Dianne Dentice

FURTHER READING

Barr, Linda. *Long Road to Freedom: Journey of the Hmong.* Bloomington, Minn.: Red Brick Learning, 2004. Account of the plight of Hmong refugees during the early twenty-first century.

Faderman, Lillian, and Ghia Xiong. *I Begin My Life All Over: The Hmong and the American Immigrant Experience.* Boston: Beacon, 1998. Collection of thirty-five Hmong immigrant narratives that emphasizes generational differences.

Keown-Bomar, Julie. *Kinship Networks Among Hmong-American Refugees.* New York: LFB Scholarly Publishing, 2004. Thorough sociological study of Hmong immigrants.

Mote, Sue Murphy. *Hmong and American: Stories of Transition to a Strange Land.* Jefferson, N.C.: McFarland, 2004. Another collection of Hmong immigrant narratives.

Parrillo, Vincent. *Strangers to These Shores.* 9th ed. Boston: Allyn & Bacon, 2008. General treatment of race and ethnic relations with a section on Laotian immigration that emphasizes Hmong immigrants.

Schaefer, Richard T. *Racial and Ethnic Groups.* 11th ed. Upper Saddle River, N.J.: Prentice Hall, 2007. General textbook on American ethnic groups that includes a case study of a Hmong community in Wausau, Wisconsin.

Sherman, Spencer. "The Hmong in America: Laotian Refugees in the Land of the Giants." *National Geographic* (October, 1988). Well-illustrated description of Hmong communities in North Carolina and California.

SEE ALSO: Asian immigrants; Immigration waves; Indochina Migration and Refugee Assistance Act of 1975; Laotian immigrants; Minnesota; Refugees; Tennessee; Thai immigrants; Vietnam War.

HOLOCAUST

THE EVENT: Systematic attempt by Germany's Nazi regime to exterminate European Jews
DATE: Late 1930's to mid-1940's
LOCATION: German-occupied European countries

SIGNIFICANCE: During World War II and the years leading up to it, European Jews were the principal victims of German chancellor Adolf Hitler's genocidal policies. Many fled eastern and western Europe, attempting to enter the United States.

Between 1933, which saw the Nazis' rise to power, and Germany's 1945 surrender that ended World War II, more than 345,000 Jews emigrated from Germany and Austria. Many of them initially fled to countries that were later occupied by Germany, and these Jews subsequently left again or were murdered. Although about 85,000 Jewish refugees reached the United States between March, 1938, and September, 1939, far greater numbers were seeking refuge. However, when U.S. president Franklin D. Roosevelt was inaugurated in 1933, the United States was preoccupied with the challenges of the Great Depression—high unemployment and widespread social disillusionment—which contributed to public resistance to any relaxation of immigration quotas. Another factor in opposing specifically Jewish immigration was anti-Semitism. Anti-Jewish sentiment was on the rise during the 1920's; it increased dramatically during the early 1930's and reached its peak in America during the late 1930's and early 1940's.

FAILED ATTEMPTS TO HELP THE JEWS

In 1939, the United States refused to admit more than 900 refugees who had sailed from Hamburg, Germany, on the SS *St. Louis.* After being turned away from Cuba, the ship appeared off the coast of Florida. After the United States denied it permission to land, the *St. Louis* returned to Europe. Great Britain, France, the Netherlands, and Belgium each accepted some of the passengers as refugees. Of the ship's 908 passengers, 254 are known to have died in the Holocaust. The event was widely publicized.

News of the true extent of the Holocaust began to reach the United States only in 1941—the year

in the United States entered World War II. Nevertheless, the U.S. Department of State placed even stricter limits on immigration due to national security concerns. The threat of enemy subversion during the war was a legitimate concern, but the State Department exaggerated the problem and used it as a reason for cutting in half the already small immigration quotas. In 1943, 400 Jewish rabbis marched on Washington, D.C., to draw attention to what was happening to Holocaust victims. Only a handful of politicians met with the marchers, but one of them, Senator William Warren Barbour of New Jersey, proposed legislation that would have permitted 100,000 Holocaust refugees to enter the United States temporarily. Barbour's bill failed to pass, and another, similar bill, introduced in the House of Representatives by Representative Samuel Dickstein of New York, also failed to pass.

In 1944, President Roosevelt, pressured by government officials and the American Jewish community, took action. He established the War Refu-

Jewish refugees aboard the St. Louis *arriving in Belgium in June, 1939, after they were turned away from Cuba. More than one-quarter of the refugees eventually died in the Holocaust.* (AP/Wide World Photos)

gee Board to facilitate the rescue of refugees in imminent danger. The American Joint Distribution Committee and the World Jewish Congress worked with the board to help rescue many thousands of Jews in Hungary, Romania, and other European nations. However, government funding for the board was so small that 91 percent of its work was funded by American Jewish organizations. The board conducted a monthlong campaign to persuade Roosevelt to offer temporary shelter to large numbers of refugees, but it yielded only one result. In the spring of that year, Roosevelt established Fort Ontario, New York, as a free port for refugees. However, only a few thousand were allowed to enter, and these were people from liberated countries who were under no immediate threat of deportation to Germany. Roosevelt's response to Holocaust immigration was strongly influenced by political concerns. During an era of strong anti-immigration sentiment, any move to increase immigration might well have cost him votes in elections.

CHANGE IN IMMIGRATION POLICIES

Harry S. Truman, Roosevelt's successor as president of the United States from 1945 to 1953, favored an immigration policy that was liberal toward displaced persons, but Congress failed to act on his proposals. On December 22, 1945, Truman issued an executive order, called the Truman Directive, requiring that existing immigration quotas be designated for displaced persons. Although total U.S. immigration figures did not increase, many more displaced persons were admitted to the United States. Between the end of 1945 and early 1947, about 22,950 displaced persons entered the United States under the new Truman Directive. About 16,000 of these refugees were Jewish.

Before existing immigration quotas could be increased, congressional action was necessary. Pressured intensely by lobbying on the part of the American Jewish community, Congress passed legislation in 1948 to admit about 400,000 displaced persons to the United States. Nearly 80,000 of those who arrived, or about 20 percent, were Jewish. Other immigrants included Christians from eastern Europe and the Baltic nations who had worked as forced laborers under the Nazi regime. American entry laws favored agricultural workers to such a degree, however, that Truman found

the new law discriminatory to Jews, few of whom were agricultural workers. By the 1950's, Congress amended the law, but by that time most of the Jewish displaced persons in Europe had entered the new state of Israel, which was established on May 14, 1948.

Thanks in large part to the influx of Jews during and after the Holocaust, the United States emerged as the largest and most culturally innovative Jewish center in the world after World War II. Smaller centers of Jewish population worldwide soon turned to the vigorous Jewish establishments in the United States for help and support. By the first decade of the twenty-first century, Jews in the United States had risen to leadership positions in government, the media, entertainment, popular culture, business, labor relations, law, and the arts.

Sheila Golburgh Johnson

FURTHER READING

Abzug, Robert H. *America Views the Holocaust, 1933 to 1945: A Brief Documentary History.* New York: Palgrave Macmillan, 1999. This book tries to shed light on such grave questions as what Americans knew about the Holocaust and how they responded as it unfolded.

Breitman, Richard, and Alan M. Kraut. *American Refugee Policies and European Jewry, 1933-1945.* Bloomington: Indiana University Press, 1987. Carefully documented study that argues that U.S. policy regarding the Holocaust was the product of preexisting restrictive immigration laws and the attitude of U.S. State Department leaders who were committed to a narrow defense of American interests.

Novick, Peter. *The Holocaust in American Life.* Boston: Houghton Mifflin, 1999. Historical overview of American attitudes toward the Holocaust. A highly controversial book that argues against misuses of Holocaust history and tries to show how contemporary consciousness was formed by political conditions.

Wyman, David S. *The Abandonment of the Jews: America and the Holocaust, 1941-1945.* New York: Pantheon, 1984. Contends that British and American political leaders turned down many proposals that could have saved European Jews from death in German concentration camps.

_____. *Paper Walls: America and the Refugee Crisis, 1938-1941.* Amherst: University of Massachusetts Press, 1968. Study of the obstacles that the U.S. Congress erected to prevent the immigration of Jews during the Holocaust.

SEE ALSO: American Jewish Committee; Anglo-conformity; Anti-Semitism; Center for Immigration Studies; Congress, U.S.; Films; German immigrants; Jewish immigrants; Quota systems; Refugee Relief Act of 1953; Refugees; World War II.

HOMELAND SECURITY, DEPARTMENT OF

IDENTIFICATION: Federal cabinet-level department created to consolidate immigration and domestic security functions
DATE: Established on March 1, 2003

SIGNIFICANCE: Formed in the wake of the September 11, 2001, terrorist attacks on the United States, this well-funded cabinet department of the federal government has exemplified a governmental response to improve the coordination and effectiveness of efforts to combat the ongoing war against terrorism. It has greatly increased the number of illegal immigrants apprehended each year in the United States.

On March 1, 2003, the Department of Homeland Security (DHS) was founded to address concerns with terrorism that were greatly heightened after the 9/11 attacks. Its creation was widely acknowledged to have prompted the largest federal government reorganization since World War II, and its creation had great implications for evolving immigration policy and practice. Two of the largest agencies that had previously been dealing with immigration issues, the Immigration and Naturalization Service and the U.S. Customs Service, were among the approximately one hundred former federal departments absorbed into the new department. Other DHS branches concerned with immigration control had been created after September 11, 2001. A prominent example is the Transportation Security Administration (TSA), whose chief mandate was to ensure airport and airline safety.

KEY IMMIGRATION-RELATED ACTIVITIES OF THE DHS

The DHS subdivision with primary responsibilities for administrative functions and decisions that affect the immigrant population is the U.S. Citizenship and Immigration Services (USCIS). The former Immigration and Naturalization Service and U.S. Customs Service were merged to form the Immigration and Customs Enforcement (ICE) agency. With more than 17,200 employees and an annual budget near $5 billion—more than 20 percent of the entire DHS budget—it is the largest DHS investigative agency. The ICE mission statement emphasizes its fight against the smuggling of goods and the entry of terrorists and other criminals into the United States. Additional priorities include combating arms and drug trafficking, fraud, pornography and related sex crimes, and white-collar crime.

ICE cooperates with corresponding agencies in many foreign countries, helped by more than fifty branch offices around the world. It has five main organizational divisions:

- Office of Detention and Removal Operations
- Office of Investigations
- Office of Federal Protective Service
- Office on Intelligence and the Office of International Affairs
- forensic document laboratory

The forensic document laboratory is an important subdivision established in 1978 but now run by ICE. Its work is focused on discovering identity and travel document fraud. Its staff includes handwriting and fingerprint specialists as well as forensic chemists. Staff members often serve as expert court witnesses, and they maintain an extensive library of relevant documents. Personnel from the laboratory provide consultative and training services to related professionals in the United States and abroad and issue intelligence alerts concerning recently detected fraudulent documents.

The DHS is charged with the responsibility of maintaining the National Security Entry-Exit Registration System (NEERS), which was established in 2002 by congressional order to monitor the more than 35 million nonimmigrants visiting the United States on a temporary basis for work, study, or tourism. These visitors are required to register with DHS authorities and must provide the DHS with written notification prior to changing their residences, jobs, or schools after they have been in the United States for more than one month. Noncompliance can lead to arrest, fines, and possible deportation. One of the main databases is the Student and Visitor Information System (SEVIS), which tracks foreign students in the United States and provides notification if they do not attend their classes.

The actual activities of ICE have been quite varied. The number of illegal immigrants who have been deported has steadily increased since the agency's formation—from 166,000 in 2004, for example, to 186,000 in 2006. There has also been a large-scale effort to apprehend fugitive aliens who seek to avoid deportation orders. ICE established "fugitive operations teams" that give priority to apprehending illegal immigrants involved in violent crimes. By 2009, one hundred such teams were operating across the United States. In fiscal year 2008, they made more than 34,000 arrests and reversed a previous trend of yearly increases in the numbers of fugitive aliens. The intelligence hub of this initiative is the Fugitive Operations Support Center (FOSC), which was established in Vermont in 2006. This unit has made use of computerized databases and close contacts with other law-enforcement agencies to increase detection and apprehension rates.

ICE runs an extensive immigration detention custody system with 370 facilities either owned by the DHS or, more commonly, operating under

Secretary of Homeland Security Janet Napolitano speaking at a press conference held at the Port of Miami in May, 2009. Behind her are representatives of the Federal Emergency Management Agency, U.S. Customs and Border Protection, U.S. Coast Guard, and U.S. Immigration and Customs. (AP/Wide World Photos)

service contracts with the DHS. This system has a 32,000-bed capacity, and a detention standards unit monitors compliance with national regulations originally promulgated in 2000 by the former Immigration and Naturalization Service. ICE personnel reviewed these standards and modified them to reflect a performance, outcome-based perspective. The goal is to foster consistency across facilities in areas such as the conditions of confinement, access to lawyers, and overall operations safety.

Spurred on by the 9/11 attacks, the DHS instituted a large-scale tracking program—called U.S. Visitor and Immigration Status Indication Technology—to monitor the millions of nonimmigrant foreign nationals who visit or pass through the United States each year. Designed for use at all land ports-of-entry, it runs fingerprints and pictures through databases of criminals and those on security "watch lists." It also records the dates the visitors enter and leave the country.

CONTROVERSIES

Much of the early twenty-first century controversy swirling around DHS handling of immigration affairs can be seen as a reflection of what some have noted to be a general orientation of "hyper vigilance" in confronting terrorism. This refers to a governmental policy of pursuing even the smallest indications of possible threats to national security, even though the vast majority of such interventions ultimately turn out to be false positives. The "one-percent doctrine" states that even a probability of another 9/11-type attack as small as 1 percent merits full preventive response measures, often at great public expense. Some have noted that this approach is reflective of a general sense of moral panic, especially following 9/11, and an unbridled desire on the part of the public at large to "feel safe," in a very deep-rooted psychological sense.

The implications of such a perspective for immigration policy and practice are profound. The tactics of the DHS have been criticized as relying unfairly on the immigration status and countries of origin of immigrants. For example, immigration raids carried out in airports and utility company plants deemed to be of "high risk" for terrorist acts have often focused in a blanket way on workers of specific ethnicities, without regard to their individual likelihoods of actual guilt. In some airports, groups of Hispanic support personnel have been arrested on the grounds that their undocumented immigration status makes them more liable to terrorist recruitment and coercion.

Approval rates for applications from asylum seekers have steadily declined since the inception of the DHS, and the decision making has at times seemed to proceed on a global country-by-country (instead of on an individual applicant) basis. For example, during the early twenty-first century, more than 60 percent of Iraqi and Cuban applications for asylum were approved, while fewer than 10 percent of those from Haiti and El Salvador were given asylum.

The decreasing approval rates are coupled with a decrease in application rates, and both can be traced to tough, seemingly blanket-type approaches to detention decisions. During various periods between 2003 and 2008, all applicants from thirty-three countries that had an al-Qaeda presence were automatically detained. This practice was carried out in spite of international regulations that mandated detention decision making on an individual, case-by-case basis and a presumption against detention for those with pending asylum applications.

These applications of "guilt by association"-type processing have raised the controversial specter of racial profiling, an alleged police practice that, when exposed, has been roundly reviled by both liberal and conservative critics. This in turn is fueled by an increasing practice of privatization with the fields of corrections and security. The DHS has spent many millions of dollars on lucrative contracts to private agencies involved in augmenting border patrols and running detention centers. Just as the privatization of prisons has raised grave concerns regarding accountability and the protection of human rights, so has its role in DHS operations. This is especially troublesome considering the fact that most of the detainees are being held for alleged immigration violations, not for violent or even for property crimes. Nationally, the number of detainees has quadrupled between 1995 and 2008, when it was estimated that 30,000 immigrants were incarcerated on any given day.

In one Rhode Island detention center formerly under contract to the DHS, for example, it was alleged in a federal lawsuit that a thirty-four-year-old Chinese computer engineer with no prior criminal record was denied medical care for what ultimately turn out to be a fatal liver cancer illness. During the period of his detention, he was taken screaming in pain to Connecticut for a mandatory meeting with ICE officials, and on the return trip guards are said to have thrown him down and dragged him by his arms and legs, breaking his back in the process. The DHS subsequently canceled its contract with this facility and several of its guards were fired or otherwise disciplined, but lengthy confinement persists for many immigrants who have pending proceedings.

In large measure, the persistence of immigrant detention wings of local jails and even entire facilities occupied by immigrants reflects a financial incentive. Even in an extremely difficult economic climate, the DHS budget for detainees in the New England region alone increased by ten million dollars between 2006 and 2008, and the national budget in 2008 was $1.7 billion. It has been estimated that financially strapped local corrections facilities can receive more than ninety dollars per day for each immigrant detainee. This translates into a lucrative source of inmates to fill all available empty beds, while injecting much needed capital into the sagging economies of most of the communities housing jails and prisons. The facilities themselves have been able to use the added revenue to undertake major renovations and expansions that would never have been possible if public funding were their sole income stream. The overall detention issue is exacerbated by open-ended periods of confinement for most detainees. Unlike their indigent criminal counterparts, they are not entitled to public counsel representation at the hearings themselves.

HIGHLIGHTS OF IMMIGRATION-RELATED DHS ACTIVITIES

Despite all inherent operational difficulties and strong political pressures influencing long-range agency policy and goals, the DHS activities in the area of immigration law enforcement have been largely successful. In terms of apprehending fugitives from deportation orders, for example, two four- and five-day operations in February, 2009, resulted in more than two hundred arrests in four southern states. The nationwide number of such arrests doubled between 2006 and 2008. During the same month, ICE attorneys won prison terms for two members of a human smuggling ring oper-

ating between Canada and Detroit. This "for profit" enterprise had attempted to send a twenty-three-year-old Albanian national and his mother from Canada to the United States across the frozen Detroit River on Jet Skis. However, the Jet Skis overturned and the Albanian man drowned. This type of incident highlights the importance of a vigorously functioning agency that should be afforded a certain degree of autonomy in its operations. In light of the issues raised earlier, however, it is clear that there is a need for considerable oversight in terms of how the DHS runs its immigration-related programs and operations. This supervision, if well planned and executed, can also have positive benefits for the agency internally, in terms of overall employee satisfaction and morale.

Clearly, there is strong potential for the DHS to build on its past track record of successful enforcement, while directly addressing the internal and external controversies that have accompanied its development and growth.

Eric Yitzchak Metchik

FURTHER READING

Ackleson, Jason. "Constructing Security on the U.S.-Mexico Border." *Political Geography* 24 (2005): 165-184. Scholarly, theoretically based analysis of the evolution of U.S. policy regarding border security with Mexico.

Bullock, Jane, and George Haddow. *Introduction to Homeland Security.* 2d ed. Burlington, Mass.: Butterworth-Heinemann, 2006. Introductory text offering a comprehensive overview of the Department of Homeland Security that explains the department's various agencies and their responsibilities.

Kerwin, Donald. "The Use and Misuse of 'National Security' Rationale in Crafting U.S. Refugee and Immigration Policies." *International Journal of Refugee Law* 17, no. 4 (2005): 749-763. Insightful due process-oriented analysis of U.S. immigration policies, as affected by changed priorities after the September 11 attacks.

Kettl, Donald F. *System Under Stress: Homeland Security and American Politics.* Washington, D.C.: Congressional Quarterly Press, 2004. Excellent introductory reading for those seeking to place post-9/11 changes in immigration policy into the broader context of U.S. counterterrorism policy.

Lehrer, Eli. "The Homeland Security Bureaucracy." *The Public Interest* (Summer, 2004): 71-85. Detailed survey of DHS organizational components and capacities.

McEntire, David A. *Introduction to Homeland Security: Understanding Terrorism with an Emergency Management Perspective.* Hoboken, N.J.: John Wiley & Sons, 2009. Extensive survey of all aspects of Department of Homeland Security tasks.

Smith, Michael W. "Denial of Asylum: Is There Organizational Justice Under the Department of Homeland Security?" *International Journal of the Diversity* 6, no. 3 (2006): 61-69. Data-oriented analysis of asylum denial rate elevations during the past decade.

Ting, Jan C. "Immigration and National Security." *Orbis* (Winter, 2006): 41-52. Details national policies that have facilitated the increase in illegal immigrants in the United States, as well as the relationship of this phenomenon to the terrorist threat.

Uehling, Greta Lynn. "The International Smuggling of Children: Coyotes, Snakeheads, and the Politics of Compassion." *Anthropological Quarterly* 81, no. 4 (2008): 833-871. Case study and interview-based analysis of the problem of unaccompanied, illegal immigrant children in the United States.

White, Richard, and Kevin Collins. The *United States Department of Homeland Security: An Overview.* Boston: Pearson Custom Publishing, 2005. Scholarly but nonetheless accessible examination of the newly formed Department of Homeland Security, providing details about the department's various agencies and the role of the Border Patrol in combating terrorism.

See also: Aviation and Transportation Security Act of 2001; Border Patrol, U.S.; Citizenship and Immigration Services, U.S.; Coast Guard, U.S.; Deportation; Disaster recovery work; Illegal immigration; Immigration law; Muslim immigrants; 9/11 and U.S. immigration policy; Patriot Act of 2001; Smuggling of immigrants.

HOMESTEAD ACT OF 1862

THE LAW: Federal legislation making public land available to settlers for free

DATE: Signed into law on May 20, 1862

SIGNIFICANCE: The Homestead Act accelerated settlement of western lands in the United States. Initiated in response to pressure for the disposition of public lands, the act transferred ownership of property to U.S. citizens or immigrants willing to establish residence on the land and to make improvements and cultivate crops. A significant number of beneficiaries of the act were immigrants from Europe.

Support for the concept of distributing public land began during the early years of the United States. A precursor to the Homestead Act, the Pre-emption Act of 1841, legitimized squatting by permitting farmers to grow crops on public land that could later be purchased from the government. Despite growing pressure to open western lands, concern over economic and political issues generated opposition to homesteading. For example, eastern factory owners believed that homesteading would lure away immigrants who were an important source of cheap labor. Opposition also came from plantation owners in southern states concerned about increasing the number of small farms whose owners were not likely to support slavery. Homesteading legislation was passed by the U.S. House of Representatives in 1852, 1854, and 1859 but each time was defeated in the U.S. Senate.

The principle of dispersing public land became a major tenet of the Republican Party during the late 1850's as a means of preventing the spread of slavery into western lands. In 1860, homesteading legislation was approved by both houses of Congress but vetoed by President James Buchanan. However, the secession of southern states at the outbreak of the U.S. Civil War brought an end to major opposition. The Homestead Act was signed into law by President Abraham Lincoln on May 20, 1862, and took effect on January 1, 1863.

The central provision of the act was to enable adult heads of households to claim 160 acres each of surveyed public land. To be eligible to file claims on the land, homesteaders had to be U.S. citizens or have submitted declarations of intent to become citizens. Title to homesteaded properties could be obtained after five years of residence on the land, provided that the claimants made improvements, including construction of houses and wells and cultivation of at least ten acres.

The opportunity to acquire free land became an important factor attracting immigrants who sold assets in their home countries to purchase passage and supplies needed upon arrival in the United States. However, leniency in administration of the homesteading program allowed many people who knew little about farming to claim land—a fact that contributed to the failure of some farms. The harsh environment also created hardships for new immigrants. While 160 acres of humid land in eastern states could support a family, the same acreage west of the hundredth meridian was often too arid to sustain crops in the absence of irrigation. With few trees available in some areas, settlers built sod homes to provide shelter from wind, hailstorms, and winter blizzards.

By 1900, title to about 80 million acres of land had been distributed to 600,000 farmers. In some cases, homestead property was later acquired by speculators who had lent money needed by homesteaders to purchase equipment and supplies. Speculators also acquired land through phony claims or by purchasing abandoned farms. In 1976, the Homestead Act was repealed through passage of the Federal Land Policy Management Act in all states except Alaska, where homesteading ended in 1986.

Thomas A. Wikle

FURTHER READING

Davis, Charles. *Western Public Lands and Environmental Politics.* Boulder, Colo.: Westview Press, 2001.
Diamond, Henry L., and Patrick F. Noonan, eds.

> **HOMESTEADER QUALIFICATIONS**
>
> *The first section of the Homestead Act of 1862 spelled out the qualifications for claiming land.*
>
> Be it enacted by the Senate and House of Representatives of the United States of America in Congress assembled, That any person who is the head of a family, or who has arrived at the age of twenty-one years, and is a citizen of the United States, or who shall have filed his declaration of intention to become such, as required by the naturalization laws of the United States, and who has never borne arms against the United States Government or given aid and comfort to its enemies, shall, from and after the first January, eighteen hundred and sixty-three, be entitled to enter one quarter section or a less quantity of unappropriated public lands, upon which said person may have filed a preemption claim, or which may at the time the application is made, be subject to preemption at one dollar and twenty-five cents, or less, per acre; or eighty acres or less of such unappropriated lands, at two dollars and fifty cents per acre, to be located in a body, in conformity to the legal subdivisions of the public lands, and after the same shall have been surveyed: Provided, That any person owning and residing on land may, under the provisions of this act, enter other land lying contiguous to his or her said land, which shall not, with the land so already owned and occupied, exceed in the aggregate one hundred and sixty acres.

Land Use in America. Washington, D.C.: Island Press, 1996.
Porterfield, Jason. *The Homestead Act of 1865.* New York: Rosen, 2005.

SEE ALSO: Civil War, U.S.; Economic consequences of immigration; Emigration; Families; History of immigration, 1783-1891; Land laws; Nebraska; Oklahoma; Political parties; Westward expansion.

HONDURAN IMMIGRANTS

SIGNIFICANCE: Honduran immigration into the United States is a relatively recent phenomenon, but the 81 percent increase of Hondurans coming into the country during the first decade of the twenty-first century, was the largest of any immigrant group. Their numbers rose from approximately 160,000 in 2000 to 300,000 in 2008.

Until the fourth decade of the twentieth century, U.S. Census data did not count immigrants from individual Central American nations. In any case, the numbers of Hondurans immigrating to the United States before 1930 was small, and even during the decade of the 1930's, only 679 Hondurans entered the country legally. The numbers of immigrants remained low into the 1960's, when a significant increase began. During that decade, 15,078 Hondurans were granted legal permanent resident status in the United States. By the last year of the twentieth century, an average of more than 7,100 new immigrants per year were coming from Honduras. The 2000 U.S. Census recorded a total of 282,852 Hondurans living in the United States legally. However, these numbers do not include the large numbers of undocumented immigrants. By the year 2008, it was estimated that nearly 1 million Hondurans resided in the United States. Of that number, as many as 70 percent were estimated to be in the country illegally.

Many of the most recent Honduran immigrants to enter the United States legally have been granted temporary protected status because of the devastation in Central America left by Hurricane Mitch in 1998. That status was extended several times, including an extension to July of 2010; it grants work authorization and protection from deportation but does not assure permanent residency. As many as 80,000 Hondurans came to the United States under temporary protected status.

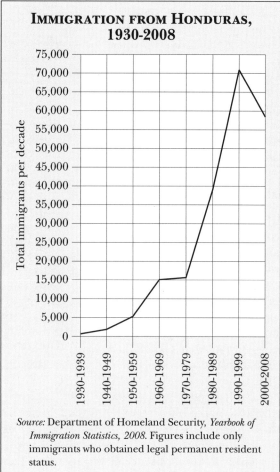

IMMIGRATION FROM HONDURAS, 1930-2008

Source: Department of Homeland Security, *Yearbook of Immigration Statistics, 2008.* Figures include only immigrants who obtained legal permanent resident status.

PROFILE OF HONDURAN IMMIGRANTS

Country of origin	Honduras
Primary language	Spanish
Primary regions of U.S. settlement	California, Washington, New York, Ohio, Illinois, Texas, Nebraska
Earliest significant arrivals	Early twentieth century
Peak immigration period	1980's-2008
Twenty-first century legal residents*	52,534 (6,567 per year)

*Immigrants who obtained legal permanent resident status in the United States.

Source: Department of Homeland Security, *Yearbook of Immigration Statistics, 2008.*

PUSH-PULL FACTORS

A combination of economic hardship and natural disasters has led to the increase in Honduran immigration. Most Hondurans are small-scale farmers with average income of only $1,700 per year. During the first decade of the twenty-first century, it was estimated that 59 percent of all Hondurans were living below the poverty line. Approximately 20 percent of adults were illiterate, and 25 percent of the children were chronically malnourished.

The 1998 arrival of Hurricane Mitch in Central America proved to be one of the worst natural disasters ever to hit Honduras. The hurricane caused great additional economic hardships in what was already a desperately poor country. Entire fruit fields were destroyed, resulting in the departure of many multinational fruit companies that were important employers. Record amounts of rainfall caused mudslides that wiped out entire villages. Back roads and bridges were destroyed, and as much as 70 to 80 percent of the national transportation infrastructure was ruined. Seven thousand people died, and more than 20 percent of the entire population were left homeless after the hurricane. During the months directly following the hurricane, the U.S. Border Patrol reported a 61 percent increase in captures of Hondurans trying to cross the border into the United States.

HONDURANS IN THE UNITED STATES

Honduran transnational communities strive to maintain ties with their hometowns while creating new homes for themselves in the United States.

The flow of migrants has a direct impact on Honduran communities in both countries, creating an exchange of cultures that changes both. Honduran residents of the United States account for 40 percent of all tourism revenue in Honduras.

Many Hondurans work in the United States in order to send remittances to relatives still in Honduras. In 2007, the Honduran foreign ministry reported that $2.8 billion in remittances were sent to Honduras by workers in the United States. Remittances directly affect the receiving families, lifting many of them out of poverty. They also add to the economic disparity in communities, creating a clear distinction between those who receive them and those who do not. However, some observers feel that remittances can create a dependence on

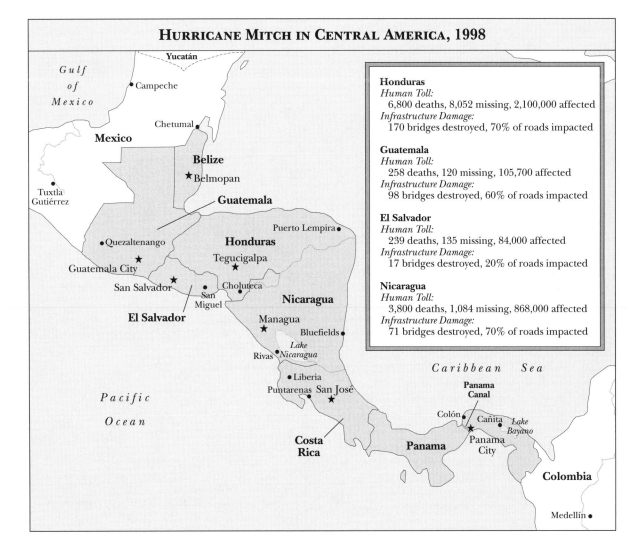

HURRICANE MITCH IN CENTRAL AMERICA, 1998

Honduras
Human Toll:
  6,800 deaths, 8,052 missing, 2,100,000 affected
Infrastructure Damage:
  170 bridges destroyed, 70% of roads impacted

Guatemala
Human Toll:
  258 deaths, 120 missing, 105,700 affected
Infrastructure Damage:
  98 bridges destroyed, 60% of roads impacted

El Salvador
Human Toll:
  239 deaths, 135 missing, 84,000 affected
Infrastructure Damage:
  17 bridges destroyed, 20% of roads impacted

Nicaragua
Human Toll:
  3,800 deaths, 1,084 missing, 868,000 affected
Infrastructure Damage:
  71 bridges destroyed, 70% of roads impacted

charity that does little to improve the economic development of Honduras.

Hondurans who try to travel to the United States to find work face difficult and dangerous journeys that require passing through Guatemala and Mexico. Peril and discomforts include rape, exposure to severe heat in desert areas, long separations from family, robbery, accidents, and even murder. Engaging professional guides known as "coyotes" can cost as much as five thousand dollars. It has been estimated that only 25 percent of the approximately 80,000 Hondurans who have tried to reach the United States each year since 1998 have succeeded.

Many of the Hondurans who have immigrated to the United States have flourished. However, a less positive result of Honduran immigration has been the development of youth gangs. During the 1990's, the U.S. government targeted undocumented residents in the penal system for deportation. Many of these former criminals were also gang members who recommenced their gangster lifestyle upon return to Honduras, creating transnational ties with gangs in the United States.

Elizabeth Ellen Cramer

FURTHER READING

Duffy, Maureen P., and Scott Edward Gillig. *Teen Gangs: A Global View.* Westport, Conn.: Greenwood Press, 2004. Discusses teen gang activity in fourteen countries, including Honduras.

González, Juan. *Harvest of Empire: A History of Latinos in America.* New York: Viking Press, 2000. General history of Latin American immigration into the United States, including that from Central and South American nations.

Nazario, Sonia. *Enrique's Journey.* New York: Random House, 2006. True story about an eleven-year-old Honduran boy's epic journey to the United States to find the mother who went north to find work when he was only five years old. Based on a prize-winning series of stories first published in the *Los Angeles Times,* for which Nazario was a feature writer.

Salgado, Sebastião, and Lélia Wanick Salgoda. *Migrations: Humanity in Transition.* New York: Aperture, 2001. Photojournalistic work depicting displaced populations of the world, including Hondurans in the aftermath of Hurricane Mitch.

Schmalzbauer, Leah. *Striving and Surviving: A Daily Life Analysis of Honduran Transnational Families.* New York: Routledge, 2005. Focusing on Honduran families in the United States, this volume investigates the role of the family in transnational communities.

SEE ALSO: El Rescate; Farm and migrant workers; Guatemalan immigrants; History of immigration after 1891; Illegal immigration; Latin American immigrants; Louisiana; Push-pull factors; Salvadoran immigrants; Sanctuary movement; Smuggling of immigrants.

HONG KONG IMMIGRANTS

SIGNIFICANCE: Immigrants from the Chinese port city of Hong Kong have differed from earlier Chinese immigrants in a variety of distinctive ways. Their arrival in the United States has drastically transformed the nature of Chinese American communities.

Located along the South China coast, Hong Kong became a British colony during the mid-nineteenth century. During a century and a half of European

PROFILE OF HONG KONG IMMIGRANTS

Country of origin	China
Primary languages	Chinese (Cantonese), English
Primary regions of U.S. settlement	West Coast, East Coast cities
Earliest significant arrivals	1960's
Peak immigration period	1970's-1990's
Twenty-first century legal residents*	35,761 (4,470 per year)

*Immigrants who obtained legal permanent resident status in the United States.

Source: Department of Homeland Security, *Yearbook of Immigration Statistics, 2008.*

colonial rule, Hong Kong culture became so different from that of the rest of China that the concept of a "HongKonger" identity arose during the 1970's. During the early 1980's, the People's Republic of China determined to take Hong Kong back from Great Britain. As European imperialism was no longer popular throughout the world, Britain eventually agreed to restore Chinese sovereignty to Hong Kong in 1997. The prospect of China's communist government assuming control of strongly capitalist Hong Kong triggered the emigration of between 500,000 and 750,000 residents of Hong Kong to other countries, including the United States.

CHARACTERISTICS OF HONG KONG IMMIGRANTS

During the 1980's and the 1990's, many of the people who emigrated from Hong Kong settled in the United States. In contrast to the peasants and contract laborers who had earlier immigrated from China to the United States, members of the late twentieth century wave of Hong Kong immigrants were primarily middle-class professionals and businesspeople, many of whom were very prosperous. More than 70 percent of the Hong Kong immigrants to the United States fell into the skilled worker and business immigrant categories. Moreover, 90 percent of them arrived in the United States already capable of conversing in English. Some observers have called these immigrants "yacht people," a facetious term that distinguishes the prosperous Hong Kongers from the desperately poor Vietnamese boat people.

In contrast to professional immigrants from other countries who have used migration as a vehicle for upward mobility, many of Hong Kong's immigrants have experienced loss of social status, reduced incomes, damage to their career development, and downward mobility in the United States. Hong Kong's emigrants might be regarded as reluctant exiles because most of them have left their homeland for political reasons, not for economic gain. Fearing they would lose political freedoms, their prosperous lifestyles, and their physical assets after communist China took over Hong Kong, many Hong Kong emigrants were anxious to obtain passports of other countries before 1997, calculating that foreign citizenship would protect them from Hong Kong's new communist regime.

Another unusual characteristic of Hong Kong emigration was its speed. Large-scale migrations of

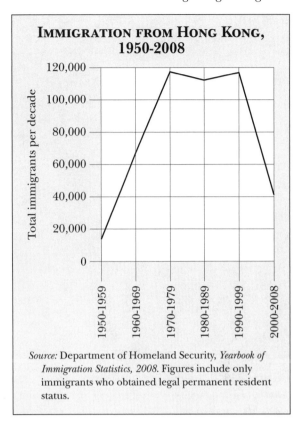

IMMIGRATION FROM HONG KONG, 1950-2008

Source: Department of Homeland Security, *Yearbook of Immigration Statistics, 2008.* Figures include only immigrants who obtained legal permanent resident status.

professional people generally take place over long time spans. In contrast, Hong Kong's middle-class migration was highly compressed. Its emigrants felt compelled to obtain foreign passports before 1997, figuring it would be too late for them to do so after the communist takeover in 1997. Consequently, the overwhelming bulk of Hong Kong immigrants to the United States arrived between the late 1980's and the late 1990's.

Another unusual characteristic of Hong Kong immigrants that set them apart from other professional immigrants was their attitude about remaining in the United States. Whereas middle-class professionals generally prefer to settle permanently after arriving in the United States, Hong Kong immigrants tended to have a "sojourner" mentality. Their paramount aim was to secure citizenship in other countries as a kind of political insurance for their futures in Hong Kong itself. With foreign passports, they could return to Hong Kong knowing that they could later leave at any time, should serious trouble arise under the coming communist government. Indeed, many Hong Kong immigrants

Seattle, Washington, restaurant owner from Hong Kong watching a parade of demonstrators marching toward the city's federal building to protest U.S. immigration policy changes in 2006. (AP/Wide World Photos)

returned to Hong Kong even before they applied for naturalization in other countries; these people sometimes stayed overseas only long enough to meet the minimal residence requirements required to secure their foreign passports.

A final characteristic of Hong Kong immigrants has been their strong sense of Hong Kong Chinese identity. They keep in touch with friends and relatives in Hong Kong and closely monitor political changes occurring there. The social lives of many Hong Kong Chinese in the United States are typically built around networks of friends who are also from Hong Kong. They speak Cantonese in their American homes, dine regularly in Chinese restaurants, regularly buy overseas editions of Hong Kong newspapers, and watch television programs on the Cantonese-language Jade Channel.

IMPACT ON CHINESE AMERICAN COMMUNITIES

The arrival of a large number of Hong Kong immigrants has helped to transform Chinese American communities. Like middle-class white Americans, middle-class Hong Kong immigrants

generally seek superior housing and living conditions. Consequently, they tend to live outside the old Chinatowns. The residential patterns of Hong Kong immigrants gave birth to many new suburban Chinatowns during the 1980's and 1990's. Whereas old Chinatowns were mostly located in city centers, the new Chinatowns were attached to newly suburban communities. Old Chinatowns are cohesive residential communities with strong ethnic organizations, but the new Chinatowns were merely clusters of shops established to service ethnic consumer demands for Hong Kong and Taiwanese immigrants.

Because middle-class Hong Kong immigrants are resourceful, they like to purchase properties for investment and speculation. Their investments have triggered rapid rises in property values within both the old and new Chinatowns, as well as nearby neighborhoods. Some established white residents have complained that the intrusion of Chinese shops into their residential areas has changed the character of their neighborhoods.

Alvin Y. So

FURTHER READING

Chabot, Richard, Oi Man Chan, and Alvin Y. So. "Hong Kong Chinese in Hawaii: Community Building and Coping Strategies." In *Reluctant Exiles?*, edited by Ronald Skeldon. Armonk, N.Y.: M. E. Sharpe, 1994. Discusses community building efforts of Hong Kong immigrants in Hawaii.

Kwong, Peter. "New York Is Not Hong Kong: The Little Hong Kong That Never Was." In *Reluctant Exiles?*, edited by Ronald Skeldon. Armonk, N.Y.: M. E. Sharpe, 1994. Examination of the various social problems that Hong Kong immigrants have created in New York City.

Li, Wei, ed. *From Urban Enclave to Urban Suburb: New Asian Communities in Pacific Rim Countries.* Honolulu: University of Hawaii Press, 2006. Collection of articles on Asian immigrants in Pacific Rim countries, including the United States.

Skeldon, Ronald. *Emigration from Hong Kong.* Hong Kong: Chinese University of Hong Kong Press, 1994. Provides much useful information on the background of Hong Kong immigrants.

Tsai, Jung-Fang. *Hong Kong in Chinese History: Community and Social Unrest in the British Colony, 1842-1913.* New York: Columbia University Press, 1993. Study of the early history of British colonization of Hong Kong.

Wong, Bernard P. "Hong Kong Immigrants in San Francisco." In *Reluctant Exiles?*, edited by Ronald Skeldon. Armonk, N.Y.: M. E. Sharpe, 1994. Detailed account of how the Hong Kong immigrants have settled in San Francisco.

SEE ALSO: Asian immigrants; Asian Indian immigrants; "Brain drain"; Chinatowns; Chinese immigrants; Immigration and Nationality Act of 1965; Page Law of 1875; Parachute children; Taiwanese immigrants.

HOUSTON

IDENTIFICATION: Largest and most cosmopolitan city in Texas

SIGNIFICANCE: Often thought of as a "boomtown" of recent origin, Houston is actually comparatively old by American urban standards. It has become a major economic center of the United States and sports a panoply of communities reflecting trends in immigration throughout American history, from a large and longstanding Hispanic presence to new arrivals from West Africa. Houston is in the top five of American cities in regard to the number of businesses owned and run by Hispanics.

The fourth most populous city in the United States, Houston was home to roughly 2,200,000 people in 2009. Of these, approximately 38 percent were Hispanic, mostly people of Mexican origin. Because Texas shares a long frontier with Mexico and was once part of that country, Houstonians of Mexican background, as with Texans in general, may be either recent immigrants, the descendents of people who fled north during periods of political unrest or financial instability in Mexico during the late nineteenth or early twentieth century, or members of families who have resided in the area for centuries. In addition to Hispanics of Mexican background, some Hispanics in Houston are of Cuban, Puerto Rican, and South American descent. Almost one-half million illegal immigrants are estimated to live in the Houston area. Most of them are of Hispanic background, but many are of Asian origin.

Much smaller in numbers than the Hispanic presence, though certainly prominent and vital, is the Asian community of Houston. The first Asians to come to Houston were the Chinese, who arrived during the early 1870's to work on local railroad lines. The number of Chinese in the city remained small until the 1960's, when political upheavals in China—from the Cultural Revolution of that decade on the mainland to the return of Hong Kong to the Beijing government in the late 1990's—led to increased emigration from China.

By the year 2000, almost 25,000 people of Chinese descent lived in Houston. A complexity of immigrant ethnic identity is highlighted by the use of the term "Chinatown" in Houston. Two different regions of the city have been labeled, both officially and unofficially, as "Chinatowns." The more important of these is a long strip along Bellaire Boulevard where many Chinese businesses, shops, churches, and homes are found. However, the American concept of "Chinatown," derived both from examples in other cities and from popular culture such as films, tends to be one of a tightly defined ethnic enclave in which Chinese Americans both live and work. The Bellaire strip in Houston contradicts this concept in significant ways: First, although there are some homes along the China-town strip, businesses predominate there. Second, a number of these businesses are owned and oper-ated by both non-Asians and Asians of other eth-nicities, such as Indians, Koreans, Japanese, and Vietnamese. These latter ethnic groups are also prominent in Houston, especially Indians and Vietnamese. In fact, Houston has the third-largest Vietnamese community in the United States, with approximately 33,000 residents at the turn of the twenty-first century.

A small but growing immigrant group in Hous-ton is that of Nigerians. The city's Nigerian com-munity, estimated at 40,000 residents, is one of the largest in the United States. In 2003, the large num-bers of Nigerians in Houston who were involved in energy-related enterprises prompted Lee Brown in 2003 to visit West Africa to establish closer ties be-tween that region's petroleum industries and those in Houston.

Thomas Du Bose

FURTHER READING

Borjas, George J. *Mexican Immigration to the United States.* Chicago: University of Chicago Press, 2007.

Powell, William Dylan. *Houston Then and Now.* San Diego, Calif.: Thunder Bay Press, 2003.

Siegel, Stanley. *Houston: A Chronicle of the Bayou City.* Sun Valley, Calif.: American Historical Press, 2005.

SEE ALSO: African immigrants; Asian immigrants; Chinese immigrants; Dallas; Empresario land grants in Texas; Illegal immigration; Mexican im-migrants; Texas; Vietnamese immigrants.

HUFFINGTON, ARIANNA

IDENTIFICATION: Greek-born author and journalist

BORN: July 15, 1950; Athens, Greece

SIGNIFICANCE: One of the most politically in-fluential immigrants of the early twenty-first century, Huffington has established herself as a centrist within a variety of media, includ-

Arianna Huffington in early 2009. (Getty Images)

ing the World Wide Web, and named one of *Time* magazine's one hundred most influen-tial people in 2006.

Born Arianna Stassinopolus in the capital of Greece, Arianna Huffington developed a slant to-ward conservative viewpoints as she grew up in her native country. However, her views shifted toward a more centrist stance after she settled in the United States, and she has called herself a progressive pop-ulist. Coming from a line of Greek journalists, she made her way to the United States in 1980 after studying at Cambridge University in England. There she lived with the English author and jour-nalist Henry Levin, who is said to have influenced her work and political positions. At Cambridge, she was the first foreign student to hold the posi-tion of president of the Cambridge Union Society.

During the 1980's, Huffington's political activi-ties leaned more to the right and introduced her to

Michael Huffington, an American politician whom she would marry in 1986. She was instrumental in supporting her husband's political career until they divorced in 1997. After becoming an American citizen, Arianna began to pursue her own career and made a swing back to more liberal views on most subjects. In 2003, she ran as an independent candidate in California's special gubernatorial election that another immigrant, Arnold Schwarzenegger, won. Although she officially withdrew from the election before it was held, her name remained on the ballot, and she finished fifth in a field of more than one hundred candidates.

Huffington's move to the news media's fourth dimension, cyberspace, came about after she had published several articles in *The National Review* and made appearances on television and public radio. In 2005, she launched her *Huffington Post* blog site on the World Wide Web. The countless blog entries she has posted there have covered events ranging from presidential politics to the dinner habits of elites and common people alike. She has also authored a number of books, ranging from biographies to messages on spirituality.

Other activities that have kept Huffington in the public's attention have included her political roundtable program on National Public Radio, *Left, Right, and Center,* which presents civil discussions of political events shaping the world. Her Detroit Project is a grassroots campaign designed to encourage American auto manufacturers to build vehicles that reduce American dependency on foreign oil. She has stated that she wants Detroit to build cars "that get Americans to work in the morning, without sending us to war in the afternoon."

Karel S. Sovak

FURTHER READING

Huffington, Arianna. *Fanatics and Fools.* New York: Miramax, 2004.

_____. *On Becoming Fearless . . . In Love, Work, Life.* Boston: Little, Brown, 2008.

_____. *Pigs at the Trough.* New York: Crown, 2003.

SEE ALSO: Greek immigrants; Jennings, Peter; Pulitzer, Joseph; Schwarzenegger, Arnold.

HULL-HOUSE

IDENTIFICATION: Settlement house for the poor founded by Jane Addams and Ellen Gates Starr

DATE: Established in September, 1889

LOCATION: Chicago, Illinois

> **SIGNIFICANCE:** Hull-House provided numerous services for the poor, many of whom were immigrants, that helped immigrants to learn about American culture and life.

The settlement house movement started in England in 1884 to provide education and assistance to the disadvantaged, while also training teachers and social workers. The first settlement house in the United States was established in 1889 in New York's lower East Side. At first staffed by men, women's settlement houses soon followed, giving young educated women an opportunity to use their knowledge and talents. In 1889, Jane Addams and Ellen Gates Starr established the most famous of the settlement houses, Hull-House, in Chicago's West Side. Settlement houses, especially in the United States and Canada, were especially important in serving immigrants who came to the cities in great numbers for work. These immigrants were

HULL-HOUSE SERVICES FOR IMMIGRANTS

- medical aid
- child care
- legal aid
- food assistance
- clothing assistance
- financial assistance
- clubs and activities for both children and adults
- English-language classes
- citizenship classes
- cultural classes in the humanities
- lecture and concert series
- University of Chicago Extension classes for credit
- vocational instruction in sewing, basket weaving, millinery, embroidery, crafts, cooking, and dressmaking

typically part of the urban poor and experienced terrible living conditions.

Although Hull-House was not the first settlement house, it became the model for virtually all others that followed. In 1889, Chicago was the second-largest city in the United States and the sixth largest in the world for industry. It offered abundant job opportunities that attracted large numbers of immigrants. Of Chicago's one million residents in 1888, approximately 78 percent were either foreign born or the children of foreign-born parents. Because of the number of potential workers, the wages were low and poverty widespread, especially among unskilled workers.

Hull-House was established on Halsted Street in the middle of an immigrant neighborhood in the Nineteenth Ward, an area considered a slum. The thirty-block area surrounding Hull-House was home to at least eighteen different nationalities that represented twenty-six different ethnic groups, including Italians, Germans, Irish, Poles, Russian Jews, Bohemians, French Canadians, and Greeks. The neighborhood contained manufacturing, small houses, apartment buildings, and tenements. City services could not keep pace with the population growth and so this neighborhood experienced the typical problems of lack of sanitation services, polluted water supply, and overcrowded, rundown housing.

Hull-House was designed to specialize in assisting immigrants, who were among Chicago's neediest residents. Its goal was to add American culture to the immigrants' native cultures, not to replace them. Serving as a neighborhood center, the settlement house provided a wide range of services. Single working women were allowed to live at the house, where they helped with day-to-day activities. Many immigrants were anxious to become Americanized and eagerly sought English and citizenship classes.

Hull-House. (University of Illinois at Chicago, University Library, Jane Addams Memorial Collection)

In addition to the social services and educational offerings, the women in the settlement house movement began to fight for social reform after witnessing at first hand the struggles of the poor. The Working People's Social Science Club offered free weekly public lectures on economic and social issues of interest to working-class people, and broke down the barriers between the middle and working classes. Activists worked to improve the overcrowded public schools, poor sanitation, health care, child labor, housing conditions, and working conditions of women and girls. Additionally, the activists worked to protect immigrants from exploitation, advocating for immigrants' rights and workers' compensation.

Virginia L. Salmon

FURTHER READING

Addams, Jane. *Twenty Years at Hull-House.* Edited by Victoria Bissell Brown. New York: Bedford/St. Martin's, 1999.

Bryan, Mary Lynn McCree, and Allen F. Davis, eds. *One Hundred Years at Hull-House.* Bloomington: Indiana University Press, 1990.

Deegan, Mary Jo. *Race, Hull-House, and the University of Chicago: A New Conscience Against Ancient Evils.* Westport, Conn.: Praeger, 2002.

Glowacki, Peggy, and Julia Hendry. *Hull-House.* Charleston, S.C.: Arcadia, 2004.

Knight, Louise W. *Citizen: Jane Addams and the Struggle for Democracy.* Chicago: University of Chicago Press, 2005.

SEE ALSO: Americanization programs; Chicago; Child immigrants; Citizenship; Education; Progressivism; Settlement houses; Welfare and social services; Women immigrants.

HUNGARIAN IMMIGRANTS

SIGNIFICANCE: Although most Hungarians who emigrated to the United States arrived between 1890 and the start of World War I in 1914, the most significant Hungarian immigration took place during the 1930's. The spread of fascism and Nazism in Europe forced thousands of highly educated scientists, scholars, artists, and musicians to leave

PROFILE OF HUNGARIAN IMMIGRANTS

Country of origin	Hungary
Primary language	Hungarian
Primary regions of U.S. settlement	East Coast
Earliest significant arrivals	Early 1850's
Peak immigration period	1880's-1914
Twenty-first century legal residents*	10,494 (1,312 per year)

*Immigrants who obtained legal permanent resident status in the United States.
Source: Department of Homeland Security, *Yearbook of Immigration Statistics, 2008.*

Hungary and Central Europe to find safe haven in America.

Although Hungarian presence in North America reaches back to 1583, when Stephen Parmenius of Buda reached American shores, the first significant Hungarian political immigration took place in the early 1850's. Following the defeat of the Hungarian Revolution of 1848-1849, several thousand Hungarians found haven in the United States. Most of them came with the intention of returning to Europe to resume their struggle against the Austrian Empire, but a new war of liberation never materialized. However, many émigrés repatriated to Hungary after the Austro-Hungarian Compromise of 1867, which transformed the Austrian Empire into the dualistic state of Austria-Hungary. Before their repatriation, however, close to one thousand Hungarians—25 percent of all Hungarians then in the United States—had served in the Union Army during the Civil War. Almost one hundred of them served as officers; among them were two major generals and five brigadier generals. Many other Hungarians never repatriated and instead joined the ranks of American professionals, businessmen, and diplomats. They were able to do so because over 90 percent of them came from the ranks of the upper nobility and the gentry, and were thus learned enough, with sufficient social and linguistic skills, to impress contemporary Americans.

EARLY TWENTIETH CENTURY ARRIVALS

The next significant wave of Hungarian immigrants were the turn-of-the-century "economic immigrants." These were mostly peasants and unskilled workers who came in huge numbers, primarily as guest workers, to work in steel mills, coal mines, and factories. Of the nearly two million immigrants from Hungary during the four decades leading up to World War I, about 650,000 were true Hungarians, or Magyars. The remaining two-thirds were Ruysins, Slovaks, Romanians, Croats, Serbs, and Hungarian Germans. Of the 650,000 ethnic Magyars, close to 90 percent were peasants or unskilled workers who had recently emerged from the ranks of the peasantry. They were drawn to America by the work opportunities that did not exist at home. Even though Hungary itself was then being urbanized and industrialized, its development was not sufficient to employ all the peasants who were being displaced from the countryside. In the course of time, about 75 percent of these "guest workers"—two-thirds of whom were young men of marriageable age—transformed themselves into permanent immigrants. They established families in the United States and became the founders of Hungarian churches, fraternal associations, and scores of local, regional, and national newspapers geared to their educational levels.

The mass European immigration that occurred during the four decades before the outbreak of World War I came to an end in 1914. Although it resumed at a slower pace after the war, the federal immigration quota laws of 1921, 1924, and 1927 put an end to this immigration, especially for those from southern and eastern Europe. This decline of immigration was furthered by the collapse of the stock market in 1929 and the resulting Great Depression. Consequently, fewer than thirty thousand Hungarians immigrated to the United States during the 1920's.

GREAT INTELLECTUAL IMMIGRATION AND WORLD WAR II

The next wave of immigrants, known as the "Great Intellectual Immigration," appeared during the 1930's, in consequence of Adolf Hitler's

---

HUNGARIANS AND THE BOMB

Hungarian émigrés constituted the most significant immigration faction among those involved in the so-called Manhattan Project that developed the atomic bomb during World War II. Laura Fermi, the widow of the Italian Nobel laureate Enrico Fermi, once asserted that the Manhattan Project's "scientific brain power was furnished by three Hungarians and one Italian." The lone Italian was Enrico Fermi himself; the three Hungarians were Leo Szilard, Eugene Wigner, and Edward Teller. Teller has also been called the "Father" of the American hydrogen bomb.

---

rise to power in Germany in 1933 and the resulting rapid increase of anti-Semitism and antiliberalism. Although only about fifteen thousand Hungarians immigrated during the 1930's, this period brought thousands of highly educated scientists, writers, artists, composers, and other professionals to the United States. Ethnic Magyars constituted only a small segment of this Intellectual Immigration, but their impact was so great and widespread that many people began to wonder about the "mystery" of Hungarian intellectual talent. The impact of this immigration on the United States was felt through the rest of the twentieth century. Several Hungarian scientists played a major role in the development of the atomic bomb during World War II. Others, such as John von Neumann, were later in the forefront of the birth of the computer, and several became Nobel laureates.

COLD WAR ERA

The post-World War II period saw the coming of several smaller immigrant waves that may have brought as many as another 130,000 Hungarians to the United States. These immigrants included about 27,000 displaced persons who represented the cream of Hungary's upper-middle-class society. Most of them left Hungary after the war for fear of the Soviet domination of their homeland. Postwar immigrants also included about 40,000 so-called Fifty-Sixers, or "Freedom Fighters," who left Hungary after the suppression of the anti-Soviet and anticommunist Hungarian Revolution of 1956.

The next three decades saw a trickle of continuous immigration of about 60,000 immigrants who escaped from Eastern Europe. The collapse of communism and Soviet rule in 1989-1990 altered the situation. With the freedom to emigrate restored, and the attractive opportunities in the United States, many highly trained Hungarians came in quest of greater economic opportunities. One German scholar called these postcommunist immigrants "Prosperity Immigrants"—people who during the Soviet era had lost much of the idealism and ethical values of their predecessors. What most of them wanted was primarily economic success. While searching for affluence in the United States, they contributed their know-how to American society, which valued and rewarded them accordingly.

By the early twenty-first century, the immigrant churches, fraternals, newspapers, and other institutions of immigrant life were in the process of disappearing. Few of the new Hungarian immigrants have shown an inclination to support the traditional institutions that were important to their predecessors. Given this reality, and the unlikelihood that there would be another major immigration from Hungary, it seemed only a question of a few years before all of these institutions would vanish. According to the 2000 U.S. Census, 1.4 million Americans claimed full or primary Hungarian descent. Of these, 118,000 (8.4 percent) still used Hungarian as a language of communication within their families. By contrast, 1.8 million claimed Hungarian ancestry in 1980, and 180,000 were still speaking Hungarian at home).

Steven Béla Várdy

FURTHER READING
Fermi, Laura. *Illustrious Immigrants: The Intellectual Migration from Europe, 1930-1941.* Chicago: Uni-

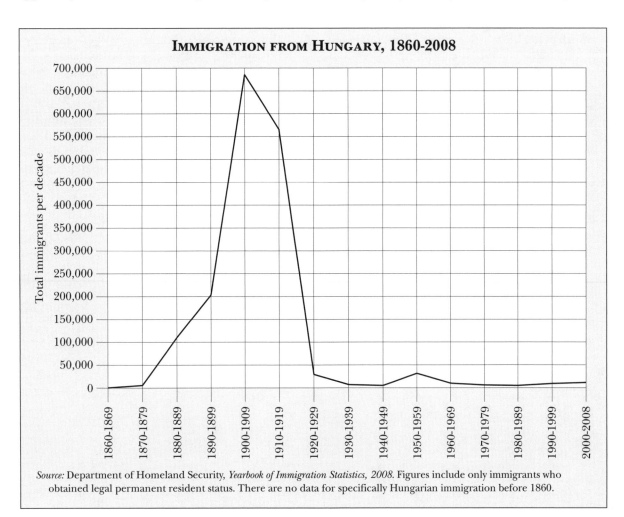

IMMIGRATION FROM HUNGARY, 1860-2008

Source: Department of Homeland Security, *Yearbook of Immigration Statistics, 2008.* Figures include only immigrants who obtained legal permanent resident status. There are no data for specifically Hungarian immigration before 1860.

versity of Chicago Press, 1969. The wife of Nobel laureate Enrico Fermi, who built the first experimental nuclear reactor, Laura Fermi provides an intimate internal view of those whom she calls Europe's "illustrious immigrants," who include such prominent Hungarians as Leo Szilárd, Eugene Wigner, and Edward Teller.

Lengyel, Emil. *Americans from Hungary*. 1948. Reprint. Westport, Conn.: Greenwood Press, 1974. Written by a prominent Hungarian American journalist, this volume is the earliest English-language synthesis of Hungarian American history and draws heavily on earlier Hungarian-language publications.

Puskás, Julianna. *Ties That Bind, Ties That Divide: One Hundred Years of Hungarian Experience in the United States*. Translated by Zora Ludwig. New York: Holmes & Meier, 2000. Scholarly, statistics-filled synthesis of Hungarian American history by a native Hungarian scholar who devoted much of her life to researching "economic" emigrants to the United States of the early twentieth century. Volume says little about post-World War II political immigrants.

Széplaki, Joseph. *Hungarians in America, 1583-1974: A Chronology and Fact Book*. Dobbs Ferry, N.Y.: Oceana, 1975. Short but useful summary of Hungarian American history by a librarian who was not a professional historian.

Várdy, Steven Béla. *Historical Dictionary of Hungary*. Lanham, Md.: Scarecrow Press, 1997. First comprehensive encyclopedic work on Hungarian history in English.

_____. *The Hungarian Americans*. Rev. ed. Safety Harbor, Fla.: Simon Publications, 2001. The first English-language synthesis of Hungarian American history by a trained Hungarian American historian.

_____. *The Hungarian Americans: The Hungarian Experience in North America*. New York: Chelsea House, 1989. Short, heavily illustrated work. Based to a large degree on the first edition of the work but also includes the Canadian Hungarian Americans. Contains an introductory essay by Daniel Patrick Moynihan.

_____. *Magyarok az òjvilágban*. Budapest: Magyar Nyelv és Kultúra Nemzetkšzi Társasága, 2000. This 840-page book on Hungarians in the New World, published by the International Association of Hungarian Language and Culture, is the largest synthesis of Hungarian American history yet published. Although still not available in English, this Hungarian edition contains a thirty-five-page English summary.

SEE ALSO: Austrian immigrants; Czech and Slovakian immigrants; European immigrants; European revolutions of 1848; Grove, Andrew; Polish immigrants; Pulitzer, Joseph; Science; Yugoslav state immigrants.

I

I REMEMBER MAMA

IDENTIFICATION: Film about a fictional Norwegian American family living in early twentieth century San Francisco

DATE: Released in 1948

SIGNIFICANCE: Director George Stevens's *I Remember Mama* offers an amiable portrayal of early twentieth century Norwegian immigrants, revealing their daily challenges, light-hearted moments, and career aspirations. Guided by a foreign-born matriarch who embraces America as she resolves problems with simple, "Old Country" wisdom, the story's Hanson family works together to manage health care and education on a tight budget and deal with problems arising from marriage, illness, eccentric relatives, and a penniless boarder.

Drawing on author Kathryn Forbes's novel *Mama's Bank Account* and playwright John Van Druten's 1944 stage adaption of the book, *I Remember Mama* utilizes an intimate narrative structure to frame the immigrant story. The film opens with Katrin (Barbara Bel Geddes), the eldest Hanson daughter—who has become a writer—typing the final words of her memoir in the attic of the Hanson's San Francisco home. At first, Katrin serves as narrator, reading from her memoir and guiding the audience back in time. Later, she joins the story as a much younger Katrin. The vignettes that follow are set mostly within the family home and feature both nuclear and extended family members, including bossy, whiny, and timid aunts, a blustery great-uncle, and a literary lodger. Meanwhile, Katrin gradually comes of age. The film ends with the family sitting around the kitchen table, with grown-up Katrin, having just received a check for the sale of her first published story, reading "Mama and the Hospital" aloud to the family.

Each time Mama reveals something about her past to Katrin in a candid conversation, she offers insights into the goals and assimilation issues of many immigrants. Family, not riches, wooed Mama and Papa from Norway. Aunts Trina, Sigrid, and Jenny had settled in San Francisco before they arrived, following Uncle Chris (Oskar Homolka), the head of the Scandinavian American clan, who ranches outside the city. Mama has become an American citizen, and her American-born children speak fluent English, without their elders' foibles or foreign accent. Going against the grain of her stodgy Norwegian sisters, Mama calls herself a San Francisco woman.

Like many immigrants, Mama and Papa Hanson and their children, Lars, Katrin, Christine, and Dagmar, stretch their limited money by making

Irene Dunne scrubbing a hospital floor in I Remember Mama. *(Time & Life Pictures/Getty Images)*

tough sacrifices. Every Saturday they gather together to apportion Papa's carpentry earnings for the landlord, grocer, and vital needs. To fund Lars's education, Papa gives up tobacco, and the siblings take on light work; to buy Katrin's graduation gift, Mama sells a family heirloom so she will not have to tap into the family bank account. However, after Katrin receives her first publication check, Mama admits that the bank account has been a fictional safety net to prevent the children from worrying.

Mama's role in the immigrant family is both traditional and pivotal. She supports, encourages, and makes peace among loved ones, often solving problems with her domestic skills. For example, she enters a hospital's off-limits, postsurgical recovery ward in which Dagmar is a frightened patient by scrubbing the floors to pass as a maid. She boosts Katrin's writing career by trading a secret homeland recipe for a celebrity writer's advice and referral. Along the way, Mama helps the family adapt Norwegian customs to America. For example, she smoothes the way for the spinster Trina to wed with neither parents nor a dowry. On porches and over cups of coffee, she curbs teasing, snubbing, and bullying behavior as life and traditions change.

I Remember Mama was popular with post-World War II Americans, first as a play, subsequently as a film, and eventually as a television series broadcast by CBS-TV from 1949 to 1957. Four of the film's actors (including Irene Dunne, who plays Mama) earned Academy Award nominations for their performances. Set in a West Coast city that was a portal to America for many newcomers, the landmark film brought widespread and positive attention to immigrant family life.

Wendy Alison Lamb

FURTHER READING

Hoobler, Dorothy, and Thomas Hoobler. *The Scandinavian American Family Album*. New York: Oxford University Press, 1997.

Zempel, Solveig. *In Their Own Words: Letters from Norwegian Immigrants*. Minneapolis: University of Minnesota Press, 1991.

SEE ALSO: California; Education; Families; Films; Health care; Marriage; San Francisco; Scandinavian immigrants; Television and radio; Women immigrants.

IDAHO

SIGNIFICANCE: Idaho's limited immigration contrasts dramatically with the immigration rates of other regions in which large numbers of immigrant groups have developed and become ingrained in the local communities. In 2008, 92 percent of the state's residents were classified as "white."

Before the United States expanded into the West, the region that would become the state of Idaho was populated by Native Americans belonging to the Bannock, Lamni, Nez Perce, Coeur d'Alene, and Gosiute nations. After the first waves of American settlers moved into the region during the early part of the nineteenth century, new immigration into Idaho slowed down considerably. The reasons for Idaho's relative lack of immigration are many. The most prominent reasons include the state's lack of both a dominant agricultural base that attracts farmworkers and major urban centers that provide employment opportunities in service industries and jobs for unskilled labor.

LATE NINETEENTH CENTURY IMMIGRATION

Most immigrants who entered Idaho after it became a U.S. state in 1890 were farmers who were able to take advantage of the region's nitrogen-rich soil, which made possible rapid crop cultivation. Limited numbers of new immigrants from Germany, England, and Russia did arrive during the nineteenth century. Some found employment in the mining and logging industries; however, many of these immigrants did not remain in the state. They instead tended to move on to California, Alaska, and Canada. Those who did remain in Idaho typically transitioned into the lucrative agricultural farming and ranching industries. Idaho's African American population before the turn of the twentieth century never exceeded five hundred persons, and the numbers of Asian Americans were similar.

TWENTIETH CENTURY ARRIVALS

During the twentieth century, Idaho remained a secondary destination for new immigrants. As late as 1940, the state registered only 5,855 foreign-born residents. The majority of Idaho's residents had relocated from eastern regions of the United States, particularly Missouri and Iowa. However, foreign immigration remained limited because of limited employment opportunities within the state, which were due to the lack of the types of heavy industries that needed large labor pools.

The only significant immigrant groups to move into the region during the early twentieth century were Canadian farmers from the neighboring province of Alberta and a very small number of people from the Basque region of Spain. The Basques—who never exceeded more than 1,000 people—typically worked as sheepherders in Idaho's hills and as general laborers for both the fledgling logging and mining industries. Many of these Spanish settlers came from the Spanish province of Bizkala. The presence of this minority population continues to be evident in Idaho's Basque restaurants and in an annual Basque festival held in Boise.

During the twenty-first century, Idaho saw a dramatic growth in population that made it one of the fastest-growing states in the union. Most new residents came from neighboring states, including a significant number from California who were attracted to Idaho's climate, employment opportunities in the technology sector, and its relatively low cost of living. Consequently, the state experienced an annual population growth of more than 13 percent between 2000 and 2006. Among these new Idaho residents were a growing number of Hispanic residents, who constituted about 10 percent of the state's population by 2009. Most of these immigrants settled in and around Boise and Twin Falls, both of which have Spanish-language media outlets.

Despite these changes, immigration into Idaho has remained limited. This may be in part due to

PROFILE OF IDAHO

Region	Northwest
Entered union	1890
Largest cities	Boise (capital), Nampa, Pocatello, Idaho Falls
Modern immigrant communities	Canadians, Hispanics, Basques

Population	*Total*	*Percent of state*	*Percent of U.S.*	*U.S. rank*
All state residents	1,466,000	100.0	0.49	39
All foreign-born residents	82,000	5.6	0.22	39

Source: U.S. Census Bureau, *Statistical Abstract for 2006.*

Notes: The U.S. population in 2006 was 299,399,000, of whom 37,548,000 (12.5%) were foreign born. Rankings in last column reflect total numbers, not percentages.

Idaho's reputation as a region that is unwelcoming of various minority or ethnic groups. This image reached a level of national notoriety during the 1990's with the highly visible actions of white-power groups, such as the Aryan Nations, and numerous highly publicized confrontations between armed militia groups and isolationists and federal law-enforcement agencies.

Robert D. Mitchell

FURTHER READING

Malone, Michael P. C. *Ben Ross and the New Deal in Idaho.* Seattle: University of Washington Press, 1970.

Peterson, Frank Ross. *Idaho, A Bicentennial History.* New York: W. W. Norton, 1976.

Weatherby, James Benjamin, and Randy Stapilus. *Governing Idaho: Politics, People and Power.* Caldwell, Idaho: Caxton Press, 2005.

SEE ALSO: Chinese immigrants; Economic opportunities; Employment; History of immigration after 1891; Italian immigrants; Labor unions; Montana; Railroads; Utah.

IDENTIFICATIONAL ASSIMILATION

DEFINITION: Late stage of assimilation in which members of a minority group, such as newly arrived immigrants, develop a sense of peoplehood based exclusively on their host society

SIGNIFICANCE: Sociologist Milton Gordon's concept of identificational assimilation helps to explain how minority groups develop a sense of peoplehood, an important stage in the assimilation of U.S. immigrants.

In his 1964 book *Assimilation in American Life,* Milton Gordon created a synthesis that delineates the multiple dimensions of assimilation, according to the various indicators of the process. He identified seven stages in which assimilation takes place: cultural, structural, marital, identity, prejudice, discrimination, and civic. These steps are not causally distinct but describe different dimensions of the same underlying process: they are subprocesses of assimilation. Gordon placed great emphasis on the first two stages—acculturation and structural assimilation. In his analysis, acculturation could occur without the other types of assimilation, and it could last indefinitely. In addition, each of the subprocesses may take place in varying degrees.

The seven stages in Gordon's synthesis offer a composite multidimensional index of assimilation that could be used to determine the extent of a group's assimilation according to both individual- and group-level criteria. Thus, Gordon's framework provides specifications for empirical indicators of assimilation, which contributed to the development of quantitative research in sociology during the 1960's.

GORDON'S FRAMEWORK

The fourth stage in Gordon's multidimensional scheme is identificational assimilation, which occurs when members of the minority group, usually newly arrived immigrants, develop a sense of peoplehood based exclusively on the host society, acquiring the memories, sentiments, and attitudes of people of the core culture. This step of assimilation became more popular in later discussions of assimilation with regard to both the descendants of European immigrants and members of the new immigrant groups.

In Gordon's framework, ethnic identity is not an undifferentiated concept. He distinguishes between historical identification and participational identity. Historical identification is a function of past and current historical events and derives from a sense of "interdependence of fate"—in sociologist Kurt Lewsin's words—which typically extends to the ethnic group as a whole. Participational identity refers to the sense of belonging to a subculture: Its members participate frequently in it and share close behavioral similarities with each other; they are also likely to be people from the same ethnic group and social class.

FURTHER RESEARCH AND CRITICISM

In 1985, Milton Yinger noted that among the several types of assimilation, the identification stage was perhaps the least well conceptualized and measured. In 1983, Richard Alba and Mitchell Chamlin tried to measure ethnic identification using a survey in which they asked people to specify the country of origin of their ancestors. In 1988, Barbara Tomaskovis-Devey and Donald Tomaskovis-Devey did similar research and established that identificational assimilation is an approximate measure of ingroup marriage in the last generation and of the intensity of current ethnic identification. In 1990, J. Allen Williams and Suzanne T. Ortega used the same conceptualization to study the fourth stage of assimilation—they asked respondents to specify if thinking of themselves as a person from the country they named was very, somewhat, or not very important to them.

Some scholars find Gordon's identificational assimilation to be ambiguous because it does not clarify if it applies to individuals or groups. Although the measurement has been applied to individuals, the overall hypothesis has been interpreted as applying to groups. Scholars like Richard Alba, Victor Nee, and Elliott Barkan find the strength of Gordon's framework in its clear articulation of some of the key dimensions of assimilation, viewed as a composite concept. They also recognize that the dimensions of assimilation can be arranged in stages to the advantage of quantitative researchers in sociology.

Elitza Kotzeva

FURTHER READING

Alba, Richard, and Victor Nee. *Remaking the American Mainstream: Assimilation and Contemporary Immigration.* Cambridge, Mass.: Harvard University Press, 2005. Sociologists Alba and Nee advance their arguments about the similarities between the immigrants of the previous century and those of the twenty-first century by providing a thorough overview of theory and history of assimilation and immigration in the United States.

Fuchs, Lawrence H. *The American Kaleidoscope: Race, Ethnicity, and the Civic Culture.* Hanover, N.H.: Wesleyan University Press, 1990. Fuchs traces the assimilation of different immigrant groups into the American mainstream during the eighteenth and nineteenth centuries to show that immigrants contribute to the ethnic diversity and civic unity of American society rather than to its divisiveness.

Gordon, Milton Myron. *Assimilation in American Life: The Role of Race, Religion, and National Origins.* New York: Oxford University Press, 1964. Seminal sociological text on assimilation in which Gordon introduces his innovative ideas on the different stages of assimilation and the stratification of American society.

Jacoby, Tamar. *Reinventing the Melting Pot: The New Immigrants and What It Means to Be American.* New York: Basic Books, 2004. Divided in five parts, the essays in the book examine the process of assimilation from a variety of perspectives and explore the new ways of thinking about America as a melting pot.

Kazal, Russell A. "Revisiting Assimilation: The Rise, Fall, and Reappraisal of a Concept in American Ethnic History." *American Historical Review* 100, no. 2 (April, 1995): 437-471. Article tracing the emergence and centrality of assimilation in the work of sociologists and concluding that a new definition of assimilation is needed.

Kivisto, Peter. *Incorporating Diversity: Rethinking Assimilation in a Multicultural Age.* Boulder, Colo.: Paradigm Publishers, 2005. Presents a set of canonical texts on assimilation theory together with writings on current immigration issues in an attempt to revise the classical perspective for the contemporary situation.

Salins, Peter D. *Assimilation, American Style.* New York: Basic Books, 1997. Examines the process of assimilation and the impacts of immigration on contemporary American society.

SEE ALSO: Anglo-conformity; Assimilation theories; Cultural pluralism; Hansen effect; Melting pot theory; Migrant superordination; Name changing.

ILLEGAL IMMIGRATION

DEFINITION: Undocumented entry into the United States in circumvention of U.S. immigration laws

SIGNIFICANCE: Although a self-professed nation of immigrants, the United States has historically shown ambivalence toward newcomers who enter the country illegally. Despite massive government efforts to curb illegal immigration, an estimated 12 million people who entered the country illegally were living in the United States during the early twenty-first century, when some sectors of the national economy would have been devastated without their labor.

The reception of illegal immigrants in the United States has ranged from open arms in a number of cities that have officially declared themselves immigrant sanctuaries to nativist hostility. Some politicians have regularly demonized illegal immigrants for their purported contributions to crime. The federal government's immigration laws contain exceptions for economic need or political persecution, but the government also maintains a large border-police apparatus that catches only a fraction of those who try to cross the borders without permission.

A SPECIAL PROBLEM

An important aspect of illegal immigration in the United States that is almost uniquely American lies in the Fourteenth Amendment to the U.S. Constitution. Its definition of citizenship makes all persons born within the United States American citizens, regardless of the citizenship of their parents. Few other countries are similarly generous in awarding citizenship, but the U.S. principle has given rise to a difficult problem in combating illegal immigration: Many children are born in the

United States to parents who are in the country illegally.

According to a 2008 study for the Pew Hispanic Center, 73 percent of all children of undocumented immigrants—the majority of whom are Hispanic—have been born in the United States and are thus American citizens. Consequently, when government immigration raids deport illegal immigrants who are parents, they often separate parents from their citizen children. This poses a contradiction in American immigration principles, as separating family members runs counter to the stated U.S. immigration goal of family unification. Immigration raids that have led to the deportation of parents while leaving their American-born children homeless have occasionally provided federal immigration agencies with public-relations embarrassments.

DEMOGRAPHICS OF ILLEGAL IMMIGRATION

Between 1990 and 2006, the numbers of immigrants who entered the United States illegally increased rapidly. After 2006, the rate stabilized, in part because depressed economic conditions in the United States reduced employment opportunities, and in part because of more stringent security controls, including a doubling of the number of U.S. Border Patrol agents working along the Mexican border, from 9,000 to 18,000.

According to early twenty-first century U.S. Census estimates, three-quarters of undocumented immigrants in the United States were Hispanic. A majority, 59 percent, had come from Mexico, with 11 percent from Asia, 11 percent from Central America, 7 percent from South America, and smaller percentages from other areas. According to estimates of the Pew Foundation Hispanic Center, of the 12.7 million Mexicans living in the United States in 2007, roughly 55 percent were in the country illegally. Illegal populations in 2006 were estimated at 2.8 million in California, 1.6 million in Texas, 980,000 in Florida, and about half a million each in New York, Arizona, Illinois, and New Jersey.

The main motivation for crossing the border has long been the quest for better employment. Undocumented immigrants, who have generally outnumbered legal immigrants, can be found in many sectors of the economy. Various surveys, including one by National Public Radio and another by *USA Today*, indicate that 3 to 4 percent of undocumented immigrants are employed in farmwork,

21 to 33 percent in service industries, 16 to 19 percent in construction and related jobs, 12 percent in sales, 15 to 16 percent in production industries, 10 percent in management, and 8 percent in transportation.

CHANGING ECONOMIC CONDITIONS

By 2005, the tide of immigration into the United States had slowed substantially, at least for a time, as increasing numbers of Mexicans and other Hispanics left the United States to return to their home countries. Between August, 2007, and August, 2008, the number of Mexicans immigrating to the United States declined by 25 percent, according to Mexico's own census figures. In 2008, the amount of money that Mexican immigrants remitted from the United States to relatives in Mexico declined by $1 billion.

By 2008, the numbers of arrests at U.S. borders had declined for three consecutive years, dropping to levels not witnessed since 1973, when the total population of the United States was much lower. In 2008, the U.S. Border Patrol reported making 724,000 arrests, 17 percent fewer than in 2007. Ninety-seven percent of these arrests took place on the southern border, and 91 percent of the persons arrested were Mexicans. The number of border arrests actually had peaked two decades earlier, in 1986, at 1.7 million. The Border Patrol credited tighter security, including the construction of fences along parts of the border, for the long-term decline.

SUPPORTERS OF ILLEGAL IMMIGRATION

A number of American communities—including the three largest cities in the United States—have declared themselves as "sanctuary cities." Their governments have instructed city employees, usually including police, to avoid cooperating with federal immigration authorities seeking illegal immigrants. Opponents say that sanctuary city measures violate federal law because the cities are in effect creating their own immigration policies, an area of law that only the U.S. Congress has authority to change. City authorities in many of these urban areas have countered by saying that undocumented immigrants have brought them more benefits than they have cost. Illegal immigrant workers pay about $7 billion per year into the Social Security system from which they will receive no benefits. According to a paper in *The Tax Lawyer*, a peer-reviewed journal of the American Bar Association, illegal immigrants pay more in taxes than they cost in social services.

During the early twenty-first century, members of a group calling itself No More Deaths patrolled the Mexican border to offer medical aid, food, and water to immigrants crossing the desert regions during hot weather. The organization's aim is to reduce deaths and serious injuries that plague many who make the difficult crossing.

OPPONENTS OF ILLEGAL IMMIGRATION

On the other side of the issue, groups such as the Federation for American Immigration Reform (FAIR), cite other studies asserting that illegal immigrants cost American governments more than the workers pay in taxes. According to this view, illegal immigration degrades public education, health care, and other services for citizens, with the heaviest burdens falling on the poor.

The Minuteman Project has lobbied Congress for increased enforcement of immigration laws as some local people, including white supremacists, have formed posses to prevent immigrants from crossing parts of the border. Sometimes these vigilante groups have assaulted people they believe to be illegal immigrants. Other people have complained that the large number of illegal immigrants have been ruining U.S. public lands on and near the border. For example, Arizona's Fish and Wildlife Service reported finding forty-five abandoned cars on the state's Buenos Aires wildlife refuge and nine tons of garbage during only two months in 2002. Park officials reported that fires set by immigrants flared out of control often enough to char more than 68,000 acres and cost $5.1 million to extinguish.

Undocumented Mexican farm workers waiting to be sent back to Mexico at Calexico in 1972, during a period when an estimated 300,000 Mexicans were entering the United States illegally every year in search of employment. (NARA)

IMMIGRATION SCAMS

The intense desire of impoverished foreigners to work in the United States legally has spawned many criminal activities that prey on would-be immigrants. Creators of these schemes have developed many ruses, all with the attitude that their victims are unlikely to complain to legal authorities. "Coyotes" routinely conduct many people across southern borders for fees ranging in the thousands of dollars per person. Entire cargo ships of illegal immigrants have arrived from Asia and unloaded people at sea after charging each of them tens of thousands of dollars. So-called Mohawk "warriors" have brought immigrants into the United States from Canada through the Akwesasne (St. Regis) reservation on the U.S.-Canadian border. These crossings have often occurred during the winter months, when the St. Lawrence River is frozen over.

On May 27, 2009, twelve Uzbekistani nationals were arrested in Kansas City, Missouri, on charges of recruiting hundreds of prospective workers from Jamaica, the Philippines, and the Dominican Republic, with promises of obtaining for them H-2B visas so they could do seasonal work legally in the United States. However, after they arrived in the country, the workers were held in debt bondage for years and charged fees for work uniforms, food, and rent as they performed menial labor in hotels and office buildings in and near Kansas City. The traffickers, having created a company they called Giant Labor Solutions, collected the workers' paychecks and turned the workers into virtual slaves.

In and near New York City, pastors of a supposed Pentecostal church in Queens, La Iglesia Roca de la Salvación Eterna, asserted that they possessed a special allocation of green cards earmarked for members of church congregations, for paperwork and an $8,000 to $16,000 processing fee. More than 120 illegal immigrants, most of them from Ecuador, were defrauded out of more than $1 million before the bogus pastors were arrested in early 2009. Many of the immigrants lost their life savings in the scam.

Bruce E. Johansen

FURTHER READING

Buchanan, Patrick J. *State of Emergency: The Third World Invasion and Conquest of America.* New York: Thomas Dunne Books/St. Martin's Press, 2006. Visceral discourse asserting that continued illegal immigration will ruin the U.S. economy and culture.

Conover, Ted. *Coyotes: A Journey Through the Secret World of America's Illegal Aliens.* New York: Vintage Books, 1987. Compelling account of the dangers of crossing the United States-Mexico border from the street level, with an emphasis on the "coyotes" who guide illegal immigrants into the United States for fees.

Frank, Thomas. "Modern Slavery Comes to Kansas." *Wall Street Journal,* June 17, 2009, p. A11. Account of a human-trafficking ring that recruited illegal workers with promises of work visas and then held them in debt bondage.

LeMay, Michael C. *Illegal Immigration: A Reference Handbook.* Santa Barbara, Calif.: ABC-CLIO, 2007. Encyclopedic reference work on many issues pertaining to illegal immigration and related subjects.

Ngai, Mae M. *Impossible Subjects: Illegal Aliens and the Making of Modern America.* Princeton, N.J.: Princeton University Press, 2004. Detailed study of illegal immigration into the United States from 1924 to 1965.

Semple, Kirk. "Green Cards, Belief, and Betrayal at a Storefront Church." *The New York Times,* June 17, 2009, p. A17-A18. Detailed account of how 120 illegal immigrants were defrauded of more than $1 million by fake preachers who promised them green cards.

Urrea, Luis Alberto. *The Devil's Highway: A True Story.* Boston: Little, Brown, 2004. Detailed account of a harrowing journey of would-be immigrants across the U.S.-Mexico border in 2001, during which at least fourteen people died.

Williams, Mary E., ed. *Immigration: Opposing Viewpoints.* Farmington Hills, Mich.: Greenhaven Press, 2004. Collection of essays presenting opposing viewpoints on the questions of whether immigration should be restricted, how serious a problem immigration is, how the United should address illegal immigration, and how U.S. immigration policy might be reformed. Also contains a directory of organizations devoted to immigration issues.

SEE ALSO: Border fence; Citizenship and Immigration Services, U.S.; Deportation; Florida illegal immigration suit; Illegal Immigration Reform and Immigrant Responsibility Act of 1996; Mexican American Legal Defense and Educational Fund; Sanctuary movement; Sweatshops.

ILLEGAL IMMIGRATION REFORM AND IMMIGRANT RESPONSIBILITY ACT OF 1996

THE LAW: Federal law designed to reduce illegal immigration and to apprehend undocumented aliens

DATE: Signed into law on September 30, 1996

ALSO KNOWN AS: IIRIRA

SIGNIFICANCE: The Illegal Immigration Reform and Responsibility Act, or IIRIRA, was enacted to prevent the flow of undocumented aliens into the United States. The law stipulated such initiatives as increased border patrol staffing for border surveillance, enhanced enforcement and penalties against alien smuggling, tougher sanctions for illegal immigrants caught inside the U.S. borders, and increased restrictions on alien employment, benefits, and assistance programs.

On September 30, 1996, President Bill Clinton signed the Illegal Immigrant Reform and Immigrant Responsibility Act into law. Before the law was passed in Congress, two sets of immigration bills had been considered in each house of Congress. One was dedicated to controlling illegal immigration, the second to managing legal immigration. If the legal-immigration bill had passed, it would have radically reduced the numbers of employment and family immigrants allowed into the United States. The other bill focused specifically on stronger border enforcement, apprehension, and deportation. Eventually, the two bills were combined in each house, only to be split again later, after arguments arose over the language of the bill's component parts. The reason for combining the bills centered on the notion that the controversial legal-immigration bill would have an easier time passing if it were connected to the more popular illegal-immigration bill. After much debate, the legal-immigration bills in each house were defeated. However, several items from them concerning legal immigration ended up in the final draft of the illegal-immigration bill. The final bill was coupled with another piece of legislation not related to immigration issues; it concerned the finances of the day-to-day operation of the entire federal government—an issue that made its immediate passage crucial.

The illegal-immigration bill that ultimately became IIRIRA 96 was divided into six broad areas and focused primarily on stronger enforcement efforts and penalties for person who attempt to enter illegally, smuggle immigrants into the country, or live inside U.S. borders without proper documentation. The six major areas of the new law included:

Six of forty-nine Salvadorans whose attempt to enter the United States illegally in 1999 failed. They are shown at El Salvador's international airport after being returned to their homeland on a plane chartered by the U.S. government. (AP/Wide World Photos)

- Title I: Improvements to border control, facilitation of legal entry, and interior enforcement
- Title II: Enhanced enforcement and penalties against alien smuggling and document fraud
- Title III: Inspection, apprehension, detention, adjudication, and removal of inadmissible and deportable aliens
- Title IV: Enforcement of restrictions against employment
- Title V: Restrictions on benefits for aliens
- Title VI: Miscellaneous provisions

One of the most controversial items in the bill, Title III, addressed the issue of undocumented aliens already inside U.S. borders. In particular, the government enacted rules calling for permanent restrictions or bans on undocumented aliens found in violation of certain legal rules. For example, the act states that any person who has been in the United States illegally for at least 180 days, but less than one year, must remain outside the United States for three years unless granted a pardon. Moreover, any person who has been in the United States illegally for more than one year must reside outside the United States for ten years unless a pardon is granted. Any such person who returns to the United States prematurely without the specified pardon will not be permitted to apply for a waiver for reentry for an additional ten years. Additionally, the language of the law applies regardless of whether a person has a spouse or children who are U.S. citizens.

Paul M. Klenowski

FURTHER READING

Hayes, Helene. *U.S. Immigration Policy and the Undocumented: Ambivalent Laws and Furtive Lives.* Westport, Conn.: Praeger, 2001.

Newton, Lina. *Illegal, Alien, or Immigrant: The Politics of Immigration Reform.* New York: New York University Press, 2008.

SEE ALSO: Border fence; Commission on Immigration Reform, U.S.; Due process protections; Illegal immigration; Immigration Act of 1990; Immigration law; Immigration Reform and Control Act of 1986; Select Commission on Immigration and Refugee Policy; Smuggling of immigrants.

ILLINOIS

SIGNIFICANCE: Illinois has had an immigration history more complex than that of many states. Its early history was characterized by movements of Native Americans and influxes of people from other parts of the United States. During the nineteenth century, the state began drawing large numbers of European immigrants to its farmlands and cities, and the twentieth century brought in new waves of immigrants from Latin American countries and Africa.

Illinois's early immigration history made it a microcosm of the north-south split within the United States as a whole. After the nation gained its independence, many southerners migrated to Illinois from Kentucky (which provided Abraham Lincoln's family), Virginia, and Tennessee. The Blackhawk War of 1832 drove most of the few remaining Native Americans out of northern Illinois, and then new arrivals from New England and New York State began dominating Illinois's commerce and politics. By 1860, the state was divided between those who approved of slavery and favored secession and those who favored abolition and preserving the Union. Illinois remained in the Union during the Civil War, but some of its southern counties remained sympathetic to the Confederacy. As late as the twenty-first century, northern and southern accents could still be observed around the state.

NINETEENTH CENTURY TRENDS

Illinois's first great influx of foreign immigrants came after 1830 with the arrival of Germans, many of whom settled across the Mississippi River from St. Louis, Missouri. Mostly classically educated, these Germans were dubbed "Latin Farmers." The aftermath of Europe's many failed revolutions in 1848 brought another wave of German immigrants known as "Forty Eighters."

During the second half of the nineteenth century Illinois's population increased by more than 20 percent every decade. A large part of this increase was due to foreign immigrants, especially Germans and Irish, along with smaller numbers of Swedes and British. Germans settled throughout most of the upper Mississippi Valley, from St. Louis in the south to Wisconsin in the north, and they also settled in Chicago and other areas in the northern part of Illinois.

Irish immigrants tended to concentrate in Illinois's cities and along the railroads and assimilated rapidly. Swedes tended to cluster in groups. In 1847, they founded a commune at Bishop Hill, near Galva. They also settled in towns such as Rock Island and Rockford, and many of them farmed. Rock Island's Augustana College originated as a Swedish institution.

The population of Illinois's largest city, Chicago, was more than half foreign born by 1860. Germans made up one-fifth of the total, followed by a slightly smaller number of Irish and even smaller numbers of Swedes. In 1870, Chicago's population of just over 300,000 included more than 50,000 Germans and more than 40,000 Irish. By 1900, Swedes made up 9 percent of Chicago's population. These groups were soon joined by a large influx of African Americans from southern states.

TWENTIETH CENTURY TRENDS

After 1920, immigrants to Illinois came from new sources, especially in Chicago. In 1900, 30,150 Italians were living in Chicago. By 1920, that figure had risen to 109,458. Poles had an established community along Chicago's Milwaukee Avenue by 1900, and they numbered almost 140,000 by 1920. World War II brought refugees who helped swell Chicago's Polish community, which fostered Polish-language newspapers, Polish-language Roman Catholic masses, and other Polish institutions, all of which were still strong into the early twenty-first century. World War II also brought a new wave of German refugees.

Mexican immigration into Illinois began just before 1920. Many of these immigrants were fleeing the violence of the Mexican Revolution, which started in 1910. At the same time, American entry into World War I drew many American workers away from Illinois's farms and factories to serve in the armed forces and war-related industry. Mexican workers took many of their places in both agricultural fields and factories. Mexicans and other Hispanic immigrants concentrated in the Chicago area. Hispanic components of Chicago's population were so important by the 1960's that bilingual signs were appearing in city trains. By the 1990's, some Chicago neighborhoods, such as Pilsen, were predominantly Spanish-speaking and were electing Hispanic representatives to the city council and the U.S. Congress. By the last decade of the twentieth century, Illinois meatpackers were facing such a shortage of workers that they were actively recruiting workers in Latin America and Africa.

By 2006, Illinois's estimated population of 12,832,000 included 1,773,000 foreign-born residents. The state's rich ethnic mix was reflected in its linguistic diversity. More than 10 percent of the state's people spoke Spanish at home, and tens of thousands of families were speaking Polish, German, Tagalog, Italian, Chinese, Korean, French, Russian, or Greek in their homes.

Timothy C. Frazer

FURTHER READING

Arredondo, Gabriela F. *Mexican Chicago: Race, Identity, and Nation, 1916-39.* Champaign: University of Illinois Press, 2008. Analysis of how the revolutionary background of Chicago's Mexican im-

---

PROFILE OF ILLINOIS

Region	Midwest
Entered union	1818
Largest cities	Chicago, Rockford, Aurora, Naperville, Peoria, Springfield (capital)
Modern immigrant communities	Mexicans, other Hispanics, Africans

Population	Total	Percent of state	Percent of U.S.	U.S. rank
All state residents	12,832,000	100.0	4.29	5
All foreign-born residents	1,774,000	13.8	4.72	5

Source: U.S. Census Bureau, *Statistical Abstract for 2006.*

Notes: The U.S. population in 2006 was 299,399,000, of whom 37,548,000 (12.5%) were foreign born. Rankings in last column reflect total numbers, not percentages.

migrants influenced their adjustment to American life.

Candeloro, Dominic. *Chicago's Italians: Immigrants, Ethnics, Americans.* Charleston, S.C.: Arcadia, 2003. Traces the contributions of Chicago's Italians to labor unions, politics, and religion, and treats changes brought to the Italian community by World War II.

Daniels, Roger. *Coming to America: A History of Immigration and Ethnicity in American Life.* New York: HarperCollins, 1990. Thorough but readable treatment of groups of immigrants from the seventeenth century through the 1980's.

Frazer, Timothy C., ed. *"Heartland" English.* Tuscaloosa: University of Alabama Press, 1987. Collection of essays describing the impact immigrants and settlement had on the spoken English of several midwestern states, including Illinois.

Pacyga, Dominic A. *Polish Immigrants and Industrial Chicago: Workers on the South Side, 1880-1922.* Chicago: University of Chicago Press, 2003. Study of Polish immigrants who labored in Chicago factories and attempted to create neighborhoods like those of their homeland.

SEE ALSO: Abolitionist movement; Bilingual education; Chicago; German immigrants; Great Irish Famine; Irish immigrants; Italian immigrants; Language issues; Mexican immigrants; Polish immigrants.

IMINGAISHA

DEFINITION: Japanese-based corporate organizations that recruited emigrant workers for Hawaii's sugar cane industry during the late nineteenth and early twentieth centuries

SIGNIFICANCE: The workers sent to Hawaii by the *imingaisha* began an era of organized Japanese economic emigration that reversed imperial Japan's long-standing restrictions on population movement outside the country and marked the beginning of the Japanese community in the United States.

During the latter part of the nineteenth century, the expansion of the sugar cane industry in the independent kingdom of Hawaii created a demand for foreign workers because the islands' native population were unable to keep up with the new demands for manpower. Of the many nationalities considered for recruitment, the Japanese were seen as most desirable. However, the Japanese government's legal restrictions on emigration posed significant obstacles.

After the failure of several unsanctioned attempts by private individuals to bring Japanese workers to Hawaii during the 1860's, an agreement was reached between Japan and the kingdom of Hawaii permitting workers to emigrate under imperial sanction while governed by ministry officials. After this initial period of Japanese government-sponsored emigration ended in 1894, a new system was set in place to address concerns of possible exploitation of Japanese workers. By that time, Hawaii's monarchy had been replaced by a republican government. In 1898, the U.S. government would annex the islands and make them an American territory. Meanwhile, the independent Hawaiian government was concerned about the danger of allowing so many Japanese workers to enter the islands that they would shift the balance of racial and ethnic groups in the population.

The new arrangement was built on fifty-one independent private corporations that were created to maintain the flow of contract workers (and the economic benefits to Japan their remittances provided), with the five earliest such firms appearing between 1891 and 1894. The original imperial ordinance of 1894 governing the trade in workers was expanded and became law on April 29, 1896, as *Imin hogoho*, the Emigration Protection Law. It defined *imin* as persons who emigrated to foreign countries other than China or Korea for the purpose of labor, and whatever members of their families accompanied or later joined them abroad. Typical *imingaisha* firms operated by negotiating with the owners of more than fifty separate Hawaiian sugar plantations to establish their manpower needs. They then sent recruiters to rural Japanese villages in selected prefectures to contract predominantly male workers, arranging their transportation to Hawaii, while making profits on the entire enterprise.

The Japanese government saw the emigrants as helping to address both the unemployment problems of rural Japan, while providing a new source of income to assist in the nation's modernization efforts. The degree of popularity of this form of overseas labor can be seen in the fact that the companies eventually transported some 124,000 Japanese workers to Hawaii. The change of Hawaii from an independent republic to an American territory on July 7, 1898, led to the extension of an 1885 U.S. law prohibiting foreign contract employment (a measure originally intended to interdict Chinese laborers) to Hawaii, over the protests of the sugar planters, who tried unsuccessfully to have their workforce exempted from this law.

Paradoxically, the end of the *imingaisha* era came when these same workers' complaints against them for violating the Emigration Protection Law resulted in the formation of the Japanese Reform Association in 1905, while many workers started coming to Hawaii unbound by labor contracts, thereby simply bypassing the organized emigration process completely. The 1907 Gentlemen's Agreement between the United States and Japan banned the movement of Japanese from Hawaii to the mainland but also eliminated the issuance of passports for laborers intending to enter the American market.

Robert B. Ridinger

FURTHER READING

Jung, Moon-Ho. *Coolies and Cane: Race, Labor, and Sugar in the Age of Emancipation.* Baltimore: Johns Hopkins University Press, 2008.

Moriyama, Alan Takeo. *Imingaisha: Japanese Emigration Companies and Hawaii, 1894-1908.* Honolulu: University of Hawaii Press, 1985.

Okihiro, Gary Y. *Cane Fires: The Anti-Japanese Movement in Hawaii, 1865-1945.* Philadelphia: Temple University Press, 1992.

Van Sant, John E. *Pacific Pioneers: Japanese Journeys to America and Hawaii, 1850-1880.* Champaign: University of Illinois Press, 2000.

SEE ALSO: Asian immigrants; Contract labor system; Farm and migrant workers; Gentlemen's Agreement; Hawaii; Immigration Convention of 1886; Issei; Japanese immigrants.

"IMMIGRANT"

DEFINITION: Broad term for a person who has moved from an original homeland to another state or country

SIGNIFICANCE: Although the United States was created through immigration and has absorbed a steady stream of newcomers from many lands throughout its history, the term "immigrant" remains an often unclear or ambiguous word for many Americans, as does its relationship to a number of kindred words and phrases. Within the United States, "immigrant" has both specific legal denotations and popular connotations that differentiate it from terms such as "migrant," "refugee," and "alien."

The roots of the English word "immigrant" go back to the Latin verb *migrare*, which meant precisely what its direct descendant "migrate" means in modern English: to move from one locality to another. Thus, movements of people or animals from one place to another are usually called "migrations," and people who periodically move from one country or region to another are spoken of as "migrants."

The Latin prefix *in-* has several uses and connotations. One is what is sometimes called in linguistics illative force, that is, the suggestion of going into a new place or state of being. Another use of *in-* is intensive in nature; it can lend forcefulness to the word to which it is prefixed. Therefore, "immigration" (in which *in-* has become *im-*) implies not only a change in location but also suggests that the change is a significant one, more than likely a permanent one. This, then, is then the definition of "immigrant" in both legal and lexicographical terms: a person who moves from one country to another to take up residence there. However, the term connotes merely a physical change in location, not any change in political allegiance or legality. Consequently, an immigrant may be a naturalized citizen of the United States, a resident alien who lives in the country but maintains citizenship in the home country and who has proper documentation in the form of a visa and green card, or an "illegal immigrant" who has no such documentation or whose documents are outdated. Resident aliens are sometimes also referred to as "landed immigrants" or "permanent residents."

Of the various words associated with, or similar to, "immigrant," "immigrant" itself is the broadest term, the generic word for a person who has changed the country of his or her residence. "Alien," from a Latin root meaning "other" or "strange," designates any person from another country and can theoretically be applied to a person from a country other than the United States who is still in that country. A "refugee" is legally defined in the United States as someone who has come to the country to avoid persecution in the country of origin on the basis of such issues as race or religion. Therefore, one person can be—and sometimes is—an alien, an immigrant, and a refugee simultaneously.

The U.S. Citizenship and Immigration Services recognize and define various subcategories of immigrants and immigration. One populous subcategory is that of family-based immigrants, people from other countries who are spouses, fiancés, children, parents, and siblings of U.S. citizens. Another large subcategory is that of employment-based immigrants. These are people who possess job skills and professional expertise that have been deemed especially desirable or needed in the United States—as well as their families. A variation of this latter group is known as investor immigrants: immigrants who are granted visas to begin new businesses in the United States, especially in parts of the country where the economy is sluggish.

Thomas Du Bose

FURTHER READING

Beasley, Vanessa. *Who Belongs in America?* College Station: Texas A&M Press, 2006.

Borjas, George J. *Heaven's Door: Immigration Policy and the American Economy.* Princeton, N.J.: Princeton University Press, 2001.

SEE ALSO: Citizenship; Families; Illegal immigration; Immigration law; *A Nation of Immigrants*; Permanent resident status; Refugees; Resident aliens.

THE IMMIGRANT

IDENTIFICATION: Silent comedy about poor European immigrants arriving in New York during the early twentieth century

DATE: Released in 1917

SIGNIFICANCE: Directed and cowritten by groundbreaking film artist Charles Chaplin, *The Immigrant* depicts obstacles and triumphs associated with the immigrant experience. In 1998, the U.S. Library of Congress selected *The Immigrant* for preservation in the National Film Registry.

Distributed by the Mutual Film Corporation and filmed on location at the Chaplin Studios in Hollywood, California, *The Immigrant* stars Charles Chaplin and Edna Purviance as unnamed immigrants, apparently—but not definitely—of Eastern European origin. The film develops various motifs, often exaggerated for comic effect, based on the harsh realities that a generation of European immigrants to the United States experienced.

The first part of the twenty-minute film takes place aboard a ship, where Chaplin, in his iconic "Tramp" persona, plays a steerage-class passenger who suffers from seasickness and endures the torments of card-playing thieves and pickpockets. Edna Purviance is also among the deck passengers. The voyage ends when the ship enters New York Harbor, and its passengers see the Statue of Liberty. Thrilled by their first glimpse of the most famous symbol of American freedom, the steerage passengers rush to the side of the ship to get a closer look. However, at that moment, they are roughly roped in by immigration officials, who pull them back, as if they were merely so many farm animals. The Tramp expresses his defiance of this exercise of authority by kicking one of the officers in the rear.

The second half of the film depicts the Tramp and Purviance's chance meeting in a restaurant. Money issues and a surly waiter (Eric Campbell) complicate the scene. In the end, however, the American Dream proves true: An artist spots the penniless couple and offers them a job. The film is notable for its command of contemporary filmmaking techniques, editing, and fluid plotline.

Cordelia E. Barrera

Charlie Chaplin's Tramp character (left) and fellow steerage-class passengers relishing their first look at the Statue of Liberty. (The Granger Collection, New York)

FURTHER READING

Chaplin, Charlie. *Charlie Chaplin: Interviews.* Edited by Kevin J. Hayes. Jackson: University Press of Mississippi, 2005.

_____. *My Autobiography.* 1964. New York: Penguin Books, 1992.

Lyons, Timothy J. *Charles Chaplin: A Guide to References and Resources.* Boston: G. K. Hall, 1979.

Robinson, David. *Chaplin: His Life and Art.* Rev. ed. New York: Penguin Books, 2001.

Schickel, Richard, ed. *The Essential Chaplin: Perspectives on the Life and Art of the Great Comedian.* Chicago: I. R. Dee, 2006.

SEE ALSO: California; Crime; European immigrants; Films; Hamburg-Amerika Line; Pacific Mail Steamship Company; Statue of Liberty; Stereotyping; Transportation of immigrants; Women immigrants.

IMMIGRANT ADVANTAGE

DEFINITION: Term used within sociology to describe distinctions among minority groups within a larger society and those peoples who immigrate to these societies voluntarily from other nations

SIGNIFICANCE: Immigrants who are considered members of ethnic groups already residing within the United States often have advantages over native-born members of those groups.

Members of resident minority groups are often "marginalized," living on the fringe of society, often in poverty, lacking education, occupational skills, political power, or the means to integrate into the mainstream. These groups, much like immigrant groups, are frequently made up of ethnic and racial minorities. However, compared with marginalized groups, immigrants have numerous advantages and often become successful, productive members of a society.

One of the primary advantages that many immigrants have is that most people who immigrate to a new country typically do so by choice and therefore arrive already motivated to succeed. Another advantage is that they often have the resources needed to relocate to a new country. National immigration services typically work at keeping out low-skilled and poorly educated immigrants.

A third advantage is that immigrants to the United States tend to believe in the "melting pot" ideal and want to join the mainstream society and learn the new language. To become citizens of the United States, for example, immigrants must speak, read, and write English and pass an examination on U.S. history and government. Therefore, although immigrants may start on the lowest rungs of the economic ladder, they often move up more quickly than members of marginalized resident minorities. In many cases, their rise is accelerated by their ability to take advantage of affirmative action programs that were originally designed to benefit native-born members of disadvantaged minorities.

Rochelle L. Dalla

FURTHER READING

Barone, Michael. *The New Americans: How the Melting Pot Can Work Again.* Washington, D.C.: Regnery, 2001.

Cook, Terrence E. *Separation, Assimilation, or Accommodation: Contrasting Ethnic Minority Policies.* Westport, Conn.: Praeger, 2003.

Jacoby, Tamar, ed. *Reinventing the Melting Pot: The New Immigrants and What It Means to Be American.* New York: Basic Books, 2004.

SEE ALSO: Affirmative action; African Americans and immigrants; Assimilation theories; Civil Rights movement; Employment; Hansen effect; "Immigrant"; Melting pot theory; "Middleman" minorities; Migrant superordination; "Model minorities."

IMMIGRANT AID ORGANIZATIONS

DEFINITION: Charitable organizations established within immigrant communities, often church affiliated, to provide financial assistance and other support to members of the communities

SIGNIFICANCE: Immigrant aid organizations played an important role in helping immigrants to establish themselves in the United States. Not only have they offered much-needed financial assistance to immigrants, many of whom have been employed in low-wage jobs, but they also have given immigrants a sense of belonging and created a sense of home by providing social activities and traditional holiday celebrations.

During the eighteenth, nineteenth, and twentieth centuries, the vast majority of immigrants coming to the United States from Europe, Latin America, and Asia were poor working-class individuals who came seeking economic opportunities and better lives for themselves and their families. Farmers, laborers, and tradespeople who have lacked formal educations have found themselves in a new country in which customs are different, working conditions are often far from ideal, and the legal system is unfamiliar. The situation of new immigrants has been made more difficult by the fact many do not speak English when they arrive, and they have missed the cultural ambiance that they had left in their native lands.

Within the various ethnic communities or groups, organizations were soon formed to help individuals through both financial assistance and moral support. Early organizations helped those in their group who were ill and in need of medical care and those who were at times unable to find work and provide for their families. The concept of self-help was a major part of these organizations. Members paid either set dues or whatever they could afford. These funds were typically used to assist members with expenses incurred in childbirth, weddings, and funerals. Aid organizations eventually began offering health and life insurance at low rates. Some organizations even established banks to provide loans to members. Many organizations were also active in maintaining traditions of the home countries by sponsoring festivals and traditional holiday celebrations. Many of these organizations have remained active into the twenty-first century. as aid societies or social organizations or both.

ETHNIC-BASED ORGANIZATIONS

The first immigrant aid organization formed in the United States was the Charitable Irish Association of Boston, which was founded in 1737. Originally, its members had to be Irish Protestants, or of Irish ancestry, and had to live in Boston. However, by 1742, the majority of the members were Irish Catholics living in Boston. The Ancient Order of Hibernians (AOH) formed organizations to aid Irish Catholic immigrants in almost all the areas of the United States in which Irish immigrants settled. The Hibernians were present in New York City, in Savannah, Georgia, and in Philadelphia.

The AOH was also active in the anthracite coal-mining region of Pennsylvania where it was purported to be associated with the Molly Maguires, a militant Irish Catholic mineworkers group that attempted to improve their working conditions by the use of intimidation and force. While members of the Molly Maguires were also members of the AOH, the latter organization itself eschewed violence, was benevolent, and provided financial assistance to members who were ill or impoverished.

The large Mexican immigrant population that was first located in the southwestern United States brought with it from Mexico a strong sense of community. *El pueblo*, the place where one lives, had a major significance in the Mexican mindset. Community aid organizations known as *mutualistas* were a part of the culture of their homeland. The membership of the *mutualistas*, which have remained very active into the twenty-first century, has varied and continues to do so. Members have included Mexicans, Mexican Americans, and non-Mexicans. The *mutualistas* provide not only financial assistance and tra-

ditional social activities but also support to members who experience workplace or political discrimination.

The Italian immigrants who came to the United States also created mutual aid organizations to provide financial assistance to the ill and impoverished. However, unlike the Irish, who emphasized nationality and religion, and the Mexicans, for whom *el pueblo*, or the community, was most important, the Italians established their societies on a narrower base. Their organizations based membership either on the families to which members belonged or the regions of Italy from which the immigrants came.

Flyer from an organization dedicated to protecting Italian immigrants from being exploited upon their arrival in America. (Center for Migration Studies)

OTHER IMMIGRANT ORGANIZATIONS

The mutual aid organizations established by the vast number of Chinese immigrants brought to the California area as laborers in the gold mines and for railroad construction were even more complex in their determination of membership. However, they also reflected the traditions and culture of the home country. Three distinct types of Chinese mutual aid associations were established. The clan associations received members having the same surname, and the tongs had a broader membership and included immigrants from different clans and districts. Membership in the *huikuan* or *huiguan* was open to all those speaking the same dialect, coming from the same district, or belonging to the same ethnic group. Other European groups such as the Belgians, Germans, and Poles also established aid organizations based on nationality.

Shawncey Webb

FURTHER READING

Candeloro, Dominic. *Chicago's Italians: Immigrants, Ethnics, Americans.* Chicago: Arcadia Press, 2003. Traces development of Italian contributions to Chicago in labor unions, politics, and religion.

Gutíerrez, David G. *Walls and Mirrors: Mexican Americans, Mexican Immigrants and the Politics of Ethnicity.* Berkeley: University of California Press, 1995. Excellent history of Mexicans and their descendants in the United States with a strong emphasis on the Mexican immigrants' maintenance of their culture and the role of *mutualistas*. Also good presentation of role of labor and political organizations.

Portes, Alejandro, and Rubén G. Rumbaut. *Immigrant America: A Portrait.* Berkeley: University of California Press, 2006. Excellent for understanding the problems and difficulties shared by immigrant groups and the need for immigrant aid organizations.

Pozzetta, George, ed. *Immigrant Institutions: The Organization of Immigrant Life.* New York: Routledge, 1991. Collection of useful articles on Italian, Jewish, and Japanese aid organizations. Many articles emphasize the roles of ethnic newspapers and of saloons as gathering places.

Reimers, David. *Other Immigrants: The Global Origins of the American People.* New York: New York University Press, 2005. Good discussion of the problems faced by non-European immigrants, with

some attention to the aid organizations that were formed.

SEE ALSO: Association of Indians in America; Chinese family associations; Chinese secret societies; Coalition for Humane Immigrant Rights of Los Angeles; El Rescate; Ethnic enclaves; Health care; Mexican American Legal Defense and Educational Fund; Social networks; Sociedad Progresista Mexicana; Welfare and social services.

IMMIGRATION ACT OF 1882

THE LAW: First comprehensive immigration law enacted by the U.S. Congress
DATE: Enacted on August 3, 1882

> **SIGNIFICANCE:** Setting the basic course of United States immigration law and policy, the Immigration Act of 1882 established categories of foreigners deemed "undesirable" for entry and gave the U.S. secretary of the treasury authority over immigration enforcement.

The 1882 Immigration Act was the first comprehensive immigration law enacted by the federal government. As such, it would have enormous consequences for future immigration legislation. The act built the framework for federal oversight over immigration and delineated categories of "undesirables" who would be barred entry to the United States. Through the first century of American independence, immigration had been relatively open, with only occasional oversight and restrictions imposed by individual states. By the 1870's, however, increasing pressure was brought to bear against immigrants, especially Chinese laborers in California. In 1875, Congress passed the Page Law, which served to reduce immigration of women from Asia. Overall immigration continued to increase, however, with the year 1882 seeing the largest number of immigrants in American history: 788,992 persons. In response, Congress passed two historic immigration acts. The first was the Chinese Exclusion Act of 1882, suspending immigration of Chinese laborers.

The second was the Immigration Act of 1882, which was enacted on August 3 of that year. This act was the first comprehensive immigration law to deal with federal oversight and categories of exclusion. As to oversight, the law gave power over immigration enforcement to the secretary of the treasury, who was already responsible for overseeing customs in U.S. ports. The Treasury Department was mandated to issue regulations for the orderly admission of immigrants and to collect a "head tax" of fifty cents for each arriving immigrant to defray administrative expenses.

The Treasury secretary was authorized to enter into contracts with individual states to administer immigration entry. As to categories of those deemed undesirable, the act prohibited the entry of "any convict, lunatic, idiot, or any person unable to take care of himself or herself without becoming a public charge." Carried over from the immigration rules of several states, the "public charge" doctrine served to bar arriving foreigners who could not show the financial ability to support themselves. Foreigners denied entry were returned to their starting points at the expense of the ship owners. Interestingly, the act made an exception for foreigners convicted of political offenses, reflecting the traditional American belief that the United States is a haven for those persecuted by foreign tyrants.

The specifics of the Immigration Act of 1882 would soon be amended, but the contours of federal oversight and categorical restrictions that it established would remain. In 1891, Congress established exclusive federal control over immigration through a superintendent of immigration, the forerunner of the Bureau of Immigration and Naturalization. States would no longer play a role in the official administration of immigration affairs.

In 1903, Congress, alarmed by the 1901 assassination of President William McKinley and by the specter of political radicalism and anarchism, acted to end the 1882 law's exemption for political offenses, forbidding immigration of persons "opposed to organized government." The exclusion of those likely to become public charges remained a fixed element of American immigration law, presenting a potential obstacle to poorer immigrants. In 1917, 1921, and 1924, Congress added exclusions by national origins to the list of undesirables. National origins quotas would be the centerpiece of immigration policy in the decades to follow. The specifics of the Immigration Act of 1882 had been

altered; however, its focus on federal oversight and exclusion by categories had set the framework for immigration law for the following century.

Howard Bromberg

FURTHER READING

Daniels, Roger. *Guarding the Golden Door: American Immigration Policy and Immigrants Since 1882.* New York: Hill & Wang, 2004.

Gunderson, Theodore. *Immigration Policy in Turmoil.* Huntington, N.Y.: Nova Science, 2002.

SEE ALSO: Alien Contract Labor Law of 1885; Bureau of Immigration, U.S.; Chinese Exclusion Act of 1882; Congress, U.S.; Immigration Act of 1891; Immigration Act of 1903; Immigration Act of 1917; Immigration Act of 1921; Immigration Act of 1924; Immigration law; Page Law of 1875.

IMMIGRATION ACT OF 1891

THE LAW: Federal legislation that increased government regulation of immigration
DATE: Enacted on March 3, 1891

SIGNIFICANCE: Beginning in 1882, responsibility for administering U.S. immigration law, excluding the Chinese exclusion law, rested with the individual states. In the Immigration Act of 1891, the U.S. Congress assigned responsibility for enforcing immigration policy to the federal government in an effort to increase the effectiveness of immigration law. The act also expanded the list of excludable and deportable aliens.

In the light of several concerns over immigration law, Congress passed the Immigration Act of 1891, which included provisions intended to secure closer inspection and provide more effective enforcement of immigration law. The 1891 act centralized responsibility for enforcement of immigration law in the federal executive branch, tightened regulation along the land borders, and expanded the list of excludable and deportable immigrants.

Of paramount importance to Congress in 1891 was the centralization of enforcement under the executive branch of the federal government. Under the Immigration Act of 1882, the secretary of the treasury was responsible for executing the provisions of the act, but he did not hire and directly oversee the agents who would regulate immigration. The law mandated that state governors determine which state agency or officials would be responsible for enforcing federal immigration law. After the governor identified the agency, the secretary of the treasury then entered into contract with that state agency. By this law, the national government had broad authority over immigration restriction. While the secretary of the treasury was nominally responsible for immigration regulation, most of the responsibility rested with the states because the state agency responsible for enforcement immigration restriction continued to be state-based.

In the Immigration Act of 1891, Congress made the secretary of the treasury responsible for prescribing rules for inspection of the nation's coastal ports and its borders with Canada and Mexico. The 1891 act created the Office of Superintendent of Immigration. The new executive or bureaucratic office would comprise three clerks and a superintendent appointed by the president, who all worked under the jurisdiction of the secretary of the treasury. By 1894, this federal bureaucracy had become the Bureau of Immigration. The 1891 act, therefore, charged officers of the U.S. government, who were employed directly by the Office of Superintendent of Immigration, with carrying out the inspection and deportation of immigrants. Local or state officials would no longer directly enforce immigration restrictions. The superintendent of immigration was responsible for hearing appeals from aliens, but Congress assigned jurisdiction over cases arising out of the act to the circuit and district courts of the United States.

While the Immigration Act of 1882 regulated coastal borders, it did not regulate the contiguous borders, and immigrants crossing either the U.S.-Canadian or the U.S.-Mexican border entered the nation largely without inspection. Reports estimated that, in six months before the passage of the Immigration Act of 1891, as many as fifty thousand immigrants entered the United States from Canada without inspection. With the Immigration Act of 1891, Congress began tightening regulation of the U.S.-Mexican and the U.S.-Canadian borders.

The 1891 act also extended the federal government's power to deport immigrants beyond Chinese workers and contract laborers. The act listed all the existing categories of excludable immigrants: "idiots," the insane, paupers, and polygamists; persons liable to become a public charge; people convicted of a felony or other crime or misdemeanor involving moral turpitude; and sufferers "from a loathsome or dangerous" contagious disease. This act connected each of these excludable categories with a deportation provision, so that all these categories were now both excludable and deportable.

Torrie Hester

FURTHER READING

Daniels, Roger. *Guarding the Golden Door: American Immigration Policy and Immigrants Since 1882.* New York: Hill & Wang, 2004.

Hutchinson, Edward Prince. *Legislative History of American Immigration Policy, 1798-1965.* Philadelphia: University of Pennsylvania Press, 1981.

Salyer, Lucy. *Laws Harsh as Tigers: Chinese Immigrants and the Shaping of Modern Immigration Law.* Chapel Hill: University of North Carolina Press, 1995.

SEE ALSO: Alien Contract Labor Law of 1885; Bureau of Immigration, U.S.; Congress, U.S.; Deportation; Geary Act of 1892; History of immigration after 1891; Illegal immigration; Immigration Act of 1882; Immigration Act of 1903.

IMMIGRATION ACT OF 1903

THE LAW: Federal legislation that increased government regulation of immigration

DATE: Enacted on March 3, 1903

SIGNIFICANCE: The Immigration Act of 1903 expanded the federal government's power to regulate immigration. In this piece of legislation, Congress codified immigration law and refined the existing classes of inadmissible immigrants. Of even greater significance to the history of immigration was the act's creation of two new inadmissible classes: The first covered immigrants involved in prostitution, and the second dealt with anarchists.

Much of the Immigration Act of 1903 dealt with preexisting immigration law. In this new act, Congress codified immigration law and increased the tax on immigrants entering the United States, excluding Canadians and Mexicans. The law refined the federal regulation of poor immigrants by amending the contract labor and public charge provisions; it also extended the time limit on deporting aliens in most inadmissible classes from one to three years. In addition, Congress added prostitutes and those associated with prostitution, as well as anarchists, to the list of excludable or inadmissible classes of immigrants.

None of the immigration laws passed between 1875 and 1902 explicitly provided for the deportation of prostitutes. The Page Law, passed in 1875, only made the importation of prostitutes a felony and, in practice, provided for tougher screening of Chinese women in Hong Kong. Before 1903, the federal government did deport a small number of Chinese women suspected of prostitution, but it deported them as manual laborers in violation of the Chinese exclusion laws rather than as prostitutes. Under the Immigration Act of 1903, however, Congress empowered the Bureau of Immigration to exclude people involved in prostitution and to deport prostitutes as well as procurers of prostitutes, if they were immigrants too.

The Immigration Act of 1903 made immigrants excludable on political grounds for the first time by adding anarchists to the list of inadmissible classes. Responding to public fears about anarchists, which were heightened by the assassination of President William McKinley in 1901, Congress included a provision in the law that made anarchists or those who advocated violence against government excludable and deportable. John Turner, a British-born labor activist and self-proclaimed anarchist who was in the United States organizing workers, was one of the first people affected by the antianarchist provision of the Immigration Act of 1903. He challenged the constitutionality of the new anarchist provision in the U.S. courts. The U.S. Supreme Court upheld the anarchist provisions in the 1904 case *Turner v. Williams*. Congress would later refine and expand the anarchist provision, which immigration authorities used in the Palmer raids following World War I and against communists during the Cold War.

Torrie Hester

FURTHER READING

Chan, Sucheng. "The Exclusion of Chinese Women, 1870-1943." In *Entry Denied: Exclusion and the Chinese Community in America, 1882-1943.* Philadelphia: Temple University Press, 1991.

Langum, David J. *Crossing over the Line: Legislating Morality and the Mann Act.* Chicago: University of Chicago Press, 1994.

Preston, William, Jr. *Aliens and Dissenters: Federal Suppression of Radicals, 1903-1933.* Champaign: University of Illinois Press, 1963.

SEE ALSO: Congress, U.S.; Espionage and Sedition Acts of 1917-1918; History of immigration after 1891; Immigration Act of 1891; Immigration Act of 1907; Immigration Act of 1917; Immigration law; Industrial Workers of the World; Page Law of 1875; Progressivism; Women immigrants.

IMMIGRATION ACT OF 1907

THE LAW: Federal legislation regulating immigration
DATE: Signed into law on February 20, 1907

SIGNIFICANCE: This law created the Dillingham Commission to collect data used in future immigration laws, further narrowed Asian immigration, limited Muslim immigration, and expanded the definition of undesirable women immigrants.

In 1905, amid continuing concerns over increased immigration, President Theodore Roosevelt called upon the U.S. Congress to increase protection from unwanted immigration, especially in the nation's largest cities, and to codify earlier legislation. Roosevelt and Congress sought to exclude immigrants who would not make good citizens. In February, 1907, Congress passed a new immigration act that expanded previous immigration restrictions by prohibiting Asians from entering the United States through the territory of Hawaii, doubled the immigration head tax to four dollars per person, broadened the excludable classes of immigrants to include contract labor and subversive and presumably immoral groups, and required ships to allow minimum amounts of deck space for each passenger and to provide manifests of their departing aliens.

Section 39 of the new law created the U.S. Immigration Commission—better known as the Dillingham Commission—to investigate immigration problems and their impact on the nation. The commission provided detailed reports to future Congresses regarding the need for refining immigration laws. The commission called on Congress to put the economic well-being of U.S. citizens above the needs of corporations that relied heavily on uneducated immigrants for cheap labor. The commission also favored further limiting immigration, implementing an alien literacy test, and continuing the Chinese exclusion policy and restricting Japanese and Korean immigration. The commissioners argued that Congress should limit the admission of unskilled aliens and implement a quota system.

The Immigration Act of 1907 was notable for several key innovations regarding immigration policy. Section 12 required ships with alien passengers departing the United States to provide complete lists of their passengers by name, age, sex, nationality, occupation, and place of residence in the United States. The information gathered through this law provided the first statistical documentation on alien departures. To combat the practice of polygamy and the keeping of concubines, the act expanded on the Immigration Act of 1891, which denied entry to polygamists, to include any persons who espoused these practices. The Ottoman Empire viewed these provisions as an attack on Islamic religious practices.

Women were a particular target of the 1907 law, which broadened the definition of prostitutes to include women arriving in the United States for any immoral purposes. The vague language of the law was used to exclude women in arranged marriages, especially those of Asian origin, and allowed for their deportation. Responding to concerns of progressive reformers, the act tightened laws targeting immigrant women suspected of being recruited to work as prostitutes. It also permitted the deportation of women who lived in known houses of prostitution or who had practiced prostitution within three years of their entering the United States. This was the first statutory provision authorizing deportation based on criminal conduct within the United States.

Linda Upham-Bornstein

FURTHER READING

Abrams, Kerry. "Polygamy, Prostitution, and the Federalization of Immigration Law." *Columbia Law Review* 105, no. 3 (2005): 641-716. Examination of the role marriage played in the development of immigration laws regarding women and Muslims.

Cott, Nancy F. *Public Vows: A History of Marriage and the Nation.* Cambridge, Mass.: Harvard University Press, 2000. Thoroughly researched account of the evolution of marriage in American legal and social practice.

Hutchinson, Edward P. *Legislative History of American Immigration Policy, 1798-1965.* Philadelphia: University of Pennsylvania Press, 1981. Survey of congressional actions on immigration, examining specific elements of those policies.

SEE ALSO: Congress, U.S.; Dillingham Commission; History of immigration after 1891; Immigration Act of 1891; Immigration Act of 1903; Immigration Act of 1917; Immigration law; Progressivism; Return migration; Women immigrants.

IMMIGRATION ACT OF 1917

THE LAW: Federal law imposing major new restrictions on categories of people allowed to immigrate

DATE: Went into effect on May 1, 1917

> **SIGNIFICANCE:** The Immigration Act of 1917 was the first federal law to impose a general restriction on immigration in the form of a literacy test. It also broadened restrictions on the immigration of Asians and persons deemed "undesirable" and provided tough enforcement provisions.

Through the first century of American independence, immigration into the United States was largely unrestricted. This open-door policy began to change during the 1870's and 1880's, with the introduction of federal legislation aimed at barring two classes of immigrants: Asian laborers to California and immigrants deemed physically and mentally "undesirable." In 1882, for example, Congress passed the Chinese Exclusion Act to bar the immigration of Chinese workers and a general immigra-

President Woodrow Wilson, with his wife, Edith, at his second inauguration in 1917. Wilson twice vetoed the Immigration Act of 1917, only to see Congress pass it over his objections. (Library of Congress)

tion act to bar the immigration of persons judged likely to become "public charges."

The general Immigration Act of 1882 also imposed a "head tax" of fifty cents on each immigrant. The U.S. Congress, which was constitutionally empowered to exercise exclusive jurisdiction over immigration, continued to increase restrictions through the late nineteenth and early twentieth centuries. The head tax was increased to four dollars by the Immigration Act of 1907. The Chinese Exclusion Act was amended and tightened in legislation enacted in 1884, 1888, 1892, and 1902. In the Gentlemen's Agreement of 1907, Japan agreed to bar its citizens from emigrating to the United States. The Immigration Act of 1891 added more categories of people to the list of "undesirable aliens," including persons with contagious diseases and polygamists. The Immigration Acts of 1903, 1907, and 1910 added rules to exclude persons with mental and physical defects, persons with tu-

berculosis, and anarchists. However, congressional provisions to add a literacy requirement to the immigration laws were vetoed by Presidents Grover Cleveland in 1896, William Howard Taft in 1913, and Woodrow Wilson in 1915.

PROVISIONS OF THE 1917 LAW

The Immigration Act of 1917 updated and codified much of the previous immigration legislation, thereby effectively repealing the Immigration Acts of 1903, 1907, and 1910. President Wilson vetoed the law, but Congress overrode his veto and the act went into effect on May 1, 1917. A long and comprehensive piece of legislation, the act contained thirty-eight subsections and took up twenty-five pages in the Congressional Session Laws.

The law was significant in five major areas; it

- increased the head tax
- expanded categories of "undesirable aliens"
- excluded South Asian immigrants
- added a literacy requirement
- contained new enforcement provisions

The new law increased the head tax levied on every adult immigrant to eight dollars and required liens to be was placed on passenger ships for nonpayment. The law's expansion of categories of "undesirables" who would be barred from entry reflected new theories of comparative psychology. The act excluded so-called "idiots, imbeciles, and feeble-minded persons;" persons of "constitutional psychopathic inferiority;" "mentally or physically defective" persons; the insane; alcoholics; persons with epilepsy, tuberculosis; or contagious diseases; paupers and vagrants; criminals; prostitutes; anarchists; polygamists; political radicals; and contract laborers.

The Immigration Act of 1917 also barred most immigration from Asia. Chinese immigrants were already barred by the Chinese Exclusion Acts and the Japanese by the Gentlemen's Agreement. In addition, the act created the "Asiatic Barred Zone," which encompassed India, Afghanistan, Persia (now Iran), Arabia, parts of the Ottoman Empire and Russia, Southeast Asia, and the Asian-Pacific islands.

Reflecting public hostility to southern and eastern European immigrants, the act required all adult immigrants to demonstrate an ability to read. Any language sufficed. Finally, the act contained

531

extensive provisions for enforcement. Penalties were imposed on any persons or corporations who encouraged or assisted the immigration of persons barred by the act or contract laborers. The act required all ships carrying immigrants to provide detailed information about each passenger's name, age, sex, physical description, literacy, nationality, destination, occupation, mental and physical health, and criminal record. Immigration inspectors, medical examiners, and Boards of Special Inquiry were authorized to carry out these regulations and decide on the admissibility of immigrants.

IMPACT OF THE LAW

The act of 1917 represented a further tightening of the immigrant restrictions begun by Congress during the 1870's. Although the 1880's witnessed the exclusion of "undesirables" and Chinese and the imposition of a head tax, the 1917 act greatly expanded these restrictions. The list of undesirables was couched in vague terms of mental and physical health, and could thus be interpreted in almost unlimited ways. The eight-dollar head tax was a significant levy on impoverished immigrants. The literacy requirement, which had been vetoed by three presidents, appeared to be a significant impediment to many immigrants. Heavy penalties and fines were imposed on any persons who seemingly assisted immigration in violation of the law. This expansion of restrictions can be explained, in part, by the rise of psychological and eugenics theories categorizing inferior individuals and races and nativist sentiments exacerbated by World War I.

The restrictions culminating in the 1917 act ultimately proved to be more qualitative than quantitative. In fact, the first two decades of the twentieth century saw the greatest numbers of immigrants up to that time: 8,795,386 people entered the United States between 1901 and 1910, and another 5,735,811 entered between 1911 and 1920. In the fiscal year between July, 1920, and June, 1921, more than 800,000 immigrants entered the country. Only about 1,450 persons were actually excluded by the literacy test. The 1917 act prefigured but differed from the immigration quotas that would be imposed by new immigration laws during the 1920's. These quotas greatly restricted immigration for the first time in American history and did so in an attempt to preserve the ethnic heritage of the United States as it was perceived at the turn of the century.

Howard Bromberg

FURTHER READING

Daniels, Roger. *Guarding the Golden Door: American Immigration Policy and Immigrants Since 1882.* New York: Hill & Wang, 2004. General history of immigration restrictions. Notes that the 1917 law represented the first major categorical restriction of immigration in American history.

Hing, Bill Ong. *Defining America Through Immigration Policy.* Philadelphia: Temple University Press, 2004. Chapter 3, on the 1917 literacy test, sees its origins in American animosity toward Italian and Jewish immigrants.

King, Desmond. *Making Americans: Immigration, Race, and the Origins of the Diverse Democracy.* Cambridge, Mass.: Harvard University Press, 2000. Scholarly study of the history of immigration that describes the 1917 act as replacing the tenet of individual selection for admission with group criteria.

Lee, Erika. *At America's Gates: Chinese Immigration During the Exclusion Era, 1882-1943.* Chapel Hill: University of North Carolina Press, 2003. Highlights the creation of the Asiatic Barred Zone as a milestone in restricting Asian immigration.

Shanks, Cheryl. *Immigration and the Politics of American Sovereignty, 1890-1990.* Ann Arbor: University of Michigan Press, 2001. Historical study of the relationship between immigration law and policy and notions of American sovereignty. Portrays the Asiatic Barred Zone as the predecessor of the quota laws of the 1920's and the literacy test as motivated by exclusionary rather than educational sentiments.

SEE ALSO: Asian immigrants; Asiatic Barred Zone; Chinese Exclusion Act of 1882; Chinese immigrants; Congress, U.S.; History of immigration after 1891; Immigration Act of 1882; Immigration Act of 1891; Immigration Act of 1903; Immigration Act of 1907; Immigration law; Literacy tests.

IMMIGRATION ACT OF 1921

THE LAW: Federal legislation limiting the immigration of aliens into the United States

DATE: Enacted and signed into law on May 19, 1921

ALSO KNOWN AS: Johnson Act; Emergency Quota Act of 1921

SIGNIFICANCE: The first federal law in U.S. history to limit the immigration of Europeans, the Immigration Act of 1921 reflected the growing American fear that people from southern and eastern European countries not only did not adapt well into American society but also threatened its very existence. The law specified that no more than 3 percent of the total number of immigrants from any specific country already living in the United States in 1910 could migrate to America during any year.

On May 19, 1921, the same day on which the law was passed by the U.S. Congress, recently inaugurated President Warren G. Harding signed the Emergency Quota Act into law. The premise of the act had been debated in the Congress for several years. Indeed, a version of the bill had passed during the previous session of Congress only to fall victim to a pocket veto by the ailing President Woodrow Wilson during the last days of his administration

The bill was a product of the Dillingham Commission, which had been chartered in 1907 and was chaired by Representative William P. Dillingham of Vermont. It represented several versions, the latest of which had been created by Representative Albert Johnson of Washington. Although concerns about undesirable immigration to the United States had been discussed for decades, and action had been taken to prevent the immi-

gration of most Asians, fears springing out of the aftermath of World War I again bestirred those who would close the floodgates of immigration.

According to federal officials scattered throughout European consulates, literally millions of Europeans hoped to emigrate to the United States in the aftermath of World War I (1914-1918). Some of these would-be immigrants could be considered as coming from the "desirable" classes of western and northern European nations, but it appeared that the vast majority of the potential immigrants would be coming from southern and eastern Europe.

Many Americans held the perception that individuals from southern and eastern Europe could not be assimilated properly into the culture of the United States. Their languages, customs, and religions were thought to be too different from those

Contemporary cartoon portraying the effectiveness of the Immigration Act of 1921 in reducing the flow of European immigrants to the United States to a mere trickle. (The Granger Collection, New York)

of preceding generations of immigrants for full-scale integration into American culture. The fear was that these newer immigrants would always be "hyphenates," or citizens who would call themselves, or be called by others, by such hyphenated names as "Polish-Americans," "Greek-Americans," and "Italian-Americans."

Beyond the fear of being swamped by unassimilable immigrants from eastern and southern Europe was the fear that these immigrants' increasing numbers would depress wages for American workers. In addition, some people feared the potential of the rising political power of the new class of immigrants. To counter the tide of uneducated, working-class immigrants, professionals were allowed to enter the United States with few restrictions, regardless of their nations of origin.

As signed into law, the 1921 bill required that no more than 3 percent of the number of persons from a nation living in the United States, as recorded in the census of 1910, could be admitted to the country in the forthcoming year. Taken to its ultimate understanding, the law allowed only about 357,000 people to immigrate to the United States during the 1922 fiscal year. Based on the 1910 population figures, the bill effectively limited emigration of northern and western Europeans to approximately 175,000 individuals. As this figure reflected almost precisely the numbers of immigrants from these regions during the years leading up to 1921, the bill had little impact on northern and western European immigration. The bill imposed no limitations on immigration from the Western Hemisphere.

The impact of the 1921 law on southern and eastern Europe was much different. Again basing its quotas on 1910 population figures, the bill effectively limited nations in these regions to about 175,000 individuals. However, in contrast to western and northern Europeans, immigrants from southern and eastern Europe had contributed approximately 685,000 persons during each of the years immediately prior to the passage of the 1921 law.

The bill was intended to be in effect for only a single year; however, it was not replaced until 1924. The significance of the 1921 bill lies in the fact that it was the first time Americans had actively and legally sought to limit European immigration.

Kimberly K. Porter

FURTHER READING

Briggs, Vernon M. *Mass Immigration and the National Interest: Policy Directions for the New Century.* Armonk, N.Y.: M. E. Sharpe, 2003.

Higham, John. *Strangers in the Land: Patterns of American Nativism.* New Brunswick, N.J.: Rutgers University Press, 1963.

Shanks, Cheryl. *Immigration and the Politics of American Sovereignty, 1880-1990.* Ann Arbor: University of Michigan Press, 2001.

SEE ALSO: Congress, U.S.; Dillingham Commission; European immigrants; History of immigration after 1891; Immigration Act of 1903; Immigration Act of 1907; Immigration Act of 1917; Immigration Act of 1924; Immigration law.

IMMIGRATION ACT OF 1924

THE LAW: Federal legislation that set immigration quotas for individual countries that were based on the number of foreign nationals living in the United States in 1890

DATE: Signed into law on May 26, 1924

ALSO KNOWN AS: National Origins Act; Johnson-Reed Act; Asian Exclusion Act

SIGNIFICANCE: The act represented the first major attempt to restrict immigration into the United States. The establishment of a quota system limited immigration from southern and eastern Europe (primarily Jewish and Slavic) while allowing significant immigration from northern and western Europe. Asians were specifically excluded from immigration.

The Immigration Act of 1924 was a continuation of the Immigration Act of 1917 and attempted to fix loopholes in immigration restriction established by the earlier law. In the decades prior to 1917, what was effectively unlimited immigration resulted in nearly ten million people legally entering the United States. Many of these people came from eastern Europe and Russia. The onset of World War I significantly reduced the ability of Europeans to enter the United States. The war itself, and the subsequent entry of the United States into the war in April, 1917, resulted in a nationalistic fervor within the American population that in turn resulted in modifications to existing immigration laws. The effect was to severely alter the demographics of those permitted to enter the country.

IMMIGRATION ACT OF 1917

Previous immigration laws, particularly those that governed immigration from Japan—Chinese were already barred, the result of the Chinese Exclusion Act of 1882—were largely restrictive solely on the basis of a "Gentlemen's Agreement": Since 1907, Japan had voluntarily restricted emigration of its citizens to the United States. The major concern of the Immigration Act of 1917 was the large influx of eastern Europeans, many of them illiterate, as well as "Asiatics"—the term used for Asians. In February, 1917, the act was passed over the veto of President Woodrow Wilson and became law. Provisions of the act included the exclusion of "undesirables" such as criminals, those deemed insane or "idiots," and alcoholics. The most controversial portion of the act, creating an "Asiatic Barred Zone," kept out immigrants from eastern Asia, particularly those from India. The Philippines were not included since the islands were an American possession, nor was Japan included.

Other provisions increased the "head tax" to eight dollars. Finally, a literacy test was imposed on future immigrants. Any persons over the age of sixteen would have to be literate. However, this particular provision was relatively loose in its restrictions. As long as a husband was literate, neither his wife nor other family members had to be literate as well. The literacy test proved to be of no more than minor significance. During the last year in which the act was law—July, 1920, to June, 1921—only some fourteen hundred immigrants were denied entry as a result of illiteracy, compared with more than one million who attempted to enter. Nevertheless, the act of 1917 represented the first broad attempt to restrict immigration into the United States.

IMMIGRATION ACT OF 1921

The recognition that more than 800,000 immigrants had been admitted to the United States during 1920-1921 illustrated the loose restrictions imposed by the immigration law of 1917. Of particular concern was the fear that many of these immigrants from Russia or eastern Europe, many of them Jewish, were Bolsheviks or other kinds of radicals. The Red Scare (1919-1920) represented a symptom of the growing concern that revolutions taking place in Europe could spread to American shores. The Immigration Act of 1921, while merely a stopgap until more encompassing legislation could be passed, reflected that fear. Unlike the 1917 law, the 1921 act limited the annual number of immigrants from each country to 3 percent of that nation's nationals present in the United States according to the 1910 U.S. Census. Total immigration was set at 357,000 persons.

THE 1924 LAW

Introduced by Congressman Albert Johnson in the House of Representatives and David Reed in the Senate, the Immigration Act of 1924 was intended to permanently restrict the immigration numbers from "undesirable" areas of the world—particularly from Russia and eastern Europe.

In addition to having fears about radicalism, congressional leaders were concerned about the large influx of workers willing to work for substandard wages; not surprisingly, among the supporters of the bill were the leaders of the growing unions among American workers. The fear of "cheap labor" was largely directed toward eastern Europeans. During World War I, large numbers of Latin American workers, particularly from Mexico, had entered the United States to supplement the labor force related to war industries or farming, especially in the sparsely populated Southwest. The importance of these workers was reflected in their exemption from the quota system as established by the act. In the years prior to implementation of the act, immigrants from Latin America represented approximately 30 percent of total immigration.

Changes in the demographics of the United States in the years between 1880 and 1920 played perhaps the most significant role in defining the language of the bill. The perception had been that the United States had been settled largely by western European stock, primarily Protestant, and nearly entirely white. Black people, freed from slavery only in recent generations, and mostly uneducated and living in poverty, were either excluded or simply ignored in the argument.

By the 1920's, nearly one-third of the American population consisted of immigrants and their families. The birthrate among this segment of the population suggested that the proportion of the

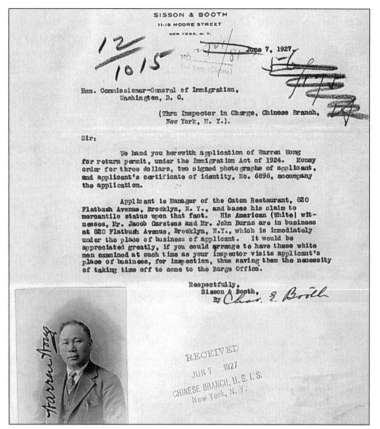

Application for the readmission to the United States of a Brooklyn restaurateur who had returned to China for a visit. The letter cites the terms of the Immigration Act of 1924. (NARA)

population they represented would continue to increase. Moreover, intelligence tests administered to U.S. Army recruits during World War I were interpreted to mean that southern and eastern Europeans were of lesser intelligence than northern Europeans. The mythology of the superiority of the Nordics, or northern and western Europeans, was addressed in a popular book written by the American anthropologist Madison Grant, *The Passing of the Great Race* (1916). Grant argued that both physical and mental characteristics of eastern European immigrants were below the standards of the dominant Protestant stock. Unless restrictions were placed on this population—and a program of eugenics was considered as a portion of such control—both the quality of life and the characteristics of a Protestant-dominated society would suffer. Limits to immigration represented the clearest support for Grant's arguments. The effect on Asian

or African immigration was even greater. The 1924 act excluded Asians "and their descendants" as well as descendants of "slave immigrants."

The greatest influx of immigrants from eastern Europe had occurred in the two to three decades prior to the start of World War I in 1914. Thus, the basis for the quota was changed from the U.S. Census of 1910 to that of 1890, when far fewer southern and eastern Europeans had resided in the United States. Furthermore, the quota was reduced from 3 percent to 2 percent of the number of foreign-born persons of each nationality resident in the United States in 1890. By 1929, the 2-percent quota was replaced by a total annual immigration cap of 150,000.

Other changes were meant to increase the monetary cost to potential immigrants, another means to restrict the poor. The head tax was increased to nine dollars. while requirements for both visas and photographs were implemented. The cost of the visa was nine dollars. This meant that families with several children might have to pay fifty dollars or more, on top of the cost of travel by ship, which might have been ten to twenty dollars per passenger. The significance of the visa was not only at the port of entry. In this manner, consulates at the country of origin also had a mechanism to regulate who was permitted to immigrate to the United States. Since members of the consulate determined which applicants could obtain visas, they exercised significant discretion as to who would be acceptable. In theory, only "desirables" would be issued such visas.

CONSEQUENCES OF THE ACT OF 1924

The most immediate impact of the new law was the restriction of eastern Europeans, particularly Jews, from entering the United States. Between 1880 and 1924, approximately two million European Jews entered the country. In the year after passage of the new immigration law, fewer than 10,000 European Jews were able to enter on an annual basis. Similar effects were observed among other eastern Europeans. Between 1921 and 1929, the average number of Poles entering the United States was reduced from an annual average of 95,000 to fewer than 10,000. The number of German immigrants, however, because of reduced restrictions—and a larger quota—increased during this period to a high of 45,000 annually, a number exceeded by British subjects to 50,000 annually. Between 1924 and the years immediately following World War II, total immigration was below three million people.

The long-term effects on European Jewry proved particularly devastating. With the limited quotas, European Jews in general, and French, Polish, and German Jews in particular, were largely unable to obtain visas during the years leading up to World War II, during which some six million Jews died at the hands of the Nazis. While Jewish refugees such as Albert Einstein were often epitomized as examples of the openness of American society to European refugees, the reality was that only several thousand Jews, mostly the highly educated, were able to enter the United States.

The national quotas were slightly modified in 1929. However, the system as established by the act of 1924 remained largely in place until 1952. Family members of U.S. citizens were not included in quota numbers, while women were not afforded equal status until the changes of 1952.

Richard Adler

FURTHER READING

Daniels, Roger. *Coming to America: A History of Immigration and Ethnicity in American Life.* New York: HarperPerennial, 2002. History of immigration beginning with the earliest settlements. The significance of various immigration acts and restrictions is explored.

_____. *Guarding the Golden Door: American Immigration Policy and Immigrants Since 1882.* New York: Hill & Wang, 2004. Synopsis of the evolution of immigration policies since the 1880's. Highlighted are specific laws associated with major immigration legislation.

Higham, John. *Strangers in the Land: Patterns of American Nativism, 1860-1925.* New Brunswick, N.J.: Rutgers University Press, 2002. Examines the history of nativism and its significance to the sociology and economics of the developing United States.

LeMay, Michael, and Elliott Robert Barkan, eds. *U.S. Immigration and Naturalization Laws and Issues: A Documentary History.* Westport, Conn.: Greenwood Press, 1999. Collection of documents that covers the history of immigration laws beginning with the colonial period. Relevant court cases are discussed.

Lowe, Lisa. *Immigrant Acts: On Asian American Cultural Politics.* Durham, N.C.: Duke University Press, 1999. Explores the significance of the Asian community in America, its history and response to prejudice.

Wenger, Beth. *The Jewish Americans: Three Centuries of Jewish Voices in America.* New York: Doubleday, 2007. Immigration, challenges, and growth of the Jewish community in America. Includes the effects of laws regulating immigration on the Jewish population.

SEE ALSO: Asian immigrants; Congress, U.S.; European immigrants; Gentlemen's Agreement; History of immigration after 1891; Immigration Act of 1907; Immigration Act of 1917; Immigration Act of 1921; Immigration and Nationality Act of 1952; Immigration law; Jewish immigrants; Quota systems.

IMMIGRATION ACT OF 1943

THE LAW: Federal legislation that lifted a government ban on Chinese immigration

DATE: Signed into law on December 17, 1943

ALSO KNOWN AS: Chinese Exclusion Repeal Act of 1943; Magnuson Act

SIGNIFICANCE: At the height of World War II, when the United States needed to promote goodwill with China, Congress repealed an 1882 federal immigration statute restricting all Chinese from entering the country and considerably eased the process of naturalization for those Chinese already residing in America.

Beginning with the discovery of gold in California in 1848, Chinese immigrants flooded into the state, driven from their home by waves of civil unrest and

Congressman Warren G. Magnuson in December, 1944. (Time & Life Pictures/Getty Images)

catastrophic famines. Even as the prospect of gold mining diminished, these immigrants found ready work building the transcontinental railroad, a massive engineering project that involved brutal work conditions in inhospitable environments. More than seventeen hundred miles of track were laid in six years, thanks largely to Chinese immigrant labor. Once the work was completed in 1869, however, as the Chinese immigrants returned to California urban areas and began working menial jobs, largely food service and laundry, they became the subject of nearly a decade of discrimination and violence driven by heated (and xenophobic) rhetoric that defined their presence as an economic hardship. In addition, because these immigrants did not share the language or religion of Americans, they were viewed with a keener hostility than were European immigrants.

By 1882, more than 300,000 Chinese had emigrated—a number viewed with alarm—fueling the passage of the 1882 Chinese Exclusion Act, which essentially closed America to any Chinese immigrants and denied citizenship to any Chinese already residing in the United States. It was the first time Congress had ever prohibited specific immigration. Initially, the ban was to last for ten years, but it was extended and ultimately made permanent in 1902. Numerous lawsuits unsuccessfully challenged the act as discriminatory, racist, and a violation of the Fourteenth Amendment.

Lifting the ban on Chinese immigration reflected political expediency during World War II. In the middle of a difficult land war in the Far East, with Japan using America's anti-Chinese sentiments as propaganda in an effort to derail China's alliance with the Allied Powers, the U.S. War Department moved to have the Chinese Exclusion Act rescinded. Sponsored by Washington State Democratic representative (later six-term senator) Warren G. Magnuson, himself a veteran of naval service in the Far East theater earlier in the war, the Immigration Act of 1943 proposed lifting the ban on Chinese immigration, setting a quota on the number of visas to be granted annually at 105. (The policy at the time was to allow annually 2 percent of that immigrant population already living in America.)

The token quota did not mollify those who feared the economic and cultural impact of any surge of Far East immigrants: Chinese immigrants could pursue entry into the country through other nations. To assuage such xenophobic fears, Congress determined that for the Chinese, immigration status would be determined not by country of origin (as it was for Europeans) but rather by ethnicity. Thus, if a Chinese family living in the Philippines applied for entry, they would be counted as Chinese.

President Franklin D. Roosevelt backed the compromise. It passed both houses of Congress and was signed on December 17, 1943. It would take more than twenty years of immigration reform legislation, culminating in the 1965 Immigration and Nationality Act, to eliminate the quota system.

Joseph Dewey

FURTHER READING

Chang, Iris. *The Chinese in America: A Narrative History.* New York: Viking Press, 2003.

Lee, Erika. *At America's Gate: Chinese Immigration During the Exclusion Era, 1882-1943*. Chapel Hill: University of North Carolina Press, 2007.

Yung, Judy, Gordon Chang, and Him Mark Lai, eds. *Chinese American Voices: From the Gold Rush to the Present*. Berkeley: University of California Press, 2006.

SEE ALSO: Angel Island Immigration Station; Anti-Chinese movement; Asian immigrants; Chinese Exclusion Act of 1882; Chinese immigrants; Congress, U.S.; Fiancées Act of 1946; Geary Act of 1892; History of immigration after 1891; Immigration Act of 1924; *United States v. Ju Toy*; World War II.

IMMIGRATION ACT OF 1990

THE LAW: Federal legislation that increased quotas for legal immigration into the United States

DATE: Enacted on November 29, 1990

> **SIGNIFICANCE:** This legislation has been seen as a return to the pre-1920's open door immigration policy of the United States. It allowed for an increase in the number of legal immigrants into the United States and waived many of the conditions that had previously restricted immigration of certain groups. The act allowed for sanctuary in the country and increased the numbers of work visas and visas awarded to immigrants hoping to become permanent residents of the United States.

The Immigration Act of 1990 allowed for an increase of those seeking immigrant visas. Such visas are given for numerous reasons, but are primarily granted to foreign workers seeking permission to work or become permanent residents of the United States. This category includes persons sponsored by American employers and by family members already in the United States, and priority and skilled workers, including college professors, athletes, and professionals in the arts, sciences, and medical fields.

The primary goal of the Immigration Act was to supplement the depleting skilled worker class of the United States. Many leaders in government feared that illegal immigration was flooding the workforce with unskilled and non-English speaking workers who threatened slowly to push skilled labor jobs out of the United States to other nations with less stringent labor laws, such as Mexico and India. The act allowed for an increase from roughly the 50,000 immigrant visas per year of the past to 140,000 visas by the end of the fiscal year 1991 for skilled positions. For the majority of these positions, employers or employees were to submit documentation showing that no skilled American workers were available for the jobs offered to immigrants. Some opponents of the law argued that this important requirement was often ignored by American employers seeking cheaper labor.

In addition to allowing skilled immigrant laborers into the United States, the act allowed for the creation of additional visas to be granted via a lottery system. This lottery system became important for immigrants from countries not regarded by the U.S. government as reliable providers of skilled and priority labor. To allow for an increase in immigrants from previously nonpriority countries, the 1990 law eased the requirements for English-language competency during the immigration phase and simplified the previously lengthy process for seeking permanent residence in the United States. Although standards were generally lowered, the United States still placed a cap on the total numbers of immigrants allowed per year. The cap was 675,000-700,000 through the first five years the law was in effect, and it remained steady at afterward. At the same time, to avoid overrepresentation from any single country, a limit of 48,000 was placed on the total number of immigrants from one nation.

The first several years after passage of the law saw a steady increase in skilled labor immigrants. The 1990 act was the first major overhaul in U.S. immigration law since the 1960's, and its passage prompted increased numbers of both skilled and nonskilled laborers from other nations to immigrate. The largest increases in legal immigration came from Mexico and the Philippines. Other nations that saw increases in numbers of immigrants during the first five years the law was in effect were India, Canada, China, and many African countries.

IMPACT OF THE LAW

The Immigration Act of 1990 was enacted primarily to increase skilled labor positions in the

United States. As a result, the medical fields (such as doctors), the arts, sciences, education (including professors), and athletes all experienced increases in the number of skilled positions in the United States. In an attempt to lure and keep these skilled workers in the country, other laws pertaining to deportation and exclusion were weakened.

This weakening of other laws, as well as new rules and regulations for accepting nonimmigrant visas, accepting immigrants of previously disallowed countries, and the increase in temporary work visas, allowed nonskilled workers to find many loopholes in the new immigration law. This unexpected event produced both positive and negative effects. First, the increase in skilled workers allowed the United States to compensate for the depletion of skilled workers in many fields. However, the parallel increase in nonskilled laborers aggravated problems already evident in the country, notably an overflow of non-English speaking, nonskilled workers. Meanwhile, the positive and negative effects of the law increased the need for policing the nation's borders and ports of entry. The overall effect of the act increased border patrol spending, safety, and procedures for handling high-priority cases for the country.

Keith J. Bell

FURTHER READING

Geyer, Georgia Anne. *Americans No More.* New York: Atlantic Monthly Press, 1996. Critical examination of the impact of the Immigration Act of 1990, which Geyer describes as the "most comprehensive reform of our immigration laws in sixty-six years."

LeMay, Michael C., and Elliott Robert Barkan, eds. *U.S. Immigration and Naturalization Laws and Issues: A Documentary History.* Westport, Conn.: Greenwood Press, 1999. Broad history of U.S. immigration laws supported by extensive extracts from actual documents.

National Immigration Project. *Immigration Act of 1990 Handbook: The Complete Practical Guide to the 1990 Act.* 9 vols. New York: Clark, Boardman, Callaghan, 1991-1999. Massively detailed guide to the 1990 law.

Shanks, Cheryl. *Immigration and the Politics of American Sovereignty, 1890-1990.* Ann Arbor: University of Michigan Press, 2001. Scholarly study of changes in federal immigration laws from the late nineteenth century through the Immigration Act of 1990. Pays particular attention to changing quota systems and exclusionary policies.

SEE ALSO: Congress, U.S.; Economic consequences of immigration; Guest-worker programs; History of immigration after 1891; Illegal Immigration Reform and Immigrant Responsibility Act of 1996; Immigration and Nationality Act of 1965; Immigration and Naturalization Service, U.S.; Immigration law; Select Commission on Immigration and Refugee Policy.

IMMIGRATION AND NATIONALITY ACT OF 1952

THE LAW: Federal legislation that removed restrictions on Asian immigration while also tightening government control over suspected subversive organizations and individuals
DATE: Enacted on June 27, 1952
ALSO KNOWN AS: McCarran-Walter Act

SIGNIFICANCE: This federal law upheld the national origins quota system established by the Immigration Act of 1924, which gave preference to individuals of northern and western European lineage. It also created a system of preferences for skilled workers and relatives of citizens and permanent residents, repealed the last of the existing measures to exclude Asian immigration, and enacted strict security provisions over suspected subversives and "undesirable aliens."

Named for its congressional sponsors and passed by Congress over President Harry S. Truman's veto, the McCarran-Walter Act, or Immigration and Nationality Act of 1952, reaffirmed the quota system designed during the 1920's that favored northern and western Europeans. At the same time, however, it also removed a racist restriction—"aliens ineligible for citizenship"—that had been used against Asian immigration for generations, while keeping the small number of quotas in place. It gave first preference to highly qualified immigrants with skills urgently needed in the United

<table>
<tr><td colspan="1">

PREFERENCES UNDER THE 1952 LAW

- First: highly qualified professionals with desirable skills

- Second: parents of U.S. citizens

- Third: spouses and unmarried adult children of resident aliens

- Fourth: other relatives, brothers, sisters, and married children of resident aliens

</td></tr>
</table>

States, along with the spouses and children of such immigrants. Other preferences depended on family relationships.

The law's quota numbers for European immigrants were raised slightly from the 1920 base of 154,000, to 158,000, and northwestern Europe was allocated 85 percent of these slots, with Great Britain (65,000), Germany (26,000) and Ireland (18,000) receiving two-thirds of the total. The number for Asian nations was set at 2,000 visas annually. No quota restrictions were placed on spouses and minor children of U.S. citizens and on immigrants from the Western Hemisphere. During the ensuing decades, the law would have a significant impact on immigration from Mexico and other Latin American nations. The legislation also made deportation easier and provided for fines and imprisonment for any person convicted of harboring an undocumented alien.

The legislation also sought to raise legal barriers, even preventing temporary visitor visas, against suspected subversives and persons regarded as "undesirable aliens." Section 212(a) of the law listed thirty-one categories of inadmissible aliens, including those

> who write or publish . . . or who knowingly circulate, distribute, print, or display, any written or printed matter, advocating or teaching opposition to all organized government, or advocating or teaching . . . the economic, international, and governmental doctrines of world communism.

President Truman and his supporters thought that any political litmus test of that nature was against America's traditions of freedom of thought and expression, and political belief.

During the 1970's and 1980's, a number of high-profile cases highlighted the "undesirable aliens" section of the McCarran-Walter Act. Under this

provision, visas were denied to such "undesirable aliens" as Colombian novelist and Nobel laureate Gabriel García Márquez, British author and later Nobel laureate Doris Lessing, Chilean poet and Nobel laureate Pablo Neruda, British author Graham Greene, and Canadian writer Farley Mowat. All these distinguished persons were denied normal visas to enter the United States because they did not meet the ideological-exclusion provisions of the Immigration and Nationality Act of 1952.

John Boyd

FURTHER READING

Bon Tempo, Carl J. *Americans at the Gate: The United States and Refugees During the Cold War.* Princeton, N.J.: Princeton University Press, 2008.

Daniels, Roger. *Guarding the Golden Door: American Immigration Policy and Immigrants Since 1882.* New York: Hill & Wang, 2004.

Tichenor, Daniel J. *Dividing Lines: The Politics of Immigration Control in America.* Princeton, N.J.: Princeton University Press, 2002.

SEE ALSO: Congress, U.S.; History of immigration after 1891; Hull-House; Immigration Act of 1924; Immigration and Nationality Act of 1965; Immigration law; Luce-Celler Bill of 1946; McCarran Internal Security Act of 1950; "Undesirable aliens."

IMMIGRATION AND NATIONALITY ACT OF 1965

THE LAW: Federal legislation that eased restrictions on non-European immigration
DATE: Signed into law on October 3, 1965
ALSO KNOWN AS: Hart-Celler Act

SIGNIFICANCE: This first major change in U.S. quota policy greatly altered the ethnic makeup of immigrants entering the United States during the late twentieth and early twenty-first centuries and prompted a massive increase in total immigration.

During the 1920's, the federal government set fixed immigration quotas for each country of origin. During the very late nineteenth century and the early twentieth century, the United States had experienced heavy immigration from southern and eastern Europe. Because earlier European American settlers had come mostly from northern and western Europe, many policy makers believed that the more recent immigrants would not fit easily into American society. Accordingly, Congress passed immigration laws in 1921 and 1924 that set quotas for the numbers of immigrants from each region who would be admitted into the country. These quotas were based on the numbers of immigrants who had arrived during earlier eras. The quota system therefore favored northern and western European immigrants.

IMMIGRATION AND NATIONALITY ACT OF 1952

The Immigration and Nationality Act of 1952, also known as the McCarran-Walter Act, retained the national-origin criterion of the 1920's. It also added an overall limit to the numbers of immigrants from each country who would be admitted and within that limit gave each country a cap equal to 1 percent of the persons of that national origin who had been living in the United States in 1920. The 1952 law also added a series of preferences to the national origins system. The first basis rested on an economic criterion, giving first preference to immigrants with valuable skills. Other preferences, however, rested on the social norm that family relationships should enjoy a special status. For example, parents of existing U.S. citizens constituted the second preference, spouses and children

President Lyndon B. Johnson signing the Immigration and Nationality Act of 1965, which substantially changed U.S. immigration policy toward non-Europeans. Johnson made a point of signing the legislation near the base of the Statue of Liberty, which had long stood as a symbol of welcome to immigrants. Lower Manhattan can be seen in the background. (Lyndon B. Johnson Library Collection/Yoichi R. Okamoto)

of resident aliens the third, and other relatives the fourth.

In 1965, Congress amended the 1952 immigration law. In part, this change was a response to the Cold War politics of the time. American lawmakers were concerned about competition with communist nations and believed that more open immigration policies would reflect well on the reputation of the United States abroad. A major stimulus to this new legislation was the opposition to racially discriminatory laws arising during the Civil Rights era. Michigan's Democratic senator Philip Hart, one of the sponsors of the 1965 reform, declared that the effort to maintain the American creed and to protect the American political heritage required that American immigration policy become more consistent with democratic moral and ethical principles.

The new immigration bill was initially introduced in the House of Representatives by New York Democratic representative Emmanuel Celler, and Hart cosponsored it in the Senate. Massachusetts Democratic senator Edward Kennedy was one of the strongest advocates for the new immigration law. President Lyndon B. Johnson also strongly favored the legislation. Other lawmakers objected that the proposed change would lead to a massive increase in immigration and that many new arrivals would be from nations other than the European countries that had historically provided most of America's immigrants. Both President Johnson and Senator Kennedy argued, in response, that the law would bring few changes in either the numbers or the origins of immigrants. The House of Representatives approved the bill by a vote of 326 to 69 and the Senate by 76 to 18. On October 3, 1965, President Johnson signed it into law at the foot of the Statue of Liberty, an important icon to immigrants.

Provisions of the 1965 Law

When the act went into effect on July 1, 1968, it established an annual ceiling of 170,000 immigrants from the Eastern Hemisphere, with each country in the Eastern Hemisphere limited to 20,000 immigrants. At the same time, however, the law initially permitted the entry of children, parents, and spouses of American citizens without limitations. Consequently, nearly three-quarters of the 20,000 immigrants permitted from each Eastern

Hemisphere country were to be admitted on the basis of family reunification. Another 6 percent were to be accepted as refugees from repressive communist regimes and 20 percent because they had special skills or other qualifications. Immigrants from the Western Hemisphere were limited to 120,000 per year, initially without the system of preferences.

Although the 1965 act was later amended several times, family reunification has continued to be the primary basis for immigrant admission. The first preference for quota immigrants is unmarried children, of any age, of U.S. citizens. Spouses of resident aliens and unmarried children of residents fall into the second preference. In practice, this means that after unmarried children of U.S. citizens who have applied for U.S. residence in a given year have been granted visas, the next quota slots are filled first by spouses and unmarried children of noncitizen alien residents. The third preference goes to professionals and persons of exceptional ability in the arts and sciences who intend to work for American employers. Married children, of any age, of U.S. citizens receive the fourth preference. The fifth preference goes to noncitizen sisters and brothers of U.S. citizens. Skilled and unskilled workers coming to take jobs for which American workers are in short supply are classified as the sixth preference.

Amendments to the law have allowed some immigrants outside the quota categories to be admitted without yearly numerical limitations. The greatest number of these are spouses of American citizens. Others, such as political refugees, can also enter the United States without being counted as part of the overall ceiling.

Consequences of the Law

Contrary to the predictions of Senator Kennedy and President Johnson, the 1965 immigration law was followed by both an enormous increase in immigration and changes in the countries of origin. From 1971 to 1980, 4,493,000 immigrants were admitted into the United States, an increase of 1,171,000 over the years from 1961 to 1970. The increase in numbers accelerated in the decades that followed. By 1990, of the estimated 21,596,000 foreign-born people living in the United States, about 43 percent had arrived during the 1980's. By the year 2007, more than 38 million immigrants lived in the United States, accounting for about 12 percent of the country's total residents.

Meanwhile, the primary countries of origin shifted from Europe to Latin America and Asia. By the late 1990's, about one-half of all immigrants in the United States were coming from Latin America and about one-quarter from Asia. During the last three decades of the twentieth century, immigration was the primary source of demographic change and population growth in the United States. As a result, scholars in this field use the term "post-1965 immigration" to refer to the new trends that followed the change in law.

Carl L. Bankston III

FURTHER READING

Capaldi, Nicholas, ed. *Immigration: Debating the Issues.* Amherst, N.Y.: Prometheus Books, 1997. Collection of essays examining current U.S. immigration policy and its effects from a variety of perspectives.

Isbister, John. *The Immigration Debate.* West Hartford, Conn.: Kumarian Press, 1996. Extended essay on issues arising from changing federal immigration policy by an economist who is himself an immigrant and the son of a former deputy minister of citizenship and immigration in the Canadian government.

LeMay, Michael C. *Anatomy of a Public Policy: The Reform of Contemporary American Immigration Law.* Westport, Conn.: Praeger, 1974. Scholarly exploration of changes in U.S. immigration policy with particular attention to the Immigration Act of 1965.

LeMay, Michael C., and Elliott Robert Barkin, eds. *U.S. Immigration and Naturalization Laws and Issues: A Documentary History.* Westport, Conn.: Greenwood Press, 1999. Collection of more than one hundred primary documents—ranging from court cases and laws to editorials—on modern immigration issues. Includes edited versions of the Immigration Act of 1965 and other laws that make them easy for students to understand.

Shanks, Cheryl. *Immigration and the Politics of American Sovereignty, 1880-1990.* Ann Arbor: University of Michigan Press, 2001. Study of the history of U.S. immigration policy showing how government criteria for admitting immigration have shifted from race to political ideology, wealth, and job skills.

Waters, Mary C., and Reed Ueda, eds. *The New Americans: A Guide to Immigration Since 1965.* Cambridge, Mass.: Harvard University Press, 2007. Study of modern trends in U.S. immigration that assesses the impact of the Immigration Act of 1965 on American society and government policy.

SEE ALSO: Asian immigrants; Congress, U.S.; History of immigration after 1891; Immigration Act of 1921; Immigration Act of 1924; Immigration and Nationality Act of 1952; Immigration law; Latin American immigrants; Quota systems.

IMMIGRATION AND NATURALIZATION SERVICE, U.S.

IDENTIFICATION: Department of Justice agency formerly responsible for upholding all immigration laws

DATE: Operated from 1933 until March 1, 2003

ALSO KNOWN AS: INS

SIGNIFICANCE: The U.S. Immigration and Naturalization Service was long the primary federal agency responsible for the protection and enforcement of laws guiding the immigration and naturalization processes. It was also responsible for investigating, arresting, prosecuting, and deporting aliens who entered the United States illegally. After the agency was dissolved in 2003, its functions were distributed among three new federal agencies.

Through its seventy-year history, the U.S. Immigration and Naturalization Service, or INS, was the branch of the U.S. Department of Justice that handled both legal and illegal immigration matters. During the eighteenth and early nineteenth centuries, the U.S. population expanded exponentially with immigrants pouring into the country from all over the world. These early immigrants entered the country without having to carry documents or meet the requirements of immigration law.

GOVERNMENT REORGANIZATION

In 1891, the federal government created the U.S. Bureau of Immigration within the Department of the Treasury to oversee the administration of immigration law. After going through several administrative reorganizations and cabinet department shifts, the bureau was combined with the previously separate Bureau of Naturalization into the Immigration and Naturalization Service within the Department of Labor. Put in charge of controlling all aspects of illegal immigration into the United States, this new agency oversaw the U.S. Border Patrol.

In 1940, President Franklin D. Roosevelt transferred the INS from the Department of Labor to the Department of Justice. Over the ensuing decades, the duties and responsibilities of the INS continued to evolve. The agency experienced a dark period during World War II, when it was put in charge of operating and maintaining internment camps and detention centers for enemy aliens and sympathizers. Through the balance of the twentieth century, the agency concentrated on cracking down on illegal immigration resulting from weak border patrol and surveillance efforts. As new laws were enacted, the INS and Border Patrol became essential tools in the fight against domestic and foreign terrorism while continuing to regulate the flow of legal immigrants into the United States.

STRUCTURE OF THE INS

After being reassigned to the Department of Justice, the INS was restructured internally. Its top administrators were commissioners appointed by the president of the United States. The commissioners reported directly to the U.S. attorneys general. A comparatively large bureaucratic agency, the INS comprised four main subdivisions: programs, field operations, policy and planning, and management. Its Programs Division handled all functions pertaining to enforcement and investigations, including arrest, detention, and deportation of undocumented immigrants as well as the regulation and processing of all legal aliens attempting to enter the country.

The Field Operations Division was accountable for the oversight of numerous INS field offices both at home and abroad. It was responsible for the implementation of policies and delegated tasks for its three regional offices. In turn, administrators from these regional offices oversaw thirty-three districts and twenty-one border-area offices throughout the United States. Globally, the Field Operations Division was also tasked with directing the INS's Office of International Affairs headquarters that provided oversight for sixteen offices in other countries. Additionally, the division worked directly with the United Nations, the U.S. Department of State, and the U.S. Department of Health and Human Services to ensure that human and civil rights of all who entered the United States, both legally and illegally would, be safeguarded.

The third major division of the INS, the Office of Policy and Planning, oversaw coordinating, housing, and distributing all information related to immigration-related services. This division was also responsible for official communications with other cooperating federal agencies and the general public, along with all research and evaluation efforts.

The fourth office of the INS was the Management Division, which provided key administrative services to all field offices, both at home and abroad. These services included offices tasked with such items as information resource and technical management, finance, human resources, and clerical support.

DISBANDMENT

On March 1, 2003, the INS was officially disbanded. Most of its original functions and responsibilities were delegated to three new federal agencies to be housed in the newly created Department of Homeland Security, a new federal department created in response to the aftermath of the terrorist attacks of September 11, 2001. All border divisions of the former INS, which included patrol, investigation, prosecution, and deportation of all illegal immigrants, were combined with branches of the U.S. Customs Service to form a new agency called U.S. Customs and Border Protection.

Paul M. Klenowski

FURTHER READING

Andreas, Peter. *Border Games: Policing the U.S.-Mexico Divide.* Ithaca, N.Y.: Cornell University Press, 2001. Academic work that offers insights into the many political elements behind the patrolling of the U.S. border with Mexico.

Boehm, Randolph, et al., eds. *Records of the Immigration and Naturalization Service.* Bethesda, Md.: University Publications of America, 1995. Revealing collection of official documents that provides a unique look at the INS throughout its history.

Cohen, Steve. *Deportation Is Freedom! The Orwellian World of Immigration Controls.* Philadelphia: Jessica Kingsley, 2005. Critical analysis of the implementation of U.S. immigration laws, with particular attention to the work of the Immigration and Naturalization Service.

Galan, Mark, and Edward Dixon. *Immigration and Naturalization Service.* New York: Chelsea House, 1990. Part of a series on federal agencies designed for young readers, this brief book covers the historical foundations of the INS and traces the evolution of the agency's changing responsibilities.

Juffras, Jason. *Impact of the Immigration Reform and Control Act on the Immigration and Naturalization Service.* Santa Monica, Calif.: RAND Corporation, 1991. Brief study of the impact of the 1986 federal immigration law on the INS in eight major cities.

Weissinger, George. *Law Enforcement and the INS: A Participant Observation Study of Control Agents.* Lanham, Md.: University Press of America, 1996. Drawing on interviews with INS investigators, this study describes the structure of the INS in its social context.

SEE ALSO: Border Patrol, U.S.; Bureau of Immigration, U.S.; Citizenship and Immigration Services, U.S.; Commission on Immigration Reform, U.S.; Drug trafficking; Goldman, Emma; Homeland Security, Department of; Immigration Act of 1891; 9/11 and U.S. immigration policy; Patriot Act of 2001.

IMMIGRATION AND NATURALIZATION SERVICE V. CHADHA

THE CASE: U.S. Supreme Court decision concerning the use of legislative vetoes on immigration rulings
DATE: Decided on June 23, 1983

SIGNIFICANCE: Based on the constitutional principles of separation of powers and bicameralism, the *Chadha* decision prohibited legislation authorizing one house of Congress from overriding a decision made by the executive branch.

One section of the Immigration and Nationality Act of 1965 authorized the attorney general to allow particular deportable aliens to remain in the United States, but the act also provided the option of a "legislative veto," which authorized a single chamber of Congress to invalidate the decision of the Immigration and Naturalization Service (INS). From 1932 until 1983, Congress included legislative vetoes in almost three hundred laws. The use of the procedure was considered an effective way of retaining legislative control over the president and regulations of the executive agencies.

Born in Kenya to Indian parents and holding a British passport, Jagdish Rai Chadha had studied in the United States with a student visa. When his visa expired, neither Great Britain nor Kenya would accept him, so he applied for permanent residence in the United States. Based on Chadha's character and "extreme hardship," the INS approved his application, but the House of Representatives voted to veto the decision.

By a 7-2 vote, the U.S. Supreme Court held that the U.S. Constitution did not authorize the use of the legislative veto. With this ruling, the Court struck down more congressional enactments than it had previously in its entire history. Speaking for the majority, Chief Justice Warren E. Burger wrote that "explicit and unambiguous provisions of the Constitution prescribe and define the respective functions of the Congress and of the Executive." Any valid congressional mandate, he explained, must include passage by both houses of Congress, followed by presentment to the president, whose veto could be overridden only by a two-thirds vote in both houses. In a vigorous dissent, Justice Byron R. White argued that if Congress could delegate powers to the executive branch, it should be able to place limitations on these powers.

Thomas Tandy Lewis

FURTHER READING
Craig, Barbara H. *Chadha: The Story of an Epic Constitutional Struggle.* Berkeley: University of California Press, 1988.
Maltz, Earl. *Chief Justiceship of Warren Burger, 1969-*

1986. Columbia: University of South Carolina Press, 2000.

SEE ALSO: Citizenship; Congress, U.S.; Constitution, U.S.; Due process protections; Immigration law; Supreme Court, U.S.

IMMIGRATION AND NATURALIZATION SERVICE v. LOPEZ-MENDOZA

THE CASE: U.S. Supreme Court decision on the constitutional rights of undocumented immigrants

DATE: Decided on July 5, 1984

> **SIGNIFICANCE:** The *Lopez-Mendoza* decision upheld very minimal application of Fourth Amendment rights to deportation proceedings, thereby allowing immigration officials to use some improperly acquired evidence when deciding whether noncitizens should be expelled from the country.

In 1976 and 1977, Immigration and Naturalization Service (INS) officials arrested Adan Lopez-Mendoza and Elias Sandoval-Sanchez, respectively, at their place of employment. Authorities disregarded rules based on the Fourth Amendment's prohibition against unreasonable searches and seizures. After both men admitted to INS officials that they had unlawfully entered the country from Mexico, their deportation was ordered in separate proceedings. On administrative appeal, the Board of Immigration Appeals (BIA) affirmed the orders, ruling that because a deportation proceeding is a civil action, the mere fact of an illegal arrest is irrelevant to a deportation order. The Ninth Circuit Court of Appeals reversed the ruling and held that the confessions, as fruit of an unlawful arrest, should be suppressed as customary in the exclusionary rule.

By a 5-4 majority, however, the U.S. Supreme Court held that the Fourth Amendment and the exclusionary rule do not apply in deportation proceedings. Writing for the majority, Justice Sandra Day O'Connor made four major arguments. First, the BIA was correct in asserting that the protec-

tions in criminal trials do not apply to civil actions. Second, the INS maintains an adequate oversight program for monitoring compliance with Fourth Amendment requirements. Third, deportation hearings, unlike criminal trials, have the function of stopping the continuation of an illegal situation, and the social costs of releasing a defendant whose mere presence in the country violated the law would be excessive in comparison to the minimal benefits of the exclusionary rule in such contexts. Finally, O'Connor affirmed that the federal courts continued to have the authority to exercise judicial review of any egregious actions of immigration officials. Justices William J. Brennan and Byron R. White both wrote strong dissenting opinions.

Thomas Tandy Lewis

FURTHER READING

Aleinikoff, Thomas A., et al. *Immigration and Citizenship: Process and Policy.* 6th ed. St. Paul, Minn.: Thomson/West, 2008.

McFeatters, Ann C. *Sandra Day O'Connor: Justice in the Balance.* Albuquerque: University of New Mexico Press, 2006.

SEE ALSO: Citizenship; Congress, U.S.; Constitution, U.S.; Deportation; Due process protections; Illegal immigration; Immigration law; Supreme Court, U.S.

IMMIGRATION AND NATURALIZATION SERVICE v. ST. CYR

THE CASE: U.S. Supreme Court decision on deportation procedures

DATE: Decided on June 25, 2001

> **SIGNIFICANCE:** The *St. Cyr* decision held that recent federal legislation did not eliminate the federal courts' jurisdiction to consider habeas corpus petitions from resident aliens who were deportable because of felony convictions.

In 1996, Enrico St. Cyr, a lawful resident alien from Haiti, pleaded guilty to selling controlled substances in Connecticut. As a result, immigration officials brought deportation proceedings against him. Two complex federal statutes of 1996, the Anti-terrorism and Effective Death Penalty Act (AEDPA) and the Illegal Immigration Reform and Immigrant Responsibility Act (IIRIRA), severely restricted the jurisdiction of the federal courts to exercise "judicial review" over immigration officials' deportation proceedings and deportation orders. Despite the statutes, St. Cyr petitioned a U.S. district court for a writ of habeas corpus, and the petition was granted.

The major issue before the U.S. Supreme Court was whether the district courts continued to have habeas corpus jurisdiction over deportable aliens, as it did before enactment of the AEDPA and IIRIRA. In a 5-4 opinion, the Court ruled in the affirmative. Arguing that the relevant wording was ambiguous, Justice John Paul Stevens argued that the terms "judicial review" and "habeas corpus" had distinct legal meanings and that denial of the opportunity of habeas corpus relief would perhaps be unconstitutional. He wrote: "if an otherwise acceptable construction would raise serious constitutional problems and an alternative interpretation is fairly possible, the statute must be construed to avoid such problems." In a strong dissent, Justice Antonin Scalia that the privilege of habeas corpus relief was not guaranteed in the U.S. Constitution and that the plain language of the two statutes stripped the district courts of jurisdiction to entertain petitions from deportable aliens.

Thomas Tandy Lewis

FURTHER READING

Gordon, Charles, Stanley Mailman, and Stephen Yale-Loehr. *Immigration Law and Procedure.* New York: Matthew Bender, 2001.

Phelan, Margaret, and James Gillespie. *Immigration Law Handbook.* 2d ed. New York: Oxford University Press, 2005.

SEE ALSO: Citizenship; Congress, U.S.; Constitution, U.S.; Deportation; Due process protections; Immigration law; Supreme Court, U.S.

IMMIGRATION CONVENTION OF 1886

THE TREATY: Hawaiian-Japanese protocol that protected Japanese agricultural workers in the independent Hawaiian Islands

DATE: 1886

ALSO KNOWN AS: Treaty of Immigration

> **SIGNIFICANCE:** As a landmark agreement between two sovereign nations designed to protect the human rights of Japanese immigrants relocating to the kingdom of Hawaii, the Immigration Convention reflected less a lofty humanitarian imperative than a pragmatic economic necessity, as it guaranteed a steady stream of cheap immigrant laborers for Hawaii's sugar plantations.

By the 1840's, sugar cane was the primary agricultural export of the kingdom of Hawaii. Sugar planting was labor-intensive; crops required year-round maintenance, and plantation work was grueling under the best circumstances—backbreaking work and long hours in scorching temperatures. Initially, uneducated native Hawaiians provided most of the labor. However, when news of the California gold strikes reached the islands during the late 1840's, waves of native Hawaiians headed to the mainland looking for easy riches, and leaving the islands' sugar plantations in need of cheap labor. At that time, Japan was itself emerging from nearly two centuries of self-imposed isolation from the West, and leaving its new Meiji government was ready to pursue Westernization. In 1867, Japan signed an accord with the government of Hawaii to send Japanese laborers to work the sugar plantations. On June 19, 1868, the first immigrants, 153 men, landed in Hawaii.

With little agricultural background and none in the exacting work of harvesting sugar efficiently, the Japanese workers were quickly unsettled by their experiences on the islands. Hampered by language differences, the Japanese workers were routinely whipped to get them to work more efficiently, and they suffered from high rates of accidents. In addition, the Japanese workers had difficulty adjusting to the tropical climate. Indeed, their working conditions recall the antebellum slave plantation system of a generation earlier in the American South. Many of the first immigrants wanted to return to Japan, and word quickly spread about the harsh conditions. The Japanese government launched an investigation into the allegations of cruelty. During the late 1870's, it threatened to stop sending workers to Hawaii.

Despite these problems, Japanese immigration to Hawaii continued to rise, largely because of Japan's own economic problems caused by the country's rush to industrialize. By the early 1880's, an estimated 28,000 Japanese laborers worked Hawaii's sugar plantations. Because plantation work was shunned by native Hawaiians, the islands' government understood that it needed to address the concerns of the Japanese government. In 1886, the Hawaiian government intervened on behalf of the Japanese workers at the urging of Katsunosuke Inouye, a special commissioner sent by Japan to investigate plantation conditions. The ensuing accord, the Immigration Convention, redefined the Japanese plantation workers as wards of the government and the planters as agents of the government, thus putting the practices on the plantations under direct government control and scrutiny.

The agreement represented an unprecedented act of intervention by a government to protect the human rights of an immigrant population. However, although the new directive provided a system for reporting abuses and a protocol for accountability, it was largely voided within a year. Nevertheless, Japanese immigration to the islands continued to increase because of bad economic conditions in Japan. By the turn of the twentieth century, nearly 60,000 Japanese worked on the islands.

Joseph Dewey

FURTHER READING

Jung, Moon-Ho. *Coolies and Cane: Race, Labor, and Sugar in the Age of Emancipation.* Baltimore: Johns Hopkins University Press, 2008.

Okihiro, Gary Y. *Cane Fires: The Anti-Japanese Movement in Hawaii, 1865-1945.* Philadelphia: Temple University Press, 1992.

Van Sant, John E. *Pacific Pioneers: Japanese Journeys to America and Hawaii, 1850-1880.* Champaign: University of Illinois Press, 2000.

SEE ALSO: Anti-Japanese movement; Asian immigrants; Asiatic Exclusion League; Gentlemen's Agreement; Hawaii; History of immigration, 1783-1891; *Imingaisha*; Immigration Act of 1882; Japanese immigrants; "Yellow peril" campaign.

IMMIGRATION LAW

DEFINITION: Branch of law that deals with the entry and settlement of alien nationals in the United States

SIGNIFICANCE: The gatekeeper of the borders of the United States, federal immigration law determines who may enter the country, how long they may stay, their status, their rights and duties while in the United States, and how they may become resident aliens or American citizens.

Under the U.S. Constiution, the U.S. Congress has complete authority over immigration. The courts have generally found issues regarding immigration to be nonjusticiable, and presidential power extends only to refugee policy. States have limited authority regarding immigration.

HISTORY

Primarily because of the need for labor and the spacious frontier, there was unrestricted immigration during the first one hundred years of the U.S. government's existence. After the Civil War, federal law began to reflect restrictions on the immigration of certain groups, and in 1875 Congress passed a law barring convicts and prostitutes from admission. These were among the first of many "quality control" exclusions based on the nature of the immigrants. The list of unacceptable types of immigrants continued to grow in subsequent legislation. The Immigration Act of 1882, considered the first-general federal immigration act, added "lunatics," "idiots," and those likely to become public charges to the exclusionary list. For the first time, the act also imposed a head tax on every arriving immigrant, which served to defray administrative expenses. As numbers of immigrants increased steadily, immigration was regarded as a threat to the economy, and Congress expanded the list of "undesirables," adding the diseased, paupers, and polygamists. Immigrants were required to take a physical examination to determine whether they were diseased.

The Bureau of Immigration was established in 1891. The forerunner of the Immigration and Naturalization Service (INS), the bureau was responsible for inspecting immigrants at all ports of entry into the United States. At the turn of the twentieth century, there was a sharp increase in immigration, which Congress attempted to control by excluding more classes of immigrants: epileptics, the insane, beggars, anarchists, the feebleminded, the tubercular, and those with a mental or physical defect that might affect their ability to earn a living. The quality controls were not easily enforced, however, and huge numbers of immigrants entered the United States from countries in southern or eastern Europe. Because the earlier quality control exclusions did little to restrict the flow of immigrants, groups favoring restrictions on immigration advocated literacy as an entrance requirement. A literacy bill was not passed, however, and a joint congressional-presidential commission to study the impact of immigration on the United States concluded that the country no longer benefited from a liberal immigration policy and should impose further restrictions, including literacy.

In 1921, Congress passed the Emergency Immigration Act, which established national immigration quotas. The Immigration Act of 1924 capped the number of permissible immigrants from each country, but this resulted in more surreptitious border crossing. Complex formulas resulted in unequal quotas that favored immigrants from northern and western Europe. The Great Depression essentially closed the country to immigration, while the post-World War II economic upswing brought an increase in immigration as President Harry S. Truman issued a directive admitting forty thousand war refugees.

MODERN IMMIGRATION LAW

The Immigration and Nationality Act (INA) of 1952, also known as the McCarran-Walter Act, eliminated racial restrictions on immigration but retained nationality-based quotas and created the Immigration and Naturalization Service to enforce the caps. When Congress passed the INA, it defined "alien" as any person lacking citizenship or status as a U.S. national. There are different categories of aliens, including resident and nonresident, immigrant and nonimmigrant, and documented and undocumented (or illegal), depending upon whether the alien has proper records and identification for admission into the United States. Those documents include a visa or valid passport, border-crossing card, permanent resident card, or reentry permit.

The need to curtail illegal immigration motivated Congress to enact the Immigration Reform and Control Act of 1986, which tightened criminal sanctions for those who hire illegal immigrants. The act also denied welfare benefits to undocumented aliens and legitimized certain aliens through an amnesty program. The Immigration Marriage Fraud Amendments of 1986 aimed to eliminate the practice of marrying to obtain citizenship. The Immigration Act of 1990 equalized the allocation of visas worldwide, and the Illegal Immigration Reform and Immigrant Responsibility Act of 1996 changed certain language dealing with the process of alien entry into the United States.

Every person in the United States, including American citizens, has an immigration status that falls under one of these major categories:

- U.S. citizens—persons born within the United States or born abroad to U.S. citizens, or who have naturalized
- lawful permanent residents—green card holders eligible to reside in the United States permanently and apply for naturalization
- asylees and refugees—persons granted asylum in the United States and persons who enter as refugees and who have not yet been granted permanent residence
- nonimmigrants—persons who enter the United States temporarily for specific purposes, such as tourism, study, short-term work, or business
- temporary protected status—persons who have obtained status as citizens of countries designated by the U.S. Congress to receive protected status because of armed conflicts, natural disasters, or other unusual circumstances
- out of status—persons who enter the United States lawfully on nonimmigrant visas that have either expired or had their terms violated
- undocumented aliens—persons who enter the country without inspection—usually from Canada or Mexico—or with a fraudulent passport

POST-9/11 IMMIGRATION REFORM

The terrorist attacks of September 11, 2001, on New York City and Washington, D.C., intensified efforts to confront problems dealing with America's moral commitment to immigrants. President George W. Bush proposed a series of sweeping measures designed to combat terrorism, including the strengthening of borders. The Uniting and Strengthening America by Providing Appropriate Tools Required to Intercept and Obstruct Terrorism (USA PATRIOT) Act was passed quickly and signed into law in October of 2001. The Patriot Act expanded the electronic surveillance powers of government and thus allowed greater intrusion on Americans' civil rights. It provided for greater surveillance of aliens and increased the power of the attorney general to identify, arrest, and deport aliens.

The Patriot Act broadened the definition of "terrorist" to include anyone who endorses or provides financial support to a terrorist organization, or who actually participates in terrorist activities. To identify possible terrorists, U.S. consulates are required to check visa applicants' names against "lookout lists" prior to issuing a visa, resulting in increased time for many noncitizens seeking admission to the United States and causing some people to be denied admission because they were incorrectly identified as terrorists.

In another reaction to the 2001 attacks, Congress enacted the Homeland Security Act in November of 2002, which established a new cabinet department—the Department of Homeland Security—to coordinate the antiterrorist activities of the government and reorganize immigration policy. Functions of the now abolished INS were divided among several agencies within the Department of Homeland Security. The federal government placed more than 300,000 aliens scheduled for deportation on a criminal list, more than doubled the number of border patrol agents, provided high-tech equipment to detect weapons that could be smuggled across Canadian or Mexican borders, enhanced the tracking of visitors to the United States, and gave the attorney general greater authority to expel anyone suspected of terrorist connections.

Americans have been deeply divided over immigration policy, and no consensus has emerged, although most people agree that policies had to be strengthened after the 2001 terrorist attacks. Opponents of these measures argue that these steps curtail civil liberties, particularly those of Muslims; supporters counter that the measures are important and significant tools in the war on global terrorism. Among other steps authorized in the name of national security, the government required special registration of certain Arab and Muslim noncitizens; arrested, detained, and interrogated large numbers of Arab and Muslim noncitizens; and engaged in their selective deportation. Special registration requirements were imposed by the executive branch on the ground that the political branches of the federal government had plenary power over immigration. Throughout history, harsh measures have been taken against unpopular groups in the name of national security. The internment of persons of Japanese ancestry during World War II is the best-known example.

Although early twenty-first century immigration laws are generally neutral on their face and do not discriminate on the basis of race, they have racially disparate effects. For example, ceilings on immigrant admissions from a single country in any year apply to all countries but have a disproportionate impact on prospective immigrants from Mexico as well as noncitizens from other developing nations such as China, India, and the Philippines because demand for immigration from those countries exceeds their annual ceilings. Increased border enforcement on the U.S.-Mexican border has had a disproportionate impact on Mexican citizens and undocumented Mexican migrant workers. Statistics from early 2006 indicated that the United States had no record of as many as twelve million undocumented immigrants, more than half of whom were of Mexican origin and representing more than double the approximately five million undocumented immigrants of the early 1990's. Because there has been a dramatic increase in the undocumented immigrant population, it can be concluded that enhanced border enforcement has largely failed.

The Intelligence Reform and Terrorism Prevention Act of 2004 overhauled the government's intelligence operations and created a director of national intelligence, answerable directly to the president, who was responsible for integrating the activities of fifteen agencies responsible for gathering intelligence information. Major provisions of the act include strengthening visa application requirements, creating a visa and passport security program within the State Department, establishing more stringent passport requirements for travel within the Western Hemisphere, developing a system to track people entering and leaving the United States, and increasing U.S.-Mexican border security. The number of detention beds for those awaiting deportation was increased, minimum standards were established for issuing driver's licenses and birth certificates and for documents required for boarding airplanes, criminal penalties for alien smuggling were increased, and the General Accounting Office was required to study weaknesses in the asylum system. By 2009, all U.S. citizens and foreign nationals entering or leaving the United States by air, sea, or land to or from Canada, Mexico, Bermuda, the Caribbean, or Central or South America were required to have a valid passport.

Marcia J. Weiss

FURTHER READING

Jasper, Margaret C. *The Law of Immigration*. 3d ed. New York: Oxford University Press, 2008. Almanac that explores immigration law, the rights and obligations of aliens, and the process of citizenship through naturalization. A useful reference for the layperson that contains sample documents and an extensive glossary.

Johnson, Kevin R., and Bernard Trujillo. "Immigration Reform, National Security After September 11, and the Future of North American Integration." *Minnesota Law Review* 91, no. 5 (2007): 1369-1407. Scholarly article with numerous references outlining security problems and possible solutions in the post-9/11 era.

Powell, John. *Immigration.* New York: Facts On File, 2007. Contains essential information for researching the issue of immigration, including chronology, glossary of terms, biographical data, and an extensive and fully annotated bibliography including periodicals and Web documents, microforms, CDs, and film resources.

Weissbrodt, David, and Laura Danielson. *Immigration Law and Procedure in a Nutshell.* St. Paul, Minn.: Thomson/West, 2005. Excellent introduction to immigration law containing summaries and references to court cases, the Constitution, and pertinent statutes.

SEE ALSO: Bureau of Immigration, U.S.; Congress, U.S.; Constitution, U.S.; Homeland Security, Department of; Immigration Act of 1882; Immigration Act of 1917; Immigration Act of 1921; Immigration Act of 1924; Immigration Act of 1990; Immigration and Nationality Act of 1965; McCarran Internal Security Act of 1950; 9/11 and U.S. immigration policy; Patriot Act of 2001; Quota systems; Supreme Court, U.S.

IMMIGRATION LAWYERS

DEFINITION: Attorneys who specialize in representing immigrants

SIGNIFICANCE: As the complexities and restrictions of U.S. immigration law have increased, the legal profession's subspecialty of immigration lawyers has flourished, extending in some cases to social-cause lawyering.

During the era of relatively open immigration that existed in the United States until the last quarter of the nineteenth century, there was little need for specialized immigration lawyers. However, as the federal government began enacting immigration restrictions during the 1870's, a new field arose in the legal profession: lawyers who specialized in helping immigrants navigate the increasing stream of regulations and restrictions emanating from the federal government.

IMMIGRATION LAWYERS ON ELLIS ISLAND

During the 1890's, the U.S. Congress established exclusive oversight over immigration to the United States. It established official immigration reception stations on Ellis Island in New York Harbor in 1892 and on Angel Island in California's San Francisco Bay in 1910. These immigration facilities were staffed by federal officials enforcing the restrictions enacted by Congress in a series of immigration acts. Immigrants responded by beginning to turn, in large numbers, to lawyers to assist them in the immigration process.

Given the almost plenary power vested in immigration officials at that time, early immigration lawyers played a mostly advisory role. Becoming expert in the administrative processes required for immigration, lawyers coached their clients on what to say to customs officials and tried, usually in vain, to appear as counsel for their clients in immigration proceedings. However, in cases that went before the immigration Boards of Special Inquiry that were authorized in 1893 to make determinations as to the entry of aliens, lawyers played more active roles.

Records have survived from about 424 appeals of decisions made by Boards of Special Inquiry in New York during the 1890's. In 277 cases—about two-thirds of the total—the immigrants involved were represented by attorneys. Of the 277 cases involving attorneys, five of the attorneys appeared in five or more appeals each, thus demonstrating a nascent immigration bar. The most notable of the five attorneys was Henry Gottlieb of the firm of MacKinley & Gottlieb, who handled eighty-five of the appeals. A lawyer named John Palmieri handled the second-greatest number of appeals, thirty-seven. Given that the 1890's represented the first great wave of Jewish and Italian immigration to New York, it is safe to conclude that Gottlieb specialized in helping Jewish immigrants and that Palmieri helped Italian immigrants.

SOCIAL CAUSE IMMIGRATION LAWYERING

Both immigration and federal immigration legislation steadily increased during the first decades of the twentieth century. With these increases came growth in the numbers of immigration lawyers. What had been part-time legal work for general practitioners was increasingly becoming full-time work for lawyers specializing in immigration cases. With this increased specialization came two developments.

The first development was the immigration bar's looking to promote its own professionalization and expertise. The American Immigration Lawyers' Association (AILA) was founded in 1946 as a national, nonprofit organization dedicated to the practice and teaching of immigration law. In 1975, it had about 600 members. By 1985, its member-

Immigration lawyer, Jessica Salsbury, hugs a domestic worker to celebrate the passage of legislation protecting the rights of domestics at a Montgomery County Council meeting in Rockville, Maryland in 2008. (AP/Wide World Images)

> ## WORK PERFORMED BY IMMIGRATION LAWYERS
>
> - Analyze the facts in the case of someone desiring to immigrate
> - Explain all benefits for which immigrants may be eligible
> - Recommend the best way to obtain legal immigrant status
> - Complete and file appropriate applications
> - Keep up with new laws affecting their clients
> - Speak for clients in discussions with federal immigration officials
> - Represent clients in court
> - File necessary appeals and waivers
>
> *Adapted from:* American Immigration and Lawyers Association, "A Guide to Consumer Protection and Authorized Representation," Washington, D.C.: AILA, 1998.

ship had grown to about 1,800 lawyers. In 2009, the association claimed more than 11,000 lawyers and law professors as its members, with thirty-six chapters and more than fifty national committees.

In the second development, some immigration lawyers began to look upon their specialty as an opportunity for social-cause lawyering. The AILA itself established in 1987 the American Immigration Law Foundation (later renamed the American Immigration Council) as a charitable organization to advocate on behalf of immigrants and to promote public awareness of immigration issues. One of the most successful examples of social-cause lawyering was that of immigration lawyers securing the right to asylum of refugees from the violence engulfing Central America during the late 1980's and early 1990's.

In alliance with members of the Sanctuary movement, immigration lawyers filed politically oriented lawsuits such as *Orantes-Hernandez v. Meese* (1988), *American Baptist Churches v. Thornburgh* (1991), and *Mendez v. Reno* (1993). After years of litigation, these lawyers helped secure the right of Salvadorans and Guatemalans to obtain asylum status in the United States, even though the governments of El Salvador and Guatemala were nominally allies of the United States, receiving extensive American support. Other groups that advocated on behalf of immigration rights and accessible borders included the American Civil Liberties Union, the Fair Immigration Reform Movement,

the Mexican American Legal Defense and Educational Fund, the National Immigration Forum, and the National Immigration Law Foundation.

PRACTICING IMMIGRATION LAW FOR PROFIT

Obtaining residency in the modern United States can be an arduous process, and most aliens seeking residency require legal services. Many lawyers have generously devoted their time to assisting immigrants for reduced fees or even no fees at all. However, as the size of the legal profession in the United States has boomed, and as more avenues have been opened for solicitation and profit-making by lawyers, the immigration bar has become plagued by allegations of corruption, scandal, and exploitation. In 1985, several high-profile immigration lawyers were convicted and disbarred. In 2003, for example, immigration lawyer Samuel Kooritzky was sentenced to ten years in federal prison for engaging in immigration fraud through his Capital Law Centers. In 2005, the federal Executive Office for Immigration Review disciplined fifty-four immigration lawyers.

Howard Bromberg

FURTHER READING

Anthes, Louis. *Lawyers and Immigrants, 1870-1940: A Cultural History.* Levittown, N.Y.: LFB Scholarly Publishing, 2003. This volume in the publisher's Law and Society series traces the connections among law, lawyers, immigrants, and cultural issues. Anthes researched the practice of immigration lawyers on Ellis Island.

Salyer, Lucy. *Laws Harsh as Tigers: Chinese Immigrants and the Shaping of Modern Immigration Law.* Chapel Hill: University of North Carolina Press, 1995. History of Chinese immigration that Salyer shows to be central to the shaping of immigration law, with a detailed account of the administration of immigration law on Ellis Island.

Sarat, Austin, and Stuart Scheingold, eds. *Cause Lawyers and Social Movements.* Stanford, Calif.: Stanford University Press, 2006. Collection of essays on lawyering activists. The essay by Susan Coutin recounts efforts of lawyers working to obtain asylum rights for Central Americans.

Serrill, Michael. "A Booming but Tainted Specialty." *Time*, July 8, 1985. Account of growth of immigration law practice, with both respected human rights advocates and fraudulent and corrupt lawyers.

Warner, Judith, ed. *Battleground Immigration*. Westport, Conn.: Greenwood Press, 2009. Compendium of immigration-related topics, with material on the role of lawyers in forming political perspectives on immigration.

SEE ALSO: Angel Island Immigration Station; Asian American Legal Defense Fund; Deportation; Ellis Island; Immigration law; Mexican American Legal Defense and Educational Fund; New York City; Sanctuary movement.

IMMIGRATION REFORM AND CONTROL ACT OF 1986

THE LAW: First federal law to impose sanctions on American employers who hired undocumented alien workers, while also providing amnesty for a specific category of aliens

DATE: Enacted on November 6, 1986

ALSO KNOWN AS: Simpson-Mazzoli Act; Simpson-Rodino Act; IRCA

SIGNIFICANCE: The Immigration Reform and Control Act (IRCA) was designed to balance public concerns about increasing illegal immigration with business's need for cheap labor and the need to address issues of racial and ethnic discrimination. The final bill focused less on restricting the numbers of immigrants than on putting existing undocumented aliens on the path to citizenship and on deterring further illegal immigration by strengthening border control and employer sanctions.

During the late 1970's, national economic problems and the increased visibility of both documented and undocumented immigrants led the U.S. Congress to focus on immigration reform. Fears traditionally associated with waves of immigration, such as the loss of jobs to lower-wage earners and unassimilated enclaves of newcomers, led Congress to create the Select Commission on Immigration and Refugee Policy in 1979. The commission reviewed existing immigration laws and produced a report in March, 1981. Two recommendations became the focal point of the Immigration Reform and Control Act of 1986: strengthening sanctions on employers who hired undocumented aliens and improving access to American citizenship for undocumented aliens within the United States.

Immigration reform was championed by Wyoming senator Alan Simpson and Missouri representative Roman Mazzoli. Several versions of the bill they based on the recommendations of the Select Commission languished in Congress throughout the early 1980's. A fragile coalition of civil rights-oriented immigrant advocacy groups and free market business groups who wanted cheap labor helped to overcome opposition from groups who supported restricting immigration to pass the Immigration Reform and Control Act in November, 1986.

IRCA had two major components. The first provided amnesty to illegal immigrants already in the United States. Long-term undocumented immigrants who could prove residency in the United States continuously since before January 1, 1972, were permitted to apply for permanent status that would lead to American citizenship. Aliens residing illegally in the country after January 1, 1982. were given the opportunity to apply for temporary status that could possibly lead to permanent residency. Congress also bowed to the pressure of agricultural interests and placed undocumented workers who had worked in the United States for three months during the fiscal year ending May 1, 1986, on the road to permanent-resident status.

The second component of IRCA focused on deterring future illegal immigration. For the first time, federal law made employers responsible for verifying and keeping records of the work-eligibility status of all employees they hired after November 6, 1986. Employers who hired undocumented immigrants faced fines of up to ten thousand dollars and six-month prison terms for each undocumented employee in their workforces. Congress also strengthened nondiscrimination provisions of the law to placate immigrant-advocacy groups who were concerned that businesses would stop hiring legally documented immigrants who happened to have "foreign-sounding" names. The final provision aimed at deterring immigration focused on improving border patrolling to prevent illegal passage into the country.

IRCA provided a mix of amnesty for undocumented immigrants already in the United States and provisions designed to deter future illegal immigration. However, by focusing on resolving the problem of undocumented aliens, the legislation did not address the issue of limiting future immigration. Ultimately those in favor of an expansive American immigration policy triumphed over immigration-control advocates. The legislation affected approximately three million undocumented workers. However, its deterrence provisions had relatively little effect on stemming the tide of illegal immigration after 1986.

J. Wesley Leckrone

FURTHER READING

Hing, Bill Ong. *Defining America Through Immigration Policy.* Philadelphia: Temple University Press, 2004.

Zolberg, Artistide R. "Reforming the Back Door: The Immigration Reform and Control Act of 1986 in Historical Perspective." In *Immigration Reconsidered: History, Sociology, and Politics,* edited by Virginia Yans-McLaughlin. New York: Oxford University Press, 1990.

SEE ALSO: Amerasian Homecoming Act of 1987; Border Patrol, U.S.; Congress, U.S.; Gay and lesbian immigrants; History of immigration after 1891; Immigration Act of 1990; Latin American immigrants; Select Commission on Immigration and Refugee Policy.

IMMIGRATION WAVES

THE EVENTS: Periods that experienced large and enduring increases in immigration to the United States

SIGNIFICANCE: With each immigration wave that the United States has experienced, the culture and context of life in the United States have changed considerably. Such changes have continued into the twenty-first century.

The first immigrants to settle in what is now the United States were the ancient ancestors of modern Native Americans. The precise routes of those first North American immigrants are disputed, but there is no uncertainty about the fact that every human being on the continent is either a recent immigrant or a descendant of earlier immigrants. Since the first immigrants came here from Asia more than thirteen thousand years ago, there have been four large and easily recognizable modern waves of immigrants into the United States.

During the seventeenth century, the first wave of European colonists began arriving. Most of them came from England and northern Europe. This wave peaked shortly before the American Revolution of 1776-1783. The second wave lasted about fifty years, through the mid-nineteenth century, and brought mostly Irish and Germans to the United States. That period was followed by the third wave, which lasted about forty years and brought in millions of Asians and southern and eastern Europeans. Finally, after U.S. immigration law abolished quotas based on nationalities in 1965, the fourth major wave began. It has continued into the first decade of the twenty-first century and has been the largest immigration wave in U.S. history. The majority of immigrants it has brought into the United States have come from Mexico, Central America, and the Caribbean islands of the West Indies.

NATIVE AMERICAN ORIGINS

Whether they came by way of a land bridge between Alaska and Siberia or crossed the ocean in junks or on rafts, it is generally agreed that the first Americans arrived on the continent at least thirteen thousand years ago. Some authorities put that date back as far as fifty thousand years. The ancestors of modern Native Americans either entered North America in more than one location or they migrated widely after arriving. Their descendants were eventually spread out over North, Central, and South America and the West Indies and had a total pre-Columbian population of between 10 and 50 million people.

As these first Americans adapted to the changes in their environment brought about by significant climate change and their own travels, they developed rich cultures, and many had what some people have viewed as an almost ideal way of life. Al-

Immigrants registering at New York City's Castle Garden reception center in 1866. (Library of Congress)

though the frequent presence of wars, slavery, and many other social injustices mar that idealistic view, the more human scale of the problems and the closeness to nature make the life of the early Americans very attractive to many citizens of the modern world.

FIRST MODERN IMMIGRATION WAVE, 1609-1775

Quests for adventure, flights from religious persecution, and hopes for brighter economic futures induced almost one-half million Europeans to leave their homeland and come to America between 1609 and 1775. Many of these new arrivals were indentured servants, under contract to work for masters from four to seven years merely to pay the costs of their transatlantic passage. The first black Africans to come to America during this period also came as indentured servants. However, almost all the Africans who followed came as chattel slaves.

Most immigrants who came during the seventeenth century were from England, with smaller numbers from France, Germany, Ireland, Italy, and other countries. By the turn of the eighteenth century, they had raised the population of Great Britain's North American colonies to 250,000. After 1700, the numbers of immigrants from Ireland, Scotland, and Germany increased dramatically, while those from England decreased. Between 1700 and the start of the American Revolution in 1775, the colonial population almost doubled, to 450,000. During that period, the principal port of entry was Philadelphia, but immigrants also entered through Baltimore, Maryland, and Charleston, South Carolina.

SECOND IMMIGRATION WAVE, c. 1820-1870

After a lull in immigration during the American Revolution and wars in Europe, a second wave of immigrants began arriving around 1820. Most of these newcomers entered the United States through New York City, instead of Philadelphia. In 1855, Castle Garden was opened at the southern tip of Manhattan Island in New York City as the nation's first immigration station.

A majority of immigrants arriving on the East Coast during this second wave were Irish and Germans. A potato famine hit Ireland during the 1840's, and as much as one-third of the immigrants during this time were Irish fleeing that famine. The newly arrived Irish tended to remain near the East Coast. Many of them arrived penniless and lacked the resources to travel further inland. Almost equal numbers of Germans arrived during the same period. However, unlike the Irish, they tended to continue inland. Many of them bought farms in the Midwest.

Gold was discovered in California in 1848, and the transcontinental railroad was begun in 1862. Both the lure of gold and the prospect of work on the railroad brought a wave of Chinese immigrants to the West Coast of the United States that dried up in 1882, only after the U.S. Congress enacted the Chinese Exclusion Act that year. That law made immigration for practically all ethnic Chinese illegal. Meanwhile, most Chinese immigrants entered the United States through the port of San Francisco. Most of them were single men who planned to make their fortunes and return to China. However, a large proportion of them ended up spending the rest of their lives in the United States, where most of them worked in low-paying jobs.

In response to fears of native-born Americans about job competition, concerns about religious and political differences, and simple, blatant racism, a political party was formed called the America Party or the Know-Nothing Party. During the 1850's, supporters of this party and other nativist movements demanded laws that would reduce immigration, particularly from Asia. The state of California, where most of the Chinese immigrants worked, enacted its own laws to discourage Chinese immigration. During the 1870's, the United States suffered an economic depression at the same time Germany and Great Britain were enjoying relative prosperity. Thanks to the combination of restrictive legislation and economic problems, immigration went through another period of decline.

THIRD IMMIGRATION WAVE, 1881-1920

During the 1880's, American states seeking to increase their populations and railroad companies seeking laborers began sending agents across the Atlantic to recruit immigrant workers. By the late nineteenth century, transoceanic transportation had become significantly cheaper and less arduous, making it easier for poor Europeans to immigrate to the United States. The period between about 1881 and 1920 brought more than 23 million new immigrants from all parts of the world, but mostly from Europe, to the United States. The first decade of this period saw most of the immigrants coming from northern and western Europe; after 1890, the majority came from southern and eastern Europe. Meanwhile, restrictive U.S. immigration laws continued to keep the numbers of immigrants from Asia very small.

Like the Chinese immigrants of the previous wave, many of the new immigrants from southern and eastern Europe encountered a good deal of hostility in their new homeland. Again feeling threatened by job competition, and concerned about racial, religious, and political differences, native-born Americans directed their new hostility primarily against Jewish immigrants, Roman Catholics, and Japanese. Before long, a general distrust and resentment of all new immigrants began to grow. Anti-immigrant sentiment found its way into federal government, and the U.S. Congress enacted a new series of restrictive immigration laws between 1917 and 1924. The Immigration Act of 1917, for example, required immigrants to demonstrate their ability to read and write. The same law also created the "Asiatic Barred Zone" to halt immigration from most of Asia.

Nevertheless, despite their chilly reception, immigrants continued to pour into the United States in search of better lives. In 1921, the U.S. Congress passed a new immigration law that set ceilings on the numbers of immigrants permitted from individual countries. Using a formula designed to slow immigration from southern and eastern Europe, the new law had the effect of ensuring that most new immigrants would come from northern and western European nations.

Immigration into the United States was further curtailed by the onset of the Great Depression of the 1930's. During the Depression years, more people emigrated from the United States than immigrated. Between 1931 and 1940, only about one-half million new immigrants arrived in the United States. After the United States entered World War II at the end of 1941, the federal government made its immigration laws less restrictive, particularly for citizens of the country's wartime ally China. Nevertheless, the third great immigration wave was already over.

FOURTH IMMIGRATION WAVE, AFTER 1965

In 1965, passage of the federal Immigration and Nationality Act ended the system of quotas based on nationality. In their place was a new, far less restrictive quota system based on hemispheres. The new system permitted 120,000 immigrants per year from the Western Hemisphere and 170,000 from the Eastern Hemisphere. In 1978, even these quotas were replaced by a single, worldwide quota of

290,000 immigrants per year from all parts of the world. From 1992 to 1994, this figure was raised to 700,000 immigrants before being reduced to 675,000 in 1995. None of these quotas placed any limits on the numbers of immediate family members of U.S. citizens who could enter the country. As a consequence, the actual numbers of immigrants who entered the United States legally were higher than the quota figures.

During the first decade of the twenty-first century, the United States was still in the midst of the largest wave of immigration in its history. One million immigrants entered the country legally every year. By the first decade of the twenty-first century, fully one-tenth of all residents of the United States were foreign born. In addition to these approximately 30 million legal immigrants in the country, the U.S. Census estimated that about 8.7 million immigrants were in the country illegally. Most new immigrants, both legal and illegal, were Hispanics from Mexico, the Caribbean, and Central America. Between 1990 and 2000, the Hispanic population of the United States increased 63 percent—from 22.4 million to 35.3 million residents. Indeed, the largest and longest-enduring movement of laborers between any two countries in the world has been from Mexico to the United States.

Wayne Shirey

FURTHER READING

Foner, Nancy. *From Ellis Island to JFK: New York's Two Great Waves of Immigration.* New Haven, Conn.: Yale University Press, 2000. Comparison of the great wave of Jewish Russian and Italian immigrants to New York City around 1900 with the late twentieth century wave of immigrants from Asia, Latin America, and the Caribbean.

Katz, Michael B., and Mark J. Stern. *One Nation Divisible: What America Was and What It Is Becoming.* New York: Russell Sage Foundation, 2006. Examines the effect of large-scale immigration on American society and the economy.

Lippert, Dorothy, and Stephen J. Spignesi. *Native American History for Dummies.* Hoboken, N.J.: Wiley, 2007. Despite its title, this volume offers a very intelligent discussion of the immigration of the earliest Americans.

Waters, Mary C., and Reed Ueda, eds. *The New Americans: A Guide to Immigration Since 1965.* Cambridge, Mass.: Harvard University Press, 2007. Collection of descriptive essays on the various immigrant groups that have made up the post-1965 immigration wave and on the key topics concerning this wave.

SEE ALSO: Economic consequences of immigration; Great Irish Famine; History of immigration, 1620-1783; History of immigration, 1783-1891; History of immigration after 1891; Illegal immigration; Immigration and Nationality Act of 1965.

IN RE TIBURCIO PARROTT

THE CASE: U.S. district court decision on racial discrimination
DATE: Decided in 1880

> **SIGNIFICANCE:** In the *Parrott* ruling, a U.S. district court in California prohibited the application of a constitutional amendment that would have prohibited the employment of Chinese persons in the state.

In 1880, section 19 of the new California constitution prohibited the employment of "any Chinese or Mongolian," and it also authorized the legislature to enact laws to this effect. Irish teamster Dennis Kearney held large rallies to promote anti-Chinese sentiments, and a resulting criminal statute made the employment of Chinese a misdemeanor. The president of a silver mining company, Tiburcio Parrott, believing the law was unconstitutional, refused to discharge his Chinese employees. Arrested and charged, he petitioned a U.S. district court for a writ of habeas corpus, which was granted.

Two district judges, Ogden Hoffman and Lorenso Sawyer, held that both the constitutional provision and the statute were inconsistent with rights guaranteed in the Burlingame Treaty with China (1868) and therefore violated Article VI of the U.S. Constitution. Because treaties were part of the "supreme law of the land," their provisions were superior to state constitutions and state statutes. Although this was a major victory for the Chinese of California, the state legislature responded by passing discriminatory laws, restricting where the Chinese might live and prohibiting them from obtaining licenses in various businesses.

Thomas Tandy Lewis

FURTHER READING

Kens, Paul. "Civil Liberties, Chinese Laborers, and Corporations." In *Law in the Western United States*, edited by Gordon M. Bakken. Norman: University of Oklahoma Press, 2000.

McClain, Charles J. *In Search of Equality: The Chinese Struggle Against Discrimination in Nineteenth-Century America.* Berkeley: University of California Press, 1994.

SEE ALSO: Anti-Chinese movement; Burlingame Treaty of 1868; California; Capitation taxes; Chinese immigrants; Citizenship; Due process protections; Immigration law; Supreme Court, U.S.

INDENTURED SERVITUDE

DEFINITION: Form of contract labor that binds employees to work for specified periods of time, usually in satisfaction of debts

SIGNIFICANCE: During the colonial period of British North America, a high proportion of British working-class immigrants to the American colonies came as indentured servants. Precise figures are unavailable, but it is estimated that 40 to 75 percent of white immigrants experienced a period of unfree labor in colonial times. The British indenture system ceased to operate after the American Revolution, but debt-slavery of migrants continued under institutions such as the Chinese credit-ticket system.

The term "indentured servitude" is distinguished from slavery by its temporary nature. The term also refers to labor contracts in which a heavily indebted worker is effectively prevented from changing employers or retaining wages beyond a subsistence level. Indentured servitude as a North American institution dates from the earliest days of the colonial period. This form of bondage preceded African slavery and existed side by side with it up until the American Revolution. When the Americas ceased to be the property of Great Britain, the formal mechanisms for recruiting or forcing individuals into indentures and shipping them across the Atlantic no longer operated, although an internal indenture system continued to operate at the state level for many decades.

In its strictest sense, indentured servitude refers to a contract transferring ownership of an individual to his or her employer for a fixed term. Indentured servants ceased to be autonomous agents. They had no control over place of residence or conditions of employment and could not marry without the owner's consent. Their persons could be bought and sold. Although colonial law and terms of contracts granted them some rights and protections, laws protecting the owners' property rights were more uniformly enforced than those promoting the welfare of the property.

The term "indentured servant" often evokes images of domestic servants. Indeed, the majority of female indentured servants, who constituted about 20 percent of all indentured immigrants during the seventeenth and eighteenth centuries, probably fell into this category. Male indentured servants were more likely to be agricultural laborers. Skilled tradesmen entered the system when they fell afoul of the law.

COLONIAL AMERICA

In theory, an indenture was a voluntary contract, at least for adult males. In practice, most contracts involved an element of coercion or deception. Just under half of the 307,400 migrants from the British Isles to the thirteen colonies between 1680 and 1775 came as free citizens. Seventeen percent were criminal convicts, and 33.7 percent were indentured servants. The convicts, who had been convicted of felonies, served their sentences of transportation as indentured servants to private individuals rather than in state-managed labor camps.

British law also allowed involuntary apprenticeship of orphans, illegitimate children, and children whose families could not support them. Such forced apprenticeship might include transportation across the Atlantic. English poor laws dictated that adults who were capable of supporting themselves, but had no visible means of support, could be compelled to work. Vagrants, beggars, prostitutes, and able-bodied paupers could be forcibly indentured. For the most part, people who made a conscious choice to immigrate to the colonies for economic gain or to take advantage of greater religious and political freedom borrowed money for relocation costs, calculating (correctly) that a person with any skill or education could redeem the debt in a shorter period and be free in the interim.

For some members of the British underclass, forcible relocation and involuntary labor provided a door of opportunity, but these were a minority. One-third of those transported did not survive until the end of their indentures. During the seventeenth century, contracts often provided for a modest land grant upon completion of service, but by 1700 good land had become scarce, and a newly freed servant who had no developed skills had few resources to begin a new life. Some settled on the frontier in Appalachia. Others remained with their old employers as ostensibly free laborers. To a large extent, their descendants remained a permanent underclass of poor whites, landless or tied to unproductive land, poorly educated, and little attached to cultural norms that had not served their forebears. Some, especially those who still had strong family ties, returned to England.

Life for indentured servants was often bleak and grueling. They worked from dawn to dusk, six days a week. In contrast to black slaves, who were encouraged to raise families, they were expected to remain celibate, and under large employers usually lived under communal conditions resembling military barracks. In theory, the indentured servant had a contractual right to adequate food, clothing, and shelter; in practice, an unscrupulous employer, having no long-term investment in his captive employee, could stint on necessities. Complaints through the civil court system rarely resulted in redress.

In Puritan New England, Sundays included a hefty dose of religious instruction to correct the presumed low moral character of transported ruffians. To some extent justified, the widespread prejudice among free settlers against indentured laborers became a self-fulfilling prophecy. Expecting teenagers and young adults of either sex to remain celibate for years on end, and to refrain from petty property crime when no legal avenue of obtaining money or goods beyond the employer's meager ration existed, was simply unrealistic. Some of the runaways featured in frequent newspaper advertisements were true runaways, but a fair proportion consisted of young men out on a spree.

An owner could flog his servants if they misbehaved. Serious breaches of contract, including running away, were punished by extension of the indenture contract. Women were liable to sexual exploitation, either by their owners or by fellow servants. Societal perception that women of this social class were inherently immoral meant that protestations of rape or seduction fell on deaf ears. If a woman became pregnant, the law automatically added three years to her indenture contract to compensate for loss of labor to the owner.

German immigrants who settled in Pennsylvania during the eighteenth century came to America under a system resembling indentured servitude, with, however, significant differences. Immigrant brokers recruited laborers in Germany, contracting to transport them to America for a set fee, and sold the debt to the American employer. Called redemptioners, these immigrants were obliged either to work for that employer until the debt was paid off or to find another source for the funds. Although brokers charged excessive fees and misrepresented the opportunities for high-paid employment, and a redemptioner could end up working for little net remuneration for years, without any realistic prospect of changing jobs, he was still a free man. A similar system operated in Ireland, where the absence of poor laws prevented coerced indenture through the court system.

AFTER THE AMERICAN REVOLUTION

After Britain recognized the independence of the thirteen colonies in 1784, the flow of legally indentured servants and transported convicts from the British Isles stopped, though not because of the U.S. Constitution or any legislative act in the United States. Britain used these people as a resource to develop its colonial possessions, and was loath to relinquish any of them to an independent state and potential rival. Anyone transported through the justice system after 1784 ended up in Canada, the West Indies, or Australia. Parliament enacted some laws restricting the activities of immigrant brokers and military recruiters during the early nineteenth century, as well as limiting the ability of people with certain critical skills to leave the country voluntarily. The laws restricting voluntary emigration were largely ineffective.

Immigrant brokers continued to operate in Germany and Ireland during the early nineteenth century. European countries with their own expanding empires (France, Spain, Portugal, Holland) or frontiers (Russia) discouraged emigration to the United States.

Railroad building and continued westward expansion created a huge demand for labor that neither voluntary immigration from Europe nor involuntary internal migration could satisfy. To make up the deficit, the growing nation looked to China as a source of cheap workers. On paper, the Chinese "coolies" appeared to be voluntary migrants enlisted by brokers in China to work for American employers who paid the broker and shipping agent and collected the debt from the Chinese employees' wages. In practice, most were forced into service in China and placed in occupations and regions in the United States where alternative employment was impossible, leaving them at the employer's mercy. This credit-ticket system, which brought 350,000 Chinese laborers to the American mainland between 1840 and 1882, embodied many features of the old indentured labor system. In contrast to earlier European immigrants, however, the Chinese were never encouraged to become permanent settlers or citizens and were prohibited from doing so after 1882.

Military service can be viewed as a form of indentured servitude. During the U.S. Civil War, recruiters for the Union Army operated in some of the German states, enlisting German nationals for a cash bonus on joining and American citizenship and a land grant if they survived the war. Young men from Ireland and other countries where open foreign recruiting was prohibited were met at the docks with the same promise. Availability of an unlimited supply of foreign recruits was a nontrivial factor in the Union's victory over the South.

INDENTURED SERVITUDE IN TWENTIETH AND TWENTY-FIRST CENTURY AMERICA

After World War I, the United States became much more selective in the numbers, classes, and nationalities of immigrants it would accept as permanent residents and potential future citizens. Accepting an exclusive and restrictive contract with a single employer in return for payment of resettlement costs is no longer a possible avenue for becoming an American, except as a means of getting a toehold.

At the same time, the U.S. Citizenship and Immigration Services (formerly the Immigration and Naturalization Service) recognizes a number of classes of temporary workers whose conditions of employment approach indenture. In addition to legal guest workers, there were, in 2004, an estimated six million undocumented foreign nationals working in the United States, some proportion of whom paid hefty fees to the agents who smuggled them into the country and connected them with their present employers. These undocumented workers risk deportation if they complain about working conditions or attempt to change jobs.

Among types of legal labor contracts embodying aspects of involuntary servitude that affect foreign nationals, labor activists have singled out the H-2 visa program, special dispensations for employees of foreign embassies and consulates, and garment sweatshops operating in the Mariana Islands, a U.S. possession.

In 2007, 120,000 workers were admitted to the United States on H-2 visas to take temporary unskilled jobs for specific employers. Charges against the program include exorbitant fees exacted from workers and employers who seize documents, holding the workers effectively prisoner, and fail to provide contractual working conditions. Employees of embassies are governed by the laws of the parent country, which may tolerate virtual slavery. The status of the Mariana Islands as a U.S. territory, their proximity to Asia, and the vagaries of American import laws have allowed multinational corporations to set up garment factories in Saipan, import contract workers from China and Southeast Asia who live as virtual prisoners, and proudly stamp the products as "Made in the USA." Unlike the immigrant garment workers who toiled in New York sweatshops in the early twentieth century, these women have no chance of attaining the benefits of American life.

Martha A. Sherwood

FURTHER READING

Jordan, Don. *White Cargo: The Forgotten History of Britain's White Slaves in America.* New York: New York University Press, 2008. A mixture of statistical and anecdotal material that highlights the involuntary nature of most indenture contracts. Illustrated.

Lancaster, R. Kent. "Almost Chattel: The Lives of Indentured Servants at Hampton-Northampton, Baltimore County." *Maryland Historical Magazine*

94, no. 3 (Fall, 1999). Scholarly study of indentured workers at an iron foundry, 1750-1800, based on company records.

Morgan, Kenneth. *Slavery and Servitude in Colonial America: A Short History.* New York: New York University Press, 2001. Extensive statistical information and discussion of legal status of immigrants.

Wokeck, Marianne. *Trade in Strangers: The Beginnings of Mass Migration to America.* University Park: Pennsylvania State University Press, 1999. Scholarly study of eighteenth century German and Irish immigration, principally to Pennsylvania.

Zipf, Karin. *Labor of Innocents: Forced Apprenticeship in North Carolina, 1715-1919.* Baton Rouge: Louisiana State University Press, 2005. Describes institutionalized involuntary servitude of poor women and teenagers in colonies, when it was a feature of immigration, and in nineteenth century America.

SEE ALSO: Alien Contract Labor Law of 1885; British immigrants; Civil War, U.S.; Contract labor system; Coolies; Credit-ticket system; Economic opportunities; Guest-worker programs; Pilgrim and Puritan immigrants; Slave trade.

INDIANA

SIGNIFICANCE: Because of Indiana's history and geographical location, its population has a higher percentage of people who originated in the American South than any other midwestern state. Indeed, Indiana is politically, culturally, and linguistically the most "southern" midwestern state. In contrast, international immigration has had less of an impact in Indiana than in most other states. In 1880, only 7.8 percent of the state's residents were foreign born, compared to 23.0 percent in Illinois and 14.0 percent in Ohio.

PROFILE OF INDIANA

Region	Midwest
Entered union	1816
Largest cities	Indianapolis (capital), Fort Wayne, Evansville, South Bend, Gary
Modern immigrant communities	Mexicans, Germans

Population	*Total*	*Percent of state*	*Percent of U.S.*	*U.S. rank*
All state residents	6,314,000	100.0	2.11	15
All foreign-born residents	264,000	4.2	0.70	22

Source: U.S. Census Bureau, *Statistical Abstract for 2006.*

Notes: The U.S. population in 2006 was 299,399,000, of whom 37,548,000 (12.5%) were foreign born. Rankings in last column reflect total numbers, not percentages.

After the United States won its independence in 1783, most of what would become the state of Indiana was considered the property of Native Americans, as stipulated by the 1795 Treaty of Greenville. However, between 1800 and 1810, Indians made land cessions in the extreme southern part of Indiana and again in 1838, when the Potawatomi people were forcibly removed from the state, in defiance of earlier treaty provisions, and removed to Kansas. Their removal made desirable land available to Kentuckians and other southern American settlers before many international immigrants arrived.

EUROPEAN IMMIGRANTS

The first substantial group of overseas immigrants to enter Indiana were Swiss, who settled in Switzerland County, along the Ohio River in the extreme southeast part of the state. Swiss surveyors arrived in 1796, and a colony was founded at Vevay in 1803. Vevay still held a Swiss wine festival as late as 2008.

Germans formed the largest immigrant group to come to Indiana before the late twentieth century, but they were not as numerous there as in many other states. Germans began a colony at New Harmony in 1814. However, they were gone by 1825, and their land was sold to Robert Owen and a group of British utopians. Political problems in

Germany in 1848, together with the scarcity of agricultural land, led to the arrival of more Germans later. Many of these immigrants settled in the southeastern part of the state, near the Swiss. That part of the state was so heavily populated by German speakers that a traveler reported leaving a boat at Madison in 1846 and going north for almost eighty miles without hearing a word of English spoken. German immigrants were most prominent in Indiana's Ripley and Dubois Counties but were outnumbered by American southerners and Ohioans.

In later decades, Indiana's German residents began moving toward the state's cities. In 1850, Germans constituted 14 percent of the population of Indianapolis, where Germans became enough of a political force to make public school instruction in German optional. In Fort Wayne, skilled German workers were recruited for local industries. By the late nineteenth century, that city's population was said to be 80 percent German. German organizations—Turners Clubs and singing societies—were still active in 2000 in Indiana.

Other Indianans of German extraction were not international immigrants. Long-established Amish communities maintained a separate existence and spoke the German dialect called Pennsylvania Dutch. According to the 2000 U.S. Census, that dialect was spoken at home by almost eight thousand Indiana residents.

LATE TWENTIETH CENTURY AND MEXICAN IMMIGRATION

In 1960, only 2 percent of Indiana's residents were foreign born, and most of these were Germans. However, the state's immigrant mix began to change during the 1970's. Failures in Mexico's economy drove many Mexicans north in search of work, and some of these people found their way to Indiana. Although fewer Mexican immigrants came to Indiana than to other midwestern states, they brought a fundamental change to the state's ethnic composition. By the year 2000, foreign-born residents constituted only 3 percent of Indiana's nearly 6,100,000 residents. However, the 185,555 residents whose primary language at home was Spanish outnumbered German speakers by more than four to one.

Timothy C. Frazer

FURTHER READING

Blakely, George T. *Creating a Hoosier Self-Portrait: The Federal Writers' Project in Indiana, 1935-42.* Bloomington: Indiana University Press, 2005.

Carmony, Donald F. *A Brief History of Indiana.* Indianapolis: Indiana Historical Bureau, 1966.

Haller, Charles R. *Across the Atlantic and Beyond: German and Swiss Immigrants to America.* Bowie, Md.: Heritage Books, 1993.

SEE ALSO: German immigrants; Illinois; Kentucky; Ku Klux Klan; Mexican immigrants; New Harmony; Ohio; Rapp, George; Swiss immigrants.

INDOCHINA MIGRATION AND REFUGEE ASSISTANCE ACT OF 1975

THE LAW: Federal legislation establishing a resettlement assistance program for Southeast Asian refugees

DATE: Enacted on May 23, 1975

SIGNIFICANCE: Strongly supported by President Gerald R. Ford and opposed by those who feared an influx of Southeast Asian refugees after the end of the conflict in Vietnam, the Indochina Migration and Refugee Assistance Act allowed some 200,000 Cambodians and Vietnamese to enter the United States under a special "parole" status and provided financial assistance for their resettlement.

After Saigon fell to the North Vietnamese at the end of the Vietnam War in 1975, thousands of people tried to flee Southeast Asia. Although many Americans feared that a large number of refugees would deflate wages and create a social burden, Congress passed the Indochina Migration and Refugee Assistance Act of 1975, which permitted refugees from Cambodia and Vietnam to enter the country and provided $455 million for resettlement. In 1976, the act was amended to include refugees from Laos. Nonprofit groups, including the U.S. Conference of Catholic Bishops, Civitan International, and the International Rescue Committee, sponsored families, providing food, clothing, and shelter until they could support themselves.

Initially, the U.S. government placed refugees in scattered locations, hoping to prevent the formation of large enclaves. Once families' lives stabilized, however, they tended to move near each other, with many settling permanently in Texas and California.

Cynthia A. Bily

FURTHER READING

Bloemraad, Irene. *Becoming a Citizen: Incorporating Immigrants and Refugees in the United States and Canada.* Berkeley: University of California Press, 2006.

Kelly, Gail Paradise. *From Vietnam to America: A Chronicle of the Vietnamese Immigration to the United States.* Boulder, Colo.: Westview Press, 1977.

Strand, Paul, and Woodrow Jones, Jr. *Indochinese Refugees in America: Problems of Adaptation and Assimilation.* Durham, N.C.: Duke University Press, 1985.

SEE ALSO: Amerasian Homecoming Act of 1987; Asian immigrants; Cambodian immigrants; Congress, U.S.; Hmong immigrants; Laotian immigrants; Refugees; Vietnamese immigrants.

INDONESIAN IMMIGRANTS

SIGNIFICANCE: Although the Southeast Asian nation of Indonesia has one of the largest populations in the world, it has sent comparatively few immigrants to the United States. However, the numbers of Indonesian immigrants began increasing rapidly during the 1980's, and their heavy concentration in Southern California gave them considerable visibility.

Indonesia is made up of a large number of populated islands located south of Southeast Asia's Malay Peninsula. It has the largest population of any nation in Southeast Asia and is home to a diverse variety of ethnic and linguistic groups. The most numerous of these groups are the Javanese, who constitute about 45 percent of Indonesia's total population. Partly because it was a Dutch colony until 1949, Indonesia has had fewer political, eco-

PROFILE OF INDONESIAN IMMIGRANTS	
Country of origin	Indonesia
Primary language	Indonesian
Primary regions of U.S. settlement	Southern California
Earliest significant arrivals	Early 1950's
Peak immigration period	1980's
Twenty-first century legal residents*	25,281 (3,160 per year)

*Immigrants who obtained legal permanent resident status in the United States.
Source: Department of Homeland Security, *Yearbook of Immigration Statistics, 2008.*

nomic, and cultural ties to the United States than many other Asian nations.

Some of the earliest American immigrants of Indonesian origin were people of mixed European and Indonesian ancestry. These mixed-background migrants left Indonesia during the late 1940's during the nation's struggle for independence. Many of them went first to the Netherlands before moving to the United States. During the mid-1950's, U.S. government scholarships enabled some Indonesian students to study in the United States. During the 1960's, political and economic turmoil in Indonesia prompted some emigration to the United States by Indonesians, especially ethnic Chinese from the archipelago.

By 1980, an estimated 26,700 Indonesian-born immigrants lived in the United States. About one-fourth of them had arrived in the United States before 1960 and close to one-third had arrived between 1960 and 1964. During the 1980's, immigration from Asia increased greatly. By 1990, the total number of foreign-born people from Indonesia in the United States doubled, reaching more than 53,600. This figure increased to close to 77,000 in 2000 and reached an estimated 86,000 by 2007.

Despite this rapid growth, Indonesian migration still remained much lower than immigration from many other parts of Asia. Even in the heavy migration years from 1999 to 2008, a time during which migrants from Asia made up about one-

Barack Obama and Indonesia

Although Indonesia's ties with the United States have historically been limited, the Southeast Asian nation has a special connection with the forty-fourth president of the United States. Between the ages of six and ten, future U.S. president Barack Obama lived in Jakarta, Indonesia, while his mother was married to an Indonesian man. Obama attended two schools in Indonesia and learned to speak some Indonesian—the only language other than English that he speaks. While he was in Indonesia, his mother gave birth to a daughter, Maya Soetoro, by her Indonesian husband. Obama's half sister holds dual American and Indonesian citizenship. She later completed her education in the United States and became a teacher in Hawaii. Adding to her family's rich ethnic mix, she married the Canadian-born son of Malaysian Chinese immigrants to Canada and became Maya Soetoro-Ng.

nesian food. Indonesian Americans employed outside the restaurant industry are most heavily represented in professional and technical occupations.

Carl L. Bankston III

Further Reading

Takaki, Ronald. *Strangers from a Different Shore.* Boston: Back Bay Books, 1998.

Taylor, Jean Gilman. *Indonesia: Peoples and Histories.* New Haven, Conn.: Yale University Press, 2003.

Vickers, Adrian. *A History of Modern Indonesia.* New York: Cambridge University Press, 2005.

See also: Asian immigrants; California; Filipino immigrants; Los Angeles; Malaysian immigrants; Muslim immigrants; Thai immigrants; Vietnamese immigrants.

Industrial Revolution

The Event: Era during which the economies of Western countries began moving away from primarily agricultural bases to industrial and commercial bases

Date: Nineteenth century

Significance: The shift from economies based largely on subsistence agriculture to economies based on industry and trade created a vast number of unskilled and semiskilled jobs that helped to attract immigrants to the United States.

The demographic revolution that began in the Western world during the eighteenth century and accelerated during the nineteenth and twentieth centuries made it imperative to develop employment for the increasing numbers of people in the developing nations. During the long period that became known as the Industrial Revolution, large numbers of Europeans moved from rural areas into cities where jobs in new industries were to be found. Many of these people crossed the Atlantic Ocean looking for work and joined native-born Americans who were moving into cities.

Changing Sources of Economic Growth

As late as the eighteenth century, the great bulk of people in Europe and North America were still

quarter of all new legal immigrants to the United States, only about 3,000 immigrants per year came from Indonesia. This figure was dwarfed by the averages of more than 60,000 Chinese and 54,000 Filipinos arriving every year.

In 2007, California was home to about 40,000 people who had been born in Indonesia. This figure accounts for nearly one-half of all Indonesians in the United States. The single-largest concentration of these immigrants was in the Los Angeles/Long Beach metropolitan area, where about 17,500 Indonesians lived. Another 6,000 had settled in the Riverside-San Bernardino area. Other Indonesians were scattered around the country, with the greatest numbers found in Washington, D.C. (about 5,000 Indonesians in 2007), the New York-New Jersey area (about 4,300), and Southern California's Orange County metropolitan area (about 3,600).

Restaurants have been an important source of employment for Indonesians, about 12 percent of whom were employed in commercial eating and drinking places during 2007, according to U.S. Census data. Indeed, roughly one of every eight Indonesian Americans worked as a cook, waiter, or waitress. The Los Angeles area, in particular, has had a significant number of restaurants owned by Indonesian immigrants and specializing in Indo-

supporting themselves and their families through their individual labor, mostly on farmlands. They relied on human and animal power to grow and harvest plant food crops and raise livestock that would sustain their lives. In some places, individual farmers made their farms more efficient by harnessing wind and hydraulic power. They had sailing vessels propelled by wind, and grain mills and lumber mills powered by waterwheels and windmills. Coal, petroleum, and electrically powered machines were still largely unknown.

The early nineteenth century saw human beings beginning to harness a new form of power: steam, which could make machines work faster and with greater power. As the century wore on, steam power was made to run trains, ships, and factory machines. By the end of the century, electricity was being harnessed to run machines even more efficiently, and new kinds of motors were being made to run off petrochemical fuels, such as gasoline.

These new forms of machinery did not suddenly spring into use. They required many years of experimentation and adaptation to reach high levels of efficiency. Steam-powered train, ferry, and shipping services began operating during the first decades of the nineteenth century, but they did not become commercially significant until around mid-century. Meanwhile, factories were beginning to adapt steam-powered machines to manufacturing. A key element of the process of modernizing manufacturing was the introduction of standardization of parts.

The importance of standardization was especially evident in the manufacture of guns, an indus-

Contemporary magazine illustration of the New York headquarters of I. M. Singer & Co. in 1857. Singer was a primary manufacturer of sewing machines, which played a major role in the Industrial Revolution and made possible the employment of many thousands of immigrants. (Library of Congress)

try that played an important role in developing the technique. Armories in Springfield, Massachusetts, and Harpers Ferry, Virginia (later in West Virginia), helped pioneer in the development of machine tools, jigs, and templates that made possible the production of multiple identical parts. Standardized parts made assembly faster and more economical and made replacement parts much easier and cheaper to obtain. Standardization was later introduced into the manufacturing of many other products for which there was increasing demand, such as clocks, sewing machines, farm machines, and transportation equipment. Before the Industrial Revolution, complicated devices such as guns, tools, and clocks had been made by hand by workers trained by long experience to produce individual parts, one at a time. Making the parts and assembling them both required high levels of skills. After techniques for manufacturing identical, and thus fully interchangeable, parts were perfected, the finished products could be assembled relatively easily by semiskilled and sometimes even unskilled workers—many of whom were recent immigrants to the United States.

CREATION OF INDUSTRIAL AMERICA

After the mid-nineteenth century, the development of machine-powered mass-manufacturing techniques powered the American economy. It had begun in the textile industry, whose mills had provided jobs for large numbers of the Irish immigrants who were then beginning to enter the United States. However, mass manufacturing extended well beyond the textile industry and became, in a sense, self-generating. As increasingly large factories required ever greater quantities of materials to operate, their needs spurred the development of other industries. For example, the railroads required steel in huge quantities for their thousands of miles of rails and for the trains themselves. The steamships and ferries that were beginning to move passengers and cargoes at previously unimagined speeds needed giant foundries to manufacture the plates that formed them and the engines that powered them.

The immense demands for the iron alloys from which to fashion the new machines created a steel industry whose size was empowered by the Bessemer process that was invented in 1855 but only widely adopted after the U.S. Civil War (1861-

1865). The Bessemer process made possible the vast steel mills of Pittsburgh and other cities, and the steel industry in turn contributed to the great expansion of the coal-mining industry, which was also beginning to supply great amounts of fuel to railroads and steamships. Through the late nineteenth century, coal mining employed huge numbers of unskilled immigrant laborers.

One of the ultimate achievements of the Industrial Revolution was the creation of assembly-line production that Henry Ford introduced to automobile manufacturing during the early twentieth century. To the system of interchangeable parts, assembly lines added the advantage of simplifying the tasks performed by individual workers to make large-scale manufacturing more profitable. Simplification of workers' tasks opened many jobs to unskilled immigrant workers.

Nancy M. Gordon

FURTHER READING

Hounshell, David A. *From the American System to Mass Production, 1800-1932*. Baltimore: Johns Hopkins University Press, 1984. Traces the development of engineering technology that underlay the Industrial Revolution.

Mayr, Otto, and Robert C. Post, eds. *Yankee Enterprise: The Rise of the American System of Manufactures*. Washington, D.C.: Smithsonian Institution Press, 1981. Collective review of the factors that created the Industrial Revolution in America.

Mokyr, Joel. *The Lever of Riches: Technological Creativity and Economic Progress*. New York: Oxford University Press, 1990. Recounts how technological innovation drove the Industrial Revolution.

Singer, Charles, et al., eds. *The Late Nineteenth Century, 1850 to 1900*. Vol. 5 in *A History of Technology*. New York: Oxford University Press, 1954-1958. Part of a classic multivolume work tracing the role played by technology in history.

Stiles, T. J. *The First Tycoon: The Epic Life of Cornelius Vanderbilt*. New York: Alfred A. Knopf, 2009. Biography of one of the major players in the ferry, shipping, and railroad industries during the nineteenth century that provides fascinating coverage of technological advances in each of the industries that Vanderbilt developed.

Temin, Peter, ed. *Engines of Enterprise: An Economic History of New England*. Cambridge, Mass.: Harvard University Press, 2000. Collection of essays by a number of scholars that examine the role played by industrial technology in New England's economy.

SEE ALSO: Coal industry; Economic consequences of immigration; Economic opportunities; European immigrants; European revolutions of 1848; Immigration waves; Iron and steel industry; Settlement patterns.

INDUSTRIAL WORKERS OF THE WORLD

IDENTIFICATION: Global labor union
DATE: Founded in June, 1905
LOCATION: Chicago, Illinois
ALSO KNOWN AS: Wobblies

SIGNIFICANCE: The Industrial Workers of the World was the first large labor union in the United States to organize as an industrial union instead of according to craft. It focused a large part of its organizing efforts on newly arrived immigrant workers, whom other union organizations ignored or overtly discriminated against.

The Industrial Workers of the World (IWW) was founded in Chicago in 1905 by unionists opposed to the policies of the American Federation of Labor (AFL), in particular its refusal to organize unskilled workers. Founding members included William D. "Big Bill" Haywood of the Western Federation of Miners, Daniel De Leon of the Socialist Labor Party, and Eugene V. Debs of the Socialist Party. Unlike most union and leftist political organizations in the United States during the early twentieth century, the IWW recognized the importance of organizing all workers regardless of race, gender, national origin, or craft. This realization stemmed from its philosophy of international worker solidarity as expressed in the IWW slogan, "One Big Union." Although many of the workforces involved in IWW organizing drives were made up primarily of European immigrants, internationalist immigrant organizing was important given the separation of communities along ethnic lines.

Other unions, especially those affiliated with Samuel Gompers and the AFL, considered immigrant workers competition for what were considered "American" jobs. The IWW sought to overcome the artificial separations enforced by governmental, economic, and religious authorities in order to create a sense of common struggle. Strikes among miners and textile workers that were organized with the help of the IWW included women, children, and men of all backgrounds and were usually successful, at least in terms of creating class solidarity, based in part on the union's opposition to the "owning classes" of all nations.

In the eastern United States, the IWW organized among textile workers (often the most exploited members of the workforce), many of whom were of southern European origin. In places such as Lawrence, Massachusetts, and other mill towns, the IWW represented multiple nationalities to create a strong, unified strike against the textile mill owners. In the western United States, the IWW was one of the first major national labor organizations to organize Asian workers. In doing so, the union stood in contrast not only to the AFL but also to radical political groups such as the Socialist Party. Asian workers were separated not only by their language differences but also by their physical and cultural differences. Consequently, they faced both de facto and de jure discrimination and the threat of deportation. The IWW worked to defend these workers' rights while organizing. In 1912, after Italian organizers Arturo Giovannitti and Joseph Ettor were arrested in the Lawrence strike, it was the IWW that led the campaign to free the men. The U.S. government responded with mass deportations of immigrants associated with the union.

In its heyday during World War I, the IWW claimed more than 100,000 members. By the first decade of the twenty-first century, it was a much smaller organization. The union has continued to organize among immigrants and other underrepresented workers and advocate for immigrant rights.

Ron Jacobs

FURTHER READING

Foner, Philip S. *History of the Labor Movement in the United States.* Vol. 4. New York: International Publishers, 1965.

Thompson, Fred W., and John Bekken. *The Indus-*

trial Workers of the World: Its First One Hundred Years—1905 Through 2005. Foreword by Utah Phillips. Chicago: Industrial Workers of the World, 2006.

See also: Economic opportunities; Employment; Espionage and Sedition Acts of 1917-1918; Garment industry; Gompers, Samuel; Industrial Revolution; International Ladies' Garment Workers' Union; Labor unions; Massachusetts; United Farm Workers.

INFECTIOUS DISEASES

Definition: Communicable human diseases caused by pathogenic microorganisms

Significance: During North America's colonial era, immigrants from Europe and Africa imported many contagious diseases that wreaked havoc on not only Native American populations but also nonimmunized colonists. Successive waves of disease-carrying immigrants during the nineteenth century set off epidemics ranging from cholera to plague, despite ever more effective public health measures, and encountered effective anti-immigrant sentiment and action. During the early twenty-first century, visitors as well as immigrants posed threats to U.S. public health as carriers of new diseases and new strains of old diseases.

Every person and every community lives in an environment filled with bacteria, viruses, fungi, and parasites, many of which carry pathogens potentially lethal to humans. People who live for many years in the same area and with the same neighbors develop effective immune system defenses against the commonly occurring pathogens. Sometimes they pass their immunity along to subsequent generations genetically. When a new pathogen is inserted into a community by changes in the environment or the intrusion of new people, the effects may be devastating, as existing members of the community may have limited or no developed biological defenses. Unlike noninfectious diseases such as diabetes or cancer, an infectious disease can be passed among members of a community by the actions of carriers of pathogens. These carriers might include tainted foods or water; insects, parasites, and their droppings; and infected people. During the centuries before germ theory made modern medicine an effective counter to most infectious diseases, there was little understanding of pathogens and carriers, and little that any human community could do to defend against them.

COLUMBIAN EXCHANGE

The early history of European and African settlement in the Western Hemisphere provides a depressingly long list of epidemics and pandemics. Many of these occurred on a large geographical scale, sparked by the contact of Native American communities with immigrant men and women who carried deadly pathogens to which the carriers themselves were immune or highly resistant. In turn, these intruders were susceptible to Native American diseases, one example of which may have been syphilis. It seems that some infected Spanish explorers contracted that sexually transmitted disease (STD) and spread it after their return to Europe. For their part, Native Americans died by the thousands of imported Old World diseases such as measles, mumps, smallpox, typhus, and influenza. This biological interaction is sometimes referred to as part of the "Columbian Exchange," taking its name from the Italian explorer Christopher Columbus.

Although early immigrants from Europe and Africa tended to share resistance to a wide range of pathogens, later generations, long removed from their homelands and isolated from certain diseases in the New World, tended to lose their natural defenses to the Old World diseases. When new immigrants arrived from the Old World, even from the same cities and regions as the ancestors of second- or third-generation colonists or slaves, their reinfusion of disease-causing pathogens could and often did trigger outbreaks—even epidemics—among the settled immigrants populations. Perhaps ironically, however, this was least likely to occur in large cities such as New York, Boston, and Philadelphia, in which steady streams of new immigrants kept levels of exposure and resistance relatively high among the urban populations.

Some imported diseases, such as mosquito-borne malaria and yellow fever, were initially and inadvertently inserted into humid coastal environments in the New World that were well suited to the insects by Spanish slavers and their human cargoes. While the African immigrant populations were generally resistant to the potentially deadly diseases, both Native Americans and Europeans proved to be highly susceptible. The insects became carriers when they sucked the blood of human carriers. In regions where human carriers diminished in number, as along the northern Atlantic coastline (thanks in part to the practice of quarantine), the incidence of the disease dropped off. Fresh arrivals of African or Caribbean slaves along the southern U.S. coasts, however, helped maintain high incidence levels. Even before Walter Reed and other researchers untangled the true nature of yellow fever during the early twentieth century, Americans sought strict limitations on immigrants and even trade from Cuba and other island sources of the disease whose carriers set off recurrent outbreaks.

EPIDEMICS DURING THE AGE OF SAIL

Traditional Western medicine had long associated disease with filth, a lack of basic hygiene, and, by the later eighteenth century, poverty. From the 1820's, ships from Europe brought trickles and then floods of immigrants from Ireland and central Europe. Many of these people were both poverty-stricken and sick with opportunistic diseases such as typhus, influenza, and typhoid fever. Cramped and unsanitary quarters, lack of clean clothing, and poor nutrition shipboard exacerbated weak constitutions and undermined the healthy. Rightly fearful of the spread of infectious diseases, civic and state authorities in North America maintained quarantines and isolation facilities at major ports for sick or suspect passengers. Although a single case of influenza might be gotten over with no lasting effects, chronic conditions such as STDs and Hansen's disease (leprosy) presented almost no possibilities of cure. Those who suffered from such maladies would be turned away, to find refuge elsewhere. They might then attempt to enter the country illicitly or simply return to their homelands.

Even due diligence could fail, especially with emerging diseases. Cholera had first broken out of its homeland in eastern India in 1817, but America was spared the ensuing first pandemic. The second pandemic proved less accommodating, and Irish immigrants brought the waterborne disease with

them to Canadian and U.S. port cities in 1832. New York City lost 3,000 residents in July and August, and New Orleans suffered 4,340 fatalities during three weeks in October. Eventually spreading to the western frontier, cholera killed an estimated 150,000 people in North America between 1832 and 1849. The year 1866 saw the final epidemic of cholera in the United States, when eastern and Gulf port cities counted 50,000 deaths.

The popular conception of Roman Catholic Irish immigrants as lazy, poor, and disease-ridden was reinforced by the huge numbers of penniless refugees who appeared as the potato famine (1845-1852) ravaged their homeland. A British government report in 1856 noted that malnutrition and starvation among the Irish were accompanied by many other medical conditions, including infectious diseases: "fever, scurvy, diarrhea and dysentery, cholera, influenza and ophthalmia." Despite the availability of vaccines, smallpox "prevailed epidemically," and typhus was nearly endemic in crowded Irish cities. Each year, hundreds of thousands of Irish died and one-quarter million Irish emigrated. Although British port authorities were supposed to screen out emigrants carrying diseases before they departed, this task was often left to American officials. As a result, many emigrants died on ships, earning the passenger vessels the nickname "coffin ships." Despite screening and quarantine procedures, many disease carriers still managed to enter the United States, and many of them settled in already overcrowded and unsanitary ethnic enclaves in American cities, inducing outbreaks as well as increased public health structures and efforts to combat the increasingly complex disease regimes.

PUBLIC HEALTH AND ANTI-IMMIGRANT SENTIMENT

The fact that a significant percentage of immigrants were Roman Catholic and, to a growing extent, Jewish, as well as poor and suffering from diseases, fed the fears and prejudices of nativist and other anti-immigrant groups. During the last decades of the nineteenth and first decades of the twentieth centuries, groups such as the Immigration Restriction League harnessed the ideas of new medical pseudosciences in their attempts to limit the diversity of immigrants. They blamed the perceived prevalence of certain diseases among east-

U.S. Health Service officers inspect Japanese immigrants as they arrive on the West Coast of the United States in the early 1920's. (NARA)

ern and central European immigrants, especially typhus and tuberculosis (TB), on natural genetic dispositions.

Tuberculosis was once widely considered to be a genteel or sensitive person's disease. However, as it spread among the working classes in large U.S. cities, it became associated with poverty, squalor, and ethnic minorities, and sufferers were rounded up for isolation. A major outbreak in 1892 in New York City led to passage of the National Quarantine Act of 1893. San Francisco's bubonic plague outbreak in 1900-1901 was very likely sparked by stowaways aboard a visiting Japanese freighter. However, its first known fatality was a Chinese immigrant who lived in a very poor Chinese neighborhood. Residents of Chinatown, fearing both mobs and the government, hid subsequent cases of plague until the outbreak could no longer be concealed. Anti-Chinese sentiment then flashed across the city, and there were calls to eradicate the Asian American

neighborhood. Cooler heads prevailed, however, and modern antiplague measures kept the number of fatalities to only 122.

The popular linkage of disease and immigrants remained a major factor in U.S. public policy. Along the U.S.-Mexican border, perfunctory visual inspections for obvious signs of diseases were replaced by mandatory flea-dip baths for large numbers of very poor laborers and immigrants who sought work or refuge from the dislocations of the Mexican Revolution after 1917. The worldwide influenza pandemic that followed World War I may have killed more than 40 million people, including 675,000 Americans—a fatality rate that was five times the annual average for that disease. Like the war itself, the pandemic underlined the metaphorical shrinkage of the world and the increasing immediacy of threats that included disease. This sentiment resulted in the federal immigration restriction acts of 1921 and 1924.

MODERN HEALTH THREATS

Twentieth century science and technology complicated ideas about the relationship between immigrants and infectious diseases. Medical researchers have found cures or effective treatments for a wide variety of potentially deadly diseases. While Americans generally have access to these, many are beyond the reach of potential immigrants. At the same time, jet aircraft have made intercontinental travel swift and relatively cheap. Visitors and U.S. travelers abroad, as well as immigrants, can and do enter America as carriers of a wide variety of pathogens.

Those who enter a country illicitly, or choose to remain undocumented, often avoid public health screening and surveillance officials who might identify them as carriers and treat their conditions. Instead, such individuals threaten members of the communities in which they settle. By the end of the twentieth century, tuberculosis was making an alarming resurgence across the globe, especially in developing countries in Asia and Africa. The United States has one of the world's lowest levels of incidence of the disease, but neighboring Mexico's rate is ten times higher. TB presents a problem that is being echoed by other diseases: the natural evolution of drug-resistant varieties that threaten to make the American pharmaceutical arsenal obsolete.

Sexually transmitted diseases, including HIV/AIDS, can be treated, but immigrant communities are often resistant to public health measures. The worldwide spread of HIV/AIDS means that immigrants from Africa or Haiti are not alone suspect. The incidences of forms of hepatitis, malaria, dengue fever, and even leprosy were on the rise across the United States during the early twenty-first century, with health practitioners often noting the prevalence of the foreign-born among their victims. Since many modern-day immigrants find work in agricultural and food preparation and service sectors, the possibilities are good for spreading diseases beyond local communities. The failure effectively to screen those who cross America's borders also opens the door for incidences of bioterrorism, as it raises the potential for other types of terrorism as well.

Joseph P. Byrne

FURTHER READING

Apostolopoulos, Yiorgos, and Sevil Sönmez, eds. *Population Mobility and Infectious Disease.* New York: Springer, 2007. Collection of analytical articles on the variety of forms of population movement and the roles they have played in the spread of disease in the early twenty-first century.

Duffy, John. *Epidemics in Colonial America.* Baton Rouge: Louisiana State University Press, 1953. Older book that remains the standard text on the causes, courses, and effects of epidemic disease in Britain's North American colonies.

Grob, Gerald N. *The Deadly Truth: A History of Disease in America.* Cambridge, Mass.: Harvard University Press, 2002. Broad overview that goes beyond imported disease and effects of disease on immigrants to chronic and occupational problems from the colonial era to the end of the twentieth century.

Markel, Howard. *Quarantine! East European Jewish Immigrants and the New York Epidemics of 1892.* Baltimore: Johns Hopkins University Press, 1997. Study of the role of Jewish immigrants in the outbreaks of cholera and typhus, the ethnically based initial responses, and the role of the events in the passage of the 1893 screening and quarantine act.

_____. *When Germs Travel: Six Major Epidemics That Have Invaded America Since 1900 and the Fears They Have Unleashed.* New York: Pantheon Books, 2004. Chronicle of the historical outbreaks of tuberculosis, plague, typhus, cholera, HIV/AIDS, and trachoma in a very readable set of analytical narratives.

Shah, Nayan. *Contagious Divides: Epidemics and Race in San Francisco's Chinatown.* Berkeley: University of California Press, 2001. Study of San Francisco's large Chinese community that emphasizes the city's bubonic plague outbreaks and the roles of and influences on popular attitudes toward Asian immigrants.

SEE ALSO: Acquired immunodeficiency syndrome; African immigrants; Ellis Island; Eugenics movement; Globalization; Great Irish Famine; Haitian boat people; Health care; Smuggling of immigrants; Sweatshops; Transportation of immigrants; "Undesirable aliens"; World migration patterns.

INTELLIGENCE TESTING

DEFINITION: Use of psychometric standards concerning verbal and nonverbal abilities as part of legislation guiding decisions regarding authorized entry of foreigners into the United States

SIGNIFICANCE: The nascent science of intelligence testing developed in confluence with growing support for more severe controls on the acceptance of foreign-born entrants to the United States. Proponents of this view were able to highlight some of the early studies of psychologists conducting intelligence testing research as part of their efforts to pass restrictive immigration legislation, even in the face of presidential vetoes.

Intelligence testing has a long, honored tradition in the United States. It originated in France, where psychologist Alfred Binet was the first researcher to categorize student performances on specific reasoning tasks in terms of what he called their "mental ages" between 1904 and 1908. When he judged that students' mental ages were substantially lower than their chronological ages, he concluded that the test result argued for special remedial programs for the students. In 1912, the German psychologist William Stern defined "intelligence quotient," or "IQ," as a ratio of mental age divided by chronological age, multiplied by 100. What began in Europe as an earnest attempt to identify the needs of students with learning disabilities became a source of labeling with serious consequences in twentieth century America.

In 1910, the American psychologist Henry H. Goddard translated Binet's work into English. Goddard invented the label "moron" for any adult with a mental age between eight and twelve and advocated that those with IQs below 70 should not be allowed to have children. This perspective fit in well with a budding eugenics movement in the United States that advocated genetic engineering to raise intelligence levels, while reducing poverty and criminality. Lewis Terman, a professor at Stanford University, adapted the Binet scale and its measured intelligence quotient into its most commonly used form. Like Goddard, however, he was heavily influenced by biological determinism and

at least initially supported the idea that there were racial differences in human intelligence that reflected differing biological makeups. He recanted this view in 1937, but not before the stage was set for changes in important immigration legislation in the United States that reflected his earlier orientation toward the understanding of intelligence.

INTELLIGENCE TESTING AND IMMIGRATION LAW

The psychological work with the closest influence on later immigration policy was performed by Robert Yerkes of Harvard University. In 1917, when the United States entered World War I, he created the Army Mental Tests and oversaw their administration to 1.75 million Army draftees. Two versions of the tests, "Alpha" and "Beta," provided written and pictorial modalities so that illiterate servicemen could be tested as well. Carl Brigham, a Princeton University psychologist, analyzed the data that were collected and concluded that native-born draftees had higher IQ scores than immigrants. Moreover, a "Nordic" (northern European) subgroup had higher scores than those from southern and eastern Europe.

Brigham's work was attacked on methodological grounds, and he recanted his conclusions in 1930. However, he published his findings in 1923, the year before the federal Immigration Act of 1924 greatly restricted foreign entry to the United States. This act initially used the 1890 census as a basis for establishing strict quotas not to exceed 2 percent of those from each country included in the census. It greatly reduced the number of southeastern Europeans allowed into the country and had an impact that would be acutely felt during World War II, when entry was largely denied to European Jews seeking a safe haven from extermination in the Nazi Holocaust. Although detailed analyses of empirical work supporting immigration restrictions do not appear in the congressional hearings concerning this law, the acceptance of biological determinism and the discriminatory treatment of minorities may well have contributed to its passage.

LATER PERSPECTIVES

Relatively soon after the Immigration Act of 1924 was passed, the popularity of using racial theories of intelligence as guideposts to immigration law and policy waned. There was an increasing realization that test performances reflected familiarity with American culture and language more often than they did an assessment of native intelligence. Meanwhile, members of the psychology-research establishment became more ethnically diverse, and during the aftermath of World War II there was more of an interest in explaining prejudicial attitudes. This was accentuated by a eugenics-oriented policy carried to horrific extremity by the German Nazi regime in Europe.

While the current intelligence testing community is much more sensitive to issues of cultural bias and attempts to develop "culture-fair" or "culture-free" instruments, elements of biological determinism have persisted. The Human Genome Project, which some people have claimed has important implications for controlling psychological disorders related to crime and homelessness, is a prominent example.

In addition, the early twenty-first century U.S. "war on terrorism," with its restriction of basic civil liberties, perpetuates an orientation toward selecting out undesirables in order to eliminate their perceived threat. Instead of classifying would-be immigrants as "feebleminded" on the basis of intelligence tests of questionable validity, there has developed a tendency to employ modern biometric technology that enforces even more restrictive policies to bolster homeland security.

Eric Yitzchak Metchik

FURTHER READING

Elliott, Stuart, Naomi Chudowsky, Barbara Plake, and Lorraine McDonnell. "Using the *Standards* to Evaluate the Redesign of the U.S. Naturalization Tests: Lessons for the Measurement Community." *Educational Measurement: Issues and Practice* 25, no. 1 (Fall, 2006): 22-26. Methodological critique of attempts by the U.S. Citizenship and Immigration Services to revise naturalization tests.

Perdew, Patrick R. "Developmental Education and Alfred Binet: The Original Purpose of Standardized Testing." In *2001: A Developmental Odyssey*, edited by Jeanne L. Higbee. Warrensburg, Mo.: National Association for Developmental Education, 2001. Comprehensive review of the historical evolution of intelligence testing in the United States, including its relationship to biological determinism and immigration law and practice.

Resta, Robert G. "The Twisted Helix: An Essay on Genetic Counselors, Eugenics, and Social Responsibility." *Journal of Genetic Counseling* 1, no. 3 (1992): 227-243. Examination of the historical implications of the eugenics movement and its most recent manifestations.

Samelson, Franz. "From 'Race Psychology' to 'Studies in Prejudice': Some Observations on the Thematic Reversal in Social Psychology." *Journal of the History of the Behavioral Sciences* 14 (1978): 265-278. Analysis of historical reasons for change in social psychological research, from studies of alleged racial differences in intelligence to causal models explaining racial prejudice.

Snyderman, Mark, and R. J. Herrnstein. "Intelligence Tests and the Immigration Act of 1924." *American Psychologist* 38, no. 9 (1983): 986-995. Critical analysis of the alleged link between viewpoints of psychologists conducting intelligence research and the passage of the Immigration Act of 1924 that greatly restricted immigration.

SEE ALSO: "Brain drain"; Eugenics movement; Higher education; Immigration Act of 1924; Immigration law; Language issues; Literacy tests; "Mongrelization"; Quota systems; Stereotyping.

INTERMARRIAGE

DEFINITION: Marriage unions between citizens and noncitizens

SIGNIFICANCE: Many Americans believe they have the right to marry whomever they wish and to live with their spouses in the United States, even when their marriages are to residents of other countries. This belief and the practice of intermarriage between immigrants and American citizens have helped shape American immigration policy and influenced the composition of American society.

Under early twenty-first century U.S. immigration policies, valid marriages of citizens of the United States of America with foreign-born persons give the citizens the right to petition for permission for their spouses to enter the United States. After approval is given by the U.S. Citizenship and Immigration Services, noncitizen spouses may apply for a K-3 visa. This preferential nonimmigrant category has a relatively short waiting period, permits the applicants to apply for work in the United States, and provides the opportunity for permanent resident status. This category of immigration has become a major vehicle for new immigrants to the United States, thanks to the fact that family reunification has become a basic goal of U.S. immigration policy.

HISTORICAL PATTERNS OF IMMIGRATION

U.S. immigration policy, and ultimately the laws pertaining to marriage between aliens and citizens, has evolved in response to the American experience with earlier immigration, fear of change, and a number of major events that have affected U.S. history. Most early immigrants to what is now the United States came from northern and western Europe. After new immigrants arrived, they, in turn, brought in family members who added more permanence to the developing society. However, many immigrants also intermingled with Native Americans and people from countries other than those from which they themselves came. The federal Naturalization Act of 1790 focused on the majority immigration group and, as such, applied exclusively to free white people. During the mid-nineteenth century, Chinese workers, many of them gold prospectors and railroad workers, arrived in the United States. Negative American reactions to the presence of this distinctly different group prompted the U.S. Congress to enact the Chinese Exclusion Act of 1882, which prevented Chinese from becoming naturalized citizens. During the late nineteenth and early twentieth centuries, Japanese and other immigrants were also prohibited from becoming naturalized citizens. However, an 1855 law gave citizenship to foreign-born women who married American men.

During the mid-nineteenth and early twentieth centuries, the pool of immigrants entering the United States grew more diversified and included large numbers of people from southern and eastern Europe. In response to this new immigration, Congress enacted a series of restrictive laws that resulted in a U.S. quota system based on early migration patterns. These laws banned members of specific ethnic groups from immigrating, including those who were spouses of U.S. citizens.

During the 1940's, some American military personnel who went overseas during World War II wanted to return home with their spouses from other countries. Under public pressure, Congress amended immigration laws for this purpose. The 1945 War Brides Act and the 1946 Fiancées Act relaxed immigration restrictions by permitting many foreign spouses and children to immigrate to the United States. Previously excluded populations were still banned from immigrating, but in 1947, the Soldiers Bride Act changed that by allowing formerly barred spouses to enter the United States. Japanese, Filipino, Korean, and other foreign-born spouses of American service personnel then began entering the United States under a nonquota system. The Immigration and Nationality Act of 1952 continued the quota system but granted some Asians immigration privileges and made family reunification a choice method for migration. Nonquota immigrants who came to the United States under this law left open quota slots for other immigrants.

CHANGES FOLLOWING THE IMMIGRATION ACT OF 1965

The Immigration and Nationality Act Amendment of 1965 brought sweeping changes to immigration policy, including the elimination of the quota system. Family reunification was now among the highest preferences for legal migration and put foreign spouses second in line after children of American citizens. This new amendment opened the door for foreign-born immigrants from nations that were barred in 1924. Consequently, Latin American and Asian immigration surged dramatically.

During the early 1970's, American citizens gained the right to petition for their fiancés to be issued nonimmigrant K-1 visas, which permitted fiancés to visit the United States for periods of up to ninety days they actually married. By this time, family reunification was a driving force in qualifying for immigration, but it was causing consternation among some Americans who feared that sham marriages, or "marriages of convenience," would proliferate as a means of avoiding the stricter immigration regulations applying to other categories of immigrants. As a result, the Immigration and Marriage Fraud Amendments (1986) made permanent residency a conditional status that required later proof of marriage validity. Ten years later, the Illegal Immigration Reform and Immigrant Responsibility Act of 1996 codified the responsibilities of American citizens who sponsor aliens.

In 2000, the Legal Immigration Family Equity Act, or LIFE Act, amended the rules for K-1 visas by permitting citizens and permanent residents to bring their spouses and children to the United States under a long-term resident category. Although this amendment raised some concerns regarding the potential for dramatic increases in immigration, it was also seen as a method of easing family dislocations, improving immigrant assimilation, and aiding social and cultural integration.

Throughout American history, men have used long-distance correspondence to find spouses, also known as mail-order brides, in other countries. Modern technology—most notably the World Wide Web and the Internet—and marriage brokers have increased this practice as a legitimate method of migrating to the United States.

Cynthia J. W. Svoboda

FURTHER READING

Bean, Frank D., and Gillian Stevens. *America's Newcomers and the Dynamics of Diversity.* New York: Russell Sage Foundation, 2003. Study of recent immigration and its impact on American society.

Constable, Nicole. *Romance on a Global Stage: Pen Pals, Virtual Ethnography, and "Mail Order" Marriages.* Berkeley: University of California Press, 2003. Research on the practice in which American men use introduction agencies to find Chinese and Filipina wives.

Cott, Nancy F. *Public Vows: A History of Marriage and the Nation.* Cambridge, Mass.: Harvard University Press, 2000. Wide-ranging study of the legal and social institution of marriage in the United States.

Gordon, Linda W. "Trends in the Gender Ratio of Immigrants to the United States." *International Migration Review* 39, no. 4 (Winter, 2005): 796-818. Provides information on recent immigration and the immigration laws that pertain to spousal migration.

Jasso, Guillermina, and Mark R. Rosenzweig. *The New Chosen People: Immigrants in the United States.* New York: Russell Sage Foundation, 1990. Analysis of marriage and family reunification among immigrants in the United States.

SEE ALSO: Amerasian children; Cable Act of 1922; Child immigrants; Families; Filipino immigrants; Mail-order brides; Marriage; "Marriages of convenience"; War brides; War Brides Act of 1945.

INTERNATIONAL LADIES' GARMENT WORKERS' UNION

IDENTIFICATION: Industrial labor union
DATES: 1900-1995
ALSO KNOWN AS: ILGWU

SIGNIFICANCE: The International Ladies' Garment Workers' Union improved working conditions for garment makers, most of whom were immigrants. Under the leadership of David Dubinsky, himself an immigrant, the union became recognized as one of the most powerful labor unions in the United States.

The International Ladies' Garment Workers' Union (ILGWU), originally formed by the amalgamation of seven unions, at first consisted mostly of eastern European Jewish immigrants, although a few of the original two thousand members were of Irish descent. For years, the union was characterized by internal strife, mainly among the immigrants, many of whom were anarchists, socialists, or members of other radical groups; each group wanted to dominate the union. Still, the union grew.

From 1909 to 1911, large-scale strikes occurred in the garment industry. Most of the people in the picket lines were Jewish women, though a number of Italian immigrants also joined the lines. As a result of the strikes, clothing manufacturers agreed to deal directly with the ILGWU. Part of the settlement of the strikes involved the Protocol of Peace, which led to improved working conditions, increased wages, and shorter workdays for garment industry workers. The agreement was a departure from the strife that many of the immigrant members had brought to the union.

Official seal of the International Ladies' Garment Workers' Union. (The Granger Collection, New York)

The ethnic makeup of the ILGWU changed over the decades. In 1919, many Italian women's unions were chartered as part of the ILGWU, and an even larger number of Italian immigrants joined the union during the 1930's. Also during that decade, immigrants from Asian countries such as Syria, Lebanon, and Armenia entered the garment trade and eventually joined the ILGWU. Later, thousands of Latin American workers, including Puerto Ricans and Mexicans, entered the garment trade and became ILGWU members.

The union thrived under the leadership of David Dubinsky, a Polish immigrant who moved to New York City in 1911, where he worked as a cloak cutter and soon joined the ILGWU. During the 1920's, the communists tried to take over the union, but the moderates, led by Dubinsky, stopped them. Dubinsky became union president in 1932 and remained in that position until he retired in 1966. While he was union president, ILGWU membership grew significantly, especially during the Great Depression and the 1940's. By 1942, the ILGWU had about 300,000 members. Many historians have argued that under Dubinsky's leadership, the ILGWU became one of the most effective American labor unions. By the 1960's, however, the number of garment workers in the United States was begining to decline as a result of cheaper clothing

imports and the offshoring of factories. After Dubinsky's retirement, the ILGWU started to lose membership.

By 1995, the union had only about 125,000 members. That year, it united with the Amalgamated Clothing and Textile Workers' Union to form the Union of Needletrades, Industrial and Textile Employees (UNITE!), representing more than 250,000 members. During its time, the ILGWU bettered working conditions for thousands of immigrants in the garment industry. It improved the sanitation, safety, and comfort of the workplace and won living wages and respect for workers.

Richard Tuerk

FURTHER READING

Bender, Daniel E. *Sweated Work, Weak Bodies: Anti-Sweatshop Campaigns and Languages of Labor.* New Brunswick, N.J.: Rutgers University Press, 2005.

Danish, Max D. *The World of David Dubinsky.* Cleveland: World Publishing, 1957.

Wolensky, Kenneth C., Nicole Wolensky, and Robert P. Wolensky. *Fighting for the Union Label: The Women's Garment Industry and the ILGWU in Pennsylvania.* University Park: Pennsylvania State University Press, 2002.

SEE ALSO: Garment industry; Great Depression; Industrial Workers of the World; Irish immigrants; Italian immigrants; Jewish immigrants; Labor unions; Mexican immigrants; Puerto Rican immigrants; Sweatshops; Triangle Shirtwaist fire; Women immigrants.

IOWA

SIGNIFICANCE: The interactive relationship between the land, immigration, and settlement patterns in the Iowa region has influenced its history, culture, and institutions. Many of the ethnic languages have faded with the third generations of immigrants, but the core values of family and community remain an ideological stronghold in Iowa.

Iowa's first settlers came from the eastern and Old Northwest states of Ohio, Pennsylvania, New York, Indiana, Kentucky, and Virginia. These groups often resided and lived in one other state before finally moving on to Iowa. Because there was a lack of timber in many parts of the state, many settlers constructed sod houses.

By the mid-nineteenth century, settlers were pouring into the region. Iowans began to plan the first railroad in the state with the development of the Illinois Central. while the Chicago and Northwestern eventually reached Council Bluffs near Omaha. Council Bluffs became the main eastern hub for the Union Pacific. A few years later, the Chicago, Milwaukee, St. Paul, and Pacific completed a line across the state for trading and shipping products and crops. The state eventually had five railroad lines, which contributed significantly to the growth of the agricultural sector for immigrant farmers.

Hoping to attract more foreign-born settlers, state government officials government arranged the publication of a booklet titled *Iowa: The Home for Immigrants* (1870). Promoting the social, political, educational, and physical attributes of the state, the ninety-six-page booklet was issued in English, Dutch, and Swedish editions. In 1870, the state's population rose from 675,000 to 1,194,000. Germans constituted the largest ethnic group. Many Germans took up such professions as shopkeepers, newspaper editors, schoolteachers, bankers, and craftsmen. Other groups whom Iowa attracted from Europe included Swedes, Danes, Hollanders, and Britons. Members of these groups tended to concentrate within specific counties. For example, Scandinavians settled in Winneshiek and Story counties, Swedes in Boone County, and Danes in southwestern Iowa.

TWENTIETH CENTURY DEVELOPMENTS

After 1900, a coal mining industry began to emerge in Buxton, located in the state's northern Monroe County. Many southern and eastern immigrant groups went into the industry's low-skilled jobs because they did not require much training. Italian men often immigrated to the United States alone, working in the coal industry until they saved

PROFILE OF IOWA

Region	Midwest
Entered union	1846
Largest cities	Des Moines (capital), Cedar Rapids, Davenport, Sioux City
Modern immigrant communities	Hispanics

Population	Total	Percent of state	Percent of U.S.	U.S. rank
All state residents	2,982,000	100.0	0.99	30
All foreign-born residents	112,000	3.8	0.29	36

Source: U.S. Census Bureau, *Statistical Abstract for 2006.*
Notes: The U.S. population in 2006 was 299,399,000, of whom 37,548,000 (12.5%) were foreign born. Rankings in last column reflect total numbers, not percentages.

enough money to send for their families. By 1925, Iowa's coal industry was beginning a steady decline. By the mid-1950's, only a few underground mines remained in the state. After World War II, the state's economy improved with a rise in the manufacturing sector, which manufactured such products as appliances, fountain pens, food products, and farm implements.

The late twentieth century saw an influx of Hispanic immigrants in Iowa. Many of them were undocumented. In May, 2008, federal immigration authorities raided Agriprocessors, Inc, the nation's largest kosher meatpacking plant. and rounded up 389 illegal immigrants, who faced deportation. The raid also found that the plant used underage workers and abused Iowa labor laws in other ways.

Gayla Koerting

FURTHER READING

Dinnen, Steve. "How an Immigration Raid Changed a Town: Tiny Postville, Iowa, Struggles to Regain Its Footing One Year After the Largest Immigration Sweep in U.S. History." *Christian Science Monitor,* May 31, 2009.

Iowa: The Home for Immigrants—Being a Treatise on the Resources of Iowa. Des Moines, Iowa: Mills, 1870.

Michaud, Marie-Christine. *From Steel Tracks to Gold-Paved Streets: The Italian Immigrants and the Railroad in the North Central States.* New York: Center for Migration Studies, 2005.

Stellingwerff, Johan. *Iowa Letters: Dutch Immigrants*

on the American Frontier. Translated by Walter Lagerwey. Grand Rapids, Mich.: William B. Eerdmans, 2004.

SEE ALSO: American Protective Association; Farm and migrant workers; Illinois; Kansas; Mississippi River; Missouri; Nebraska; Railroads.

IRANIAN IMMIGRANTS

SIGNIFICANCE: Iranian immigration to the United States is a recent phenomenon and has taken place primarily since 1975. The Islamic fundamentalist revolution of the late 1970's that transformed Iran into a theocratic state was a major world event that increased Iranian migration to the United States and created some negative stereotypes of Iranians among Americans. Some large Iranian American communities have developed, most notably in the region of Los Angeles.

The first recorded immigrants from Iran to the United States arrived during the 1920's, when 208 people from Iran (or Persia, as the country was then generally known) came to the United States. Their numbers increased over the next four decades but still remained comparatively small. Im-

PROFILE OF IRANIAN IMMIGRANTS

Country of origin	Iran
Primary language	Farsi
Primary regions of U.S. settlement	California
Earliest significant arrivals	1920's
Peak immigration period	1979-2008
Twenty-first century legal residents*	93,195 (11,649 per year)

*Immigrants who obtained legal permanent resident status in the United States.

Source: Department of Homeland Security, *Yearbook of Immigration Statistics, 2008.*

migration and Naturalization Service data show only 9,059 people coming from Iran during the 1960's. In the 1970's through the 1990's, Iranian immigration shot up dramatically. Between 1970 and 1979, 33,763 Iranians immigrated legally to the United States. During the 1980's, this figure went up to 98,141 and decreased only slightly, to 76,899, during 1990's. Between 2000 and 2008, 67,915 new residents came from Iran.

By 1980, the Iranian-born population of the U.S. amounted to 130,000 people, compared to only about 24,000 a mere ten years earlier. More than 70 percent of this 1980 population had arrived during the second half of the 1970's, so they were an extremely new group. They were concentrated on the West Coast, with four out of ten Iranian residents of the United States living in California alone and one out of five living in the Los Angeles-Long Beach metropolitan area. The Iranian-born population continued to expand into the twenty-first century, growing from slightly more than 204,000 in 1990 to more than 290,000 in 2000 and to about 328,000 in 2007.

REVOLUTION AND IMMIGRATION

Much of the immigration from Iran to the United States resulted from political unrest in Iran and as a consequence of people fleeing the Iranian Revolution of 1978-1979 and the creation of the Islamic Republic in 1980. As a state devoted to the majority religion of the Shia form of Islam, the Iranian republic has been intolerant of minority religions. While an estimated 98 percent of Iranians are Shia Muslims, immigrants to the United States have disproportionately contained adherents of Iran's minority religions, which include Sunni Muslims, Zoroastrians, Jews, Baha'is, and Christians. Between the time of the revolution and 1990, the easiest way for an Iranian to obtain legal permission to enter the U.S. was by obtaining refugee status. Even after that time, Iranian refugees entered the United States at a rate of about 2,700 per year. From 1990 to 2008, nearly 50,000 people from Iran were admitted to the United States as refugees. However, not all these people were included in the official immigration statistics, because they were all accepted as refugees receiving legal permanent resident status.

Another important way that Iranians have entered the United States has been to come as stu-

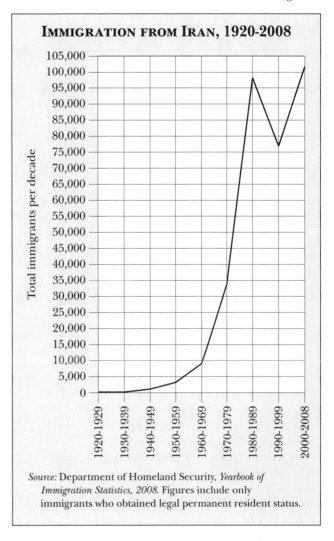

dents and then apply for legal residence. Generally, Iranians who have sought student or other types of visas have usually gone to Turkey first, became the United States closed its embassy in Iran after 1979. Before the revolution, Iran went through a rapid period of development, so that it has many well-educated people. In addition, many Iranian high school students had already studied English by the early 1970's, and knowledge of this language has made it easier for Iranian students to gain admission to American colleges and universities.

The period of tension between the United States and Iran immediately following the revolution created some problems for Iranians living in the United States. With the tacit approval of their new government, Iranians seized the American embassy in the capital of Tehran. They held Americans captive there for 444 days, creating an international crisis that contributed to U.S. president Jimmy Carter's electoral defeat in 1980 and caused strong anti-Iranian sentiments to sweep across the United States. The U.S. responded by instituting an "Iranian Control Program," which scrutinized the immigration status of nearly 60,000 people studying in the United States. In addition, even Iranian immigrants who were opposed to the new government in their country sometimes experienced open expressions of public hostility.

IRANIANS IN THE UNITED STATES

By 2007, the geographic concentration of Iranian immigrants had grown greater. About 60 percent of them lived in California, with more than one-third of Iranian-born people in the United States living in the Los Angeles-Long Beach metropolitan area and another 7 percent in nearby Orange County. Outside California, the largest numbers of Iranians could be found in Texas (home to about 6 percent) and in New York State (also about 6 percent). However, there were at least some Iranians in most of the states.

Because of their generally high levels of education, Iranians in the United States have tended to work in white-collar, professional occupations. In 2007, more than one-fifth of them worked as managers, officials, or proprietors. Other common occupations included salespeople, professional and technical workers, and physicians and surgeons. The most common industrial concentrations were in educational services or medical services. However, compared to native-born American women, Iranian women have shown relatively low labor force participation. In 2007, only about half of Iranian-born women in the United States were in the labor force.

Carl L. Bankston III

FURTHER READING

Ansari, Maboud. *The Making of the Iranian Community in America.* New York: Pardis Press, 1992. Useful overview of the growth of the Iranian immigrant community in the United States.

Bozorgmehr, Mehdi. "Iran." In *The New Americans: A Guide to Immigration Since 1965,* edited by Mary C. Waters, Reed Ueda, and Helen B. Marrow. Cambridge, Mass.: Harvard University Press, 2007. Best available short overview of Iranian immigration, written by a highly respected authority on this topic.

Dumas, Firoozeh. *Funny in Farsi: A Memoir of Growing Up Iranian in America.* New York: Villard, 2003. Warmly personal memoir of the experiences of an Iranian American.

Karim, Perssis, and Mehid M. Khortami, eds. *A World in Between: Poems, Stories, and Essays by Iranian-Americans.* New York: George Braziller, 1999. Anthology of literary works by Iranian immigrants that illustrate the experiences of Iranians in the United States.

Naficy, Maid. *The Making of Exile Cultures: Iranian Television in Los Angeles.* Minneapolis: University of Minnesota Press, 1993. Examination of how Iranian television has influenced group identity in the large ethnic community in Los Angeles.

Sharavini, Mitra K. *Educating Immigrants: Experiences of Second Generation Iranians.* New York: LFB Scholarly Publishing, 2004. Emphasizes the importance Iranian immigrants place on education for their children and looks at the relative success of Iranian ancestry students in American schools.

SEE ALSO: Arab immigrants; California; Israeli immigrants; Los Angeles; Muslim immigrants; Pakistani immigrants; Refugees; Religions of immigrants.

IRISH IMMIGRANTS

SIGNIFICANCE: During the early nineteenth century, Ireland was one of the main sources of immigration to the United States. Irish immigrants provided much of the labor for American cities and transportation systems and helped to establish Roman Catholicism in the United States.

The first identifiable wave of Irish migration to the United States began in 1729, when a poor harvest and a depression in the linen trade created economic hardship in Ireland. By 1784, just after the American Revolutionary War, an estimated 400,000 Irish lived in the new United States. During the six decades leading up the U.S. Civil War (1861-1865), the Irish became one of the nation's largest and most recognizable minority groups. Despite a decline in migration from Ireland in the twentieth century, Irish immigrants and their descendants have continued to play an important part in American history.

EARLY IRISH IMMIGRATION

The majority of the Irish in America before the nineteenth century were those who later became known as Scotch-Irish, descendants of people from Scotland who had moved to the northern part of Ireland in earlier centuries. These northern Irish were mainly Protestant, and distinctions between the them and other Irish immigrants came into popular usage in the nineteenth century when much larger numbers of Roman Catholic Irish began to arrive. Northern Irish migration peaked between the 1750's and the early 1770's, with an estimated 14,200 people from Northern Ireland reaching America during the 1750's, 21,200 during the 1760's, and 13,200 during the first of the 1770's, leading up to the American Revolution. Most of the pre-Revolutionary War immigration from Ireland took place between 1760 and 1775, when about 25,000 new arrivals came to the colonies.

The first U.S. Census in 1790 may have underestimated the proportion of the population that was of Irish background. However, in 1931 scholars who studied the linguistic and national background origin of the American people at the time of that first U.S. Census estimated that about one out of every ten Americans in 1790 was of Irish ancestry, including both Protestants and a smaller numbers of Catholics. The 1931 estimates indicated that people of Irish ancestry could be found in all parts of the new nation, but that they made up the largest proportions of populations in the South. According to these figures, in 1790, people of Irish background made up 15 percent of residents in Georgia, 14 percent in South Carolina, 12 percent in Kentucky and Tennessee, and 11 percent in Virginia and North Carolina. As immigration from Ireland and other parts of Europe increased during the first half of the nineteenth century, however, the new immigrants tended to settle in the North and in the most urbanized parts of the country, rather than in the rural South.

EARLY NINETEENTH CENTURY IMMIGRATION

Movement from Ireland to the United States continued into the nineteenth century and began to increase in response to new opportunities. Notably, the U.S. began to build up its first transportation infrastructure, in the form of canals. The Erie Canal in New York State, perhaps the best known of these waterways, was under construction from 1818 to 1825. That project drew heavily on immigrant Irish labor, beginning the long history of building the American transportation infrastructure with Irish workers. The success of the Erie Canal stimulated the digging of canals in other parts of the country, creating a growing demand for workers who were willing to endure the hard labor required in canal building. Somewhat later, the Illinois & Michigan Canal, created between 1837 and 1848, employed hundreds of Irish laborers. To the south, Irish workers dug the canal system of swampy New Orleans.

Reliable data on how many Irish reached American shores date only from 1820. In 1819, the United States passed the Steerage Act. It gave the U.S. government information on immigration by requiring that all vessels reaching American shores deliver passenger lists to customs officials, who then sent copies to the U.S. State Department. That department would, in turn, submit the lists to Congress. As a result, 1820 became the first year in which the U.S. systematically collected data on new arrivals. During that same year, the Irish made up the single largest immigrant group, accounting for 43 percent of all arrivals to the United States.

Irish immigration continued at high levels throughout the decades leading up to the Civil War. The numbers of Irish immigrants rose from 51,617 during the 1820's to 170,672 during the 1830's, increasing still further to 656,145 during the 1840's. During the decade of the 1850's, the number of people arriving in the United States from Ireland reached its historical peak at 1,029,486.

One reason that the flow from Ireland increased during these years was that the demand for their labor continued to rise. The railroads made up the second major part of the American transportation

PROFILE OF IRISH IMMIGRANTS

Countries of origin	Ireland, United Kingdom
Primary language	English
Primary regions of U.S. settlement	All regions
Earliest significant arrivals	1729
Peak immigration period	1830's-1920's
Twenty-first century legal residents*	12,379 (1,547 per year)

*Immigrants who obtained legal permanent resident status in the United States.
Source: Department of Homeland Security, Yearbook of Immigration Statistics, 2008.

system, after the canals. In 1830, the United States had only 23 miles of railroad. Only one decade later, this figure had grown to 2,818 miles. It increased to 9,021 miles in 1850 and then to 30,626 miles in 1860. Immigrants from Ireland, in particular, laid these miles of tracks.

The Irish were also pushed out of their native land by poverty and hunger as the middle of the century approached. The Potato Blight created famine in Ireland in the years 1845 to 1850. Continuing hardship, in addition to the existence of established Irish communities around the United States, pushed immigration from Ireland to its record level in the 1850's.

By the middle of the nineteenth century, Irish Americans were an urban and working class group. Only 16 percent of people born in Ireland lived on farms in the United States in 1850, compared to well over one-half of all Americans. A majority of the Irish in the United States (53 percent) lived in urban areas, at a time when urban areas were home to only 15 percent of the people in the nation. While only about 15 percent of all workers in the country were listed as laborers by occupation, about half the Irish natives in the census of that 1850 were so identified.

Anti-Irish feeling among other groups in the United States resulted, in part, from the concentration of many Irish immigrants in lower-income districts of cities, which caused the Irish to be associated with urban slums. Prejudice against this group also resulted from religious differences. Most Irish immigrants who arrived after 1830 were Roman Catholics. The established population of the United States was mainly Protestant. Suspicion of Catholics in general and of Irish Catholics in particular led to the creation of a number of anti-Catholic organizations. The Native American Party, later renamed the American Party and popularly known as the "Know-Nothing" Party, was the most prominent of these. Fear that floods of Catholics from Ireland and other locations threatened to overwhelm the native-born, Protestant population produced widespread victories for this anti-immigrant and anti-Catholic party in elections across the nation in 1855 and 1856.

Irish Immigrants during the U.S. Civil War

By 1860, a year before the Civil War broke out, well over 1.5 million people born in Ireland were living in the United States; they constituted about 6 percent of the country's total population and about 40 percent of its foreign-born population. New York State held the greatest number of Irish immigrants. Its 500,000 Irish residents made up about 13 percent of its entire population. More than 200,000 Irish immigrants lived in New York City alone, and Brooklyn, then still separate from New York City proper, was home to another 60,000.

Massachusetts had the second-largest number of residents who had been born in Ireland in 1860. Its nearly 200,000 Irish immigrants accounted for just over 16 percent of the whole population of the state. The city of Boston in Massachusetts held nearly 50,000 Irish-born people One out of every five of the people in tiny Rhode Island in 1860 had come from Ireland.

Although most of the Irish immigrants settled in the northeast, they could be found in almost all U.S. states. The southern states that were about to secede from the Union were home to about 100,000 Irish-born people. Louisiana alone was home to more than 26,000 people from Ireland during the last year before the war. The Irish were living on both sides of the divide when the Southern states attempted to secede from the Union, but they were more heavily represented in the North. An estimated 150,000 Irish served in the Union Army, while about 30,000 are believed to have fought for the Confederacy.

The best-known Irish fighting force during the Civil War was the New York Irish Brigade, which saw service from the time of the Battle of Bull Run in July, 1861. Nearly forty other Union regiments had "Irish" in their names. On the Confederate side, Irish fighting forces included the First Virginia Battalion and the Tenth Tennessee Regiment. Irish immigrants and descendants of Irish immigrants also served as individual soldiers in most of the other forces of both sides.

The heavy representation of the Irish in the Civil War was not always voluntary. Both sides drafted soldiers, drawing most heavily among poorer people, such as the Irish. In the North, the Enrollment Act of 1863 enabled any drafted person who paid a fee of three hundred U.S. dollars to hire a substitute draftee. Many low-income Irish immigrants believed that they were fighting on behalf of rich men.

Congress passed the Enrollment Act at a time when many Irish in northern cities were already becoming disenchanted with the war. Irish soldiers had suffered heavy casualties by 1863. As urban laborers, Irish workers were also competing with black workers. When President Abraham Lincoln announced the Emancipation Proclamation on January 1, 1863, many of these workers began to believe that the primary goal of the war was to free black slaves, rather than to preserve national unity. When local authorities used black workers to break a mainly Irish dock strike in New York in the spring of 1863, the anti-war and anti-black feelings of many New York Irish intensified.

On July 10, 1863, government officials posted the first list of draftees under the Enrollment Act. In New York, it seemed evident that the Irish wards were supplying more conscripts than other parts of the city. In response, protesters marched on the city recruiting station. The protests turned into riots, during which blacks became especially targeted. The rioters burned the Colored Orphan Asylum and beat up and lynched a number of New York's black residents. During the week that followed, more than one hundred riot victims died, and another 1,500 suffered serious injuries. The New York draft riots ended only after Union troops returned from the Battle of Gettysburg to reestablish order, and the city voted $2.5 million to buy exemptions.

Despite the draft riots and the resentment they

revealed, Irish immigrants fought in every battle of the Civil War. With the end of the war, the United States entered a new period of rapid industrialization and soon began welcoming a great tide of new immigrants. The Irish continued to be a significant part of immigration after the Civil War; however, the vast numbers of immigrants coming from other countries meant that Ireland no longer dominated international movement to the United States as it had done before the Civil War.

IMMIGRATION DURING AND AFTER THE GREAT WAVE

The Civil War was enormously destructive, but it also helped to stimulate the American economy and to push the United States toward more industrialization. As the nation entered the 1880's, it en-

tered into a remarkable period of economic expansion that transformed the United States into one of the world's greatest industrial powers by the time of World War I (1914-1918). It also began a dramatic rise in immigration as part of this economic expansion. Sources of immigration also began to shift, from northern and western European countries to southern and eastern European countries.

During this great immigration wave, immigrants continued to arrive from Ireland in significant numbers, but these numbers never again reached their peak of the 1850's. Irish migration actually began to decrease gradually around the turn of the twentieth century, even as overall numbers of immigrants to the United States were rapidly growing. As Irish immigration slowed, the Irish-born population of the United States gradually decreased

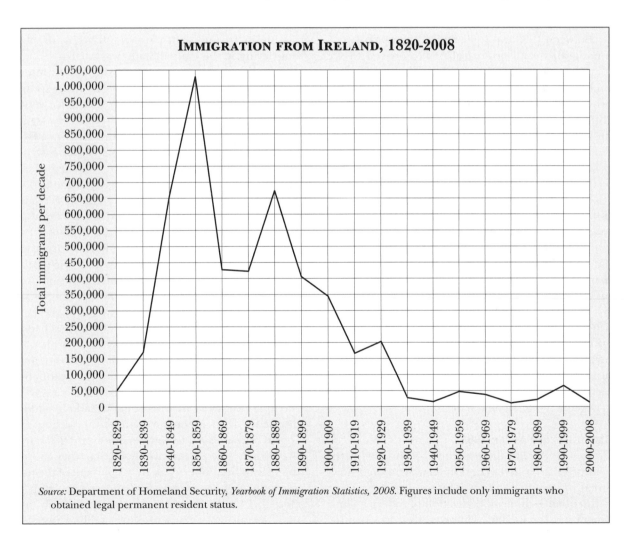

IMMIGRATION FROM IRELAND, 1820-2008

Source: Department of Homeland Security, Yearbook of Immigration Statistics, 2008. Figures include only immigrants who obtained legal permanent resident status.

from its maximum of about 1,870,000 people in 1880.

The heavy immigration of earlier years still meant that many locations in the United States had large Irish communities at the opening of the twentieth century. By 1900, the Irish-born population of the New York City metropolitan area had grown to an estimated 366,000 people. Another 650,000 residents of the New York area were children of Irish immigrants. Nearly 200,000 of the people in metropolitan Boston were from Ireland, and another 320,000 were children of Irish immigrants. In many cities across the United States, the existence of Irish American communities provided a basis for ethnically based politics and economic activity. The Kennedy family, which later produced America's first Roman Catholic president in the person of John F. Kennedy, arose from the Irish community of Boston.

Between 1900 and 1909, only 4.2 percent of new immigrants came from Ireland, compared to 43 percent one-half century earlier. The proportion of foreign-born people living in the United States who were from Ireland dropped from 44 percent in 1850 to 15.8 percent in 1900 and about 7.2 percent in 1920. In 1880, 10 percent of all Americans had at least one parent who had been born in Ireland. By 1910, this figure had dropped to 5.7 percent. Nevertheless, the latter figure meant that even as late as 1910, after decades of heavy southern and eastern European immigration, more than one of every twenty people in the United States was the child of an Irish immigrant. People from Ireland or with family links to Ireland still made up a substantial part of the American population in the early twentieth century.

The great wave of immigration came to an end when the United States adopted restrictive immigration policies during the 1920's. Afterward, the overall number of immigrants decreased steadily until the late 1960's. Irish immigration also dropped sharply, both in absolute numbers and as a percentage of all new arrivals.

IMMIGRATION AFTER 1965

During the last three decades of the twentieth century, the United States began welcoming a new great wave of immigrants. This was in large part a consequence of the liberalization of American immigration law in 1965. However, Ireland's contribution to this new wave was relatively small. During the 1970's, people from Ireland made up only 0.2 percent of immigrants to the United States. During the 1980's, they made up only 0.4 percent.

The government of Ireland helped to keep this migration at a relatively low level. The nation's leadership had become concerned about the loss of young people from Ireland's relatively small population during the middle of the twentieth century. During the early 1960's, the government in Dublin persuaded the administration of U.S. president John F. Kennedy to reduce the number of American visas available to potential Irish migrants. In addition, the Immigration and Nationality Act of 1965 gave first preference to immigrants who had immediate family members living in the United States. Because Irish immigration had been relatively small for decades and was then limited by agreement between the two nations, the number of people in Ireland with parents, children, or siblings living in the United States was small.

Irish immigration surged in the 1990's after Connecticut congressman Bruce Morrison sponsored a special green card lottery system for visas that became known as "Morrison visas." New legal residents from Ireland jumped from 4,767 in 1990 to 12,226 in 1991 as Morrison visas became available. However, the Morrison lottery ended after only three years and Irish immigration began to decrease again. The temporary increase in arrivals did not change the historical trend of a decreasing Irish-born population in the United States. By 2007, fewer than 170,000 people born in Ireland were living in the United States, less than one-tenth the number of the Irish-born residents during the late nineteenth century, even though the total American population was much larger at the beginning of the twenty-first century than it had been a century earlier.

Despite the comparatively small numbers of immigrants from Ireland at the end of the twentieth century and beginning of the twenty-first century, the long history of Irish settlement had created a distinctive Irish American identity. According to census estimates made between 2005 and 2007, by the first decade of the twenty-first century more than 22 million Americans, or 7.5 percent of the total population, gave their first ancestry as "Irish"; close to 14 million, or 4.6 percent, gave "Irish" as their second ancestry. Close to 4 million people gave Scotch-Irish as their first ancestry and another 1.5 million gave that as their second ancestry. Altogether, more than 41 million Americans, 14 percent of the total population, traced at least part of their heritage to the Emerald Isle during the early twenty-first century.

Carl L. Bankston III

FURTHER READING

Dolan, Jay P. *The Irish Americans: A History.* New York: Bloomsbury Press, 2008. History of Irish Americans from the early eighteenth through the early twenty-first centuries. The author examines Irish American history by focusing on the four themes of politics, religion, labor, and nationalism.

Griffin, William D. *The Irish Americans: The Immigrant Experience.* New York: Beaux Arts Editions, 2001. Lavishly illustrated history of Irish Americans, with more than two hundred black-and-white and color paintings and photographs.

Ignatiev, Noel. *How the Irish Became White.* New York: Routledge, 1996. Influential work that argues that the Irish were an oppressed social class and were even seen as members of a distinct race before the Civil War. Ignatiev maintains that the Irish became recognized as "white" in large part by embracing the antiblack racism of other Americans.

Laxton, Edward. *The Famine Ships: The Irish Exodus to America.* New York: Henry Holt, 1998. Based on research in Ireland and compilations of stories passed down to Irish immigrant descendants in America, the author tells the histories of Irish immigrants from 1846 to 1851.

Lee, J. J., and Marion R. Casey, eds. *Making the Irish American: History and Heritage of the Irish in the United States.* New York: New York University Press, 2006. Massive compilation of articles on the Americanization of the Irish, containing both original research and classic articles on this topic. An excellent resource on Irish settlement in America.

McCarthy, Cal. *Green, Blue and Grey: The Irish in the American Civil War.* Cork, Ireland: Collins Press, 2009. Detailed history of Irish soldiers fighting on both sides in the Civil War.

Miller, Kerby, and Patricia Mulholland Miller. *Journey of Hope: The Story of Irish Immigration to America.* San Francisco: Chronicle Books, 2001. Uses letters, journals, and diaries of immigrants to recount the history of Irish immigration and the experiences of Irish immigrants in America.

SEE ALSO: Anti-Catholicism; Boston; British immigrants; Civil War, U.S.; European immigrants; Fenian movement; Flanagan, Edward J.; Great Irish Famine; History of immigration, 1783-1891; Know-Nothing Party; Molly Maguires; Philadelphia anti-Irish riots.

IRON AND STEEL INDUSTRY

DEFINITION: Enterprises involved in the mining of iron ore, its smelting and processing, its conversion to steel, and its distribution to other industries

SIGNIFICANCE: Immigrants to the United States were in many ways responsible for the rise and success of the nation's large iron and steel industry. Most important, their labor made it possible for the significant growth and prosperity of steel manufacturing in America during the late nineteenth and early twentieth centuries.

The growth of the iron and steel industries in the United States has seen a corresponding rise in the employment of European immigrants in the manufacturing of these products. Before 1880, workers in iron and steel facilities of the United States had derived primarily from northern and western Europe, particularly from Great Britain. These mostly English, Welsh, and Scottish ironworkers, engineers, and other metalworkers arrived in the United States during the early to mid-nineteenth century. These skilled migrants, after having weighed their opportunities, chose to emigrate from the British Isles to take advantage of rising opportunities in America, which included the option of owning farmland. Not only did they sustain the development of the American iron industry, they also accelerated the implementation of new technological aspects in its production. Many of these immigrants worked and settled among the diverse iron industries located in Pennsylvania, the largest iron-producing state through much of the nineteenth century.

Pittsburgh, Pennsylvania, steelworkers in 1905. (The Granger Collection, New York)

LATE NINETEENTH CENTURY IMMIGRANTS

The iron and steel industry continued to progress after the U.S. Civil War, and an increasing need for labor corresponded to this growth. During the late nineteenth and early twentieth centuries in particular, steel companies increasingly employed various eastern and southern Europeans in the production and fabrication of steel products. These immigrants included large numbers of Slovaks, Hungarians, and Ukrainians who performed unskilled work in the mills and furnaces in the northern United States, particularly around such cities as Pittsburgh, Pennsylvania.

During this period, the size and scale of manufacturing facilities increased dramatically. The use of more machinery prompted producers to recruit additional unskilled laborers from eastern Europe. About 30,000 new steelworkers were working in American factories by 1900. The motivation of many of these new arrivals was to make enough money to return to Europe and live well in their native vil-

lages and towns. The majority migrants who eventually stayed hoped for advancement from the lowest-paid and hardest jobs in the mills to better positions. Many of these men came alone and lived in the boardinghouses and company towns operated by mill owners. As their economic condition improved, they sent for their families, who gradually displaced earlier northern and western European immigrants and their descendants in the steel factories and communities. Meanwhile, they existed a well as they could while working long, hazardous hours with low pay.

STRUGGLE TO UNIONIZE

Many native-born American workers believed that immigrants and their families would not fight against workplace and community injustice on their own accord, and that they would not strike or organize for better working conditions against an overwhelmingly powerful industry. Consequently, craft unions belonging to the American Federation of Labor were reluctant to recruit foreign-born laborers because of skill and ethnic prejudice. However, immigrant workers and their families proved many observers wrong with their participation during the Homestead, Pennsylvania, strike of 1892 and their spontaneous 1909 uprising against Pressed Steel Car in McKees Rocks, Pennsylvania. In the latter conflict, immigrant leaders seized the initiative and recruited organizers from the newly formed Industrial Workers of the World. They won some measure of success, until company officials set native-born against foreign-born workers and broke the unity of the strike.

Later struggles, especially the steel strike of 1919, witnessed even larger immigrant participation, despite successful corporate employment of nativist prejudice and armed force. It was the formation of the Steelworkers' Organizing Committee and the support of the Congress of Industrial Organizations during the 1930's, along with a government that did not support the use of armed intervention, that led to the second and third generations of workers enjoying the fruits of unionized labor into the 1960's.

LIFE IN THE STEEL COMMUNITIES

Second- and third-generation immigrants and their families built more comfortable lives in steel communities such as Johnstown and Pittsburgh, Pennsylvania. and Youngstown, Ohio, from the 1940's through the 1960's. However, as succeeding generations were assimilating into American society, the nation also experienced a severe economic malaise beginning during the early 1970's that corresponded with corporate decisions to relocate entire steel facilities away from the northern United States. This deindustrialization of the steel industries during the 1970's and 1980's led to the wholesale closing of steel production in Youngstown and Pittsburgh that caused devastating unemployment. This, in turn, forced subsequent generations of immigrant children to struggle to survive in what was left of the industry in their communities or to search for other work elsewhere, away from their ancestral homes. Many of the hard-hit communities remained economically devastated into the twenty-first century. Some have survived to host other forms of employment and newer generations of ethnic families. All, however, still bear the imprints of their original immigrant communities.

James C. Koshan

FURTHER READING

Bell, Thomas. *Out of This Furnace: A Novel of Immigrant Labor.* Pittsburgh: University of Pittsburgh Press, 1976. Originally published in 1941, this classic historical novel is set in the steel mills and communities of Braddock, Pennsylvania, and based on Bell's family of largely Slovak heritage. It covers three generations, from the 1880's through the 1940's.

Brody, David. *Steelworkers in America: The Nonunion Era.* Champaign: University of Illinois Press, 1998. First published in 1960, this informative and well-researched account of iron and steel workers during the early decades of the twentieth century continues to fill in the gaps of the history of pre-unionized steelworkers and their struggles before the 1930's.

Hinshaw, John. *Steel and Steelworkers: Race and Class Struggle in Twentieth-Century Pittsburgh.* Albany: State University of New York Press, 2002. Analytical approach to the unfolding social problems engendered by working in the Pittsburgh steel industry and its effects on subsequent working-class families and communities as the industry declined.

Kleinberg, S. J. *The Shadow of the Mills: Working-Class Families in Pittsburgh, 1870-1907.* Pittsburgh, Pa.: University of Pittsburgh Press, 1989. Narrative work focusing on the lives of mill workers and their families away from the shop floors that utilizes primary sources to build a portrait of working-class life.

Krause, Paul. *The Battle for Homestead, 1880-1892: Politics, Culture, and Steel.* Pittsburgh, Pa.: University of Pittsburgh Press, 1992. Far-reaching, archival- based book on the struggles surrounding the community of Homestead that also provides the necessary context for understanding the infamous strike of 1892.

SEE ALSO: Alabama; Coal industry; Czech and Slovakian immigrants; Economic consequences of immigration; Economic opportunities; Employment; Goldman, Emma; Industrial Revolution; Industrial Workers of the World; Labor unions; Ohio; Pennsylvania.

ISRAELI IMMIGRANTS

SIGNIFICANCE: The state of Israel was established only in 1948, and much of its own population growth has come about through Jewish emigration from the United States and Europe. This makes analyses of migration *from* Israel to the United States uniquely complex. Many ostensible immigrants to the United States from Israel have been Jews who originated in the United States, emigrated to Israel, and later returned to North America. Some of these same returnees have even returned to Israel again. The subject is also complicated by the fact that immigrants to the United States from Israel have included Muslim and Christian Palestinians, who may or may not have been Israeli citizens. Moreover, some Palestinian immigrants who were legally Israeli citizens may not have identified with the Jewish state.

The number of immigrants to the United States whose last country of residence was Israel has grown steadily over the decades. From 1950 to 1959, 21,376 legal migrants from Israel were admitted into the United States. During the 1960's, that figure increased to 30,911 and in the 1980's to 43,669. After a slight dip to 41,340 during the 1990's, a total of 47,873 new immigrants arrived from Israel between 2000 and 2008. Estimates from U.S. Census data indicate that numbers of people born in Israel, or Palestine, in the United States grew from 94,500 in 1990 to 123,000 in 2000 and reached 154,000 in 2007.

According to the sociologist Steven J. Gold, a widely recognized authority on Israeli immigrants, Jewish Israelis in the United States have shown a number of distinctive characteristics. They have tended to have high levels of education and to work in professional fields, most notably in educa-

PROFILE OF ISRAELI IMMIGRANTS

Country of origin	Israel
Primary languages	Hebrew, English
Primary regions of U.S. settlement	California, New York State
Earliest significant arrivals	1950's
Twenty-first century legal residents*	36,516 (4,565 per year)

*Immigrants who obtained legal permanent resident status in the United States.
Source: Department of Homeland Security, *Yearbook of Immigration Statistics, 2008.*

tional services. According to early twenty-first century U.S. Census figures, about one-quarter of Israeli immigrants have been managers, officials, and proprietors. Other common occupations have been in sales, teaching, and professional and technical jobs. However, most Jewish Israeli immigrants have come to the United States in order to escape political unrest in the Middle East, not to seek improved economic opportunities. Consequently, although they have generally adapted well to American life and generally speak English fluently, a substantial number of them have avoided describing themselves as "Americans" and have expressed a desire eventually to return to Israel. Many continue to speak Israel's national language, Hebrew, at home.

Jewish Israelis live throughout the United States, but they are most heavily concentrated in New York City and Los Angeles. These two cities alone contain about half of all Jewish Israelis living in the United States. Other popular destinations for many Israeli immigrants have included Michigan, Florida, and Illinois. Israeli immigrants are frequently drawn to large established Jewish neighborhoods, such as Brooklyn and Queens in New York City and West Hollywood and the San Fernando Valley in the Los Angeles area.

Carl L. Bankston III

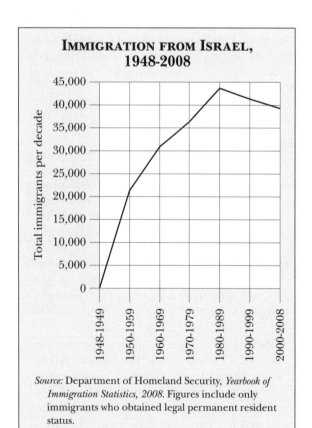

IMMIGRATION FROM ISRAEL, 1948-2008

Source: Department of Homeland Security, *Yearbook of Immigration Statistics, 2008.* Figures include only immigrants who obtained legal permanent resident status.

FURTHER READING

Gold, Steven J. *The Israeli Diaspora.* Seattle: University of Washington Press, 2002.

Gold, Steven J., and Bruce A. Phillips. "Israelis in the U.S." In *American Jewish Yearbook, 1996*. New York: American Jewish Committee, 1996.

O'Brien, Lee. *American Jewish Organizations and Israel*. Washington, D.C.: Institute for Palestine Studies, 1986.

Sobel, Zvi. *Migrants from the Promised Land*. New Brunswick, N.J.: Transaction Books, 1986.

Telushkin, Rabbi Joseph. *The Golden Land: The Story of Jewish Immigration to America*. New York: Harmony Books, 2002.

Worth, Richard. *Jewish Immigrants*. New York: Facts On File, 2005.

SEE ALSO: *Afroyim v. Rusk*; American Jewish Committee; Anti-Defamation League; Anti-Semitism; Arab immigrants; Dual citizenship; Emigration; Holocaust; Jewish immigrants; Los Angeles; Muslim immigrants; New York City.

ISSEI

IDENTIFICATION: First-generation Japanese immigrants

SIGNIFICANCE: During the mid-nineteenth century, after more than two centuries as a closed nation, Japan began permitting emigration to the United States. The Issei, the first generation of immigrants in the United States, quickly became a crucial element in the development of Pacific states' agricultural economies. However, because they were Asians and maintained tight-knit cultural neighborhoods with other Issei, they were perceived as a threat and faced bigotry as well as discriminatory legislation. Consequently, most Issei never had all the benefits of immigration enjoyed by members of many other immigrant groups.

The first Japanese to enter what is now the United States came to Hawaii in 1885, when the islands were still an independent kingdom. These first immigrants were mostly well-educated working-class men. Many were students and accomplished artisans who were interested in learning at first hand Western agricultural techniques and economic practices so they could help modernize their eco-nomically distressed homeland when they returned to Japan, which was then emerging from two centuries of rigid military rule that had closed off the nation from the international community. These immigrants were welcomed by the Hawaiian government as cheap labor to maintain the islands' extensive sugar cane and pineapple plantations.

These Issei immigrants quickly extended their range, as subsequent waves of migrants went to the Pacific Coast states, most notably California. There, the Issei faced significant challenges. They did not share the language, customs, religions, or history of the established first- and second-generation European immigrants. They were therefore viewed with considerable hostility even as their hard work and the quiet temperaments, derived from their Buddhist training in stoic endurance, made them important contributors to the economic success of the Pacific region. They were especially important in farming, fishing, mining, and railroad construction. By 1910, nearly 180,000 Issei were working in the Pacific coastal areas.

That influx, perceived to be just the beginning by conservative anti-Asian xenophobes, led to popular sentiments that Asian "hordes" would take away jobs belonging to Americans. Indeed, Asian immigrants faced violence as well as a coordinated campaign of bigoted rhetoric from organized labor. Ultimately they faced harsh government restrictions. For example, the controversial 1882 Chinese Exclusion Act was the first national legislation that prohibited a specific ethnic group from immigrating. Ironically, this law initially encouraged Japanese immigration, as the American labor force needed to replace the Chinese. However, the act also denied all Asian immigrants the right to become American citizens, thus ensuring that the Issei would be perpetual aliens in the United States.

In 1907, President Theodore Roosevelt negotiated the so-called Gentlemen's Agreement with Japan in which the Japanese government agreed to issue passports only to military personnel, diplomats, and merchants, thus eliminating working-class immigrants from Japan. In 1910, California passed the Alien Land Law, which prohibited "aliens" from purchasing farmland at a moment when Issei controlled roughly one-half million acres in the state. Anti-japanese sentiments were not nationally held; indeed, Japanese art and culture was a Jazz Age fad. However, the U.S. Congress enacted the Immigration Act of 1924, which aimed at ending all Japanese immigration.

After imperial Japan launched a surprise attack on the U.S. naval base at Pearl Harbor in Hawaii in December, 1941, bringing the United States into World War II, the federal government interred nearly one-third of the Issei living along the West Coast of the United States. Denied the right to vote or own land, segregated into ethnic schools, and branded as untrustworthy aliens, the Issei had only their Nisei children who were born in the United States to enjoy the benefits of American citizenship and economic prosperity.

Joseph Dewey

FURTHER READING

Ichioka, Yuji. *The Issei: The World of the First Generation Japanese Immigrants, 1885-1924.* New York: Free Press, 1988.

Nakane, Kazuko. *Nothing Left in My Hands: The Issei of a Rural California Town, 1900-1942.* Berkeley, Calif.: Heyday Books, 2009.

Tamura, Linda. *The Hood River Issei.* Champaign: University of Illinois Press, 1994.

SEE ALSO: Anti-Japanese movement; Asian American Legal Defense Fund; Asian immigrants; Asian Pacific American Labor Alliance; Gentlemen's Agreement; Immigration Act of 1924; Japanese American Citizens League; Japanese American internment; Japanese immigrants; Little Tokyos; "Yellow peril" campaign.

ITALIAN AMERICAN PRESS

DEFINITION: American news publications targeted at Italian American and immigrant Italian communities

SIGNIFICANCE: Newspapers, magazines, and journals designed to appeal to the Italian community in America, often published in Italian, provided new immigrants and succeeding generations important information about both the United States and Italy, helping immigrants acclimate to their new homeland while remaining in touch with their roots.

News vehicles for Italian immigrants in America were available as early as 1836, when *El Correro Atlantico* appeared in New Orleans. New York City had its first Italian-language paper, *L'Eco d'Italia*, in 1850, and even before the great influx of Italians into the United States between 1880 and 1920 several other major cities could boast of having one or more publications that catered to this ethnic group.

Because Italian immigrants generally clustered together in neighborhoods that were dubbed "Little Italies," it was easy for publishers to distribute their newspapers to waiting audiences, most of whom were poor and ignorant of American customs. Many publications contained stories about events in Italy as well as news about America, enabling immigrants to stay in touch with the old country while adjusting to their new home. Such publications were also convenient media in which employers could advertise job openings. Newspapers also served as forums for individuals to vent their frustrations about life in what they called *La Merica* that to many was proving less rosy than they had anticipated.

CHARACTERISTICS OF THE ITALIAN AMERICAN PRESS

The explosion of Italian immigration to America after 1880 saw a concurrent rise in Italian American news publications. New York City alone had dozens of small Italian papers, and cities such as Boston, Philadelphia, Chicago, Pittsburgh, and San Francisco also had multiple news organs. Many of these publications competed with one another for the same readers, however, and fierce competition ensured that many would be short-lived. Most readers were working-class men and women to whom the papers delivered a great deal of news and opinions on labor issues. The better-financed papers tended to promote conservative interests. For example, Carlo Barsotti's *Il Progresso Italo-Americano* in New York, Charles Baldi's *L'Opinione* in Philadelphia, and Mariano Cancelliere's *La Trinacria* in Pittsburgh were decidedly promanagement. These conservative papers even went so far as to carry management advertisements for strikebreakers when unions conducted work stoppages.

At the same time, quite a number of papers were controlled by various unions and workers' rights groups; for example, the International Workers of the World used *La Questione Sociale* and later *L'Era*

Editor of an Italian-language newspaper in New York correcting proofs in 1943. (Library of Congress)

Nuova as propaganda tools to influence Italian workers. Publications such as *Il Proletario* in Philadelphia and *La Plebe* in Pittsburgh advocated for workers' rights and promoted civil disobedience, a stance that got them in trouble with authorities on occasion. A typical government tactic used to stymie these radical organs was to have the U.S. Post Office declare them seditious and refuse to grant their publishers mailing privileges, thereby curtailing circulation. Nevertheless, between 1880 and 1940, more than a hundred radical papers appeared. Their impact on the working classes was significant.

RISE OF FASCISM

The passionate interest of Italians in their homeland was at the root of the greatest controversy involving the Italian American press. Beginning during the 1920's Italian American papers ran articles and editorials praising the Fascist Italian dictator Benito Mussolini, whose efforts they thought would unite Italy and bring justice and prosperity to the peasantry. Chief among Mussolini's Italian American supporters was Generoso Pope, a businessman who bought several newspapers, including the New York papers *Il Progresso Italo-Americano* and *Corriere d'America*, both of which enjoyed wide circulation. Pope had personal access to both Mussolini and U.S. president Franklin D. Roosevelt and used his newspapers to promote the Fascist agenda. He was not alone, however. Most mainstream publications, including many supported by the Roman Catholic Church, were ardent Fascist supporters—until Mussolini's bellicose imperialist ventures in Africa and Spain during the mid-1930's turned American opinion against him. Even then, some Italian papers ran articles critical of Mussolini in their English-language sections while continuing to print favorable pieces about him in Italian.

Support for Mussolini was not universal, however. In Detroit, *La Voce de Popolo* editor Monsignor Joseph Ciarrocchi ran articles exposing the Italian dictator's propaganda campaign being waged in America. Many left-leaning publications were highly critical. One of the most vocal anti-Fascist publications was *Il Martello*, owned and edited by Carlo Tresca, a lifelong activist who had fought for workers' rights since arriving in the United States in 1904. Frequently, those publishing unfavorable material on Mussolini before the outbreak of World War II were intimidated or even assaulted by pro-Fascist elements in the United States. After the United States entered World War II against Japan, Germany, and Italy at the end of 1941, open support for Fascism in the Italian American press was replaced by calls for the overthrow of Mussolini's regime.

POSTWAR PRESS

By the end of World War II in 1945, many Italian Americans had begun to assimilate into the mainstream culture. Dwindling populations in Little Italies and waning interest among second- and third-generation Italian Americans in their ancestral home and language led to a decline in publications targeted specifically at their ethnic interests. Nevertheless, a number of magazines and journals published by various civic groups such as the Italy-America Society and the National Italian-American Foundation enjoyed wide readership into the twenty-first century. Most of these publications promoted pride in the Italian American heritage and celebrated customs from the old country that had become part of the larger melting-pot culture of the United States.

Laurence W. Mazzeno

FURTHER READING

Diggins, John N. *Mussolini and Fascism: The View from America*. Princeton, N.J.: Princeton University Press, 1972. Discusses the fascination of Italian Americans with Mussolini, explains the role of the mainstream Italian American press in promoting a favorable view of him, and describes efforts of anti-Fascist publications to counter positive Fascist images.

Mangione, Jerre, and Ben Morreale. *La Storia: Five Centuries of the Italian-American Experience*. New York: HarperCollins, 1992. Extensive history of Italian immigration to America, outlining contributions of Italian Americans to the United States. Includes a brief commentary on the role of the Italian American press.

Moreno, Barry. *Italian Americans*. Hauppauge, N.Y.: Barron's Educational Series, 2003. Describes the history and customs of Italian immigrants; briefly sketches the role of the Italian American press within these communities.

Park, Robert E. *The Immigrant Press and Its Control*. New York: Harper, Collins, 1922. Provides a sense of the concerns mainstream America had with ethnic newspapers, including those published by Italian Americans, which were perceived as potentially subversive to American values.

Pericone, Nunzio. *Carlo Tresca: Portrait of a Rebel*. New York: Palgrave Macmillan, 2005. Biography of the activist and newspaper editor influential in promoting the cause of labor and combating favorable views of fascism within the Italian American community.

SEE ALSO: Ethnic enclaves; German American press; Immigration waves; Italian immigrants; Labor unions; Little Italies; Spanish-language press.

ITALIAN IMMIGRANTS

SIGNIFICANCE: The late nineteenth and early twentieth centuries saw a large-scale influx of Italian immigrants to the United States. Most of them settled in East Coast cities such as New York and Philadelphia. By the early twenty-first century, people of Italian heritage constituted 6 percent of the total American population and ranked as the fifth-largest ethnic group in the United States.

Italians began immigrating to North America during the early colonial period, but massive Italian immigration began only during the late nineteenth century. The new immigrants faced prob-

Italian immigrants arriving at Ellis Island in 1911. (Library of Congress)

lems similar to those encountered by earlier waves of foreign immigrants, such as the Irish. Most of them tended to gravitate to the eastern cities, in which they created "Little Italies." Their assimilation progressed slowly and was often hampered by the perception that many Italians were members of the criminal Mafia. By the late twentieth century, however, Italian Americans occupied prominent positions in most sectors of American life.

EARLY IMMIGRATION

Immigration from Italy to the United States was only a trickle before the 1880's. The British colonies contained small pockets of Italians, who brought Italian horticulture and winemaking to North America as early as the seventeenth century. During the late eighteenth century Revolutionary War era and in the early days of the independent American republic, political philosopher Filippo Mazzei was probably the most prominent Italian in the United States. He was a close friend of Thomas Jefferson and had a plantation near Jefferson's Virginia home. The two men conversed in Italian, and Mazzei is believed to have given Jefferson the phrase "that all Men are created equal," which Jefferson famously rendered "all Men are created equal" in the Declaration of Independence.

Later Italian immigrants were important in the development of the early wine industry in California. During the nineteenth century, Italian artists and musicians made significant contributions to art, architecture, and music, especially opera. However, their numbers were small until late in the century.

LATE NINETEENTH CENTURY IMMIGRATION

The political unification of Italy in 1879 did not bring better lives to the majority of Italians, who began to emigrate in large numbers to Brazil, Argentina, and the United States. Life for the new immigrants was difficult in all these countries, but Italians continued to emigrate. Many hoped to accumulate enough money to return to Italy to buy land and lead better lives in their homeland. Most sent remittances to family members in Italy in the meantime. By 1900, about 500,000 Italians were living in the United States, mostly in New York, Pennsylvania, New Jersey, and New England. About 150,000 Italians lived in New York City alone, and Philadelphia and Chicago also had growing Italian communities.

TWENTIETH CENTURY TRENDS

Anti-Italian sentiments among native-born Americans grew along with the burgeoning numbers of Italian immigrants. Propaganda against the Italian immigrants usually focused on fears of the Mafia. Throughout the United States, Italian immigrants were targets of violence, even lynching, by anti-immigrant nativist groups that were alarmed by the new wave of immigration. To help mitigate their difficult situations, Italians established mutual aid societies that provided services ranging from medical care to funerals to members. Many immigrants cities got moral support from living in Little Italies, in which they were surrounded by fellow countrymen (*paesani*) and could enjoy many of the trappings of the culture of their homeland. Italian grocery stores and other services helped in the transition, especially among those still unable to speak English.

Some immigrants returned to Italy, but most remained in the United States permanently. Male heads of families generally arrived in the United States first. As they became established, they sent for the rest of their families. Over time, notions of returning to Italy faded. Occasionally, however, some family members remained in the United States while others returned to Italy, traveling back and forth whenever possible. This was especially true after World War II.

Immigrants who came to the United States during the twentieth century, especially after World War I (1914-1918), enjoyed a brief period of relative prosperity. However, the Great Depression of the 1930's proved an especially difficult time. By then, Italy was under Benito Mussolini's Fascist rule, so returning to Italy was out of the question for many immigrants. In 1939, Italy followed Nazi Germany into World War II and became a declared enemy of the United States.

ITALIAN RELIGION AND CULTURE

Historically, most Italians have been Roman Catholics, and immigrants have continued in that religious faith in the United States. However, early Italian immigrants were not entirely comfortable in American Catholic churches, which were dominated by Irish American clergy. In cities in which Italians were concentrated, the immigrants gravitated toward predominantly Italian parishes, which tried to keep alive the Italian language and culture.

Although a majority of Italian Americans have remained Catholics, they have not occupied a place in the leadership of the American church that reflects their numbers. Some Italian American men and women entered the Catholic clergy and religious orders but not in the same numbers as Irish Catholics have done. Consequently, the American church has continued to have a predominantly Irish imprint. Despite the large numbers of Italians in New York City, there has never been an Italian American cardinal in the city's archdiocese.

Not all Italians were or are Catholic. Some have joined Protestant churches in small communities lacking Catholic churches. Others have left the Roman Catholic Church after getting divorced and remarrying—practices on which Catholics frown. By the early twenty-first century, Italian Americans were prominent in a variety of Protestant denominations.

FAMILIES

An important center of Italian immigrant life has been the family. Family members have tended

PROFILE OF ITALIAN IMMIGRANTS

Country of origin	Italy
Primary language	Italian
Primary regions of U.S. settlement	Northeast
Earliest significant arrivals	Seventeenth century
Peak immigration period	1880's-1920's
Twenty-first century legal residents*	21,028 (2,629 per year)

*Immigrants who obtained legal permanent resident status in the United States.
Source: Department of Homeland Security, *Yearbook of Immigration Statistics, 2008.*

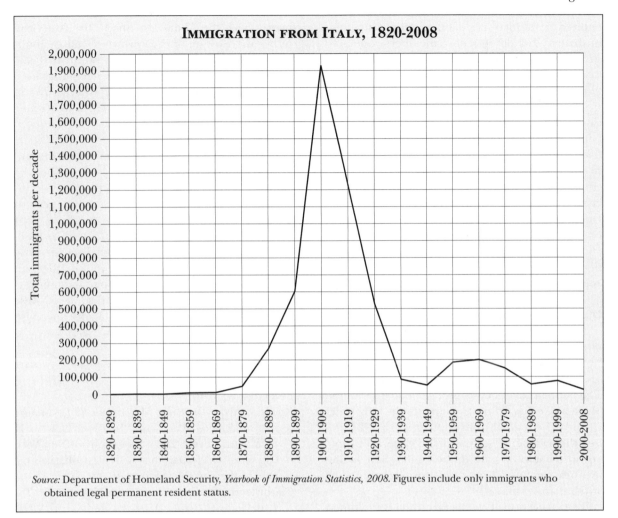

IMMIGRATION FROM ITALY, 1820-2008

Source: Department of Homeland Security, *Yearbook of Immigration Statistics, 2008.* Figures include only immigrants who obtained legal permanent resident status.

to live near one another, especially with the big cities' Little Italies. Italian youths were encouraged to marry not only within the Roman Catholic faith but also within the Italian community. Marrying outside the Italian community was rare among early immigrants, but it became more common after several generations had passed. First-generation immigrant families strongly discouraged marriage with "Americans"—the general designation for anyone not of Italian descent.

The Americanization of an Italian family is a subtheme of Francis Ford Coppola's *Godfather* film trilogy. The films trace the evolution of an Italian family from the youthful Vito Corleone's initiation into the harsh criminal world of New York City's Little Italy to his son Michael Corleone's lavish lifestyle in the Far West, showing how the family's customs and lifestyle changed. After a poverty-stricken beginning as an immigrant orphan, Vito eventually prospered but hung onto a traditional Italian lifestyle. In contrast, Michael lived like an American millionaire on a large estate with few signs of Italian culture.

Women played a major role in Italian immigrant families and in the workplace. Although men were usually the first to come to the United States, many Italian women also immigrated alone, either as single women seeking better lives or as heads of households. When whole families immigrated together, the women tended to assume matriarchal roles within the families, allowing their husbands to retain their traditional Italian roles as family heads. Some women did part-time piecework at home for wages, while others worked in factories, entered domestic service, or, together with their husbands and other family members, operated small businesses. Some families ran small grocery stores, or similar establishments, attached to their homes.

The Italian immigrant culture encouraged education as a central part of the goal of achieving better lives. Consequently, Italian Americans have had higher-than-average graduation rates from high schools and average to above-average rates of completion of higher degrees. The Italian family culture subscribed to the concept of the "American Dream," and encouraged their children to pursue education as a way of getting ahead in the new society. Families in the Little Italies tended to be competitive and were proud to boast of their children's achievements.

ITALIAN STEREOTYPES

Few European immigrant groups have faced as much ethnic prejudice as Italians. Epithets such as "wop," "dago," and even "*Eye*-talian" have been only surface manifestations of anti-Italian sentiments. The popular tendency to associate Italians with the Mafia and other criminal elements was long widespread. The federal Immigration Act of 1924 limited the number of southern and eastern Europeans who could migrate to the United States. The measure can be seen as at least partly motivated by anti-Italian sentiment.

The conviction of Nicola Sacco and Bartolomeo Vanzetti for robbery and murder in 1927 has often been cited as an example of anti-Italian xenophobia because the evidence used against them was weak. Their long trial process was highly politicized. Instead of concentrating on the evidence concerning the crimes of robbery and murder, the trial focused on the defendants' anarchist political views, which probably played a greater role in their conviction and eventual execution than the actual evidence in their case.

As time passed and Italians moved into the American cultural mainstream, groups such as the Italian American Civil Rights League (formerly the Italian American Anti-Defamation League) and the National Italian-American Foundation worked to combat negative stereotypes. The fact that criminals in films and television dramas often had Italian surnames contributed to the stereotypes. However, the *Godfather* films that seemed to

romanticize the Mafia also made the American public more aware of the warmth of Italian family life and family values. By the early twenty-first century, stereotyping of Italians was declining, even though the popular cable television series *The Sopranos* was keeping alive public perceptions of criminal Italians.

ITALIAN CONTRIBUTIONS TO AMERICAN CUISINE

The art of cooking has always been part of the Italian domestic landscape. From their earliest arrivals, Italian immigrants have brought vineyards and other forms of horticulture to the United States. Later immigrants, particularly those from southern Italy, also contributed such dishes as pizza, spaghetti, meatballs, and lasagna to the American cuisine. Many immigrants opened restaurants within Italian neighborhoods, and some of these acquired national reputations. Italians have also contributed espresso, cappuccino, and lattes to American coffeehouses.

Norma Corigliano Noonan

FURTHER READING

Brodsky, Alyn. *The Great Mayor: Fiorello LaGuardia and the Making of the City of New York*. New York: St. Martin's Press, 2003. Biography of New York City's famous Italian mayor that emphasizes his role in the city's development.

Cannistrero, Philip, and Gerald Meyer, eds. *The Lost World of Italian American Radicalism*. Westport, Conn.: Praeger, 2003. Collection of essays about the various facets of Italian radicalism, especially after World War I.

Ciongoli, A. Kenneth, and Jay Parini. *Passage to Liberty: The Story of Italian Immigration and the Rebirth of America*. New York: Regan Books, 2002. Glossy and engaging history of Italians in America, going back to the eras of Christopher Columbus and Filippo Mazzei.

Guglielmo, Thomas A. *White on Arrival: Italians, Race, Color, and Power in Chicago, 1890-1945*. New York: Oxford University Press, 2003. History of Chicago's Italian community that focuses on racial aspects of the Italian experience, from characterizations of Italians by themselves and other groups to their relations with the African American community.

Iorizzo, Luciano J., and Salvatore Mondello. *The Italian Americans*. 3d ed. Youngstown, N.Y.: Cambria Press, 2002. Well-written scholarly history of the evolution of the Italian American community in the United States.

Poe, Tracy N. "The Labour and Leisure of Food Production as a Mode of Ethnic Identity Building Among Italians in Chicago, 1890-1940." *Rethinking History* 5, no. 1 (2001): 131-148. Study of Italians in Chicago that focuses on food, culture, and residential patterns.

Vecchio, Diane C. *Merchants, Midwives and Laboring Women: Italian Migrants in Urban America.* Champaign: University of Illinois Press, 2006. Brief history of Italian immigrant women in the United States.

Vecoli, Rudolph J. "European Americans: From Immigrants to Ethnics." *International Migration Review* 6, no. 4 (Winter, 1972): 403-434. Analysis of the historiography of European immigration that reviews the approaches of some of the major immigration historians, revealing the interpretations that evolved over time.

SEE ALSO: Anti-Catholicism; Argentine immigrants; Atlas, Charles; European immigrants; Films; *Godfather* trilogy; History of immigration after 1891; Immigration waves; Italian American press; Little Italies; Ponzi, Charles; Sacco and Vanzetti trial; Tammany Hall.

J

JAPANESE AMERICAN CITIZENS LEAGUE

IDENTIFICATION: Voluntary organization formed to protect and promote the rights of Japanese Americans
DATE: Established in 1929
ALSO KNOWN AS: JACL

SIGNIFICANCE: The Japanese American Citizens League was founded to protect the civil rights of Japanese Americans but quickly became a champion of all civil rights issues affecting people of all backgrounds.

The Japanese American Citizens League (JACL) was founded in California in 1929 in response to the anti-immigration fervor and legislature that was gaining popularity and support. The organization's mission was to protect the civil rights and liberties of all people, regardless of their race, ethnicity, nationality, or gender.

Early twentieth century California had the largest Japanese American population of any state in the United States. It also had more than one hundred statutes limiting the rights of residents of Japanese ancestry. Groups such as the Grange and the Native Sons of the Golden State used their power both at the state level and in the U.S. Congress to pass legislation that limited the rights and political participation of Japanese and Japanese American citizens. Far more extreme were organizations such as the Asiatic Exclusion League, whose purpose was to purge the West of all Asian residents, including those born in the United States. Although the organization was inexperienced, the JACL challenged not only anti-Asian organizations but also the discriminatory congressional legislation that limited Asian rights.

The importance of the JACL came to a head on December 7, 1941, after the attack on Pearl Harbor. Hours after the attack, U.S. government officials raided offices and homes of Japanese in Hawaii and along the West Coast of the United States, imprisoning many leaders of the Japanese community, including senior JACL members. Junior members of the organization then had to defend their colleagues and fellow citizens under a climate of fear and anger toward all things Japanese. The JACL ensured that the interned were protected and enjoyed a reasonable level of physical comfort. It also kept the Japanese American community aware of developments through its newspaper, *Pacific Citizen*, and won the right for Japanese Americans to serve in the U.S. armed forces during World War II.

Following the release of internees after World War II ended in 1945, the JACL continued to be a champion for civil rights. In 1946, the group began a painstaking campaign to repeal California's alien land law, which prohibited Asian immigrants from owning land in the state. This was followed by the formation of the Leadership Conference on Civil Rights in 1948 and support of the federal Evacuation Claims Act during the same year in its quest for compensation for Japanese who had been interned during World War II. JACL's work on the Immigration and Nationality Act of 1952 allowed women to gain entry into the democratic process, and the organization lobbied strongly for the passage of the federal Civil Rights Act of 1964.

In 1978, the JACL launched an investigation into the losses suffered by Japanese and Japanese Americans who had been sent to relocation camps. The organization supported the formation of a government commission, which was sponsored by President Jimmy Carter, to study the issue. In 1982, the commission declared that the federal government's actions during the war had been unconstitutional and recommended payment of a monetary redress. The redress was awarded under the Civil Liberties Act of 1988, providing compensation and a presidential apology to victims.

During the early twenty-first century, the JACL continued to lobby for civil rights. One of the issues that it has championed is the right for humans to marry, including marriage for same-sex couples.

Sara Vidar

FURTHER READING
Gruenewald, Mary Matsuda. *Looking Like the Enemy: My Story of Imprisonment in Japanese American In-*

ternment Camps. Troutdale, Oreg.: NewSage Press, 2005.

Harth, Erica. *Last Witnesses: Reflections on the Wartime Internment of the Japanese.* New York: Palgrave Macmillan, 2003.

Japanese American Citizens League. *The Journey from Gold Mountain: The Asian American Experience.* San Francisco: JACL, 2006.

SEE ALSO: Anti-Japanese movement; Asian American Legal Defense Fund; Asian Pacific American Labor Alliance; Asiatic Barred Zone; Asiatic Exclusion League; California; Japanese American internment; Japanese American press; Japanese immigrants; World War II.

JAPANESE AMERICAN INTERNMENT

THE EVENT: Federal government's forced evacuation and relocation of Japanese Americans living on the West Coast to internment camps during World War II

DATE: 1942 to 1945

LOCATION: Relocation centers in western states between California and Arkansas

SIGNIFICANCE: In February, 1942, President Franklin D. Roosevelt issued Executive Order 9066, which authorized U.S. military officials to remove persons from areas of the American mainland designated as military zones. More than 110,000 Japanese Americans were considered security risks and forced to dispose of their West Coast homes, businesses, and property and move into ten desolate relocation camps from California to Arkansas. The internment deprived the affected Japanese Americans of their civil liberties as U.S. citizens or residents.

As the start of World War II, about 120,000 Japanese Americans resided in the United States. Most lived in California and other Pacific coast states. The 40,000 first-generation immigrant Japanese, or Issei, were generally over the age of fifty and excluded from citizenship by the Immigration Act of 1924. The 80,000 second-generation Nisei were under age eighteen, and most were American citizens.

Immediately after the Japanese attack on Pearl Harbor on December 7, 1941, the U.S. government detained 2,000 Japanese Americans who were considered security risks. The shock of the Pearl Harbor attack; the Japanese military takeover of Guam, Hong Kong, Manila, and Singapore; and reports of Japanese atrocities in the Philippines created an atmosphere of hysteria on the West Coast. Many Americans feared that a bombing attack on the West Coast might be next. They also believed that Japan had resident spies living on the coast and feared that Japanese Americans would aid their racial brothers. Numerous inflammatory and invariably false reports of Japanese attacks on the American mainland flashed through coastal communities. However, no reports of attacks on the American mainland were authenticated until the Japanese shelled an oil refinery near Santa Barbara, California, on February 22, 1942, and the Oregon coast near Fort Stevens on June 21. Neither attack did much damage.

The biggest impetus for internment came with the release in late January of a government investigation of the Pearl Harbor attack. The report, compiled by U.S. Supreme Court justice Owen Roberts, claimed without documentation that Hawaii-based espionage agents, including Japanese American citizens, had aided the Japanese striking force. The press and interest groups further spread fear and prejudice that denied the constitutional rights of Japanese Americans.

EVACUATION ORDER

Assistant Secretary of War John McCloy was responsible for a military decision on the fate of Japanese Americans and ordered Colonel Karl Bendetsen to prepare a final recommendation for General John DeWitt, chief of the Army's Western Defense Command. In early February, DeWitt officially requested authority to remove all Japanese Americans from the West Coast because they belonged to an "enemy race" whose loyalty was suspect. Secretary of War Henry Stimson, Attorney General Francis Biddle, Assistant Attorney General James Rowe, and Edward Ennis, director of the Alien Enemy Control Unit, questioned the internment on racial grounds as unconstitutional and unnecessary. Stimson warned that removal of Japanese Americans on a racial basis would "tear a tremendous hole in our constitutional system." Biddle told Stimson that the Justice Department would not evacuate any American citizen.

The internment strategy was finalized on the evening of February 17, 1942, in the living room of Biddle's Washington home. Biddle had told Stimson that afternoon that he no longer opposed internment after being assured that the Army, not the Justice Department, would handle the mass roundup and detention programs. McCloy persuaded Biddle to participate in publishing the executive order and confronted Rowe and Ennis, who were furious about Biddle's reversal of position on internment. Despite having reservations, Stimson advised Roosevelt that DeWitt should be authorized to proceed.

On February 19, President Roosevelt signed Executive Order 9066, which authorized U.S. military officials to remove any and all persons from areas of the United States designated as military zones. The order did not apply to persons living outside the Western Defense Command. No explicit reference to Japanese Americans was necessary. The secretary of war was authorized to establish detention centers to protect West Coast military facilities from sabotage and espionage. The original order did not specify what should happen to the evacuees or exclude voluntary withdrawal. Japanese Americans were encouraged to leave the prohibited Pacific coast military zone voluntarily. About 15,000 moved in with midwestern or eastern relatives or friends. Roosevelt established the War Relocation Authority (WRA) to administer the voluntary resettlement and designated Milton Eisenhower as its director. Many inland states warned that the eastward movement of Japanese immigrants posed problems. The governors of Wyoming, Idaho, and Kansas adamantly opposed resettlement of Japanese Americans.

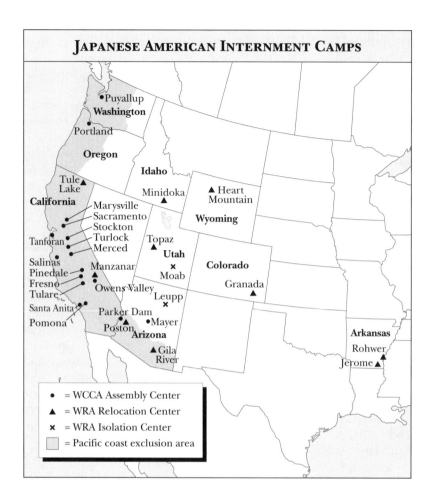

EVACUATION AND INTERNMENT

On March 27, 1942, the Army stopped voluntary withdrawal and began evacuating the remaining Japanese Americans. Within weeks, more than 100,000 Japanese Americans were given forty-eight hours to dispose of their businesses, homes, and property and report to makeshift assembly centers at fairgrounds and racetracks. At Santa Anita Race Track in Arcadia, California, detainees were jammed into hastily converted horse stalls until they could be transferred to permanent relocation centers.

The War Department moved internees to ten inland internment camps from California to Arkansas. All ten sites were located on barren, federally owned land, usually Indian reservations. The first evacuees were sent in June to Manzanar, California—a desolate, 6,000-acre site surrounded by guard towers, searchlights, machine-gun installations, and barbed-wire fencing. The internees endured boiling summer heat and frigid winter cold and sandstorms, confined without any recognition of their constitutional rights.

Each family was crammed into a spartan, 20-by-20-foot uninsulated cabin. The residents tried to live as normally as possible, organizing farm plots, markets, schools, newspapers, and police and fire departments. Eisenhower, deeply troubled by the involuntary internment, resigned as WRA director. In 1943, many internees bristled when Dillon Meyer, Eisenhower's replacement, forced all internees to undergo interrogation to establish their loyalty to the United States. About 8,500 internees, mostly young Nisei men, refused to forswear allegiance to the Japanese emperor or indicate willingness to serve in the U.S. military forces; they were deemed disloyal and sent to a camp at Tule Lake, California. About 3,000 of those considered loyal were recruited into the 442d Regimental Combat Team, an all-Japanese military unit that battled bravely in Italy.

Many internment camps operated through the remainder of the war. The WRA found homes and jobs for 17,000 Japanese Americans in 1943. Late that year, Biddle pressed Roosevelt for accelerated releases of internees from the camps. Secretary of Interior Harold Ickes warned Roosevelt in June, 1944, about the negative historical legacy of the detention centers. Stimson favored freeing the loyal Japanese Americans after the 1944 presidential election. The WRA had relocated about one-quarter of the internees by August, 1945.

CONSTITUTIONAL CHALLENGES

War Department officials observed anxiously as several lawsuits challenged the constitutionality of the relocation program. Surprisingly, only three cases involving Japanese Americans contesting the internment orders reached the U.S. Supreme Court. The three challengers came from varied backgrounds. Minoru Yasui, a lawyer and Army Reserve officer, broke the curfew order in Portland, Oregon. Gordon Hirabayashi, a Quaker pacifist and college student in Seattle, Washington, violated the curfew and exclusion orders on religious grounds. Fred Korematsu, a twenty-three-year-old American-born Nisei shipyard welder, dodged the exclusion order in San Leandro, California, and hoped to escape the West Coast with his Italian American friend.

In each case, the U.S. Supreme Court ruled that the war powers granted to the president and Congress by the U.S. Constitution eclipsed the due process and equal protection claims of the three Japanese Americans. On June 24, 1943, the Court rendered unanimous decisions in *Hirabayashi v. United States* and *Yasui v. United States* supporting the government's stance on the curfew orders (and avoiding the coerced evacuation and compulsory internment issues). In the former case, Justice Frank Murphy, however, warned that the relocation program tested constitutional powers by substantially restricting the personal liberty of American citizens based on the accident of race or ancestry.

An Army document defending the evacuation became an issue in *Korematsu v. United States* (1944). Colonel Bendetsen, DeWitt's deputy, drafted the *Final Report: Japanese Evacuation from the West Coast, 1942*. The 618-page report listed "military necessity" as DeWitt's official explanation for the internment program. Justice Department lawyers initially saw the report in January, 1944, when preparing their briefs for the *Korematsu* case. The *Final Report* stirred a spirited debate between the Justice and War departments. Bendetsen cited hundreds of examples of subversive activities on the West Coast in 1942 to defend the forced evacuation as both militarily necessary and constitutional. The Justice Department, however, soon discovered that Bendetsen had distorted his facts about a raid by the Federal Bureau of Investigation (FBI) turning up more than sixty thousand rounds of ammunition and many rifles, shotguns, and maps that had come from a sporting goods store and about espionage involving supposedly illicit radio transmissions.

The Justice Department attorneys, in a footnote, sought to disavow the *Final Report* when arguing the *Korematsu* case. They questioned both the military's factual assertions that the evacuation was a military necessity and the allegations of espionage, sabotage, and treason by the Japanese Americans. McCloy insisted that the footnote be deleted because it would shatter the consensus the Supreme Court had patched together in the other two cases and would probably prompt the Court to rule the entire relocation program unconstitutional. The top Justice Department officials yielded to McCloy's pressure after two days of spirited debate and deleted the footnote, depriving the Court of grounds upon which to challenge the *Final Report* assertions. The Court otherwise might have ruled in Korematsu's favor.

In the *Korematsu* case, the Supreme Court on December 18, 1944, upheld the detention program. The case provided the greatest challenge to the constitutionality of the evacuation program. Justice Hugo L. Black's majority opinion affirmed Korematsu's original conviction for violating the evacuation decree but carefully avoided ruling on the legality of his subsequent internment. Black argued that strict scrutiny must be given to all legal restrictions that curtail the civil rights of a single racial group and decided that military necessity provided ample grounds to believe that the government's actions met the strict scrutiny test. Justices Roberts, Murphy, and Robert Jackson sharply dissented. Jackson protested that the Court majority was affirming the principle of racial discrimination.

The previous day, the West Coast military authorities rescinded DeWitt's original evacuation order and permitted the remaining camp residents to reenter the Western Defense Command. Beginning in January, 1945, those Japanese Americans who had passed loyalty test screenings were gradually released from the camps. Several thousand who were considered disloyal were detained until after World War II ended.

LEGACY OF SHAME

The internment of Japanese Americans left a legacy of shame. The Japanese American internees suffered about $400 million in property losses because of the evacuation. In 1948, Congress paid them a paltry $37 million in reparations. Four de-

Internees eating a meal at the Manzanar Relocation Center in California's eastern Sierras. (NARA)

cades later, it responded to calls for redress by passing the Civil Liberties Act of 1988, which awarded $20,000 in reparations to each detainee who was still alive. Meanwhile, the Commission on Wartime Relocation and Internment of Civilians reviewed the factors that led to Executive Order 9066 and examined its consequences. In 1983, the commission concluded that "race prejudice, war hysteria, and a failure of political leadership" by the Roosevelt administration led to Executive Order 9066 and a "grave injustice" to Japanese Americans.

The commission's findings and newly discovered evidence from government files prompted legal efforts to remove the criminal records of the wartime defendants. A federal judge rescinded Korematsu's conviction, holding that the Supreme Court had approved Roosevelt's order on the basis of "unsubstantiated facts, distortions, and misrepresentations" to the Court by high-ranking officials. In 1998, President Bill Clinton bestowed the Presidential Medal of Freedom, the nation's highest civilian honor, on Korematsu. The detention undermined the cultural authority of the elderly Issei, liberated their Nisei children from provincial tradition and cultural isolation, and expedited the Nisei's assimilation into the larger society. Younger Japanese Americans rapidly ascended the ladder of social mobility and became among the best-educated Americans, with incomes substantially above the national average. Roosevelt's Executive Order 9066 created what the American Civil Liberties Union (ACLU) termed "the greatest deprivation of civil liberties by government in this country since slavery." Roosevelt mobilized the country for ultimate victory in World War II, but the internment program remains a stigma on his wartime record.

The Japanese internment decried American ideals of justice. The ceaseless uneasiness of government officials with their own policy and the cautious manner with which the Supreme Court treated the evacuation cases testify to the awkwardness with which American culture dealt with the internment incident. The internment of Japanese Americans refuted the nation's best image of itself as a tolerant, inclusive, fair-minded melting pot society—a vision long nourished in American lore and one strongly reaffirmed by the World War II conflict.

David L. Porter

FURTHER READING

Commission on Wartime Relocation and Internment of Civilians. *Personal Justice Denied.* Washington, D.C.: Government Printing Office, 1983. The commission concluded that "race prejudice, war hysteria, and a failure of political leadership" resulted in "grave injustice" to the Japanese Americans.

Daniels, Roger. *Prisoners Without Trial: Japanese Americans in World War II.* New York: Hill & Wang, 1993. Describes and analyzes the decision to remove Japanese Americans from the West Coast, their confinement, their reaction to their unjust treatment, and the repercussions of the internment.

Hayashi, Brian Masaru. *Democratizing the Enemy: The Japanese American Internment.* Princeton, N.J.: Princeton University Press, 2004. Questions whether racism, wartime hysteria, and a failure of political leadership fully explain the U.S. government incarceration of Japanese Americans and offers revealing new interpretations of their internment.

Irons, Peter. *Justice at War: The Story of the Japanese American Internment Cases.* Berkeley: University of California Press, 1993. Well-researched work examining the *Yasui, Hirabayashi,* and *Korematsu* court cases, exposing the government's coverup of data that could have disproved its claims of "military necessity" for evacuation and internment.

Ng, Wendy. *Japanese American Internment During World War II: A History and Reference Guide.* Westport, Conn.: Greenwood Press, 2002. This reference work provides six thematic essays on the history and meaning of the Japanese internment, short biographies of the major personalities in the internment, and a selection of primary documents.

Tateishi, John, ed. *And Justice for All: An Oral History of the Japanese American Detention Camps.* New York: Random House, 1984. This poignant, bitter, inspiring oral history gives the personal recollections and experiences of thirty Japanese Americans who were part of the only group of American citizens ever confined to detention camps in the United States.

War Department. *Final Report: Japanese Evacuation from the West Coast, 1942.* Washington, D.C.: Government Printing Office, 1943. This report, requested by John DeWitt, lists "military necessity" as the official government explanation for the evacuation and internment.

See also: Anti-Japanese movement; Asian American literature; Hawaii; Japanese American press; Japanese immigrants; Japanese Peruvians; Loyalty oaths; Oregon; Prisoners of war in the United States; World War II.

JAPANESE AMERICAN PRESS

Definition: Publications issued in both Japanese and English languages that cater primarily to Japanese immigrants and their descendants

Significance: The Japanese American press provided a means whereby Japanese Americans dealt with the prejudicial treatment they received in America. The idea that the Nisei, or second-generation Japanese Americans, should embrace "Americanism" received major impetus. Newspapers also provided an outlet for incarcerated Issei, or first-generation Japanese immigrants, and Nisei during World War II.

The golden era of the Japanese American ethnic press occurred during the 1920's and 1930's, when the ethnic populations in West Coast cities had grown large enough to support several competing newspapers. The Los Angeles *Rafu Shimpo* provided local and regional news to a large West Coast readership, while the competing but shorter-lived *Doho* gave emphasis to progressive, pro-labor news and opinion. The San Francisco press included the *Nichi Bei Shinbun* and the *Shin Sekai*. Under publisher Kyutaro Abiko, *Nichi Bei* published both San Francisco and Los Angeles editions during the 1920's. However, a labor strike closed the latter paper in 1931. *Nichi Bei* was the highest-circulation Jap-

anese American newspaper. The East Coast press included New York City's *Japanese American News*.

The Japanese-language papers also published articles in English, but not on a regular basis until 1925, in *Nichi Bei*. By this time, the publishers realized the need to cater to English-speaking Nisei. Other English-language sections soon appeared, followed by English-language weeklies, including *Japanese American Weekly*, introduced by Abiko in 1926, and the Seattle-based *Japanese American Courier*, introduced in 1928. Although the *Courier* achieved only a fraction of the circulation of the Japanese-language papers, its editor, James Yoshinori Sakamoto, exerted considerable influence and was instrumental in the development of the Japanese American Citizens League.

Japanese American residents of Manzanar Relocation Center reading newspapers produced within the internment camp during 1943. (Library of Congress)

Several newspapers, especially Sakamoto's *Courier*, fostered the attitude that an ethic of hard work and loyalty would lead to the eventual absorption of Japanese Americans into the mainstream of American life. The press was far from unified in reacting to the times, however. Whereas the Issei press heavily supported Japan in the Sino-Japanese War that began in July, 1937, *Doho* criticized Japan for creating havoc in Asia. Differences of opinion also split the Japanese-language and English-language staffs within individual newspapers.

The Japanese press suffered severely in the aftermath of the Japanese attack on Pearl Harbor on December 7, 1941. U.S. military officials desired total suppression of Japanese-language publishing, while civilian authorities merely urged its control. Nevertheless, all Japanese American papers on the West Coast were shut down by mid-May, 1942. In contrast, the inland press, including the *Rocky Nippon*, *Colorado Times*, *Utah Nippo*, and the relocated *Pacific Citizen*, continued and to some degree thrived during the war. Newspapers also quickly developed within internment camps.

Although officially sanctioned, internment camp newspapers enjoyed some autonomy. The *Manzanar Free Press*, for example, was headquartered in the Office of Official Reports and was subject to censorship by the camp director. In practice, however, the paper's editors received little interference. The director even authorized a Japanese-language edition during the paper's second year. While barred from directly criticizing federal policies that had led to the mass Japanese American incarceration, *Free Press* editors were allowed to print factual stories on legal challenges to those policies. The *Free Press* was circulated by mail to all the internment camps.

The Japanese American press was restored to vitality by the end of the war, with the new *Nichi Bei Times* established in 1946 to reconnect individuals separated by incarceration. As had the *Nichi Bei Shinbun*, the *Times* became the leading U.S. Japanese American newspaper.

Mark Rich

FURTHER READING

Hosokawa, Bill. *Nisei: The Quiet Americans*. New York: William Morrow, 1969.

Mizuno, Takeya. "The Federal Government's Decisions in Suppressing the Japanese-Language Press, 1941-42." *Journalism History* 33, no. 1 (2007): 14-23.

Ng, Wendy. *Japanese American Internment During World War II: A History and Reference Guide*. Westport, Conn.: Greenwood Press, 2002.

Yoo, David K. *Growing Up Nisei: Race, Generation, and Culture Among Japanese Americans of California, 1924-49*. Champaign: University of Illinois Press, 2000.

SEE ALSO: Anti-Japanese movement; Chinese American press; Filipino American press; Japanese American Citizens League; Japanese American internment; Literature; Little Tokyos; San Francisco; Television and radio.

JAPANESE IMMIGRANTS

SIGNIFICANCE: From the 1880's, Japanese immigration to Hawaii and the western states made the Japanese one of the largest Asian ethnic groups in the United States. Though mostly blocked by legislation between 1924 and 1965, some Japanese immigration continued through those years. Japanese Americans completely integrated and became very successful in government, business, the sciences, and cultural enterprises.

The first immigrants from Japan began to arrive in the Hawaiian Islands between 1885 and 1895, following on the heels of the Chinese Exclusion Act of 1882. Plantation owners who were forbidden from hiring Chinese workers hired thousands of Japanese citizens to work in the sugar cane and pineapple fields. About half of these Japanese eventually migrated to California, Oregon, and Washington State. More than 100,000 Japanese people made the journey across the Pacific to Hawaii before 1900, making the Japanese the dominant immigrant group in the islands. The new Meiji emperor of Japan had opened up the country and finally allowed citizens to emigrate. The working conditions were not good in Hawaii, but Japanese laborers were lured to the islands by the prospects of earning ten times more than was possible in their home country.

LIFE IN HAWAII

During the 1880's, Hawaii was technically still a monarchy but was mostly controlled by American businessmen and plantation owners who farmed sugar cane, coffee, and pineapple on large estates throughout the islands. This required huge workforces. The native Hawaiians had fled or died out due to the diseases brought by American and European missionaries and white settlers, thus creating a labor market for the Chinese and Japanese. As a part of its new openness to foreign trade, the Meiji government formulated an agreement with Hawaii that made it easier for agricultural workers to leave Japan to work in the plantations. The agreement took the form of a labor contract that allowed American plantation owners to pay for transportation costs to Hawaii. The Japanese were required to work for up to a year to repay the debt.

In 1885, approximately 30,000 Japanese workers immigrated to Hawaii. The first-generation Japanese born outside America were known as the Issei. They had few chances for education or good-paying jobs at home and hoped to save some of the money they earned working in Hawaii. Almost all the Japanese immigrants to Hawaii worked the sugar cane fields and were paid low wages. Some returned to Japan after one year, but many stayed in Hawaii until the opportunity arose to immigrate to the West Coast of the United States.

The number of Japanese moving to Hawaii through labor contracts and also through repayment arrangements made between immigrants and their home villages greatly increased during the last years of the nineteenth century. The official census of Hawaii counted 12,610 Japanese citizens in 1890, and that number had increased to more than 60,000 by the turn of the century. The new Japanese residents of Hawaii set up communities that resembled Japanese villages around the boundaries of plantations. The influx of Japanese to the islands was mutually beneficial because it provided jobs to those displaced by the Meiji Restoration. The thousands of new workers helped increase the productivity of the sugar cane and pineapple fields. The working conditions were unsurprisingly not good: The plantation workers spoke only English and treated the Japanese workers like horses or cattle, forcing them to get up at 4:00 A.M. to begin working the fields at 6:00 A.M., seven days a week.

In 1900, Hawaii became a U.S. territory, which meant that it would be governed by U.S. law, under which contract labor arrangements were illegal. When the Japanese who came to Hawaii under such a contract finished their obligation with the plantation owner, they were free to return to Japan. Many chose to go to California to look for better opportunities, while about one-third decided to remain in Hawaii and continue in agricultural labor. Since the majority of Japanese workers were men, some had to wait for future wives to be sent from Japan through arranged marriages, which were still common during the early years of the twentieth century. Some women traveled to Hawaii to join brothers or husbands already working there.

The longer the Japanese stayed in Hawaii, the more likely they were to marry and have children, thereby increasing the size of their community. As fear of the immigrants increased, in 1908 Japanese workers staged protests against the long hours and harsh conditions, demanding better wages and safer working conditions. The strike did not change the plantations' working conditions but served as a testament to increased immigrant political power and community action. With little prospect of change in Hawaii, Japanese workers left the islands to search for better jobs, mostly in California. About 40,000 Japanese traveled from Hawaii in

PROFILE OF JAPANESE IMMIGRANTS	
Country of origin	Japan
Primary language	Japanese
Primary regions of U.S. settlement	Hawaii, West Coast
Earliest significant arrivals	1880's
Peak immigration period	1900-1920's
Twenty-first century legal residents*	62,096 (7,762 per year)

*Immigrants who obtained legal permanent resident status in the United States.

Source: Department of Homeland Security, *Yearbook of Immigration Statistics, 2008.*

the years after the labor strike of 1908, becoming the first large group of Japanese immigrants to reach the mainland.

JOURNEY TO THE MAINLAND

By 1908, a labor shortage had been created by anti-immigrant laws such as the Chinese Exclusion Act of 1882, which prohibited Chinese from becoming U.S. citizens, making it easy for the Japanese workers to find jobs. Chinese workers had taken many of the lowest-paying jobs in railroad construction, farming, logging, mining, and fishing, but now those jobs were available to new immigrants. Some Japanese looked for work in cities such as San Francisco and Los Angeles, but many had grown up on farms in Japan or Hawaii, so they decided to pursue agricultural work. They were especially keen on the possibility that they might eventually be able to buy the land themselves. The large and productive valleys of California presented unlimited possibilities.

Japanese workers, like the Chinese before them, soon developed the reputation for accepting physically demanding work for low pay. They took to the fields and factories, working long hours and putting up with challenging conditions. Farmworkers who harvested produce were paid by the bushel of produce picked. Japanese workers proved that they could earn twice the pay of others because they were quick and efficient. They came from a small country with limited farm resources, so they were accustomed to getting the most produce from the lowest-quality farmland. In California, where the land was fertile and abundant, Japanese farmers could outproduce other farmers with techniques such as growing strawberries between rows of grapevines. They were also good at saving their earnings, so eventually farmworkers could combine their individual savings and buy land for the benefit of one another.

PRESSURE BUILDS TO EXCLUDE JAPANESE

The Japanese immigrants' willingness to work long hours and work together in order to purchase farmland made them one of the most successful ethnic groups, but some Americans resented their success. Some people felt that the Japanese were taking away jobs from white Americans. Labor unions such as the American Federation of Labor (AFL) refused to allow Japanese workers to join

their organizations. Businesspeople and farmers were afraid of the Japanese workers' success, and they began to pressure the government to take action. In 1905, the Asiatic Exclusion League (AEL) was formed in California to prevent more immigrants from coming to the United States from Japan. The AEL and other racist groups pressured President Theodore Roosevelt to stop further immigration, but Roosevelt did not want to needlessly irritate the Japanese government. Roosevelt vetoed several new laws modeled after the 1882 Chinese Exclusion Act, but he did accept the Gentlemen's Agreement with Japan in 1907, which prohibited male workers from emigrating to Hawaii or the mainland. While new immigration was banned, the agreement allowed the Japanese to send family members (children, wives, or parents) of workers already living in the United States to join them.

More anti-Japanese laws were passed in the years after the Gentlemen's Agreement because of ethnocentrism and negative attitudes about immigrants from places other than northern Europe. The Immigration Restriction League (IRL) was led by Prescott Hall, who argued that people from northern Europe were energetic, free, and progressive while southern Europeans, Jews, and Asians were downtrodden, primitive, and lazy. These racist attitudes were common during the early twentieth century. Both the AEL and the IRL posited that the Japanese were taking away unskilled, low-paying jobs from Euro-Americans, but in fact the industrious Japanese were rapidly leaving agricultural work and beginning to own land and lease it to others.

In 1913, however, California enacted its first Alien Land Law, which made it illegal for noncitizens to purchase land. A Japanese immigrant named Takao Ozawa resented this law and fought against it all the way to the U.S. Supreme Court, which declared in 1922 that naturalized citizenship was limited to whites and African Americans. However, children of Japanese immigrants born in the United States would be considered citizens. The Immigration Act of 1924 prevented almost all immigration from Japan for three decades. Despite these barriers, Japanese immigrants continued to work hard and prosper, combining resources to create social organizations such as savings and loans, banks, and social assistance groups. The slew

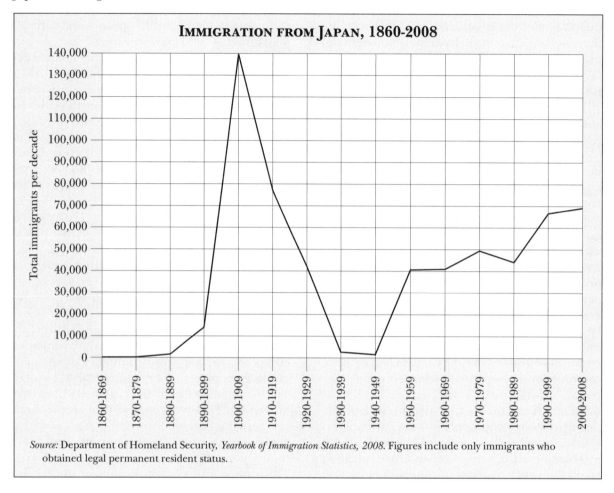

IMMIGRATION FROM JAPAN, 1860-2008

Source: Department of Homeland Security, *Yearbook of Immigration Statistics, 2008.* Figures include only immigrants who obtained legal permanent resident status.

of anti-Japanese laws was not completely effective because the new laws did not apply to those born in the United States.

WORLD WAR II AND JAPANESE IMMIGRANTS

During the 1930's, as the United States struggled through the Great Depression, Japan's government became increasingly militaristic. With Emperor Hirohito on the throne, Japanese leaders elevated the traditional Shinto religion, transformed the emperor into a religious figure, and demanded total obedience to the state. Japan turned away from the path of modernization and democracy, spreading a doctrine of world domination and propaganda about its racial superiority. Japan's army invaded China's Manchuria region in 1931 to begin a path of destruction that would not end until the atomic bombs were dropped on Hiroshima and Nagasaki in August, 1945. After the Jap-

anese surprise attack on Pearl Harbor on December 7, 1941, the United States declared war on Japan and its allies, including Adolf Hitler's Germany and Benito Mussolini's Italy.

Like other Americans, the Japanese Americans in the western states viewed the rise of the military government in 1930's Japan with savage indignation, and they could not understand the godlike reverence for Hirohito. After many years of anti-Japanese laws in California, some people were still suspicious of the Japanese citizens who worked hard, owned houses and farms, and attended churches and schools like other Americans. Soon after Pearl Harbor, western states enforced curfews that required Japanese Americans to stay inside their homes between 8:00 P.M. and 6:00 A.M. The Federal Bureau of Investigation (FBI) went to work arresting suspicious "enemy aliens" who might be leaders in the Japanese community such as Shinto and Buddhist priests, businesspeople, teachers, and professionals. In 1942, California fired all state employees of Japanese ancestry without reason or due process of law. Most were American citizens with rights guaranteed by the U.S. Constitution. Secretary of War Henry Stimson believed that Japanese American citizens were more loyal to their race than to their adopted country.

In February, 1942, President Franklin D. Roosevelt issued Executive Order 9066, which empowered the military to remove any persons from any area in the country where national security was at risk. Even though the executive order did not mention the Japanese by name, it was effectively designed to contain Japanese Americans in California, Oregon, and Washington State. Roosevelt's order displaced some 120,000 Japanese Americans from their homes, relocating the immigrants to internment camps for the duration of the war. About 70,000 of this group were U.S. citizens. Most of the Japanese were surprised by the forced resettlement because they thought of themselves as Americans. The Army's Western Defense Command set up makeshift assembly centers at old fairgrounds, horse racetracks, rodeo grounds, and farm labor camps, from which internees were later transferred to permanent detention camps in scattered locations throughout the United States, from Manzanar, California, to Rohwer, Arkansas.

As the tide of World War II began to change and the Allies won battles in Europe and in the Pacific, Americans started to reconsider the internment camps and their view of Japanese Americans. Many Japanese Americans stayed in the camps from 1942 until the end of 1944, but some took a loyalty test and were allowed to leave as long as they resettled away from the West Coast. Some Japanese Americans were disgusted by the loyalty tests and refused to submit to them since they were already legal citizens.

FROM THE 1950'S THROUGH THE 1970'S

With the tragic conclusion of World War II, a difficult period for Japanese Americans ended. The Evacuation Claims Act of 1948 allowed Japanese Americans who had lost property during the internment to claim 10 percent of every dollar lost, but this small amount of compensation was difficult to obtain. During the 1950's, many Japanese immigrants had dispersed to other cities, but the majority still lived in Los Angeles, San Francisco, and San Jose, which had their own Little Toykos. The largest group of new Japanese immigrants was made up of "war brides," women who had married American soldiers during the occupation of Japan. In some ways, the war brides had a more difficult

Japanese immigrants awaiting processing at the federal government's immigrant reception center on San Francisco Bay's Angel Island during the 1920's. (NARA)

time than the first Japanese immigrants because they lacked a social network and moved to places where few if any Japanese people were living.

During the early 1960's, John F. Kennedy called for reform of exclusionary immigration policies, namely those of the Immigration Act of 1924. After Kennedy's assassination in 1963, President Lyndon B. Johnson carried out Kennedy's wishes with the enactment of the Immigration and Nationality Act of 1965, which resulted in more than doubling Japanese immigration to the United States from less than 2,000 to about 4,500 per year. The Civil Rights movement, led by Martin Luther King, Jr., also influenced Japanese Americans, as they began to question the violation of their rights by the government during the 1940's. Some Japanese Americans published memoirs about their experiences in the internment camps and made a pilgrimage to Manzanar. Bowing to pressure from Japanese Americans, Gerald R. Ford signed a proclamation in 1976 admitting that internment had been a "national mistake."

LATE TWENTIETH AND EARLY TWENTY-FIRST CENTURIES

According to the 1980 U.S. Census, more than 600,000 Japanese Americans were living in the United States, still mostly in the western states. Third- and fourth-generation Japanese Americans were well integrated into American society. Surveys revealed that about half of the married Japanese Americans living in large California cities were married to non-Japanese. Japanese Americans were successful in many professional careers and were represented at many levels of local, regional, and national politics. In 1980, Congress established the Commission on Wartime Relocation and Internment of Civilians to hold hearings, allowing many Japanese Americans to speak about their experiences in the internment camps for the first time. In 1988, President Ronald Reagan signed a bill that gave payments of $20,000 to each surviving Japanese American detainee, and the law also provided money for education of their descendants. Although it took more than forty years, justice was finally realized.

The 2000 U.S. Census documented about 800,000 citizens who claimed Japanese ancestry. Most Japanese who came to the United States during the late twentieth century tended to be either university students or high school students who stayed about five years, or Japanese businessmen, who stayed for a shorter time. In the early twenty-first century, the number of Japanese immigrants to the United States is relatively small compared with the influx in the early twentieth century, but the impact of Japanese culture has been tremendous. In the late twentieth and early twenty-first centuries, Japanese corporations started to build factories in the United States as car companies such as Honda, Toyota, and Nissan became increasingly popular. Japanese consumer electronics companies such as Sony, Hitachi, Toshiba, and Panasonic became household names in America. Japanese popular culture, including anime and manga, and Japanese cuisine also became widely popular with Americans. The rapid acceptance of Japanese culture is all the more astonishing given the rampant racism and anti-immigration laws of the 1920's and 1930's. Japanese Americans have become one of the most assimilated and successful groups of immigrants in the United States.

Jonathan L. Thorndike

FURTHER READING

Daniels, Roger. *Asian America: Chinese and Japanese in the United States Since 1850.* Seattle: University of Washington Press, 1988. Well-written, scholarly account of the experiences of Japanese and Chinese immigrants in America.

Duus, Peter, ed. *The Twentieth Century.* Vol. 6 in *The Cambridge History of Japan.* New York: Cambridge University Press, 1989. Essays discuss the rise of Japanese nationalism and the push toward colonial expansion and World War II.

Gordon, Andrew. *A Modern History of Japan: From Tokugawa Times to the Present.* New York: Oxford University Press, 2003. An excellent overview of Japan in relation to world history and immigration.

Ingram, W. Scott. *Japanese Immigrants.* New York: Facts On File, 2005. Juvenile book with good-quality photographs and sidebars about Japanese culture and individuals' stories.

Jansen, Marius B., ed. *The Nineteenth Century.* Vol. 5 in *The Cambridge History of Japan.* New York: Cambridge University Press, 1989. Standard scholarly work that chronicles Japan's transformation from a feudal society to a modern democratic state during the Meiji Restoration.

Takaki, Ronald. *Strangers from a Different Shore: A History of Asian Americans.* Boston: Little, Brown, 1989. An account of the systematic racism and discrimination that Chinese, Japanese, and later immigrants from East Asia and Southeast Asia faced in the West.

SEE ALSO: Anti-Japanese movement; Asiatic Exclusion League; Gentlemen's Agreement; Gospel Society; Issei; Japanese American Citizens League; Japanese American internment; Japanese Peruvians; Little Tokyos; North American Free Trade Agreement; *Ozawa v. United States*; "Yellow peril" campaign.

JAPANESE PERUVIANS

IDENTIFICATION: Peruvians of Japanese descent who were deported to the United States during World War II

SIGNIFICANCE: Although Peruvians would elect a Japanese man, Alberto Fujimori, the president of their country in 1990, earlier generations of Peruvians resented and distrusted the Japanese living in their country. In an effort to send all its Japanese people to Japan during World War II, the Peruvian government began shipping them to the United States, where most of the deportees were interned for the duration of the war, along with many Japanese Americans.

During the late nineteenth and early twentieth centuries, the deteriorating economic situation in Japan prompted many young Japanese to migrate to the Americas. When the Japanese were legally barred from entering the United States, they turned their attention to South American nations. In 1899, the first Japanese began settling in Peru.

Although initially hired by Peruvian agricultural landowners, many Japanese immigrants eventually migrated to Peru's cities to work as small-scale merchants. South Americans did not wholeheartedly welcome the Japanese immigrants, however. This distrust and hostility deepened during the 1930's, partly because of the perceived affluence of the Japanese during the Great Depression and partly because of Japan's aggressive empire building.

During the 1930's and early 1940's, the Peruvian government enacted discriminatory laws directed against Japanese immigrants.

In May, 1940, rumors that the Japanese in Peru's capital city, Lima, were planning to take over the country led to anti-Japanese riots. Anti-Japanese sentiments combined with the December, 1941, Japanese attack on Pearl Harbor, the U.S. naval base in Hawaii, to lead the administration of President Manuel Prado y Ugarteche to view the internment of Japanese as both politically popular and expedient. However, in order to intern more than six thousand people, the government would need money that it did not want to spend. Prado found it easier and cheaper to send the Japanese to the United States.

On the grounds of "military necessity," Peru deported about 1,800 first-generation Issei and second-generation Nisei to the United States. The first ship, the *Etolin*, left Callau in April, 1942, with 141 male Japanese Peruvians. No legal charges had been brought against any of these people, none of whom had criminal records. Designated as prisoners of war, the deportees were taken to temporary camps in Panama before debarking in New Orleans, Louisiana. From there, they were sent to internment camps in Texas and Montana.

Engaged in a version of ethnic cleansing, the Peruvian government expected that the Japanese whom it was deporting would eventually be sent to Japan. Meanwhile, U.S. secretary of state Cordell Hull and U.S. Armed Forces chief of staff George C. Marshall supported the collection of Japanese Peruvians, anticipating that they might be exchanged for American civilians interned in Japanese-occupied territories in Asia. No internees were ever exchanged, but 342 of the Japanese Peruvians did return to Japan in 1942. A lack of shipping hampered Peru's internment program from its start and limited the number of deportees to 1,800.

After World War II ended in 1945, and U.S. internment camps were closed, about 100 Japanese Peruvians who had been interned in the United States returned to Peru. About 300 remained in the United States. The rest went to Japan.

Caryn E. Neumann

FURTHER READING

Kikumura-Yano, Akemi, ed. *Encyclopedia of Japanese Descendants in the Americas: An Illustrated History of the Nikkei.* Walnut Creek, Calif.: AltaMira Press, 2002.

Masterson, Daniel M., and Sayaka Funada-Classen. *The Japanese in Latin America.* Champaign: University of Illinois Press, 2004.

SEE ALSO: Anti-Japanese movement; Asian immigrants; Japanese American internment; Japanese immigrants; Latin American immigrants.

JENNINGS, PETER

IDENTIFICATION: Canadian-born American television journalist
BORN: July 29, 1938; Toronto, Ontario, Canada
DIED: August 7, 2005; New York, New York

SIGNIFICANCE: As an immigrant news broadcaster, Jennings was exceptionally conscious of America's place in the world community. With his international focus, he led his Amer-

ican Broadcasting Company (ABC) network to top ratings and coauthored two books that illumine the American experience.

Peter Jennings was the son of Elizabeth Osborne and Charles Jennings. His father was Canada's first network television news anchor and later a Canadian Broadcasting Corporation executive. Peter himself was initially so little motivated by formal education that he dropped out of high school. After obtaining some media experience in Canada, he moved to New York when he was given the opportunity to become American television's youngest network news anchor. Feeling unprepared for that assignment, he instead turned to international reporting, at which he excelled. In 1971, he established the first American television news bureau in any Arab country. Six years later, he became ABC's first chief foreign correspondent and was respected for his preparation, research, and eagerness to meet people of all backgrounds.

In 1978, Jennings became part of a three-person

Peter Jennings during the early 1980's. (AP/Wide World Photos)

ABC anchor team for *World News Tonight*. In 1983, he became the program's sole anchor. His documentaries and other specials often covered international problems. As an immigrant and traveler, he was increasingly fascinated by the uniqueness of America, which he described as the only nation founded on ideas written into a constitution. With Todd Brewster he wrote *The Century* (1998), exploring the impact of twentieth century events upon Americans. In 2002, he followed that book with *In Search of America*, an exploration of how constitutional ideals still shape American identity. Both books accompanied television documentary series.

In 2003, Jennings became an American citizen. Through the last two years of his life, he held dual Canadian/American citizenship.

Betty Richardson

FURTHER READING

Darnton, Kate, Kayce Freed Jennings, and Lynn Sherr, eds. *Peter Jennings: A Reporter's Life*. New York: Public Affairs, 2007.

Fensch, Thomas. *Television News Anchors: An Anthology of Profiles of the Major Figures and Issues in United States Network Reporting*. Woodlands, Tex.: New Century, 2001.

SEE ALSO: Canadian immigrants; Dual citizenship; Huffington, Arianna; Pulitzer, Joseph; Television and radio.

JEWISH IMMIGRANTS

IDENTIFICATION: Adherents of Judaism and their ethnic kin who derived from many different European nations, particularly those in eastern Europe

SIGNIFICANCE: By the turn of the twenty-first century, about 5.1 million Jews were living in the United States, primarily in larger cities and their suburbs. Most Jews are considered part of the U.S. middle class, and do every type of work. A high percentage are business executives, professionals, or skilled workers, and many are in the fields of art, literature, and theater. Among Jews' primary concerns are education and philanthropy.

Jews were present in what is now the United States as early as the colonial period of the seventeenth century. The earliest Jewish communities consisted of Sephardic Jews of Spanish and Portuguese ancestry, who had migrated to Brazil before moving on to North America in 1654 aboard a ship named *Sainte Catherine.*

Early settlers in New Amsterdam confronted religious prejudice and discrimination by Governor Peter Stuyvesant, who did not wish them to remain. The Jews petitioned the Dutch West Indies Company, however, and were permitted to settle in the area. Governor Stuyvesant made life difficult for them by restricting their rights and exempting them from military service. However, the Jews were not denied the opportunity to practice their religion in private. The first Jewish congregation in North America, Shearith Israel (Remnant of Israel) dates from April 26, 1655.

After Dutch-ruled New Amsterdam fell to the British and became New York City in 1664, Jewish religious services continued in homes until 1695, when the Jewish immigrants were given permission to build a synagogue. This was finally accomplished in 1728. English became the standard language of these immigrants, and until the early 1820's Jewish immigrant religious practices reflected the Sephardic tradition, and Shearith Israel was regarded as the "mother synagogue." Sephardic rituals were also adopted by Ashkenazi Jews from Germany and Poland.

COLONIAL LIFE

Business was the occupation of the early Jewish settlers. Some were traders and craftsmen; others were wealthy merchants. Eventually, some of them were not satisfied to remain in New York and left for other colonies. Jewish settlements were established in Rhode Island, where Newport became the center of the country's whale oil, candle, and soap industries. By the start of the American Revolution in 1775, Newport had become the most important center of Jewish life in the country. Of the approximately 1,500 Jews in the colonies at that time, the largest concentration—about 200—lived in Newport, where they established what would become the oldest surviving synagogue in the United States.

The lifestyles of colonial Jews generally mirrored those of their neighbors, except in their ritu-

Editorial cartoon in an early 1881 issue of Frank Leslie's Illustrated Newspaper *showing "Columbia" welcoming Jewish refugees from German persecution.* (Library of Congress)

als and religious practices. Following kosher dietary laws, keeping proper Jewish homes, observing holidays, and educating children constituted significant challenges for Jews living outside the large cities. By the end of the eighteenth century, only about 3,000 Jews lived in the entire United States. More than half of them lived in the South. Georgia elected the country's first Jewish governor, Daniel Emanuel. Jews were becoming assimilated into American society and were continuing to thrive, but through intermarriage with Christians and religious conversions, their numbers were actually declining.

With the Louisiana Purchase in 1803, the country's boundaries expanded, and a number of Ashkenazi immigrants went westward. Jews helped to found St. Louis, Nashville, Detroit, and Cincinnati. Many of the Ashkenazi Jews who arrived during the early nineteenth century settled in the large cities of the East where they first landed, but some traveled inland to smaller cities such as Rochester, Pittsburgh, Chicago, and Cincinnati. Because they were generally poor and uneducated with little English-speaking ability, these immigrant tended to live close together in cities and ply trades that did not require special knowledge or education, such as garment-making and peddling.

NINETEENTH CENTURY TRENDS

Jewish immigration began increasing significant during the mid-nineteenth century, Between 1840 and 1860, the Jewish population of the United States rose to about 200,000, due in large part to an influx of immigrants from central Europe seeking refuge from the strife surrounding the failed revolutions of 1848, worsening economic conditions, and anti-Jewish legislation in many of the German-speaking states. These new immigrants were generally better educated and more financially secure than earlier Jewish immigrants, and brought with them higher culture, a tradition of charity, and reform Jewish practices to their new homes. Among these new immigrants were trained physicians who opened Jews Hospital (later known as Mount Sinai Hospital) in New York City, beginning a tradition of Jewish-sponsored hospitals in American cities. Founded to provide places in which Jewish physicians could work, these hospitals evolved into well-respected community institutions for all members of society. Other Jews eventually became government officials in their communities, as well as industrialists and financiers. Many Jewish merchants became successful department store moguls.

By 1880, approximately 250,000 Jews were living in the United States. Many of them were highly educated and largely secular German Jews. Reformers among these immigrants became the foundation of the emerging reform Jewish movement in the United States. Rabbi Isaac Mayer Wise, who had been born in Bohemia in 1819, is credited with founding the reform movement, creating the Union of American Hebrew Congregations, and establishing the rabbinical school Hebrew Union College in Cincinnati, Ohio.

Other immigrants during that era came from the poor rural Jewish populations of Russia, Poland, Lithuania, and Ukraine, fleeing religious persecution in eastern Europe. The primarily Yiddish-speaking Ashkenazi Jews had little in common with the upper-class German Jews, who remained segregated in worship and business dealings. The Ashkenazi Jews founded their own Orthodox synagogues and tended to associate mainly with other members of their own community.

Mass Exodus

During the nineteenth century, most Russian Jews lived in confined areas as laborers and small merchants. Anti-Semitism, suspicion, and hatred were ever present, and deadly government-sponsored pogroms against Jews created a permanent atmosphere of fear among Russian Jews. The goal of the Russian government was to force one-third of all Russian Jews to leave Russia, another third to convert to Christianity, and the final third to starve to death. In response to this catastrophic government plan, Russian Jews flooded European port cities, from which they sailed to America.

After reaching the United States, many Russian Jews gravitated to New York City's lower East Side, where newcomers sought out others from their Russian village and regions. Eventually, the lower East Side became a melting pot of Yiddish speakers. Similar developments occurred in smaller cities, such as Boston and Philadelphia. To aid new immigrants, *Landsmanschaften*, organizations based on geographic ties to home villages, assumed the role of extended family and provided health insurance, interest-free loans, and medical and burial assistance. Despite their difficulties in becoming

assimilated into the new culture, the newly arrived Jews wrote letters to relatives and friends with glowing accounts of America, urging them to follow them there.

Between 1881 and 1890, 3.7 percent of all immigrants to the United States were Jews. By the first decade of the twentieth century, Jews constituted more than 10 percent of all immigrants, and by 1920, 23 percent of the world's Jews lived in the United States. Two million Jews had arrived from eastern Europe alone by 1924. As distrust of immigrants grew after World War I, the Immigration Act of 1921 and the national origins quota system established by the Immigration Act of 1924 severely restricted immigration from southern and eastern Europe after that time.

Yiddish Culture and Its Demise

A dialect of German written in Hebrew characters, the Yiddish language united Jewish immigrants of all classes and backgrounds. Immigrants were comforted by its familiarity in the cities and the theater, in newspapers and vaudeville. Performers such as Groucho Marx, Jack Benny, Walter Winchell, George Jessel, and Molly Picon, among many others, had their start in vaudeville and went on to success in radio and television. More than twenty Yiddish newspapers, the best known of which was the *Jewish Daily Forward*, were published in New York City alone.

Because the borders of the United States were effectively closed to new Jewish immigrants, the earlier immigrants were becoming Americanized and assimilated more quickly. Consequently, Jewish ghettoes, the Yiddish press, and the Yiddish theater steadily declined. Growing anti-Semitism attacked Jews, their patriotism, and their character. During the 1920's, some prestigious universities established quotas limiting the numbers of Jewish students they would admit. Jewish graduates also faced discrimination as they attempted to attend graduate and professional schools; some were forced to attend foreign medical schools or change their career goals. Some changed their names, hiding their Jewish backgrounds to gain admission to restricted institutions. Blatant discrimination in housing existed, as did discrimination in employment, private clubs, and private schools.

Nevertheless, Jews made their mark in many areas. Jewish Americans achieved success in entertainment. Levi Schubert, Albert Zukor, Marcus Loew, and Louis B. Mayer founded theaters and film production companies; Jewish composers/songwriters George and Ira Gershwin and Irving Berlin achieved phenomenal success. Business entrepreneur Helena Rubenstein founded a giant cosmetics company, and Rose Schneiderman, a labor activist and political leader seeking to improve working conditions, was the only woman appointed by President Franklin D. Roosevelt to the labor advisory board of the National Recovery Administration. Baseball star Hank Greenberg, the first baseman for the Detroit Tigers, broke several long-standing records and was inducted into the Baseball Hall of Fame.

THE EUROPEAN HOLOCAUST

After Adolf Hitler became chancellor of Germany in 1933, he began to put anti-Semitic policies into effect and vowed to exterminate the entire Jewish race. Concentration camps were opened at Dachau, Buchenwald, and Sachsenhausen. The plight of the Jews in Germany grew steadily worse, and many European Jews were convinced that their only chance for survival was to emigrate to the United States. Restrictive U.S. immigration laws were in effect, however, and immigrants had to prove that they either had sufficient resources to sustain themselves in the United States or had families to support them.

Austrian Jews were also forced from their homes and sent to a camp called Mauthausen after Germany occupied Austria in 1938. On November 9-10, 1938, Nazi troops destroyed Jewish homes and synagogues and brutally beat and murdered Jews during *Kristallnacht* (night of the broken glass). The event spurred U.S. president Franklin D. Roosevelt to ease immigration restrictions and permit more Jewish immigrants to enter the United States. Between 1938 and 1941, more than 100,000 European Jews immigrated to the United States.

After Poland fell to the Nazis in September 1939, Jews were forced to leave their homes and move into large cities. Many died from lack of food or proper housing; others were taken to the Auschwitz concentration camp, which opened in 1940. Nazi troops continued to march across Western Europe, conquering many nations. In early 1942, Nazi officials met and discussed what they called the "Final Solution to the Jewish Ques-

tion"—a genocide that had as its goal the total extermination of the Jews. Other concentration camps were erected in Poland in which guards used poisonous gas to execute inhabitants.

By the middle of 1942 confirmed reports came out of Poland about the mass executions of Jews by the Nazis. Jewish charitable organizations worked to aid and transport the Polish Jews; in 1944 the War Refugee Board bribed Nazi officials to release 200,000 from the concentration camps. A total of approximately 6 million Jews were slaughtered during the Holocaust.

AFTER WORLD WAR II

New U.S. laws enacted after the war greatly increased the number of displaced persons permitted to enter the United States. Between 1946 and 1952, more than 80,000 Jews came to America. Assisted by the Hebrew Immigrant Aid society and the National Council of Jewish Women, the immigrants received temporary housing, food, clothing, medical care, and instruction in English. As laws outlawing discrimination in housing were passed during the 1950's, Jews moved to urban suburbs, established new temples and synagogues, and started new religious schools and community centers. During the last two decades of the twentieth century and the first years of the twenty-first century, approximately 400,000 new Jewish immigrants came to the United States, many to seek educational opportunities.

Marcia J. Weiss

FURTHER READING

Diner, Hasia. *The Jews of the United States, 1654-2000.* Berkeley: University of California Press, 2004. Survey of American Jewish history that emphasizes religious issues, while also covering economic and cultural issues.

Finkelstein, Norman H. *American Jewish History.* Philadelphia: Jewish Publication Society, 2007. Introduction to the historical, cultural, and religious heritage of American Jews. Contains numerous photographs, maps, and charts.

Friedman, Saul A. *No Haven for the Oppressed: United States Policy Toward Jewish Refugees, 1938-1945.* Detroit: Wayne State University Press, 1973. Examination of anti-Semitic hostility toward Jews fleeing from the Holocaust during Germany's Nazi era.

Howe, Irving. *World of Our Fathers: The Journey of the East European Jews to America and the Life They Found and Made.* New York: Simon & Schuster, 1976. Story of the eastern European Jews who came to America and their efforts to retain their Yiddish culture.

Telushkin, Rabbi Joseph. *The Golden Land: The Story of Jewish Immigration to America.* New York: Harmony Books, 2002. Tells the story of Jewish immigration to America through removable documents and artifacts.

Wenger, Beth. *The Jewish Americans.* New York: Doubleday, 2007. Comprehensive history of Jews in the United States. Includes numerous first-person accounts of the Jewish experience and numerous photographs.

Worth, Richard. *Jewish Immigrants.* New York: Facts On File, 2005. Concise history of Jewish immigration written for young readers. Well illustrated.

SEE ALSO: American Jewish Committee; Anti-Defamation League; Anti-Semitism; Berlin, Irving; Einstein, Albert; Former Soviet Union immigrants; Garment industry; Holocaust; Israeli immigrants; Name changing; Polish immigrants; World War II.

JORDAN V. TASHIRO

THE CASE: U.S. Supreme Court decision concerning privileges in treaties

DATE: Decided on November 19, 1928

> **SIGNIFICANCE:** One of a series of rulings relating to the tension between U.S. treaties with Japan and California's alien land laws, the *Tashiro* decision gave a broad and liberal interpretation of the privileges guaranteed by treaties, emphasizing the common meanings of the words in a 1911 commerce treaty.

The U.S.-Japanese Treaty of Commerce and Navigation of 1911 authorized citizens of Japan to participate in commerce, which included everything "incident to or necessary for trade upon the same terms as native citizens." The treaty put significant limits on the extent to which California was able to enforce the discriminatory Alien Land Law, passed in 1913. In interpreting the treaty, the Supreme Court had ruled that the treaty protected the right

to operate a pawnbroker business but that it did not extend to manufacturing or agricultural production.

K. Tashiro and other citizens of Japan residing in California petitioned the state government for the incorporation of a Japanese hospital in Los Angeles. State officials refused to consider the petition on the grounds that treaty rights did not extend to the operation of a business corporation. Tashiro and his associates challenged the refusal in state court. When the court agreed with Tashiro's position, the secretary of state of California petitioned the Supreme Court for a writ of certiorari, which was granted.

The Supreme Court unanimously upheld the ruling of the lower court. Writing the opinion of the Court, Justice Harlan F. Stone followed the precedent of liberally construing the privileges enumerated in treaties, and he concluded that the ordinary meanings of the words in the 1911 treaty necessarily included three relevant privileges: (1) conducting a business in corporate form, (2) providing medical services for a fee, and (3) leasing an appropriate amount of land needed for the purpose of a commercial business.

Thomas Tandy Lewis

FURTHER READING

Hyung-chan, Kim, ed. *Asian Americans and the Supreme Court: A Documentary History.* Westport, Conn.: Greenwood Press, 1992.

LeMay, Michael, and Elliott Robert Barkan, eds. *U.S. Immigration and Naturalization Laws and Issues: A Documentary History.* Westport, Conn.: Greenwood Press, 1999.

SEE ALSO: Alien land laws; California; History of immigration after 1891; Japanese immigrants; Supreme Court, U.S.

THE JUNGLE

IDENTIFICATION: Novel by Upton Sinclair about an immigrant Lithuanian family in Chicago and the corrupt meatpacking industry

DATE: First published in 1906

> **SIGNIFICANCE:** In preparation for the writing of *The Jungle,* Sinclair visited Chicago meat-

Upton Sinclair. (Library of Congress)

packing plants disguised as a worker in order to experience at first hand the brutal working conditions and the contamination of the meat products for America's dinner tables. Although his intention was to bring attention to the plight of exploited workers, public outcry focused on the unsanitary conditions of the meat industry and led to the passage of federal food-inspection laws.

Upton Sinclair's muckraking novel *The Jungle* offers a devastatingly bleak picture of the lives of Lithuanian immigrants lured from their homeland to the dark heart of America—Chicago and the meatpacking industry that destroys them physically and spiritually. From nineteenth century

French naturalists such as Émile Zola, the socialist Sinclair borrowed the concept of the individual rendered powerless by immense natural and sociopolitical forces that reduce humans to animals caught in a trap.

The Jungle begins with the wedding reception of Jurgis Rudkus and Ona Lukoszaite, who postponed marrying to save for this expensive but cherished ritual in their culture. Soon the scene will seem a poignant reminder of lost happiness as the family is ground down by drudgery, deception, and death. Jurgis will witness the deaths of his father, Antanas, then Ona along with their second child, and eventually their toddler son, who drowns in a mud puddle. In addition to these losses, Jurgis comes to recognize the full dimensions of the jungle metaphor, or its variant, the slaughterhouse. The immigrants are lambs drawn to the slaughter by oppressive capitalism, exploiting them as "wage-slaves," fleecing them of their hard-earned wages and savings, then condemning them to death by starvation, accident, or disease, just as callously as the meatpackers butcher animals for meat.

Although a mediocre novel as a work of literature, *The Jungle* was a best seller that is still widely read in the twenty-first century, and it became a primary force behind the passage of the Pure Food and Drug Act of 1906, which led in turn to creation of the Food and Drug Administration.

Earl G. Ingersoll

FURTHER READING

Musteikis, Antanas. "The Lithuanian Heroes of *The Jungle*." *Lithuanus* 17, no. 2 (1971): 27-38.

Øverland, Orm. "*The Jungle*: From Lithuanian Peasant to American Socialist." *American Literary Realism* 37, no. 1 (2004): 1-23.

Subacius, Giedrius. *The Lithuanian Jungle*. Amsterdam, Netherlands: Rodopi, 2006.

SEE ALSO: Chicago; Former Soviet Union immigrants; Goldman, Emma; Literature; Presidential elections.

K

KANSAS

SIGNIFICANCE: Kansas's central position on migration and cattle trails and railroads during the nineteenth century made it a region through which large numbers of immigrants passed on their way west. Many of them went no farther.

The first European to lead an exploration of the region that would become the state of Kansas was Francisco Vásquez de Coronado in 1541. Three centuries later, the Santa Fe Trail was cut across the territory to facilitate the transporting of manufactured goods, silver, and furs from neighboring Missouri to New Mexico. Abilene, Kansas, became the final destination for cattle drives following the Chisholm Trail. Railroads soon followed. Cattle loaded onto railcars were carried to Chicago meatpacking plants. By 1880, 8,720 miles of railroad tracks crisscrossed the state.

The first permanent white settlers began dribbling into the territory during the 1830's. The pace of their settlement accelerated after the passage of the Kansas-Nebraska Act in 1854. By the mid-1850's, both abolitionists from the New England states and proslavery settlers from Missouri poured into Kansas to compete for dominance in the struggle to determine whether the territory would become a free or a slave state. Second-generation pioneers coming from Ohio, Indiana, and Illinois tended to settle in the middle section of the territory, while its upper southern region was settled mostly by those coming from Missouri, Kentucky, and southern Indiana. This mix of settlers with violently opposing views on slavery brought an era of chaos and violence that became known as "Bleeding Kansas." Eventually, however, the abolitionists prevailed, and Kansas entered the Union as a free state on January 29, 1861.

After the Civil War (1861-1865), many military veterans, along with European immigrant groups, settled and constructed homesteads in Kansas. Swedes constituted a major concentration near Lindsborg, which is south of Salina. Germans settled west of Maryville; German-Russian Mennonites north of Newton; German-Russian Catholics near Hays; and Czechs west of Ellsworth.

TWENTIETH CENTURY DEVELOPMENTS

More English-speaking immigrants from Ireland, Wales, and Scotland settled in southeast Kansas than in any other Great Plains state, but Germans have remained the largest European immigrant component of the state's population. Farmers in Kansas have led the United States in wheat, sorghum, and sunflower production, but the state's agricultural industry has faced the problem of finding farmworkers, as young Kansans have moved from the rural areas into the cities. Not surprisingly, Johnson County, which contains metropolitan Kansas City, has become the state's fastest-growing county. Meanwhile, the need for farmworkers has contributed to an increase in foreign immigration.

During the late twentieth century, the Hispanic population had an increasing impact on the demographics of the Great Plains.

PROFILE OF KANSAS

Region	Midwest
Entered union	1861
Largest cities	Wichita, Overland Park, Kansas City, Topeka (capital)
Modern immigrant communities	Mexicans, Central Americans

Population	Total	Percent of state	Percent of U.S.	U.S. rank
All state residents	2,764,000	100.0	0.92	33
All foreign-born residents	173,000	6.3	0.46	31

Source: U.S. Census Bureau, *Statistical Abstract for 2006.*
Notes: The U.S. population in 2006 was 299,399,000, of whom 37,548,000 (12.5%) were foreign born. Rankings in last column reflect total numbers, not percentages.

Meatpacking and construction companies began to recruit and hire Mexicans and Central Americans in large numbers to offset union forces by paying the immigrants lower wages. In 2006, Kansas had 173,000 foreign-born residents, who constituted 6.3 percent of the total population of the state. Hispanics are most numerous around the southeast portion of the state. The large influx in Latin American immigrants has brought with it an increase in the numbers of undocumented aliens in the state. U.S. immigration officials have responded with raids on plants employing immigrants that have resulted in mass deportations. During the first decade of the twenty-first century, legislatures in both Kansas and neighboring Nebraska began grappling with economic and social issues that have arisen from illegal immigration. Both states have seen proposals for major changes in the document-verification systems used by companies to stop unscrupulous hiring practices.

Gayla Koerting

FURTHER READING

Blouet, Brian W., and Frederick C. Luebke. *The Great Plains: Environment and Culture.* Lincoln: University of Nebraska Press, 1979.

Gjerde, Jon. *The Minds of the West: The Ethnocultural Evolution of the Rural Middle West, 1830-1917.* Chapel Hill: University of North Carolina Press, 1979.

Webb, Walter Prescott. *The Great Plains.* New York: Ginn, 1931.

Wishart, David J., ed. *Encyclopedia of the Great Plains.* Lincoln: University of Nebraska Press, 2004.

SEE ALSO: Czech and Slovakian immigrants; German immigrants; Iowa; Latin American immigrants; Missouri; Nebraska; Scandinavian immigrants.

KENTUCKY

SIGNIFICANCE: Kentucky has taken in fewer foreign immigrants than more urban states. Most nineteenth and twentieth century immigration was urban or, in the case of Kentucky's eastern coal region, industrial in nature. However, during the last decade of the twentieth century and the first decade of the

next century, immigration to Kentucky began to increase; undocumented Hispanic workers have come in unprecedented numbers.

Although early immigration to Kentucky was dominated by people of Scotch-Irish and English ancestry, immigrants from other parts of Europe were represented as well. Germans—particularly settlers who came by way of Pennsylvania—were not uncommon, and significant numbers of Welsh, French Huguenot, and other groups also came. As early as the 1780's, Dutch settlers from Pennsylvania arrived in Kentucky and near Harrodsburg erected an archaic Dutch Reformed Church meeting house of timbered wattle and daub that still survives. Slaves, too, migrated to frontier Kentucky, and in their veins ran the blood of various, mostly West African, ethnicities.

After 1848, famine and political unrest drove large numbers of Germans and Irish to the United States. While most headed for the Northeast or joined the growing tide of settlement in the American Midwest, a number entered the urban centers of the South. In Kentucky, this meant the Ohio River cities of Covington, Newport, and Louisville. Louisville especially received large numbers of Irish and Germans. In 1850, members of these groups constituted 11,000 of the city's total white population of 36,224. In Louisville, a combination of raw xenophobia, anti-Catholicism (many of the newcomers were Roman Catholics) and the popularity of a short-lived national nativist movement called the Know-Nothing Party finally erupted in the "Bloody Monday" antiforeign riots on election day, August 6, 1855. Twenty-two people were killed and much property was destroyed, but the incident was not to be repeated in Kentucky.

As occurred in a number of other southern states during the late nineteenth century, some Kentuckians feared that the state was not receiving sufficient immigration to support its economic growth. The state legislature took action, creating an immigration commission in 1880. The commission launched a campaign to attract northern Europeans to the state and met with some success. A number of Swiss, Germans and Austrians did arrive. By 1885, these newcomers had established a sprinkling of small colonies, spanning the region between Lyon County in western Kentucky to Laurel in the east. Although none of these settlements thrived as much as hoped, some have survived into the twenty-first century as small communities.

TWENTIETH CENTURY DEVELOPMENTS

As American industry began tapping in earnest the vast timber and mineral resources of the eastern Kentucky mountains during the early twentieth century, new immigrants entered the state. Indeed, as coal mines and company towns arose during the first two decades of the century, Hungarians, Poles, Italians, Yugoslavs, and a veritable Ellis Island of other groups entered the Kentucky coal fields. These immigrants never outnumbered native-born white miners in the region, but they become a large contingent. Immigrants, along with African Americans, were typically assigned the dirtiest and most dangerous of jobs. By 1930, immigrants had begun to leave Kentucky's depressed coal fields, but a handful stayed and their descendants were absorbed into the local culture.

Into the twenty-first century, Kentucky's population has remained predominantly white and native born. Nonetheless, during the 1990's, Kentucky experienced the nation's third-fastest growth in immigrant population. By 2000, about 2.5 percent of Kentucky's total residents were documented immigrants. Immigrants from Vietnam and China were among the two fastest-growing groups to enter the state during this period. Most of these new immigrants did not come to Kentucky directly from their original homelands but instead migrated from elsewhere in the United States. They were evidently hoping to make their livelihoods in a less crowded state.

Hispanics have long worked as laborers in Kentucky. They have had a particularly long-standing presence in central Kentucky's famous thoroughbred horse industry. During the 1990's and early twenty-first century, Latin Americans began entering Kentucky in unprecedented numbers. By 2006, Mexicans alone accounted for nearly one-quarter

of the state's foreign-born population. By this period, a large but unknown number of illegal immigrants—mostly from Mexico but also from other Latin American countries—had entered the Kentucky workforce. Most worked in agriculture, agricultural processing and the service sector. While these undocumented workers are not as numerous as those in some other southern states, their numbers have been sufficiently large to attract political controversy.

Jeremiah Taylor

FURTHER READING

Barrett, Tracy. *Kentucky.* 2d ed. New York: Marshall Cavendish Benchmark, 2008.

Cantrell, Doug. "Immigrants and Community in Harlan County, 1910-1930." *Register of the Kentucky Historical Society* 86 (1988): 119-141.

Klotter, James C., ed. *Our Kentucky: A Study of the Bluegrass State.* 2d ed. Lexington: University Press of Kentucky, 2000.

Ray, Celeste, ed. *The New Encyclopedia of Southern Culture.* Vol. 6. *Ethnicity.* Chapel Hill: University of North Carolina Press, 2007.

SEE ALSO: British immigrants; Coal industry; Economic opportunities; European immigrants; German immigrants; Irish immigrants; Know-Nothing Party; Mexican immigrants; Ohio; Swiss immigrants.

PROFILE OF KENTUCKY

Region	Eastern central United States
Entered union	1792
Largest cities	Lexington-Fayette, Louisville, Owensboro, Bowling Green
Modern immigrant communities	Vietnamese, Asian Indians, Mexicans

Population	Total	Percent of state	Percent of U.S.	U.S. rank
All state residents	4,206,000	100.0	1.40	26
All foreign-born residents	112,000	2.7	0.29	35

Source: U.S. Census Bureau, *Statistical Abstract for 2006.*
Notes: The U.S. population in 2006 was 299,399,000, of whom 37,548,000 (12.5%) were foreign born. Rankings in last column reflect total numbers, not percentages.

KISSINGER, HENRY

IDENTIFICATION: German-born U.S. secretary of state

BORN: May 27, 1923; Fürth, Bavaria, Germany

SIGNIFICANCE: As national security advisor and secretary of state under Presidents Richard M. Nixon and Gerald R. Ford, Kissinger helped shape American foreign policy during the latter half of the Vietnam War.

The son of a middle-class Bavarian Jewish family, Henry Kissinger fled to the United States with his family in 1938 after it became clear that Nazi Germany's hostility toward Jews was no ordinary pogrom to be weathered. In the United States he changed his first name from Heinz to Henry and succeeded in school even while working long hours to help support his family. Drafted into the U.S. armed services in 1943, he worked as an interpreter during the Allied occupation of Germany, where he helped track down and prosecute former Gestapo agents. After the war ended in 1945, he returned to school and earned a doctoral degree in political science at Harvard University in 1954. He later joined the faculty of Harvard and went on to make his mark as an authority on international relations. The books he wrote in that field offered penetrating insights on American nuclear policy that attracted attention at very high levels.

In 1969, President Richard Nixon wooed Kissinger away from academia to accept an appointment as national security advisor. Nixon was so satisfied with Kissinger's work that he elevated Kissinger to secretary of state, making him the nation's top diplomat and the primary shaper of U.S. foreign policy. Although disliked by critics of the Vietnam war, Kissinger survived the Watergate scandal of the early 1970's and remained at his posts under Gerald R. Ford. After Ford lost the presidential election of 1976, Kissinger retired from public service. He became an elder statesman, offering advice to Republican politicians and conservative think tanks.

Leigh Husband Kimmel

FURTHER READING

Berman, Larry. *No Peace, No Honor: Nixon, Kissinger and Betrayal in Vietnam.* New York: Free Press, 2001.

Dallek, Robert. *Nixon and Kissinger: Partners in Power.* New York: HarperCollins, 2007.

Hanhimäki, Jussi. *The Flawed Architect: Henry Kissinger and American Foreign Policy.* New York: Oxford University Press, 2004.

Kissinger, Henry A. *Ending the Vietnam War: A History of America's Involvement in and Extrication from the Vietnam War.* New York: Simon & Schuster, 2003.

SEE ALSO: Albright, Madeleine; Anti-Semitism; German immigrants; Holocaust; Jewish immigrants.

Henry Kissinger. (© The Nobel Foundation)

KNOW-NOTHING PARTY

IDENTIFICATION: Nativist, anti-Roman Catholic political organization

DATE: 1852-1860

ALSO KNOWN AS: Native American Party; National Council of the United States of North America

SIGNIFICANCE: During the nineteenth century, the United States experienced an influx of Roman Catholic immigrants from Europe. These immigrants differed from earlier European immigrants, most of whom had been Protestants. Religious differences between Protestant Americans and Roman Catholics created economic, social, and political strains as the United States became a more diversified country. The Know-Nothing movement emerged in opposition to Catholic immigration.

During the 1830's and 1840's, the United States witnessed an influx of immigrants from Europe. From 1831 to 1840, approximately 538,000 individuals migrated to the United States; one-third of these were Catholics. The decade of the 1840's saw another 1.7 million immigrants come to the United States. Approximately 50 percent of these immigrants were Catholic, primarily from Ireland and Germany. By 1850, approximately 10 percent of the U.S. population was Roman Catholic. Many native-born Protestant Americans began to fear that the United States was being overwhelmed by Catholic immigrants, and some even believed that the pope wanted to colonize the United States in order to extend his authority.

KNOW-NOTHING MOVEMENT

As more and more Catholics came to the United States, they settled in the cities of the North. These immigrants were generally unskilled workers who competed with working-class Protestants for low-wage jobs. Ten-sions between the two groups were compounded by the Panic of 1837, as jobs became scarce and the wages of the working class suffered. Also, as Catholics settled in the cities, disputes arose concerning public aid to parochial schools. At the same time, Catholic parents resisted paying taxes for public schools to which they were unwilling to send their children. Amid growing anti-Catholic sentiment, the Know-Nothing movement would emerge and capitalize on the decline of the major parties—the Whigs and the Democrats—during the 1850's.

During the 1840's, several nativist organizations were established in reaction to Catholic immigration. In 1852, these groups merged to form the National Council of the United States of North America, which later became known as the Know-Nothing Party. Members referred to the organization as the Supreme Order of the Star-Spangled Banner. Membership in the society was limited to native-born citizens who were twenty-one years of

KNOW-NOTHINGISM IN BROOKLYN.

"None but citizens of the United States can be licensed to engage in any employment in this city."
Brooklyn Board of Aldermen.

Editorial cartoon from an 1881 issue of Frank Leslie's Illustrated Newspaper *lampooning a nativist policy of Brooklyn's municipal government.* (Library of Congress)

age or older; Protestant, born of Protestant parents, or raised under Protestant influence; and not married to a Catholic. The stated purpose of the organization was to protect American citizens in the legal and proper exercise of their civil and religious rights, to use legal methods to resist the Catholic Church and other foreign influences against American institutions, and to elect only native-born Protestant Americans to public office. The organization also advocated a twenty-one-year residency requirement for citizenship. It developed an elaborate ritual with signs, handshakes, and passwords, and members were required to maintain the secrecy of the group and its activities. When questioned about the organization, members would answer "I don't know"—hence the by-name. The group's secrecy was eventually shed, however, as it rose to political prominence.

POLITICAL ACTIVITIES

By 1855, the party had established state councils in approximately thirty-three states, and the movement claimed one million members. Initially, the organization secretly endorsed candidates from one of the major parties; however, by 1854 it had founded its own party and begun to nominate candidates. It held its first open national convention in New York City during that same year and officially abandoned its fraternal secrecy. The apex of the Know-Nothing Party was in 1854 and 1855. During this time, the party elected mayors in Boston, Chicago, and Philadelphia, as well as governors in Rhode Island, New Hampshire, Connecticut, Massachusetts, California, and Kentucky. In Massachusetts, the Know-Nothing Party received 63 percent of the vote and won every state senate seat and all but 3 of the 378 state house seats. In addition, Know-Nothing candidates were elected to all eleven Massachusetts seats to the House of Representatives. It was estimated that at least fifty-one members of the Thirty-fourth U.S. Congress were members of the Know-Nothing Party.

In February, 1856, delegates met in Philadelphia before the nominating convention of their rennamed national party, the American Party. However, members split over the issue of slavery, and delegates from Ohio, Pennsylvania, Illinois, Iowa, and the New England states walked out. The remaining delegates persuaded former President Millard Fillmore to be their party's candidate for president. Fillmore, however, disavowed anti-Catholicism and transformed the American Party from a nativist organization to an anti-Democratic and prounion party. In the election of 1856, Fillmore received just over 20 percent of the vote and carried only one state, Maryland. Following the election, the American Party and the Know-Nothing movement quickly disappeared. While several enclaves remained in border states until 1860, anti-Catholicism was relegated to secondary importance as the issue of slavery became the major concern of the American people.

William V. Moore

FURTHER READING

Bennett, David H. *The Party of Fear: From Nativist Movements to the New Right in American History.* Chapel Hill: University of North Carolina Press, 1988. Discusses the background to nativism and has several chapters on the Know-Nothing movement and party.

Lipset, Seymour Martin, and Earl Raab. *The Politics of Unreason: Right-Wing Extremism in America, 1790-1970.* New York: Harper & Row, 1970. Uses status politics to explain right-wing movements, including the Know-Nothing movement.

Mulkern, John R. *The Know-Nothing Party in Massachusetts: The Rise and Fall of a People's Movement.* Boston: Northeastern University Press, 1990. Analysis of the Know-Nothings in Massachusetts.

Richardson, Darcy G. *Others: Third Party Politics From the Nation's Founding to the Rise and Fall of the Greenback-Labor Party.* New York: iUniverse, 2004. Includes information on the nativist movement and the emergence of the Know-Nothing Party.

Voss-Hubbard, Mark. *Beyond Party: Culture of Antipartisanship in Northern Politics Before the Civil War.* Baltimore: Johns Hopkins University Press, 2002. Includes an analysis of nativist culture as well as the Know-Nothing movement.

SEE ALSO: American Protective Association; Anti-Catholicism; Employment; Great Irish Famine; History of immigration, 1783-1891; Ku Klux Klan; Nativism; Philadelphia anti-Irish riots; Religions of immigrants; Xenophobia.

KOREAN IMMIGRANTS

SIGNIFICANCE: Until the late twentieth century, Korean immigration to the United States was relatively small. However, the Korean War of 1950-1953 prompted a major wave of immigration from South Korea, and the liberalization of American immigration laws during the 1960's brought an even larger wave of immigrants. By the turn of the twenty-first century, Koreans were one of the fastest-growing ethnic groups in the United States. By the year 2008, about 1.5 million people of Korean descent were residing in the country, and Koreans constituted the fifth-largest Asian immigrant group in the United States, after Chinese, Filipinos, Asian Indians, and Vietnamese.

In 2003, Korean American communities throughout the United States celebrated the centennial anniversary of Korean immigration. However, the history of Korean immigrants in America actually started during the late nineteenth century. In 1882, Korea and the United States signed a treaty of amity and commerce that permitted Koreans to immigrate to the United States. Afterward, close political, military, and economic relations between the two countries helped shape Korean immigration to the United States. After the 1882 treaty, Korean diplomats, political exiles, students, and merchants began visiting, but they did not settle in the country. The first significant wave of Korean immigrants came to the American territory of Hawaii as sugar cane plantation workers in 1903.

KOREAN IMMIGRATION TO HAWAII

During the late nineteenth century, famine and poverty had driven many rural Koreans to urban centers, where they were exposed to Christianity and Western cultural influences. During that period, Korea was feeling the pressure of Chinese and Japanese efforts to dominate its government, and many Koreans were becoming more sympathetic to the idea of emigrating. Meanwhile, friendly political and economic relations between Korea and the United States were opening the possibility of having Korean workers go to the U.S. territory of Hawaii. This idea was facilitated by both Hawaiian planters and American missionaries in Korea. The Chinese Exclusion Act of 1882 had contributed to a labor shortage in Hawaii. Hawaiian sugar cane planters relied mostly on Japanese laborers. However, as labor unrest among the Japanese increased in Hawaii, the planters contemplated the possibility of bringing in laborers from other Asian countries and invited Koreans to come to Hawaii as strikebreakers.

Horace Allen, an American medical missionary working in Korea, played a significant role in initiating Korean immigration to Hawaii. During a visit in the United States in 1902, he met with Hawaiian planters and afterward used his political influence as a missionary to send Koreans to Hawaii. Few Koreans were initially willing to go to Hawaii, so missionaries in Korea personally recruited workers from among their own Christian congregations. In contrast to the Japanese and Chinese workers who had come from confined geographical areas in their home countries, early Korean immigrants had diverse geographical backgrounds, and nearly half of them were Christian converts. In December, 1902, 56 men, 21 women, and 25 children left Korea on the SS *Gaelic*. They arrived in Honolulu, Hawaii, on January 13, 1903. Over the next two years, nearly 7,500 Koreans went to Hawaii to work on sugar cane plantations.

KOREAN IMMIGRATION, 1905-1945

That first wave of Korean immigration came to an abrupt end in 1905, when the Korean government received reports of mistreatment of Korean laborers in Mexico and stopped permitting its people to go to either Mexico or the United States. Japan's government also pressured the Korean government to close its emigration bureau because it was concerned with the condition of its own citizens who were working in Hawaii. In 1907, the United States and Japan signed a Gentlemen's Agreement that stopped immigration of Japanese laborers to the United States. By that time, Korea was effectively ruled by Japan, so Korean workers were also banned from emigrating. After Korea was forcibly annexed by Japan in 1910, Korean immigration to the United States virtually halted.

Most of the early Korean immigrants were engaged in agricultural labor in Hawaii on three-year contracts. After their contracts expired, many Koreans went from Hawaii to the mainland United

States or returned to Korea. Some of those who made their way to the United States found success in the West Coast states, where they bought farms and started agricultural enterprises. However, California's Alien Land Law of 1913 prevented all Asian immigrants, including Koreans, from owning land and limited their leases in California. Some of the Koreans who left Hawaii worked on railroads on the West Coast, and some of these people were recruited to work as farm laborers.

Between 1907 and 1924, a small number of picture brides, students, and political exiles from Korea were admitted to the United States. Approximately 1,100 picture brides joined their prospective husbands between 1910 and 1924, when the new U.S. Immigration Act instituted discriminatory quotas based on national origins. This new law greatly reduced immigration from southern and eastern Europe and virtually ended it from Asia. Even after 1924, however, small groups of Korean political exiles and students continued to arrive in the United States, fleeing from the Japanese colonial rule in their homeland.

The U.S. government was sympathetic toward Korean political refugees from Japanese rule and admitted them to the United States as nonquota immigrants. Between 1925 and 1940, about 300 Korean students entered the United States on Japanese-issued passports. Most of them remained in America after completing their studies because they feared persecution by the Japanese government if they returned to Korea. Many of them participated in organizations and demonstrations for Korean independence. Female immigrants, though small in number, also took part in the efforts. As many of the early Korean immigrants were Christians, churches became important gathering places for them and helped fulfill not only their religious but also political and social needs.

KOREAN IMMIGRATION, 1945-1965

After World War II ended in 1945, the Japanese were ousted from Korea, which was effectively partitioned between the Soviet Union and the United States. The United States occupied the southern part of the Korean Peninsula until 1948, when the Republic of Korea was established under president Syngman Rhee. Meanwhile, the Soviet Union helped set up a communist government in the north.

PROFILE OF KOREAN IMMIGRANTS

Country of origin	North and South Korea
Primary language	Korean
Primary regions of U.S. settlement	California and New York State
Earliest significant arrivals	1880's
Peak immigration period	1965-2008
Twenty-first century legal residents*	189,144 (23.643 per year)

*Immigrants who obtained legal permanent resident status in the United States.
Source: Department of Homeland Security, *Yearbook of Immigration Statistics, 2008.*

As the Korean War broke out in 1950, the United States supplied military and economic assistance to South Korea and eventually negotiated the peace settlement with the Soviet Union. After an armistice was declared in 1953, Korea remained divided at the thirty-eighth parallel. The United States continued to provide military and economic aid to South Korea with the goal of containing the spread of communism in Asia. South Korea also depended heavily on U.S. aid to finance its postwar reconstruction.

The Korean War was both directly and indirectly responsible for the immigration of Koreans to the United States. Many people, traumatized by the war experience and looking for political and economic stability, left the war-ravaged country. Because of its close ties to Korea, the United States became the primary destination of many emigrants. The most visible groups of Korean immigrants to the United States after the war were wives of American servicemen, war orphans, and professional workers and students. These people differed from earlier Korean immigrants in many ways, especially in the proportion of women immigrants. The earlier wave of Korean immigration had a ratio of about ten men to every woman. After the arrival of "picture brides" during the 1910's and 1920's, the Korean immigrant population became 66 percent male during the 1930's. During the second wave of

Korean immigration, however, women accounted for more than 70 percent of all Korean immigrants to the United States.

The U.S. War Brides Act of 1945 allowed wives of American soldiers to enter the United States as nonquota immigrants. Korean war brides began to arrive in the United States during the Korean War and continued to come afterward as nonquota immigrants. Every year from 1953 until the end of the decade, about 500 Korean war brides were admitted to the United States. Passage of the Immigration and Nationality Act of 1952 repealed racial exclusion and relaxed the national quota criteria. Although the law was not fully liberalized, it opened a window of opportunity for many Koreans to come to the United States. Along with the wives of American servicemen, babies of servicemen and war orphans entered the United States as nonquota immigrants. Direct products of the Korean War, these typically forlorn-looking people dominated popular images of Korea in the United States during the 1950's. In 1955, Harry and Bertha Holt, American evangelists from Oregon, popularized the adoption of Korean orphans and the abandoned babies of American servicemen. Between 1955 and 1977, American families adopted about 13,000 Korean orphans. Every year during the 1980's, Americans adopted 7,000 to 8,000 Korean children. In contrast to popular images of Korean war orphans, many of the adoptees were not true orphans at all but were children who had been given up for adoption because of Korean racial prejudice against mixed-race babies or because their unwed or impoverished mothers could not afford to raise them.

Along with the military brides and adoptees who came to the United States from Korea were students and professional workers. Between 1945 and 1965, about 6,000 Korean students came to the United States to seek higher education at colleges and universities. After completing their studies some returned to South Korea to work as academicians and professionals, but many became permanent residents in the United States. This period of Korean immigration provided a steppingstone for the third wave of Korean immigrants. Many of the Koreans who immigrated to the United States before 1965 were naturalized as American citizens and were thus able to sponsor relatives who followed them under the family reunification preferences of the Immigration and Nationality Act of 1965.

IMMIGRATION AFTER 1965

The U.S. Immigration and Nationality Act of 1965 (also known as the Hart-Cellar Act) eliminated national origins quotas and gave priority to immigrants with skills. In addition, the law allowed the spouses, unmarried minor children, and parents of U.S. citizens to enter as nonquota immigrants. With the passage of the 1965 law, the third and largest wave of Korean immigration began. While early immigrants were mostly farmers, most post-1965 immigrants have come from urban, middle-class backgrounds and have exhibited considerable diversity in their occupations and social classes.

After 1965, South Korea's own government began actively encouraging emigration as a means to reduce the pressures of its growing population and

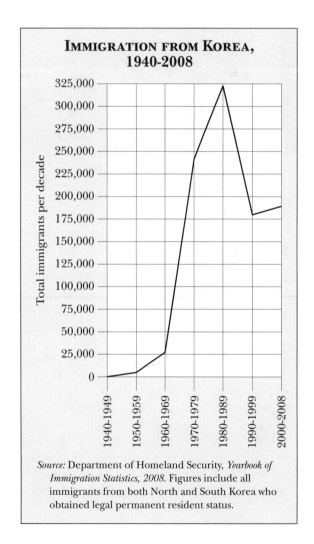

IMMIGRATION FROM KOREA, 1940-2008

Source: Department of Homeland Security, *Yearbook of Immigration Statistics, 2008.* Figures include all immigrants from both North and South Korea who obtained legal permanent resident status.

Residents of Los Angeles's Koreatown watching a parade with floats supporting political candidates in South Korea's presidential elections during the late 1980's. (Korea Society/Los Angeles)

to reap economic benefits from emigrants earning money abroad. Industrialization and modernization in Korea motivated its people to move to cities and to other countries, such as the United States and Germany, to find better opportunities and higher-paying jobs. Moreover, remittances from the immigrants have played a significant role in the growing Korean economy. The close military, political, and economic ties between the United States and South Korea have favored America as the primary destination for many Koreans.

The Korean immigrants who arrived before 1965 were not a highly visible group because of their small numbers and sparse distribution across the United States. However, with the rise of immigration after 1965, Korean immigrants have become one of the fastest-growing immigrant groups in the United States. Between 1970 and 1990, the Korean population in the country rose from

70,000 residents to almost 800,000. By the year 2000, that number had grown to 1.1 million.

KOREAN BUSINESS VENTURES IN THE UNITED STATES

During the 1960's, South Korea rose from the ravages of the war and gained economic strength and stability, aided by U.S. economic support and export-oriented economic policies. The living standards of South Koreans improved, and higher education expanded rapidly. During the early 1960's, only about 6 percent of Korean Americans were classified as professionals and managers. The immigrants who have come to the United States since 1965 have been more highly educated and had more professional job skills than their predecessors. However, despite their educational attainments and technical skills, many new immigrants found themselves confined to the lower rungs of the occupational ladders in their fields and prevented from practicing their professional skills due to language barriers and their unfamiliarity with American customs. In response, many of them turned to self-employment, running liquor stores, greengroceries, and other small shops in urban centers throughout the United States. Unfamiliar with the American banking system, many Koreans have joined Korean-run rotating credit associations.

Korean immigrants have done well as small merchants throughout the United States. During the 1980's, they began winning praise as a hardworking, law-abiding "model minority." However, their economic success and educational attainments did not always reflect the reality of their lives, and tended to conceal mounting troubles within their Korean American communities. During the 1980's and 1990's, tensions between Korean merchants and the largely black and Hispanic clientele of their innercity stores began rising. In New York City, Washington, D.C., Philadelphia, and Chicago, African Americans launched protest demonstrations and boycotts against Korean businesses, which they believed were exploiting their communities. These tensions reached an exploding point in Los Angeles in April, 1992, when much of the city erupted into rioting after the white police officers who had savagely beaten the black motorist Rodney King were acquitted of wrongdoing. The devastating riots exposed racial and economic hostilities between African Americans and Korean immigrants. During three days of violent rioting, fifty-eight people were killed and more than one billion dollars in property damage was done. A disproportionately large number of Korean stores were destroyed during the rioting, and the media brought to the fore tension and conflicts between Korean immigrants and African Americans.

The Los Angeles riots revealed deeply ingrained racism and economic disparities in American society and Korean ethnic communities. However, in the aftermath of the riots, Koreans made efforts to resolve the conflicts and form alliances with other minority groups. Meanwhile, Korean immigrants discovered greater solidarity within their own community. Like members of other Asian communities, Koreans have been noted for shunning involvement in political organizations and activities.

However, after the riots, they became more outgoing, and national organizations began playing more important roles in Korean immigrant communities.

Ji-Hye Shin

FURTHER READING

Abelmann, Nancy, and John Lie. *Blue Dreams: Korean Americans and the Los Angeles Riots.* Cambridge, Mass.: Harvard University Press, 1995. Study of race relations of Korean Americans analyzed through the Los Angeles riots of 1992.

Hurh, Won Moo, and Kwang Chung Kim. *Korean Immigrants in America: A Structural Analysis of Ethnic Confinement and Adhesive Adaptation.* Rutherford, N.J.: Fairleigh Dickinson University Press, 1984. Overview of Korean immigration to the United States from a sociological perspective.

Kim, Hyung-Chan, and Wayne Patterson, eds. *The Koreans in America, 1882-1974.* Dobbs Ferry, N.Y.: Oceana, 1974. Chronology and fact book that examines the history of Korean immigration to the United States.

Kim, Nadia Y. *Imperial Citizens: Koreans and Race from Seoul to LA.* Stanford, Calif.: Stanford University Press, 2008. Study with a global framework to examine racial ideas Koreans had prior to and after their immigration to the United States.

Lee, Mary Paik. *Quiet Odyssey: A Pioneer Korean Woman in America.* Seattle: University of Washington Press, 1990. First-hand account of a Korean woman who immigrated to Hawaii as a young child with her family. It narrates early years of Korean immigration in the United States.

Min, Pyong Gap. *Caught in the Middle: Korean Communities in New York and Los Angeles.* Berkeley: University of California Press, 1996. Sociological study of post-1965 Korean immigrants in the United States that focuses on lives and challenges of Korean merchants.

SEE ALSO: Alaska; Amerasian children; Chinese immigrants; Gentlemen's Agreement; Hawaii; Immigration and Nationality Act of 1952; Immigration and Nationality Act of 1965; Japanese immigrants; Korean War; Missionaries; "Model minorities"; Push-pull factors.

KOREAN WAR

THE EVENT: Unresolved military conflict between North and South Korea that drew the United States and communist China into the fighting

DATE: June 25, 1950-July 27, 1953

LOCATION: Korean Peninsula

> **SIGNIFICANCE:** The Korean War caused a massive displacement of people in both North and South Korea that left many thousands of Koreans in need of new homes. The close military, political, and economic ties between the United States and South Korea's government during and after the war facilitated the immigration of large numbers of Korean war refugees, war brides, and war orphans to America.

From the early twentieth century until the end of World War II in 1945, Japan ruled Korea as a colony. Japan's defeat in the war ended its control over Korea, but the Korean Peninsula was then politically divided at the thirty-eighth parallel. The northern portion of the peninsula was occupied by the communist Soviet Union, and the southern portion was occupied by the United States. In 1948, each part of Korea established its own independent government: the Democratic People's Republic of Korea in the north, and the Republic of Korea in the south. Vast differences in the political ideology of the communist north and the Western-leaning south generated friction that eventually escalated into a full-scale war that would involve both the United States and the People's Republic of China.

The Korean War officially began on June 25, 1950, when North Korea launched a surprise attack across the thirty-eighth parallel in an attempt to reunify the peninsula under its rule. Under United Nations (U.N.) auspices, the United States sent combat troops and military assistance to South Korea. Despite massive American and Chinese involvement, the conflict became a stalemate, and the United States eventually played a leading role in negotiating an armistice that ended the fighting on July 27, 1953. The settlement reestablished the thirty-eighth parallel as the border between North and South Korea. With the war technically never officially ended, the so-called demilitarized zone surrounding the border was heavily guarded by both sides and remained tense into the twenty-first century.

Meanwhile, the war itself had a devastating impact on the peoples of both North and South Korea. Particularly hard hit were large numbers of women and children who lost their families and were left without any means to support themselves.

KOREAN IMMIGRATION DURING THE 1950's

Both during and after the war, many people fled from both North and South Korea to other countries, including China and the United States. The close military and political ties between South Korea and the United States led the majority of emigrants to choose America. Even North Korean refugees who lacked strong family or regional ties in South Korea generally preferred to go to the United States. A small number of Korean prisoners of war, who refused to be repatriated to either North or South Korea were sent to the United States as well. In fact, the war opened opportunities to all Koreans to emigrate to America. Wives of American servicemen and orphans represented the largest groups of Korean immigrants during and immediately after the war.

WIVES OF AMERICAN SERVICEMEN

The military relations between the United States and South Korea created a new group of immigrants: war brides. After the war, the United States continued to station large numbers of American troops throughout South Korea. Many American service personnel married Korean women. U.S. immigrant quotas based on national origin remained in force, but the Korean wives of American servicemen could enter the United States legally as nonquota immigrants under the term of the Immigration and Nationality Act (McCarran-Walter Act) of 1952.

From 1953 until 1960, about 500 Korean war brides arrived in the United States annually. In Korea, these women were ostracized by their relatives and neighbors for marrying non-Koreans. After they reached the United States, many of them encountered prejudice from Americans who stereotyped them as prostitutes and barmaids. Married to white and black Americans, most of these women had little contact with other Korean immigrants. Out of touch with fellow Koreans and handicapped by limited English-language skills and unfamiliarity with American culture, they led culturally isolated lives. Consequently, many of their marriages did not last long. Because many of them came from lower-class backgrounds and had limited educations and few professional skills, they generally found it hard to support themselves and their children after their marriages failed. Nevertheless, most of these war brides became American citizens, and they would later sponsor the immigration of other Korean family members under the terms of the family reunification preferences of the Immigration and Nationality Act of 1965.

G.I. BABIES AND WAR ORPHANS

Other products of the Korean War were the births of thousands of so-called G.I. babies fathered by U.S. service personnel and the orphaning of thousands of Korean children. During the 1950's, these children became another major category of Korean immigrants to the United States. They also formed the first wave of Korean adoptees in America. G.I. babies and war orphans included children of both white and black American fathers and Korean mothers and orphans of Korean fathers and mothers. Despite the popular images of Korean War orphans at the time, many of the children adopted by American parents were not actually orphans. Most were given up by their natural parents for various reasons. Some were abandoned because of Korean racial prejudice against mixed-race babies. Others were give up by unwed mothers and by families too poor to care for them.

The number of Korean children needing parents was so great that the South Korean government created a special agency to place them for overseas adoption. This effort gained wide publicity when Harry and Bertha Holt, American evangelists in Oregon, adopted eight Korean children in 1955 and started their own international adoption service. Between 1955 and 1977, 13,000 Korean children were adopted by American families.

The Korean immigrants who came to America after the Korean War were noted for their remarkable heterogeneity. However, most Korean immigrants from that period were directly or indirectly connected with the U.S. military and American economic involvement in the Korean War. For many Americans, the Korean War was a quickly forgotten war, but it left a lasting imprint on both American and Korean society.

Ji-Hye Shin

FURTHER READING

Bergquist, Kathleen Ja Sook, et al., eds. *International Korean Adoption: A Fifty-Year History of Policy and Practice*. New York: Haworth Press, 2007. Collection of multidisciplinary essays on Korean adoption with several articles on Korean adoptees in the United States.

Blair, Clay. *The Forgotten War: America in Korea, 1950-1953*. New York: Times Books, 1987. Well-researched and comprehensive examination of the origins and conduct of the Korean War.

Edwards, Paul M. *The Korean War.* Westport, Conn.: Greenwood Press, 2006. Part of Greenwood's Daily Life Through History series, this book by a Korean War veteran and prolific scholar details the experiences of the individual troops fighting in Korea.

Hastings, Max. *The Korean War.* New York: Simon & Schuster, 1987. Detailed examination of military operations of the nations involved in the Korean War, from a British military historian. Includes a chronology of the war.

Hurh, Won Moo. *The Korean Americans*. Westport, Conn.: Greenwood Press, 1998. Historical, cultural, and socioeconomic study of Korean Americans.

Keller, Nora Okja. *Fox Girl*. New York: Penguin Books, 2002. Novel about a group of Korean children abandoned after the Korean War and their coming-of-age experiences near American military bases in Korea.

Oh, Arissa. "A New Kind of Missionary Work: Christians, Christian Americans, and the Adoption of Korean G.I. Babies, 1955-1961." *Women's Studies Quarterly* 33, nos. 3-4 (2005): 161-188. History of Korean adoption in America that examines adoption as a new missionary work shared by Christians and Christian Americanists.

Yuh, Ji-Yeon. *Beyond the Shadow of Camptown: Korean Military Brides in America*. New York: New York University Press, 2002. First detailed study of Korean military brides in the United States and their oral histories.

SEE ALSO: Amerasian children; Korean immigrants; McCarran Internal Security Act of 1950; Vietnam War; War brides; War Brides Act of 1945; Women immigrants; World War II.

KU KLUX KLAN

IDENTIFICATION: Secretive white nativist organization

DATE: First formed in 1866

SIGNIFICANCE: Founded in the American South by a Confederate general to suppress the freedoms of African American former slaves, the Ku Klux Klan disbanded after only five years but reemerged in 1915 as a secret fraternal organization dedicated to racial purity. Throughout its intermittent existence, it has been actively opposed to the immigration of nonwhite peoples.

Thomas Nast cartoon published by Harper's Weekly *in 1874 vilifying the Ku Klux Klan's mistreatment of African Americans.* (Library of Congress)

Months after the formation of the Ku Klux Klan in Tennessee, former Confederate general Nathan Bedford Forrest became the organization's first "grand wizard." During the Klan's first brief incarnation, its southern Democrat members warred against the Reconstruction policy of the federal government. They particularly resented what they regarded as the policy of allowing citizens without substantial property assets to control the manner in which propertied citizens used their own possessions. Meanwhile, they terrorized newly freed African Americans, lynching them and burning their homes to discourage them from voting.

The original Klan had disappeared by the time Reconstruction ended during the 1870's. However, it reappeared in Atlanta, Georgia, in 1915, and began directing its hate campaigns against new immigrants in the name of "Americanism."

The Klan enjoyed its greatest popularity during the 1920's, when many Americans were growing uneasy about the great surge in immigration from eastern and southern European countries. The Klan added its voice to others charging that Italian, Irish, and Polish Catholics; Russian and Slavic Jews; and Asians were threatening to destroy the white Anglo-Saxon Protestant base of the American population. Klan hate literature depicted Roman Catholics and Jews as threats to traditional religious American values and American racial purity. Klan literature found Asians particularly easy to stereotype and denigrate; like African Americans, Asians simply looked different.

Klan propaganda against these immigrant groups attracted millions of new members across the United States. However, the Klan's membership was strongest in the South, from Florida to Texas, and in the Midwest, especially in Indiana. Members came from all strata of white male society.

The Klan's program reflected the anti-immigrant feelings of many Americans during the 1920's, the decade during which the federal government added restrictions to immigration from southern and eastern Europe to those already in force against Asian immigration. In 1924, the Klan helped elect eleven state governors and sixteen congressmen, and in 1928 it helped defeat the Roman Catholic presidential candidate Alfred E. Smith.

After again fading away during the 1930's, the Klan made its third appearance in 1946 and remained active into the twenty-first century. In its most recent incarnation, the Klan has worked to improve its public image while continuing to campaign against immigration into the United States.

A. W. R. Hawkins III

FURTHER READING

Blee, Kathleen M. *Women of the Klan.* Berkeley: University of California Press, 1991.

MacLean, Nancy. *Behind the Mask of Chivalry.* New York: Oxford University Press, 1994.

Trelease, Allen W. *White Terror: The Ku Klux Klan Conspiracy and Southern Reconstruction.* Baton Rouge: Louisiana State University Press, 1971.

SEE ALSO: African Americans and immigrants; Anti-Catholicism; Anti-Defamation League; Anti-Semitism; Crime; Jewish immigrants; Nativism; Xenophobia.

L

LABOR UNIONS

DEFINITION: Worker organizations formed to seek improvements in their members' wages, benefits, and working conditions

SIGNIFICANCE: During the eras when American labor unions were most powerful, the majority of immigrants to the United States were members of the working class, and many immigrants played major roles in labor organizations. Many immigrants have joined national, industry-based unions; others have created race-specific labor unions. Historically, the racial heterogeneity of the American labor force has been a source of both conflict and solidarity.

Since the end of the U.S. Civil War in 1865, an incredibly diverse mix of races has taken part in the labor movement that has helped to shape the United States. During the Reconstruction era after the war, emancipated African American slaves and their descendants joined the ranks of agricultural and industrial laborers. Meanwhile, the numbers of immigrants flooding into the United States was rising to unprecedented levels. From the last decades of the nineteenth century until 1924, more than 25 million new immigrants, primarily from Asia and Europe, poured into the nation in response to the call for laborers to fill positions in expanding factories, mines, and mills. The later decades of the twentieth century saw even more immigrant laborers join those previous arrivals, but most of these immigrants were from other parts of the world, primarily Mexico, the West Indies, Central and South America, Pacific Rim nations, and South Asia.

HETEROGENEITY IN THE AMERICAN LABOR FORCE

Cultural and racial heterogeneity has long been the unique hallmark of laborers in the United States, but this very diversity has had both negative and positive consequences for the American labor movement as a whole. Individual immigrant groups have sometimes asserted their racial identities in their struggles for recognition in the American working class. This tendency has generated conflicts among workers from different immigrant groups. Many employers, seeking to marginalize their employees to keep wages down, have inflamed those racial tensions to reduce their employees' ability to organize.

At the same time, however, racial and ethnic identification can be a powerful mobilizing force. Immigrant laborers have sometimes realized that their commonality of work experience can bridge their unique cultural understandings, creating points of mobilization for protection and advancement. Both the tendency toward interracial conflict and the tendency toward racial solidarity have coexisted within some of the key national American labor unions, and the ebb and flow of those tendencies have affected their immigrant membership even into the early twenty-first century.

KNIGHTS OF LABOR, THE AFL, AND THE CIO

The Noble Order of the Knights of Labor (KOL) was organized in 1869 with the goal of uniting all those who worked for wages into a single, huge national union that would produce and distribute goods on a cooperative basis. Recognizing the need for broad-based labor solidarity to achieve this goal, the Knights of Labor offered membership to men and women of all races.

Through the 1870's and 1880's, KOL leader Terence Powderly traveled throughout the United States to recruit members. His campaign was successful to the extent that he helped establish more than thirty cooperative enterprises. Peak membership in the KOL included about 70,000 African American workers and 40,000 Asians and Europeans. The organization's multiethnic solidarity helped to improve the conditions of Missouri Pacific Railroad workers in 1885. KOL-led work stoppages ultimately forced railroad mogul Jay Gould to restore the wages he had cut the previous year, and he begrudgingly recognized his employees' union.

Formed in 1886 to organize craft unions encompassing laborers in specific trades, the American Federation of Labor (AFL) was much more racially restrictive and divisive than the Knights of Labor.

In his own membership recruitment campaigns, AFL leader Samuel Gompers appealed only to the elite male members of the working class—the most skilled workers. During the late nineteenth century, few members of minority groups fit that description, and even those who did were excluded from membership. Although Gompers himself was an immigrant from England, he believed that if the AFL allowed members of certain immigrant groups to join, the federation would become caught up in racial controversy. Convinced that his organization had more imperative and concrete issues on its agenda, he avoided racial entanglements by simply prohibiting minority workers from joining the AFL.

The AFL's "aristocracy of labor" continued to deny membership to unskilled and semiskilled immigrant labor through the 1930's. Persistent racist and nativist ideologies led many AFL leaders to see immigrant groups as individual nationalities whose differences were potentially subversive to the American labor movement, rather than as potentially valuable allies in the advancement of labor's interests.

In 1935, John L. Lewis and seven other top AFL leaders broke from the AFL to form the Congress of Industrial Organizations (CIO). These men believed that their new union would make itself strongest by welcoming semiskilled and unskilled workers of all races, who had been ignored by the AFL. The CIO made good use of the more than 1.8 million workers whom it brought under its umbrella. In 1937, successful sitdown strikes against General Motors, Chrysler, and U.S. Steel won the CIO recognition as the bargaining agent for millions of workers previously regarded as unorganizable.

AFRICAN AMERICAN WORKERS

Even before the CIO split from the AFL in 1935, labor organizer A. Philip Randolph had organized the many African Americans working on the nation's passenger railroads into a powerful union. His Brotherhood of Sleeping Car Porters won significant concessions from the Pullman Company during the 1930's and later provided a solid base from which black workers could challenge racial discrimination on a variety of fronts. In 1941, his union helped persuade President Franklin D. Roosevelt to issue an executive order forbidding employment discrimination by defense contractors. Seven years later, Randolph and his union helped persuade President Harry S. Truman to issue an order outlawing racial segregation in the American armed forces.

During the 1960's, African Americans began working to extend connections between labor activism and civil rights. They began at the local level with strikes by sanitation workers in Memphis, Tennessee, and hospital workers in Charleston, South Carolina. Undertaken by previously unorganized, heavily exploited, poverty-wage workers, these actions for higher wages and safer working condi-

Cover of an 1886 magazine depicting a convention of the Knights of Labor in Richmond, Virginia. (The Granger Collection, New York)

tions gained the attention and support of larger national industrial unions, including the United Auto Workers and the United Steelworkers. However, despite the success of the individual strikes, white workers have supported African American labor actions only halfheartedly, reflecting the continued divide between race relations and working-class solidarity.

HISPANIC WORKERS

Responding to the demand for manual laborers after the United States entered World War II, the United States and Mexico instituted the bracero program in 1942. Thousands of impoverished Mexicans, lured by higher wages, headed north to thin sugar beets, pick cotton, and weed and harvest cucumbers, tomatoes, and other crops on American farms. As experienced farm laborers, the more than 350,000 braceros who crossed the border annually helped to develop North American agriculture. The bracero program contract between the United States and Mexico was ended in 1964, pressured by Latino labor activist César Chávez's description of the program as "legalized slavery."

The son of migrant farmworkers, Chávez helped to raise awareness of the plight of braceros and other agricultural workers, and became the head of the United Farm Workers union (UFW) after it formed in 1965. Until his death in 1993, he used strikes and national boycotts against fruit- and vegetable-raising agribusinesses to win wage and working conditions concessions for mostly migrant agricultural laborers. The UFW later became an independent affiliate of the AFL-CIO and helped win passage of a California law recognizing the right of farmworkers to engage in collective bargaining. By the 1980's, about 45,000 farmworkers labored under the protection of UFW contracts, and the union was bargaining on behalf of farmworkers in states across the country.

The majority of farmworkers who have benefitted from UFW labor organizing have been Mexican Americans and Mexicans. Workers from other Hispanic groups, particularly Puerto Ricans and Cubans, have found representation in another major union that protects such service employees as janitors, nursing home aides, hospital aides, security guards, and building service maintenance. Although the membership of the Service Employees International Union (SEIU) is largely Hispanic, the union itself is not a race-specific organization. It merely happens that the majority of public service sector jobs are filled by Hispanic workers, many of whom are foreign immigrants. The SEIU has united more than 1.5 million workers and has become the North American union with the largest number of immigrant members.

ASIAN WORKERS

To an extent that may have been greater than that experienced by any other ethnic group, Asian immigrants have historically been excluded from American labor organizations. This has been true even though Asian immigrants have worked in some of the most dangerous occupations that laborers have faced. For example, the early mining industry in the Far West was one of the first to employ the Chinese, who dug for gold, hauled coal, and worked with explosives. Chinese immigrants also helped to build the railroad lines that connected the West to eastern markets and did some of the most dangerous work with explosives to excavate tunnels. Japanese immigrants also worked on the railroads, first in construction, and later as porters and foremen.

Despite the difficult and often dangerous work that Chinese and Japanese laborers performed, these immigrants were resented and badly treated by native-born American workers and employers. State laws were passed to limit their rights, and federal laws were enacted to limit further Asian immigration. Asian workers responded by organizing at the community level and embracing wider cultural and racial demands for justice and dignity. They also formed their own race-based unions.

Since the early 1990's, one of the most active Asian unions has been the Asian Pacific American Labor Alliance (APALA). This organization was founded in 1992 to address the special needs of Asian and Pacific Islander garment factory workers, hotel and restaurant workers, longshoremen, nurses, and supermarket workers, and to connect those local alliances to the national American labor movement. The APALA has actively promoted the formation of AFL-CIO legislation to create jobs, ensure national health insurance, and reform labor law. It has also supported national governmental action to prevent workplace discrimination against immigrant laborers and to prosecute perpetrators of racially motivated crimes.

The successful creation of race-specific labor unions and the inclusion of immigrant groups in the larger project that is the American labor movement have not resolved the debate about the role of immigrant and minority workers in American labor. However, these developments have helped ensure a continuing discussion about issues that have captured the attention of labor organizers since the late nineteenth century—higher wages, safer working conditions, increased respect—and have raised awareness of the importance of immigrant groups toward realizing those goals for all workers.

Cynthia Gwynne Yaudes

FURTHER READING

Asher, Robert, and Charles Stephenson, eds. *Labor Divided: Race and Ethnicity in United States Labor Struggles, 1835-1960.* Albany: State University of New York Press, 1990. Collection of case studies exploring how racial heterogeneity in the American labor movement has created the potential for both divisiveness and unity.

Briggs, Vernon M. *Immigration and American Unionism.* Ithaca, N.Y.: Cornell University Press, 2001. Evaluates the effects that immigration has had on union membership throughout American history and adds to the current debate about how industries should deal with documented and undocumented immigrant workers.

Milkman, Ruth. *Organizing Immigrants: The Challenge for Unions in Contemporary California.* Ithaca, N.Y.: Cornell University Press, 2000. Analyzes recent California labor history and evaluates prospects for organizing among immigrant labor in America's most populous state.

Ness, Immanuel, ed. *Immigrants, Unions, and the New U.S. Labor Market.* Philadelphia: Temple University Press, 2005. Collection of case studies of worker collective action that explains why and how immigrant workers organize.

Walker, Thomas J. Edward. *Pluralistic Fraternity: The History of the International Worker's Order.* New York: Garland Press, 1991. Examines the seemingly unique ability of communist-backed labor organizations to create worker solidarity across racial and national lines.

SEE ALSO: Asian Pacific American Labor Alliance; Bracero program; Coal industry; Economic consequences of immigration; Employment; Goldman, Emma; Industrial Workers of the World; International Ladies' Garment Workers' Union; United Farm Workers.

LAHIRI, JHUMPA

IDENTIFICATION: British-born American author of Asian Indian descent
BORN: July 11, 1967; London, England

> **SIGNIFICANCE:** Lahiri's focus on cultural displacement highlights the Asian Indian immigrant experience from an intergenerational perspective. Her Pulitzer Prize-winning short-story collection, *Interpreter of Maladies* (1999), concentrates on Indian immigrants searching for cultural connections and love. At a personal level, Lahiri considers herself American, but feels somewhat displaced herself, having been raised with a keen sense of her Indian heritage.

Born Nilanjana Sudeshna Lahiri in London, England, to parents from Bengal, India, Jhumpa Lahiri moved to the United States at the age of three and grew up in Rhode Island. She became an American citizen at the age of eighteen. Immersed in immigrant culture, she also spent a great deal of time in India, where her family made frequent visits to relatives in Calcutta (now called Kolkata).

Lahiri began writing in childhood to stave off the loneliness of feeling like an outsider because she looked different from her classmates. She wrote fiction throughout college. After graduating from Barnard College in 1989 with a bachelor's degree in English literature, she went on to earn three master's degrees and a doctorate from Boston University. Her fiction won both accolades and awards after she finished her doctoral degree.

While Lahiri was still in school, she began consciously examining the immigrant experience, though she was initially seeking to understand her own identity. She used fiction to illustrate the Asian Indian immigrant experience, ranging from conflicts between Hindu and Christian lifestyles to an Indian immigrant's loneliness and longing for "home." She collected her stories into a book, *Interpreter of Maladies* (1999), which won the Pulitzer Prize in 2000. The title story is about an interpreter for an Indian physician who literally interprets the doctor's diagnoses for patients. Three of the nine stories are set in India, and the other six are set in the United States and feature Indian immigrants. Her work concentrates on cultural displacement, Hindu family structures, and the Westernization of second- and third-generation immigrants.

American reviewers have almost universally praised Lahiri's work for its depictions of the Indian American experience. Her work also had an immediate popular appeal in the United States, where the literature of other Indian Americans such as Bharati Mukherjee appealed more to academics and intellectuals. Critics in India, by contrast, have given her work a mixed reception, and some have criticized her for writing flat Indian characters, saying that she writes better about the general Indian immigrant experience.

Lahiri followed *Interpreter of Maladies* with a novel, *The Namesake*, in 2003, and again drew widespread critical acclaim. The novel concentrates on the issues faced by second-generation Indian immigrants and the importance of names to identity. Her second short-story collection, *Unaccustomed Earth* (2008), also focuses on Indian immigrants, concluding with three linked short stories focusing on both American and Indian customs regarding love, including arranged marriages.

Lahiri has proved to be one of the strongest voices for Indian American immigrants of several generations, capturing their unique struggles to achieve an American identity without surrendering their Indian culture.

Jessie Bishop Powell

FURTHER READING

George, Sheba Mariam. *When Women Come First: Gender and Class in Transnational Migration.* Berkeley: University of California Press, 2005.

Kafka, Phillipa. *On the Outside Looking In(dian): Indian Women Writers at Home and Abroad.* New York: Peter Lang, 2003.

SEE ALSO: Anglo-conformity; Asian American literature; Asian Indian immigrants; Association of Indians in America; Families; History of immigration after 1891; Intermarriage; Lim, Shirley Geok-lin; Literature; Mukherjee, Bharati; Sidhwa, Bapsi.

LAND LAWS

DEFINITION: Federal legislation pertaining to the transfer of public lands to private ownership

SIGNIFICANCE: From the time that the United States was established as an independent nation in 1783, the U.S. Congress has passed land laws defining the procedures by which new territory can pass from public ownership to individual ownership. While agriculture was a major source of employment during the nineteenth century, the acquisition of land became a fundamental inducement to immigrants to come to the United States. Many were pushed off their lands in Europe as population rose dramatically during the late eighteenth and throughout the nineteenth century. Owning land individually became in the eyes of many immigrants the pathway to a secure future.

When European immigrants first came to what became the United States, they brought with them a concept of land ownership fundamentally different from that held by the aboriginal Native American inhabitants. The concept of individual ownership, in Europe restricted by the surviving elements of feudal society, stood in sharp contrast to the concepts prevailing among the Indian tribes, which favored communal ownership with individual rights to use land temporarily. However, striving for land over which they had full control had propelled the first European discoveries in America. Although titles to New World lands were first vested in the monarchs whose subjects "discovered" them, as governments developed into their more modern forms, they found themselves constrained by shortages of funds during an era when possession, or control, of land was considered the primary measure of wealth. As governments sought to expand their territories, they began to use the granting of ownership to pieces of land as a means to collect revenue.

ORIGINS

Some of the major grievances that eighteenth century North American colonists had about British rule concerned government restrictions on their freedom to settle and farm lands in the vast open spaces between the Atlantic seaboard colonies and the Mississippi River to the west. Great Britain, which had acquired control over those western lands when it defeated France in the French and Indian War (1756-1763), had tried to block settlement by individuals migrating from the colonies along the Atlantic Coast. In its Proclamation of 1763, the British government forbade new settlements in lands west of the Alleghenies that were reserved for use of Native Americans. Attempts by settlers from the coastal colonies to move into that western area became one of the bones of contention in the American Revolution (1775-1783). After the war, the United States gained title to the area in the 1783 peace treaty with Great Britain. Settling in the region then became a priority for the new nation.

Within the British North American colonies, which had ben populated overwhelmingly by immigrants from Great Britain, laws pertaining to land ownership were determined largely by the individual colonial governments. Although it was technically vested in the British monarch, land ownership was quickly devolved to those who managed the colony in America—either as a company such as the Massachusetts Bay Colony, or as individuals, who through wealth or connections, secured from the British monarchs grants of land in North America. These agents in turn passed over control either to large landowners or to new communities, as was the case in Massachusetts. The latter tended to pass subordinate control to new settlements with provisions for dividing the allotted lands to early settlers.

Homesteaders crossing the Plains during the 1880's, looking for land in the West. (Getty Images)

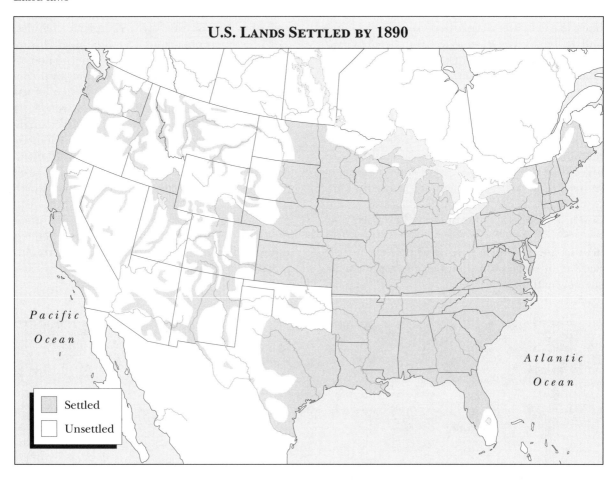

U.S. LANDS SETTLED BY 1890

Pacific Ocean

Atlantic Ocean

- Settled
- Unsettled

LAND LAWS OF THE UNITED STATES

One of the earliest problems faced by the new Congress of the United States was how to organize the distribution of land west of the Alleghenies. In 1784, Congress appointed a committee, of which Thomas Jefferson was the leading member, to draw up a plan. The proposal the committee produced set forth the outlines of the plan that followed in the Land Ordinance of 1785. The plan required several things:

- resolution of Indian claims to the land through treaties with local tribes
- surveying of the land into rectangular townships six miles on a side, each township to be then subdivided into 36 sections, one mile square and comprising 640 acres
- reservation of some of the land for military bounties granted during the Revolution
- subsequent sale of the land to private individuals

This subdivision of the United States into units of thirty-six square miles was followed throughout the settlement of the west. When Congress was passing the Land Ordinance of 1785, it added some new wrinkles. It reserved one section of each township to be offered for sale for the schools of the future community; it ruled that the secretary of war could claim some of the sections for payment to veterans of the Revolutionary War; it provided that the townships would be distributed to the various states on whom would fall responsibility for selling the land by sections or as whole townships; and it required that sales should be conducted through public auctions after at least seven (later reduced to four) of the survey (range) lines had been run. By 1787, relatively few sales had actually occurred, so Congress then authorized the sale of large aggregates to wealthy individuals who were prepared to take on the task of finding settlers to work the lands.

PEOPLING OF THE WEST

Although settlers from the seaboard colonies poured into the new Ohio Territory, formal settlement was held up by the slow progress of the survey lines and by the need to secure treaties from the Indians then resident in Ohio. Several unsuccessful clashes with tribes that resisted the flood of settlers led, finally, to the conclusive victory of an American force at the Battle of Fallen Timbers in 1794. In the ensuing Treaty of Greenville, the Indian tribes then resident in northwest Ohio ceded all their Ohio lands to the United States. The conditions of the Land Ordinance continued to be fulfilled in future years as more victories over the Indian tribes and cession of their rights by treaty were met.

It is not known how many immigrants were attracted to the United States by the availability of public land because U.S. immigration records were not kept until 1821. However, there is little doubt that the prospect of securing large plots of land at minimal costs drew many immigrants from Europe. Initially most came from the British Isles, including Ireland, but as the nineteenth century wore on, many more came from continental Europe. Early sales of public lands were intended for citizens of the United States, but over the course of the nineteenth century sales were opened to immigrants who began the naturalization process, thereby affirming their intention to become American citizens. Although U.S. debts from the Revolution and the War of 1812 had been paid off with the proceeds from land sales by the 1830's, Congress continued to seek revenue from further sales.

The large number of land laws passed by Congress indicates that the federal government continued to view selling public lands as a major source of revenue. One obstacle to sales was quickly changed: the need to bid at a single, central auction place. As early as the year 1800, Congress designated several on-the-ground sites for land auctions in Ohio—Cincinnati, Chilicothe, Marietta, and Steubenville. Afterward, auctions were held near the sites of the land being sold. Special officials were appointed to handle the sales, and rules spelled out how payments were to be made to the U.S. Treasury. Initially, land was sold for one to two dollars per acre under four-year payment plans. In later years, the prices and payment systems were regularly changed. In 1820, Congress acknowledged that a great deal of land had been occupied by "squatters" and allowed them to "preempt" title to the lands they occupied by paying part of their costs in advance of the auctions.

Meanwhile, Congress often tied land grants to other government programs. For example, by the mid-nineteenth century, its policy of awarding lavish land grants to railroads was becoming notorious. Congress granted large tracts of land to the railroads in the hope that the railroads would pass the land along to settlers. In the 1862 Homestead Act, Congress gave both citizens and prospective citizens a "preemption" right, enabling them to settle on public lands and secure title to those lands after five years for payments of two dollars per acre. The Timber Act of 1873 gave settlers up to ten years to claim title to the land they occupied if they planted substantial numbers of trees on the land. Homesteaders willing to develop desert lands in the West that were unsuitable for agriculture could buy title to their lands for only twenty-five cents per acre.

By the 1890's, Congress was beginning to recognize that public lands suitable for homesteading were becoming scarce, restricting purchasers to those who had not previously claimed land under the Pre-emption or Homestead Acts. It was still unclear to what extent the availability of public land was drawing foreign immigrants. During the early nineteenth century, the attraction of land was no doubt great, and immigration from Germany and Scandinavia undoubtedly was encouraged by the availability of cheap land.

Much of the public land was actually taken up by speculators who had no intention of settling it themselves; they planned to sell it to latecomers. News also got out that the costs of turning public land into useful farms could be high, which meant that immigrants with limited capital would have difficulty developing any land they could afford to purchase. Most immigrants who came to the United States to farm probably arrived during the first half of the nineteenth century; however, major settlement of Wisconsin and Minnesota did not begin until after the U.S. Civil War. Many Europeans who immigrated during the 1850's and 1860's settled in the Upper Midwest.

The goal that propelled many immigrants to come to the United States was the prospect of acquiring land for themselves. The federal land acts strengthened that resolve, by making vast tracts of land available at low cost to those prepared to settle and take up farming. Creating farms out of wild lands, however, was not an easy task, and many immigrants who tried failed. Consequently, many immigrants who left farms in Europe to farm in the United States wound up as industrial workers in cities.

Nancy M. Gordon

FURTHER READING

Dunham, Harold J. "Some Crucial Years of the Land Office, 1875-1890." In *The Public Lands: Studies in the History of the Public Domain*, edited by Vernon Carstensen. Madison: University of Wisconsin Press, 1968. Long the primary source of material on the public lands, the many useful articles remain relevant.

Freund, Rudolf. "Military Bounty Lands and the Origins of the Public Domain." In *The Public Lands: Studies in the History of the Public Domain*, edited by Vernon Carstensen. Madison: University of Wisconsin Press, 1968. Close study of the vexing problem that Congress faced in dealing with military bounty lands.

Rasmussen, R. Kent, ed. *Agriculture in History*. 3 vols. Pasadena, Calif.: Salem Press, 2010. Collection of essays on specific historical events, including many relevant to U.S. land issues.

Rasmussen, Wayne D., ed. *Agriculture in the United States: A Documentary History*. 4 vols. New York: Random House, 1975. Reprints the land laws of the United States, mostly contained in volume 1.

Rohrbough, Malcolm J. *The Land Office Business: The Settlement and Administration of American Public Lands, 1789-1837*. London: Oxford University Press, 1968. Exhaustive account of how American public lands were sold to settlers.

SEE ALSO: Alien land laws; Economic opportunities; Empresario land grants in Texas; European immigrants; History of immigration, 1783-1891; Homestead Act of 1862; National Road; Railroads; Settlement patterns; Westward expansion.

LANGUAGE ISSUES

DEFINITION: Issues concerning the special problems that non-English-speaking immigrants face in the United States and legislative attempts to address these problems

SIGNIFICANCE: Language issues affect all aspects of an immigrant's life in the United States. The ability to speak English correlates highly with the ability to function well. Access to information, health care, and cultural assimilation are often dependent on an immigrant's ability to speak English.

Since its very beginning, the United States has been a country of many languages. Native Americans spoke at least fifty-five distinct languages, and as immigrants arrived they continued to speak the languages of their home countries. Even though the English language became paramount, there long was a general tolerance of other languages. After the Mexican War, when Mexico ceded large tracts of land to the United States in February of 1848, Mexico and the United States signed the Treaty of Hidalgo, which gave American citizenship to all Mexican nationals who remained in the ceded lands. The treaty also guaranteed certain civil, political, and religious rights to these new Spanish-speaking American citizens. Along with those protections, it was assumed that the former Mexican nationals would keep their language. There were suggestions to restrict this freedom in the early years of the country, but laws of this kind were considered a threat to civil liberties.

In later years, however, various events began to change this tolerant attitude. For example, California's gold rush attracted to the West Coast easterners who ignored the language guarantees of the Mexican-American treaty. In the East, anti-Roman Catholic attitudes and fear of foreign radicals supported a feeling of "national superiority." It was God's design, many thought, that Americans were a chosen people and that foreigners had no place in the United States. A famous late nineteenth century editorial cartoon by Thomas Nast, depicted Roman Catholic bishops as crocodiles swimming ashore with the intention of destroying the public school system.

The onset of World War I brought language issues further to the fore. A great number of American citizens had come from Germany. Many had kept their native language, and German was used in their schools. However, with the onset of the war, those who spoke German were regarded with suspicion as unpatriotic and somehow less than totally "American." In a speech that former president Theodore Roosevelt delivered in 1917, the year that the United States entered the war, he said:

> We must have but one flag. We must also have but one language. That must be the language of the Declaration of Independence, of Washington's Farewell Address, of Lincoln's Gettysburg Speech and Second Inaugural. We cannot tolerate any attempt to oppose or supplant the language and culture that has come down to us from the builders of this Republic with the language of any European country. The greatness of this nation depends on the swift assimilation of the aliens she welcomes to her shores. Any force which attempts to retard that assimilative process is a force hostile to the highest interests of our country. . . . We call upon all loyal and unadulterated Americans to man the trenches against the enemy within our gates.

Two years later, President Woodrow Wilson gave a speech in which he warned against those who continued to speak the languages of their original homelands or to practice their former customs. Wilson complained about what he called "hyphenated" Americans, stating that

> any man who carries a hyphen about him carries a dagger which he is ready to plunge into the vitals of the Republic. If I can catch a man with a hyphen in this great contest, I know I will have got an enemy of the Republic.

By 1919, fifteen U.S. states had decided to make English the sole language of instruction in all their primary schools—both public and private. In some states, bills were introduced that would have prohibited the teaching of foreign languages in elementary schools. These legislative efforts were, in part, expressions of public fear of foreign influences. From 1920 to 1964, American citizenship gradually became dependent upon the ability to read and write the English language, which was increasingly becoming the language of government and education. One result of this tendency was that minority language speakers began to hide their ethnic origins and to forget their ancestral languages. Millions of people were taught to be ashamed of their ancestral languages, their parents, and their foreign origins. Even people whose ancestors who had come to America before the Revolutionary War were told that they could not keep their mother tongues and still be good American citizens. Speaking more than a single language was regarded as a sign of divided allegiance.

FOREIGN WORKERS

At various times in its history, the United States has imported people from other countries to work. For example, thousands of workers were brought from China to do menial work during the California gold rush after 1848. Even more were brought to work on the transcontinental railroad, which was completed in 1869. Like the members of many immigrant groups, Chinese immigrants have tended to stay together within their own ethnic communities and speak their own language. A popular modern argument against permitting foreign immigration is that newcomers tend to isolate themselves within their own communities and refuse to learn the local language.

After the United States signed the Geneva convention relating to the status of political refugees in 1980, the nation opened its borders more widely to new immigrants. Russians, Bulgarians, Vietnamese, Mexicans, and many others entered the United States to find work. Some immigrants have entered the United States seeking asylum because of dangerous situations in their home countries. These people are at greater risk of deportation if they can not speak English because of their restricted ability to explain their situations to immigration officials. Immigrant victims of crime also often face greater dangers because of language barriers.

EDUCATION

In 1968, the Bilingual Education Act became the first piece of federal legislation that addressed the issue of minority language speakers. The bill was introduced in 1967 by Texas senator Ralph Yarborough to provide school districts with federal funds to increase language skills in English. It was originally intended for Spanish-speaking students, but in 1968 it was merged into the Bilingual Education Act, or Title VII of the Elementary and Secondary Education Act (ESEA). This law gave public school districts the opportunity to provide bilingual education programs to remedy the high rates of school failure. However, its real goal was to direct speakers of other languages into English-speaking programs. The bill provided federal funding for resources for educational programs, teacher training, development of materials, and parent involvement projects.

A central question that needed to be resolved was whether immigrants should learn to speak English before beginning to learn other subjects, or should children begin their formal educations in their own languages so they would not be too old to participate in grade-level activities by the time they developed proficiency in English. The federal law gave individual school districts the freedom to choose whichever approach they believed warranted, so long as their programs were designed to meet the special educational needs of the students. However, President Reagan slashed the funding for bilingual education by $35.4 million. Many native English speakers believed that the national interest is served when all members of society can speak English. In 2006, the U.S. Senate passed an amendment to the Comprehensive Immigration Reform Act designating English as the official national language. However, the amendment never became law.

HEALTH CARE

The Civil Rights Act of 1964 ensured that federal money would not go to any institution that discriminates on the basis of race, color, or national origin. In addition, the U.S. Department of Health and Human Services has stated that health care organizations must offer and provide language assistance services, including bilingual staff members and interpreter services at no cost to people with limited English proficiency. Despite this federal law, as many as twenty-three million people in the United States may be at risk of receiving substandard health care merely because they are not fluent in English. This is due in part to conflicts in understanding. Thirty states have designated English as their official language and require all state services to be conducted in English. When state laws conflict with federal laws, health care professionals can be at a loss in knowing how to react. State laws cannot override the entitlement of the federal Civil Rights Act.

Lack of communication between immigrants and health care providers because of language differences can cause great harm to persons seeking health care. When doctors do not speak their patients' languages and interpreters are not available, misunderstandings can lead to misdiagnoses, incorrect treatments, the inability of patients to understand instructions for medications and therapy, and inability to obtain information about financial assistance. In such situations, many immigrants are understandably reluctant to seek needed medical care. In extreme situations, misunderstandings between medical professionals and non-English-speaking patients can lead to deportation, financial loss, or even death.

TECHNOLOGY

Another area in which language issues make life more difficult for non-English-speaking immigrants is the field of information technology, known popularly as IT. As IT has played a growing role in workplaces, immigrants in general and Hispanics in particular are often at a disadvantage when they search for jobs. More than one-half of immigrants from Latin America have fewer than twelve years of education and are consequently often inadequately educated to work with modern computers and electronic communications. For example, a great majority of pages on the World Wide Web are in English, making them difficult for people with limited English proficiency to understand.

Another difficulty is that many Hispanics do not have social networks that greatly value information technology. Even among native speakers of English, poor language skills can be a barrier to information technology usage. A study of former Soviet-bloc countries also reveals that workers who can speak English are more likely to work with computers and earn more money because of it. In addition to having greater access to better-paying jobs, it has become increasingly important for immigrants to be able to use the Internet for daily living in the United States. Indeed, the World Wide Web can be especially valuable to immigrants as a source of information on immigration law and legal assistance.

Cultural Attitudes and Language Suppression

During the early twentieth century, many Americans began accepting the idea that people who could not speak English could not be true, patriotic Americans. The large number of immigrant Italians, German Jews, and Slavic peoples entering the United States from eastern and southern European countries evoked fears among American citizens that new immigrants were not learning English quickly enough, and therefore not assimilating into American culture. In 1911, the Dillingham Commission, led by Senator William P. Dillingham of Vermont, proposed a reading and writing test as a method for barring undesirable aliens from entering the country. The federal Immigration Act of 1924 introduced strict immigration rules that explicitly excluded members of ethnic and racial groups deemed to be genetically inferior. This law sharply restricted the flow of eastern and southern Europeans and totally excluded Asians. It was the first permanent limitation on immigration to the United States.

By the early twenty-first century, most immigrants appeared to believe it was in their own interest to learn to speak English. By this time, members of most Hispanic immigrant families were learning English within two generations, whereas in the past it took about three generations. Consequently, many children of first-generation families now speak English as their primary language.

Winifred O. Whelan

Further Reading

Kibler, Amanda. "Speaking Like a 'Good American': National Identity and the Legacy of German-Language Education." *Teachers College Record* 110, no. 6 (June, 2008): 1241-1268. Survey of the history of German language teaching in the United States, showing how it flourished before World War I and declined afterward.

Ono, Hiroshi, and Madeline Zavodny. "Immigrants, English Ability, and the Digital Divide." *Social Forces* 86, no. 4 (June, 2008): 1455-1479. Study showing how immigrants are both financially and culturally disadvantaged by their limited access to information technology, which is overwhelmingly in English.

Pöllabauer, Sonja. "Interpreting in Asylum Hearings: Issues of Role, Responsibility and Power." *Interpreting* 6, no. 2 (2004): 143-80. Findings of a study undertaken in Graz, Austria, where immigrants were asking for asylum in the United States. Translators and interpreters were found to shorten and paraphrase statements, leave out certain information, and otherwise distort the evidence given by the asylum seekers.

U.S. Commission on Civil Rights. *The Excluded Student: Educational Practices Affecting Mexican Americans in the Southwest.* Washington, D.C.: Government Printing Office, 1972. Study revealing how the educations of Spanish-speaking students in southwestern states have been damaged by language differences.

Youdelman, Mara K. "The Medical Tongue: U.S. Laws and Policies on Language Access." *Health Affairs* 27, no. 2 (March/April, 2008): 424-433. Article providing statistics on state laws that deal with language access in health care facilities, and how states are held accountable for providing interpreters and translators.

See also: Anglo-conformity; Bilingual education; Education; English as a second language; English-only and official English movements; Hayakawa, S. I.; *Lau v. Nichols*; Linguistic contributions; Literacy tests; Multiculturalism; Name changing.

Laotian immigrants

Significance: Significant numbers of Laotian immigrants first came to the United States in the wake of the Vietnam War. They have often been lumped together with Vietnamese refugees, but the Laotians have differed in generally having less education, fewer skills, and more assimilation challenges. The Hmong, who fought against communism in Laos, are often included among Laotian immigrants, but these mountain people come from throughout Southeast Asia.

Laos is situated in the center of the Indochinese peninsula at the heart of the Mekong Basin, with Vietnam to the east. The location of the country ensured that it would become caught up in the turmoil of the Vietnam War during the 1960's and early 1970's, when its own people were also fighting

Laotian refugee children at a refugee camp in Thailand in 1979. (AP/Wide World Photos)

a civil war. As the United States withdrew from Southeast Asia in 1975, Laotian refugees began to make their way to America. The U.S. government labeled all refugees as "Indochinese" regardless of their countries of origin. As a result, Laotians have been lumped together with the much larger number of Vietnamese refugees who poured into the United States. Consequently, some of the available government information does not represent the pattern of Laotian immigration.

The Laotian refugees came in two major waves, which included ethnic Chinese, Lao minorities (chiefly Lao Theung and Mein), and the Hmong among their numbers. The first wave, from 1975 to 1977, consisted largely of boat people and overland refugees who had spent considerable and often harrowing time in refugee camps in Southeast Asia. Many of these people were Hmong who had fled Laos for refugee camps in Thailand after the communist government of the Pathet Lao took control in December, 1975.

The second wave, consisting largely of Lao minorities who began to arrive in the United States in 1978, resulted from attempts by the new Lao government to consolidate its control over ethnic minorities who had fought earlier for the U.S. Central Intelligence Agency. In 1978, the U.S. government offered "parolee" status to Hmong and other Laotians who had been employees of the U.S. government, with priority given to people who had been persecuted by communists. The 1980 Refugee Act gave the refugees resident-alien status and enabled more Laotians to enter the United States.

The Laotian immigrants who arrived as the result of the Vietnam War tended to be less educated than previous Southeast Asian immigrants. The 20,000 or so Hmong who arrived during the late 1970's were, for the most part, illiterate. The Hmong and Laotian ethnic minorities tended not only to be illiterate, but also to have skills in few fields other than slash-and-burn agriculture. The fact that the Hmong and Mein peoples had no writ-

PROFILE OF LAOTIAN IMMIGRANTS

Country of origin	Laos
Primary language	Lao
Primary regions of U.S. settlement	California, upper Midwest
Earliest significant arrivals	1978
Peak immigration period	1978-1980
Twenty-first century legal residents*	13,953 (1,699 per year)

*Immigrants who obtained legal permanent resident status in the United States.

Source: Department of Homeland Security, *Yearbook of Immigration Statistics, 2008.*

ten language further complicated their ability to adjust to life in the United States. The refugees tended to be young, with most coming as part of large family groups.

By the end of the 1980's, about 266,000 Laotians had immigrated to the United States. Most settled in California but a significant number have established lives in the upper Midwest, chiefly in Minnesota.

Caryn E. Neumann

FURTHER READING

Goudineau, Yves, ed. *Laos and Ethnic Minority Cultures: Promoting Heritage.* Paris: UNESCO, 2003.

Kelly, Gail P. "Coping with America: Refugees from Vietnam, Cambodia, and Laos in the 1970's and 1980's." *The Annals of the American Academy of Political and Society Science* 487 (September, 1986): 138-149.

Lee, Joann Faung Jean. *Asian Americans in the Twenty-first Century: Oral Histories of First- to Fourth-Generation Americans from China, Japan, India, Korea, the Philippines, Vietnam, and Laos.* New York: New Press, 2008.

SEE ALSO: Asian immigrants; Burmese immigrants; History of immigration after 1891; Hmong immigrants; Indochina Migration and Refugee Assistance Act of 1975; Thai immigrants; Vietnam War; Vietnamese immigrants.

LATIN AMERICAN IMMIGRANTS

SIGNIFICANCE: Throughout U.S. history, Latin Americans have immigrated in waves to North America. Halfway through the first decade of the twenty-first century, about 44 million residents of the United States traced their ancestry to Hispanic immigrants; of these, about 17.7 million had been born in Latin American nations. Early Hispanic immigrants tended to congregate in western and southwestern states in the U.S. However, by the turn of the twenty-first century, Latin American immigrants were settling throughout the entire country—in large urban centers, suburban areas, and small towns—and they were becoming one of the fastest-growing ethnic groups in the United States.

In response to changing historical conditions, immigration from Latin America to the United States ebbed and flowed through the nineteenth and twentieth centuries. The late twentieth century surge in Hispanic immigration was a product of many factors, including the increasing economic globalization of labor markets, the long shared border between the United States and Mexico, and increasingly attractive economic opportunities for immigrants in the United States.

Any consideration of "Latin American" immigration must keep in mind the wide diversity and heterogeneous nature of the many Hispanic, or Latino, peoples living in the United States. Immigrants have come to the United States from nineteen Spanish- and Portuguese-speaking countries of the Western Hemisphere, bringing with them a wide variety of cultural backgrounds. They have settled in almost every region of the United States, doing so under a variety of circumstances and for different reasons.

PRE-TWENTIETH CENTURY TRENDS

During the eighteenth and nineteenth centuries, most Hispanics lived in the southwestern region of what is now the United States. This region constituted the northern part of Spain's New World empire until Mexico became independent in 1821. Afterward, it was part of Mexico until the Mexican War of 1846-1848, when the region passed

PROFILE OF LATIN AMERICAN IMMIGRANTS

Countries of origin	Mexico and nations of Central America, South America, and the Caribbean islands
Primary languages	Spanish, Portuguese
Primary regions of U.S. settlement	Southwest, New York State
Earliest significant arrivals	Sixteenth century
Peak immigration period	1965-2008
Twenty-first century legal residents*	3,301,935 (366,881 per year)

*Immigrants who obtained legal permanent resident status in the United States. Figures do not include Puerto Ricans.

Source: Department of Homeland Security, *Yearbook of Immigration Statistics, 2008.* See also articles on immigrants of individual nations and the West Indies.

to the United States. Most of the Hispanic residents of the region remained after 1848 and became American citizens. Initially, Mexicans and other Hispanics continued their historical patterns of moving back and forth between Mexico and the American Southwest in order to work and conduct trade, but they had to cross a new international border to do so. That border would later become the major crossing point for new Hispanic immigration into the United States.

Around the turn of the twentieth century, the United States began receiving Hispanic immigrants from other countries. After the Spanish-American War of 1898, small numbers of Puerto Ricans and Cubans began coming to the eastern United States to work temporarily and later return home. These two patterns of nineteenth century immigration would frame, to a large extent, the continued movement of Latin Americans into the United States during the twentieth century.

TWENTIETH CENTURY DEVELOPMENTS

Immigration from Latin America continued steadily into the twentieth century, a pattern due to changing political and economic conditions in Latin America. During the first decades of the century, Latin Americans came to the United States in search of work. As jobs grew scarce in their own countries, U.S. economic stability drew them into the large urban centers of the Northeast, Midwest, and Southwest. While immigration levels dipped slightly during the Great Depression of the 1930's, they began to rise again immediately after World War II ended in 1945. At that time, the U.S. government began playing an active role instituting policies to encourage an already cyclical migration pattern in which Latin Americans traveled to the United States on a temporary basis to earn money and later return to their home countries. As a result, the already existing movement from regions such as Mexico and the Caribbean continued, with the majority of immigrants being men who worked to support families whom they left at home. Upon finishing their job contracts or seasonal work, some settled in the United States and others returned to Mexico.

A turning point in twentieth century immigration came about when the U.S. Congress passed the Immigration and Nationality Act of 1965. This legislation, combined with late modifications in U.S. immigration policy, including tighter control of the U.S.-Mexican border, and changing political relations between the U.S. and other hemispheric governments, fundamentally transformed the nature of Latin American immigration. Whereas Hispanics had historically tended to immigrate to a limited number of U.S. urban regions, they were now spreading out all over the United States. Moreover, because the 1965 immigration law placed more emphasis on the reunification of families, increased numbers of women, children, and entire families were beginning to enter the United States to work and settle permanently. In a process known as "chain migration," Hispanic communities developed strong social networks linking their new American communities with their home regions in other countries. Latin American began organizing and participating more fully in the civic and political lives of their new communities, and were becoming visible at both the local and national levels.

Many Latin American immigrants have maintained dual citizenship, which allows them to vote in elections in both the United States and their home countries and to continue to remain connected with the social and cultural facets of life in their home countries. Latin American immigrants have tended to travel frequently to their home countries, and many of them send remittances, primarily monetary, to family members outside the United States.

Large-scale Latin American immigration has had a measurable impact on the demographic structure of the United States. Hispanics are, on average, younger than the general population. Moreover, they are adding significant numbers of young people to labor forces in regions of the United States where native-born populations are aging. By expanding the pool of those who work labor-intensive and, typically, low-wage jobs, they have helped to reinvigorate parts of the United States that had been experiencing net population losses. Because many of them are also settling in rural, as well as urban, areas, their sheer numbers are causing local communities to rethink how they will integrate the newly arrived groups into the civic and cultural lives of their towns and cities. Increased Hispanic participation in political processes has helped to shift emphases to issues important to immigrant communities and to change voting patterns in many regions.

PUSH-PULL FACTORS

The reasons why Latin Americans have immigrated to the United States have changed since the early nineteenth century. In the past, and particularly during the mid-nineteenth century, educated upper- and middle-class Latin Americans tended to migrate to the United States either to work as professionals and then return home or to send their children to U.S. schools. This was especially true among Hispanics in the island countries of the Caribbean. During the late nineteenth and twentieth century, however, members of other socioeconomic classes began arriving in the United States, a trend that has continued up to the twenty-first century. Latin America can be viewed as divided into four distinct zones:

- Mexico
- Caribbean basin, or West Indies
- Central America
- South America

MEXICAN IMMIGRANTS

Historically, most Latin American immigrants have come from Mexico. During the nineteenth and early twentieth centuries, movement across the U.S.-Mexican border was fluid; people from both sides could cross with little obstruction. Consequently, Mexicans could travel north to work and return home easily. During the first decades of the twentieth century, the numbers of people moving north across the border began to increase significantly, and larger numbers of immigrants from Mexico's lower and middle classes began arriving on the U.S. side in search of political stability and economic opportunity.

During the 1940's, the U.S. and Mexican governments negotiated agreements such as the bracero program in order to create more orderly systems of bringing workers into the United States. Under these programs, large numbers of Hispanic migrant workers traveled north to the United States to work in the construction and agricultural sectors of the U.S. economy. After completing their contracts, they generally returned home; however, some remained permanently in the United States. Contract labor programs continued into the 1960's, and through these programs, the U.S. government recognized and formalized an already existing migration pattern.

The border between the United States and Mexico extends approximately 1,920 miles along the southern edges of California, Arizona, New Mexico, and Texas and the northern edges of the Mexican states of Baja California, Sonora, Chihuahua, Coauila, Nuevo León. and Tamaulipas. The border runs through mostly arid terrain ranging from sandy flatlands to rugged mountains.

CARIBBEAN IMMIGRANTS

The West Indies islands of Puerto Rico, Cuba, and Hispaniola—which is shared by the Spanish-speaking Dominican Republic and French-speaking Haiti—constitute the second region of Latin America. Though separated by open expanses of sea, these islands share a geographic proximity to the United States that accounts in part for the movement of many West Indians to the U.S. mainland. During the nineteenth century, upper- and middle-class Hispanic islanders traveled in small numbers from the Caribbean to the United States. By the beginning of the twentieth century, their numbers had gradually increased but still remained small in actual numbers. The 1920's and 1930's saw an increase in West Indian immigration as job opportunities were becoming scarcer in the Caribbean.

During the mid-twentieth century, West Indian immigration numbers increased substantially. The economic and political circumstances varied among the Hispanic islands, but all these islands were experiencing growing populations and shrinking job bases. People from the Dominican Republic and Puerto Rico—which by then was a U.S. dependency—continued to go to the United States primarily to work, and they formed large communities, primarily in the Northeast. Cuban immigration surged during the 1960's as a result of the island's communist revolution, and it continued to be strong into the 1980's and 1990's.

CENTRAL AMERICAN IMMIGRANTS

Significant immigration from Central American nations did not begin until the late twentieth century, but immigrants from those nations have dispersed over a wide area of the United States, particularly the South, Midwest, and Far West. Political upheavals during the 1970's and 1980's impelled many people from Guatemala, El Salvador, and Nicaragua to migrate north. A large part of these immigrants were members of the working classes and had less education than other Latin American immigrants. Consequently, they have tended to experience higher levels of poverty after settling in

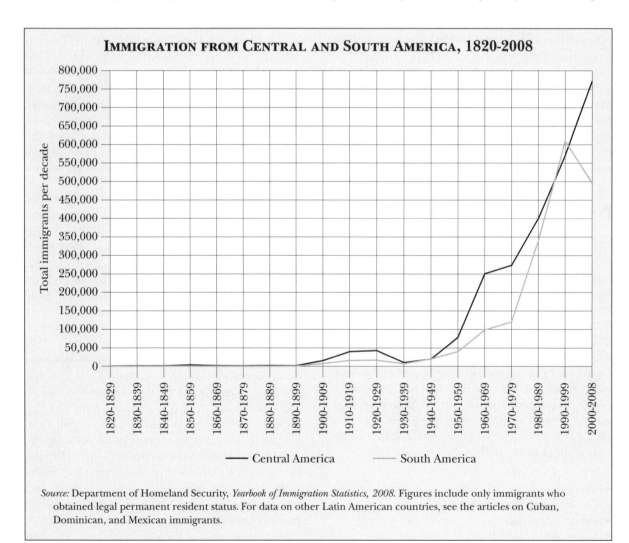

IMMIGRATION FROM CENTRAL AND SOUTH AMERICA, 1820-2008

Source: Department of Homeland Security, *Yearbook of Immigration Statistics, 2008.* Figures include only immigrants who obtained legal permanent resident status. For data on other Latin American countries, see the articles on Cuban, Dominican, and Mexican immigrants.

Protestor waving a Honduran flag at a Miami, Florida, demonstration that was one of many across the United States during a national day of protest against government crackdowns on illegal immigration on May 1, 2006. The predominantly Latin American protestors sought to call attention to the positive economic contributions that undocumented immigrants make to the United States. (AP/Wide World Photos)

the United States. In contrast, immigrants from the more politically stable Costa Rica have tended to be more highly educated and better equipped to find success in the United States. Even after political unrest had largely abated in Central America by the early twenty-first century, immigrants continued to come to the United States in large numbers.

SOUTH AMERICAN IMMIGRANTS

Although South America has the largest population of any of the four Latin American zones, it has historically supplied the fewest immigrants to the United States. However, during the last decade of the twentieth century and the first decade of the twenty-first, the rate of immigration from South American nations more than doubled. The countries sending the most people to the United States have been Brazil, Peru, Ecuador, and Colombia. The numbers of immigrants from Colombia have been particularly high because of political instability

in that country. Meanwhile, increasing numbers of immigrants have come from Argentina, Venezuela, Chile, and Bolivia. Immigrants from South America have settled throughout the United States, but they have tended to concentrate in the Northeast and along the East Coast. Among Latin American nations, the countries of South America are the most distant from the United States. Because of the great distances immigrants from those countries travel to reach the United States, the immigrants have worked especially hard to develop social and support networks to facilitate their journey.

South American immigrants have traditionally brought higher levels of education, and their emigration from their homelands has created serious "brain drains" in their home countries. However, by the early twenty-first century, increasing portions of immigrants were coming from the working classes of their countries. Chilean immigrants have generally had higher levels of education and professional skills, while Paraguayan and Bolivian immigrants have tended to be less educated. Paraguay's high rate of population growth has made the immigrants coming from that country younger than those of most other Latin American nations.

CHANGING PATTERNS IN IMMIGRATION

With the large increase of Latin American immigration to the United States after the 1960's, extended family and kinship networks have grown apace. They, in turn, have facilitated the development of chain migration links. Whereas in the past, most Latin Americans coming to the United States were men planning to work and save money before returning home, the late twentieth century saw a large increase in the numbers of women, children, and families following established migration routes to live and work in American communities in which Hispanic family and social contacts were already established.

These social and kinship networks have also led to generally more participation in local civic organizations, clubs, and churches, as well as a renewed use of mutual aid societies to assist and support new immigrants. At the same time, the Spanish-language media and press have become increasingly important disseminators of news, culture, entertainment, and advertising to Spanish-speaking markets.

William A. Teipe, Jr.

FURTHER READING

González, Juan. *Harvest of Empire: A History of Latinos in America.* New York: Viking Press, 2000. Useful general historical overview of the many Hispanic peoples who have immigrated to the United States from all regions of Latin America.

Mahler, Sarah J. *American Dreaming: Immigrant Life on the Margins.* Princeton, N.J.: Princeton University Press, 1995. Close study of Central and South American immigrants in New York's Long Island, who might be viewed as a microcosm of Latin American immigrants in the United States.

Meier, Matt S., and Feliciano Rivera. *Mexican Americans/American Mexicans: From Conquistadors to Chicanos.* 2d ed. Toronto: HarperCollins Canada, 1993. Thorough overview of Mexican immigration into what is now the United States, from the time of early Spanish conquests to the modern American Chicano movement.

Rodriguez, Gregory. *Mongrels, Bastards, Orphans, and Vagabonds: Mexican Immigration and the Future of Race in America.* New York: Pantheon Books, 2007. Broad overview of Mexican immigrants that attempts to assess its implications for future American developments.

Rodríguez, Havidán, Rogelio Sáenz, and Cecilia Menjívar. *Latinas/os in the United States: Changing the Face of America.* New York: Springer, 2008. Broad study of Hispanic communities in the United States, emphasizing their diversity.

Suro, Roberto. *Strangers Among Us: Latino Lives in a Changing America.* New York: Vintage Books, 1999. Balanced view of immigration by Latin Americans.

SEE ALSO: Brazilian immigrants; Chain migration; Colombian immigrants; Cuban immigrants; Dominican immigrants; Ecuadorian immigrants; Guatemalan immigrants; Honduran immigrants; Japanese Peruvians; Latinos and immigrants; Mexican immigrants; Nicaraguan immigrants; Puerto Rican immigrants; Salvadoran immigrants; Spanish-language press; Telemundo.

LATINOS AND IMMIGRANTS

SIGNIFICANCE: American citizens of Latino descent have long had a special relationship with Latin American immigrants, with whom they have shared a common culture and a common language. In addition to these cultural affinities, the geographical proximity of the United States and Latin American nations—particularly Mexico—has helped to foster close ties between Latinos in the United States and the nations from which new immigrants have emigrated. However, while Latinos in the United States have often helped immigrants adjust to life in the United States, others have felt threatened by Latin American immigration.

As Latin American immigrants poured into the United States in increasing numbers during the late twentieth century, many of them were absorbed into established American Latino communities. Many Latinos around the United States have organized their own social-service agencies to aid immigrants. For example, El Centro de la Raza, in Seattle, has hosted many services for new immigrants of all ethnicities since it was founded in 1972. It began as a Latino-led center but broadened its mission in a multiethnic community. Immigration, especially among Latinos, is a family affair, and El Centro often parses its mission in familial terms.

El Centro and other community centers also have actively maintained Latin American connections, as well as relationships with diplomatic offices in Mexico and other Spanish-speaking countries. Some people at El Centro say that it is a community center with a foreign policy. El Centro, for example, has played a key role in forging Seattle's sister-city relationship with Managua, Nicaragua.

ANTI-IMMIGRATION SENTIMENTS

A minority of Latino immigrants who have become U.S. citizens (or their children) oppose further immigration. An example has been provided by Roberto Suro, the author of *Strangers Among Us: How Latino Immigration is Transforming America* (1998). The son of Puerto Rican and Ecuadorean parents and a reporter for the *Washington Post*, Suro has argued for strengthening U.S. border security, imposing stricter penalties for those immigrants who enter the United States illegally more than once, and restricting aid to countries, such as Mexico, that do not do enough to restrain emigration of their own citizens to the United States.

Suro's views have been criticized for ignoring immigration's motive forces throughout history. Most immigrants, including the parents of Latinos who came into the United States in earlier years, did not leave their original homes until economic necessity or political repression compelled them. Thus, the flow of illegal immigration can be solved only by fundamental political and economic changes in the countries whose people are leaving in large numbers. However, critics have charged that this line of reasoning ignores the safety-valve function of emigration from countries that cannot provide employment for all their citizens.

Suro's book focuses not on Latin American immigrants like himself who have succeeded in the United States, but rather on those whom, he asserts, wallow in the culture of poverty, fail to learn English, and feed on the illegal drug trade and other forms of criminal activity. His perception is selective, critics charge, as he perpetuates stereotypes that fuel much anti-immigrant activity. Suro speaks for a segment of the immigration debate whose advocates believe that the expanding, open economy of earlier years in the United States has stagnated, and that further immigration will only worsen tensions among ethnic groups, causing more problems for already resident Latinos by increasing competition for limited jobs.

Another example of the differing attitudes held by various Latinos vis-à-vis immigration is evident at the U.S.-Mexican border, where a large proportion of the federal agents who enforce laws keeping the border secure are themselves Latinos.

Bruce E. Johansen

FURTHER READING

González, Juan. *Harvest of Empire: A History of Latinos in America.* New York: Viking Press, 2000. Good overview of the histories of the many Latino immigrant groups that have come to the United States.

Hopfensperger, Jean. "Hard Times Send Latinos Back Across the Border: Fewer Jobs, Tougher Immigration Rules Force Some Immigrants to Return Home." *Minneapolis Star-Tribune*, May 29, 2009. Extensive examination of Latino immigrants' return to their home countries following economic difficulties in the United States, especially in Minnesota's Twin Cities.

Schrader, Esther. Review of *Strangers Among Us* by Roberto Suro. *Washington Monthly*, October, 1998. Detailed examination of issues raised in Suro's book on Latino immigration, which is reconfiguring North American politics and culture. Suro opposes illegal Latino immigration.

Segura, Gary M., ed. "Latino Immigration and National Identity." *Perspectives on Politics* (June, 2006). Rebuts assumptions that Latino immigrants generally fail to succeed and adapt to social norms in the United States; it finds that public discourse on Latinos and immigration often relies on stereotypes and inaccurate information.

Suro, Roberto. *Strangers Among Us: How Latino Immigration Is Transforming America.* New York: Alfred A. Knopf, 1998. A *Washington Post* reporter, Suro explores immigration issues and concludes that older Latino immigrants sometimes oppose easing of laws for those who come after them.

SEE ALSO: Bilingual education; Bracero program; Chicano movement; Drug trafficking; Employment; Farm and migrant workers; Illegal immigration; Latin American immigrants; Mexican immigrants; Puerto Rican immigrants; West Indian immigrants.

LAU V. NICHOLS

THE CASE: U.S. Supreme Court decision on the education of children with limited English-language skills

DATE: Decided on January 21, 1974

SIGNIFICANCE: Based on the Civil Rights Act of 1964, *Lau v. Nichols* required school districts to provide compensatory training for students with limited proficiency in the use of the English language, but the ruling left it up to educational authorities and school districts to decide which methods of instruction to utilize.

In 1971, San Francisco's school district was racially integrated by court order. At that time, the school district had about 2,800 students of Chinese ancestry who were unable to communicate in the English language. The district provided 1,000 of these students with special instruction in English but provided no such instruction for the remaining 1,800 students. The parents of those not receiving special instruction went to court in a class-action suit, arguing that the district's policy violated Title VI of the Civil Rights Act of 1964, which prohibited educational discrimination based on national origin. In addition, the parents asserted that the district's policy was contrary to the requirements of the equal protection clause of the Fourteenth Amendment.

Although the lower federal courts ruled against the parents, the Supreme Court unanimously held that the district's failure to provide the students with appropriate language instruction denied them equal educational opportunity on the basis of ethnicity. In writing the opinion for the Court, Justice William O. Douglas relied entirely on the Civil

Rights Act of 1964 and wrote that there was no need to consider whether the district's actions might also be inconsistent with the Fourteenth Amendment. To buttress his position, Douglas observed that the district received a substantial amount of federal financial assistance and that a 1970 antidiscrimination guideline of the Department of Health, Education, and Welfare required federally funded school districts to rectify the "linguistic deficiencies" of students from non-English-speaking homes. While requiring "affirmative steps" to overcome the language barrier, Douglas did not prescribe any particular means toward that end, whether bilingual instruction, English as a second language (ESL) training, or another approach.

The *Lau* decision significantly expanded the rights of limited-English-proficient (LEP) students throughout the nation. Among other things, it popularized the notion that language is so closely interwoven with a group's national culture that language-based discrimination constitutes a form of national-origin discrimination. The decision helped encourage the Department of Health, Education, and Welfare to issue the "Lau Remedies" of 1975, which required bilingual instruction in elementary schools where enough LEP students of the same language made it practical. Enforced by the Office of Civil Rights, five hundred school districts adopted bilingual programs within the next five years. Experts disagreed, however, about the effectiveness of such programs. The Republican administrations of the 1980's allowed a more flexible, case-by-case approach, and most districts abandoned bilingualism and attempted to help LEP students with ESL classes.

Thomas Tandy Lewis

FURTHER READING

Epstein, Lee, and Thomas Walker. *Constitutional Law for a Changing America: Rights, Liberties, and Justice.* 6th ed. Washington, D.C.: CQ Press, 2006.

O'Brien, David M. *Constitutional Law and Politics.* 7th ed. New York: W. W. Norton, 2008.

SEE ALSO: Bilingual education; Bilingual Education Act of 1968; Citizenship; Constitution, U.S.; Due process protections; Education; English as a second language; History of immigration after 1891; Multiculturalism; Supreme Court, U.S.

LEM MOON SING V. UNITED STATES

THE CASE: U.S. Supreme Court decision on habeas corpus petitions by aliens
DATE: Decided on May 27, 1895

SIGNIFICANCE: The *Lem Moon Sing* decision upheld a federal law prohibiting district courts from reviewing habeas corpus petitions, thereby empowering immigration authorities to exclude or deport alien immigrants without any concern that judges might find fault with their procedures.

A businessman who had resided many years in California, Lem Moon Sing was born in China to Chinese parents, which made him ineligible for naturalized American citizenship. In 1894, he visited his native land with the intention of returning in a few months to resume living and working in the United States. During his absence, however, the U.S. Congress passed an appropriation act with a provision that immigration officials' decisions were final when excluding aliens from admission into the United States under the Chinese Exclusion Act of 1882. Decisions were subject to review by the secretary of the treasury. When arriving in San Francisco later that year, Sing appeared to meet the qualifications for reentry. He presented two credible witnesses testifying that he had conducted business as a merchant and was not a laborer excluded by the Scott Act of 1888. Immigration officials, nevertheless, denied him permission to enter the country.

Arguing that the exclusion was an unconstitutional denial of due process and that it violated treaties with China, Sing petitioned the U.S. district court for a writ of habeas corpus, which would have allowed a judge to review the decision. Based on the 1894 law, the petition was denied. The Supreme Court, by an 8-1 margin, upheld the judgment of the lower court. Speaking for the majority, Justice John Marshall Harlan reviewed the Court's precedents concerning the power of Congress to make immigration policy. While recognizing the duty of immigration officials to faithfully follow provisions in both laws and treaties, Harlan insisted that the U.S. Constitution empowered Congress to decide that the final judgment would be made by officials within the executive department of the government.

Thomas Tandy Lewis

FURTHER READING

Hyung-chan, Kim, ed. *Asian Americans and the Supreme Court: A Documentary History*. Westport, Conn.: Greenwood Press, 1992.
McClain, Charles J. *In Search of Equality: The Chinese Struggle Against Discrimination in Nineteenth-Century America*. Berkeley: University of California Press, 1994.

SEE ALSO: Chinese Exclusion Act of 1882; *Chinese Exclusion Cases*; Chinese immigrants; Congress, U.S.; Due process protections; History of immigration, 1783-1891; *Immigration and Naturalization Service v. St. Cyr*; *Nishimura Ekiu v. United States*; Supreme Court, U.S.; *United States v. Ju Toy*.

LENNON, JOHN

IDENTIFICATION: English musician and political activist
BORN: October 9, 1940; Liverpool, England
DIED: December 8, 1980; New York, New York

SIGNIFICANCE: After winning international fame as one of the lead singers of the British rock band called the Beatles, Lennon moved to the United States in 1971 and joined in a number of radical leftist causes. In 1972, President Richard M. Nixon attempted to have him deported for political reasons.

Upon the breakup of John Lennon's world-famous rock group the Beatles, he and his Japanese-born wife, Yoko Ono, used their celebrity to promote the anti-Vietnam War movement. In 1969, they staged quixotic protests such as "Bed-ins for Peace," and Lennon was denied entry to the United States. Lennon and Ono moved to New York City in 1971, associating with such radicals as Jerry Rubin and Abbie Hoffman. Lennon and Ono also advocated a number of leftist causes in their protest album *Sometime in New York City* (1972).

President Richard M. Nixon, fearing that Lennon's influence on young voters could undermine his reelection and that there could be a Lennon-led disruption of the 1972 Republican National Convention, ordered Lennon's deportation. In March of that year, Lennon was served a deportation notice by the Immigration and Naturalization Service citing a 1968 misdemeanor drug conviction in England. Lennon appealed the order, which was eventually overturned in 1975. Despite Lennon's radical associations, the Federal Bureau of Investigation's surveillance of him determined the often intoxicated Lennon to be a minimal subversive threat. He gained permanent resident status in 1976 but was killed by a mentally deranged American fan four years later.

Luke A. Powers

John Lennon (left) with his Japanese wife, Yoko Ono, in New York City, in 1972. (AP/Wide World Photos)

FURTHER READING

Norman, Philip. *John Lennon: The Life.* New York: Ecco Press, 2008.

Wenner, Jann. *Lennon Remembers.* 1971. New ed. New York: Verso, 2000.

Wiener, Jon. *Gimme Some Truth: The John Lennon FBI Files.* Berkeley: University of California Press, 1999.

SEE ALSO: Citizenship and Immigration Services, U.S.; Drug trafficking; Due process protections; Films; "Moral turpitude"; Music; New York City.

LIBERIA

IDENTIFICATION: West African nation that originated as a refuge for freed American slaves

SIGNIFICANCE: Since its founding, Liberia has had a unique relationship with the United States. Its history is closely linked with American slavery and the abolitionist movement in the United States, and the West African nation was founded as a colony for former African American slaves and free blacks, who were encouraged to emigrate from the United States during the early nineteenth century. During the early twentieth century, a black nationalist movement in the United States attempted to send more settlers to Liberia.

Liberia's first American settlers were eighty-eight free-born African Americans who went there in 1820 and settled at Cape Mesurado, at the mouth of the St. Paul River. Most of these people were educated and free, and many owned property in Maryland and Virginia. Although they had not been born into slavery in the United States, they had not enjoyed full citizenship rights as Americans. By the time Liberia declared its independence in 1847, several thousand more free-born African Americans and former slaves had joined them in the new nation. These original immigrants and their descendants were afterward known as Americo-Liberians.

LIBERIA'S EARLY IMMIGRANTS

By 1824, the original Cape Mesurado Colony was home to several hundred settlers and had been renamed the Liberia Colony. Throughout the 1820's, other colonies were established along the coast. These included New Georgia, which was settled by Africans from other parts of the continent who had been liberated from slave ships by U.S. naval vessels while they were being carried to the Western Hemisphere. After these people were set free in the new colony, they became known as "Congos."

Meanwhile, several additional colonies were established under the sponsorship of colonization societies, including the American Colonization Society, and the state legislatures of Kentucky, Maryland, Mississippi, New York, Pennsylvania, and Virginia. The colonies expanded along Liberia's coast throughout the 1830's and 1840's. The population of the region was made up of three distinct groups of people: the original settlers from America, enslaved Africans who had been liberated from slave ships, and the region's indigenous peoples, primarily from Malinké-speaking societies. Americo-Liberians and Congos would always constitute a small minority of the total population of Liberia, but they dominated the politics and economy of Liberia through the nineteenth century and most of the twentieth century. By the twenty-first century, however, average Liberians no longer made distinctions among descendants of the original settlers of Liberia.

By 1847, when the Republic of Liberia declared its independence, approximately 15,000 Americans had settled in the country, along with a few thousand newly so-called Congos. Several European nations quickly established diplomatic relations with Liberia, but the United States did not recognize the new nation until 1862.

TWENTIETH CENTURY LIBERIA

Liberia was long an anomaly in sub-Saharan Africa, most of which was colonized by European nations during the late nineteenth century. By the twentieth century, Liberia and Ethiopia were the only sub-Saharan countries that had not been colonized by Europe, but Liberia differed from Ethiopia, on the other side of the continent, in being politically dominated by non-African settlers, most of whom came from the United States. The country's Americo-Liberian rulers did not even recognize members of Liberia's indigenous societies as citizens of the new nation until 1904. During the 1920's, Marcus Garvey's Universal Negro Improvement Association tried to start a new resettlement program to send African Americans to Liberia, but only a small number of people emigrated to the country.

Meanwhile, Liberia developed painfully slowly. Even its borders with its colonial neighbors remained poorly defined until well into the twentieth century. In his 1936 book, *Journey Without Maps*, author Graham Greene trekked 350 miles through Liberia's rain forests. The only map available at the time from the U.S. government showed a wide swath of Liberia as being unexplored, with a vast, empty space fancifully labeled "cannibals."

The Americo-Liberians governed Liberia through a single party. Although their governments were often corrupt, the country remained relatively stable until 1980, when an army sergeant named Samuel K. Doe brought down the govern-

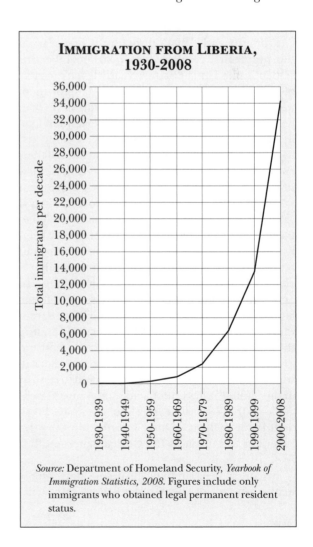

IMMIGRATION FROM LIBERIA, 1930-2008

Source: Department of Homeland Security, *Yearbook of Immigration Statistics, 2008.* Figures include only immigrants who obtained legal permanent resident status.

ment in a swift coup and had its Americo-Liberian leaders executed. Afterward, ethnic tensions increased until 1989, when Doe's former chief of procurement, Charles Taylor, invaded Liberia from neighboring Côte d'Ivoire and took control of the government. Taylor's regime was marked by a long, bloody civil war, during which 200,000 Liberians died, and about one-third of the nation's population fled to neighboring countries. Thousands of Liberians who had the means to do so fled their war-torn nation and sought refuge in the United States, essentially reversing the trend of Americans returning to the shores of West Africa. Liberia's civil war officially ended in August, 2003, when all the warring parties agreed to a cease-fire. However, by then, much of Liberia lay in ruins, and a massive humanitarian disaster existed.

LIBERIAN IMMIGRATION TO THE UNITED STATES

From the early 1990's through the first years of the twenty-first century, nearly 20,000 Liberians settled in the United States. Nearly three-quarters of them resided in Rhode Island. Many of them were descendants of African American slaves who had long maintained ties with their extended family members in the United States. In seeking refuge, they began returning to the homeland of their ancestors, the United States. To afford these new immigrants legal protection, the U.S. government began granting them temporary protected status (TPS) in 1991. By 2005, TPS had been extended to thousands of Liberians, many of whom had been living in the United States for a decade or more and had either renewed or established new family, social, and economic ties with the United States. In September, 2006, the U.S. Department of Homeland Security announced that the TPS program would stop on October 1, 2007, effectively ending the refugee status Liberian immigrants had enjoyed in the United States. However, Liberians already registered under TPS were allowed to remain in the United States under a new status into March, 2009. As that extension was about to expire, President Barack Obama signed an order allowing the Liberians to remain in the United States another year.

Because Liberia remains a fragile state with a weak economy and nearly nonexistent infrastruc-

ture, many U.S. government leaders believe that forcing the return of nearly 20,000 immigrants to Liberia could easily overwhelm the frail nation. To address the issue, the Liberian Refugee Immigration Fairness Act of 2007 was introduced in the U.S. Senate in February, 2007. A similar bill, the Liberian Refugee Immigration Protection Act of 2007, was introduced in the U.S. House of Representatives in April. 2007. Both forms of legislation were designed to permit eligible Liberians living in the United States to apply for permanent resident status. However, both bills were still awaiting passage in 2009.

Terry A. Anderson

FURTHER READING

Clegg, Claude Andrew. *The Price of Liberty: African Americans and the Making of Liberia.* Chapel Hill: University of North Carolina Press, 2004. Comprehensive history of the origins and early development of Liberia.

Koser, Khalid, ed. *New African Diasporas.* New York: Routledge, 2003. Describes the waves of immigration of the late twentieth century from Africa to the United States and to northern Europe and the United Kingdom.

Murdza, Peter J., Jr. *Immigrants to Liberia, 1865 to 1904: An Alphabetical Listing.* Newark, Del.: Liberian Studies Association of America, 1975. Detailed list of all the African American families who settled in Liberia during the late nineteenth century.

Ndubuike, Darlington. *The Struggles, Challenges, and Triumphs of the African Immigrants in America.* Lewiston, N.Y.: Edwin Mellen Press, 2002. Discusses the struggles of African immigrants in adapting to American society.

Smith, James Wesley. *Sojourners in Search of Freedom: The Settlement of Liberia by Black Americans.* Lanham, Md.: University Press of America, 1987. Another interesting history of the founding of Liberia by African Americans.

SEE ALSO: Abolitionist movement; African Americans and immigrants; African immigrants; American Colonization Society; "Brain drain"; Emigration; Maryland; Remittances of earnings; Slave trade.

LIM, SHIRLEY GEOK-LIN

IDENTIFICATION: Malaysian American author and academic

BORN: December 27, 1944; Malacca, Malaya (now Malaysia)

SIGNIFICANCE: A feminist professor and prolific poet, short-fiction writer, novelist, and literary critic, Shirley Geok-lin Lim researches and writes from the margins as a woman, an English-speaking Malaysian Chinese/Peranakan, and an immigrant Asian American. Her work on language, gender, nation, and ethnicity as engines of cultural production is particularly valuable for an understanding of the identity creation of immigrants.

Shirley Geok-lin Lim was born during World War II at a time when the Japanese army forces had overpowered the British colonial rulers for control of Malaya. Her Chinese father was fluent in Hokkien (a Chinese dialect), Malay, and English. His father had emigrated from Fujian Province, China, to Malaya for work. Lim's Peranakan (Malayan-native Chinese who adopted Malay and Western cultures) mother was fluent in Teochew (another Chinese dialect), Malay, and English. Lim, whose first language was the Malay of her mother, quickly became a predominantly English speaker both at home and at school by the age of six, when she went to a convent school run by Roman Catholic nuns. As a child in Malacca, Lim suffered abuse, poverty, and abandonment—her mother left Lim's father and her five brothers when she was eight years old. She comes from a family of eight brothers (three half brothers) and one half sister.

Lim moved away from her family to Kuala Lumpur to attend the University of Malaya, graduating with a bachelor's degree in 1967 and a master's degree in 1969, both in English literature. In 1969, she moved to the United States to attend Brandeis University on Fulbright and Wien International scholarships. As a new international student from a tropical country, she initially suffered both loneliness and culture shock. Nevertheless, she completed a master's degree (1971) and a doctorate (1973) in English and American literature. In No-

vember, 1972, she married Charles Bazerman, a Jewish New Yorker who also had a doctorate in English and American literature from Brandeis, and they had a son. While pregnant, Lim became a U.S. citizen on February 14, 1980. Her son's American identity solidified her connection to the United States, although she struggled as an immigrant mother to be a part of her local community. Lim has taught at Hostos Community College, City University of New York (1973-1976); Westchester College, State University of New York (1976-1990); and the University of California, Santa Barbara (1990-   ).

Lim's major areas of teaching and research are women's studies, Asian American literature, and Southeast Asian literature. Her poetry and fiction are populated by characters who live in the multilingual, multicultural, multireligious, and multiracial society of her country of origin. Her novels *Joss and Gold* (2001) and *Sister Swing* (2006) deal with characters who have moved from one country to another: Malaysia to Singapore and America to Singapore in the former; Malaysia to America in the latter. Her nonfiction works include *The Forbidden Stitch: An Asian American Women's Anthology* (1989; coeditor), which won an American Book Award/Before Columbus Award in 1990, and her prominent memoir, *Among the White Moon Faces* (1996), which won an American Book Award in 1997.

Lydia Forssander-Song

FURTHER READING

Lim, Shirley Geok-lin. *Among the White Moon Faces: An Asian-American Memoir of Homelands.* New York: Feminist Press at the City University of New York, 1996.

_____. *Sister Swing.* Singapore: Marshall Cavendish, 2006.

Newton, Pauline T. *Transcultural Women of Late Twentieth-Century U.S. American Literature: First Generation Migrants from Islands and Peninsulas.* Burlington, Vt.: Ashgate, 2005.

SEE ALSO: Asian American literature; Lahiri, Jhumpa; Literature; Malaysian immigrants; Mukherjee, Bharati; Sidhwa, Bapsi; Women immigrants.

LINGUISTIC CONTRIBUTIONS

DEFINITION: Contributions to American English made by immigrant speakers of other languages

SIGNIFICANCE: English has long had the largest lexicon, or roster, of vocabulary items, of any language on Earth, in large part because of frequent borrowings from other tongues, especially from Latin, Greek, Old Norse, and French. However, the multicultural nature of the United States, especially from the mid-nineteenth century onward, facilitated the adaptation of borrowed words and phrases into American English at an even greater rate than had been the case in England, the country from which the language derived.

Before the English language was implanted in North America, most of its foreign linguistic influences had been the inadvertent results of military conquests or had come from deliberate attempts at language-engineering by scholars. In the North American colonies and later in the independent United States, changes in the language were more spontaneous and more organic. They were natural outgrowths of the intermingling of peoples from all over the world. The scope of immigrant influences on American English is perhaps best illustrated by examining contributions from the Romance languages of immigrants from countries such as France, Spain, Portugal, Italy, and the many Latin American nations and from the Germanic languages of immigrants from German-, Dutch-, and Scandinavian-speaking countries. Most of the words that have entered American English from the Romance languages pertain to folkways, food, and place names of both natural and artificial locations.

Folklorists employ the term "folkways" to encompass a wide array of professions, social roles, lifestyle issues, customs, dress, recreation, and folk beliefs. Many French terms that have found their way into American English reflect the lifestyles and beliefs of immigrants in regions bordering on Quebec in the northeast and in Louisiana in the south. Examples include

- *voyageur,* trapper or trader who travels long distances
- *traiteur,* folk healer or herbalist
- *lagniappe,* gift or act of kindness extended to guests as a token of cordiality
- *fifolet,* spirit or witch manifesting a nighttime phosphorescence
- *loup garou,* werewolf or similar creature of the night
- *gris-gris,* protective magic devices

Similar terms from Spanish include

- *quincienera,* celebration of a girl's fifteenth birthday
- buckaroo, term for cowboy adapted from the Spanish *vaquero,* literally "cattler"
- *curandero,* folk-healer, the Spanish equivalent of *traiteur*

Words for items of apparel also feature prominently in Spanish loanwords in American English. Examples include poncho, serape, and "ten-gallon hat." The latter originated when English-speakers mistook the Spanish word *galan* for the braid on a hatband for the English word "gallon" for a liquid measurement. Many other words related to the folkways of Spanish-speaking immigrants pertain to items used in ranching, such as "lariat" from Spanish *la reata* for rope or noose. Folk music also has contributed many words, such as "mariachi" for the exuberant form of Mexican music featuring string and wind instruments originally played at marriages—the English word to which the name of the music is directly related. Names of instruments used in mariachi music have also found their way into English. "Guitar" comes from the Spanish *guitaron* for large guitar.

Among the most readily recognized words from Italian are names for crime syndicates, such as "Mafia" and "Cosa Nostra." During the late nineteenth century, American English adopted the Italian *paisano* (sometimes rendered *paisan* in English) for peasant or worker as a jocular term for buddy or compatriot.

ROMANCE FOOD AND FORMATIONS

Words from Romance languages denoting foodstuffs and structures have flooded American English since the founding of the United States, but most especially since the nineteenth century. Italian words for pasta dishes such as "macaroni" and "spaghetti" entered the English language in England, but after millions of Italians immigrated to the United States during the nineteenth century, Italian restaurants became so commonplace that such Italian terms become more common in American usage than in British English. During the early twentieth century, "pizza" became an American staple, as did a number of coffee drinks of Italian origin such as "espresso," "cappuccino," and "latte."

Spanish gave American English words such as "taco," "tequila," "enchilada," and "burrito." In numerous cases, the dishes were as much American-European hybrids as were the words themselves. For example, enchiladas are a Mexican-American creation, neither fully Spanish nor even wholly Mexican. American pizza has little in common with the Italian dish after which it is named. Many of the Franco-American food terms in American English come from French, French Caribbean, and French Canadian cooking in the American South, especially in Louisiana. Examples include roux, a rich stock for sauces and gravy, and jambalaya, a meat-and-rice dish whose name came into English from Catalan by way of Spanish into Louisiana French. The thick, rich soup known as chowder is a French Canadian innovation in New England cooking terminology.

PLACE NAMES

As numerous as cuisine-related loanwords are in American English, Romance language names for types of places—both geographical and architectural—are equally common. Mexican Spanish has given southwestern American English terms such as

- "hoosegow" (jail), which comes from *juzgado* (place of the judged ones)
- "arroyo," a direct Spanish borrowing for a type of dry riverbed common in the Southwest
- "mesa," a flat, raised area of land from the Spanish word for table

From Cajun French, the dialect of French Canadian immigrants to Louisiana, contributed "bayou" for swamp and "levee" for the earthworks used to protect lowlands from flooding. Another French contribution that has much wider usage in American English is "bureau." The word originally was used for a bedroom desk or dresser; then it was extended to a piece of office furniture, and finally to an office and the agency it housed. In this later sense, both "bureau" and its derivative, "bureaucracy," were borrowed not only by international English but also by a number of other languages.

GERMANIC CONTRIBUTIONS

Borrowings into American English from the Germanic languages followed pathways similar to those from Romance languages. Food-related words have been common. From German have come "strudel," "noodle," "sauerkraut," "pretzel," and the coffee-related equivalent of English "teatime," "kaffeeklatsch." Dutch has given American English "cruller" for a type of pastry and the even more commonly used word "cookie," which was unknown in British English before it was introduced from American English. The equivalent British term has long been "biscuit." The British "biscuit" came from an Old French word for "twice-baked" pastries. In American English, the same word underwent a semantic shift to designate round, scone-like portions of bread. The Dutch *cookie* then filled the niche vacated by "biscuit."

A surprisingly large number of Germanic borrowings have been words denoting types of people; many of these words are derogatory in nature. German examples include "bum" for a lazy or idle person, from the verb *bummeln* (to loaf). Yiddish, the German dialect used primarily by Jews, gave American English a veritable flood of insulting terms. "Yekl," "klutz," "schlemiel," "schlimazel," "schmo," "schmuck," and "schnook" all connote stupidity or ineptitude to some degree. However, perhaps the most enduring and widespread insult from Germanic immigrant languages is the ubiquitous "dumb." For centuries, the homonymic English word "dumb" had meant mute; however, in every other populous Germanic language, spoken collectively by millions of immigrants, a near-identical word meant stupid or foolish. Examples include German's *dumm* and Swedish and Danish's *dum.* The Old English word "dumb" simply borrowed the meaning of its many Germanic cousins.

Not all such Germanic borrowings are negative. "Boss" from Dutch and "ombudsman" from Swedish are both neutral. Yiddish's "mensch" for a good-hearted individual is positive. At the same time, the Romance languages have contributed some insulting terms. American English's "bimbo" for an attractive but unintelligent person is from *bambino*, Italian for baby. "Boob" and "booby" probably derive from Spanish *bobo* for a fool or clown.

OTHER TYPES OF CONTRIBUTIONS

The Romance and Germanic languages are not the only immigrant languages that have made significant contributions to American English. For example, "egg foo young" and "chow mein" are examples of words derived from Chinese for food dishes that were actually devised by Chinese immigrants in the United States. Likewise, "kolache," a pastry popular among Czechs and Slovaks, has evolved in the United States into a sweeter sort of treat reminiscent of American cinnamon rolls while at the same time developing a name that is a singular form in English although derived from a plural form in Czech.

Immigration has left traces on facets of American English that go beyond mere items of vocabulary. For example, among English speakers in areas where dialects of French have long been common, for example, Louisiana, one sometimes hears questions formulated without insertion of the default auxiliary verb "do." Instead of asking "How did your clothes get wet?" a person might say "How your clothes got wet?" The latter sentence structure imitates French syntax. Another example of imitating French phrasing is the rapid-fire repetition of an adjective to suggest intensity, as in "It is hot-hot today."

In regions in which many Americans are bilingual English and Spanish or else in close contact with such speakers, one often hears "leave" used with "to" to indicate a destination, for example, "They are leaving to school" instead of the standard "They are leaving for school," a structure imitative of Spanish, which employs the single-letter preposition *a* (to) in such circumstances.

Another phrase-structure affected by languages of immigrants may be the tag question—making a statement and immediately adding a brief yes/no question seeking confirmation or denial. In formal English, such questions involve complex formulations. For example, the tag on the simple statement, "Roger is drunk" requires copying over the verb ("is"), choosing the appropriate pronoun ("he"), and reversing the polarity of the statement (positive in this case) to negative, thus yielding,

"Roger is drunk, isn't he?" In contrast, most European languages, including members of the Romance and Germanic families, forego such linguistic acrobatics by simply appending to a declarative statement a single word meaning "yes" or "no," for example *si* or *no* in Spanish, *ja* or *nein* in German. During the twentieth century, informal variants of tag questions became increasingly popular in American English, as in "Roger is drunk, right?" Such practices are likely patterned after similar constructions in many immigrant tongues. A peculiarity of grammar in the speech of the American South, the so-called "double modal" constructions such as "might could" or "might should" instead of "might be able" and "perhaps should," may be legacies of Scottish immigrants, as such wording was once common in Scotland.

MORPHOLOGY

American morphology—aspects of English pertaining to roots and stems of words—and pronunciation also bear the imprint of immigration. For example, American English has borrowed the common noun ending -*o* from Romance languages to append to English roots, yielding such hybrids as "weirdo" and "wino." During the late 1990's, the Italian/Spanish noun suffix -*ista* came into similar use, yielding hybrid words such as "fashionista," a term for a person obsessed with clothing trends.

Thomas Du Bose

FURTHER READING

Baron, Dennis. *Grammar and Good Taste*. New Haven, Conn.: Yale University Press, 1982. Definitive discussion of the trends in what is considered appropriate and inappropriate in American English and the forces that have shaped American concepts of linguistic correctness and propriety.

Baugh, Albert, and Thomas Cable. *A History of the English Language*. 5th ed. Upper Saddle River, N.J: Prentice Hall, 2002. Chapter 11 of this book offers a thorough assessment of the forces that have shaped American English and the place of American English in relation to world English.

Bryson, Bill. *Made in America*. New York: Perennial, 1996. Highly enjoyable best-seller about American English with much information about the contributions of various groups of immigrants.

Finegan, Edward, and John Rickford, eds. *Language Variation in North American English*. New

York: Cambridge University Press, 2004. Scholarly but accessible overview of variations within North American English.

Marckwardt, Albert. *American English.* New York: Oxford University Press, 1971. Although originally published during the 1950's, this book remains the standard study of the English language in the United States.

Millward, Celia. *A Biography of the English Language.* 2d ed. Orlando, Fla.: Harcourt, 1996. Exemplary textbook on the history of the English language. Chapter 9 provides a concise review of the special features of American English.

SEE ALSO: Dutch immigrants; Foodways; French immigrants; German immigrants; Italian immigrants; Language issues; Louisiana; Mexican immigrants; Multiculturalism; Scandinavian immigrants.

LITERACY TESTS

DEFINITION: Tests of reading and writing fluency administered to immigrants seeking to attain U.S. citizenship

SIGNIFICANCE: Literacy tests have been a focal point of the controversy between those who would require a minimum standard of educational competence for attaining American citizenship and those who decry what they view as arbitrary restrictiveness. Literacy tests have been a key component of proposed immigration laws and a reason cited for presidential vetoes of legislation that would have instituted them.

Literacy tests as a decision-making barometer have a long heritage dating from their role during the Middle Ages as part of the process to extend "benefit of clergy" status to wayward priests. They afforded preferential treatment in a separate ecclesiastic system of justice to priests who could successfully read the "neck verse" from Psalms. This practice was abolished in the United States in 1827, but the importance of literacy as a gateway

Cartoon in a March, 1916, issue of Puck *magazine lampooning the literacy test requirement in the bill that would become the Immigration Act of 1917.* (Library of Congress)

to success in mainstream American life (for both criminal-offender and law-abiding populations) has persisted into the twenty-first century.

The Immigration Act of 1917 was the first major piece of federal legislation to include a literacy test, but earlier attempts to include such tests were vetoed by Presidents Grover Cleveland, William Howard Taft, and Woodrow Wilson in 1897, 1913, and 1915, respectively. The 1897 bill vetoed by Cleveland would have required tests of both reading and writing, while the two later bills included tests for reading only. The wording of the 1917 law, which was eventually passed, precluded admission into the United States for those who were physically able to read but did not have the requisite skills to read English or another language, including Hebrew or Yiddish. The proposed test was made up of thirty to forty commonly used words, and examinees were allowed to choose the language or dialect they preferred. Although the law did not set limits on the numbers of immigrants per year or national quotas, it was clearly designed to lower immigration rates, particularly from countries with high levels of illiteracy.

The attitude of President Woodrow Wilson when he vetoed the proposed 1917 legislation restricting immigration is particularly instructive (his veto was ultimately overridden, resulting in passage of the law). Although he had been accused of holding biases against certain minority groups who he felt could not assimilate into a homogenous American middle class, Wilson strongly protested the inclusion of a literacy test. He saw it as a measure of prior educational opportunity, which could result in the rejection of citizenship applications from those with limited educational backgrounds. Their character and motivations would nonetheless render them highly desirable additions to an American middle-class "melting pot" characterized by hard work, dedication to a common set of goals, and ultimate achievement.

Since the early twentieth century, debate about how literacy tests would affect immigration law and policy has continued unabated. Empirical evidence has shown a strong link between fluency in English reading and later vocational success. An attempt initiated in 2001 by the U.S. Citizenship and Immigration Services (USCIS) to revise the naturalization tests was been harshly criticized by a committee under the auspices of the National Research Council. The basis of these criticisms were both methodological and substantive, including the lack of a clearly stated rationale for the literacy tests as well as the process used to develop their content. A new naturalization test was completed for all applicants from October 1, 2009, onward. It includes units on civics and English speaking, reading, and writing.

Eric Yitzchak Metchik

FURTHER READING

Elliott, Stuart, Naomi Chudowsky, Barbara Plake, and Lorraine McDonnell. "Using the *Standards* to Evaluate the Redesign of the U.S. Naturalization Tests: Lessons for the Measurement Community." *Educational Measurement: Issues and Practice* 25, no. 1 (Fall, 2006): 22-26.

McSeveney, Sam. "Immigrants, the Literacy Test, and Quotas: Selected American History College Textbooks' Coverage of the Congressional Restriction of European Immigration, 1917-1929." *The History Teacher* 21, no. 1 (1987): 41-51.

Vaught, Hans. "Division and Reunion: Woodrow Wilson, Immigration, and the Myth of American Unity." *Journal of American Ethnic History* 13, no. 3 (1994): 24-50.

SEE ALSO: Citizenship; Dillingham Commission; Education; English as a second language; Higher education; Immigration Act of 1907; Immigration Act of 1917; Immigration law; Intelligence testing; Language issues; Quota systems; World War I.

LITERATURE

SIGNIFICANCE: Successive waves of immigration to the United States have produced myriad literary works by immigrants. Likewise, native-born writers have also traveled and lived abroad throughout the country's history and have written from the unique perspective of being far from home. In both fiction and nonfiction, the literature of immigration highlights issues that are at the heart of the American experience: the search for self, the conflict between ethnic or national roots and individual identity, and the clash between cultures and generations.

Whatever metaphor is used to describe the ethnic makeup of the country—symphony, salad bowl, or patchwork quilt—the United States has been a nation of immigrants since its founding, and immigration has been a constant subject and theme of its literature. The very first works of American literature—such as John Smith's *The Generall Historie of Virginia, New England, and the Summer Isles* (which was first published in 1624 and included the story of Pocahontas) or William Bradford's *Of Plymouth Plantation* (1630)—were accounts of immigration and settlement in the New World.

Many of the classic works of American literature were in fact written by Europeans first venturing to America: J. Hector St. John de Crevecoeur, whose *Letters from an American Farmer* (1782) so accurately

According to John Smith's account of the settling of Virginia, the Native American chief Powhatan was about to have him executed when Powhatan's daughter Pocahontas intervened to save his life. This story became part of American lore, but some modern scholars believe that Pocahontas may merely have acted out a prearranged role in a tribal ritual that Smith did not understand. (Gay Brothers)

describes the new country and its inhabitants, was born in France. Thomas Paine, who wrote effectively in support of the American Revolution, was born in England. Anne Bradstreet, considered the first American poet, was also born in England and immigrated to Massachusetts with her husband in 1630. *The Interesting Narrative of the Life of Olaudah Equiano: Or, Gustavus Vassa, the African* (1789) was the start of a long line of African American literature, much of it the story of forced immigration during slavery. Even some of the classic works of the nineteenth century are tales of immigration. One of the most popular works by the poet Henry Wadsworth Longfellow was *Evangeline* (1847), which recounts the expulsion of French Canadians from Nova Scotia and their move to Louisiana during the eighteenth century, while the three central characters in Nathaniel Hawthorne's classic novel *The Scarlet Letter* (1850) are all recent English immigrants working out their fates in early Boston.

LITERATURE OF SECOND-WAVE IMMIGRATION

The first great wave of immigration after the founding of the republic occurred between 1830 and 1860 and was northern European in origin, including English, Irish, and German settlers. However, it was during the second major wave—from the 1880's to the 1920's and mainly from southern and eastern Europe—that the literature of immigration became a distinct literary form. The Statue of Liberty was dedicated in New York Harbor in 1886, and the lines from the Jewish American poet Emma Lazarus graced its base:

Give me your tired, your poor
Your huddled masses yearning to breathe free.

In 1892, Ellis Island began operating as the port of entry, and millions of immigrants from Greece, Italy, Poland, and other Slavic countries poured into East Coast ghettos.

Clearly, to the more established residents of the United States, these new travelers—darker complexioned and speaking different languages—were the true immigrants, and the literature they produced only confirmed their foreign origins. Books by and about the new immigrants highlighted their struggles. One of the first works of American realism was Rebecca Harding Davis's "Life in the Iron Mills" (1861), a story of Welsh factory workers in Virginia and the first in a line of exposés of the industrial exploitation of immigrants that would lead to Upton Sinclair's *The Jungle* (1906), the story of Lithuanian immigrants scraping out a living in the meatpacking industry in Chicago (and a novel that helped enact the country's first Pure Food and Drug Act).

Works such as Mary Antin's autobiography *The Promised Land* (1912) described how the dream of Americanization could come true for European immigrants. Most accounts of immigration during the late nineteenth century tended to focus on the hardships of the process: The Danish-born journalist Jacob Riis's *How the Other Half Lives* (1890), for example, documented unsafe conditions in crowded New York City tenements. Even when life was not physically hard, as in Kate Chopin's novel *The Awakening* (1899), set in Creole areas around New Orleans, the conflict of different cultural codes could cause tragedy.

In 1916, the critic Randolph Bourne wrote in his essay "Trans-national America" that the idea of the melting pot was misleading. The first settlers did not have to assimilate into any existing culture, Bourne argued; immigrant cultures have always given vitality and variety to the country, and recent immigrants should hold on to their distinctive cultural habits. Many of the literary works of the period confirmed Bourne's assumptions, even while most Americans ignored his plea. The protagonists in Abraham Cahan's *Yekl* (1896) and *The Rise of David Levinsky* (1917) are Russian Jews who end up lost between two worlds, their culture of origin and the country where they dream of success. Anzia Yezierska's stories and novels, such as *Hungry Hearts* (1923), depict similar difficulties of assimilation, especially for eastern European Jews. Willa Cather's *My Ántonia* (1918) fictionalizes the hardships of Bohemian (Czech) immigrants trying to eke out a living on the Western plains, while O. E. Rölvaag's *Giants in the Earth* (1927) is also set on the Western prairie and involves the difficulties for Norwegian immigrants trying to farm that harsh land.

ASSIMILATION AND CELEBRATION

Restrictive federal legislation enacted in 1921 and 1924 limited immigration through more than one-half century. When immigration picked up again after 1965, the main points of debarkation were not European but Asian, Caribbean, and Central American. At the same time, the Civil Rights movement after the 1940's had created a new ethnic awareness, a consciousness of ethnic contributions to so many areas of life in America.

This new pride in turn spawned the rediscovery of older works of immigrant literature, and the creation of a new generation of ethnic writers. Both Mike Gold's *Jews Without Money* (1930) and Henry Roth's *Call It Sleep* (1934), for example, strongly autobiographical accounts of immigrant Jewish family life in New York's lower East Side, were rediscovered during the 1960's, while a decade later Carlos Bulosan's classic autobiography of Filipino immigration, *America Is in the Heart* (1943), was first reprinted (1973). During that same period, Maxine Hong Kingston's powerful fictional memoirs *The Woman Warrior* (1976) and *China Men* (1980) were published, as well as Ernesto Galarza's *Barrio Boy* (1971), an account of his family's migration from Mexico to the United States.

Historians started to question the underlying assumptions and the very terms used to describe immigration and assimilation: Namely, Nathan Glazer and Daniel Patrick Moynihan in *Beyond the Melting Pot: The Negroes, Puerto Ricans, Jews, Italians, and Irish of New York City* (1963) and Michael Novak in *The Rise of the Unmeltable Ethnics: Politics and Culture in the Seventies* (1971). The renewed interest in ethnic and immigrant literature led to new studies—for example, Marcus Klein's *Foreigners: The Making of American Literature* (1981) and Werner Sollors's *Beyond Ethnicity: Consent and Descent in American Culture* (1986)—which in turn led to a number of new ways of viewing American literature. Ethnic literature, Sollors argued, is the pattern for American literature; according to Klein, most twentieth century American writers are "foreigners," immigrants or the heirs of immigrants who reshaped the century's literature.

During the last decades of the twentieth century, the American literary canon was transformed, as publishers rushed to include forgotten or rediscovered writers in their anthologies. Ethnic writers stepped forward to claim literary prizes: N. Scott Momaday won the Pulitzer Prize in fiction in 1969 for *House Made of Dawn* (1968), Alice Walker in 1983 for *The Color Purple* (1982), and Toni Morrison five years later for *Beloved* (1987). Writers emerged to tell the stories of every ethnic thread in the historical quilt of the United States. This discovery of ethnicity's centrality in American life, as in the literary canon, meant that Americans increasingly embraced their immigrant backgrounds, often making or maintaining close contact with their countries of origin. Rather than producing stories of being torn between cultures, as in so many earlier twentieth century accounts of immigration, writers by the end of the century increasingly celebrated their ability to live in two cultures, to transcend borders and boundaries. Frank McCourt's popular memoir of his impoverished Irish childhood, *Angela's Ashes* (1996), was both a celebration of the strengths of his Irish mother in the face of grinding poverty and a tribute to his success in the United States. Increasingly, writers could view both their pasts and their futures without fear or tension.

Any survey of American literature of the previous century or so confirms these trends. Such an examination might begin with the English Jewish writer Israel Zangwill's popular 1908 play *The Melting-Pot*, which described the immigration process at the same time that it coined a misnomer to describe it. Finley Peter Dunne, the Chicago newspaper columnist, created the fictional Irish bartender Mr. Dooley, who commented on every social and political event up to World War I, including immigration. A Dutch immigrant to the United States called his autobiography *The Americanization of Edward Bok* (1920), while an immigrant from Slovenia, Louis Adamic, published *Laughing in the Jungle: The Autobiography of an Immigrant in America* in 1932 and *My America* in 1938. Irish immigration was touched on in James T. Farrell's *Studs Lonigan* trilogy (1935); Italian American life in Pietro di Donato's *Christ in Concrete*

(1939) and John Fante's *Wait Until Spring* and *Bandini* (1938). Thomas Bell wrote *Out of This Furnace* (1941), a novel detailing the hardships of immigrant Slovak laborers in western Pennsylvania steel mills, while William Saroyan made comedy out of the difficulties of his Armenian family in Fresno, California, in *The Daring Young Man on the Flying Trapeze* (1934) and *My Name Is Aram* (1940). All of these works explored, in various degrees, the struggles of assimilation, the loss of individual identity in that process, and the pain of being torn between two cultures.

With the rise of a new ethnic consciousness after World War II, immigrant literature underwent an enormous transformation. The change was marked by the publication of *Roots: The Saga of an American Family* (1976), which traced Alex Haley's ancestors back to Africa before slavery, became an enormously popular television series and helped to encourage similar discoveries in other ethnic histories. After Haley, new ethnic literary groups emerged,

Israel Zangwill, author of the 1908 play that introduced the concept of the "melting pot" to the English language. (Library of Congress)

669

and new attitudes toward immigrant history were born. Older European immigrant groups would continue to be represented in the more diverse American literary range—for example, Polish American Jerzy Kosinski's novel *The Painted Bird* (1965) or Italian American Mario Puzo's *The Godfather* (1969)—but more immigrant literature was coming from other continents.

CARIBBEAN LITERATURE

Caribbean immigration actually rose during the 1920's, when the flow from Europe was slowing. Early writers such as Claude McKay, who migrated from Jamaica in 1912, became a part of the African American literary boom of the Harlem Renaissance of the 1920's. McKay's poetry was collected in *Harlem Shadows* (1922), and his novel *Home to Harlem* was published in 1928. The next generation helped to carve out a more distinctive Caribbean identity. Paula Marshall's *Brown Girl, Brownstones* (1959) is her best-known novel, but she published fiction for the next four decades, novels and short stories in which her characters (often women) work out their identities in a conflict between New York City and the West Indies.

The literary outpouring since the 1960's has been even more prolific, and almost every Caribbean island-state has been represented. Cuban American writers have included Cristina Garcia, whose novel *Dreaming in Cuban* appeared in 1992, and Paula Fox, who has written adult fiction (such as her novel *A Servant's Tale*, in 1984) but who is better known as a children's writer. Her book *The Slave Dancer* (1973) received the Newbery Medal. Oscar Hijuelos has written a series of novels set in both Cuba and the United States, and *The Mambo Kings Play Songs of Love* (1989) won the Pulitzer Prize in fiction. Writers who have immigrated from the Dominican Republic include Julia Alvarez, who wrote the novel *How the García Girls Lost Their Accents* (1991), and Junot Díaz, whose short-story collection *Drown* (1996) was favorably reviewed, and whose first novel, *The Brief Wondrous Life of Oscar Wao* (2007), won the Pulitzer Prize in fiction.

Jamaica Kincaid was born in Antigua in the West Indies in 1949 and came to the United States when she was seventeen. She has written often of the Caribbean immigrant experience: in the novels *Annie John* (1985), *Lucy* (1990), and *The Autobiography of My Mother* (1996), as well as in short stories (*At the Bottom of the River*, 1983) and essays (*A Small Place*, 1988). Haitian Americans have been represented by Edwidge Danticat, the highly respected writer whose novel *Breath, Eyes, Memory* was published in 1994, whose collection of short stories *Krik? Krak!* (1995) was nominated for a National Book Award, and whose memoir of her family's dual citizenship, *Brother, I'm Dying* (2007), was given the National Book Critics Circle Award.

Puerto Rican writers have included Piri Thomas, whose *Down These Mean Streets* (1967) has become a classic coming-of-age urban memoir, and Nicholosa Mohr, whose *El Bronx Remembered* (1975) and *In Nueva York* (1977) fictionalized the coming-of-age struggles of poor Puerto Rican women in New York. Judith Ortiz Cofer published poetry, a novel (*The Line of the Sun*, 1988), and a memoir (*Silent Dancing: A Partial Remembrance of a Puerto Rican Childhood*, 1990) in which two cultures and languages are only part of the mix of ethnic, class, and gender issues.

ASIAN LITERATURE

Even greater diversity and richness have characterized immigrant Asian American literature of the last decades of the twentieth century and into the twenty-first century, as the numerous anthologies and studies of this ethnic literature attest: for example, Jessica Hagedorn's collection *Charlie Chan Is Dead: An Anthology of Asian American Fiction* (1993) and Shirley Geok-lin Lim and Amy Ling's *Reading the Literatures of Asian America* (1992). Although Chinese immigrants have long been a part of American history, their literature was not always available (for example, *Island: Poetry and History of Chinese Immigrants on Angel Island, 1910-1940*, published in 1980). It was not until the appearance of Maxine Hong Kingston and then Amy Tan that Chinese American literature blossomed. Tan's popular novels *The Joy Luck Club* (1989) and *The Kitchen God's Wife* (1991) highlighted the conflicts between assimilation and the desire for ethnic identity, and between generations. A flurry of Chinese American fiction dealing with these immigrant conflicts quickly followed: Gish Jen's *Typical American* (1991), Gus Lee's *China Boy* (1991), David Wong Louie's *Pangs of Love* (stories, 1992), and Fae Myenne Ng's *Bone* (1993).

These themes of dual identity, the conflict between the desire for both ethnic roots and individual identity, characterize other Asian American literatures as well. The hardships of immigrant life were magnified for the Japanese Americans, who were interned in camps in the West during World War II, and that horrific experience has colored the fiction since then, including Jeanne Wakatsuki Houston and James Houston's *Farewell to Manzanar* (1973), Hisaye Yamamoto's *Seventeen Syllables, and Other Stories* (1988), and Cynthia Kadohata's *The Floating World* (1989).

Korean American literature—such as Ronyoung Kim's *Clay Walls* (1987) and Chang-Rae Lee's *Native Speaker* (1995)—has highlighted the hardships of immigration and the difficulties of dual identity. The same can be said for Indian American fiction—namely Bharati Mukherjee's *Jasmine* (1989), and the works of Jhumpa Lahiri, whose collection of stories, *Interpreter of Maladies* (1999), won the Pulitzer Prize in fiction in 2000, and whose novel *The Namesake* (2003) was made into a popular film.

IMMIGRATION AND THE AMERICAN LITERARY CANON

Literature and art do not recognize national borders as walls or fences but, like ideas, flow easily back and forth from one country or continent to another, and this is particularly true in the literature of immigration and emigration. In addition to immigrants writing about their experiences coming to the United States, writers throughout American history have emigrated to other countries and written from that perspective. For example, Henry James based many of his novels and stories in Europe, often dramatizing the clash between nineteenth century American innocence and European experience. Both Ezra Pound and T. S. Eliot spent most of their careers writing in Europe. James and Eliot eventually became British subjects; Pound died in Italy. African American writers Richard Wright and James Baldwin found France a more congenial environment after World War II than an America they experienced as racially oppressive.

Both immigrant and emigrant fiction and memoir record the lasting tension between ethnic or national roots and the desire for assimilation, the sense of living between two worlds. In the increasingly globalized, shrinking world of the twenty-first century, the literature of immigration can describe the movement of people between countries and cultures and thus make the journey for readers before they attempt their own. For this and other reasons, the literature of immigration will undoubtedly continue as a valuable and vital form in the American literary canon.

David Peck

FURTHER READING

Ferraro, Thomas J., ed. *Ethnic Passages: Literary Immigrants in Twentieth-Century America.* Chicago: University of Chicago Press, 1993. Includes essays on Mario Puzo, Anzia Yezierska, and Maxine Hong Kingston, among other immigrant writers.

Fine, David M. *The City, the Immigrant, and American Fiction, 1880-1920.* Metuchen, N.J.: Scarecrow Press, 1977. Fine studies the literature of the early twentieth century, when European immigrants crowded into urban ghettos—for example, Abraham Cahan's *The Rise of David Levinsky* (1917).

Klein, Marcus. *Foreigners: The Making of American Literature, 1900-1940.* Chicago: University of Chicago Press, 1981. Literary history of the first half of the twentieth century from a radical perspective, which emphasizes its ethnic and proletarian nature. Concludes with detailed analyses of Mike Gold, Nathanael West, and Richard Wright.

Payant, Katherine B., and Toby Rose, eds. *The Immigrant Experience in North American Literature.* Westport, Conn.: Greenwood Press, 1999. Contains a dozen essays, including studies of O. E. Rölvaag and Paule Marshall, Jewish immigrant women's autobiographies and Asian American narratives.

Prchal, Tim, and Tony Trigilio, eds. *Visions and Divisions: American Immigration Literature, 1870-1930.* Piscataway, N.J.: Rutgers University Press, 2008. Anthology of selections from key writers of the Progressive Era, when immigration increased and debates about it likewise rose.

Simone, Roberta, ed. *The Immigrant Experience in American Fiction: An Annotated Bibliography.* Lanham, Md.: Scarecrow Press, 1994. More than six hundred entries describe individual authors, anthologies, and secondary sources for more than forty immigrant groups—from Armenian, through Irish and Italian and Jewish, to West Indian.

Whitlark, James, and Wendell Aycock, eds. *The Literature of Emigration and Exile*. Lubbock: Texas Tech University Press, 1992. Includes essays on American female immigrants in Canada, Maxine Hong Kingston's *China Men*, and a dozen other topics and writers.

SEE ALSO: Alvarez, Julia; Antin, Mary; Art; Asian American literature; Danticat, Edwidge; *The Jungle*; Lahiri, Jhumpa; Lim, Shirley Geok-lin; Mukherjee, Bharati; *My Ántonia*; Santiago, Esmeralda; Sidhwa, Bapsi; Tocqueville, Alexis de; Yezierska, Anzia.

LITTLE HAVANA

IDENTIFICATION: Cuban enclave within Miami, Florida

SIGNIFICANCE: Little Havana was the focal point for Cuban immigration to the United States following the Cuban Revolution of 1959. The neighborhood still maintains a large Cuban-born population and distinct culture and politics. The residents, in large part, see themselves more as a community in exile than as assimilated Americans.

Miami, Florida's "Little Havana" (*La Pequeña Habana*) has been the cultural and political center not only of Miami's Cuban American immigrant community but also of the Cuban community of the entire United States. The neighborhood has been home to everything from political organizations hatching plots against Fidel Castro's communist regime to Latino music bands, art festivals, and religious parades. Formed after 1960 following the exodus from Cuba of hundreds of thousands of exiles from Castro's revolution of 1959, Little Havana continues to play an important part in the political life of Miami, the state of Florida, U.S. presidential elections, and even the anti-Castro dissident movement in Cuba. Unlike other immigrant communities in the United States, such as New York's Little Italy, it has lost neither its original ethnic composition nor political power over time.

Although officially designated as a "neighborhood" by the U.S. Census of 2000, with the Miami River, Southwest Eleventh Street, Southwest Second Avenue, and Interstate 95 for boundaries, Little Havana is best located and understood by both residents and outsiders by its landmarks and places of historical importance. Calle Ocho (Southwest Eighth Street), which Cuban Americans call *La Saguacera* in the hybrid argot of Spanglish, is the gateway to the neighborhood. A giant mural overlooking the Eighth Street entrance to Little Havana depicts crucial scenes from pre-Castro Cuban history, reinforcing the notion that this is a community in exile, and not, culturally speaking, an integrated part of the United States. Another cultural and political signpost is the Versailles Restaurant, which many residents consider the epicenter of Little Havana. Here, over dishes of chicken, rice, beans, and plantains—Cuban staples—conversations often turn to exile politics. The neighborhood economy rests largely on small shops selling everything from guayaberas—the white linen, short-sleeved shirts traditionally worn by Cuban men—to statues and talismans associated with Santería, the Afro-Cuban syncretic religion of African deities and Roman Catholic saints.

Little Havana has changed little demographically since the first wave of exiles arrived in 1960. More than 90 percent of its population is Latino, with Cubans constituting almost the entire Hispanic bloc. Many residents still occupy the same homes and own the businesses they purchased during the 1960's. The area is more politically conservative than the rest of Cuban Miami, and the population is less willing to engage in any sort of dialogue with the Castro regime.

The graying, and physical demise, of many of the first-generation Cubans and the boom in tourism to the neighborhood, bringing other Latinos and non-Hispanic Americans to spend their money in local enterprises, have the potential to alter the political and cultural features that have made Little Havana distinct. At the beginning of the twenty-first century, the obsession of the locals with anti-Castro politics is slowly giving way to the notion that most residents will never see their homeland again, and tourist dollars have transformed traditional political and religious festivals into street parties rather than evocations of Cuban history. Little Havana seems destined to be incorporated into a new *patria* (homeland), the United States.

Julio César Pino

FURTHER READING

García, Cristina María. *Havana USA: Cuban Exiles and Cuban Americans in South Florida, 1959-1994.* Berkeley: University of California Press, 1996.

Poey, Delia, and Virgil Suárez, eds. *Little Havana Blues: A Cuban-American Anthology.* Houston: Arte Público Press, 1996.

Rieff, David. *The Exile: Cuba in the Heart of Miami.* New York: Simon & Schuster, 1993.

SEE ALSO: Cuban immigrants; Ethnic enclaves; Florida; Freedom Airlift; González case; Haitian immigrants; Latin American immigrants; Latinos and immigrants; Mariel boatlift; Miami; Settlement patterns.

LITTLE ITALIES

DEFINITION: Ethnic enclaves in American cities that have transplanted village communities from Italy

SIGNIFICANCE: Within major urban cities such as New York, Philadelphia, Boston, and Chicago, "Little Italy" communities formed to provide Italian immigrants with a sense of unity and Italian nationalism that they did not have in Italy.

Many of the first Italians who immigrated to the United States landed and then settled in New York City. However, many immigrants also populated Italian enclaves in other cities throughout the United States. Arriving in large numbers between 1880 and 1920, the Italian immigrants tended to rely on *padrones*, or more established immigrants, who helped them adjust to their new environment. However, *padrones* often took advantage of illiterate newcomers by exacting heavy payments for housing and employment services.

CAUSES OF IMMIGRATION

During the 1840's and 1850's, small groups of emigrants from northern Italy sought financial security in the United States. Unlike members of the later migration of southern Italians, members of this earlier group proudly identified themselves as Italians. After Italy itself was finally unified in 1870, these early Italian immigrants gloried in their new-found national identity. Southern Italians, by contrast, left Italy in great numbers after unification. For them, Italy was a nation in name only. Although the Risorgimento strengthened Italy overall, the northern provinces alone experienced its economic and political benefits. To immigrants from the southern regions of Abruzzo, Molise, Campania, Basilicata, Apulia, Calabria, and Sicily, northern Italy was as foreign as America.

For southern Italians who suffered the pangs of starvation, high taxes, and dislocation under Italy's unification government, the possibility of employment and a better place in which to live was worth the journey across the Atlantic. Thanks to cheaper and safer oceanic transatlantic transportation and the promise of riches overseas, more than five million southern Italians immigrated to the United States and countries in South America and North Africa between 1876 and 1930. Plagued with outbreaks of cholera in the Italian countryside that killed more than 55,000 people, many southern Italians left their homeland only to be turned away at the various ports of entry, the most famous being Ellis Island in New York.

THE NORTH

Although Italian immigrants suffered degradation in America from native-born residents who believed that southern Europeans were too ignorant to assimilate, the newcomers compensated for their unfriendly reception by forming their own communities in small enclaves in major American cities. Dubbed "Little Italies" in most cities, these neighborhoods were essentially transplanted Italian villages, or *paesi*.

After arriving in New York Harbor, Italian immigrants moved from the port to Manhattan, and then on to that island's crime-ridden Five Points district. The immigrants soon staked their claims within the enclave. Many earned their livings as organ grinders, street performers, and rag pickers. Despite the fact that the majority of the immigrants had been farmers in their homeland, most accepted work in crowded East Coast American cities to avoid having to travel great distances inland in the unfamiliar land.

Italians who settled in New York City eventually moved beyond Manhattan's Point to other boroughs, such as Queens, the Bronx, and Staten Island. Some went much farther and toiled in the coal mines in Pennsylvania, Illinois, and West Virginia, while others followed the rails farther west.

Although Italians had settled in Philadelphia even before the American Revolution, they did not immigrate *en masse* to the United States until the 1850's. Within fifty years, 45,000 Italians from Calabria and Sicily were making their homes in Philadelphia. By the first decade of the twentieth century, the southern Italians outnumbered their compatriots from the north. Introducing the pushcart to the local neighborhood, Italians pedaled their merchandise on the streets of the city; they opened restaurants, and made their livings as tailors and construction workers. Nonetheless, they still suffered indignities. Segregated sections were designated for Italians in movie theaters, and the filthy streets of their neighborhoods became breeding grounds of disease.

Following the Great Irish Famine of the late 1840's, Boston, like Philadelphia, became a port of call for immigrants. Italians from Genoa, Campania, and Sicily arrivng in Boston settled first in the north end of the city, which they dominated by the time of World War I (1914-1918). Many Sicilians who had been fishermen in their native land took up fishing in Boston. As the city's population increased, the Italian immigrants moved from its North End to the suburbs in Lawrence, Massachusetts. Significantly, New England Italians engaged in fierce rivalry with the Irish, who had already established themselves in Democratic politics. This prompted a number of Italians to gravitate toward the Republican Party, which enticed them with the promise of a full dinner pail and minor recognition—at least until Irish Democrats were willing to share their political opportunities with them.

MIDDLE AMERICA

Following the national Panic of 1873, many southern Italians followed a general migration from

Mulberry Street, the heart of New York City's Little Italy, around 1900. (Library of Congress)

New York City to Chicago to look for work and, as a result, supplanted the Irish and Swedes in Chicago's so-called Little Hell section. Because workers were in such demand, especially during World War I, Italians were a welcome source of cheap labor for employers. Although dreadful conditions in Little Hell predated the Italian migration, native-born Americans began identifying Italians with the area's criminal environment. This caused many Italians to join labor unions and fight for better conditions and wages.

RESULTS

Little Italies provided Italian immigrants with familiar communities within an unfamiliar country. Although some Italians never learned to speak the English language, others acclimated easily to their new surroundings and achieved wealth in America. Because farming land was becoming more scarce, many Italians who immigrated to America had no choice but to settle in the cities. They also migrated to the South and West Coast, earning notoriety and profiting by operating wineries in San Francisco's Little Italy and fisheries in San Diego. Establishing colonies throughout the United States, from Providence, Rhode Island to New Orleans, Louisiana, the Italians made significant contributions to American culture.

Debra A. Mulligan

FURTHER READING

Barkan, Elliott Robert. *From all Points: America's Immigrant West, 1870's-1952.* Bloomington: Indiana University Press, 2007. Excellent source on Little Italies in the West.

Dinnerstein, Leonard, and David M. Reimers. *Ethnic Americans: A History of Immigration.* 4th ed. New York: Columbia University Press, 1999. Textbook that provides an excellent outline on the trends of migration in the United States.

Iorizzo, Luciano J., and Salvatore Mondello. *The Italian Americans.* Boston: Twayne, 1980. Concise narrative of the Italian American experience.

Mangione, Jerre, and Ben Morreale. *La Storia: Five Centuries of the Italian-American Experience.* New York: Harper Perennial, 1992. Informative study of Italian immigration and Italian contributions to American culture and government.

SEE ALSO: Chicago; Criminal immigrants; Ethnic enclaves; *Godfather* trilogy; Italian American press; Italian immigrants; Nativism; New York City; Philadelphia; Rhode Island.

LITTLE TOKYOS

DEFINITION: Japanese ethnic enclaves that developed within existing U.S. cities, especially along the West Coast, during the late nineteenth and early twentieth centuries

SIGNIFICANCE: Urban enclaves provided a source of social and economic stability for Japanese immigrants, despite the fact that the difficulty of finding employment led many toward rural and agricultural pursuits. The cultural conservatism fostered within these enclaves helped deepen the gap between Issei, or first-generation immigrants, and the fast-changing national culture of Japan. It also deepened the gap between Issei and Nisei, the second-generation immigrants.

Little Tokyos, or "Japantowns," arose in cities and towns across the United States for reasons that reflected the natural needs of a new immigrant population. Their greatest concentration occurred along the West Coast. The continued robust existence of these enclaves into the 1930's and early 1940's, however, was partly the result of the sometimes severe racial prejudice and discrimination against Asians, and specifically the Japanese, that prevailed in the United States during the late nineteenth and early to mid-twentieth centuries.

Among the influences leading to the formation of Little Tokyos, the dormitory-style boardinghouses run by early Japanese had particular importance. In Seattle, for example, sixty-five such boardinghouses were in operation by 1905. In addition to providing welcoming living quarters for new arrivals, these houses provided centers of operation for *keiyaku-nin*, the Japanese contractors who acted as agents between immigrant laborers and American railroad, farm, and cannery employers.

Although the enclaves proved important for community reasons, the tendency of many Japanese immigrants to work at agricultural occupa-

Shop in Los Angeles's Little Tokyo that was forced to sell out its entire stock before its proprietor was sent to an internment camp during World War II. (AP/Wide World Photos)

tions encouraged their moving away from urban areas. The Nisei tendency to distance themselves from their Japanese heritage, moreover, worked against the long-term success of the enclaves as active communities. The enclaves' existence remained strong up to the time of World War II, however, due to prejudicial land-ownership policies in California and elsewhere, and also to the difficulty Nisei encountered in obtaining jobs elsewhere, even when possessing college degrees. A large percentage of Nisei ended up working for their parents, temporarily stemming the flow of populace away from the enclaves.

Little Tokyo, Los Angeles

The Japanese enclave located a few blocks south of the Los Angeles city hall became the one most strongly associated with the "Little Tokyo" name, although it was also called "J-Town." Founded during the 1890's, it had a resident population of some 30,000 Japanese Americans at its peak.

The equivalent enclave in San Francisco was usually called "Nihonmachi," or "Japantown." In the United States as a whole, forty-three Japantowns came into existence before the United States entered World War II in 1941. That number included small, rural enclaves. The enclaves provided important centers for Japanese-language schools, newspapers, Buddhist temples, Christian churches, and, in a few communities, hospitals.

Enclaves were of importance not only for the mutual economic support but for nurturing a nascent Japanese American culture. The literary magazine *Leaves*, for example, was the work of Los

Angeles Nisei, as was the Sunday literary supplement, in English, of Japanese daily *Kashu Mainichi*. Amateur theater also thrived, with groups including the Little Tokyo Players in Los Angeles.

In contrast to the forward-thinking Nisei, the Issei developed a mode of life within the Japanese enclaves based on their memories of traditional Japanese life that was already becoming outmoded in Japan itself. This conservatism among the Issei led to a growing gap not only between Issei culture and Japanese national culture, but also between Issei and Nisei attitudes toward life in America. By 1930, the Nisei constituted a significant percentage of the Japanese American population, and outnumbered the Issei in California. Given that the Nisei were more inclined to pursue assimilation into American culture, however difficult it was to achieve, this demographic shift further worked against the expansion of Japantowns.

With the forced removal of Japanese Americans from coastal areas in the aftermath of the Japanese attack on Pearl Harbor on December 7, 1941, the continued existence of most U.S. Japantowns was rendered nearly impossible. Promises that personal property of internees would be safeguarded during their internment often proved empty. In Los Angeles, a reported three thousand African Americans moved into housing vacated by Japanese internees in Little Tokyo in July, 1943, tripling their ranks as the war progressed, and leading to the neighborhood's being rechristened "Bronzeville." Although the 1943 Little Tokyo crisis related to ethnic conflict, it involved non-Japanese residents. Peaceful race relations later would mark Japanese and African American interactions, after the incarcerated Japanese began returning.

The wartime propaganda film titled *Little Tokyo, USA*, gave the "Little Tokyo" name nationwide currency, and created an association between the ethnic enclaves and subversive politics. The Hollywood film mixed actual newsreel footage with invented action in portraying Japanese Americans as sources of treachery against the United States, even while using actors of miscellaneous Asian descent to portray Japanese Americans.

Resettlement policies in the wake of World War II led to the intentional geographical dispersal of large numbers of Japanese Americans, upon their release from prison camps. This dispersal accelerated the integration of the Nisei into larger American society and acted as a further element in the diminution of importance of the Japantowns in Japanese American life.

By the early twenty-first century, only three officially designated "Japantowns" still existed. These included Los Angeles's Little Tokyo, which was declared a National Historic Landmark District in 1995; Japantown, San Francisco; and Japantown, San Jose, California.

Mark Rich

FURTHER READING

Daniels, Roger. *Asian America: Chinese and Japanese in the United States Since 1850*. Seattle: University of Washington Press, 1988. Solid overview of the immigration histories of the two Asian immigrant groups.

Hosokawa, Bill. *Nisei: The Quiet Americans*. New York: William Morrow, 1969. Written by an important Japanese American journalist, this book provides a broadly inclusive, fact-filled portrait of an American generation and remains a definitive study.

Lyman, Stanford Morris. *Chinatown and Little Tokyo: Power, Conflict, and Community Among Chinese and Japanese Immigrants in America*. Millwood, N.Y.: Associated Faculty Press, 1986. Illuminating comparison of Chinese and Japanese immigrant populations, documenting their differences of cultural outlook and the impact this had on the assimilation of each group into American society.

Takahashi, Jere. *Nisei/Sansei: Shifting Japanese American Identities and Politics*. Philadelphia: Temple University Press, 1997. Examination of the complicated relationship between first-, second-, and third- (Sansei) generations of Japanese Americans.

Yoo, David K. *Growing Up Nisei: Race, Generation, and Culture Among Japanese Americans of California, 1924-49*. Champaign: University of Illinois Press, 2000. Valuable account that provides a detailed examination of life in Japantowns, with notable focus on the press.

SEE ALSO: Alien land laws; Anti-Japanese movement; Ethnic enclaves; Japanese American press; Japanese immigrants; Los Angeles; Settlement patterns.

Los Angeles

IDENTIFICATION: Cosmopolitan Southern California city that is the largest in its state and the second largest in the United States

SIGNIFICANCE: A major world city with a population of 3.8 million people in 2009, Los Angeles has the largest concentration of immigrants of any American city. An estimated 38 percent of its residents were born outside the United States, and they have come from more than 140 different countries, making Los Angeles one of the most ethnically diverse cities in the world.

Founded in 1781 as a Spanish port city, Los Angeles became a Mexican city after Mexico won its independence from Spain in 1821. After the United States defeated Mexico in the Mexican War of 1846-1848, Los Angeles became an American city, but was slow to grow as most of the new state of California's growth was concentrated in the north.

The arrival of the first railroads was the first catalyst to attract significant numbers of people to Los Angeles. During the 1880's, the Santa Fe Railroad made Los Angeles its western terminus, and city officials paid the Southern Pacific Railroad to extend a rail line from San Francisco to Los Angeles. The railroads hired thousands of Chinese immigrants to work on rail lines. By 1880, one-quarter of all workers in California were Chinese men. Passenger fare wars between competing rail companies brought many new residents to the area, including European immigrants from the Midwest.

After a series of federal immigration laws began restricting immigration from Asia, the railroads recruited Mexicans to maintain rail lines in the Southwest and were consequently instrumental in drawing Mexican immigrants to Los Angeles. During the early twentieth century, Los Angeles's Mexican population virtually exploded, growing from 5,000 people in 1900 to more than 150,000 in 1930. However, nearly one-third of these Mexican immigrants were deported from the region during the early years of the Great Depression by U.S. Labor Department officials. Mexicans began returning to the region during the 1940's, after the United States inaugurated a new bracero program to bring Mexican workers into the United States to help during the wartime labor shortage.

As Los Angeles became industrialized during the 1930's, its automobile, airplane, and other industries attracted numerous different immigrant groups. The rapidly expanding factories gave jobs to thousands of non-English-speaking immigrants and were influential in expanding the city's borders.

LATE TWENTIETH CENTURY TRENDS

The city's immigration patterns underwent a major shift after 1960, as the numbers of European immigrants began to decline and non-European immigration began rising rapidly. In 1965, the U.S. Congress passed the Immigration and Nationality Act, which abolished the country-based quota system formerly in place. The new law benefited many nationalities—most notably Asians—who had previously been unable to come to the United States because of the quotas. Before the passage of the 1965 law, Asians accounted for only 7 percent of all immigrants arriving in the United States. By the 1980's, about 44 percent of all immigrants were coming from Asian countries. Many of these new immigrants settled in Los Angeles, which experienced a four-fold growth in Asian population between 1970 and 1990. Immigrants from Vietnam, Cambodia, and Laos arrived in greater numbers after the Vietnam War ended in 1975. They were followed by an influx of Filipinos during the 1980's. By the early twenty-first century, Los Angeles was second only to New York City in the size of its Asian population.

The years following 1970, also saw a large rise in immigration from Mexico and other Latin American countries, and Hispanics became the single largest category of foreign immigrants to Los Angeles. Due in part to the city's nearness to the Mexican border, the Greater Los Angeles region became home to nearly 2 million Mexican immigrants—the single largest concentration of Mexican nationals within the United States.

As Mexicans continued to immigrate in large numbers to Los Angeles and other parts of California, they faced increasing scrutiny from anti-immigration activists. In March, 2006, Los Angeles was the site of the largest immigration rally in the country, as similar rallies took place across the country to protest proposed federal legislation designed to increase penalties for undocumented immigrants.

Bethany E. Pierce

FURTHER READING
Abu-Lughod, Janet L. *New York, Chicago, Los Angeles: America's Global Cities.* Minneapolis: University of Minnesota Press, 1999.
Ochoa, Enrique C., and Gilda L. Ochoa, eds. *Latino Los Angeles: Transformations, Communities, and Activism.* Tucson: University of Arizona Press, 2005.
Rieff, David. *Los Angeles: Capital of the Third World.* New York: Simon & Schuster, 1991.
Sawhney, Deepak Narang, ed. *Unmasking L.A.: Third Worlds and the City.* New York: Palgrave, 2002.
Waldinger, Roger, and Mehdi Bozorgmehr, eds. *Ethnic Los Angeles.* New York: Russell Sage Foundation, 1996.

SEE ALSO: Asian immigrants; *Born in East L.A.*; California; Captive Thai workers; Coalition for Humane Immigrant Rights of Los Angeles; El Rescate; Little Tokyos; Mexican immigrants; Proposition 187.

LOUISIANA

SIGNIFICANCE: One of the most culturally diverse of all American states, Louisiana is well known for its French colonial heritage, which has remained evident in the southern parts of the state, especially in New Orleans. However, immigrants from many other countries have also contributed to the state's rich heritage, and the northern part of the state is noted for its Scotch-Irish heritage.

Located at the mouth of the Mississippi River, which would become a major trade and transportation route into the heartland of the United States, Louisiana originated as a colony of France. In 1699, Pierre le Moyne, Sieur d'Iberville, and his brother, Jean Baptiste, Sieur de Bienville, built Fort Maurepas, near the mouth of the Mississippi River, and brought in Canadian settlers to develop a colony. However, the place proved to be so unhealthy

that it had to be abandoned. In 1717, Bienville began to developed another post at what would eventually become the city of New Orleans.

At first, the French government forced convicts, vagrants, and prostitutes to go to Louisiana, but many of these people were too unhealthy, too unwilling to work, or too unfamiliar with agriculture to make satisfactory colonists. The government then tried offering generous grants, but the French farmers they hoped would go to Louisiana would not emigrate. However, so many German and Swiss peasants were willing to seize this opportunity that an area along the Mississippi River north of New Orleans became known as the German Coast. The name survived, even though the descendants of these immigrants adopted French culture and made French their language.

During the early years of French colonization, Native American tribes often attacked new settlements. Eventually, however, tribal infighting and European diseases reduced their numbers until they were no match for the superior military strength of the invaders. Nevertheless, some communities of the Houma, Koasati (Coushatta), Choctaw, and Apalachee peoples still survived in Louisiana in the early twenty-first century.

After Spain acquired Louisiana in 1762, new land grant policies attracted large numbers of European immigrants to the colony, but few of them were from Spain. Thousands were French-speaking Acadians who had been driven out of Nova Scotia. Some of these people, who became known in Louisiana as Cajuns, have maintained their distinctive language and customs.

U.S. OCCUPATION

The United States purchased the vast Louisiana Territory from France in 1803, and the state of Louisiana entered the union shortly afterward. These developments attracted more Anglo-American settlers. Many immigrants with Scotch-Irish backgrounds became small farmers in the northern part of the state, while those whose ancestries were Scottish and English became merchants and planters in the south. Development of the state's agricultural plantation system began the importation of slaves from Africa and the West Indies. However, since the period of French rule, there had always been free blacks in Louisiana; most of them lived in New Orleans.

During the 1840's and 1850's, many Irish and German immigrants came to Louisiana to work as manual laborers. Later in the nineteenth century, Americans from midwestern states relocated to Cajun Louisiana to raise rice and to work on the railroads; many of them were quickly absorbed into the Cajun way of life. However, the Croatians who established the oyster industry in Plaquemines Parish retained their distinct identity, as did Italians, primarily from Sicily, who would begin immigrating into Louisiana during the early twentieth century.

During the mid-twentieth century, thousands of Honduran immigrants from all levels of society arrived in New Orleans. Some came to acquire convent educations, others to work in casinos and restaurants. During the 1970's, Vietnamese immigrants began settling in the coastal areas, where they worked in the fishing industry, and in New Orleans, where they opened small businesses. Louisiana also became home to immigrants from India, China, and the Philippines. Meanwhile, increasing numbers of Latin Americans were moving into the state. By 2006, almost one-half of all foreign-born residents in Louisiana were Hispanic. About 17 percent of these immigrants had been born in Mexico. One reason for the influx of Mexicans into the state was that after hurricane Katrina, there were good jobs in the construction industry. Since many of these workers were undocumented, it was unclear how many would remain in the state permanently.

Rosemary M. Canfield Reisman

FURTHER READING

Brasseaux, Carl A. *French, Cajun, Creole, Houma: A Primer on Francophone Louisiana*. Baton Rouge: Louisiana State University Press, 2005.

Garvey, Joan B., and Mary Lou Widmer. *Beautiful Crescent: A History of New Orleans*. Rev. ed. New Orleans: Garmer Press, 1997.

Lowe, John, ed. *Louisiana Culture from the Colonial Era to Katrina*. Baton Rouge: Louisiana State University Press, 2008.

Taylor, Joe Gray. *Louisiana: A History*. New York: W. W. Norton, 1984.

SEE ALSO: African Americans and immigrants; Alabama; Disaster recovery work; French immigrants; German immigrants; Honduran immigrants; Irish immigrants; Italian immigrants; Linguistic contributions; Mississippi; Mississippi River; Vietnamese immigrants.

PROFILE OF LOUISIANA				
Region	Gulf coast			
Entered union	1812			
Largest cities	New Orleans, Baton Rouge (capital), Shreveport, Metairie, Lafayette			
Modern immigrant communities	Mexicans, Hondurans, Vietnamese			
Population	*Total*	*Percent of state*	*Percent of U.S.*	*U.S. rank*
All state residents	4,288,000	100.0	1.43	25
All foreign-born residents	125,000	2.9	0.33	34

Source: U.S. Census Bureau, *Statistical Abstract for 2006.*
Notes: The U.S. population in 2006 was 299,399,000, of whom 37,548,000 (12.5%) were foreign born. Rankings in last column reflect total numbers, not percentages.

LOYALTY OATHS

DEFINITION: Required expressions of allegiance to a country or government that are often employed to test the loyalty of immigrants

SIGNIFICANCE: Popular during times of war, loyalty oaths and their variants have been imposed upon immigrants as conditions of admission and eventual citizenship, as well as requirements for certain types of public employment.

As formal expressions of allegiance to a given country or government, loyalty oaths have a long history in North America. For example, Puritan settlers required loyalty oaths from community members. After the U.S. Civil War (1861-1865), loyalty oaths were a condition for the reintegration into American political life of former Confederate states during Reconstruction. Modern American political officeholders, such as the president of the United States, take loyalty oaths when they are sworn into office. During the Cold War, many U.S. states tried to suppress communist sympathies by requiring loyalty oaths of public employees, most notably teachers. However, many of these efforts were later deemed unconstitutional by the U.S. Supreme Court. In general, the prevalence of loyalty oaths in the United States has risen during times of war and upheaval, including the Revolutionary War, the Civil War, both world wars, and the Cold War.

Immigrants to the United States have also frequently been targets of loyalty oaths and tests. This is due in part to popular fears of divided country loyalties, combined with the perception, particularly during the early twentieth century, that immigrants were responsible for bringing dangerous political ideologies, such as anarchism and socialism, into the United States. The very first federal Naturalization Act, passed by the U.S. Congress in 1790, included an oath of allegiance as a requirement for citizenship. It was followed eight years later by the Alien and Sedition Acts, which empowered the president of the United States to deport immigrants with unpalatable political views.

It was only after the assassination of President William McKinley by an avowed anarchist in 1901 that Congress added mandatory political screening of arriving immigrants, barring the admission of all those suspected of advocating anarchism or the overthrow of the government of the United States. This requirement was followed nearly two decades later by the World War I-era Espionage and Sedition Acts and the infamous Palmer raids, which included the deportation of thousands of immigrants due to their radical political activities and beliefs.

Loyalty oaths also played an important role during the internment of Japanese Americans during World War II. Military boards required the completion of loyalty examinations by all internees over the age of seventeen. To qualify for release from internment, male internees had to agree to serve in the U.S. armed forces—women in the Women's Army Corps. All had to renounce all forms of allegiance to the Japanese government and swear to abide by the laws of the United States, even if they had not yet been granted American citizenship.

Since the passage of the Naturalization Act of 1790, loyalty oaths affirming support for the United States and the U.S. Constitution have been a consistent requirement for the granting of citizenship to resident aliens. In 2009, this requirement was still in place, demanding that prospective citizens take a public oath "to support and defend the Constitution and the laws of the United States against all enemies, foreign and domestic," to renounce any foreign allegiances, and to offer military or other service if required.

Sarah Bridger

FURTHER READING

Hyman, Harold. *To Try Men's Souls: Loyalty Tests in American History.* Berkeley: University of California Press, 1958.

Levinson, Sanford. "Constituting Communities Through Words That Bind: Reflections on Loyalty Oaths." *Michigan Law Review* 84, no. 7 (1986): 1440-1470.

Preston, William S. *Aliens and Dissenters: Federal Suppression of Radicals, 1903-1933.* 2d ed. Champaign: University of Illinois Press, 1994.

SEE ALSO: Alien and Sedition Acts of 1798; Citizenship; Deportation; Dual citizenship; Espionage and Sedition Acts of 1917-1918; Immigration Act of

---

U.S. OATH OF CITIZENSHIP

I hereby declare, on oath, that I absolutely and entirely renounce and abjure all allegiance and fidelity to any foreign prince, potentate, state, or sovereignty of whom or which I have heretofore been a subject or citizen; that I will support and defend the Constitution and laws of the United States of America against all enemies, foreign and domestic; that I will bear true faith and allegiance to the same; that I will bear arms on behalf of the United States when required by the law; that I will perform noncombatant service in the Armed Forces of the United States when required by the law; that I will perform work of national importance under civilian direction when required by the law; and that I take this obligation freely without any mental reservation or purpose of evasion; so help me God.

1903; Japanese American internment; Naturalization; Naturalization Act of 1790; Red Scare; Science; World War I; World War II.

LUCE-CELLER BILL OF 1946

DATE: Signed into law on July 3, 1946
THE LAW: Federal law that eased immigration sanctions on Asian Indians and Filipinos
ALSO KNOWN AS: Immigration Act of 1946

SIGNIFICANCE: The Luce-Celler Bill overturned several decades of federal immigration laws that discriminated against specific Asian nationalities by reopening immigration from India and the Philippines and granting the right of naturalization to immigrants from those countries.

Before entering World War II in late 1941, the U.S. government sought to enlist the assistance of a number of countries to join forces against the expansionist German regime that threatened to destroy much of Europe. Filipinos and Asian Indians were enlisted in the cause, but they soon found they were not allowed to immigrate to the United States and become citizens because of legal restrictions imposed on even those who served the United States during the war.

The Luce-Celler Bill permitted Filipinos and Indians who had entered the United States legally to be naturalized as citizens. At the same time, the law imposed a quota of one hundred Indian immigrants per year, effectively activating a provision of a federal law enacted earlier during the twentieth century. When a wave of Indian people began during the late nineteenth century, the United States responded with the Naturalization Act of 1870, which denied Asians the right to gain citizenship. The discrimination that followed the Indian race stemmed from the word "caucasian" and the courts' interpretation of what race was "white enough" to gain citizenship.

The Luce-Celler Bill also permitted the naturalization of Filipinos, who had lost their status as American nationals with the passage of the Tydings-McDuffie Act of 1934, when the Philippines took its first legal step toward independence from the United States. President Harry S. Truman signed the bill into law on July 3, 1946—the day before the Philippines became fully independent.

Karel S. Sovak

FURTHER READING

Daniels, Roger. *Guarding the Golden Door: American Immigration Policy and Immigrants Since 1882.* New York: Hill & Wang, 2004.

Jensen, Joan M. *Passage from India: Asian Indian Immigrants in North America.* New Haven, Conn.: Yale University Press, 1988.

Karnow, Stanley. *In Our Image: America's Empire in the Philippines.* New York: Random House, 1989.

Leonard, Karen Isaksen. *The South Asian Americans.* Westport, Conn.: Greenwood Press, 1997.

Stern, Jennifer. *The Filipino Americans.* New York: Chelsea House, 1989.

SEE ALSO: Asian immigrants; Asian Indian immigrants; Asiatic Barred Zone; Asiatic Exclusion League; Congress, U.S.; Filipino immigrants; Filipino Repatriation Act of 1935; History of immigration after 1891; Immigration Act of 1943; Immigration and Nationality Act of 1965; Immigration law; *United States v. Bhagat Singh Thind.*

M

McCarran Internal Security Act of 1950

The Law: Federal legislation requiring the registration of communist organizations

Also known as: Subversive Activities Control Act

Date: Enacted on September 23, 1950

> **Significance:** An outgrowth of the anticommunist hysteria during the early Cold War known as McCarthyism, the law prohibited individuals who were or had been members of registered communist organizations from entering the United States. It also allowed for the deportation of communists and other individuals deemed subversive by the federal government.

During the early Cold War period, the United States entered a period of intense fear and persecution of communism. The successful Soviet test of an atomic weapon in 1949, the establishment of a communist government in China that same year, and the outbreak of the Korean War in 1950 contributed to these fears. Wisconsin senator Joseph McCarthy is generally associated as the demagogue most responsible for exacerbating these tensions. Indeed, the anticommunist witch hunt of the early 1950's is known as McCarthyism, but others in the federal government supported a similar agenda.

Pat McCarran, the Democratic senator from Nevada, was one of these supporters, and he sponsored the Internal Security Act of 1950 as a means of combating communism in the United States. The major thrust of the law was to prevent communist sympathizers from obtaining employment in defense industries. In order to accomplish this goal, organizations sympathetic to communist objectives were required to register with the newly created Subversive Activities Control Board (SACB). Past or present members of those organizations were then denied federal employment. The law also denied registered individuals from obtaining passports so that they were unable to leave the country.

McCarran also opposed immigration, and portions of the law directly targeted immigrants. Specifically, it prevented past or present members of communist organizations from entering the United States or from obtaining citizenship. The law had poorly defined standards for what constituted support of communism. As a result, members of foreign labor organizations or citizens of nations with communist governments could be denied entry without actually being practicing communists. Additionally, the law allowed the deportation of communist immigrants already within the United States, and it provided for the creation of detention centers where individuals deemed subversive could be held during times of emergency without trial. In effect, it changed the deportation from a punishment for actual crimes committed into a tool for eliminating political dissent in the immigrant community.

President Harry S. Truman vetoed the security measures as a threat to civil liberties, but the next

Senator Pat McCarran in 1947. (Library of Congress)

day, Congress overrode his veto by a substantial majority. Truman's objections proved prophetic, and cases challenging the act quickly appeared before the U.S. Supreme Court. The first, *Carlson v. Landon* (1952), challenged the right of the government to detain immigrants without bail pending deportation hearings. The court ruled that while the U.S. Constitution protected naturalized citizens, it provided no such protections for resident aliens. The subsequent Immigration and Nationality Act of 1952, which was also sponsored by McCarran, further regulated immigration of communists and individuals deemed subversive by the government. Meanwhile, the Internal Security Act required the registration of communist organizations until the Supreme Court ruled in *Albertson v. Subversive Activities Control Board* (1963) that communists could not be required to register with the government because that violated the Fifth Amendment rights to avoid self-incrimination.

John K. Franklin

FURTHER READING

Oshinsky, David M. *A Conspiracy So Immense: The World of Joe McCarthy*. New York: Oxford University Press, 2005.

Patenaude, Marc. *The McCarran Internal Security Act, 1950-2005*. Saarbrücken, Germany: VDM Verlag, 2008.

SEE ALSO: Deportation; History of immigration after 1891; Immigration and Nationality Act of 1952; Immigration law; Industrial Workers of the World; Korean War; Labor unions; Loyalty oaths.

MCCREARY AMENDMENT OF 1893

THE LAW: Amendment to the Geary Act of 1892 to extend the registration period for Chinese living in the United States by an additional six months

ALSO KNOWN AS: McCreary Act

DATE: Enacted on November 3, 1893

SIGNIFICANCE: The McCreary Amendment made unncessary the wholesale deportation of Chinese persons from the United States and marked a significant change in U.S. immigration policy by requiring for the first time that photographic identification be included on all registration certificates.

The Geary Act passed in 1892 was much harsher than the original Chinese Exclusion Act of 1882. In addition to extending exclusion, the Geary Act required that all Chinese laborers register for certificates of residence that proved their right to remain in the United States. The Chinese community organized extensive opposition to the law. They refused to register and challenged the constitutionality of the Geary Act in the U.S. Supreme Court. To avoid immediate massive Chinese deportation, the Senate passed the McCreary bill, proposed by Representative James B. McCreary, into law on November 3, 1893, extending the required registration time for six more months. The bill stipulated that after that time, a Chinese person could be held without bail pending deportation.

The McCreary Amendment required compliance by Chinese persons who resided in the United States prior to its passage who sought reentry into the United States. It defined laborers to include merchants, laundry owners, miners, and fishers. Although the McCreary Amendment received little historical attention, it significantly changed existing immigration policy by requiring photographs on all identity certificates. This was the first statutory requirement for photographic identification on immigration documentation and remained part of subsequent immigration policy.

Alvin K. Benson

FURTHER READING

Cassel, Susie Lan, ed. *The Chinese in America: A History from Gold Mountain to the New Millennium*. Walnut Creek, Calif.: AltaMira Press, 2002.

Lee, Erika. *At America's Gates: Chinese Immigration During the Exclusion Era, 1882-1943*. Chapel Hill: University of North Carolina Press, 2003.

SEE ALSO: Chinese Exclusion Act of 1882; *Chinese Exclusion Cases*; Chinese immigrants; Geary Act of 1892; Gresham-Yang Treaty of 1894; Taiwanese immigrants.

MACHINE POLITICS

DEFINITION: Nonideological form of local politics dominated by small and typically corrupt elites and based on exchanges of material benefits for political support

SIGNIFICANCE: At its peak during the late nineteenth and early twentieth centuries, machine politics was a response to the needs of the growing urban populations. Operating under a spoils system, many late nineteenth century political machines offered new immigrants jobs and housing in exchange for votes.

The birth of the American political machine can be traced to the waves of immigration to the United States during the late nineteenth century. Following the U.S. Civil War (1861-1865), America saw tremendous expansion in industry and a rapid increase in urbanization. Many immigrants who entered the United States between 1860 and 1890 were poorly educated and unable to speak English. Urban political machines emerged to help alleviate abject poverty, as they could address the needs of the immigrants better than government agencies could. Many immigrants needed jobs and resources faster than traditional means could provide them. Thus, in large cities such as Chicago, New York City, and Kansas City, Missouri, political machines were created to meet these needs.

Machine "bosses," as the leaders of the machines came to be known, provided immigrants help with naturalization, finding jobs, and negotiating rent agreements. Although not often in charge of hiring immigrants directly, bosses persuaded elected officials to give jobs to immigrants or to ensure that government contracts were made with businesses that would employ the faithful immigrants. Machine bosses were seen as beacons of hope for the downtrodden and in many cases took on paternalistic roles. In return for their patronage they expected unwavering loyalty at the voting booth. Although this system has been difficult to enforce during the twenty-first century, it was simple to maintain during the nineteenth century. At that time, privacy in voting booths was limited. Many immigrants arrived at polling places, where they received already marked ballots that they dropped into ballot boxes to be counted—all under the watchful eyes of machine bosses. In many cases, the undemocratic methods of political machines were the only means immigrants had to get jobs. Many immigrants became party leaders within their own neighborhoods and thus helped draw new immigrants into established political machines.

TOM PENDERGAST

A famous example of a machine boos was Tom Pendergast of Kansas City, Missouri. Pendergast's older brother Jim ran a saloon and hotel in Kansas City. As a bartender Jim heard about people's problems and did what he could to help them. Later, when a friend of Jim ran for political office, Jim asked his customers to vote for his friend. The friend won, and shortly thereafter Jim ran for political office himself as an alderman; he also won. Tom Pendergast saw the potential political influence that could be gained from helping needy voters. He found people jobs, gave them food, and persuaded them to vote for his favored candidates. In 1900, the Pendergast machine helped elect Kansas City's mayor, and Pendergast himself was able to oversee the appointments of two hundred workers for a street-paving program. By the early 1920's, Pendergast was spending six hours a day listening to people's needs, and the rest of his time was spent meeting those needs in exchange for votes.

In 1922 and 1926, Pendergast got future U.S. president Harry S. Truman elected to county positions. This relationship with Pendergast would later cause trouble for Truman when he ran for the U.S. Senate and for president. By 1932, Pendergast was able to swing votes for Missouri state and national offices. In return for his assistance in supporting Franklin D. Roosevelt for president, Roosevelt directed five million dollars worth of federal aid to Pendergast through New Deal programs.

The Pendergast machine was practically invincible within Missouri and might have lasted decades longer had not the immigration pattern in Kansas City changed. Most immigrants settling in Kansas City during the 1930's were Italians who resented the Irish leaders and party workers who made up a large percentage of the Pendergast machine. Physical fights ensued, and a once purely political machine began to evolve into a gangster-related mafia. Pendergast himself was later jailed for tax evasion, and his political career came to an abrupt end.

Kathryn A. Cochran

FURTHER READING

Cornwell, Elmer E., Jr. "Bosses, Machines, and Ethnic Groups." *Annals of the American Academy of Political and Social Science* 353, no. 1 (1964): 27-39. Traces the influence of ethnic groups on politics after the decline of the machines during the 1920's.

Gerstle, Gary, and John H. Mollenkopf. *E Pluribus Unum? Contemporary and Historical Perspectives on Immigrant Political Incorporation.* New York: Russell Sage Foundation, 2005. Highlights the struggles of immigrants to assimilate into American political society.

Heidenheimer, Arnold J., and Michael Johnston. *Political Corruption: Concepts and Contexts.* 3d ed. New Brunswick, N.J.: Transaction Publishers, 2002. This compilation explores the historical concept of political corruption via the nineteenth century political machines.

McCullough, David. *Truman.* New York: Simon & Schuster, 1992. Chapters 5 and 6 give a detailed account of how the Pendergast machine selected Harry S. Truman for the U.S. Senate.

Roosevelt, Theodore. "Machine Politics in New York City." *The Century* 33, no 1 (1886): 74-83. Timely look at political machines operating in New York City and a rationalization of why they exist.

Royko, Mike. *Boss: Richard J. Daley of Chicago.* New York: Penguin Books, 1971. Classic work in the field of machine politics, Royko explores the only major political machine to survive in the second half of the twentieth century.

SEE ALSO: Employment; Irish immigrants; New York City; Political parties; Presidential elections; Progressivism; Tammany Hall.

MAIL-ORDER BRIDES

DEFINITION: Women involved in marriages with residents of the United States that are arranged through postal correspondence, Internet connections, and international dating and introduction services

SIGNIFICANCE: Mail-order brides are women who marry their partners after having responded to advertisements for wives or having been selected from their own personals that were posted in newspapers, catalogs, Internet sites, or through marriage broker services. This practice has been used as a legal method of migrating to the United States since the early colonial era.

In the history of the United States, men traditionally immigrated to the new colonies and across the frontiers in far greater numbers than did women. As they settled and began building communities, they wanted marital partners. Single men, who often could not find spouses, needed alternative methods of introduction to women. Finding women who were willing to migrate to remote areas and become spouses to men they hardly knew required effort. Sometimes, men hoped to find a wife through the creation of advertisements or by responding to them. Long-distance location of spouses through advertisements continues to be practiced in America in the early twenty-first century.

EARLY AMERICAN HISTORY

During the American colonial era, in locations where the population of women was low, some colonies brought in women who were eager for a new start in the New World. An early known incidence of this was in 1619, when the Virginia Company of London sent its first ship that carried "mail-order brides" to colonists. Interested men reimbursed the company by paying 120 pounds of tobacco for the women's transportation. During the early eighteenth century, France began shipping women to New Orleans. Later, during the western frontier and California gold rush days, bachelors from the West sought women from the eastern states and other countries to join them. Some men contacted friends and church groups, while others advertised in newspapers.

During the nineteenth century, mail-order catalogs advertising prospective brides as well as marriage brokerage services emerged. Like seeds and clothing, women could be ordered through catalogs; hence, they were dubbed "mail-order brides." While some men who lived in remote areas used these services because of a continued lack of women in the vicinity, others chose mail-order services as a convenient method of selecting particular characteristics in their spouses. At the turn of the twentieth century, for example, Japanese and other Asian immigrants often resorted to selecting mates from pictures; those chosen "picture brides" then migrated to the United States. These men hoped to marry women from similar cultural backgrounds.

LATE TWENTIETH CENTURY DEVELOPMENTS

By the 1970's, career options were moving more and more American women away from the traditional role of the stay-at-home wife. Many Western men adapted to and supported these changes, while others met traditional wives, but other men chose to seek an alternative option through the use of mail-order bride services. These men were in search of a spouse from a traditional or non-Western background. They purchased advertisement literature that described eligible women, selected their choice from among those depicted, and worked toward obtaining their brides. Most of the bridal candidates who advertised were underprivileged women from developing countries. Poverty and other woes enticed them to seek their fortunes in an entirely new culture.

Throughout the 1980's, the majority of the women who sought fiancé visas, ninety-day entry permits for marriage purposes, were Southeast Asians, particularly women in the Philippines. During the 1990's, deteriorating economic conditions in Russia and Ukraine dramatically increased the interest of Russian and Ukrainian women in becoming mail-order brides. They hoped to enrich their lives, escape socioeconomic depression, and make new starts. By that time, mail-order bride services had replaced most of the print catalogs with similar advertisements that were available via the Internet on the World Wide Web. With this new technology, couples could much more readily exchange pictures and correspondence than in the past.

The mail-order bride practice has a long tradition in the United States. The practice has supporters who believe it is an acceptable custom and opponents who consider the process to be unethical trafficking of women. A high percentage of mail-order brides remain married to their original domestic partners, but some have been trapped in abusive relationships. In an effort to reduce potential problems, President George W. Bush signed the International Marriage Broker Regulation Act in 2006. This law required that candidates for mail-order brides be at least eighteen years old, be given criminal and marital background check information on the men with whom they wished to correspond, and be provided with legal rights and contact information regarding domestic violence. Mail-order brides make up only a small percentage of the total number of immigrants to the United States, but they remain an important part of the country's history.

Cynthia J. W. Svoboda

FURTHER READING

Belleau, Marie-Claire. "Mail-Order Brides in a Global World." *Albany Law Review* 67, no. 2 (Winter, 2003): 595-608. Discusses the laws in the United States and Canada and makes recommendations for changes.

Constable, Nicole. *Romance on a Global Stage: Pen Pals, Virtual Ethnography, and "Mail Order" Marriages.* Berkeley: University of California Press, 2003. An anthropologist reviews the myths, fairy tales, political economy, and history of mail-order brides.

Enss, Chris. *Hearts West: True Stories of Mail-Order Brides on the Frontier.* Guilford, Conn.: TwoDot, 2005. Relates true accounts of mail-order brides during the nineteenth and early twentieth centuries.

Lindee, Kirsten M. "Love, Honor, or Control: Domestic Violence, Trafficking, and the Question of How to Regulate the Mail-Order Bride Industry." *Columbia Journal of Gender and Law* 16, no. 2 (Summer, 2007): 551-602. Discusses international marriage brokerage rationale for regulation and the International Marriage Broker Regulation Act of 2006.

So, Christine. "Asian Mail-Order Brides, the Threat of Global Capitalism, and the Rescue of the U.S. Nation-State." *Feminist Studies* 32, no. 2 (Summer, 2006): 395-419. Cites several mail-order bride publications and concludes that Asian mail-order brides are perceived as tools for obtaining traditional families.

SEE ALSO: Chinese immigrants; Families; Fiancées Act of 1946; Filipino immigrants; Japanese immigrants; Marriage; "Marriages of convenience"; Picture brides; Russian and Soviet immigrants; War brides; Women immigrants.

MAINE

SIGNIFICANCE: A predominantly white state, most of whose immigrants have come from nearby parts of Canada, Maine has also become the home of small but increasingly significant numbers of African and Asian immigrants, who have become economic and cultural assets.

Most inhabitants of Maine lived on farms at the time Maine became a state during the early nineteenth century. Early immigrants helped produce dairy products and crops such as hay, potatoes, apples, and blueberries. Aroostook County became one of the major potato-producing areas of the United States. Most of the state's early immigrants were French Canadians, many of whom worked in the lumber industry. Newcomers from the Canadian coastal region found opportunities in fishing along the state's extensive Atlantic coast and in another important Maine industry, shipbuilding, especially in Bath. Before 1870, however, these northern immigrants formed a very small part of the total population.

IMMIGRANTS IN THE MILLS

The first large textile mill was built in 1826 in Saco. Lewiston later became the main textile center in the state. Earlier nineteenth century immigrants tended to be Irish but were less numerous than in other New England states, and they tended to leave the mills for other types of work. Between 1870 and 1930, with a peak during the 1880's, French Canadian workers with relatively short routes to travel arrived in railroad stations in southwestern Maine towns such as Biddeford and Lewiston. Many of them planned later to return to Canada, but continuing economic troubles in their former homeland often made them stay in Maine. Some immigrants worked in paper-making, one of the state's largest industries after the early 1880's.

Franco-Americans became steady and reliable workers who expected their children to follow in their footsteps, but they limited the educational opportunities of the next generation. This limitation and linguistic difficulties with English impeded social development of younger immigrants. As late as 1970, 43 percent of Maine's Franco-American residents had only grade-school levels of education or less. During the late twentieth and early twenty-first century, however, cultural centers were established in public colleges at Fort Kent, near the Canadian border, and in Lewiston. Special television programs were also established for Franco-American children.

EARLY TWENTY-FIRST CENTURY DEVELOPMENTS

Fabric mills and the towns that depended on them declined sharply during the late twentieth century. An unusual form of integration has provided new life for Lewiston, a town generally perceived to be dying. Hundreds of African immigrants, particularly from Somalia, began arriving after 2000. Many opened restaurants and small businesses, and some introduced their own versions of textile arts. African immigrants have energized the state's cultural life with their oral poetry, music, and colorful clothing. Some Sudanese and Congolese have followed the Somali initiative. A large increase in the number of people studying English as a second language indicates that they are also accommodating themselves to their new linguistic situation.

PROFILE OF MAINE

Region	New England
Entered union	1820
Largest cities	Portland, Lewiston, Bangor
Modern immigrant communities	Somalis, Cambodians, Chinese

Population	Total	Percent of state	Percent of U.S.	U.S. rank
All state residents	1,322,000	100.0	0.44	40
All foreign-born residents	42,000	3.2	0.11	44

Source: U.S. Census Bureau, *Statistical Abstract for 2006.*
Notes: The U.S. population in 2006 was 299,399,000, of whom 37,548,000 (12.5%) were foreign born. Rankings in last column reflect total numbers, not percentages.

Immigrants from China and Cambodia have injected Asian culture into Maine's largest city, Portland. Although Maine natives have been thought of as distant to outsiders, they seem to have welcomed these African and Asian newcomers.

Robert P. Ellis

FURTHER READING

Brault, Gerard J. *The French-Canadian Heritage in New England.* Hanover, N.H.: University Press of New England, 1986.

Fairfield, Roy P. *Sands, Spindles, and Steeples.* Portland: York Institute, 1956.

Judd, Richard William, et al. *Maine: The Pine Tree State from Prehistory to the Present.* Orono: University of Maine Press, 1995.

Rivard, Paul E. *A New Order of Things: How the Textile Industry Transformed New England.* Hanover, N.H.: University Press of New England, 2002.

SEE ALSO: African immigrants; Asian immigrants; Canadian immigrants; Connecticut; Language issues; Massachusetts; Rhode Island; Vermont.

MALAYSIAN IMMIGRANTS

SIGNIFICANCE: Immigrants from the Southeast Asian nation of Malaysia began entering the United States in significant numbers after Malaysia (called Malaya until 1963) became independent in 1957. Malaysian immigration to the United States has never been large, but Malaysian immigrants have established significant communities in a number of western American cities. Malaysian immigration has tended to rise and fall with economic fluctuations in Southeast Asia.

When the British-ruled Federation of Malaya became independent in 1957, it was beset with political instability because its much larger neighbor Indonesia initially objected to creation as an independent state. Internal strife, combined with the outbreak of armed hostilities between the new government and various groups of Chinese communist guerrillas, prompted many Malayan citizens to emigrate to the United States.

American business interests in Malaysia go back

PROFILE OF MALAYSIAN IMMIGRANTS

Country of origin	Malaysia
Primary languages	Malay, English
Primary regions of U.S. settlement	West Coast states and Hawaii
Earliest significant arrivals	1959
Peak immigration period	1990-2000
Twenty-first century legal residents*	16,757 (2,095 per year)

*Immigrants who obtained legal permanent resident status in the United States.

Source: Department of Homeland Security, *Yearbook of Immigration Statistics, 2008.*

---

to the era of British rule. Numerous large American corporations have large investments in Malaysia; these include General Electric, Chevron, and Coca-Cola. During the late twentieth century, the United States became Malaysia's primary trading partner, and the two countries have generally had friendly relations.

Since the 1960's, Malaysian immigration to the United States has generally fluctuated with economic ups and downs in Malaysia and Southeast Asia. In fact, economic forces have been the primary factor drawing Malaysians to the United States. Frustrated by limited investment opportunities in Malaysia, many immigrants come to the United States to invest in small businesses. Emigration to the United States became even more appealing after Malaysia's currency was revalued in 2005. Many Malaysians believed they would be better off in the long run by investing their capital in American dollars.

During the last decade of the twentieth century, the number of Malaysians who immigrated to the United States was three times greater than it had been during the previous decade. The global recession of the early twenty-first century prompted even greater levels of immigration as unemployment and inflation rates in Malaysia rose. By 2008, approximately 50,000 Malaysians were living in the United States. Evidence of the growing numbers of Malaysians in the United States could be seen in the development of sizable Malaysian enclaves such cities as Los Angeles, San Francisco, and Boston.

Robert D. Mitchell

FURTHER READING

Gould, James W. *The United States and Malaysia.* Cambridge, Mass.: Harvard University Press, 1969.

Lim, Lin Lean. *Impact of Immigration on Labor Markets in Peninsular Malaysia.* Tokyo: Nihon University Population Research Institute, 1986.

Yeoh, Michael, ed. *Twenty-first Century Malaysia: Challenges and Strategies in Attaining Vision, 2020.* London: ASEAN Academic Press, 2002.

SEE ALSO: Asian immigrants; Economic opportunities; Filipino immigrants; History of immigration after 1891; Indonesian immigrants; Lim, Shirley Geok-lin; Thai immigrants; Vietnamese immigrants.

MARIEL BOATLIFT

THE EVENT: Massive influx of Cuban refugees who reached the United States on small boats
DATE: April 1-September 25, 1980
LOCATION: Cuba; Florida; Florida Straits

> **SIGNIFICANCE:** The sudden arrival in South Florida of approximately 125,000 Cuban refugees in the Mariel boatlift may have been the largest single migratory influx in one region in American history. It elicited a reappraisal of U.S. refugee policy and provoked a negative public reaction to Cuban refugees.

During the first decades after Fidel Castro's communist government took power in 1959, emigration from Cuba brought more than 300,000 refugees to the United States. Most of them settled in South Florida. However, while the largest Cuban exodus, between 1965 and 1973, was due mostly to the federal government's Cuban Adjustment Act of 1965, which gave Cuban immigrants special consideration, it was not the most dramatic. The most divisive and disruptive Cuban immigration wave occurred in the Mariel boatlift of 1980.

By the late 1970's, pressures on Cuban opponents to leave their homeland were reaching new levels. In April of 1980, about 10,000 Cubans sought political asylum in the Peruvian embassy in Havana. The Cuban government responded by opening the port of Mariel to allow all who wanted to emigrate to do so. From then until September, approximately 125,000 Cubans sailed for Florida on more than two thousand mostly small boats owned or chartered by Cuban Americans.

The bulk of the people who left Cuba on boats were young male members of the working class. A small number were political prisoners, petty criminals, substance abusers, and people known to have mental disorders. Initially, the refugees were affectionately dubbed "Marielitos." However, the term eventually became a pejorative term associated with depravity, violent behavior, and laziness, and the American media and some politicians characterized the Mariel boatlift refugees as having been made up of "lower-class" deviants and criminals. However, fewer than 2 percent of the refugees were found to have been convicted of felony crimes.

When the Mariel refugees began arriving, South Florida's large Cuban American community rushed to their aid with the full backing of their highly organized private charitable institutions. In Dade County alone, the Cuban Americans raised more than $2 million to assist their compatriots. However, growing concern that this new wave of Cubans would tarnish the image of the established, family-oriented Cuban American community prompted some business and political leaders to withdraw the support.

In June, 1980, President Jimmy Carter ordered all Mariel refugees who had not found relatives or others to sponsor them to be placed in federal detention camps in Wisconsin, Pennsylvania, and Arkansas. In Pennsylvania and Arkansas, the refugees, bored and fearful about their future, rioted. By October, the majority of the Marielitos had been released into various communities, and the detention camps were closed. Meanwhile, the riots created a public backlash against the Mariel refugees. The much-publicized presence of criminals among the refugees also helped generate a feeling of revulsion against the entire group: Marielitos were blamed for the upsurge in violent crime in Miami in 1981. In 1980, a year of economic downturn,

Florida shrimpboat returning from Mariel, Cuba, loaded with Cuban refugees as it lands at the U.S. Navy's Key West naval base in April, 1980. (AP/Wide World Photos)

many people in the United States feared that more Cuban refugees would mean higher unemployment.

In 1985, President Ronald Reagan secured a promise from Castro to take back Marielito criminals. However, after a few hundred had been returned to Cuba, Castro's government became enraged at U.S. sponsorship of the anti-Castro Radio Martí and canceled the agreement. In November, 1987, the United States reached a new agreement with Cuba that provided for deporting to Cuba known Marielito criminals in return for U.S. acceptance of Cuban political prisoners. Some Marielitos held in federal prisons in Louisiana and Georgia rioted and took hostages. The riots ended after the Reagan administration promised that no prisoners would be returned to Cuba without individual reviews of their cases and that those whose offenses were minor would be released into the community. However, hundreds of Marielitos remained in federal prisons several years later.

Despite the difficult reception that many of the Marielitos experienced, many of them went on to achieve economic success in the United States.

Darius V. Echeverría

FURTHER READING

Diaz, Guarione M. *The Cuban American Experience: Issues, Perceptions, and Realities.* St. Louis, Mo.: Reedy Press, 2007.

Engstrom, David W. *Presidential Decision Making Adrift: The Carter Administration and the Mariel Boatlift.* Lanham, Md.: Rowman & Littlefield, 1997.

Larzelere, Alex. *The 1980 Cuban Boatlift: Castro's Ploy, America's Dilemma.* Washington, D.C.: National Defense University Press, 1988.

SEE ALSO: Criminal immigrants; Cuban immigrants; Education; Florida; Freedom Airlift; Haitian boat people; Immigration and Nationality Act of 1965; Miami; Push-pull factors; Stereotyping.

Marriage

DEFINITION: Socially recognized institution whereby two adults are joined in a special kind of social and legal dependence

SIGNIFICANCE: From the earliest years of the United States, marriage has been a central part of American immigration policy and practice. Marrying American citizens or residents has become the easiest and most common way to enter the United States legally—a fact that has attracted additional government scrutiny to so-called marriages of convenience. The rise of same-sex marriage as a social issue has also posed difficult new legal questions about marriage and immigration.

The first major piece of federal legislation on immigration, the Chinese Exclusion Act of 1882, barred most immigration from China to the United States. Chinese born in the United States were still regarded as American citizens. However, Chinese-born workers then already residing in the United States could reenter the United States after leaving the country only with reentry certificates issued by American customs collectors. This early legislation involved marriage because the wives of Chinese-born laborers were prohibited from entering the country, even if the men had valid reentry certificates, and because women were defined by the status of their husbands. This meant that a U.S.-born woman could lose her citizenship by being married to a Chinese man without citizenship.

PREFERENCES FOR SPOUSES BEFORE 1965

Although the Chinese Exclusion Act treated marriage as a basis for exclusion, American immigration policies have historically used marriage as a basis for inclusion. The Emergency Immigration Act of 1921 established a national origins quota by temporarily limiting the annual number of immigrants from any country to 3 percent of the number of persons from that country who had been living in the United States in 1910. The Immigration Act of 1924, also known as the Johnson-Reed Act, made quotas permanent and pushed them back to 2 percent of the number of people from a given country living in the United States in 1890. However, the new immigration law also recognized

preference quota status for spouses of U.S. citizens aged twenty-one and older and for immigrants skilled in agriculture, together with their wives and their dependent children under the age of sixteen, as well as for parents of citizens. Citizens, wives and unmarried children under age eighteen could enter outside the quotas, as could people in several other categories.

The Immigration and Nationality Act of 1952, also known as the McCarran-Walter Act, retained the national origin criterion, but it also strengthened the preference system. The first basis was economic, as immigrants with special skills were given first preference. Other preferences, however, rested on the social norm that family relationships enjoy a special status. Parents of U.S. citizens constituted the second preference, spouses and children of resident aliens the third, and other relatives the fourth.

Spouses, usually wives, were also able to enter the United States through special provisions for the marital partners of members of the U.S. armed forces. An estimated 150,000 to 200,000 European women married U.S. soldiers between 1944 and 1950. During the same period of time, 50,000 to 100,000 Asian women married U.S. servicemen. American immigration laws were very restrictive, and made it especially difficult for Asians to enter the United States, so on December 28, 1945, the U.S. Congress passed the War Brides Act, which waived most of the immigration requirements for women who had married members of the American armed forces serving overseas. Later, marriages with U.S. soldiers brought significant numbers of spouses into the country from Korea, the Philippines, and Vietnam.

PREFERENCES FOR SPOUSES AFTER 1965

Thirteen years after the McCarran-Walter Act, a new amendment to American immigration law pushed preference categories to the forefront and largely removed the national origins restrictions. Under the new system of categories, family reunification became the central principle of American immigration law. Moreover, the unification of spouses became the most important form of family reunification. In addition, spouses of U.S. citizens could be admitted to the United States outside the preference system altogether.

By 1986, the first year for which categories of admission are available in the U.S. Census Bureau's *Yearbook of Immigration Statistics*, spouses of residents admitted under the preferences and spouses of citizens together accounted for more than 41 percent of all legal immigrants. Even as overall numbers of immigrants grew in the succeeding years, spouses continued to make up more than one-third of all those admitted. Moreover, spouses of U.S. residents made up the largest category of people permitted to enter the country under any preference, and in most years they constituted the majority of family-sponsored immigrants.

American immigration law also has enabled people from other countries to form marriages leading to permanent residence. U.S. citizens may petition U.S. Citizenship and Immigration Services (known as Immigration and Naturalization Services before 2002) for K-1, fiancé visas, so that foreign fiancés can enter the country and apply for a marriage license in one of the states.

Because American immigration law so strongly favors marriage as a reason for inclusion, marriages of convenience—those conducted only in order to obtain permanent legal residence—have become a matter of serious concern. The 1986 Immigration Marriage Fraud Amendments amended the Immigration and Nationality Act of 1952 to impose residency requirements and heightened scrutiny and to provide penalties for marriage fraud.

SAME-SEX MARRIAGE

The rise of same-sex marriage as a social issue at the end of the twentieth century raised questions about whether gay and lesbian U.S. citizens and permanent residents should be eligible for marital immigration benefits for their partners of the same sex. In the case of *Adams v. Howerton* in 1982, an American citizen named Richard Adams argued, in his home state of Colorado, that his partner, Andrew Sullivan, should be classified as his spouse for immigration purposes. However, U.S. law excluded homosexual immigrants until 1990. In denying Adams his bid for marital immigration rights, a federal circuit court cited as evidence that the U.S. Congress did not intend spousal benefits to extend to same-sex couples. With the 1990 end of exclusion on the basis of same-sex involvement, some observers felt that the legal grounds for denying marital immigration benefits to same-sex partners had been removed. Accordingly, advocates

maintained that denying same-sex couples the same immigration opportunities as opposite-sex couples constituted unfair discrimination. Against this, other commentators responded that the opposite-sex couple was the foundation of American social order and that it should receive special recognition and support in national immigration policy.

The recognition of same-sex marriage in some states raised the possibility that debates over marriage and immigration policy could intensify. Historically, what constitutes "marriage" has been defined by individual states, not by the federal government, and states have usually recognized marriages conducted in other states. However, while same-sex marriage has been recognized in a few states, a majority of states passed statutes or constitutional amendments during the 1990's and the early twenty-first century defining marriage as limited to unions between two opposite-sex individuals. Moreover, a federal law known as the Defense of Marriage Act of 1996 specified that no state needed to recognize another state marriage between members of the same sex and that the federal government itself now defined marriage as a union of one man and one woman. This legislation made it unlikely that marital immigration benefits would be extended to same-sex partners, even though U.S. immigration policy no longer blocked entry on the basis of homosexuality.

Carl L. Bankston III

FURTHER READING

Badgett, M. V. Lee. *When Gay People Get Married: What Happens When Societies Legalize Same-Sex Marriage.* New York: New York University Press, 2009. Examination of how same-sex marriage influences societies that includes some consideration of implications for immigration.

Bray, Ilona. *Fiancé and Marriage Visas: A Couple's Guide to U.S. Immigration.* 5th ed. Berkeley, Calif.: Nolo, 2008. Intended as a how-to book, this volume provides a good, easy-to-follow guide to immigration policies on fiancé and marriage visas.

Constable, Nicole. *Romance on a Global Stage: Pen Pals, Virtual Ethnography, and "Mail Order" Marriages.* Berkeley: University of California Press, 2003. Anthropological study of the ways in which American men have searched for wives from other countries, with special attention to the business of mail-order brides.

Cott, Nancy F. *Public Vows: A History of Marriage and the Nation*. Cambridge, Mass.: Harvard University Press, 2002. Comprehensive history of marriage in American law and society.

Shanks, Cheryl. *Immigration and the Politics of American Sovereignty, 1880-1990*. Ann Arbor: University of Michigan Press, 2001. Excellent overview of American immigration policy that includes some discussion of marriage issues.

SEE ALSO: Cable Act of 1922; Families; Gay and lesbian immigrants; *Green Card*; Immigration and Nationality Act of 1965; Intermarriage; Mail-order brides; "Marriages of convenience"; Page Law of 1875; Picture brides; War brides; War Brides Act of 1945; Women immigrants.

"MARRIAGES OF CONVENIENCE"

DEFINITION: Marriages entered into for reasons other than permanent union, such as gaining permanent resident status in the United States

SIGNIFICANCE: Often contracted to evade immigration law, "marriages of convenience" have become an increasingly common method by which immigrants have obtained permanent resident status in the United States. Because marriage is a basic social institution, U.S. immigration policy has been designed to keep married people together. Immigrants traveling to the United States have been encouraged to bring their spouses. Other immigrants, however, have found a route to permanent residence and even citizenship through marriages of convenience.

The concept of "marriages of convenience" has given rise to terms such as "sham marriages," "fraudulent marriages," and "green card marriages." In the context of immigration law, all these terms pertain to essentially the same thing: marriages undertaken for the purpose of circumventing legal requirement for obtaining permanent residency status. It should also be understood that such marriages differ from marriages to so-called mail-order brides. Although women may enter the latter type of marriage for the purpose of immigrating the United States, they do so in the knowledge that their American husbands are seeking permanent marriage partners.

Since the mid-twentieth century, U.S. immigration policy has actively championed marriage and family unification as vital to a stable society. However, marriages are not always undertaken to unite couples who are deeply in love and committed to sharing their lives together. In many societies, families join couples together in arranged marriages, promoting unions between people who may not even know each other in advance, but they do not do this to skirt immigration policies. In contrast, marriages of convenience do exactly that.

One of the easiest ways to become a naturalized American citizen has been to marry a citizen to avoid major immigration difficulties. The immigrant spouses do not need to wait for visa numbers or even need labor certificates. Marriage to an American citizen automatically makes an alien eligible for the legal status of a permanent resident. During the 1980's, the numbers of immigrants who entered the United States after marrying American citizens rose from 87,221 in 1981 to 124,093 in 1985, and 140,000 in 1986. However, the Immigration and Naturalization Service (INS) estimated that 30 percent these immigrants' marriages were fraudulent. In many cases, the American citizens were knowing parties to sham marriages. In others, however, they entered their marriages in good faith only to learn later that they were not the true objects of their immigrant spouses' affection, but instead merely their spouses' means to permanent residency status, one step away from full citizenship.

Arranging sham marriages, which costs an immigrant from two hundred to five thousand dollars, has become a business. In August, 1986, the INS deported the head of a West Coast company that had arranged seventy sham marriages after charging immigrants from three to five thousand dollars for each wedding. Single mothers were particular targets of immigrant seeking "green card marriages."

IMMIGRATION MARRIAGE FRAUD AMENDMENTS OF 1986

Concerned about the increasing numbers of aliens receiving permanent residency status through marriage and convinced that more than one-third of such marriages were fraudulent, Congress enacted the Immigration Marriage Fraud Amendments (IMFA) on November 10, 1986. This law created a two-year "conditional" permanent residency status for immigrants marrying American citizens. During the ninety days leading up the end of the two-year period, couples were required to submit joint petitions for permanent legal status. So couples could prove their marriages were still valid, INS officials were authorized to make home visits. To verify that couples were living as man and wife, officials interviewed apartment managers, employers, friends, and neighbors. They also interviewed the spouses themselves—separately—asking questions about their weddings, division of household chores, home furnishings and decor, and other matters to see whether the couples were cohabiting. Although instructed not to do, some INS officials have asked intimate questions about the couples' relationships. These interviews have led to a number of law suits about invasion of privacy. When investigators determine that a marriage is fraudulent, they may rescind the immigrant partner's permanent resident status or citizenship, order the immigrant's deportation, or even instigate criminal proceedings against both spouses.

MARRIAGE FRAUD IN THE MEDIA

The magnitude of the sham-marriage problem was so great during the 1980's that television's *Nightline* program broadcast a special on the subject in August, 1985. The program featured an interview with Senator Alan Simpson, the chair of the Senate Subcommittee on Immigration. Sham marriages have also been treated lightly in the media. The 1990 film *Green Card* is a romantic story about an American woman and a French man entering a completely fraudulent marriage for different purposes. The woman needs to be married to lease the apartment of her dreams; the Frenchman needs to marry a citizen so he can gain permanent resident status. The couple's efforts to fool INS officials become the subject of levity. A story line for a 2009 episode of the popular television series *Desperate Housewives* included a scheme for "green card marriage."

Although marriages of convenience may be treated humorously in fiction, the reality has been less than comic. The sham-marriage business has continued to thrive into the twenty-first century, arranging marriages for immigrants for hefty fees and coaching couples on how to respond to official immigration investigations. The news media are filled stories about marriage-fraud rings. Immigrants seeking marriages and the "green cards" come from all over the world. With many aliens willing to pay thousands of dollars for marriages, American citizens in desperate need of money may find sham marriages tempting.

After the terrorist attacks of September 11, 2001, the issue of sham marriages took on another aspect: Fully one-half of thirty-six foreign-born suspected terrorists who were in the United States from the early 1990's to 2004 gained their legal resident status by marrying Americans. Consequently, government agencies began stepping up efforts to uncover sham marriages. In 2008, U.S. Immigration and Customs Enforcement agents rounded up three dozen suspects in Operation Knot So Fast. Government efforts to curtail marriage fraud has continued, but marriage has remained a major route to immigration into the United States.

Marcia B. Dinneen

FURTHER READING

Chau-Eoan, Howard G. "Tightening the Knot." *Time*, December 15, 1986, 35. Brief discussion of how the Immigration Marriage Fraud Amendments of 1986 were expected to be tougher on marriage fraud.

Farrell, Mary H. J. "For Immigrants Trying to Obtain the Coveted Green Card, Marriage May Be a Treacherous Strategy." *People Weekly*, February 25, 1991, 93-96. Story that includes examples of green card marriages.

Glasser, Jeff. "The Benefits of Marriage." *U.S. News & World Report*, April 2, 2001, 18. Article showing how a new law may actually promote marriage fraud.

Lopez, Elena Maria. "Marriage Fraud." *USA Today*, April 7, 2006, p. 13A. Discusses the ease, through marriage, of getting permanent access to the United States.

Pear, Robert. "In Bureaucracy, Aliens Find Another Unprotected Border." *The New York Times*, October 19, 1986. Statistics show the increase in marriages as a way to enter the United States.

SEE ALSO: Citizenship; Citizenship and Immigration Services, U.S.; *Green Card*; Green cards; Immigration and Naturalization Service, U.S.; Immigration Reform and Control Act of 1986; Intermarriage; Marriage; Permanent resident status.

MARYLAND

SIGNIFICANCE: Between the time of the American Revolution and World War I, more than one million immigrants entered the United States through the port of Baltimore. One reason for this traffic through Baltimore was that the city was the westernmost port on the East Coast, which made it closer to the inland areas where many new immigrants wished to settle. Completion of the National Road to the Ohio River in 1818 and the construction of the Baltimore and Ohio Railroad a decade later also contributed to western movement. However, there were also many opportunities for work in nineteenth century Maryland, particularly in Baltimore.

Small numbers of Germans and Irish migrated to colonial Maryland, and French political refugees came during the 1790's, but the first large-scale immigrant waves that began during the 1830's brought Germans and Irish. By 1860, 32,613 Germans were living in Baltimore, a city whose population was one-quarter foreign born. Germans worked as furniture and piano makers, butchers, brewers, and skilled craftsmen generally. The German Society of Maryland, founded in 1783, provided German newcomers with clothing, fuel, jobs, health care, and even legal assistance. By mid-century the city had German newspapers and German cultural organizations. Jews from southern Germany also found refuge in this community.

The Irish found work building railroads and cities. Baltimore was growing especially fast, with as many as two thousand new buildings being erected every year by mid-century. The Irish also found work as shopkeepers, clerks, and tavern owners. During the 1850's seven Roman Catholic churches had opened in Baltimore; four of them were predominantly Irish. The Irish also opened their own schools. Their devotion to Catholicism led to oppression by the Know-Nothing Party in Maryland, as in many other states in this period.

POST-CIVIL WAR IMMIGRATION

After the Civil War ended in 1865, cooperation between a German shipping line and a Germanic Maryland businessman named Albert Schumacher led to a large increase of Northern European immigrants who entered the United States through Baltimore on their way to western locations. However, many stayed in Baltimore. As the century waned, they were joined by Poles, Czechs, Ukrainians, and Greeks. Many Italian immigrants came to Baltimore from Philadelphia by rail and created a section of the city that became known as Little Italy. Significant numbers of Jews began arriving during the 1880's, fleeing religious persecution in Russia and Poland. Many of them established sweatshops, whose numbers reached two hundred in 1890. The shops also employed Lithuanians and Bohemians.

As in many other eastern states, foreign immigration into Maryland peaked shortly before World War I began in 1914. The war itself and new federal restrictions on immigration enacted during the 1920's severely retarded im-

PROFILE OF MARYLAND

Region	Atlantic coast
Entered union	1788
Largest cities	Baltimore, Columbia, Silver Spring
Modern immigrant communities	Mexicans, Chinese

Population	Total	Percent of state	Percent of U.S.	U.S. rank
All state residents	5,616,000	100.0	1.88	19
All foreign-born residents	683,000	12.2	1.82	12

Source: U.S. Census Bureau, *Statistical Abstract for 2006.*
Notes: The U.S. population in 2006 was 299,399,000, of whom 37,548,000 (12.5%) were foreign born. Rankings in last column reflect total numbers, not percentages.

migration into Maryland until after World War II. However, it would not be until the 1980's that foreign immigration again became significant in the state's development.

TWENTY-FIRST CENTURY TRENDS

In the year 2000, 10 percent of Maryland's residents were foreign born. This was the same percentage that the state had had in 1870. However, in 2000, 35 percent of the immigrants were Asians and 34 percent were Latin Americans. The bulk of the latter were Mexicans, who numbered about 40,000. Another change from nineteenth century immigration patterns was that the majority of newcomers settled not in Baltimore but in counties to its south and southwest. Prince George's and Montgomery Counties had the largest portions of foreign-born residents.

During the early years of the twenty-first century, Latin Americans—including Puerto Ricans who were already American citizens—overtook Asians as the largest immigrant group. However, Asians continued to enter the state in large numbers, and they were joined by African immigrants, who accounted for more than one-fifth of all new immigrants.

China has supplied the largest number of Asian immigrants during the twenty-first century, followed by Korea and Vietnam. The Latin American group contains the heaviest concentration of immigrants who do not speak English well. Hispanic immigrants have been especially evident in the construction trades. Asians are most often found in the professional, scientific, and technical areas.

Robert P. Ellis

FURTHER READING

Bode, Carl. *Maryland: A Bicentennial History.* New York: W. W. Norton, 1978.

Miller, Kerby A., et al. *Irish Immigrants in the Land of Canaan: Letters and Memoirs from Colonial and Revolutionary America, 1675-1815.* New York: Oxford University Press, 2003.

Olson, Sherry H. *Baltimore: The Building of an American City.* Baltimore: Johns Hopkins University Press, 1997.

Powell, Barbara M., and Michael A. Powell. *Mid-Maryland History: Conflict, Growth and Change.* Charleston, S.C.: History Press, 2008.

SEE ALSO: Asian immigrants; Chinese immigrants; German immigrants; Irish immigrants; Know-Nothing Party; Maryland; Virginia; Washington, D.C.

MASSACHUSETTS

> **SIGNIFICANCE:** Before New York Harbor's Ellis Island became the major East Coast immigration reception center in 1892, many European immigrants entered the United States through Boston, Massachusetts. Irish immigrants predominated during the middle decades of the nineteenth century, with large numbers of Italians arriving during the decades surrounding the turn of the twentieth century. Later immigration became much more diverse, with large influxes of Jamaicans, Portuguese-speaking peoples, and Chinese entering the state during the late twentieth century.

Populated chiefly by English settlers during its century-and-a-half existence as a British colony, Massachusetts attracted more immigrants from England, British North America, and Ireland during the early decades of the nineteenth century. By the 1840's, famine conditions in Ireland were provoking tens of thousands of Irish people to cross the Atlantic Ocean; most of them entered the United States through New York and Boston. These immigrants were mostly poor and had no means of traveling beyond the American cities in which they first arrived, but most of them had farmed small plots of land and had no experience working in an urban environment. In 1845, nearly one-third of all people living in Boston were either foreign born or children of foreign-born immigrants; many of these were from English backgrounds. By 1850, a large Irish influx had helped raise this figure to 45.7 percent in 1850. By 1855, more than one-half the people in Boston were immigrants and their children. Through most of that period, Irish immigrants outnumbered all other ethnic groups combined.

LATER IMMIGRANTS

Irish Americans gradually moved out of Boston into rural Massachusetts as men found work as farmhands and day laborers, but others became smiths, hostlers, stablers, carpenters, and waiters. Because these newcomers trusted and understood one another, many of them found work serving their neighbors as butchers, grocers, and tailors. One field of endeavor particularly open to Irish women was domestic help. In contrast to many other immigrants, Irish immigrants arrived in the United States already speaking English, and many young single women were satisfied to work for little more than their board and lodging.

The Irish who remained in poor and overcrowded conditions in Massachusetts cities increased disease and crime. Within the predominantly Protestant state, the immigrants' Roman Catholic religion was viewed with suspicion. In 1834, an Ursuline convent in Charlestown was attacked by a Protestant mob and burned to the ground. During the 1850's, a nativist movement known as the Know-Nothing Party raised fears that the devotion of Catholics to the pope would challenge American democracy. This movement was short-lived, but the fear of Catholics that it engendered persisted until 1960, when John F. Kennedy, of the Irish Catholic descent, ran for the presidency.

Catholic immigrants in Massachusetts generally maintained their religious affiliations, but Protestant immigrants often did not. Swedish immigrants, for example, were mostly Lutherans when they arrived, but when they could not easily find Lutheran congregations, they were inclined to turn to more convenient churches of other Protestant denominations. Other features of immigrants' culture reshaped and became part of the mainstream, but immigrants also shed features of culture that did not fit into the pattern of life in Massachusetts. Immigrants generally adopted mainstream clothing, food, music, and games, even when these differed considerably from those of their homelands.

The growth of large fabric mills throughout the nineteenth century brought many French Canadians into Massachusetts. Their form of Roman Catholicism was less unpopular in Massachusetts than that of the Irish, but their French-speaking children exerted a strain on an educational system with little experience of absorbing non-English-speaking children.

EARLY TWENTIETH CENTURY DEVELOPMENTS

During the years immediately preceding and following 1900, new waves of immigrants began entering Massachusetts: Jews from Russia, and non-English-speaking newcomers from southern and eastern Europe. The largest number came from Italy, and most of these came from southern Italy. Italians tended to live in ethnic enclaves in big cities, such as Boston's North End. They did not readily mix with established communities—either native-born residents or other immigrants. The Italians' darker skins set them apart from the Irish and German immigrants whom Massachusetts natives had already encountered.

Many first-generation Italian immigrant men worked at pick-and-shovel jobs in various locations. The women generally did not work outside their homes but often did piecework and sewing at home to supplement their husbands' incomes. Children were sent out to work as soon as they were old enough to take jobs. Some were taken out of school so they could go to work as early as possible.

Many immigrant workers determined that the Industrial Workers of the World (IWW)

PROFILE OF MASSACHUSETTS

Region	New England
Entered union	1788
Largest cities	Boston, Worcester, Springfield, Lowell, Cambridge
Modern immigrant communities	Mexicans, Brazilians, Portuguese, Chinese

Population	Total	Percent of state	Percent of U.S.	U.S. rank
All state residents	6,437,000	100.0	2.15	13
All foreign-born residents	908,000	14.1	2.41	8

Source: U.S. Census Bureau, *Statistical Abstract for 2006.*
Notes: The U.S. population in 2006 was 299,399,000, of whom 37,548,000 (12.5%) were foreign born. Rankings in last column reflect total numbers, not percentages.

French Canadian immigrants working at a Winchendon, Massachusetts, mill in 1911. (Library of Congress)

served their needs better than the American Federation of Labor. After the mostly unskilled immigrant workers received a pay cut in mills along the Merrimack River in Lawrence, the IWW organized a general strike on their behalf. The strike lasted two months during the winter of 1912 and led to violence and prosecution of workers. Before it ended, hundreds of Russian, Italian, and French Canadian laborers went back to their homelands.

Prospective immigrants, many of whom were family members and relatives of those who had come earlier, found new federal laws blocking them during the 1920's, particularly the Immigration Act of 1924, which reduced the number of admissible immigrants to 2 percent of the population from any country already living in the United States in 1890. This law virtually excluded new immigrants from southern and eastern European countries. The law also included an act specifically banning Asian populations entirely. Thus immigration for the next few decades consisted mainly of northern and western Europeans.

Late Twentieth Century Developments

In 1965, the U.S. Congress replaced the 1924 immigration law with one that based immigration standards not on race or nationality but on skills. This allowed many more southern and eastern Europeans to enter the country, as well as educated Asians who would make important contributions to the nation.

After 1965, immigration from the Caribbean increased, particularly from the English-speaking island nation of Jamaica. Many Jamaican professionals and skilled workers settled in Massachusetts. By the year 2000, most of the state's immigrants were coming from the Caribbean, Portugal, and Canada. A Northeastern University study covering

1999-2001 found that 47 percent of Massachusetts's immigrants possessed some post-secondary education, and 25 percent engaged in professional services. Among all skilled and semiskilled blue-collar workers in Massachusetts. 45 percent were foreign born.

A Census Bureau community survey in 2006 established Brazil, China, and Portugal (including Portuguese islands) as the top sources of Massachusetts immigration. Early during the twenty-first century only Florida attracted more Brazilians than Massachusetts. Brazilian immigrants found many jobs in food services, but a large portion of them were in professional services.

Robert P. Ellis

FURTHER READING

Handlin, Oscar. *Boston's Immigrants*. Cambridge, Mass.: Belknap Press, 1969. Study of Boston's immigrants up to the time of the Civil War by one of the leading scholars of American immigration history.

Puleo, Stephen. *The Boston Italians*. Boston: Beacon Press, 2007. Well-researched book on the history of one ethnic group settling in one large city.

Rivard, Paul E. *A New Order of Things: How the Textile Industry Transformed New England*. Hanover: University Press of New England, 2002. Detailed study of immigrant textile workers in Massachusetts by a former official of the American Textile History Museum in Lowell.

Solomon, Barbara Miller. *Ancestors and Immigrants: A Changing New England Tradition*. Cambridge, Mass.: Harvard University Press, 1956. Exploration of the development of restrictions on New England immigration between the 1850's and 1920's.

Ueda, Reed, and Conrad Edick Wright, eds. *Faces of Community: Immigrant Massachusetts, 1860-2000*. Boston: Massachusetts Historical Society, 2003. Collection of essays demonstrating how several immigrant groups adapted to their Massachusetts environment during the later nineteenth century.

Watson, Bruce. *Bread and Roses: Mills, Migrants, and the Struggle for the American Dream*. New York: Viking Press, 2005. Detailed look at the situation that confronted immigrant textile workers in Lowell during the early twentieth century.

SEE ALSO: Anti-Catholicism; Boston; Brazilian immigrants; Connecticut; German immigrants; Industrial Workers of the World; Mexican immigrants; Pilgrim and Puritan immigrants; Religions of immigrants; Women immigrants.

MELTING POT THEORY

DEFINITION: Idea that immigrants to the United States would be fused into one culture

SIGNIFICANCE: An idealistic view of cultural assimilation that was forced upon groups of immigrants during the early twentieth century, the melting pot theory was later discredited as more realistic perspectives concerning immigration prevailed.

The concept of the "melting pot" originated in the English Jewish dramatist Israel Zangwill's play *The Melting-Pot*, which was first performed in Washington, D.C., in 1908. Zangwill's play advanced the idea that a special social and cultural integration of immigrants occurred in America. In its reprocessing of William Shakespeare's sixteenth century play *Romeo and Juliet*, Zangwill's play depicts a pair of lovers from feuding Russian families who emigrate to the United States, where they find themselves and their families in a "crucible," in which all old antagonisms fall away and they become "refined" in their new American identity.

ASSIMILATION PRESSURES

Inspired by the notion that different cultural groups would be combined and blended to form a new composition, like metals being melded at great heat to become stronger alloys, the melting pot theory was enormously popular. Accordingly, the United States had been transformed repeatedly by earlier waves of immigrants, who, as loyal, patriotic Americans, contributed to America's progress. To facilitate this end, immigration laws were passed during the 1920's that restricted the immigration of members of ethnic groups that were more difficult to assimilate—those who would not "melt" together with Americans of western and northern European heritages.

American expectations of immigrants included a commitment to all things American. There was little tolerance of "hyphenated Americanism," such as "German-Americans." Immigrants were expected to learn to speak English and to divorce themselves completely from the countries of their birth. This "melting" into an American identity was embraced by many European immigrants, who, fleeing from poverty and prejudice, proclaimed intense loyalty to America in World War I and renounced their own ethnic identities.

The federal Immigration Act of 1924 severely restricted the immigration of Asians, southern and eastern Europeans, and Jews, ensuring that future immigration would come mostly from northern and western Europe. Consequently, the American identity resulting from the melting pot through the first half of the twentieth century retained an essentially white face. After World War II, however, federal immigration policy became less restrictive, allowing new ethnic variations.

Attitudes concerning assimilation had also modified, with more people supporting the idea of cultural pluralism that was first advanced by Horace Kallen and Randolph Bourne in 1915-1916. Cultural pluralism, in which smaller ethnic groups band together within a larger nation, allows members of the smaller groups to take pride in their own ethnic identities while remaining loyal to the host nation. Later, other assimilation theories appeared that included the "salad bowl" theory, suggesting the lettuce is the host country and the other ingredients represented various ethnic groups being assimilated into the dominant group.

AFTER 1965

Following the federal Civil Rights Act of 1964, which legally ended discrimination against members of racial minorities in public accommodations and other areas, and the expanded Immigration and Nationality Act of 1965, Americans held more tolerant attitudes toward other ethnicities and also had more negative views of the melting pot idea. Indeed, many prominent Americans began to denounce the "Americanization" of immigrants, and others, such as Nathan Glazer and Daniel P. Moynihan, made a major contribution to the national perspective

with their bestselling book *Beyond the Melting Pot* (1963), which argues that the melting pot had "never really happened." To support this argument, the book cites the ethnic enclaves in New York.

The 1965 immigration reform act that abolished the immigrant quotas and aimed at family reunification, allowed drastic increases in the number of immigrants and an extreme shift in the countries of their origin. During the late 1960's and 1970's, immigrants began coming in huge numbers from Latin America, the Philippines, and Asia—regions whose immigrants in the past had

Poster issued by the federal government during World War II reminding Americans of the positive contributions made to the nation by immigrants, while drawing upon the concept of the "melting pot." (NARA)

been restricted from entering the United States. However, assimilation has continued to occur in some form, although less it is less forced than it was during the early twentieth century, despite the resistance of some immigrants to being absorbed.

Among the factors that influence the rate of assimilation of immigrants are the education levels and resources that the immigrants bring with them. Not all who come to America are impoverished, uneducated, or persecuted. While the formal schooling of many Latin American immigrants is limited to an average of six or seven years, many immigrants from Asia, particularly those from India, have doctoral and medical degrees that permit them to move quickly into scientific and entrepreneurial positions. Korean immigrants have ranked high in ownership of independent businesses.

Multiculturalism, a controversial idea based on the idea that all cultures are of equal worth, has not been totally embraced in the United States. This has been particularly true since the terrorist attacks on the United States of September 11, 2001, that were made by Muslim extremists. Also, the American public has become increasingly concerned about the massive influx of Spanish-speaking Latin American and the impact they are having on American society. In fact, during the early twenty-first century, the issue of immigration was again becoming a contentious one, with several writers denouncing multiculturalism as a barrier to a return to the melting pot idea with its insistence upon the continuity of American beliefs and values.

Mary G. Hurd

FURTHER READING

Jacoby, Tamar, ed. *Reinventing the Melting Pot: The New Immigrants and What It Means to Be an American.* New York: Perseus Books Group, 2004. Collection of essays reflecting diverse attitudes toward assimilation.

Namias, June. *First Generation: In the Words of Twentieth-Century American Immigrants.* Rev. ed. Champaign: University of Illinois Press, 1992. In their own words, American immigrants recount the issues that compelled them to come to America.

Sanabria, Robert. *Stewing in the Melting Pot: The Memoir of a Real American.* Sterling, Va.: Capital Books, 2002. Relates the author's childhood experience of being forced to assimilate in a Methodist-operated orphanage for Latino children in Los Angeles during the Great Depression.

Sue, Derald Wing, and David Sue. *Counseling the Culturally Diverse: Theory and Practice.* Hoboken, N.J.: John Wiley & Sons, 2002. Controversial study that aims to raise awareness of discriminatory and racist behavior in the United States as the basis of counseling individuals from diverse cultures.

Susser, Ida, and Thomas C. Patterson, eds. *Cultural Diversity in the United States: A Critical Reader.* Hoboken, N.J.: Wiley Blackwell, 2001. Collection of essays that explore cultural diversity through examining complex connections between race, ethnicity, class, and gender.

SEE ALSO: Assimilation theories; Cultural pluralism; Ethnic enclaves; European immigrants; Hansen effect; Identificational assimilation; Immigration and Nationality Act of 1965; Multiculturalism; *A Nation of Immigrants.*

MEXICAN AMERICAN LEGAL DEFENSE AND EDUCATIONAL FUND

IDENTIFICATION: National nonprofit whose mission is to protect the civil rights of Latinos in the United States

DATE: Founded in 1968

SIGNIFICANCE: The Mexican American Legal Defense and Educational Fund advocates for the nearly 45 million Latinos living in the United States, providing legal assistance, educational support, and employment assistance. It is the leading Latino civil rights organization in the United States.

The Mexican American Legal Defense and Educational Fund (MALDEF) was founded in 1968 by Pete Tijerina, a civil rights attorney working with the League of United Latin American Citizens (LULAC). Impressed with the work of the Legal Defense Fund, a project of the National Association for the Advancement of Colored People

(NAACP), he concluded that Mexican Americans needed a similar source of organization and funding to protect their civil rights. With a five-year, $2.2 million grant from the Ford Foundation, Tijerina and a board of directors established MALDEF, with headquarters in San Antonio, Texas, and offices in Arizona, California, Colorado, and New Mexico. The grant was to support the legal defense of Mexican Americans' civil rights, with $250,000 set aside for scholarships to Chicano law students. MALDEF also received a pledge of support and guidance from the more experienced Legal Defense Fund. By 2009, MALDEF had additional offices in Chicago, Atlanta, and Washington, D.C.

According to its mission statement, MALDEF works to ensure "that there are no obstacles preventing [Latinos] from realizing [their] dreams" and "to secure the rights of Latinos, primarily in the areas of employment, education, immigrants' rights, political access, and public resource equity." To accomplish its goals, MALDEF operates several targeted programs. Its Employment and Equal Opportunity Program helps Latino workers obtain fair wages and benefits by educating workers about their rights and by litigating against illegal discrimination. The Parent School Partnership and Community Education and Leadership Development programs help people understand and advocate for their rights. The Public Resource Equity Program works to ensure that Latino communities receive their fair share of public funding and other public resources; to support child-care programs, domestic violence shelters, health clinics, and other programs; and to see that there are enough bilingual staff members at appropriate agencies to assist Latinos in understanding their rights and responsibilities.

MALDEF's legal division has won several important cases, helping to protect the rights of Latinos on issues of language and access to medical care and housing. It successfully fought to overturn California's Proposition 187 (1994), which was designed to bar illegal immigrants from public education, health care, and social services. MALDEF also fought against the expansion of authority of the U.S. Border Patrol and against illegal voter redistricting in Los Angeles that would have weakened Latino political power. It has convened meetings and litigated cases regarding the rights of guest workers and has filed suits to clarify and limit the authority of the Immigration and Naturalization

Service (later U.S. Citizenship and Immigration Services) to conduct searches. In addition to legal work, MALDEF has sponsored radio spots in Spanish to help new immigrants navigate their new environment.

Cynthia A. Bily

FURTHER READING

Acosta, Teresa Palomo, and Ruthe Winegarten. *Las Tejanas: Three Hundred Years of History.* Austin: University of Texas Press, 2003.

Chavez, Linda. *Out of the Barrio: Toward a New Politics of Hispanic Assimilation.* New York: Basic Books, 1991.

Storey, John W., and Mary L. Kelley. *Twentieth-Century Texas: A Social and Cultural History.* Denton: University of North Texas Press, 2008.

SEE ALSO: Border Patrol, U.S.; Chicano movement; Civil Rights movement; Guest-worker programs; Immigrant aid organizations; Immigration and Naturalization Service, U.S.; Latinos and immigrants; Mexican immigrants; Proposition 187; Sociedad Progresista Mexicana.

MEXICAN DEPORTATIONS OF 1931

THE EVENT: Mass deportations of Mexican immigrant workers in order to redistribute jobs to U.S. citizens during the Great Depression

DATE: January-September, 1931

LOCATION: Primarily Los Angeles County, California

> **SIGNIFICANCE:** The deportations highlighted white Americans' anti-immigrant sentiments and encouraged resentment on behalf of both Mexican nationals and Mexican Americans.

After the Great Depression struck in 1929, rapidly rising unemployment provoked white Americans to perceive Mexican nationals and even Mexican Americans as the main source of competition for jobs. Anti-immigrant, and particularly anti-Mexican, sentiment was on the rise, as white Americans deemed themselves more worthy of relief aid and jobs than "foreigners" in the country.

In order to quell white Americans' anxiety and desperation during the Great Depression, Secretary of Labor William N. Doak, under the administration of President Herbert Hoover, enacted various policies to repatriate at least 100,000 deportable Mexicans of the 400,000 undocumented Mexican immigrants in the United States. The purpose of repatriation was to send idle Mexican workers back to their homeland, save social welfare agencies money, and produce jobs for white Americans. The first nine months of 1931 saw the greatest numbers of Mexicans leaving the United States at once, especially from the Los Angeles area. Authorities such as Charles P. Visel, director of the Los Angeles Citizens' Committee on Coordination of Unemployment Relief, took actions to create a hostile environment for Mexican immigrants to "encourage" their repatriation. Consequently, both ordered and "voluntary" repatriations ensued, as some Mexican nationals sought refuge from increased unemployment and discrimination in the United States, while others were forced to leave.

THE DEPORTATIONS

The mass exodus may have affected as many as two million people of Mexican ancestry, half of whom had been born in the United States. Authorities ignored the fact that some of the repatriated people were naturalized U.S. citizens and that others were citizens by virtue of birth in the United States. Merely having a Spanish surname could subject a person to screening. Deportation raids of public and private spaces occurred all over the country, as Mexicans were not isolated to specific regions, working in both industrial sectors as well as migrant farmworker communities.

The federal government allowed cities, counties, and states to manage repatriation as deemed necessary. Nativism and xenophobia during this period caused inhumane treatment of Mexicans in the United States, as people were repatriated ruthlessly via various modes of transportation, including ships, trains, cars, trucks, and buses. Parents were torn from their children, and husbands and wives were separated. Hospital patients, mentally ill people, and elderly people were also repatriated. Altogether, Mexican families and even those with American citizens as their members were torn apart.

Nonetheless, some American groups were opposed to these repatriations, especially the ranchers and agricultural growers in the Southwest who needed Mexicans as a source of cheap and exploitable labor. Mexicans, these growers claimed, did the work that other Americans were unwilling to do. The repatriation policy threatened the businesses of these growers, as they could lose crops. Merchants too realized that Mexicans were integral to their businesses. During the repatriations, merchants lost profits from their loyal Mexican customers. Moreover, bankers were concerned as Mexicans withdrew their money as they anticipated repatriation. Despite such opposition, repatriates continued to be pushed southward.

Sara A. Ramírez

FURTHER READING
Acuña, Rodolfo F. *Occupied America: A History of Chicanos.* 6th ed. New York: Pearson Longman, 2007.
Balderrama, Francisco, and Raymond Rodríguez. *Decade of Betrayal: Mexican Repatriation in the 1930's.* Rev. ed. Albuquerque: University of New Mexico Press, 2006.
Vargas, Zaragosa. *Labor Rights Are Civil Rights: Mexican American Workers in Twentieth-Century America.* Princeton, N.J.: Princeton University Press, 2005.

SEE ALSO: Border Patrol, U.S.; Bracero program; Chicano movement; Contract labor system; Deportation; El Paso incident; Great Depression; Guestworker programs; Los Angeles; Mexican immigrants; Operation Wetback; Xenophobia.

MEXICAN IMMIGRANTS

SIGNIFICANCE: Mexican immigrants represent the largest minority ethnic group in the United States and differ from other immigrant groups in the nearness of their home country, which makes movement back and forth easier and makes their culture more visible within American society.

Mexico was originally inhabited by Native American peoples who originated in Asia many millennia before the first European explorers and settlers

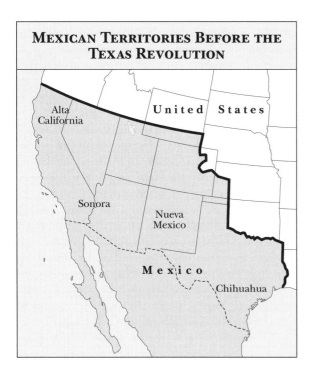

MEXICAN TERRITORIES BEFORE THE TEXAS REVOLUTION

arrived in the Western Hemisphere. The Native American peoples developed advanced cultures that gave rise to civilizations such as those of the Aztecs and Mayas in what are now Mexico and Central America that were responsible for impressive achievements in technology and mathematics. These civilizations were eventually conquered by Spain during the early sixteenth century. The Spanish introduced their language and the Roman Catholic religion to the original inhabitants of Mexico. Over time, the newcomers mixed with the Native peoples and created the mestizo, or mixed-race, peoples who would become known as modern Mexicans.

Spanish Mexico, or New Spain, extended well into the southwestern parts of what is now the United States, and those regions became part of Mexico when that country won its independence in 1821. However, American settlers wrested Texas from Mexico during the 1830's, and the American victory in the Mexican War of 1846-1848 cost Mexico California, Arizona, New Mexico, and parts of what would become other U.S. states. In one stroke, the Treaty of Guadalupe Hidalgo that settled the war transformed about 85,000 Mexican citizens into the largest minority ethnic group in U.S. territory.

PUSH-PULL FACTORS

Beginning in 1910 with the building of the railroad across the Sonoran Desert, the first wave of Mexican migration was ushered in with the flow of Mexicans "pushed" by the lack of jobs in Mexico under the president-dictator Porfirio Díaz. Moreover, with the large-scale irrigation project of the Colorado Desert in California, agriculture became a lucrative business in the Southwest. Many Mexicans were enticed to the area for jobs in agribusiness, where fruit and vegetable pickers were required in the San Joaquin Valley of California, the Lower Rio Grande Valley of Texas, and the Salt River Valley of Arizona. In addition, similar agribusinesses created jobs for picking sugar beets in Minnesota, Colorado, and Michigan. Besides the sugar beet, Michigan's car industry drew Mexican workers toward the assembly lines of Detroit, where in 1914 Henry Ford paid a daily wage of five dollars.

Another factor pushing Mexicans to go north was the Mexican Revolution that began in 1910 and kept Mexico in a state of virtual civil war into the late 1920's and devastated the country. In the face of violent upheavals, unemployment, and hunger, as many as 2 million Mexicans may have immigrated to the United States by the late 1920's. During the year 1923 alone, an average of 1,000 people crossed the border every day.

WORLD WAR I

In August, 1914, World War I began in Europe, pitting Germany against Great Britain and France and other nations. The United States remained neutral, but in early 1917, an incident involving Mexico occurred that helped to draw the United States into the war. Germany's foreign secretary, Arthur Zimmerman, sent a telegram to Mexico's President Venustiano Carranza in which he offered Germany's pledge to restore to Mexico the U.S. states of Texas, New Mexico, and Arizona in return for Mexico's cooperation with Germany in the event that the United States entered the war. The telegram was intercepted by the British, who passed it along to the U.S. government. The government had the contents of the telegram published in newspapers across the United States. In addition to helping President Woodrow Wilson take the United States into the war, the telegram helped launch a new era of American distrust of Mexicans.

Later that same year, the U.S. Congress passed the Immigration Act of 1917, which imposed an eight-dollar head tax on each immigrant—a hefty impost on Mexican immigrants. The new law also added a literacy test, which made it even more difficult for many Mexicans to enter the United States legally. However, although American suspicions of Mexicans were high, the U.S. entry into World War I created a worker shortage in the United States that forced American employers to look to Mexico for labor. After relaxing the literacy requirement and the head tax, the U.S. Department of Labor set up a system with the agribusiness companies, in which each company could apply for the number of Mexican laborers it required, thereby creating a government-controlled guest-worker program. This arrangement differed from later bracero programs in that it did not guarantee worker protections or wage increases. To ensure that Mexican workers returned to Mexico, the Labor Department held part of their pay until they were back in Mexico.

REPATRIATION

The 1920's saw the first major wave of Mexican immigration, but after the stock market crash of 1929 started the Great Depression, those numbers began reversing. Mexicans became the scapegoats for job losses in the United States, and impover-

---

PROFILE OF MEXICAN IMMIGRANTS

Country of origin	Mexico
Primary language	Spanish
Primary regions of U.S. settlement	California, Texas, southwestern states
Earliest significant arrivals	Pre-1776
Peak immigration periods	1923-1930, 1992-1996
Twenty-first century legal residents*	1,389,201 (173,650 per year)

*Immigrants who obtained legal permanent resident status in the United States.

Source: Department of Homeland Security, *Yearbook of Immigration Statistics, 2008.*

---

ished American farmers in the Midwest, which was devastated by dust bowl conditions, began migrating west in search of seasonal agricultural work that had previously been done mostly by immigrants. By 1934, more than half of California's crop pickers were white American migrant workers.

Meanwhile, additional resentment fell on American citizens of Mexican descent who were receiving federal benefits in New Deal programs during the Depression, and Mexican Americans were blamed for using taxpayer money. The federal government came under pressure to send Mexicans back to Mexico. Deportation required time-consuming legal proceedings, so the government engaged in tactics designed to intimidate Mexicans into leaving the country voluntarily. However, in 1931, the government began instituting legal proceedings to deport Mexicans who were found to have violated the conditions of their visas.

In February, 1931, agents of the U.S. Department of Labor began staging public raids across California's Los Angeles County, using local police to help identify Mexicans. Persons who could not produce documentation of their American citizenship or valid passports were bused to the Mexican border. In their haste to round up suspected Mexican nationals, government agents sent some American citizens and persons of Asian ancestry to Mexico.

The mass deportations had the desired effect of creating the fear of expulsion in the minds of Mexican immigrants, many of whom began accepting offers of free passage to Mexico. Eventually, Los Angeles set up county-sponsored trains that provided free transportation to all the Mexicans who wished to leave the country voluntarily. Many of those sent to Mexico were later unable to prove their American citizenship, which they consequently lost.

BRACERO PROGRAM

After the United States entered World War II at the end of 1941, Mexican workers were again persuaded to migrate north to fill jobs left by American workers who had entered the armed forces or gone to work in the expanding defense industry. Since 1917, the Mexican government had tried, with little success, to ensure that Mexicans working in the United States would receive better treatment. By 1942, however, the U.S. government was

Mexican immigrants passing through the border station at El Paso, Texas, in 1938. (Library of Congress)

finally ready to pay attention to the Mexican demands. In July, 1942, the U.S. and Mexican governments signed an accord in Mexico City to create the bracero program, in which the U.S. government would take responsibility for overseeing and protecting Mexicans working in the United States under the program. Between 1942 and 1947, more than 200,000 bracero workers were employed across the United States; more than half of them worked in California's agricultural fields.

Criticisms of the bracero program soon emerged. Most of the conditions for workers that Mexico had set were not met. Substandard housing of the workers was a particular problem, but this was remedied in 1943 when new housing units were built by the federal government. Another criticism was the failure of wage rates to increase along with those in areas where braceros were not working, such as Texas. Another criticism of the program was that it encouraged illegal immigration by workers who did not return to Mexico when they completed their contracts. When the program was finally ended by the U.S. government in 1964, Mexico was left with the problem of having large numbers of workers who needed employment.

OPERATION WETBACK

During the early 1950's, the U.S. Immigration and Naturalization Service (INS) was urged by President Dwight D. Eisenhower to begin deporting illegal immigrants. In June, 1953, the INS began a series of surprise raids in the program dubbed "Operation Wetback." The program continued into the following year and was publicized. In contrast to the mass repatriations of the early 1930's, the INS made sure that the people sent back to Mexico were released at points five hundred to one thousand miles south of the border to discourage them

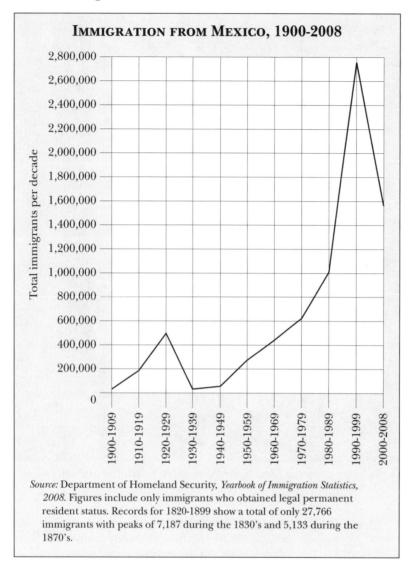

IMMIGRATION FROM MEXICO, 1900-2008

Source: Department of Homeland Security, *Yearbook of Immigration Statistics, 2008.* Figures include only immigrants who obtained legal permanent resident status. Records for 1820-1899 show a total of only 27,766 immigrants with peaks of 7,187 during the 1830's and 5,133 during the 1870's.

groups, Mexicans are often stereotyped as scofflaws and miscreants. At ports of entry along the border, Mexicans were historically forced to undergo humiliating body searches. Moreover, Mexican border posts were the only ports of entry into the United States that forced new arrivals to undergo delousing. During the swine flu outbreak in 2009, fears of Mexicans bringing the disease over the border were common throughout the United States, with many Americans renewing calls for the erection of a border wall.

Shannon Oxley

FURTHER READING

Andreas, Peter. *Border Games: Policing the U.S.-Mexico Divide.* Ithaca, N.Y.: Cornell University Press, 2001. Scholarly study of issues surrounding the policing of the U.S.-Mexican border.

Gutierrez, David G. *Walls and Mirrors: Mexican Americans, Mexican Immigrants, and the Politics of Ethnicity.* Berkeley: University of California Press, 1995. Discusses the issue of race in Mexican and Mexican American identities.

from returning to the United States. Once again, many of the people who were deported were American citizens, and again families were torn apart by the deportations. At least 300,000 people were returned to Mexico, and as many as 1 million more were stopped from entering the United States at the border.

ANTI-MEXICAN SENTIMENTS

Stereotypes about "wetbacks"—a derogatory term for illegal Mexican immigrants—stealing American jobs are perpetuated in political circles, and they increase in frequency during economic recessions. Like members of other immigrant

Hoffman, Abraham. *Unwanted Mexican Americans in the Great Depression: Repatriation Pressures, 1929-1939.* Tucson: University of Arizona Press, 1974. Comprehensive study of the massive repatriation of Mexicans during the Great Depression, with detailed data from each state that was involved

Jones, Maldwyn A. *American Immigration.* 2d ed. Chicago: University of Chicago Press, 1992. Objective historical summary of immigration in the United States, providing general information about Mexican immigration.

Meier, Matt S., and Feliciano Ribera. *Mexican Americans/American Mexicans: From Conquistadors to*

Chicanos. 2d ed. Toronto: HarperCollins Canada, 1993. Thorough summary of Mexican immigration, from the earliest Spanish conquests to the modern Chicano movement. Includes concise accounts of the Depression-era repatriation and the bracero program.

Moquin, Wayne, and Charles Van Doren, eds. *A Documentary History of the Mexican Americans.* New York: Praeger Publishers, 1971. Detailed history of Mexican ties to the United States, with full histories of Mexicans in New Mexico, California, and Texas.

Rodriguez, Gregory. *Mongrels, Bastards, Orphans, and Vagabonds: Mexican Immigration and the Future of Race in America.* New York: Pantheon Books, 2007. Broad overview of immigration law and Mexican identity in United States history.

Telles, Edward, and Vilma Ortiz. *Generations of Exclusion: Mexican Americans, Assimilation and Race.* New York: Russell Sage Foundation, 2008. Good investigation of four decades of the Mexican American experience.

See also: Border fence; Bracero program; Chicano movement; Farm and migrant workers; Latin American immigrants; Latinos and immigrants; Mexican American Legal Defense and Educational Fund; Mexican deportations of 1931; Mexican Revolution; Operation Wetback; Sociedad Progresista Mexicana; Spanish-language press.

Mexican Revolution

The Event: Political and military struggle that overthrew Mexico's dictator and prompted a mass migration to the United States
Date: 1910 to 1928
Location: Mexico

Significance: Aimed against the ruling classes, the violent Mexican Revolution overthrew a dictatorship that had lasted thirty-four years and ushered in more than a decade of political and social disorder that impelled many Mexicans to seek sanctuary in the United States.

Mexico experienced a violent revolution from 1910 to 1928. Initially, rebels sought to overthrow the dictator Porfirio Díaz, who had been in power since 1876. The disparity between rich and poor was significant in the country, with 75 percent of the population living off agriculture but owning only 5 percent of the land. Díaz had essentially placed control of the country in the hands of the landed class, foreign companies, and the Roman Catholic Church, which was allowed to control its extensive landholdings. The revolution erupted in 1910 under the leadership of an idealistic banker named Francisco I. Madero, whose supporters included the famous peasant warriors Emiliano Zapata and Pancho Villa. Those surrounding Díaz were primarily white elitist Mexicans who rejected the contributions of the 80 percent majority of the population who were Indians or mixed-blood mestizos. The goal of the revolution was to implement land reform, expel dominant foreign companies, and limit the power of the Church. Díaz was quickly defeated, but Madero's assassination in 1913 was followed by a violent struggle among the remaining leaders.

During a decade and a half of almost constant civil war—resulting in the death of more than 250,000 Mexicans, the burning of farms and factories, and the destruction of villages and cities—Mexico's economic stability was shattered. Both revolutionaries and those of the former ruling classes were left in disarray. As a result, a wave of immigrants began to cross into the United States. In 1909, fewer than 5,000 Mexicans had immigrated to the United States. However, after the revolution began during the following year, that figure jumped to nearly 90,000 immigrants per year. The revolution caused a state of constant turmoil in Mexico, especially among the landless peasants, but from 1914, when the fiercest period of fighting began, even the upper classes began to immigrate in significant numbers. By 1920, more than 900,000 Mexicans had fled north.

U.S. Reaction

During this same period, the U.S. Congress was concerned with the mass of immigrants coming into the United States from southern and eastern Europe. As a result, Congress passed the Immigration Act of 1917, which required immigrants over the age of sixteen to be literate in English or in their own languages. American agricultural interests successfully lobbied the government to exempt Mexican immigrants from the law's provisions; thus, the flow of Mexicans to serve as agricultural laborers and railroad workers continued unimpeded. Because the Immigration Act of 1921 did not set quotas for immigrants from Latin America, thousands of Mexicans entered the United States on permanent visas annually, with 1924 being the peak year, when 100,000 Mexican immigrants arrived.

In 1917, Mexico's revolutionary government enacted a new constitution that gave to the state control of all land distribution and outlawed foreign ownership of land. It also severely limited the rights of the Roman Catholic Church. It nationalized all Church lands, prohibited the Church from any role in education, and limited the power of the clergy, requiring priests to register with the state. Under revolutionary president Plutarco Elías Calles (1924-1928), the new constitution was harshly implemented, resulting in a revolt of the clergy and their followers in a second stage of the revolution that became known as the Cristero War (1926-1929). This conflict continued the large emigrant flow into the United States, with many immigrants considering themselves to be religious refugees.

The eighteen years of the Mexican Revolution resulted in the first major wave of Mexican immigrants into the United States, totaling nearly two million. These immigrants found life in the United States somewhat natural, as the Southwest, where most of them eventually settled, had for two hundred years been part of Spain or Mexico.

Raymond J. Gonzales

FURTHER READING

Gonzales, Michael J. *The Mexican Revolution, 1910-1940.* Albuquerque: University of New Mexico Press, 2002.

Meyer, Jean A. *The Cristero Rebellion: The Mexican People Between Church and State, 1926-1929.* New York: Cambridge University Press, 1976.

Womack, John. *Zapata and the Mexican Revolution.* New York: Alfred A. Knopf, 1968.

SEE ALSO: Bracero program; Chicago; History of immigration after 1891; Illinois; Immigration Act of 1921; Latin American immigrants; Latinos and immigrants; Mexican immigrants.

MIAMI

IDENTIFICATION: Largest city in South Florida and a major transportation and immigration hub

SIGNIFICANCE: Miami is the major hub of Latin American and Caribbean immigration to the United States, and the immigrant communities have both transformed the city and turned it into a nexus between the United States and its southern neighbors. The city is a hybrid of American and Latino cultures, with many immigrants maintaining close economic and political ties to their native lands.

Miami is the third-largest immigrant city in the United States, after New York and Los Angeles, but differs significantly from those two metropolises in that the immigrant population is still largely concentrated into enclaves, with the Cuban contingent outnumbering the others by a significant margin. Cuban immigration after Fidel Castro's revolution of 1959 transformed the city's economy, society, and politics. Cuban migration to the United States usually involved three generations of parents, children, and at least one elderly relative. The typical Cuban immigrant to Miami was born in a large urban center. Havana alone was home to more than half of those who arrived between 1959 and 1963. One-third of the heads of households who arrived in the United States between 1960 and 1962 had been proprietors or managers back in Cuba, while others came from the ranks of lawyers, doctors, judges, and skilled or semiskilled workers. More than 96 percent were Hispanic whites.

The 1970 U.S. Census estimated that of the one million Cubans who had migrated to the United States since 1959, more than 80 percent had settled in Miami. The exiles of this generation mainly settled in the Riverside neighborhood that came to be known as Little Havana. The biggest consignment came to Miami during the first three years of the Castro regime, and next during the so-called freedom flights of 1965-1973. A huge wave of immigration, estimated at 200,000, occurred in 1980 with the Mariel boatlift. However, after 1980 Cuban immigration once again slowed down to a trickle, until the rafters' crisis of 1994, when Cubans tried to make their way to Miami by using small, makeshift boats; eventually, some thirty thousand were granted permanent residence in the United States, mostly in the Miami area.

Cuban American immigration to Miami gave an enormous boost to a city that as late as the 1940's was seen as only a vacation spot. Cuban Americans became architects, bankers, doctors, and teachers, as well as blue-collar workers. By 2006, close to 800,000 Cubans were living in Miami-Dade County, constituting three-quarters of the Cuban American population in the United States. Ties of language, religion, and the experience of exile led many to see themselves not as part of a larger Latino or Hispanic community but rather as Cuban residents of Miami. The average Cuban adult in Miami by the end of the twentieth century earned an annual income greater than his Anglo-American neighbors, and Cuban women were more likely to participate in the labor force than any other Hispanic females. Graduation rates for both high school and college also surpassed those of the rest of the city population. As more Cuban immigrants became naturalized citizens, they flexed their political muscle. Their anti-Castro politics persuaded most Cubans to vote Republican in local, state, and national elections. In 1985, Miami elected its first Cuban American mayor, Xavier Suarez, who delivered on his promise to make the city a nexus of trade between the United States and Latin America in everything from luxury cars to shoes.

LATIN AMERICAN AND CARIBBEAN IMMIGRATION AFTER 1980

Political upheaval in Latin America and the Caribbean after 1980 brought new immigrant groups to Miami in large numbers. Nicaraguans fleeing their country's Sandinista revolution of 1979 arrived by the thousands, but many were forced by the U.S. government to return home following the defeat of the Sandinistas in elections in 1990. However, others stayed on, particularly in the downtown neighborhoods around Flagler Street. Colombians seeking refuge from the thirty-year-old civil war at home also migrated to Miami, taking up many of the blue-collar jobs previously held by Cubans. However, it was Haitian immigration during the 1990's, following the installation and then overthrow of President Jean-Bertrand Aristide, that had the greatest impact on the city's ethnic composition. Concentrated in a northeastern neighborhood of the city that soon came to be dubbed Little Haiti, Haitian immigrants faced ostracism from both the Hispanic and African American communities—the stigma associated with the spread of AIDS in Haiti was particularly harmful—but some were able to climb into the Miami middle class and even attain elected office.

At the start of the new millennium, Miami still resembled the salad bowl rather than melting pot model of immigration and settlement in the United States. Nevertheless, outright physical friction between immigrant groups was rare, and the city's reputation as the economic capital of the Caribbean continued to draw tens of thousands of migrants per year, making Miami one of the largest Latin American cities in the Western Hemisphere.

Julio César Pino

FURTHER READING

Allman, T. D. *Miami: City of the Future.* New York: Atlantic Monthly Press, 1987. History of the city during the twentieth century that stresses the ability of immigrants to assimilate while maintaining a separate cultural identity.

Didion, Joan. *Miami.* New York: Simon & Schuster, 1987. The famed novelist presents a nonfiction account of Miami as a Third World city located in the United States that holds Cuban immigrants responsible for extremist politics.

Grenier, Guillermo J., and Alex Stepick, eds. *Miami Now! Immigration, Ethnicity and Social Change.* Gainesville: University Press of Florida, 1992. This collection of essays stresses how Latin American immigration has turned Miami into a de facto capital city of Latin America, with frequent racial and political upheaval but also cooperation among groups.

Portes, Alejandro, and Alex Stepick. *City on the Edge: The Transformation of Miami.* Berkeley: University of California Press, 1993. Optimistic look at how the post-1980 wave of Cuban immigrants and later arrivals, including Haitians and Nicaraguans, has forged a more tolerant Miami.

Shell-Weiss, Melanie. *Coming to Miami: A Social History.* Gainesville: University Press of Florida, 2009. History of immigration to Miami since 1880 that emphasizes the struggle of Cubans, Haitians, and other Latin American peoples for citizenship and labor rights.

Michigan

SEE ALSO: Colombian immigrants; Cuban immigrants; Florida; Freedom Airlift; González case; Haitian immigrants; Latin American immigrants; Little Havana; Mariel boatlift; West Indian immigrants.

MICHIGAN

SIGNIFICANCE: Michigan's closeness to Canada has always made Canada its chief source of foreign immigrants. The harshness of the land and weather on the Upper Peninsula made farming impossible, so that immigrants did not come in large numbers until mining and logging became profitable.

French fur traders and missionaries from Montreal began working in what is now the state of Michigan during the seventeenth century. France later built forts at the Straits of Mackinac in 1671 and at the site of Detroit in 1701. After the American Revolution, several hundred French Canadian farmers settled at Detroit. Political difficulties in Ontario and a financial depression in Canada led to the immigration of more Canadians. By 1870, Canadians constituted the largest out-of-state group in Michigan's "thumb" area between Saginaw Bay and Lake Huron; they were also numerically predominant in the northern half of the Lower Peninsula. German immigrants were also numerous, especially after the failed European revolutions of 1848. However, Yankees, who came from New York and New England via the Erie Canal and the lakes via steamship after 1832, often dominated politics and business.

The Upper Peninsula's economy boomed during the last years of the nineteenth century and the first decades of the twentieth. Iron mining in the western part of the peninsula brought Finns, and logging brought Swedes, Irish, Italians, various eastern Europeans, and more Canadians. Most of the latter were French Canadian lumberjacks. During the early twentieth century, newspapers in the Upper Peninsula were published in Italian, Finnish, Swedish, and other languages. However, the forests and mines were exhausted by 1920, and many immigrants moved elsewhere. The region lost population between 1920 and 1930, from around 333,000 to 319,000.

With the growth of the automotive industry, Detroit's position on the Great Lakes, close to transportation from steel mills, led to a new wave of immigration. By 1930, Poles were the largest group of international immigrants, followed by Italians, Russians, Hungarians, Romanians, and Greeks. They were also joined by African Americans eager to leave the segregated South, and by whites from southern Appalachia.

LATE TWENTIETH CENTURY DEVELOPMENTS

In 1960, Michigan counted almost 400,000 residents who still spoke their ancestral languages at home. Half of them lived in Detroit. There, Polish was the most common foreign language, followed by German, Italian, French, and Hungarian. About 26,000 German speakers lived between Detroit and Saginaw Bay, and 26,000 Dutch speakers remained in the Holland colonies. In the Upper Peninsula remained between seven and nine thousand speakers each of Russian, Swedish, Ukrainian, and Finnish. In southern Michigan, the English that was spoken often re-

PROFILE OF MICHIGAN

Region	Upper Midwest
Entered union	1837
Largest cities	Detroit, Grand Rapids, Warren, Flint, Sterling Heights, Lansing (capital), Ann Arbor
Modern immigrant communities	Canadians

Population	Total	Percent of state	Percent of U.S.	U.S. rank
All state residents	10,096,000	100.0	3.37	8
All foreign-born residents	599,000	5.9	1.59	15

Source: U.S. Census Bureau, *Statistical Abstract for 2006.*
Notes: The U.S. population in 2006 was 299,399,000, of whom 37,548,000 (12.5%) were foreign born. Rankings in last column reflect total numbers, not percentages.

flected Yankee influences, but farther north Canadian accents could be heard.

Michigan's location continued to make the state an attractive target for Canadians even after World War II. As late as 1980, Canada was the largest source of foreign-born residents. In 2000, almost 39,000 Michigan residents—most probably from Canada's Quebec province—reported speaking French at home.

Timothy C. Frazer

FURTHER READING

May, George S. *Michigan: A History of the Wolverine State.* Grand Rapids, Mich.: William B. Eerdmans, 1995.

_____. *Michigan: The Great Lakes State.* Sun Valley, Calif.: American Historical Press, 2005.

Michigan: Collected Works of the Federal Writers' Project. Bel Air, Calif.: Reprint Services Corporation, 1991.

SEE ALSO: Arab immigrants; Canadian immigrants; Dutch immigrants; German immigrants; Labor unions; Linguistic contributions; Muslim immigrants; New York State; Polish immigrants.

"MIDDLEMAN" MINORITIES

DEFINITION: Members of an identifiable ethnic, religious, linguistic, or cultural group that occupies an intermediate economic and social prestige position between the domestic minority and the dominant majority

SIGNIFICANCE: "Middleman" minorities form significant economic bridges between generally poorer classes of consumers and generally wealthier classes of producers. Such minorities are often involved in small-scale retail operations or other entrepreneurial activities to provide goods and services to underserved populations.

The term "middleman minority" first became common among American sociologists during the 1960's. It describes the status and function of minority groups, whether recent immigrants or long-standing residents, who serve the retail and small commercial needs of dominant minority groups, whose members themselves have little access to the economic and social status of the majority group. The term "petty retailers" has historically been applied to middleman minorities in the United States who open small retail stores to provide basic commodities in low-income and predominantly minority neighborhoods that larger retailers and service providers tend to avoid.

DISTRIBUTION AND CHARACTERISTICS

Middleman minorities can be found around the globe. Their ethnic and cultural designations vary among the groups that form the dominant minorities within any given society. Middleman minorities throughout the world exhibit several shared characteristics. For example, members of primarily middleman minorities tend to be self-employed or work for members of their own ethnic groups until they begin their own entrepreneurial activities. Their businesses tend to be small and financed initially by ethnic aid groups. Middleman minorities have limited access to the dominant majority to buy resources, but the access they do have tends to be greater than that of the dominant minority. The middleman minorities resell these goods and services to minority populations with whom they have only transactional relationships. Members of middleman minorities rarely attempt to form social ties with members of the larger minority group in a culture.

Members of middleman minorities share a number of personal characteristics as well. For example, they tend to be hard workers and long-term planners and savers. They also tend to have strong beliefs in the value of education for their children, even when they themselves have had little formal education or opportunity to penetrate the social networks of the majority group in a culture. Education is rarely the success factor for first-generation middleman minorities. Likewise, neither is political activism. Hard work and capital accumulation provide the means for success for these people in their quest to provide educational opportunities for their children.

IMAGE OF MIDDLEMAN MINORITIES

Despite providing essential goods and services to neighborhoods that would otherwise lack them, members of middleman minorities are generally viewed with hostility by members of the minority and majority groups. They have often been the targets of discrimination and physical violence. As members of minority classes with little access to members of wealthier and more powerful majority groups, members of middleman minorities offer convenient targets on whom others may vent their frustration and feelings of anger for having being taken advantage of economically. Middleman minorities do not themselves produce the commodities they sell, but they profit from selling what others have produced. Their prosperity relative to the minority group is resented by their lower-income customers who do not share in that prosperity.

Members of middleman minorities and their children tend to outperform other minority group members in both capital accumulation and educational levels. Rather than imitate the behavior patterns of middleman minorities, other minority group members often view the entire economic and social system as be deliberately stacked against them. Thus, middleman minority businesses are often the first businesses to suffer damage during instances of urban unrest.

With the United States, members of various different ethnic and cultural group have held the status of middleman minorities. During the nineteenth and early twentieth centuries, for example, Jews of a variety of ethnic backgrounds, as well as a variety of European immigrants, constituted the bulk of middleman minorities. Members of these groups were generally able to assimilate into the economic and social mainstream by the second generation. By contrast, immigrants of Asian ethnic background have retained their middleman minority labels for much longer periods of time. Their assimilation has been slower and more difficult than that of European immigrants because of greater language barriers and physical appearances that have served as marks of differentiation from members of the majority group. Middleman minorities of Asian ethnicity have suffered hostility from other members of their own minority groups, as Asian entrepreneurs have progressed economically, and their children have assimilated socially through education leading to higher job status. While education has not been a primary factor in the success of first-generation middleman minority members, it has traditionally had a strongly positive impact on their children. As these entrepreneurs have enjoyed success, they have generally been able to release their children from having to work in their family businesses so they can concentrate on their educational activities.

One of the most obvious hostile situations for members of middleman minorities in the United States has involved Korean owners of convenience stores in predominantly low-income minority neighborhoods. Resident minorities have tended to resent the success of the Korean middlemen, with whom they have few social connections and whom they tend to regard as exploitative outsiders. Moreover, resident minorities also tend to see favoritism in government programs that assist small business owners. The more the Korean middleman prospers seemingly by taking money from resident minorities, the more powerful and potentially lethal the hostility. Such hostility was especially evident in the April, 1992, Los Angeles rioting that followed the acquittal of the police officers who beat Rodney King. Much of the violent anger felt by African Americans was directed against Korean American entrepreneurs operating within predominantly black communities.

Victoria Erhart

FURTHER READING

Butler, John. *Immigrant and Minority Entrepreneurship: The Continuous Rebirth of American Communities.* Westport, Conn.: Praeger, 2004. Examines how different ethnic minorities behave in their attempts to enter the American economic mainstream.

Kaufman, Eric. *Rethinking Ethnicity: Majority Groups and Dominant Minorities.* New York: Routledge, 2004. Studies patterns of ethnic migration caused by the pressures of globalization as various ethnic groups try to improve their status.

Sowell, Thomas. *Black Rednecks and White Liberals.* New York: Encounter Books, 2005. Sociological study of various middleman minorities around the globe and their psychological characteristics. Pays particular attention to Afro-American cultural history.

_____. *Migrations and Cultures: A World View.* New York: Basic Books, 1997. Study of various ethnic groups within different cultures to see which cultures are better at accumulating human capital based through various behaviors.

SEE ALSO: Asian immigrants; Family businesses; Korean immigrants; Stereotyping.

MIGRANT SUPERORDINATION

DEFINITION: Process through which immigrants use force to overwhelm and subdue the original inhabitants of the territories they settle

SIGNIFICANCE: Migrant superordination occurs principally in countries that are colonized by outsiders, and U.S. history provides a classic example of this process.

The superordinate/subordinate relationships that result from migrant superordination processes can take economic, political, and cultural forms. Such relationships are characterized by the institutionalization of dominant-minority relations in which the migrants enjoy disproportionate power, resources, and prestige. Power relationships are then justified by systems of beliefs that rationalize the superiority of the immigrant groups in relation to the indigenous peoples.

Reactions to migrant superordination on the part of the indigenous peoples may range from physical resistance and rebellion to accommodation and assimilation. Historical examples of migrant superordination include the European conquest of Native Americans in the Western Hemisphere and of Africans in South Africa.

M. Bahati Kuumba

FURTHER READING

Cook, Terrence E. *Separation, Assimilation, or Accommodation: Contrasting Ethnic Minority Policies.* Westport, Conn.: Praeger, 2003.

Zølner, Mette. *Re-imagining the Nation: Debates on Immigrants, Identities and Memories.* New York: Peter Lang, 2000.

SEE ALSO: History of immigration, 1620-1783; History of immigration, 1783-1891; Westward expansion; World migration patterns.

MILITARY CONSCRIPTION

DEFINITION: Actions by the U.S. government to direct immigrants to perform military service

SIGNIFICANCE: Efforts by the federal government at various periods in American history to conscript immigrants who had not yet been granted citizenship were met with mixed reaction among ethnic communities; while some groups resisted the draft in principle or protested against its being unfairly administered, many others welcomed the opportunity to serve and took advantage of provisions in the various draft laws that allowed them to become citizens more quickly.

During the Revolutionary War, the War of 1812, and the Mexican War of 1846-1848, the U.S. government filled the ranks of its fighting forces through voluntary enlistments. That practice was seen to be in keeping with the country's professed belief in respecting individual liberties; the general feeling was that no person should be forced to serve the country, even in times of national distress. However, the outbreak of the U.S. Civil War in 1861 changed the dimensions of military conflict in America, as both the Union and the Confederacy instituted conscription to build up the massive armies required to carry on the war. Moreover, both governments decided that both citizens and resident aliens who had declared their intention of becoming citizens should be eligible for conscription.

Authorities reasoned that those who wished to enjoy the benefits of citizenship—even at a future date—were obligated to defend their adopted homeland in times of crisis. This practice was not common among European nations, however, and many European governments protested, claiming that their own citizens should not have to fight for another country until they became full-fledged citizens of that country. The requirement for mandatory military service was also not well received by many recently arrived immigrants, many of whom had come to America to escape similar practices in their native countries.

CIVIL WAR PROTESTS

The Confederacy was the first of the Civil War combatants to establish a draft. Its 1862 law provided for many exemptions, however, and most aliens were able to avoid conscription even though the South relied heavily on conscripts to fill the ranks of its army. When the Union passed its first draft law one year later, in 1863, protests were mounted throughout the North almost immediately. New immigrants were especially suspicious of plans for conscription; many were certain that the poor would be drafted in greater numbers, and because most new immigrants were poor, that would mean they had a much greater chance of being inducted into the armed forces involuntarily. Their fears were fueled by two provisions in the Union law that favored those with greater financial means: Men who were drafted could either pay three-hundred-dollar bounties to the government to avoid service or hire substitutes to take their places.

Although protests were organized in several cities—the first one in Buffalo, New York, and later riots in Wisconsin—by far the most violent demonstration against the draft occurred in New York City in July, 1863, just days after officials began drawing names for conscription. The majority of the protesters were Irish immigrants, who suddenly discovered that their willingness to get involved in the political process by signing up to vote in local elections—usually as Democrats—was being used against them by Republican lawmakers responsible for draft legislation. Registering to vote was considered a sign of one's intent to remain permanently in America, and those who had registered were automatically considered eligible for the draft.

Thousands of immigrants volunteered to join the Union's Irish Brigade that was formed in New York, but many other Irish feared that if the North won the war, slaves freed from plantations in the South would migrate north and compete for jobs then being done by Irishmen. That concern, coupled with the perception that the Irish and other immigrant groups would be overrepresented among draftees, sparked a violent outburst against city and state officials. Over a five-day period, mobs roamed the streets of New York City, looting business establishments and burning buildings, including the mayor's home and several police stations. Damage to property was later estimated at one million dollars. The protesters' anger quickly focused on African Americans living in the city; shootings and lynchings claimed more than a hundred lives. Lo-

cal police units proved incapable of quelling the violence. In fact, the city's police commissioner himself suffered serious injury in an assault. The governor of New York was forced to call back militia units that had been serving with the Union forces at the Battle of Gettysburg to put down the riots.

A retrospective look at the practice of conscription during the Civil War reveals two great ironies. First, records indicate that the percentage of resident aliens who were drafted during the conflict was no greater than that of citizens. Second, many of the substitutes hired by draftees were immigrants, who evidently found the payments a way to put aside some savings that would help secure their futures, should they make it through the war.

WORLD WAR I

The first federal government draft was allowed to expire at the end of hostilities in 1865 and was not reinstated until 1917, when the United States entered World War I. After the United States entered war in April, 1917, the administration of President Woodrow Wilson determined that conscription would be necessary for the nation to assemble an expeditionary force to assist its European allies. This time, officials were careful to craft a draft law that corrected some of the inequities of the laws passed during the Civil War. Most resident aliens found the Selective Service Act of 1917 much more palatable than earlier mandates for service. The new law offered no provisions for hiring substitutes or paying bounties to avoid service. Additionally, local draft boards were established to examine each potential inductee, determine his fitness for service, and consider granting an exemption. Generally, exemptions were granted on the basis of occupation or health. When resident aliens asked for exemptions by citing their citizenship in other countries, they were told that accepting exemptions would make them ineligible for future U.S. citizenship. In general, most immigrants felt that the process was fair.

Nevertheless, as had occurred during the Civil War, pockets of resistance sprang up in various ethnic communities. Some activists attempted to convince immigrant groups, particularly Italians and Jews, to resist conscription because the war was being waged merely to further international or national business interests at the expense of the working poor. The Irish were especially skeptical because the United States was entering the conflict on the side of Great Britain, whose government was at that time resisting the movement for Irish independence.

A ploy used to turn European immigrants against conscription was the claim that the draft displayed a dangerous tendency toward "Prussianization"—a reference to the militaristic German regime that many Americans blamed for having started the war. In general, however, immigrants drafted during World War I reported for duty without demur. Moreover, many did not wait to be called but instead chose to enlist. They often did this in units organized locally along ethnic lines, allowing young men to serve alongside others with whom they shared a common heritage. At the same time, however, draftees were typically assigned to units in which men of various ethnic and socioeconomic classes served side by side; this practice actually proved beneficial to many immigrants, because it provided them experiences that allowed them to assimilate more quickly into the general population.

WORLD WAR II

The Selective Service Act of 1940 was virtually identical to that of 1917, but perhaps because America's enemies in World War II were perceived as particularly threatening, virtually no protests were raised to drafting noncitizens. Any hesitancy about the draft that existed among immigrant groups during World War I virtually evaporated by the time the United States reinstituted conscription on the eve of its entrance into the new world war in late 1941. Immigrants of virtually every nationality perceived the Axis powers of Japan, Germany, and Italy as threats to liberty for both their adopted country and their native homelands.

Xenophobic feelings that had caused some German Americans to suffer discrimination during World War I were virtually absent. Although many Japanese Americans were interned throughout the war—ostensibly to prevent espionage—thousands of their young served honorably in the U.S. armed forces, including many who were drafted. As had happened twenty-five years earlier, the experience of serving with a variety of individuals of different backgrounds from other parts of the country allowed immigrants who had been drafted to assimi-

late more rapidly into the mainstream of American society. One immigrant group that benefited notably from this opportunity for assimilation was Mexican Americans.

POST-WORLD WAR CONSCRIPTION

Although the Selective Service Act of 1940 expired in 1947, a new act was passed a year later, and immigrants once again found themselves subject to conscription as the United States built up its armed forces as a defensive measure against the threat of communism. Because the new law continued the provision that resident aliens were eligible to be drafted, immigrants were called up for service in the Korean War between 1950 and 1953 as well.

During the 1950's and 1960's, the newest wave of immigrants from Europe, many from Germany and Eastern European countries, found themselves subject to the draft. Some chose to enlist in the National Guard or military reserves to guarantee they would be able to fulfill the bulk of their six-year military obligation near family members who may have come to America with them. Resident aliens were also subject to conscription during the Vietnam War. Most served willingly, and those who protested their induction usually did so because they had scruples about the war itself, not because they felt they were being discriminated against because they were not yet citizens.

CONSCRIPTION AND CITIZENSHIP

Although federal penalties for resisting the draft have often been harsh, many immigrants found that being conscripted into the military has provided significant benefits as well. Since the American Revolution, aliens who agreed to take up arms for the United States have been allowed to accelerate their journey toward becoming American citizens. Routinely, immigrants applying for citizenship could point to their honorable service as sufficient proof of good moral character, one of the requirements for naturalization.

After World War I, aliens who served in the military, including those drafted during peacetime, were granted waivers of several years on the time required for residence in the United States before being eligible to apply for citizenship. This practice was continued even after the United States did away with the draft during the 1970's. In fact, after

2001, several proposals were put forward in Congress to provide a mechanism for granting citizenship to immigrants—including those who entered the country illegally—who chose to enlist in the armed forces.

Laurence W. Mazzeno

FURTHER READING

Anbinder, Tyler. "Which Poor Man's Fight? Immigrants and the Federal Conscription of 1863." *Civil War History* 52, no. 4 (December, 2006): 344-372. Carefully researched essay demonstrating that, despite concerns that they would be singled out for conscription, immigrants were not selected in disproportionate numbers for military service during the Civil War.

Anderson, Martin, ed. *The Military Draft: Selected Readings on Conscription.* Stanford, Calif.: Hoover Institution Press, 1982. Comprehensive analysis of the history of American drafts. Includes essays on conscription law and on the political theory justifying conscription of resident aliens.

Bergquist, James M. *Daily Life in Immigrant America 1820-1870.* Westport, Conn.: Greenwood Press, 2008. Describes living conditions for immigrants, many of whose lives were disrupted by the Civil War. Comments briefly on the 1863 draft by the Union and the rioting that followed.

Bernstein, Iver. *The New York City Draft Riots: Their Significance for American Society and Politics in the Age of the Civil War.* New York: Oxford University Press, 1990. Describes social and political conditions that prompted segments of the urban poor to mount violent protests against the 1863 draft law.

Flynn, George Q. *The Draft, 1940-1973.* Lawrence: University Press of Kansas, 1993. Examines the impact of the draft on the armed forces and American society from the establishment of a draft prior to World War II through the Vietnam War.

Hay, Jeff, ed. *Military Draft.* Farmington Hills, Mich.: Greenhaven Press, 2008. Collection of essays describing the history of the draft and the government's operations to enforce conscription laws during several periods of armed conflict and in peacetime.

Jacobs, James B., and Leslie Anne Hayes. "Aliens in the U.S. Armed Forces: A Historico-Legal Analysis." *Armed Forces and Society* 7, no. 2 (Winter, 1981): 187-208. Detailed examination of the federal government's recruitment and conscription of noncitizens from the time of the Civil War to the establishment of modern all-volunteer army.

Moore, Albert B. *Conscription and Conflict in the Confederacy.* New York: Hillary House, 1963. Examines the impact of conscription in the Confederate States of America and outlines options open to immigrants who had not yet become citizens.

Sterba, Christopher. *Good Americans: Italian and Jewish Immigrants During the First World War.* New York: Oxford University Press, 2003. Assesses the responses of two ethnic communities to American involvement in the war, including their willingness to serve in the armed forces.

SEE ALSO: Citizenship; Civil War, U.S.; Irish immigrants; Korean War; New York City; Prisoners of war in the United States; Vietnam War; World War I; World War II.

MINNESOTA

SIGNIFICANCE: Growing populations, land shortages, and rigid political and social systems prompted many northern Europeans to immigrate to Minnesota during the nineteenth century. The state was made especially attractive to European immigrants by the availability of cheap land under the federal Homestead Act of 1862. The late twentieth century, however, saw the arrival of immigrants from other parts of the world.

Minnesota is well known for its many residents of Scandinavian ancestry. Scandinavian immigration began during the nineteenth century, when Sweden and Norway were experiencing rapid population growth and began sending emigrants to North America. Both countries had limited arable land, and rich farmland could be purchased cheaply in Minnesota, making the midwestern territory, and later state, an attractive destination for settlement. Persecution by Sweden's state Lutheran church and the country's military draft were additional incentives for emigration.

Minnesota monthly newspaper serving two of the state's immigrant communities with articles in English, Spanish, and Somali. (AP/Wide World Photos)

Norwegians moved to Minnesota for the same economic and demographic reasons as the Swedes. Another factor contributing to Norwegian emigration was the country's rigid class system, which limited voting to members of the upper classes.

Minnesota also attracted many German immigrants who shared the Scandinavians' quest for cheap farmland. German immigration was also fueled by the failed revolutions of 1830 and 1848. Other midwestern states absorbed most of the German immigrants, but many of the immigrants settled in southern Minnesota. Smaller numbers settled in northern parts of the state.

LATE TWENTIETH CENTURY

By 1990 the largest immigrant groups in Minnesota were Latin Americans and Hmong from Southeast Asia, Both groups were part of a surge in immigration that began during the late 1970's. Financial and agricultural crises brought Mexicans

to Minnesota. Between 1990 and 2000. the numbers of Latinos in Minnesota tripled to 143,382. By 2004 the Minnesota State Demographic Center estimated the state's Latino population at about 175,000.

The Hmong are a non-Vietnamese people from Laos and Vietnam who sided with the United States during the Vietnam War and afterward became political refugees. The approximately 60,000 Hmong living in Minnesota in 2004 made Minnesota home to the largest number of Hmong in the United States. The state also had about 25,000 ethnic Vietnamese residents, along with smaller numbers of immigrants from Laos, Burma, and Cambodia.

World events also brought other nationalities to Minnesota. For example, during the 1990's, the collapse of the Soviet Union brought many Russians to Minnesota, and the civil wars following the breakup of Yugoslavia brought Bosnian refugees. In 2002, the collapse of the government in Somalia

719

brought a surge of Somalis to the state. Minnesota's need for high-tech workers also brought immigrants from India, Pakistan, and China.

The influence of Scandinavian immigrants has remained evident in the varieties of English spoken in Minnesota. The 1996 motion picture *Fargo* satirizes Scandinavian accents in the state. In one scene, a young Minnesota man of apparent Asian ancestry enters a restaurant in Minneapolis. When he speaks, he uses a strong Scandinavian accent exactly like that of the modern descendants of Minnesota's early Swedish and Norwegian immigrants.

Timothy C. Frazer

PROFILE OF MINNESOTA

Region	Upper Midwest
Entered union	1858
Largest cities	Minneapolis, St. Paul (capital), Duluth, Rochester, Bloomington
Modern immigrant communities	Hispanics, Hmong, Somalis, Russians

Population	Total	Percent of state	Percent of U.S.	U.S. rank
All state residents	5,167,000	100.0	1.73	21
All foreign-born residents	339,000	6.6	0.90	21

Source: U.S. Census Bureau, *Statistical Abstract for 2006.*
Notes: The U.S. population in 2006 was 299,399,000, of whom 37,548,000 (12.5%) were foreign born. Rankings in last column reflect total numbers, not percentages.

FURTHER READING

Blegen, Theodore C. *Minnesota: A History of the State.* St. Paul: University of Minnesota Press, 1963.

Lass, William E. *Minnesota: A History.* New York: W. W. Norton, 1998.

Nelson, Helge. *The Swedes and Swedish Settlements in North America.* 1943. Reprint. New York: Arno Press, 1979.

Nordstrom, Byron, ed. *The Swedes in Minnesota.* Minneapolis: T. S. Denison, 1976.

SEE ALSO: German immigrants; Hmong immigrants; Homestead Act of 1862; Language issues; Linguistic contributions; Mexican immigrants.

MISSIONARIES

DEFINITION: Representatives of Christian denominations who work abroad, seeking converts to their faiths

SIGNIFICANCE: The proselyting and educational work of various Christian missionary groups in countries around the world has often had the unintended effect of encouraging foreign converts to immigrate to the United States. Consequently, rates of immigration have been higher from countries with American missionaries than from those not missionized.

American missionaries of all Christian denominations have used a wide assortment of programs to make converts in other countries, particularly those of developing nations and the newly liberated countries of the former Eastern Bloc. Their activities have included work in underdeveloped and undeveloped countries, and countries plagued by natural disaster and ethnic rivalry such as the Sudan. Their approaches have differed from country to country, and the extent of their success is not fully known. However, an unintended consequence of missionary work has been for many new converts to immigrate to the United States.

MISSIONARY TOOLS

Many of the tools employed by Christian missionaries have been used for centuries; others have only recently become available. The various different denominations have employed different tactics in their missionary work, but it is not always easy to generalize about specific denominations. A few broad points can, however, be made confidently. All Christian denominations preach to the oneness of humankind. As part of their teachings, missionaries proclaim Jesus Christ as the Lord and offer the universalism of the Christian gospel. The concepts of resurrection and the forgiveness of sin are elements used in an effort to convert people.

MOTIVATIONS FOR IMMIGRATION

Because the great passion of many Christian converts is to enjoy the benefits of a stable society that are preached by missionaries, immigrating to the United States is a natural attraction. As part of their proselyting work, missionaries preach the virtues of democracy, which many of their converts cannot enjoy in their native lands. Missionary schools tend to foster high levels of expectations among converts, who are inculcated with American values. To some extent, this results from deliberate missionary planning. For example, the Episcopal Church sends missions to Central America yearly to construct and maintain an infrastructure whose purpose is to "civilize" local peoples. Representatives of the Roman Catholic Church—the

dominant religion in Central America—and of other denominations compete with Episcopal missionaries in the effort to "save souls for Christ." Missionaries of all denominations teach hygiene and Bible studies, promote attitudes of self-confidence among members of religious minorities, and work to create atmospheres conducive to learning.

MEDICAL AND AGRICULTURAL WORK

An important part of missionary work in many developing countries is the introduction of modern Western medicine among the indigenous peoples. The Roman Catholic Church has excelled in this work, and other denominations, such as the Mormons, also send equipment and trained personnel on missions. To increase local acceptance of Western medicine, missionaries typically provide documentation written in the local languages and make sure that medicines they distribute are labeled in the local languages. Within communities

Mormon missionary reading scripture to members of a Tongan family in 2007. Thanks to the strong missionary program of the Church of Jesus Christ of Latter-day Saints, Tonga has one of the highest percentages of Mormons of any nation in the world, and many Mormon Tongans immigrate to the United States. (Getty Images)

lacking modern medical services, health restoration can be viewed as a miracle and contribute to acceptance of the religious messages.

Missionary preaching about the importance of modern health care can also contribute to converts' interest in immigrating to America. However, in areas where missionaries send professional medical personnel and equip and maintain permanent health care facilities, access to health care becomes less of an incentive for immigration. The Denton Program, a nondenominational missionary organization. uses American military aircraft to transport medical personnel and equipment and works with various federal government departments and agencies and the Agency for International Development as well as individual missionary bodies. American churches are careful to send people fluent in the local languages.

The Christian missionary movement has also offered agricultural training in other countries, particularly in unfertile regions. Some groups stress self-help and teach local farmers in the use of modern fertilizers, feeds, shelters, and farm equipment. Agricultural training often leads to encouraging converts to immigrate to regions of the United States that need agrarian workers.

MODERN COMMUNICATION TOOLS

One of the most striking developments in modern missionary work is the availability of powerful tools of communication, many of which are available at little or no cost. Missionary action is supported internationally by a chain of sites on the World Wide Web designed to provide support. In India, for example, missionaries use a Web site that assists in language learning and helps to understand diverse cultures. Christian missionary work in that predominantly Hindu and Muslim country has been sufficiently successful to move the national government to suppress it.

Some companies, such as the on-line SOON ministries, provide evangelical movements with computer hardware at bargain prices, or even for free, for dissemination in developing countries. Missionary ham radio operators also assist novices in other countries to become acquainted with American culture, often helping converts prepare for immigration.

Evangelical missionary bodies have audio and video services that provide free support to many churches. For example, missionaries can download electronic texts of the Bible in 140 different languages. Some missionary bodies also provide information and assistance to foreign converts who wish to immigrate to the United States.

The Episcopal Church and other denominations sponsor retreats for converts considering immigration to the United States. Those aspiring to come to America attend sessions designed to strengthen the converts in their new religious beliefs and to teach them about life in the United States. A special aspect of the training is to inculcate a sense of community.

Arthur K. Steinberg

FURTHER READING

Addison, Steve. *Movements That Change the World.* Smyrna, Del.: Missional Press, 2009. Examination of the dynamics of successful missionary movements by the Australian director of Church Resource Ministries. Written for readers who are already believers, but also useful for insights into missionaries' minds.

Haddad, Yvonne Yazbeck, Jane I. Smith, and John L. Esposito, eds. *Religion and Immigration: Christian, Jewish, and Muslim Experiences in the United States.* Walnut Creek, Calif.: AltaMira Press, 2003. Collection of articles examining the religious backgrounds and religious experiences of modern immigrants to the United States.

Hiebert, Paul. *Anthropological Insights for Missionaries.* Grand Rapids, Mich.: Baker Book House, 1985. Handbook for Christian missionaries by a professional anthropologist who attempts to show missionaries how to understand the people among whom they are working. Provides helpful insights into the cultural challenges faced by missionaries in foreign lands.

Levitt, Peggy. *God Needs No Passport: Immigrants and the Changing American Religious Landscape.* New York: New Press, 2007. Sociological study that emphasizes the ways in which religious identities ensure strong self-identification with native countries.

Reed, James. *The Missionary Mind and American East Asia Policy, 1911-1915.* New York: New York University Press, 1983. Scholarly study of missionary work during a brief but critical phase in U.S.-China relations, when missionary views played an important role in American foreign policy.

Sanneh, Lamin. *Translating the Message: The Missionary Impact on Culture.* 2d ed. Maryknoll, N.Y.: Orbis Books, 2008. A Christian perspective on the history of how missionary messages are understood by converts in other cultures. Emphasis is given to translations of the Scriptures and to post-Reformation missionary work in Africa, the author's area of special expertise.

Walls, Andrew F. *The Missionary Movement in Christian History: Studies in Transmission of Faith.* Maryknoll, N.Y.: Orbis Books, 1996. Broad study of missionaries throughout the full history of Christianity. Many chapters address aspects of missionary interactions with non-Western cultures.

SEE ALSO: Gospel Society; Korean immigrants; Mormon immigrants; Religion as a push-pull factor; Religions of immigrants.

MISSISSIPPI

SIGNIFICANCE: Compared to many other states, Mississippi has experienced relatively little foreign immigration over the course of its modern history. Nevertheless, the state does have several immigrant communities whose members have faced unique conditions and problems. Vietnamese and Mexican immigrants began to increase in numbers during the late twentieth century.

Mississippi has always had much lower levels of immigration than most of the rest of the United States. However, its immigrant population began to growing more rapidly toward the end of the twentieth century and the beginning of the twenty-first century, particularly along the state's Gulf coast. Among the earliest immigrants to the state, who began arriving during the first half of the nineteenth century, Germans and Irish figured most prominently. Members of these groups generally entered the United States through the port of New Orleans, Louisiana, and then moved eastward to enter Mississippi. Many of the early German-speaking immigrants were Jews from the Austro-Hungarian Empire fleeing religious oppression in their native land.

LATE NINETEENTH CENTURY IMMIGRATION

After the U.S. Civil War ended in 1865, Chinese immigrants began entering Mississippi, particularly in the state's Delta region. As newly freed African American slaves in that region began trying to better their lives during the Reconstruction era (1865-1877), many of them not only attempted to assert their political rights but also started moving among plantations in search of higher wages. Plantation owners sought to reduce their dependence on the labor of former slaves by campaigning to bring in Chinese workers, believing that Asian laborers would be easier to control than their former slaves. However, many of the Chinese workers who came to Mississippi proved less tractable than expected by abandoning agricultural work and establishing small stores.

The end of Reconstruction in the late 1870's also saw the reestablishment of white dominance over black Mississippians, reducing the demand of white plantation owners for Chinese manual labor. This development increased opportunities for the Chinese to become members of what sociologists would later call a "middleman minority"—people

PROFILE OF MISSISSIPPI

Region	Gulf coast
Entered union	1817
Largest cities	Jackson (capital), Gulfport, Biloxi, Hattiesburg
Modern immigrant communities	Vietnamese, Mexicans

Population	Total	Percent of state	Percent of U.S.	U.S. rank
All state residents	2,910,000	100.0	0.97	31
All foreign-born residents	51,000	1.8	0.14	42

Source: U.S. Census Bureau, *Statistical Abstract for 2006.*
Notes: The U.S. population in 2006 was 299,399,000, of whom 37,548,000 (12.5%) were foreign born. Rankings in last column reflect total numbers, not percentages.

Manuel, a five-year-old shrimp-picker who understands no English, stands amid a mountain of oyster shells at a Biloxi, Mississippi, company in 1911. (Library of Congress/Lewis Wickes Hine)

who purchased wholesale goods from white suppliers and resold them to a customer base that included many African Americans. Often these Mississippi Chinese immigrants became caught in the middle in another sense under the regime of segregation, fitting neither the categories of "black" nor "white" in Mississippi society.

Another group of foreign immigrants who began settling in Mississippi during the half century following the U.S. Civil War was Arab Lebanese immigrants. The Lebanese found work in the state mainly as peddlers, traveling from place to place selling goods. They established communities in some of the larger cities, such as Vicksburg, Jackson, and Clarksdale.

LATE TWENTIETH CENTURY ARRIVALS

Through most of the years between the end of World War I in 1918 and the twenty-first century,

foreign immigration to Mississippi remained extremely low. However, the growth of the seafood industry along the Gulf coast did attract some Italian immigrants, who came mainly by way of New Orleans. During the late 1970's and early 1980's, Vietnamese refugees who had resettled in the South began moving to Mississippi's Gulf coast, especially around Biloxi, seeking work in the seafood-processing industry. As these Southeast Asian immigrants settled in the region during the 1980's, they entered the fishing and shrimping industry, which became an ethnic niche business for them. During the following decade, Gulf coast Vietnamese moved into a new ethnic occupational concentration as casino gambling became a major industry that provided them with jobs. However, at the same time this new industry provided them with employment, it also drove up housing prices within the areas in which they had settled.

The 1990's also saw a significant increase in the Mexican population of Mississippi, and Mexicans became the state's fastest-growing immigrant population during the early twenty-first century. Members of this group tended to concentrate in the construction and restaurant industries. Damage wrought by Hurricane Katrina along the Gulf coast, particularly to the Gulfport-Biloxi region in August, 2005, greatly increased the need for workers in the building trades, thereby attracting more Mexican immigrants to the construction industry. The arrival of these new immigrants also brought new problems. An unknown but apparently substantial number of these Mexican immigrant workers were undocumented, and some of the immigrants reported problems in being paid for their work by contractors.

Carl L. Bankston III

FURTHER READING

Bond, Bradley G., ed. *Mississippi: A Documentary History.* Jackson: University Press of Mississippi, 2005.

Do, Hien Duc. *The Vietnamese Americans.* Westport, Conn.: Greenwood Press, 1999.

Durrenberger, E. Paul. *Gulf Coast Soundings: People and Policy in the Mississippi Shrimp Industry.* Lawrence: University Press of Kansas, 1996.

Herrmann, Denise von, ed. *Resorting to Casinos: The Mississippi Gambling Industry.* Jackson: University Press of Mississippi, 2006.

SEE ALSO: African Americans and immigrants; Alabama; Arab immigrants; Arkansas; Chinese immigrants; German immigrants; Louisiana; Mexican immigrants; Mississippi River; Vietnamese immigrants.

MISSISSIPPI RIVER

IDENTIFICATION: Primary waterway of the central United States

SIGNIFICANCE: A mighty river whose watershed forms the continent's heartland, the Mississippi provided inexpensive transit for immigrants bound for the Midwest and the western frontier. Many settled in the riverfront cities or on nearby lands. Their work increased the output of the region's fields and factories, whose products were then shipped out via river transit. Unique cultural features evolved from the mix of immigrant settlers in major riverfront cities such as New Orleans.

The Mississippi River functioned as a magnet for immigrants even before becoming part of the United States. Discovered by the sixteenth century Spanish explorer Hernando de Soto and explored by the seventeenth century French nobleman Sieur de La Salle, both the river and its vast watershed were alternately claimed by France and Spain during the seventeenth and eighteenth centuries. The upper reaches remained the preserve of Native Americans and a few trappers until the American Revolution, but the economic and strategic importance of the river's Delta region was recognized early. New Orleans was founded in 1719. Its eighteenth century population grew to ten thousand, including Spanish soldiers, West African slaves, refugees from Caribbean plantations, Portuguese fishermen, French Creoles, and entrepreneurs from the newly independent United States.

In the surrounding Delta country, French Acadians settled after being expelled from Canada in the wake of its British takeover in the mid-eighteenth century. Isleños, former Canary Islands inhabitants, migrated to the Delta during the region's Spanish rule, also bringing their culture and fishing-based economy to the bayous. The many coves and islands of the region provided shelter for legendary pirates such as Jean Lafitte.

IMPACT OF THE LOUISIANA PURCHASE

President Thomas Jefferson's purchase of the Louisiana Territory in 1803 not only gave an expanding nation a huge new storehouse of natural resources but also secured a water route that eased transit to all the areas that bordered the river and its major tributaries. Both immigration and shipping benefited from no longer having to make onerous overland trips through the wilderness. After the Battle of New Orleans (1815) cut short a British land-grab attempt in the region, the territory was secured for settlers who wanted to build new lives there. The North American continent now offered unpopulated lands and opportunities, just as many European countries were entering an era of economic and political crises.

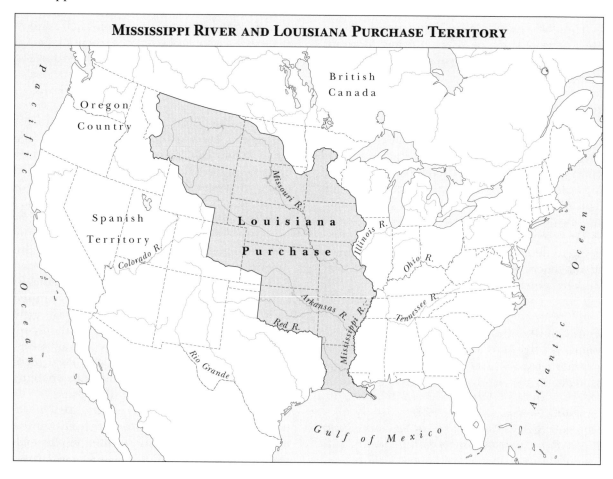

MISSISSIPPI RIVER AND LOUISIANA PURCHASE TERRITORY

One early aspect of the Louisiana Purchase was that it granted automatic U.S. citizenship to those already living in the territory. These people included a fairly large population in the Delta region, and scattered settlements in the more sparsely inhabited areas upriver. In the first decade after the purchase, more than 10,000 new French-speaking immigrants poured into New Orleans, refugees from the Haitian revolution and other slave uprisings on French Caribbean islands.

French immigrants also predominated at this time in the river's upper reaches. St. Louis and some other river cities had been founded by French voyageurs during the eighteenth century, first as an outpost for fur traders, then serving as a supply base and port for the settlers in the countryside. Lead mining began early in the city's hinterland, and by 1723 French entrepreneur Philip Francois Renault was shipping lead down the Mississippi to diverse foreign markets. Other metals,

furs, and timber were gathered or produced by the largely French early immigrants to the mid-Mississippi region.

Early during the nineteenth century, the wilderness was partially cleared and states were established in the former Northwest Territory. Their settlers often came via the Mississippi's eastern tributaries such as the Ohio River. New towns sprang up, peopled by both these internal migrants and European immigrants who arrived via the Mississippi route. Throughout most of the mid-nineteenth century, immigrants tended to come from northern or western European countries: Scandinavia, the British Isles, France, and Germany. Many were rural folk. Some of these joined the burgeoning populations of the states on the river's eastern bank, notably Illinois and Indiana, where town life and farms were already flourishing. Others set out to farm the rich, virgin soil of trans-Mississippi states, including Iowa, Minnesota, Missouri, Kansas, and Nebraska. Still others settled in riverfront cities and became shopkeepers, or carried on the crafts, ranging from tailoring to metalwork, which they had followed in their homelands.

Like the French migrants to the Mississippi Delta, many other immigrants came as refugees from disasters in their homeland. The Irish faced starvation at home from the potato blight of the mid-nineteenth century. France and Germany churned with political turbulence and the uprooting of a centuries-old social order. If the Mississippi Valley was "untamed" in comparison, it still offered the chance to build a new life without being caught up in civic unrest.

POST-CIVIL WAR EXPANSION

With prospective statehood on the horizon during the early 1850's, Kansas and Missouri were caught in the struggle over slave- versus free-state status. During the ensuing Civil War (1861-1865), it was clear that control of the Mississippi was vitally important to both sides. The war endangered ordinary river traffic, and immigration slowed drastically. There was a fair amount of immigrant participation in the war, however, supporting both sides. St. Louis, for example, had large communities of both German and Irish immigrants. Open clashes occurred between the two during the war. Many from the city's Irish Roman Catholic community joined the Confederate forces, along with Father John Bannon, who accompanied them as a chaplain and later served as a Confederate emissary to the Vatican. The Germans, with their strong martial tradition and marching societies, were staunchly antislavery and enlisted in the Union cause.

In the post-Civil War North, industry expanded to become the driving engine of the U.S. economy. The West was transformed from frontier to an integral part of the nation. The Homestead Act of 1862 offered free land to settlers for farming. Once again, immigrants, mostly from Europe, arrived in large numbers to work the farms and factories in the Mississippi Valley. Those with special skills—coopers and blacksmiths, for example—were targeted by pamphleteers, and sometimes businessmen or state governments even paid their passage to the sponsoring area. Arkansas, Iowa, and Minnesota were among the states directly or indirectly offering such aid.

Most of the first wave of post-Civil War immigrants, like their predecessors, came from northern and western Europe and assimilated fairly well into the existing river towns. The raw materials they produced—hardwood lumber, ore, grain, and other agricultural produce from the upper Mississippi basin, and rice, cotton, pine and cypress wood, and cane sugar from its lower reaches—were shipped in great quantities down the river and to far-flung markets. The craftsmen's work, in contrast, tended to stay localized. Every town needed metalworkers and carpenters, for example, and their need to deal with customers and sponsors meant that these immigrants rapidly acquired rudimentary knowledge of the English language and American customs.

By 1890, the midwestern and Great Lakes states were becoming industrial powerhouses, and the composition of the immigrant flow changed. More than 18 million migrants were to enter the United States in the next thirty years, a rate double that of earlier times. These immigrants came largely from eastern and southern Europe: from Italy, Slavic areas and other parts of the Austro-Hungarian Empire, Russia, and the Baltic region. They immigrated to find work in factories and mines, and their mores and culture were different enough from those of established inhabitants to arouse suspicion. For example, a low-lying district called Bohemian Flats sprang up in Minneapolis. While it was inhabited by hardworking families, the fact that most residents were Czechs or Slovaks was nearly as suspect as the shantylike houses and frequent floods that predominated there.

During this period too, some unexpected immigrant enclaves developed. In Mississippi, immigrant Italians set up fishing and canning enterprises; others became wholesalers of seafood and imported food items. Into the same area moved Lebanese, who often started as itinerant peddlers and then worked their way up to the ownership of groceries and specialty restaurants. In Arkansas, Chinese men were imported as laborers in the cotton fields to serve as replacements for the lost slave labor. When this program did not work out, the Chinese stayed and became grocers despite exclusionary laws aimed at them. Further north, Belgian and Greek workers moved into the Quad Cities area of Iowa, drawn by the many unskilled jobs in the John Deere factory and those in similar assembly-line factories that were part of the new industrial America.

NEW PATTERNS AND PEOPLES

World War I drastically slowed the inflow of migrants. Although a certain number of Europeans still came as refugees from the war and its aftermath, its net effect put a lid on mass migration to the Mississippi Valley as well as the rest of the nation. During the early 1920's, there was a rebound in immigration from the war-torn European countries, but this was cut off by legislation in 1924 that established national quotas and for the first time limited the total number of immigrants allowed to enter the United States. It is notable that the only strong opposition to these measures was in the northeastern states, not the Mississippi Valley, which had also benefited much from immigrants' contributions. In fact, anti-German sentiment that accompanied the war was intense in the Middle West. It probably sped up the assimilation process in this region for the many residents of German or middle European origin. Because it was no longer acceptable to speak the German language, much less express any solidarity with their (or their ancestors') homeland, such residents redoubled their efforts to blend into the "melting pot."

With the Great Depression of the 1930's, World War II, and the quota system all contributing, the region experienced a dearth of new immigrants for several decades. Those who did come were often the beneficiaries of special provisions based on world events: war brides in the wake of U.S. servicemen's wide deployment during World War II and after, or refugees from such events as the Hungarian uprising of 1956 and the Cuban Revolution in 1959. Members of the first two groups might end up in Mississippi Valley towns depending on their own personal situation. Although most Cubans settled in Florida, a significant minority found refuge in New Orleans and the Delta region, relatively close to their Caribbean origins.

Immigration possibilities changed drastically with passage of the Immigration and Nationality Act of 1965. This law repealed the existing quota system and based most immigration decisions, in theory, on family-related or skills-related considerations. Air travel and the automobile had replaced riverboats as a way for immigrants to reach their destination. For the first time, large numbers of migrants came to America's heartland from Asia and Latin America. These new migrants had a wide variety of work and educational backgrounds. Like native-born Americans, they went where the jobs were.

The Vietnam War's aftermath brought thousands of Vietnamese to America. Many found work in the Gulf coast shrimp industry. Others scattered up and down the whole Mississippi Valley, working in various occupations from health care to agricultural processing. During the 1980's and 1990's, Mexican and Central American immigrants, legal and illegal, moved to midwestern towns. They found work not only in agriculture but also in meatpacking and construction. After Hurricane Katrina devastated the Gulf coast in 2005, Mexican workers were the single largest group involved in reconstruction efforts. Within a few months, the Latino population of New Orleans soared from 3.1 percent to an estimated 9.6 percent. Most of these new Delta residents were not newly arrived in the United States, but came from other U.S. locations.

Emily Alward

FURTHER READING

Ambrose, Stephen E., and Douglas G. Brinkley. *The Mississippi and the Making of a Nation.* Washington, D.C.: National Geographic Society, 2002. Lavishly illustrated volume written by two distinguished historians. Shows the river as both a channel for commerce and a natural resource. Biographical sketches of many famous immigrants.

McDermott, John Francis, ed. *Frenchmen and French Ways in the Mississippi Valley.* Champaign: University of Illinois Press, 1969. Studies of the contributions of French explorers and immigrants to the Mississippi region.

_____. *The Spanish in the Mississippi Valley, 1762-1804.* Champaign: University of Illinois Press, 1974. Papers on the era of Spanish ownership and maximum influence.

Massey, Douglas S., ed. *New Faces in New Places: The Changing Geography of American Immigration.* New York: Russell Sage Foundation, 2008. Symposium articles showing how non-Western and Latino immigrants have brought a new diversity to American life since the 1960's. Includes studies of midwestern and southern destinations.

Thornell, John. "Struggle for Identity in the Most

Southern Place on Earth: The Chinese in the Mississippi Delta." *Chinese America: History and Perspectives* (January, 2003): 63. Scholarly but lively article tracing the survival strategies of the Chinese community from 1870 on.

SEE ALSO: Louisiana; Mississippi; Missouri; Mormon immigrants; National Road; Natural disasters as push-pull factors; Transportation of immigrants; Westward expansion.

MISSOURI

SIGNIFICANCE: Located by the Mississippi River on the threshold of the western frontier, Missouri has had a somewhat different immigrant experience from those of neighboring midwestern states. Nevertheless, like many other states, it attracted significant numbers of European immigrants during the nineteenth century, and it has had similar experiences with illegal immigration since the late twentieth century.

Most early settlers in Missouri were Americans of English origin who entered the territory from Kentucky, Tennessee, Ohio, Indiana, and Illinois. These groups spread into the river valleys into the central part of Missouri during the 1820's and into western Missouri during the 1830's. Meanwhile, the Mississippi River port of St. Louis emerged as the gateway to the western frontier. Over the next twenty years, the state's population tripled, from 19,783 to 66,586, while trading posts in both Kansas City and St. Joseph outfitted wagons trains heading west along the Santa Fe and Oregon trails.

Substantial overseas immigration began during the 1830's with the arrival of Germans, who established farms west of St. Louis and south of the Missouri River. On the eve of the U.S. Civil War, more 15 percent of the state's residents were foreign born—mostly Germans and Irish. By the end of the nineteenth century, the state was beginning to attract Italian, Greek, Polish, and east European Jewish immigrants.

TWENTIETH CENTURY IMMIGRATION

The basis of Missouri's economy gradually shifted from agriculture to industry through the early twentieth century. Between 1900 and 1970, the state's rural population dropped from 70 to less than 30 percent of the state total. However, Missouri differed from other midwestern states whose metropolitan centers grew significantly through that period. In fact, its major cities shrank. St. Louis lost almost half its population between 1950 and 1980. St. Louis and Kansas City responded by undertaking massive urban renewal programs during the 1980's to deal with air pollution, traffic, crime, and dilapidated housing, and Missouri's economy slowly began to improve. By the twenty-first century, more than half of the state's residents were clustered within its two largest metropolitan areas, St. Louis and Kansas City.

By the turn of the twenty-first century, Missouri's immigrant heritage was reflected in large numbers of people of German, Irish, English, and French descent. During the 1990's, they were joined by approximately 40,000 to 60,000 immigrants from war-torn Bosnia. By the year 2004, the state was home to 195,000 foreign-born residents, about 5 percent of

---

PROFILE OF MISSOURI

Region	Midwest
Entered union	1821
Largest cities	Kansas City, St. Louis, Springfield, Independence
Modern immigrant communities	Bosnians

Population	Total	Percent of state	Percent of U.S.	U.S. rank
All state residents	5,843,000	100.0	1.95	18
All foreign-born residents	194,000	3.3	0.52	28

Source: U.S. Census Bureau, *Statistical Abstract for 2006.*
Notes: The U.S. population in 2006 was 299,399,000, of whom 37,548,000 (12.5%) were foreign born. Rankings in last column reflect total numbers, not percentages.

whom spoke languages other than English in their homes.

Missouri was also home to between 35,000 and 65,000 undocumented immigrants, who represented less than 1 percent of the estimated 12 million undocumented immigrants believed to be living in the United States. In 2009, state lawmakers decided to crack down on illegal immigration by requiring all public employers, including state and local agencies, to use a database that searches records from the Social Security Administration and the Department of Homeland Security to determine whether potential employees are in the country legally.

Gayla Koerting

FURTHER READING

Aron, Stephen. *American Confluence: The Missouri Frontier from Borderland to Border State.* Bloomington: Indiana University Press, 2006.

Blouet, Brian W., and Frederick C. Luebke. *The Great Plains: Environment and Culture.* Lincoln: University of Nebraska Press, 1979.

Foley, William E. *A History of Missouri.* Columbia: University of Missouri Press, 2000.

Gjerde, Jon. *The Minds of the West: The Ethnocultural Evolution of the Rural Middle West, 1830-1917.* Chapel Hill: University of North Carolina Press, 1979.

Kamphoefner, Walter D. *The Westfalians: From Germany to Missouri.* Princeton, N.J.: Princeton University Press, 1987.

Thelen, David. *Paths of Resistance: Tradition and Dignity in Industrializing Missouri.* Columbia: University of Missouri Press, 1991.

SEE ALSO: Arkansas; German immigrants; Illinois; Kansas; Machine politics; Mississippi River; Nebraska; Westward expansion.

"MODEL MINORITIES"

DEFINITION: Popular conception of certain minority groups whose members tend to attain educational and economic success and achieve high degrees of assimilation into the mainstream society

SIGNIFICANCE: The term "model minority" has most often been applied to Asian Ameri-

cans, particularly Japanese, Chinese, and, more recently, Indian Americans. This issue is a significant one because it sets up strata within the category of minorities that imply that those who are most easily "assimilated" are the "best." This hierarchy allows the majority group to apply criteria of acceptance to other groups. It also is significant because the existence of this concept puts great pressure on younger members of groups labeled "model minorities" to reach high levels of achievement.

"Model minority" is a label applied to an ethnic, racial, or otherwise identifiable group, many of whose members achieve higher levels of success—as identified by the majority group—than average members of society. Measures of success may include household incomes, living conditions, or educational levels. Researchers who have studied minority groups have labeled "model minorities." Some of them consider the concept to be a myth and a form of racial and ethnic stereotyping. In the United States, Asian Americans and Asian immigrants are often given this label, as are some immigrants from India.

REACTIONS TO THE LABEL

Members of groups that have been called model minorities have varied in their responses to this label. Some are naturally proud to be considered high achieving. However, as more scholarly study has been applied to the concept, the model minority stereotype has been shown to be detrimental to many members of affected ethnic groups. It has, for example, played a role in disqualifying individuals from receiving aid from assistance programs.

Moreover, as with any stereotype, "model minority" tends to become a label that is applied to all members of a group, only some of whom are actually high achievers. This tendency can create unnecessary pressure on individuals to succeed or attempt to force individuals into molds in which they do not fit. This has been especially been a problem among Asian immigrants, whose many subgroups are very different from one another. The tendency to group all Asians together is a form of stereotyping and works to hide problems that do exist.

The label "model minority" might also lead Asians to think that their battles for equality within

American society have been won. Demographers have pointed out that this is not the case. For example, Asian Americans are highly underrepresented in political officeholding in the United States. They are also underrepresented as chief executive officers, board members, and high-level supervisors in the American corporate world.

STATISTICAL PERSPECTIVES

The concept of "model minority" depends on the computation of an average—a mathematical entity involving the addition of values attributed to everyone and divided by the number of individuals included. This statistic often hides the truth when a distribution is bimodal (that is, when many individuals are at either end of a continuum, not concentrated in the middle). In the case of a "model minority," a group might look very affluent given statistical averages, but this appearance might hide the fact that the group is actually a collection with many individuals clustered at both the high and low ends of the economic continuum.

Most of the stereotypical concepts related to the "model minority" label are most easily applied to Asians who have immigrated from China or Japan. Most of these immigrant populations derive from the middle and upper classes in their home countries. These immigrants tend to arrive in the United States already sharing the values of middle- and upper-class American society. Meanwhile, it is often forgotten that the group considered "Asian" includes such populations as Laotians, Hmong, Cambodians, Vietnamese, and Indonesians who have higher-than-average levels of poverty in the United States.

IMPLICATIONS FOR AFFIRMATIVE ACTION

The myth of the model minority works against any efforts to extend any affirmative action benefits or policies to Asian Americans, and in some cases Indian Americans. As the concept itself is a myth, many people have suggested that affirmative

Students of a Japanese-language school in Sacramento, California, around 1910. A long tradition of strong family support for education has contributed to the image of Asian Americans as "model minorities." (Sacramento Ethnic Survey, Sacramento Archives and Museum Collection Center)

action programs should work to disaggregate the Asian population in the United States and determine which populations' members do need assistance. There have also been calls to examine the areas in which Asian Americans have hit the so-called "glass ceiling" in corporate and political leadership with a view toward removing obstacles to their advancement in those fields.

Mary C. Ware

FURTHER READING

Chou, Rosalind S., and Joe R. Feagin. *The Myth of the Model Minority: Asian Americans Facing Racism.* Boulder, Colo.: Paradigm, 2008. Debunks the model minority myth by showing the depth of racism that Asian Americans actually encounter.

Fong, Timothy. *The Contemporary Asian American Experience: Beyond the Model Minority.* 3d ed. Upper Saddle River, N.J.: Prentice Hall. 2008. Focuses on how gender, race, and class intersect to affect Asian Americans.

Lee, Stacey. *Unraveling the "Model Minority" Stereotype: Listening to Asian American Youth.* New York: Teachers College Press, 1996. Drawing on interviews with many Chinese American, Japanese American, and Hmong youths, Lee uses the words of the young people themselves to show how mythic the model minority concept is by revealing the differences among Asian Americans that the stereotype works to hide.

Min, Pyong Gap, ed. *Asian Americans: Contemporary Trends and Issues.* Thousand Oaks, Calif.: Pine Forge Press, 2005. This book is distinguished from many others by focusing on issues directly affecting contemporary Asian Americans.

Takaki, Ronald. *Strangers from a Different Shore: A History of Asian Americans.* San Francisco: Back Bay Books, 1998. Popular history of Asian Americans, written by a well-known expert in the field. who illustrates the history with many primary sources.

SEE ALSO: Affirmative action; Amerasian children; Anti-Japanese movement; Asian immigrants; Assimilation theories; Chinese immigrants; Education; Immigrant advantage; Japanese immigrants; Korean immigrants; Stereotyping.

MOLLY MAGUIRES

IDENTIFICATION: Secret society of Irish miners
DATE: 1860's to 1878
LOCATION: Primarily eastern Pennsylvania

SIGNIFICANCE: The Molly Maguires illustrate the frustrations and disappointments that certain groups of immigrants encountered in the United States as they found harsh working conditions and a quality of life little better than that in their homeland.

The Molly Maguires were a secret brotherhood of Irish Roman Catholic miners who were believed to have used threats, bashings, and murder to intimidate mining supervisors in the anthracite coalfields of eastern Pennsylvania in the 1860's and 1870's. The Molly Maguires sought both revenge for unfair treatment and better working conditions. Molly Maguirism in the region came to an end when the leaders were arrested, tried, and executed for murder in a court proceeding that took place entirely under the authority of the coal companies.

Franklin B. Gowen, president of the Philadelphia and Reading Railroad and the Philadelphia and Reading Coal and Iron Company, hired Allan Pinkerton's detective agency to investigate the activities of the miners and paid a private police force to arrest them. The agency sent James McParlan to infiltrate the Molly Maguires and gather evidence regarding their activities. Posing as James McKenna, McParlan succeeded in gaining the trust of the miners and testified at the trials that he had participated in their meetings and activities. McParlan's testimony, corroborated by other witnesses who were employees in the mines, stated that the accused men committed the murders. Gowen served as special prosecutor at the trials. The jury, containing not a single Irish Catholic but made up primarily of non-English-speaking Pennsylvania Dutch, found the men guilty. In 1878, they were sentenced to death by hanging. The execution of the convicted Molly Maguires not only eliminated the violence in the coal mining region but also brought union activity to a halt.

According to McParlan, all the society members were Irish or sons of Irishmen and were Catholics. Members also belonged to the Ancient Order of Hibernians (AOH), a benevolent society whose purpose was to provide financial aid to any of their members who were in need. In addition, they belonged to the Workingmen's Benevolent Association (WBA), the union founded by John Siney in 1868. Both the AOH and the WBA were dedicated to improving the lives of the miners and their families, but neither advocated the use of violence and terrorism. There were accusations that the AOH was simply a front organization for the Molly Maguires. McParlan stated that any Molly Maguire who had a grievance against a mine supervisor or official could ask for retribution in the form of beating or murder. The membership voted and a Molly was assigned to carry out the punishment.

This was usually a Molly from another county in the region.

Historians fail to agree as to the actual existence of the Molly Maguires in the eastern Pennsylvania mining region. The Molly Maguires left no tangible evidence of their existence. Molly Maguires did exist in Ireland as a secret society of Irish Catholic tenant farmers who retaliated against wealthy Protestant landowners, both Irish and English, in the agrarian conflict over land usage. The Molly Maguires dressed in disguise as women, painted their faces with cork, and used intimidation and violence. Many of the Irish miners in Pennsylvania were from the regions of Ireland where the society was active. As mine laborers, they faced much of the same hardships and lack of fair treatment that they had fled. Dangerous working conditions, frequent disasters resulting in deaths, long hours, low wages, payment in scrip, and the policy of firing any miner who dared to complain appear reason enough for these workers to again unite as Molly Maguires.

Shawncey Webb

FURTHER READING

Dubofsky, Melvyn, and Foster Rhea Dulles. *Labor in America: A History*. Wheeling, Ill.: Harlan Davidson, 2004.

Kenny, Kevin. *Making Sense of the Molly Maguires*. New York: Oxford University Press, 1998.

SEE ALSO: Coal industry; Employment; Fenian movement; Great Irish Famine; Immigrant aid organizations; Irish immigrants; Labor unions; Pennsylvania; Pinkerton, Allan; Settlement patterns.

"MONGRELIZATION"

DEFINITION: Nonscientific theory that racial interbreeding causes degeneration of the human species

SIGNIFICANCE: As an expression of a conservative nationalist vision of America as a Protestant northern European country, ideas about "mongrelization" represented an entrenched mind-set that opposed extending open immigration to countries and races that were perceived to sully bloodlines of Nordic purity, which was regarded as the noblest manifestation of the American character.

Although from its inception America had been shaped by virtually unrestricted immigration, late nineteenth century conservatives began expressing their fears that allowing peoples such as Irish Catholics, eastern and southern Europeans, and Asians into the country threatened the American identity. The incendiary rhetoric surrounding controversial legislation curbing—or in some cases eliminating altogether—immigration from specific countries and regions deemed alien was based on the argument hat such immigrants compromised the racial makeup of the nation. Proponents of this view, who regarded themselves as fierce nationalists, defined American identity as based on western and northern European stock—which was white in skin color and primarily Protestant in religious beliefs.

The argument insisted that characteristics intrinsic to that Nordic American identity—intelligence, moral character, self-reliance, faith in democracy, sobriety, virtue, honesty, and a committed work ethic—adhered to some racial and ethnic groups but not to others. According to the argument, groups routinely designated as inferior would inevitably pollute the Nordic American bloodlines, creating "mongrel" generations of hyphenated ethnicity. The designation most often used to describe the immigration flow of these peoples was "hordes." Africans, Asians, and Mexicans were the peoples most commonly referred to as "hordes," but the term was also applied to Italians, Poles, Jews, Slavs, and other peoples from the Mediterranean basin. Advocates of the "mongrelization" theory wanted the immigration of all these peoples to be stopped or restricted.

The 1882 Chinese Exclusion Act and nearly six decades of subsequent legislation aimed at eliminating Asian immigration were manifestations of this argument. Unlike other types of immigrant restrictions—those based on the potential for political subversion or the potential for a health threat—the argument of mongrelization played to the bigotry and racist fears of the white Protestant American majority by designating certain ethnicities as undesirables.

The controversial eugenicist and self-proclaimed anthropologist Madison Grant published *The Pass-*

ing of the Great Race in 1916. In print for more than thirty years, this book made the unapologetic argument that the greatest evil facing the burgeoning American empire came from unrestricted immigration. Drawing on the metaphors—if not the science—of Charles Darwin, proponents of the mongrelization theory argued a kind of scientific racism. In proposing eugenics as a way to maintain American racial integrity, these vocal and impassioned public figures, most notably Senators Benjamin (Pitchfork Ben) Tillman of South Carolina and J. Thomas Helfin of Alabama, saw unrestricted immigration of such unsavory ethnicities as doing irreparable damage to the racial makeup and hence the moral integrity of Nordic America.

Mongrelization was largely discredited first by the groundbreaking work of professionally trained anthropologists during the 1930's who railed against such biological generalizations as the mongrelization theory as forms of fear-mongering. They argued for the influence of environment on shaping character and later cited the rise of Nazism in Adolf Hitler's Germany as an example of the dangers of notions of Nordic racial purity.

Joseph Dewey

FURTHER READING

Bennett, David H. *The Party of Fear: From Nativist Movements to the New Right in American History.* Chapel Hill: University of North Carolina Press, 1988.

Gerstle, Gary. *American Crucible: Race and Nation in the Twentieth Century.* New Brunswick, N.J.: Rutgers University Press, 2001.

Tirman, John, ed. *The Maze of Fear: Security and Migration After 9/11.* New York: New Press, 2004.

SEE ALSO: Anti-Chinese movement; Anti-Japanese movement; Anti-Semitism; Asian immigrants; Eugenics movement; European immigrants; History of immigration after 1891; Quota systems; Stereotyping; Xenophobia.

MONTANA

SIGNIFICANCE: Montana's links to immigration have a great deal to do with the mining industry. As the state's mines developed and became specialized, immigrant labor was frequently brought in to work the mines and to service the mining industry in supporting roles. Immigration into Montana has been limited since the late twentieth century. A rising number of newcomers are entering the state to take advantage of its economic and social benefits.

At the time Montana became a state in 1889, the mining industry had been well established throughout the territory for thirty years. Prospectors began working the hills of southern Montana during the 1850's. In 1862, the discovery of gold in Grasshopper Creek began a small gold rush that brought miners and speculators from California, Wyoming, and Colorado. Another gold strike was made during the following year, near the location of modern Virginia City, increasing the flow of people into Montana. As the mining industry developed, laborers were brought in to perform the demanding and dangerous work of extracting ore from the ground.

LATE NINETEENTH CENTURY IMMIGRATION

During the nineteenth century, much of the difficult and dangerous mining work in Montana was done by Chinese immigrants and African Americans. These workers were generally paid at much lower rates than white workers and were frequently given perilous and demeaning tasks that other workers refused to do. Immigrants from Ireland, England, Germany, and the Scandinavian nations also entered the region to work as miners, merchants, and investors, hoping to strike it rich during Montana's boom years. As the twentieth century approached, different regions of Montana began to specialize in certain ores. For example, Butte became a primary copper supplier for the entire United States, and Philipsburg specialized in silver production. Butte's copper mines employed workers from Greece, Bulgaria, Romania, Serbia, Poland, Czechoslovakia, Finland, and Italy.

Twentieth Century Developments

During the twentieth century, Montana's population began to stabilize as the boom-and-bust mining and land speculation industries became secondary to the state's agricultural and ranching industries. With the revisions to the Homestead Act of 1862 during the early twentieth century, immigrants were attracted to Montana by the availability of 320-acre plots of farmland for low prices. Many of these new arrivals relocated from areas in the American Midwest, particularly from Illinois and Indiana, and moved into southern and western Montana in search of good farmland and sites for home construction. The people moving into Montana were also increasingly foreign. By 1910, more than 25 percent of Montana's population was classified as foreign born. New immigrants not involved in the mining industry typically worked in agriculture, growing Montana's primary crops—wheat, barley, sugar beets, and rye. Some became ranchers, raising cattle and sheep. Throughout the twentieth century, agriculture dominated Montana's economy.

By the early twenty-first century, Montana's population was typical of states in the northern Rocky Mountain region. More than 92 percent of the population were classified as "white," with very small numbers of African Americans, Asians, and Pacific Islanders. Native American accounted for about 4 percent of all Montanans, with a growing Hispanic population making up another 3 percent. The largest Hispanic concentration was located within the urban region of Billings.

Robert D. Mitchell

Further Reading

Lee, Rose Hum. *The Growth and Decline of Chinese Communities in the Rocky Mountain Region.* New York: Arno Press, 1978.

Montana Writers' Program. *Copper Camp: Stories of the World's Greatest Mining Town, Butte, Montana.* New York: Hastings House, 1943.

Murphy, Mary. *Mining Cultures: Men, Women and Leisure in Butte, 1914-41.* Champaign: University of Illinois Press, 1997.

Profile of Montana

Region	Northwest
Entered union	1889
Largest cities	Billings, Missoula, Great Falls
Modern immigrant communities	Hispanics, Chinese

Population	Total	Percent of state	Percent of U.S.	U.S. rank
All state residents	945,000	100.0	0.32	44
All foreign-born residents	18,000	1.9	0.05	47

Source: U.S. Census Bureau, *Statistical Abstract for 2006.*
Notes: The U.S. population in 2006 was 299,399,000, of whom 37,548,000 (12.5%) were foreign born. Rankings in last column reflect total numbers, not percentages.

See also: African Americans and immigrants; Chinese immigrants; Economic opportunities; Employment; History of immigration after 1891; Idaho; Italian immigrants; Labor unions; Railroads.

"Moral turpitude"

Definition: Loosely defined term that is generally construed to encompass any behavior that gravely shocks or violates the sentiments or accepted standards of a community

Significance: In American immigration law, the term "moral turpitude" first appeared in the Immigration Act of 1891, in which it was provided as a basis for excluding immigrants suspected of possessing low morals from entering the country or as grounds for deporting previously admitted immigrants.

The concept of "moral turpitude" can be traced to a Middle English expression term with Latin roots that means "shame" and connotes immoral behavior. In modern legal parlance, moral turpitude suggests behavior that is evil in and of itself and not merely because it is prohibited by law. For example, drunk driving is not a crime of moral turpitude, but drunk driving without a license is.

An elusive concept related more to cultural concepts of sin than to statutory law, moral turpitude is sometimes associated with the sins outlined in the Old Testament's Ten Commandments. Ambiguity in the meaning of the term has allowed U.S. immigration officers such a wide latitude that they can rule to exclude or deport persons whom they personally dislike, including those presumed to engage in victimless crimes, such as consensual sexual conduct and substance abuse.

For example, immigrants suspected of being homosexuals were usually rejected before 1973, when the American Psychiatric Association stopped calling homosexuality a mental disorder. However, gay people can still be excluded because the law allows exclusion of "psychopathic personalities" apart from crimes of "moral turpitude." Foreigners who marry Americans in same-sex ceremonies have, for example, been excluded. Border agents have the power to stop persons from entering the country on the basis of a list of about thirty "indicators" of homosexuality while they survey visitors lined up at immigration checkpoints. Those who enter and are subsequently deemed sexual psychopaths may have their passports stamped "sexual deviate" as they leave the country, thereby subjecting them to the possibility of being incarcerated upon arrival in their home countries.

CATEGORIES OF CRIMES

The term "moral turpitude" encompasses a wide variety of actual crimes, which fall under four headings:

- Crimes against property, such as fraud and robbery and even shoplifting
- Crimes against government, most notably bribery, counterfeiting, and perjury
- Crimes against persons, including victimless offenses
- Aiding, abetting, or engaging in conspiracies to commit crimes of moral turpitude

The Immigration and Nationality Technical Corrections Act of 1994 increased the number of "aggravated felonies" that can provide grounds for deportation. In 1996, the law was amended to permit the attorney general of the United States to deport, without a prior hearing, any person convicted of any recent crime of "moral turpitude."

Michael Haas

FURTHER READING

Freilich, Joshua D., and Graeme Newman, eds. *Crime and Immigration.* Burlington, Vt.: Ashgate, 2007.

New York State Defenders Association. *Representing Immigrant Defendants in New York.* 4th ed. New York: Author, 2008.

Weissbrodt, David, and Laura Danielson. *Immigration Law and Procedure in a Nutshell.* 5th ed. St. Paul, Minn.: Thomson/West, 2005.

SEE ALSO: *Boutilier v. Immigration and Naturalization Service*; Congress, U.S.; Deportation; Gay and lesbian immigrants; Immigration Act of 1891; Immigration Reform and Control Act of 1986; Lennon, John.

MORMON IMMIGRANTS

IDENTIFICATION: Converts to the Church of Jesus Christ of Latter-day Saints who immigrated to North America

SIGNIFICANCE: Immigration of Mormon converts from outside the United States was an important part of the building of the Mormon Church into an international organization. The immigration of tens of thousands who saw the United States as a "New Zion" is another example of immigrants seeking religious freedom in the United States.

One of the first major religious movements entirely indigenous to the United States, the Church of Jesus Christ of Latter-day Saints—who are better known as Mormons—was founded in New York State by Joseph Smith in 1830. Almost immediately after the church was organized, Smith began sending missionaries to Europe to recruit new members. At a time when many Europeans were already warming to the idea of emigrating to North America, the missionaries' message of a "New Zion" was warmly received. The missionaries found thousands of converts in northern and western European nations during the 1840's and 1850's, creating a vibrant Mormon movement in Europe. However, because the religion was founded on the belief that the United States represented a New

Zion, Mormon leaders began making plans to transport European converts across the Atlantic.

IMMIGRANT GROUPS

One of the first significant groups of European converts to come to North America were English immigrants who arrived on the British ship *Britannia* in 1840. Its passengers immediately went to the main Mormon settlement in Nauvoo, a booming Illinois town on the Mississippi River. The leader of this group, John Moon, soon sent glowing reports back to England that convinced other Mormon converts to start for the United States. In 1849, by which time church headquarters had relocated to Salt Lake City, Utah, the church's new president, Brigham Young, founded the Perpetual Emigration Fund Company. Financed by church donations, this body paid for the transatlantic passages of impoverished converts. It also provided money for transportation, food, clothing, and wagons to help the immigrants travel overland to settlements in the West.

The peak years of Mormon immigration occurred between the 1850's and 1890's, during which tens of thousands of European converts came to the United States. Among these were more than 50,000 British converts and about 20,000 Scandinavians. The largest group of Scandinavians were Danes, who began emigrating in 1852 during a period of domestic turmoil and military conflict between Denmark and nearby German kingdoms. The Mormon leader in Denmark, Erastus Snow, organized transport for more than 10,000 Danish converts. Europeans always constituted the largest portion of Mormon immigrants, but some came from other parts of the world, most notably Australia.

IMMIGRATION ROUTES

Most European converts reached North America by way of Liverpool, England, from which to they sailed to New Orleans, Louisiana. A Mormon agent in Liverpool helped converts to find ships and provided them with contacts in the United

Mormon immigrants moving west on the Oregon Trail. Some immigrants who were unable to afford draft animals crossed the plains pushing and pulling handcarts. (Library of Congress)

States. Some Mormon-chartered boats were also used for immigrants. New Orleans was the favored port of entry into the United States because it was on the mouth of the Mississippi River, up which immigrants could ride steamboats to Nauvoo during the 1840's. After most Mormons relocated to the West, new immigrants could take steamboats up the Mississippi to the Missouri River, on which they could continue west on steamboats. However, many immigrants faced arduous overland journeys to reach New Zion until the first transcontinental railroad was completed in 1869. Passing through northern Utah, the railroad provided fast, safe, and direct transportation to Mormon territory from points in the East. Consequently, increasingly numbers of European immigrants reached Utah by sailing to New York City.

HAZARDS OF TRAVEL

Sailing across the North Atlantic and Pacific in passenger ships was generally a hazardous undertaking in mid-nineteenth century sailing ships, but most Mormon immigrants enjoyed relatively safe journeys. In 1854, however, the ship *Julia Ann* was en route from Australia to North America with several Mormon immigrants when it struck a coral reef and sank. Although casualties were limited, the sinking was a reminder of the dangers facing all transoceanic immigrants. Moreover, the perils of travel did not end when the immigrants landed in North America. Cross-country overland journeys were full of perils, and freshwater transportation had its own deadly perils. In April, 1852, a large number of Mormon converts from Wales and England were traveling up the Missouri River on the steamboat *Saluda*, when its boilers exploded near Lexington, Missouri. The explosion quickly sank the boat, killed scores of passengers, and left several orphaned children.

MORMON STRUGGLES

The Mormons' success in settling and developing the Utah Territory may have had the ironic effect of harming their immigration efforts. Under Brigham Young's leadership, many church members practiced plural marriage. The growing size of the church and the development of Utah attracted widespread attention to Mormon polygamy in the East. Criticisms of polygamy and other unusual Mormon practices prompted the federal government to pay closer attention to the administration of Utah Territory. The government shut down the church's immigration fund, slowing Mormon immigration by making it more difficult for European immigrants to reach the country. Federal officials also closely questioned many Mormon immigrants and sent some back to their home countries. As government pressures on the Mormon polygamy mounted, some polygamist families emigrated to colonies in Mexico and Canada.

Eventually, however, the church officially abandoned its support for plural marriage, and Utah was admitted to the union as a state in 1896. During the twentieth century, the church continued an aggressive missionary program throughout the world but did not make a practice of encouraging new converts to immigrate to the United States.

More than a century after the great wave of Mormon immigration ended, the church created the Mormon Immigration Index, a list of more than 90,000 converts who came to the United States during the nineteenth century. The compilation of names includes the diaries and other writings of immigrants detailing their journeys to their new Zion.

Douglas Clouatre

FURTHER READING

Abanes, Richard. *One Nation Under Gods: A History of the Mormon Church.* New York: Four Walls Eight Windows, 2002. Well-documented book that covers the Mormon Church's struggles with the U.S. government and its efforts to convert followers.

Arrington, Leonard J. *Brigham Young: American Moses.* New York: Alfred A. Knopf, 1985. Biography of one of the founding leaders of the Mormon Church. Includes details of Brigham Young's efforts to spread the religion around the world.

Mulder, William. *Homeward to Zion: The Mormon Migration from Scandinavia.* Minneapolis: University of Minnesota Press, 2000. Recounts stories of survival and tragedy as Mormons migrated from Scandinavia through the United States and into Utah.

Roberts, David. *Devil's Gate: Brigham Young and the Great Mormon Handcart Tragedy.* New York: Simon & Schuster, 2008. Account of the Mormon handcart migration from Iowa to Utah, a tragic trek across the inhospitable American West.

Stegner, Wallace. *The Gathering of Zion: The Story of the Mormon Trail.* New York: McGraw-Hill, 1964. Overview of the Mormon Church that includes sections on Mormon migration.

SEE ALSO: British immigrants; Congress, U.S.; Immigrant aid organizations; Missionaries; Nativism; Pacific Islander immigrants; Utah; Westward expansion.

MOTEL INDUSTRY

DEFINITION: Guest-accommodation industry that arose during the twentieth century to serve people traveling on highways

SIGNIFICANCE: Due to changing economic conditions in the United States and changes in immigration laws, immigrants from South Asia—particularly Indians—began to dominate the middle tier of the American motel industry during the last two decades of the twentieth century.

The path of South Asians to the United States has been a convoluted one. During the long era of the British Empire, the British sent many people from their Indian possession to other colonies in regions such as East Africa and the West Indies. In these places the transplanted Indians performed many types of labor, particularly in service industries. After Great Britain lost most of its colonies, most of the transplanted Indians remained in their new homes, continuing to work as tradespeople, civil servants, and clerks. However, during the late twentieth century, political instability in many of the former British colonies made it difficult for Asians to live and work safely. Some of these people relocated to Great Britain, but others came to the United States.

Around the same period that Indians were immigrating to the United States from other countries around the world, the American budget motel industry was becoming economically distressed. Immigrants often found that they could purchase a roadside motel for as little as forty thousand dollars. This was an amount that many Indian immigrants could afford. Moreover, the motel business was particularly well suited to Hindus, who accounted for the vast majority of Indian immigrants. Operating restaurants catering to American tastes would have been problematic, as Hindus are not allowed by their religion to handle meat. Grocery stores required large investments, and many other businesses required licensing or special training. Consequently, the budget motel industry seemed almost ideal for Indian immigrants. Motel managers could live at their places of business, thereby minimizing their personal housing costs. The language barrier was not overly difficult for Indians to surmount. Indeed, most motel managers have reported that the most important criterion for business success was a willingness to work long hours.

The depth of Asian Indian involvement in the American accommodations industry can be seen

---

THE PATEL CLAN

Throughout the United States, travelers taking rooms in public accommodations such as Days Inn, Motel 6. and other economical middle-tier motel chains might wonder why nearly all the motel managers and owners whom they encounter appear to be immigrants from India. They also might wonder why the most common surname among these individuals is "Patel." To a casual observer, it might seem that nearly all motels are owned and managed by someone who appears to be from India and is named Patel. This has not been far from the true.

The Patel clan was one of the largest clans represented among the South Asians who have immigrated to the United States, and its members have been particularly entrepreneurial. Members of the Patel clan were such prominent shopkeepers and businesspeople in their native India and in East Africa that it was jokingly said of them that they carried a "commerce gene." During the 1960's and 1970's, Patels began coming to the United States and Canada in large numbers. At that time, U.S. immigration laws allow anyone willing and able to invest forty thousand dollars in a business enterprise to apply for permanent residence that could lead to citizenship. It was thus natural for many of them to move into the motel industry.

in the size of the Asian American Hotel Owners Association, a professional organization whose members operated more than twenty thousand motels and hotels across the United States in the year 2009. These twenty thousand establishments represented than 50 percent of all middle-tier public lodging in the country, and association members also owned or managed 40 percent of all American hotel properties, including upscale hotels. These numbers represent a remarkable entrepreneurial achievement by members of the Indian American population, who collectively account for fewer than 1 percent of the total U.S. population. Equally remarkable is the fact that Indian Americans reached this level of involvement in fewer than three decades.

Mary C. Ware

FURTHER READING

Asian American Hotel Owners Association Annual Report. Atlanta, Ga.: AAHOA, 2008.

Duttagupta, Ishani. "March of the Indian Entrepreneurs." *The Economic Times* (Mumbai, India), February 6, 2009.

Helweg, Arthur W. *Strangers in a Not-So-Strange Land: Indian American Immigrants in the Global Age.* Florence, Ky.: Wadsworth, 2004.

SEE ALSO: Asian immigrants; Asian Indian immigrants; Association of Indians in America; Congress, U.S.; Economic opportunities; Employment; History of immigration after 1891.

MUIR, JOHN

IDENTIFICATION: Scottish-born American writer, naturalist, and conservationist

BORN: April 21, 1838; Dunbar, Scotland

DIED: December 24, 1914; Los Angeles, California

SIGNIFICANCE: Muir loved the wilderness in North America, which contrasted with the rocky, bare coast of his native Dunbar, Scotland. He helped found the conservation movement in the United States and cofounded the Sierra Club, originally dedicated to the protection of Yosemite National Park and later to the preservation of wilderness in the United States.

John Muir. (Library of Congress)

In *The Story of My Boyhood and Youth* (1913), John Muir wrote that he felt no regret when his father moved the family in 1849 from Scotland to America, as he immediately fell in love with the North American wilderness. Initially headed for Canada, the Muir family settled in southeastern Wisconsin. In 1880, Muir married Louisa Wanda Strentzel, the daughter of a Polish immigrant father and an American-born mother.

Muir explored and lived for a while in the Sierra Nevadas in California. He made several expeditions to Alaska and wrote numerous articles and books about his travels. He had a particular affinity for the Yosemite region in east central California. Indeed, Muir was largely responsible for the establishment of Yosemite as a national park in 1890, and through his efforts other national parks were set up. Considered the "father of the national parks," Muir also cofounded the environmental organization Sierra Club in 1892.

Richard Tuerk

FURTHER READING

Cohen, Michael P. *The Pathless Way: John Muir and American Wilderness.* Madison: University of Wisconsin Press, 1984.

Miller, Sally M., and Daryl Morrison, eds. *John Muir: Family, Friends, and Adventures.* Albuquerque: University of New Mexico Press, 2005.

Turner, Frederick. *Rediscovering America: John Muir in His Time and Ours.* New York: Viking Press, 1985.

SEE ALSO: Assimilation theories; British immigrants; Canada vs. United States as immigrant destinations; Intermarriage; Wisconsin.

MUKHERJEE, BHARATI

IDENTIFICATION: Indian-born American teacher and author

BORN: July 27, 1940; Calcutta (now Kolkata), India

SIGNIFICANCE: A writer, professor, and forceful speaker on immigration, Mukherjee is best known for her fictional works about Indian immigrants in North America. Through 2008, she had published seven novels, several collections of short stories, and a number of nonfictional essays and books, many of which touch on immigration issues.

Born in India in 1940, Bharati Mukherjee was the daughter of a pharmaceutical chemist. At an early age, she demonstrated literary ability. She could read and write by the age of three and decided to be an author by the age of ten. Life in Calcutta meant sharing a home with her father's extended family, with as many as fifty relatives living in one establishment. In 1947, her family emigrated to Great Britain, where she lived for more than three years. After returning to India, she earned bachelor's and master's degrees in English and ancient Indian culture in her home country. She then became an immigrant again, when she went to the United States to earn a master of fine arts degree in creative writing and a doctorate in English and comparative literature at the University of Iowa. In 1963, she married Canadian writer Clark Blaise after a two-week acquaintance.

After completing her doctorate in 1969, Mukherjee immigrated to Canada, where she became a naturalized citizen in 1972. Many of her writings describe her years in Canada as a time of discrimination, as she found Canadian citizens generally antagonistic toward Asian immigrants. This view can particularly be seen in her first collection of short stories, *Darkness* (1985), which echoes the occurrences of ethnic division she observed and underwent while living in Canada.

In 1980, Mukherjee moved to the United States, where she became a permanent resident. She regarded her immigration status in the United States as triumphant and embraced the "melting pot" philosophy that allowed her to become an American citizen in 1987. In becoming a citizen of the United States, she eschewed the idea that she was an "Asian American" or an "Indian American" as racist. Instead, she called herself an American with Bengali Indian origins.

Mukherjee's work has often been criticized for its inclusion of immigration issues, and she has challenged the stereotypes of immigrants that she has often seen reinforced in academic and publishing realms. Although her characters are typically female immigrants who have experienced discrimination in some form, her stories provide a powerful survival theme as their characters overcome the handicaps of their foreign backgrounds, experiences, and sorrows to find new directions.

In an attempt to break the stereotype that all Indian immigrants come from the same cultural background, Mukherjee stresses the individuality of each of her characters, rather than the overall immigrant experience. Moreover, rather than allowing herself to be absorbed into the postcolonial tradition, her objective in writing is not only to show that a person can be influenced by past experiences, culture, and beliefs, but also to demonstrate that the present experiences, culture, and beliefs play an integral part of who one will become in the future. To show the realistic span of ideas about immigration, Mukherjee incorporates characters from a range of immigration experiences, including characters who behave as postcolonials and expatriates—holding onto their pasts with nostalgic fervor—as well as characters who embrace a new life despite their race or ethnicity.

Theresa L. Stowell

FURTHER READING

Alam, Fakrul. *Bharati Mukherjee.* New York: Twayne, 1996.

Kumar, Amitava. *Away: The Indian Writer as an Expatriate.* New York: Routledge, 2004.

Zhou, Xiaojing, and Samina Najmi. *Form and Transformation in Asian American Literature.* Seattle: University of Washington Press, 2005.

SEE ALSO: Asian American literature; Asian Indian immigrants; Association of Indians in America; Lahiri, Jhumpa; Lim, Shirley Geok-lin; Literature; Sidhwa, Bapsi.

MULTICULTURALISM

DEFINITION: View that no single ethnic group should impose its culture onto the rest of the population of a diverse country but instead will benefit from greater familiarity with and respect for contributions of all cultural groups.

SIGNIFICANCE: Since the mid-1960's, multiculturalists have worked to counter tendencies of immigrant groups and minorities to be denigrated. They have succeeded in gaining adoption of on-the-job cultural sensitivity programs and educational curricula presenting positive images of nonmainstream groups. Government agencies have implemented multicultural reforms in response to pressure from minorities to decrease discrimination and prejudice, much of which resulted from ignorance of the contributions and customs of diverse cultural groups in American society.

In July, 1941, as World War II was being waged by ultranationalists in Germany and Japan, an obscure book review in the *New York Herald-Tribune* advocated "multiculturalism" as an antidote to nationalism. The term reappeared in a Canadian government report on bilingualism in 1965 that recommended that "multiculturalism" replace the "bicultural" policies of Canada that had been granting linguistic equality to English and French.

CIVIL RIGHTS MOVEMENT

Meanwhile, in the United States, the federal Civil Rights Act of 1964 outlawed discrimination in employment, government facilities and programs, public accommodations, and voting, thereby outlawing racial segregation in most areas of public life. In an executive order the following year, President Lyndon B. Johnson mandated government contractors to engage in "affirmative action" by hiring qualified members of minority groups previously excluded. Discrimination was also outlawed in the Immigration and Nationality Act of 1965, which resulted in a considerable increase in non-European immigrants.

The movement that produced civil rights legislation also pressured American universities to establish ethnic studies programs, on the premise that the historical status of nonmainstream cultures in the United States had been neglected, consistent with a policy of assimilationist Anglo-conformity, so the research agenda was to uncover the contributions of diverse minority groups to the United States, document patterns of discrimination, and otherwise enrich American scholarship by focusing on the cultural diversity of the United States. Educational institutions then voluntarily adopted programs of affirmative action, even though they were not required by law to do so.

Because not all employers voluntarily complied with affirmative action and nondiscrimination requirements, members of minority groups felt as frustrated as government officials who monitored that lack of progress. Concrete programs were needed to overcome resistance attributable to stereotypes and other factors. Immigrants with cultural practices that did not conform to the mainstream were particularly disadvantaged. For example, members of minority groups traditionally known for being employed in menial labor had difficulty being hired for white-collar jobs. In addition, federally funded mental health programs serviced few minorities, partly because many members of minorities were recent immigrants from countries in which the concept of mental illness was not understood as a treatable medical condition. To overcome favoritism toward members of the majority group, employers and directors of mental health and other government-funded programs were urged to adopt cultural sensitivity training, which relied heavily on the scholarship of ethnic studies researchers.

Cultural sensitivity training was designed for adults, and it appeared it would be needed as long as children grew up with mistaken and stereotypical ideas about ethnic groups based on ignorance. Accordingly, curriculum reform from kindergarten to college was on the education agenda during the 1970's to ensure that young people would have more respect for minority cultures that would translate into better utilization of government programs and nondiscrimination in employment. In *Lau v. Nichols* (1972), the U.S. Supreme Court ordered schools to assist language minority children, primarily immigrants, through bilingual and English-as-a-second-language programs.

Multiculturalism soon enjoyed many new forms of government support: approval of radio and television stations in minority languages, funding for minority arts and music, financial aid to minority businesses, scholarships for minority students, voting on ballots in minority languages, and acceptance of holidays for minorities. The establishment of African American civil rights leader Martin Luther King, Jr.'s birthday as a federal holiday in 1983 is an example of the latter.

Focus on the special needs of underrepresented groups broadened in scope. Women were the first to benefit, as employment discrimination based on gender was outlawed in the Civil Rights Act of 1964. Other forms of discrimination were banned in subsequent years. The term "multicultural" was soon interpreted to encompass respect for people of different ages, physical and mental capabilities, and sexual orientations.

Commercially, multiculturalism has been profitable. From the sale of traditional furniture and items such as "Black Is Beautiful" sweatshirts, marketing campaigns directed at members of different cultural groups has been successful. At the same time, owners of cinemas have converted single-screen theaters into multiplex operations that can offer films to multiple niche markets simultaneously.

BACKLASH AGAINST MULTICULTURALISM

Perhaps inevitably, some multicultural innovations were badly designed or implemented. How-

In one of the most multicultural naturalization ceremonies in U.S. history, 14,000 immigrants from 111 different countries were sworn in as American citizens in Fort Lauderdale, Florida, in September, 2000. (Getty Images)

ever, the general, incremental progress of multiculturalism gradually rankled many people in the mainstream who resented being labeled as "Americentric," "Eurocentric," "parochial," or "prejudiced," or who otherwise felt that they were being vilified. The main premise of the counterattack was that the United States was basically a product of Western civilization, so any attempt to divert attention from that foundation imperiled national unity and undermined fundamental values. For the critics, multiculturalism had gone too far.

One of the endangered values was said to be respect for competence. Some beneficiaries of affirmative action, notably students at leading universities, were told that they had been admitted to the institution merely because of their ethnicity, not because they were qualified. When private businesses were pressured to fill what they perceived as ethnic quotas in their workforce, white male job applicants cried out against "reverse discrimination." The same was true of many disappointed applicants for entry to prestigious universities.

Whereas cultural pluralists view each culture as making unique and valuable contributions to a collectively shared mainstream, multiculturalists were accused of being more concerned with preserving the distinctions among cultures. Accordingly, the aim of bilingual education morphed from serving as a transition to English-language literacy for immigrants into a permanent track in elementary and secondary education in which the entire educational curriculum might be learned in a language other than English, thereby stunting the ability of immigrants to rise in social mobility. In Hawaii, for example, residents with Native Hawaiian ancestry were provided opportunities to attend schools in which the initial language of instruction was Hawaiian, with English introduced for the first time in the fourth grade.

Another criticism of multiculturalism was that the teaching of basic American history was being eclipsed by too much attention to minority history. Because fundamental principles of American culture and democracy were treated as an orthodoxy that needed to be challenged, the result, according to critics, was cacophony and confusion in the minds of students, including members of minority groups themselves.

Multiculturalism was said to unleash identity politics and political correctness. Identity politics involved the pursuit of public policies by each ethnic group without cooperating with other ethnic groups, sometimes resulting in advocacy of conflicting solutions and lack of progress for all groups. Political correctness meant that one would be accused of being a racist for making factual statements about group characteristics or for posing hypotheses about differences among various ethnic groups. Multiculturalists responded that such statements created a "hostile environment" for students and workers, producing a chilling effect on what could be said in public, according to their critics.

Philosophically, multiculturalists were attacked for advocating a relativism in which everything is both true and not true, depending on one's cultural perspective. Social science was questioned as inherently ideological, so college debates regarding differences of opinion on public policy issues were no longer focused on achieving consensus but instead on mobilizing support among minorities to prevail over the traditional mainstream view or vice versa.

ALTERNATIVES TO MULTICULTURALISM

Both monoculturalism and multiculturalism were eventually challenged by interculturalism. The latter view holds that members of different cultures should learn from one another, rather than have one culture prevail or allow diverse cultures to become separatist. Interculturalists strive to find commonalities and consider differences as subcultures.

Another alternative, polyculturalism, insists that the world's cultures have been in flux in part because they have influenced one another for centuries, are interrelated, and therefore possess common values that should be stressed. Those who have long said that they are "citizens of the world," rather than nationalists, now reside under the banner of polyculturalism.

The election of Barack Obama to the U.S. presidency in 2008 may have opened a new chapter on multiculturalism, as many expect that this first African American president will adopt "postracial" public policies that bring Americans together after decades of "culture wars." Obama spent the first eighteen years in his life in Indonesia and Hawaii, outside the American mainland, and with relatives on four continents as well as in the mid-Pacific. His values were shaped by multicultural experiences. He also taught American constitutional law with a focus on civil rights. His apparent interculturalist message was that diverse Americans should listen to one another in order to achieve pragmatic solutions to festering problems. Many observers hoped that his message would be translated into action during his presidency.

Michael Haas

Further Reading

Bennett, Milton J. *Basic Concepts of Intercultural Communication.* Boston: Intercultural Press, 1998. Develops a methodology for intercultural communication.

Bloom, Allan. *Closing of the American Mind: How Higher Education Has Failed Democracy and Impoverished the Souls of Today's Students.* New York: Simon & Schuster, 1989. By the most prominent early opponent of the multiculturalist ethos, which the author compares to the malaise in pre-Hitler Germany. Bloom was concerned that multiculturalists saw all "truth" as relative, while the best-financed entertainers promoted mindless hedonism and narcissism.

Haas, Michael, ed. *Multicultural Hawai'i: The Fabric of a Multiethnic Society.* New York: Garland Press, 1998. Collection of articles on aspects of multiculturalism in Hawaii, ranging from literature and music to education and politics. Contributions describe a form of multiculturalism that developed not from government intervention but from social necessity. Some of the state's diverse cultural groups were historically bitter rivals and had to learn to live together in close proximity on Hawaii's small islands.

Kivisto, Peter, and Georganne Rundblad, eds. *Multiculturalism in the United States: Current Issues, Contemporary Voices.* Thousand Oaks, Calif.: Pine Forge Press, 2000. Anthology of article presenting nearly fifty diverse views on aspects of multiculturalism.

Kymlicka, Will. *Multicultural Citizenship: A Liberal Theory of Minority Rights.* Oxford, England: Clarendon Press, 1995. Written by a Canadian, a classic statement supporting multiculturalism.

Okin, Susan M. *Is Multiculturalism Bad for Women?* Princeton, N.J.: Princeton University Press, 1999. Focuses on how the preservation of cultural diversity may overshadow or even block the effort to dismantle male dominance in American society by marginalizing women's rights issues, including the right to an abortion and to avoid the humiliating roles assigned to women in traditional non-Western cultures.

Prashad, Vijay. *Everybody Was Kung Fu Fighting: Afro-Asian Connections and the Myth of Cultural Purity.* Boston: Beacon Press, 2001. Classic statement of polyculturalism.

Schlesinger, Arthur M., Jr. *The Disunitinig of America: Reflections on a Multicultural Society.* Rev. ed. New York: W. W. Norton, 1998. While accepting cultural pluralism, in which diverse cultures join together in a democratic culture, Schlesinger attacks the "cult of ethnicity" for endangering national unity by focusing on crimes committed by Western civilization on non-Western cultures while ignoring the positive elements of Western heritage.

See also: Affirmative action; Anglo-conformity; Assimilation theories; Civil Rights movement; Cultural pluralism; Education; Immigration and Nationality Act of 1965; Language issues; *Lau v. Nichols*; Stereotyping.

Music

Significance: As successive waves of immigrants arrived in North America, their musical traditions provided a link with their homelands and served as an aspect of group identity. With time, these traditions changed in response to new contexts and merged with other traditions as new forms of music were created.

During the period of European colonization of America, settlers, missionaries, and traders from Spain, Holland, England, France, and other nations began to interact with some of the many Native American nations and communities that they encountered, initially in the Atlantic, Pacific, and Gulf coastal regions. Often an integral part of ceremonies, Native American musical styles reflect the various belief systems, environments, and narratives of diverse Amerindian cultures. After the voice, which is used in group singing as well as in solo genres, the most common indigenous instruments are drums and other percussion instruments.

Despite dislocations, genocide, and assimilation, many Native Americans maintained musical practices along with language and rituals, and sometimes adopted instruments and forms from nonnative communities, especially in rural areas. During the latter half of the twentieth century, activists in the pan-Indian movement utilized music, occasionally blending native elements with familiar rock and country styles, to raise political consciousness. The institution of the powwow often includes traditional music and dance performances in large cultural gatherings. Native American music has also been associated with meditation and the environmental movement. Nonnative American music has been influenced by native concepts of individuality in music, in that certain songs come into existence through private experiences associated with personal growth.

SPANISH SETTLERS AND HISPANIC COMMUNITIES

Spanish settlements in Florida, in Texas, and along the California coast during the sixteenth through eighteenth centuries brought Roman Catholic liturgical music to the area as part of the mission system, and eventually settlers brought secular Spanish music as well, including stringed instruments such as the *vihuela*, guitar, and violin. Over time, cultural blending between Spanish and Native Americans resulted in syncretic practices, especially with regard to religious festivals. During the nineteenth century, Mexican song genres such as the *ranchera* and *corrido* were sung and accompanied by traveling groups, who also incorporated musical elements from central European immigrant cultures.

Mexicans waiting to find day jobs in East Los Angeles play mariachi tunes, perhaps the most emblematic form of Mexican music. (Getty Images)

After the northern parts of Mexico became part of the United States in 1848, Hispanic and mestizo (blended) musical culture continued to develop in those regions and was further augmented by continued immigration from Latin America to the United States. In addition to the older communities in the American Southwest, newer immigrants from Puerto Rico and other areas created vibrant enclaves in many American cities, particularly in New York, and contributed to the development of salsa, Latin rock, and other genres.

NORTHERN EUROPEAN SETTLERS AND COMMUNITIES

English and Dutch colonists brought their music with them as they established settlements in Virginia, in Massachusetts, and along the Hudson River during the seventeenth century. Congregational hymn singing was very important, especially in the Plymouth Bay settlement that was originally established as a religious community. Singing schools, taught by traveling musicians known as singing masters, became a way for communities to enjoy social gatherings as people learned part-singing, often with the aid of "shape notes" (solfeggio symbols combined with staff notation). Singing schools spread throughout the United States during the nineteenth century and led to the development of Sacred Harp singing in the South.

Secular music and instruments were also brought from England and other northern European countries. Often, the secular music was associated with social dancing (usually country dancing, square dancing, and quadrilles). During the nineteenth century, band music was cultivated, and the piano became an important instrument for middle- and upper-class families, who often gathered around the piano for recreational singing. As in England, women were encouraged to learn piano for playing within the home but discouraged from public performances. Concerts of classical music were sometimes given by European musicians for American audiences. Less sophisticated Anglo-American audiences enjoyed humorous minstrel shows, which portrayed derogatory stereotypes of African Americans to the accompaniment of lively music. French-speaking settlers who had been removed from eastern Canada during conflicts of the late eighteenth century eventually settled in western Louisiana, which alternated being a French and Spanish colony. They became known as Cajuns (or Acadians), maintained their language, and developed a unique musical style known as zydeco.

AFRICAN AMERICAN COMMUNITIES

Beginning in the early seventeenth century, West African captives were forcibly brought to the American colonies as part of the Atlantic slave trade, and in reaction to physical and cultural oppression, they developed powerful forms of musical expression. The primary vocal tradition became known as spirituals: religious songs that also carried coded messages for escape and community support. Themes of redemption and justice in spirituals were both transcendent and concrete.

A secondary genre was functional vocal music to accompany manual labor. Both forms utilized West African concepts of "call and response," in which musical phrases would alternate between a solo voice and group singing. Often, repetition would be used, with emotional intensity increasing through embellishment and inflection. Although drums were forbidden (with the notable exception of Spanish- and French-controlled areas), the banjo was reconstructed from African prototypes and eventually entered into the rural American mainstream.

After the U.S. Civil War ended and slavery was finally abolished in 1865, newer immigrants of African descent came voluntarily to the United States from the Caribbean region and, eventually, from Africa itself. Gospel music, an extension of spirituals and hymnody within African American churches, rose to prominence during the twentieth century. Blues, a secular style with melodic similarities to African American sacred music, became well known at about the same time. In the blues, a rhymed couplet, with the first line repeated, is set to a three-phrase musical structure, often with the second phrase harmonized with the subdominant. The blues was also used in instrumental music, forming an essential element of jazz and becoming the foundation for rock and other popular genres.

Near the beginning of the twentieth century, African American musicians in New Orleans and other cities spearheaded the creation of ragtime, followed by what is often regarded as the quintessential American music style: jazz, which incorporates many elements from European as well as West African musical practices. African Americans rose to fame as popular music stars—at first in jazz, later in rock, and especially in rhythm and blues (R&B), among other styles. Spirituals continued to be an important African American tradition during the twentieth century, inspiring classical settings and arrangements by Harlem Renaissance composers and being referenced in writing by W. E. B. Du Bois and in speeches by the Reverend Martin Luther King, Jr. Spirituals inspired solidarity and courage during the Civil Rights movement of the 1950's and 1960's. During the late twentieth and early twenty-first centuries, new urban styles developed, including rap, which built on African and African American traditions of incorporating rhythmic designs into speech, and hip-hop, which was begun by disc jockeys manipulating recorded music and superimposing their own sounds in live performances.

CELTIC MUSICAL TRADITIONS

During the eighteenth century, immigrants from Ireland, Scotland, Wales, and other regions settled in the Appalachian mountains. Fiercely independent and living in relative isolation, they cultivated narrative song and instrumental dance music traditions that they had brought from their homelands. In some cases, Appalachian ballads remained almost unchanged from their counterparts in Europe. Over time, the instrumental dance music acquired some African American inflectional and rhythmic influences, eventually leading to the development of bluegrass. During the nineteenth century, newer waves of immigrants from Ireland arrived but settled primarily in large communities within major cities such as New York and Boston. Because of these communities, Irish music was well documented and preserved in the United States, and some of the repertoire was eventually brought back to Ireland.

OTHER EUROPEAN IMMIGRANTS

During British North America's colonial period, German settlers, often escaping religious persecution and war, settled in many areas, especially in Pennsylvania, where they became known as the Pennsylvania Dutch. Most of their music was religious, but Germans also added musical dance forms such as the waltz to North American and Latin American music. In smaller ensembles, the accordion became a mainstay, and an inexpensive and highly portable German instrument, the harmonica, was introduced in the United States in 1868, where it was received with great enthusiasm. The harmonica was adaptable to many musical styles, including blues and country, and its plaintive, lonesome sound became identified with travelers such as cowboys, and fortune seekers who rode the railroads in search of opportunities.

German and other central European communities contributed to the development and popularity of brass band music, and another lively dance form, the polka, echoed in the large German and Polish communities of American cities. Euro-American descendants of earlier generations of immigrants often looked to Europe for guidance in matters of culture, and until the twentieth century they frequently preferred exotic new European immigrants with classical training over their homespun American counterparts for teaching posts, compositions, and concerts. During the early twentieth century, immigration from Ashkenazi Jewish communities in eastern Europe increased, bringing Klezmer music and Yiddish theater to the United States. Many first- and second-generation immigrant musicians from Yiddish-speaking communities in Europe participated in the development of musical theater, music publishing, and the emergence of the popular music industry.

In American urban centers, Italian, Greek, and other immigrant communities created ethnic enclaves during the late nineteenth and early twentieth centuries. Music, along with language, cuisine, religious worship, and other shared experiences, contributed to community identity. Eventually, through assimilation and relocation to the suburbs, some of the enclaves became less distinct, but music and dance forms were cultivated, especially the Italian *tarantella* and Greek *rebetiko* music. Americans from outside these groups are sometimes invited to experience this music and dance in cultural festivals sponsored by city governments.

ASIAN IMMIGRANTS

Most of the first Asian immigrants to the United States were from southern China. During the mid-nineteenth century, they were primarily male gold prospectors and manual laborers coming through San Francisco and other western ports. Cantonese opera and other southern Chinese music genres were occasionally supported as Chinatown enclaves grew in the cities, and Chinese Christian churches shared hymn repertoire with missionary churches in China. During the twentieth century, immigrants from other Asian nations arrived, especially in Hawaii, where Asian musicians contributed to the island's multicultural heritage. During the late twentieth century, newer immigrants from Asia were often highly educated and supported elite forms of music, often inviting visiting musicians from their home countries.

COMMUNITIES IN EXILE

The twentieth century brought unprecedented upheavals and relocations to the world, from the Armenians fleeing genocide in Turkey in 1915 through World War I, global depression during the 1930's, the Holocaust, World War II, the Cold War, wars in Vietnam and Cambodia, the Iranian revolution, and more. Many of those who were displaced or threatened by these events sought refuge in the United States. In some cases, music traditions that would have otherwise been destroyed were preserved. Although tolerance was not always a factor in America's musical history, the increasing recognition of music as a marker of personal and community identity, and the increasing value placed on musical diversity, bode well for the future.

John E. Myers

FURTHER READING

Bohlman, Philip Vilas, Edith Blumhofer, and Maria Chow, eds. *Music in American Religious Experience.* New York: Oxford University Press, 2006. Collection of detailed chapters (based on presentations for a conference at the University of Chicago) highlighting specific dimensions of the topic and spanning many ethnic groups, religious faiths and/or denominations, and historical periods.

Chase, Gilbert. *America's Music, from the Pilgrims to the Present.* 3d ed. Champaign: University of Illinois Press, 1987. Spans classical, folk, and popular music.

Roberts, John Storm. *The Latin Tinge: The Impact of Latin American Music on the United States.* 2d ed. New York: Oxford University Press, 1999. Encompasses the evolution of Latin American musical forms as well as their influence in the United States.

Rubin, Rachel, and Jeffrey Paul Melnick. *Immigra-tion and American Popular Culture: An Introduction.* New York: New York University Press, 2007. Includes extensive treatment of music, spanning the 1930's to the early twenty-first century.

Southern, Eileen. *The Music of Black Americans: A History.* 3d ed. New York: W. W. Norton, 1997. Comprehensive study includes all major genres and figures.

SEE ALSO: Art; Berlin, Irving; Cultural pluralism; Lennon, John; Linguistic contributions; Literature; Multiculturalism; Television and radio.

MUSLIM IMMIGRANTS

SIGNIFICANCE: By the early twenty-first century, approximately two million Muslim immigrants were living in the United States. The Muslim immigrant community is diverse, encompassing followers of different Islamic sects and people from virtually all regions of the world. In the face of increasing American hostility, especially since the terrorist attacks on the United States of September 11, 2001, members of this diverse immigrant community have begun to recognize their commonalities and mobilize for their rights.

Common data collection methods make it difficult to provide concise demographic information about the Muslim immigrant community in the United States. While the U.S. Census Bureau reported that approximately 0.6 percent of all people living in United States during the early twenty-first century were Muslims, that figure was derived from a survey of a representative population sample. The Census Bureau does not collect information on individual respondents' religions in the census itself and therefore cannot provide overall population numbers based on religious affiliation.

Estimates of the numbers of Muslims in the United States produced by other organizations usually range between 5 and 8 million individuals, and common consensus places the number at approximately 6 million. Since immigrants are estimated to constitute about one-third of the Muslims in the United States, the number of people who are both Muslims and immigrants is approximately 2 million. This figure is consistent with the numbers of immigrants who have come to the United States from predominantly Muslim countries, after adjusting for the proportions of non-Muslims in those countries.

EARLIEST MUSLIM IMMIGRANTS

Some of the earliest Muslim immigrants to come to what is now the United States were slaves who traveled with Spanish explorers during the sixteenth century. Some of the African slaves brought to British colonies during the seventeenth century were also slaves. Scholars have estimates that as many as 10 to 20 percent of all slaves imported to the United States practiced some forms of Islam in their homelands. Estimates on the size of this population range in number from as few as 40,000 Muslim slaves in the United States to 3 million Muslim slaves in all the Americas.

One of the most comprehensive records of the experiences of these early Muslim immigrants is the autobiography of Omar ibn Sayyid, who was brought to North Carolina from West Africa as a slave during the late nineteenth century. Omar ibn Sayyid was literate in Arabic; in 1831, he wrote a detailed account of his experiences. Slaveholders valued Muslim slaves for their literacy skills, but their religious practices were usually discouraged. Consequently, Islamic practices were not passed along to later generations of slaves. However, Islamic practices did survive in a few small and isolated communities. During the early twentieth century, oral historians found evidence of Muslim cultural and religious influences in African American communities living on islands off the coast of Georgia.

The first documented Muslim immigrants to come to the United States voluntarily came during the late nineteenth and early twentieth centuries. During the 1880's thousands of Muslims immigrated from the Ottoman Empire, mainly from parts of what are now the independent countries of Syria and Lebanon. Between 1890 and 1910, several hundred South Asian immigrants, who included some Muslims, came to the United States to work on railroads and in lumber mills in the American West. The early midwestern auto industry also had many Arab immigrant employees, many of whom were Muslims. Some of the first social and religious Muslim immigrant institutions in the United States were established by these people.

Changes in U.S. immigration laws that restricted

NATIONS WITH PREDOMINANTLY MUSLIM POPULATIONS

Countries are grouped below by the estimated percentages of Muslims within their total populations. Within each group, the countries are listed alphabetically.

96-99 PERCENT	Somalia	Bangladesh	**50-59 PERCENT**
Afghanistan	Tunisia	Guinea	Burkina Faso
Algeria	Turkey	Indonesia	Chad
Azerbaijan	Uzbekistan	Kyrgyzstan	Kazakhstan
Comoros	Western Sahara	Oman	Lebanon
Djibouti	Yemen	Tajikistan	Nigeria
Iran			
Iraq	**90-95 PERCENT**	**70-79 PERCENT**	**40-42 PERCENT**
Jordan	Egypt	Albania	Bosnia-Herzegovina
Libya	Gambia	Qatar	Guinea-Bissau
Maldives	Kuwait	Sierra Leone	
Mauritania	Mali	Sudan	**30-36 PERCENT**
Morocco	Syria	United Arab Emirates	Eritrea
Niger	Turkmenistan		Ethiopia
Pakistan		**60-69 PERCENT**	Ivory Coast
Saudi Arabia	**80-89 PERCENT**	Brunei	Macedonia
Senegal	Bahrain	Malaysia	Tanzania

Muslim immigrants praying at the Karbalaa Islamic Center in Dearborn, Michigan, in early 2003. The center provides a variety of services to help new immigrants adjust to life in the United States. (AP/Wide World Photos)

the entry of non-Europeans and established a system of national origins quotas slowed down the rate of Muslim immigration to the United States during the early to mid-twentieth century. From the 1920's to the 1950's, most Muslim immigrants arriving in the United States came from eastern European regions. By the time the national origins quota system was abolished by the Immigration and Nationality Act of 1965, only between 100,000 and 150,000 Muslims were living in the United States.

POST-1965 IMMIGRATION

The 1965 immigration law replaced national origin quotas and with new criteria for admitting immigrants based on family relationships, work skills, and refugee status. After this law went into effect, Muslims began immigrating to the United States

from countries all over the world. Research conducted by the Center for Immigration Studies suggests that the largest numbers of Muslim immigrants immediately after 1965 came from South Asian countries, particularly Pakistan, Bangladesh, and India. Immigrants from these former British colonies had the advantage of having learned English in school and were consequently highly competitive applicants for immigration based on their skills needed to fill American jobs. Large numbers of Muslims also came to the United States from the Middle East and Central Asia during this time.

During the late 1980's and 1990's. increasing numbers of Muslims came to the United States as refugees. Some were fleeing ethnic conflicts in Africa; others were escaping from religious persecution in South Asia and the Middle East. Many were refugees who had been displaced by military conflicts in Iraq, Israel, Kuwait, Lebanon, Pakistan, Somalia, Sudan, and the successor states to Yugoslavia.

POST-9/11 ISSUES

Negative stereotypes of Muslims and Muslim immigrants have been common in the United States since the colonial era. International events, particularly wars and other conflicts, have clearly contributed to negative American views of Muslims. Since the early 1970's, airplane hijackings and terrorist actions have strengthened negative public perceptions of Muslims, especially when such actions have directly affected Americans, such as the late 1970's Iranian hostage crisis. However, the Muslim extremist attacks on the United States of September 11, 2001 ("9/11") elevated negative American views of Muslims to a new level and inaugurated a new era of discrimination and violence directed against Muslims in the United States. The Federal Bureau of Investigation's annual survey of hate crimes for 2001 recorded a dramatic increase in crimes against Muslims: from 28 reported incidents directed against Muslims in 2000 to 481 in 2001—a seventeen fold increase.

The first decade of the twenty-first century has also seen the involvement of the United States in seemingly intractable wars in the predominantly Muslim countries of Afghanistan and Iraq. According to post-9/11 public opinion polls conducted by both the Pew Research Center and the Council on American-Islamic Relations, a majority of Americans have come to associate Islam with violence. Most Christian Americans also do not recognize commonalities between their own religious beliefs and those held by Muslims. Meanwhile, hate crimes directed against Muslims have continued to rise. According to data collected by the Council on American-Islamic Relations, the number of assaults and incidents of discrimination against Muslims in the United States rose from 1,019 documented cases in 2003 to 1,972 cases in 2005.

Both immigrant and nonimmigrant Muslims have been victims of hate crimes and discrimination since 9/11, but immigrants have been more frequently targeted. Significantly, many persons who have committed hate crimes seem to believe that *all* Muslims in the United States are immigrants, as many of their hate crimes are accompanied by cries of "Go Home."

In addition to the threat of hate crimes faced by Muslim immigrants, there are numerous allegations of post-9/11 legal discrimination against this community. The Patriot Act of 2001 required many immigrants from Muslim-majority countries to register with the federal government, and it enacted new restrictions on travel by individuals from those countries. By 2003, fewer green cards and visas were being issued to people in Muslim-majority countries, particularly people from Pakistan, Morocco, and Iran. Muslim immigrants generally have faced increased problems traveling as they report being profiled for more rigorous security checks than other passengers in airports.

Although there is little demographic data about the impact that these crimes and legal discrimination have had on the number of Muslim immigrants in the United States, anecdotal evidence suggests that many Muslim immigrants have chosen to return to their countries of origin or to move on to other countries, such as Canada, rather than remain in the hostile social and political climate of the United States. At the same time, however, many of the Muslims who have remained in the United States have begun to organize to educate the American public about Islam and Muslim people, and they have also worked to educate members of their own communities about their legal rights in the United States.

U.S. CIVIL SOCIETY AND POLITICAL LIFE

During the first decade of the twenty-first century, more than 1.5 billion Muslims lived in countries around the world, and forty-seven different nations had populations that were more than 50 percent Muslim. Moreover, several large countries in which Muslims accounted for much smaller percentages of total populations nevertheless had large numbers of Muslims, including India, Russia, and China. Indeed, India had the third-largest Muslim population in the world, even though its 160,945,000 Muslims accounted for only 13.4 percent of its total population.

Although Muslim immigrants have come to the United States from a wide variety of countries and cultural backgrounds, Muslims living in the United States have been able to organize around common social and religious interests. The first national Muslim conference was held in Iowa in 1952. This conference was attended by only 400 Muslims from the United States and Canada, but it marked the inception of the International Muslim Society. At a later conference in 1954, American Muslims, including a sizable number of immigrants, formed the Federation of Islamic Associations of the United States and Canada (FIA). The primary organizational goal of FIA was to address religious and cultural issues in the United States. However, members of this organization also worked as an advocacy group for the U.S. Muslim community. The FIA also provided a forum in which Muslim immigrants could come together to develop a sense of shared identity across cultural boundaries. However, although these organizations fulfilled an important role in the Muslim community, they always had small memberships. Indeed, as late as the 1980's and 1990's, Muslim Americans appear to have had fewer political organizations than other ethnic and religious groups of similar sizes.

After 9/11, Muslim immigrants and other Muslims in the United States began to participate more actively in civil organizations that would represent their concerns and work as advocates for their community. Education and advocacy groups were formed to oppose the backlash against Muslims living in the United States. According to the American Muslim Task Force on Civil Rights and Elections, a number of grassroots organizations worked to register Muslim voters, educate Muslim immigrants about their rights, and lobby against federal policies that were harmful to Muslim immigrants. Islamic centers have expanded their social programs to offer English classes and free legal assistance to Muslim immigrants. Groups such as the Council on American-Islamic Relations have collected data on hate crimes against Muslims, offered advice on promoting community safety, and increased outreach work to address negative stereotypes about Muslims and Muslim immigrants in the United States.

Jacqueline H. Fewkes

FURTHER READING

Curtis, Edward E., IV, ed. *The Columbia Sourcebook of Muslims in the United States.* New York: Columbia University Press, 2008. Comprehensive collection of primary sources and essays about Muslims and Islam in the United States. Covers diverse viewpoints within the Muslim community and includes reflections on Muslim experiences in post-9/11 America.

D'Alisera, JoAnn. *An Imagined Geography: Sierra Leonean Muslims in America.* Philadelphia: University of Pennsylvania Press, 2004. Study of attempts by Sierra Leonean Muslims to retain their religion, customs, and ethnic identity in the United States. Sierra Leone is a small West African country with a 71.3-percent Muslim population.

Ewing, Katherine Pratte, ed. *Being and Belonging: Muslims in the United States Since 9/11.* New York: Russell Sage Foundation, 2008. Eight ethnographic essays exploring how issues of identity and assimilation have been addressed in contemporary Arab Christian and Muslim communities in the United States.

Haddad, Yvonne Yazbeck, ed. *The Muslims of America.* New York: Oxford University Press, 1993. Collection of essays about Muslim communities in both the United States and Canada, written by both non-Muslim and Muslim authors. Most focus on Muslim American institutions, and many discuss the role that American foreign policy has played in the lives of Muslim immigrants.

Lawrence, Bruce B. *New Faiths, Old Fears: Muslims and Other Asian Immigrants in American Religious Life.* New York: Columbia University Press, 2002. Compares religious backgrounds of Asian immigrants to examine what role they play in the integration of Asian immigrants into American religious life, with a particular focus on Muslims from Asia.

Mohammad-Arif, Amminah. *Salaam America: South Asian Muslims in New York.* New York: Anthem Press, 2002. Ethnographic study of South Asian Muslims living in New York. Provides a strong historical background and pays particular attention to the impact of 9/11 on this community.

Rajagopalan, Kavitha. *Muslims of Metropolis: The Stories of Three Immigrant Families in the West.* New Brunswick, N.J.: Rutgers University Press, 2008. Stories of three different Muslim immigrant families, from Palestine, Iraq, and Bangladesh, that immigrated to England, Germany, and the United States.

Shaheen, Jack. *Reel Bad Arabs: How Hollywood Vilifies a People.* New York: Olive Branch Press, 2001. Fascinating source of information on portrayals of Arabs and other Muslims in more than eight hundred alphabetically arranged films, with special attention given to scenes in which negative stereotyping occurs.

SEE ALSO: Arab immigrants; Asian immigrants; Indonesian immigrants; Iranian immigrants; 9/11 and U.S. immigration policy; Pakistani immigrants; Religion as a push-pull factor; Religions of immigrants; Stereotyping; Turkish immigrants.

MY ÁNTONIA

IDENTIFICATION: Novel by Willa Cather depicting the lives of nineteenth century European immigrants in rural Nebraska

DATE: First published in 1918

SIGNIFICANCE: A novel about pioneers, *My Ántonia* recounts stories of European immigrants who sought prosperity in Nebraska at the end of the nineteenth century, focusing on how these immigrants transformed America and how America changed them.

The title character of Willa Cather's 1918 novel *My Ántonia* is Bohemian immigrant Ántonia Shimerda. Narrator Jim Burden first encounters the Shimerda family as a boy traveling from Virginia to Black Hawk, Nebraska. The family is indicative of many eastern Europeans who began new lives in Nebraska. As the English tutor of the teenage Ántonia, Jim learns about the hardships endured by the Shimerdas and other neighboring families, who are subjected to discrimination from Anglo-Saxon Americans and more established immigrant families from western and northern Europe.

Often, new immigrants are exploited in business, as the Shimerdas are by the fellow countryman who sells them their farm. They are also criticized for what is perceived to be their primitive culture and superstitious religious beliefs. Nevertheless, the European cultures of the immigrant families brighten the tapestry of Great Plains life for Jim. From the Austrian stories told by Otto Fuchs, the Burdens' hired man, to the brazen sensuality of young Norwegians such as Lena Lingard, to the raucous dance hall run by the Italian Vannis family, Jim comes to understand the rich vitality of ethnic life. Jim's view of European immigrants imbues the novel with a message of cultural pluralism rather than assimilation. In Lena, the American ideal of succeeding and blending into society is typified, but in Ántonia, who retains her culture and speaks her language with her American-born children, a multicultural ideal is emphasized.

Hugh Burkhart

FURTHER READING

Prchal, Tim. "The Bohemian Paradox: *My Ántonia* and Popular Images of Czech Immigrants." *MELUS* 29, no. 2 (2004): 4-25.

Smith, Christopher, ed. *Readings on "My Ántonia."* San Diego, Calif.: Greenhaven Press, 2001.

SEE ALSO: Anglo-conformity; Assimilation theories; Czech and Slovakian immigrants; European immigrants; Literature; Multiculturalism; Nebraska.

N

NAME CHANGING

DEFINITION: Voluntary and involuntary changing of family surnames by immigrants

SIGNIFICANCE: Modern Americans researching their family histories have often been stymied by name changes made when their ancestors immigrated to the United States. For many, it can be unsettling to learn that a family name held in much pride is little more than one century old. Some Americans have changed their names back to their ancestors' original surnames, but understanding the reasons for the name changes can help in providing a better understanding of what ancestors experienced when they immigrated.

It is sometimes difficult for twenty-first century Americans to understand why immigrants of the past were willing to change their surnames when they entered the United States, as name changing tended to cut them off from their ancestors and even from their contemporary relatives. However, connections between immigration and name changing are not merely from the past. As late as the early twenty-first century, the very first section of the U.S. government form on which immigrants apply for naturalization still contained a space for name-change requests. Its location near the top of the form highlights the continuing connection between changing one's citizenship and changing one's name. However, while the motivations of modern immigrants for changing their names are seldom as strong as they were for immigrants a century earlier, many immigrants still choose to start their new lives in the United States with new names.

INVOLUNTARY NAME CHANGES

Many modern Americans believe that their family names were changed by lazy or careless immigration officials at immigration reception centers such as Ellis Island in New York Harbor and Angel Island in San Francisco Bay. This idea has become entrenched in American thought by family traditions, popular literature, films, and even some scholarly works. However, a close study of the procedures followed at these immigration centers shows that casual name changes were rare. Government regulations were not always followed by immigration officers, but it is important to note that a federal regulation specifically prohibited officials from altering the names of immigrants. However, this regulation was not drafted to protect the integrity of ancestral histories, but to prevent the entry of undesirable aliens into the country.

One reason behind misconceptions about name changing at immigration reception centers is the false notion that immigration officials asked immigrants what their names were and then simply wrote down something phonetically close to what they heard without bothering to ask the immigrants how to spell their names. In reality, however, immigration officials did not get the names from the immigrants, but from the passenger lists of the ships on which the immigrants arrived. Many photographs of newly arrived immigrants at Ellis Island show them standing in long lines wearing what appear to be name tags. In fact, the tags the immigrants were wearing bore the names of their ships and the numbers of the lines on the ships' manifests on which they were listed. Immigration officer simply copied the names from the passenger lists, including whatever errors may have been on those lists.

Language differences can certainly cause confusion with names, particularly when the languages are written in different alphabets or systems. However, immigration officials at major centers such as Ellis Island usually spoke the languages of the immigrants to whom they were assigned. In fact, around the turn of the twentieth century, one-third of all Ellis Island officials were themselves immigrants. A small army of translators were also on duty, available to assist in getting correct information. Because immigrants later often described their entire immigration processing simply as "Ellis Island" or "Angel Island," it was easy for family traditions to incorporate the idea that their surname had been changed at one of those reception centers.

There is little doubt that many immigrant name changes were involuntary; however, it is much more likely that such changes can be attributed to errors

FATE OF THE PASSENGER LISTS

During the 1940's and 1950's, the National Archives and Records Administration placed all passenger lists of ships used by immigration reception centers on microfilm. Because microfilming was a new technology during those decades, some of the older passenger lists are difficult to decipher. However, because the original lists were later destroyed, the microfilms are the only copies that remain. In 2003, Ancestry.com began a project to digitize the information on the microfilm and to make it available online to their subscribers.

in the ships' passenger lists than to mistakes made by immigration officials. Errors could find their way into those lists several different ways. For example, some surnames had no single spelling that was recognized as standard at the time they were recorded. Moreover, many immigrants were illiterate and could not spell their own names if they were asked when they boarded the ships taking them to America. Those who could spell their names may not have been asked for the preferred spellings by shipping line clerks.

Some involuntary name changes came after the formal immigration process was completed. In one representative case, when a child of Polish immigrants reached school age, a school refused to register the child unless the long Polish family name was simplified. The child took the mother's maiden name as a family name and later passed it on to his own descendants. In another case, a well-meaning teacher persuaded the parents of the only Jewish boy in a small school to call him "Jack" instead of "Israel," his real name. She was concerned that the boy would be teased by the Christian children. The parents complied but made sure the boy understood that "Jack" was short for "Jacob," who took on the name "Israel" in the Bible. During the twenty-first century, such actions by schoolteachers would bring on lawsuits and firings, but until the late twentieth century, immigrants were rarely in a position to argue against changing their names.

VOLUNTARY NAME CHANGES

Immigrants arriving in America actually changed their names voluntarily much more often than they did involuntarily. The vast majority of them had al-

ready left their homes and relatives behind and made an arduous journey across the ocean to build new lives in a country whose main language many of them did not even speak. During the early twentieth century, few employers had qualms about discriminating against prospective employees for any reason they chose. If an immigrant's name was difficult to pronounce or spell, many employers would simply hire someone else with a more "American" name. While changing a family name may seem an extreme step to modern, native-born Americans, it was probably seen as a minor sacrifice by impoverished early immigrants who had already given up so much simply to reach America.

ETHNIC NAMING CONVENTIONS

Confusion caused by differences in naming conventions among different ethnic groups has often been the cause of immigrant name changes. Even during the twenty-first century, such differences cause some immigrants sufficient problems to move them to change their names.

Chinese naming conventions place family names first, followed by given names. Sometimes given names include generation names, which are shared by other members of the same generation. Generation names fall between the family and individual given names. For example, the name "Lee Qin Chun" indicates a person in the Lee family and the Qin generation with the given name "Chun." If Lee Qin Chun were to have two sons, they might be called "Lee Han Li" and "Lee Han Chou." Because Western naming conventions have no equivalent for generation names, opportunities for confusion are obvious.

Another Chinese convention that causes confusion for Westerners is the practice of Chinese women retaining their own family names when they marry. However, they sometimes add their husbands' family names to their own given names. Children take the family names of their fathers. Western women have only recently begun to retain their maiden names after marriage, but this relatively new custom has done little to eliminate Westerners' misunderstandings of Chinese married names. A question faced by married Chinese women when they immigrate to the United States is whether they will retain their maiden names or take their husbands' family names.

Before the nineteenth century, German Jews

did not use surnames. Fathers' first names were used in a form that would translate into English as "Jacob the son of Isaac." In 1808, Napoleon I decreed that all Jews living within his empire must adopt family names. In some places, the government gave them a list of names from which to choose and assigned names to those who failed to make selections. When these European Jews came to America, their attachment to the family names imposed on them was often tenuous, making them more prone to change their names after arriving. In addition, Jewish merchants quickly learned that in America their gentile customers were more likely to patronize stores with Anglo-Saxon-sounding names than those with Jewish names. Discrimination in hiring, housing, and other aspects of everyday life also made name changing acceptable to Jewish immigrants.

By the early twenty-first century, a large portion of immigrants to the United States were Hispanics, making the naming conventions used in Spanish-speaking countries important. Traditional Spanish names combine the surnames of both mothers and fathers. Full names are usually made up of two given names and two surnames. For example, the name "José Rafael Sepulveda Calderon" indicates a person whose mother's surname is Calderon and whose father's surname is Sepulveda. However, confusion arises from the practice of omitting the mother's surname in informal usage. Small differences such as these can cause problems when filling out forms such as employment applications.

SPELLING AND PRONUNCIATION

The Cyrillic alphabet is used by dozens of Central Asian and eastern European languages, most notably Russian. Created during the early nineteenth century, this alphabet has many characters that resemble characters in the Latin alphabet used by English and many other languages. However, some of the characters that appear to be the same actually represent different sounds, and each alphabet has characters not in the other. Because Cyrillic and Latin characters do not match perfectly, names transliterated from Cyrillic forms often have several different possible spellings in the Latin alphabet. Moreover, some transliterated names appear to Westerners to be missing vowels,

such as the name "Aleksandr." Spelling and pronunciations of Slavic names are particularly difficult for Americans and non-Slavic people. Recognizing this fact, many Slavic immigrants chose to simplify the spellings of their own names or to change their names entirely to avoid problems in their newly adopted country.

Chinese languages present even more difficult pronunciation challenges. Cantonese and Mandarin are tonal languages in which the meanings of words depend on their rising or falling tones when spoken. Mandarin, for example, uses four different tones to give meaning to spoken words: mid-level, low falling, high rising, and high creaky-rising. For a Westerner used only to placing stress on some syllables more than others, subtle tonal variations used to convey differences of meaning of a word open the door to considerable confusion. Consequently, some Chinese immigrants avoid such problems by simplifying their names.

Wayne Shirey

FURTHER READING

Belli, Melvin, and Allen P. Wilkinson. *Everybody's Guide to the Law: All the Legal Information You Need in One Comprehensive Volume.* New York: Harper-Collins, 2003. Contains a good chapter on the legalities of name changing.

Morgan, George G. *How to Do Everything with Your Genealogy.* New York: McGraw-Hill Osborne, 2004. Excellent guide to genealogical research; contains a good section on name changing.

Szucs, Loretto Dennis, and Luebking Hargreaves. *Guidebook to American Genealogy.* Provo, Utah: Ancestry Publishing, 2005. Informative book on genealogy with sections on immigrant name changing.

Wilton, David, and Ivan Brunetti. *Word Myths: Debunking Linguistic Urban Legends.* New York: Oxford University Press, 2004. Contains an informative section on the myths surrounding involuntary name changing.

SEE ALSO: Angel Island Immigration Station; Anglo-conformity; Anti-Semitism; Atlas, Charles; Chinese immigrants; Ellis Island; Employment; Identificational assimilation; Jewish immigrants; Stereotyping.

A NATION OF IMMIGRANTS

IDENTIFICATION: Posthumously published survey of U.S. immigration policy by John F. Kennedy

DATE: First published in 1958; first expanded and revised edition published in 1964

SIGNIFICANCE: *A Nation of Immigrants*, written while John F. Kennedy was still a senator, espouses reform of exclusionary immigration policies. After Kennedy was elected president of the United States in 1960, he called on Congress to reform immigration law.

In 1958, the Anti-Defamation League asked Senator John F. Kennedy, Pulitzer Prize winner for *Profiles in Courage* (1955), to write an essay advocating reform of U.S. immigration policy. Politically, Kennedy hoped to ensure support from Jewish and other immigrant communities for his 1960 bid for the presidency. He used the occasion to compose a meditation on the United States as "a nation of immigrants."

John F. Kennedy. (John F. Kennedy Library)

For Kennedy, the leveling effects of Old World oppression shaped the egalitarian nature of American democracy, built upon successive waves of immigration. In the book, Kennedy skirts the economic issues associated with cheap immigrant labor, but he eloquently documents the abuses of nineteenth and twentieth century nativist movements. He summarizes exclusionary U.S. immigration policy from the Naturalization Act of 1790 to the Immigration Act of 1924. According to Kennedy, America is not a "melting pot" for immigrants. Rather, invoking the language of cultural pluralism, he promotes immigration as the engine of democracy that allows new ideas in the arts, politics, economics, and the sciences to challenge the status quo. The book calls for legislative action to remove the immigration quota system—which was achieved after his assassination in 1963 in the Immigration and Nationality Act of 1965.

Luke A. Powers

FURTHER READING

Giglio, James. *The Presidency of John F. Kennedy.* 2d ed. Lawrence: University Press of Kansas, 2006.

Kennedy, John F. *A Nation of Immigrants.* Expanded ed. Introduction by Edward Kennedy. Foreword by Abraham Foxman. New York: HarperPerennial, 2008.

Melhman, Ira. "John F. Kennedy and Immigration Reform." *The Social Contract* 1, no. 4 (Summer, 1991): 201-206.

SEE ALSO: Anti-Defamation League; Commission on Immigration Reform, U.S.; Cultural pluralism; Immigration Act of 1924; Immigration and Nationality Act of 1965; Jewish immigrants; Melting pot theory; Nativism; Naturalization Act of 1790; Xenophobia.

NATIONAL ROAD

IDENTIFICATION: First federally funded interstate transportation project

DATE: 1811-1840

LOCATION: Maryland, Pennsylvania, West Virginia (then part of Virginia), Ohio, Indiana, and Illinois

SIGNIFICANCE: This trans-Appalachian highway provided both employment for new immigrants in its construction as well as a central artery for their westward migration, traveling across mountains and rivers and through the state capitals of Columbus and Indianapolis. Although originally planned to extend to St. Louis, political wrangling, the advent of the railroad, and the end of congressional support caused the road to terminate in central Illinois.

As early as 1802, U.S. Treasury secretary Albert Gallatin articulated the need for a National Road. In 1806, and with the support of President Thomas Jefferson, Congress passed a bill that provided for such a highway between Cumberland, Maryland, and the Mississippi River with the provision that it run through state capitals along its route. In 1811, the work began on the western edge of Cumberland, Maryland, on a twenty-foot-wide roadway with a sixty-six-foot right-of-way, built initially of stone, earth, and gravel, and later of macadam. There was no provision for eminent domain and no compensation provided to landowners, since the course of the road itself was considered sufficient recompense.

Although local citizens and farmers were employed on the project, there was a significant coterie of recent Irish immigrants who followed the westward course of the road, some of whom worked as well on the building of the Erie (completed 1825) and other canals. Mail delivery was facilitated as sections of the National Road were completed, connecting literate immigrants with family and friends on the East Coast and in Europe. The final federal appropriation was in 1838, and construction concluded in 1840 in Vandalia, Illinois.

Richard Sax

FURTHER READING

Dunaway, Wilma A. *The First American Frontier: Transition to Capitalism in Southern Appalachia, 1700-1860*. Chapel Hill: University of North Carolina Press, 1996.

Raitz, Karl B., ed. *A Guide to the National Road*. Baltimore: Johns Hopkins University Press, 1996.

SEE ALSO: Canals; German immigrants; History of immigration, 1783-1891; Iron and steel industry; Land laws; Mississippi River; Railroads; Transportation of immigrants; Westward expansion.

NATIVE AMERICANS

IDENTIFICATION: Aboriginal inhabitants of North America

SIGNIFICANCE: Although Native Americans had occupied the Western Hemisphere for at least thirteen millennia before the first modern Europeans, Africans, and Asians arrived, they, like the immigrant peoples who would follow them, originally came to the New World as immigrants.

There is substantial agreement among historians, anthropologists, archaeologists, and other scholars that the native peoples of North America originated in Asia. Most researchers believe that the ancestors of modern Indians, as they have come to be known, migrated from Siberia across the Bering Strait to Alaska. These early immigrants must have come to North America during periodic ice ages that caused the sea level to drop far enough to create a landmass approximately nine hundred miles wide that connected the Eurasian and North American continents. These early migrants probably followed the migratory mammals they hunted into North America. They eventually traveled southward and eastward until they populated most parts of the North American continent and continued advancing into Central and South America.

Despite widespread agreement on this basic theory of the origin of Native Americans, there is great disagreement concerning the timing of the migration. Furthermore, some Native American historians and writers have questioned the basic idea of explaining their origins with scientific theories that discredit the creation stories of many tribes. Indeed, such theories call into question the very idea that Native Americans are "native," implying instead that they are merely another immigrant group that happened to arrive very early.

SCIENTIFIC THEORIES

The theory that Native Americans migrated from Asia was first suggested long before scientific evidence was collected to support it. Christopher Columbus and other early European explorers and settlers in the New World assumed that Asia and North America were connected. After the vast distance between Eurasia and North America was

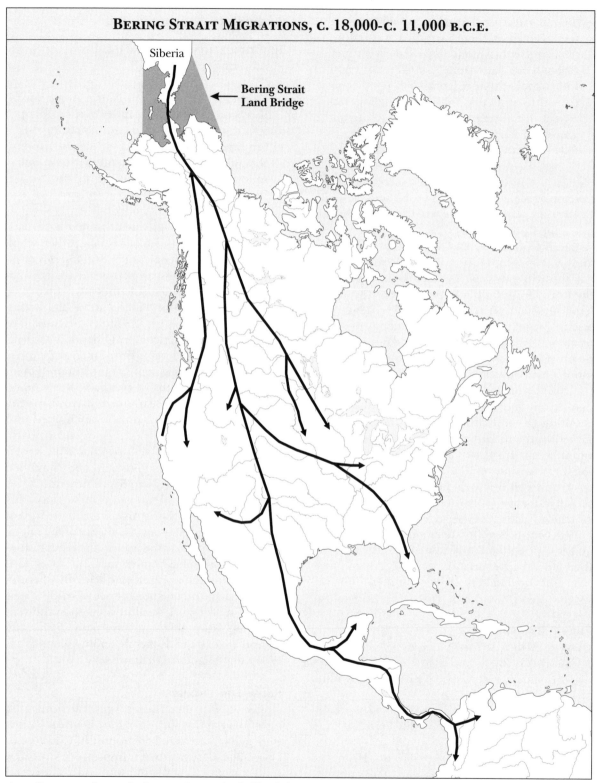

BERING STRAIT MIGRATIONS, C. 18,000–C. 11,000 B.C.E.

Siberia

Bering Strait
Land Bridge

According to one theory, the first people to arrive in North America traveled over a land bridge between modern-day Siberia and Alaska. Once on the continent, they gradually spread southward and eastward.

later understood, scholars recognized that the presence of Native Americans in what they called the New World contradicted the biblical account of Creation, which says that human beings were created in one and only one place. During the late sixteenth century, the Spanish Jesuit missionary José de Acosta proposed a migration theory to explain the existence of Native Americans, thereby vindicating the biblical account of creation. In 1728, when Vitus Bering discovered the strait between Siberia and Alaska that would later be named after him, Acosta's migration theory was discredited because no one believed that primitive peoples could have crossed the strait by boat.

During the twentieth century, scientists finally found evidence to support Acosta's theory despite the existence of the Bering Strait. During several periods within the Pleistocene period, glaciers interrupted the normal flow of water back into the ocean, causing the sea level to drop as much as three hundred feet. During the last period of glaciation, which occurred between 70,000 and 12,000 years ago, a land bridge linked the coast of Siberia with the coast of Alaska. Archaeologists named this land bridge Beringia because it follows the course of the Bering Strait. Furthermore, there is general agreement that the geologic record suggests that Beringia would have provided a practical route for human migration between 70,000 and 45,000 years ago and again between 25,000 and 14,000 years ago. However, disagreement on two points remains: exactly when human migration occurred and whether there was a single period of migration or multiple migrations over a longer period of time.

ASIAN-NATIVE AMERICAN TIES

During the twentieth century, scientists assembled overwhelming evidence proving that a migration from Eurasia to North America did, in fact, occur. In addition to the geological evidence showing that the existence of a land bridge made migration possible, anthropologists have shown that Native Americans share many characteristics with Asians, particularly the inhabitants of northern Siberia. In his 1998 book *The Origins of Native Americans*, anthropologist Michael Crawford points to four types of evidence for Asian-Native American connections: genetic, morphological, craniometric, and cultural.

Modern studies of deoxyribonucleic acid (DNA) have demonstrated that Native Americans have close genetic ties to several modern Asian peoples. Moreover, some genetic markers that appear in Native Americans appear in only one other genetic group: Asians. Crawford traces this connection down to something as mundane as earwax, pointing out that both New World and Asian peoples exhibit a high incidence of dry and brittle ear wax that is unlike the sticky and wet variety that characterizes other populations of the world. One practical result of this similarity is an unusually high level of ear infections among populations in Alaska and Siberia.

Even before the migration theory had real scientific evidence to back it up, it shared with modern science what Crawford calls "morphological" and "craniometric" evidence. Consequently, it had from its start a kind of plausibility. In simple terms, the Native Americans whom José de Acosta saw during the sixteenth century looked to him as if they had come from Asia. Among other facial and bodily characteristics, the Native Americans shared these physical features with Asians:

- straight black hair
- sparse facial and body hair
- high cheek bones
- flat faces
- skin folds (in some cases) covering upper eyelids

Modern science and archeology have added to these similarities dental evidence. Craniometric measurements of Asian and Native American skulls have also supported the migration theory, as skull characteristics tie Native Americans to Asians, not to western Europeans or Africans.

Among the cultural similarities between Native Americans and Asians are beliefs in a natural world that is animated by spirits of animals and plants that must be placated at various times and in holy men and medicine men who have visions and can cure the sick. Even a cursory knowledge of Native American spirituality suggests that it has much more in common with Eastern religions that it does with Western religious beliefs.

NATIVE AMERICAN ORIGIN STORIES

The Native Americans' traditions of their own origins contain no hints of migration from Asia. In fact, they almost entirely dispute the notion of Native peoples wandering into North America from anywhere else. Instead, traditional stories suggest that Native peoples emerged from the earth. The modern Kiowan writer N. Scott Momaday recounts the Kiowan story of origin in his 1969 book *The Way to Rainy Mountain*:

> You know everything had to begin and this is how it was: the Kiowas came one by one into the world through a hollow log. There were many more than now, but not all of them got out. . . . They looked around and saw the world. It made them glad to see so many things. They called themselves Kwuda, "coming out."

The Choctaw writer Valjean McCarty Hessing tells a similar creation story from the Pacific Northwest region of the United States. In his version, a lonely raven saw a bubbling clamshell come out of the sand. As the raven watched, people emerged from the shell. The raven was delighted that he had company on this lonely earth. In the Zuñi creation story, a lonely Sunfather hears the cries of his children in Mother Earth as he wanders the sky. Seeing two columns of foam at the base of a waterfall, he engenders life in them, ordering that they become gods who will descend into the womb of Mother Earth and bring his children up into the light. Edmund J. Ladd, a member of the Shiwi tribe, has observed that "Most, if not all" traditions of origin "teach that human beings were born out of mother earth."

Scientific research has shown that Native Americans wandered into North America from Asia in search of food and in search of a home. Native American stories suggest that Native Americans were so much a part of this continent that they emerged from beneath it. Rather than seeking a home as so many others who came to America, they were already home—a part of the very soil.

POLITICAL IMPLICATIONS

The Sioux writer Vine Deloria, Jr. has called the Bering Strait theory of Native American origin "a triumph of doctrine over facts." He points out that "there are no well-worn paths which clearly show migratory patterns," and even if there were, there would be no indication of where the footprints were heading. Deloria has also pointed out the irony in the fact that the basic Western story of ori-

gin, the biblical account of Creation, undergirds modern scientific accounts in interesting ways.

Jose de Acosta could not reconcile the existence of Native Americans with the biblical account of Creation, so he theorized that Native Americans came from Asia. In so doing, he found a place for them in the story of Creation that he had brought with him to the New World, confirming that human beings were essentially exiles, wandering from a paradise from which they had been expelled for having sinned. Whether the explanation for the wandering is expulsion from the Garden of Eden or a desperate search for food leading human beings across the Bering Strait, the outcome is the same: All of human life is wandering in search of a lost home, a journey that can only end when the wandering ceases in death. In such a context, the land itself is a prison, a place where one must toil to survive until the better world arrives. In contrast, Native American stories of origin suggest that Paradise is below the feet of Native people, that it is the very earth from which they emerged. They do not have to wander to find it—they have merely to live in its context and understand it.

Much like Deloria, James Wilson in his 1999 history of Native America, *The Earth Shall Weep*, argues that in explaining Native Americans, western science and western religion have worked hand in hand. Modern scientists have even traced the genetic history of man back to a single woman, whom they have named "Eve" after the biblical mother of humankind. They have also theorized that humankind originated in one place, Africa, from which it spread into other parts of the world. Thus, whether the account is tilted toward the biblical or the scientific view of creation, the conclusion is the same: All Americans are wanderers who wound up here in this alien land and must somehow learn to live together as immigrants. Moreover, no one is "native," not even *Native* Americans.

CONCLUSIONS

Just as for many, there is no reconciling of the biblical account of Creation with modern scientific theories of creation, such as evolution or the Big Bang, so Native American stories of creation will likely never be reconciled with the science of the migration theory of Native American origins. More importantly, however, Native American stories of creation carry with them an idea of rootedness and belonging that contradicts the biblical story of Creation as well as the science of the migration theory or even the science of evolution. In so doing, these stories dramatize for native people why they are a part of the land, "natives" in a land of immigrants.

H. William Rice

FURTHER READING

Ballantine, Betty, and Ian Ballantine. *Native Americans: An Illustrated History*. Atlanta, Ga.: Turner, 1992. Well-illustrated book that includes a Native American account of Native American origins.

Crawford, Michael H. *The Origins of Native Americans: Evidence from Anthropological Genetics*. New York: Cambridge University Press, 1998. Detailed examination of the scientific evidence for Native American origins. Although the book is written for anthropologists, nonspecialists can grasp its basic arguments.

Hoxie, Frederick E. *Encyclopedia of North American Indians*. Boston: Houghton Mifflin, 1996. Encyclopedic reference work containing entries on Native American origins from the perspectives of both modern science and Native American cultures.

Kehoe, Alice B. *North American Indians: A Comprehensive Account*. Englewood Cliffs, N.J.: Prentice-Hall, 1981. Traces the evolution of the first inhabitants of North America, region by region, from prehistory to the present. Contains recommended readings and sources at the end of each chapter.

Momaday, N. Scott. *The Way to Rainy Mountain*. Albuquerque: University of New Mexico Press, 1969. A Kiowan Indian, Momaday reconstructs not only the stories of the origin of his people, but also the stories of their migration from the Great Plains to Oklahoma.

Underhill, Ruth M. *Red Man's America: A History of Indians in the United States*. Rev. ed. Chicago: University of Chicago Press, 1971. Concise volume surveying origins, history, and definitive accounts of social customs, material culture, religion, and mythology. Written from the perspective of the first peoples of North America.

Wilson, James. *The Earth Shall Weep: A History of Native America*. New York: Grove, 1999. Comprehensive and highly readable history of Native Americans whose first part covers origins from the perspectives of both modern science and Native American traditions.

SEE ALSO: Alaska; Asian immigrants; Nativism; Natural disasters as push-pull factors; Pilgrim and Puritan immigrants.

NATIVE SONS OF THE GOLDEN STATE

IDENTIFICATION: Immigrant support group and benevolent organization
ALSO KNOWN AS: Chinese American Citizens Alliance (1927 on)
DATE: Founded in 1895; rechartered in 1915

SIGNIFICANCE: Organized initially in California to provide its Chinese American immigrants community support and to encourage them in the process of assimilation at a time when they faced entrenched bigotry and government-sanctioned discrimination, the Native Sons of the Golden State (not to be confused with the white nativist organization "Native Sons of the Golden West") became a national model for immigrant organizations interested in promoting good citizenship through respect for and commitment to the ideals of their adopted country.

By the closing decade of the nineteenth century, Chinese American immigrants in California were facing unprecedented discrimination. Initially welcomed as cheap labor during the gold rush era and then later during the massive enterprise of completing the transcontinental railroad, Chinese immigrants quickly became objects of hostility and violence by Californians convinced the Chinese were a particular threat both economically in an era of heated competition for work and culturally as the Chinese shared neither language, religion, nor social customs with the larger community of mostly European descendants.

After the landmark federal Chinese Exclusion Act of 1882 banned Chinese immigration for ten years, the Chinese community already in California struggled to find stability amid an environment of escalating bigotry that saw the steady removal of their civil rights through a succession of discriminatory state laws. Moreover, with immigration effectively curtailed, the Chinese American community faced the threat of rapid cultural extinction unless some movement was made toward assimilation.

In response to this, in 1895 a small but determined group of second-generation and English-speaking Chinese Americans met in San Francisco to found an organization designed to provide Chinese immigrants the kind of fraternal club routinely denied them because of their ethnicity. However, their specific goal was to help Chinese Americans assimilate by providing avenues through which members might participate in community activities. Members pledged to uphold the ideals of American democracy and adopted as their organization's name "Native Sons of the Golden State" to emphasize the fact they were born in California and were thus Americans by birth.

Against vocal hostility from some Chinese Americans concerned that such a mission would deprive the next generations of any sense of their Chinese heritage, members of the Native Sons nevertheless championed having Chinese Americans take leadership roles in their neighborhoods as a way to direct them into positions of authority and trust. By encouraging community participation and the moral instruction of youth, the organization quickly made national headlines and spread to other cities, first in California but nationwide within a decade. In 1915, the Native Sons of California was rechartered as the Chinese American Citizens Alliance.

Joseph Dewey

FURTHER READING

Lee, Erika. *At America's Gate: Chinese Immigration During the Exclusion Era, 1882-1943.* Chapel Hill: University of North Carolina Press, 2007.

Lien, Pei-te. *The Making of Asian Americans Through Political Participation.* Philadelphia: Temple University Press, 2001.

Pfaelzer, Jean. *The Forgotten War Against Chinese Americans.* Berkeley: University of California Press, 2008.

SEE ALSO: Anti-Chinese movement; Asian immigrants; Assimilation theories; Chinese American Citizens Alliance; Chinese Exclusion Act of 1882; Chinese immigrants; Citizens Committee to Repeal Chinese Exclusion; History of immigration after 1891; Immigration Act of 1943; "Yellow peril" campaign.

NATIVISM

DEFINITION: Negative form of ethnocentrism that is typically expressed by opposition to what is perceived as alien contamination by members of minority and immigrant groups

SIGNIFICANCE: Throughout the history of the United States, nativism has been an ideology that has driven Americans to strong, and frequently harsh, reactions against members of groups, particularly immigrants, who are perceived to be different. During the nineteenth and early twentieth centuries, nativist movements were influential in helping to pass restrictive immigration laws.

Since the founding of the United States, Americans has frequently shown ambivalence toward immigrants. Because the country has been built on immigration, it has generally welcomed new immigrants as necessary additions to the labor force and as sources of new economic growth. On the other hand, immigrants have also been feared and resented because of their alien ways and their competition with native-born Americans for jobs and political power. Nativists, the most outspoken critics of immigration, feared that the American way of life, and even the republic itself, was in danger from the constant stream of newcomers. They developed an ideology of nativism that comprised three identifiable strains:

- anti-Catholic nativism
- racial nativism
- antiradical nativism

These three strains often overlapped in the various nativist organizations that emerged in the nineteenth and twentieth centuries.

ANTI-ROMAN CATHOLIC NATIVISM

Anti-Catholic nativism had its roots in the religious views of the earliest English settlers in the American colonies. As products of the Protestant

Reformation in Europe, the early colonists viewed the pope as a foreign monarch who exercised dangerous influence through the Roman Catholic Church. The large influx of Irish Catholic immigrants during the early nineteenth century fueled an upsurge of anti-Catholic propaganda, which alleged that Irish Catholics were agents of the pope intent on undermining republican institutions. During the 1830's, inventor Samuel F. B. Morse wrote a tract, *Foreign Conspiracy Against the Liberties of the United States* (1834), in which he called for the formation of the Anti-Popery Union to resist the papal plot. His tract became required reading in many Protestant Sunday schools. In 1834, an anti-Catholic mob burned the Ursuline Convent in Charlestown, Massachusetts. Ten years later, riots erupted in Philadelphia when Irish Catholics opposed the use of the Protestant King James version of the Bible in public schools.

The American Protective Association (APA), organized in 1887, was the most visible manifestation of anti-Catholic nativism during the late nineteenth century. Its members swore they would never vote for Catholic candidates, employ Catholic workers over Protestants, or join with Catholic strikers. The APA drew strong support from workers in the midwestern and Rocky Mountain states who feared competition from cheap Irish labor. By the late 1890's, however, as Irish and German Catholics became an important part of the electorate, the more extreme anti-Catholic sentiment dissipated. The APA itself disappeared during the 1890's.

RACIAL NATIVISM

During the late nineteenth century, a racial strain of nativism, cultivated by the self-professed guardians of Anglo-Saxon culture and apparently supported by scientific research, began to be di-

Short-lived nativist newspaper published in Boston in 1852. (Library of Congress)

rected against immigrant groups. Ever since colonial times, white settlers had viewed themselves as culturally and physically different from, and superior to, Native Americans and African Americans. Some intellectuals adapted the research of Charles Darwin on biological evolution to argue that certain races would inevitably triumph over others because of their inherent superiority. English and American intellectuals confidently trumpeted the superiority of the Anglo-Saxon "race" and its institutions, and researchers set out to "prove" their cultural assumptions by measuring the cranial volumes of skulls from members of various ethnic groups and devising crude intelligence tests. As a new wave of immigrants from Asia and southern and eastern Europe began to arrive, these newcomers were quickly labeled racially inferior.

Racial nativism reached its zenith during the early twentieth century. Influenced by the European eugenics movement, with its emphasis on breeding the right racial groups, American nativists expressed alarm over the impact of the new immigrants. Madison Grant's widely read *The Passing of the Great Race* (1916) summarized many of the racial nativist arguments. Grant argued that the superior Nordic "race" was being destroyed by the influx of southern and eastern Europeans, and warned that race mixing would result in an inferior hybrid race and the destruction of Anglo-Saxon civilization. Jewish and Italian immigrants, in particular, were often singled out for criticism in nativist publications because of their alleged racial inferiority.

ANTIRADICAL NATIVISM

Immigrants also came under attack for political reasons during the late nineteenth century. Nativist writers worried that most immigrants came from nondemocratic societies, harbored socialist or anarchist sympathies, and would foment revolution in the United States. The participation of some immigrants in the labor agitation of the period seemed to confirm these fears of alien radicalism. Antiradical nativism intensified following the 1917 Russian Revolution and the onset of an economic crisis in the United States. Although most immigrants were not socialists, immigrants nevertheless constituted a majority of the membership of the American Socialist Party. During the Red Scare of 1919-1920, when many Americans feared that a communist revolution was imminent, immigrants and radicalism became synonymous in the public mind.

IMPACT ON PUBLIC POLICY

Nativism had its most significant impact on public policy in the area of immigration restrictions designed to discriminate against Asians and southern and eastern Europeans. In 1882, the federal Chinese Exclusion Act cut off further immigration by Chinese laborers. During World War I, Congress overrode a presidential veto to enact literacy tests for all immigrants, which discriminated against southern and eastern Europeans who had less access to basic education. During the 1920's, the United States adopted a system of quotas based on national origins for European immigration, imposing a maximum annual limit of 150,000 and allocating most of the slots to northern and western European countries. The national origins quota system formed the basis of immigration law until it was abolished in 1965.

Richard V. Damms

FURTHER READING

Bennett, David H. *The Party of Fear: From Nativist Movements to the New Right in American History.* Chapel Hill: University of North Carolina Press, 1988. Scholarly study of evolution of nineteenth century nativism into twentieth century political conservatism.

Billington, Ray Allen. *The Protestant Crusade, 1800-1860: A Study of the Origins of American Nativism.* New York: Macmillan, 1938. Classic historical work on early nineteenth century nativism.

Curran, Thomas J. *Xenophobia and Immigration, 1820-1930.* Boston: Twayne, 1975. Overview of the historical background behind restrictive immigration policies throughout U.S. history, focusing on nativism and such groups as the Ku Klux Klan.

Gabaccia, Donna R. *Immigration and American Diversity: A Social and Cultural History.* Malden, Mass.: Blackwell, 2002. Survey of American immigration history, from the mid-eighteenth century to the early twenty-first century, with an emphasis on cultural and social trends, with attention to ethnic conflicts, nativism, and racialist theories.

Higham, John. *Strangers in the Land: Patterns of American Nativism, 1860-1925.* New Brunswick, N.J.: Rutgers University Press, 2002. Classic account of anti-immigrant hostility in the United States from the Civil War to the final victory for restriction during the 1920's.

Lee, Erika. *At America's Gates: Chinese Immigration During the Exclusion Era, 1882-1943.* Chapel Hill: University of North Carolina Press, 2003. Study of immigration from China to the United States from the time of the Chinese Exclusion Act to the loosening of American immigration laws during the 1960's, with an afterword on U.S. immigration policies after the terrorist attacks of September 11, 2001.

Navarro, Armando. *The Immigration Crisis: Nativism, Armed Vigilantism, and the Rise of a Countervailing Movement.* Walnut Creek, Calif.: AltiMira Press, 2008. Comprehensive history of the politics of immigration to the United States since the early colonial era, focusing on the role played by nativist movements.

SEE ALSO: American Protective Association; Americanization programs; Anti-Catholicism; Anti-Chinese movement; Anti-Filipino violence; Anti-Japanese movement; Anti-Semitism; Eugenics movement; Know-Nothing Party; Ku Klux Klan; Xenophobia.

NATURAL DISASTERS AS PUSH-PULL FACTORS

DEFINITION: Natural occurrences such as hurricanes, earthquakes, volcanic eruptions, pandemics, and other disasters that prompt human migrations

SIGNIFICANCE: Permanent or temporary migration to a safer environment is the traditional survival strategy of populations faced with overwhelming natural or environmental disasters. Often such disasters not only result in destruction of living environments, but also destroy the social and economic fabrics of a society, forcing entire communities to seek new social, economic, and cultural environments in which to thrive.

Natural disasters often function as initiatives to push populations to migrate to new, more favorable living conditions. Less frequently, areas struck by natural disasters may serve to pull in small group populations if they believe the post-disaster living conditions can be exploited to their advantage. A broad and extensive record of migrations, both forced and voluntary, exists in the geological, archeological, and written historical records documenting human culture.

DISASTERS AND HISTORICAL MIGRATIONS

Evidence exists suggesting environmental change initiated the first humanoid migrations out of the African continent as early as 60 to 70 millennia in the past, dispersing human ancestry northward in an attempt to find more favorable living conditions. Geological evidence from about 70 millennia ago indicates that a super-volcanic eruption of the Lake Toba Caldera on the Indonesian island of Sumatra resulted in a massive climate-changing event. The dating of this eruption coincides with fossil evidence and DNA indexing suggesting that a massive reduction in the human population of the time from estimates of 60 million to as few as 10,000 survivors globally. The resulting bottlenecking of human evolution precipitated an outward radiation of survivors to new habitats.

In much more recent times, a massive flooding of the Black Sea through the Bosporus Straits around 5600 B.C.E. devastated the near-shore cultures and resulted in a mass migration out of the area populating new regions of Asia Minor. This flood was mythologized in both the Tale of Gilgamesh and the biblical Book of Genesis. More recently still, the super-volcanic eruption of the Santorini Caldera in the southern Aegean Sea around 1600 B.C.E. caused the downfall of the Minoan and other Bronze Age cultures, and the climatic outfall from the eruption severely stressed Egyptian and early Greek cultures. Survivors of the eruption dispersed throughout the Mediterranean basin to repopulate new territories and give rise to new cultures. In North and South America, inclusive evidence has linked droughts caused by climatic changes to the collapse and migration of native cultures, including the ancient Pueblo peoples of the American Southwest, the Maya and Olmec peoples of Mexico and Central America, and the Nazca culture of the South American Andes.

DISASTER-DRIVEN MIGRATIONS TO NORTH AMERICA

During the late tenth century, the Vikings of northern Europe were pushed to explore and settle North America after their colonies had deforested Greenland. However, they had to abandon their North American colonies when the Little Ice Age developed and new Arctic ice floes blocked sailing routes. The Little Ice Age, which lasted from the mid-thirteenth to the early seventh centuries, worked as a major push-pull factor in human migrations. Cooling in the northern hemisphere resulted in severe long-term crop losses, food shortages, and prolonged famines. It also led to the outbreak of numerous diseases, most notably the bubonic plague. The freezing of shipping lanes devastated trade. Sustained droughts ensued, forests were cut down for heating fuel, and warfare became almost constant among communities competing for shrinking resources. All these condi-

tions resulted in massive disruptions of social and cultural systems.

Northern European and Asian peoples migrated to escape the harsh climatic conditions or to fill living niches left by deaths and emigration. By the late fifteenth century, the need to search out resources and flee social upheavals gave rise to an era of exploration. Over the next several hundred years, large numbers of Europeans were pushed and pulled into emigrating to North America.

During the mid-nineteenth century, two large-scale famines proved major push factors in North American immigration: the Great Irish Famine between 1845 and 1852, and the Great Northern China Famine of 1877-1878. Survivors of both famines were pushed out of their homelands by the deteriorating economic and social conditions, and pulled to the prospects of a better life in North America. In the same manner, during the late twentieth century, severe drought, desertification,

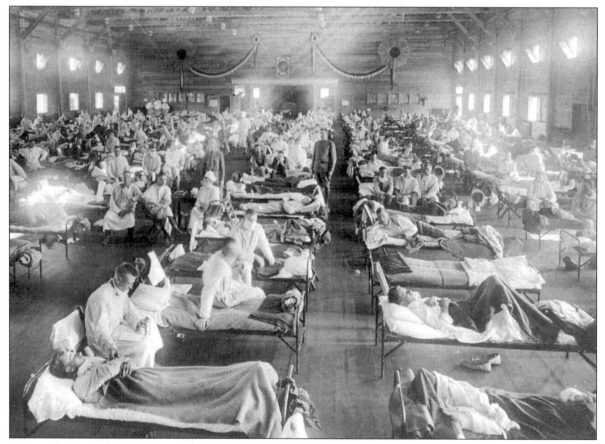

Victims of the 1918 influenza pandemic in a Kansas emergency hospital. (AP/Wide World Photos)

and famine resulted in large migrations of peoples from central and sub-Saharan Africa. As global climate changes have continued to advance during the twenty-first century, rising sea levels, climatic variations, and habitat loss will most likely bring about major new population migrations in the future.

DISASTER-DRIVEN MIGRATIONS WITHIN NORTH AMERICA

An early twentieth century disaster that directly affected North America was the great influenza pandemic of 1918-1919, in which more than 500 million people were infected and 100 million died worldwide, mostly young adults. Between 700,000 and 1 million people are estimated to have died from influenza within the United States. Influenza deaths became a pull factor that drew people to migrate to new regions to fill jobs and properties previously held by influenza victims. Another early twentieth century disaster that prompted a massive internal migration was the Great Mississippi Flood of 1927, in which more than 700,000 persons were displaced from their homes. It helped propel the Great Migration of African Americans from the South to northern cities, particularly Chicago and Detroit.

The disastrous North American hurricane season of 1928, while devastating vast areas of southern Florida, became a pull for migration as rebuilding efforts promoted the region as a vacation destination. The Dust Bowl years of the 1930's, brought on by poor farming practices and drought, pushed people from the Great Plains to northern cities and West Coast states.

In 2005, Hurricane Katrina destroyed large portions of Louisiana, Mississippi, and Alabama, most notably the city of New Orleans. The hurricane resulted in the evacuation of more than 1,000,000 people, the largest migration of Americans since the Dust Bowl years. Of these people, 700,000 became displaced persons from New Orleans, and after two years only 40 percent had returned home; the remaining number relocated to other cities throughout the United States. On a smaller scale, a tornado in Picher, Oklahoma, in 2008 resulted in the town being destroyed to such an extent it was abandoned in 2009, forcing all its residents to migrate to new locations.

Randall L. Milstein

FURTHER READING

Bullard, Robert D., and Beverly Wright, eds. *Race, Place, and Environmental Justice After Hurricane Katrina.* Boulder, Colo.: Westview Press, 2009. Revealing look at the roles of different ethnic communities in the rebuilding of the Gulf coast after Hurricane Katrina struck.

Clark, Jeffrey J. *Tracking Prehistoric Migrations: Pueblo Settlers Among the Tonto Basin Hohokam.* Tucson: University of Arizona Press, 2001. Of the migrations of early Native American groups in the American Southwest.

Diamond, Jared. *Guns, Germs, and Steel.* New York: W. W. Norton, 1997. Extended essay on world history offering many ideas on how physical geography has influenced human events such as population movements.

Fagan, Brian. *The Little Ice Age: How Climate Made History, 1300-1850.* New York: Basic Books, 2000. Interesting study of the relationship between climatic changes, food supply, and population movements during the Little Ice Age.

Gregory, James N. *American Exodus: The Dust Bowl Migration and Okie Culture in California.* New York: Oxford University Press, 1989. History of the migrants from Oklahoma and other southern Great Plains states who fled to California to escape the Dust Bowl conditions of the 1930's.

Gribben, Arthur, ed. *The Great Famine and the Irish Diaspora in America.* Amherst: University of Massachusetts Press, 1999. Collection of twelve essays commemorating the 150th anniversary of the Great Irish Famine that drove more than 1.5 million people to leave Ireland.

Levey, Richard, and Daniel Franck. *Dust Bowl! The 1930's Black Blizzards.* New York: Bearport, 2005. Graphic account of the effects of dust storms in the Midwest.

Rain, David. *Eaters of the Dry Season: Circular Labor Migration in the West African Sahel.* Boulder, Colo.: Westview Press, 1999. Encroaching desertification has made West Africa's Sahel region one of the most precarious human environments in the world. This work explores the dynamics of the population that lives in the Sahel, from the seasonal migrants to the farmers and herders.

Rosario, Kevin. *The Culture of Calamity: Disaster and the Making of Modern America.* Chicago: University of Chicago Press, 2007. Broad survey of the role of natural disasters in U.S. history.

Williams, A. R. "After the Deluge: Central America's Storm of the Century." *National Geographic*, November, 1999, 108-129. Well-illustrated account of Hurricane Mitch, which devastated Central America in 1998 and drove tens of thousands of people to emigrate to the United States.

SEE ALSO: Disaster recovery work; Economic opportunities; Great Depression; Great Irish Famine; Mississippi River; Push-pull factors; Refugees; Return migration; Salvadoran immigrants.

NATURALIZATION

DEFINITION: Process by which aliens become citizens of the new countries in which they reside

SIGNIFICANCE: The naturalization process in the United States has offered citizenship to persons born in other countries but the process itself has historically raised issues about fairness, national security concerns, and public perceptions of certain immigrant groups.

The issue of citizenship is so important that naturalization is mentioned within the foundation law of the United States, the U.S. Constitution. Article I, section 8 of that document authorizes the U.S. Congress to "establish an uniform Rule of Naturalization." In 1790, the year after the Constitution was ratified, Congress enacted its first naturalization law. The Fourteenth Amendment, which was ratified in 1868, expanded the constitutional definition of citizenship. Since that time, additional legislation has continued to refine the legal rules concerning naturalization.

EARLY YEARS OF THE REPUBLIC

When the Framers of the U.S. Constitution considered the issue of naturalization, they decided that Congress should have the power to establish uniform laws and procedures governing the process by which citizens of other countries could become American citizens. Before the Constitution was ratified, naturalization procedures were conducted by the courts of individual states, but the members of the Constitutional Convention of 1787 decided that leaving such an important matter to the states would create confusion. They agreed that decisions concerning naturalization should be ruled upon only by courts with common law jurisdiction. It was also necessary for the procedures to be conducted with prothonotaries (court clerks) and official seals.

Congress's passage of the Naturalization Act of 1790 created guidelines for U.S. citizenship. In limiting citizenship to "free white persons," the law denied the possibility of citizenship to indentured servants, free blacks, Native Americans, and, later, Asians. The law also stated that white immigrants of "good moral character" could petition state courts for citizenship after they had been residents of the United States for two years and were residents of the states to which they made their petitions. Only five years later, that law was superseded by the Naturalization Act of January 29, 1795. The new law increased the period of residence from two to five years. It also mandated that immigrants wanting to become American citizens had formally to declare their intention to become citizens three years before they formally applied. New citizens were also required formally to renounce all allegiance to their former countries.

In 1798, Congress again increased the period of residence necessary to apply for citizenship, from five to fourteen years. Although proponents of this new requirement argued that it was necessary for issues of national security, many historians believe that the change was made for political reasons—to limit the number of new citizens who might support and vote for Thomas Jefferson's Democratic-Republican Party and against the ruling Federalist Party. Indeed, naturalized citizens from Ireland and France did tend to side with the Democratic-Republicans. Considered part of the Alien and Sedition Acts of 1798, this law was repealed in 1802, when Jefferson was president.

NINETEENTH CENTURY LEGISLATION

The Fourteenth Amendment to the U.S. Constitution extended citizenship to all persons born within the territory of the United States, regardless of their parents' citizenship:

All persons born or naturalized in the United States and subject to the jurisdiction thereof, are citizens of the United States and of the State wherein they reside. No State shall make or en-

Swearing in of a new citizen before a New York judge in 1910. (Library of Congress/George Grantham Bain Collection)

force any law which shall abridge the privileges or immunities of citizens of the United States . . .

Although the words "All persons born . . . in the United States . . . are citizens" seem unequivocal, there are actually two exceptions to this principle—children of foreign diplomats and children of occupying enemy military personnel.

The Naturalization Act of 1870 made explicit the principle articulated in the Fourteenth Amendment by providing for the naturalization of all African Americans born in the United States, including former slaves.

The 1870 law also established new penalties for fraudulent naturalization applications, and it specified that Asians living in the United States were not eligible for American citizenship. The Chinese Exclusion Act of 1882 further codified these restrictions by forbidding further immigration from China and making even more explicit the ban on naturalization for Chinese residents of the United States. However, a significant challenge to Chinese exclusion came in 1898, when the U.S. Supreme Court ruled in the case of *United States v. Wong Kim Ark* that citizenship had to be granted to children born in the United States to Chinese parents. Meanwhile, the Geary Act of 1892 continued to enact the ban on naturalization by Chinese residents.

In 1862, Congress had passed a law allowing immigrants who had served honorably in the U.S. Army to apply for naturalization after only one year of residence. In 1894, this privilege was extended to honorably discharged veterans of the U.S. Navy and Marine Corps who had served a minimum of five years. These measures allowed a significant number of Irish immigrants who had served in the Mexican War and the U.S. Civil War to become citizens and helped make possible a strong Irish presence in the politics of such cities as New York, Boston, and Chicago.

The Immigration Act of 1882 sought to exclude "convicts (except those convicted of political offenses), lunatics, idiots and persons likely to become public charges" from entry into the United States. Such persons already in the country were excluded from the naturalization process. The law set up a series of immigration offices at various ports of entry and levied a fifty-cent tax on all immigrants landing at these ports.

TWENTIETH CENTURY LEGISLATION

The Naturalization Act of 1906 tightened the requirements for naturalization. Prospective citizens had to produce verification of their entry into the United States and verification of the identities of their spouses and children. They also had to demonstrate their ability to speak English. The Emergency Quota Act of 1921 set national quotas for entry into the United States based on 3 percent of the number of residents from each country who had been residing in the United States during the year 1890. The quota system effectively limited immigration from eastern and southern European countries but, perhaps oddly, set no quotas on immigration from Latin America. Consequently, the numbers of immigrants from Mexico and other Latin American countries who applied for naturalization dramatically increased over the next two decades. Meanwhile, the Nationality Act of 1940 sought to clarify the status of those born in United States territories and made residence in the United States a key to retaining citizenship for those born in the United States of foreign parents.

The Chinese Exclusion Act was finally repealed by the Immigration Act of 1943, which was also known as the Magnuson Act. Afterward, a steady stream of Cantonese-speaking immigrants began to enter the United States who were likely to learn to speak English and apply for naturalization. Repeal of the Chinese Exclusion Act also paved the way for Chinese nationals already living in the United States to apply for naturalization. The Immigration and Nationality Act of 1952, also known as the McCarran-Walter Act, added some new restrictions to immigration but granted U.S. citizenship by birth to persons born in the U.S. territories of Guam, the Northern Mariana Islands, Puerto Rico, and the U.S. Virgin Islands. Before this law

was passed, persons born in those territories had to apply for naturalization to become U.S. citizens. The Immigration and Nationality Act of 1965 allowed residents of any country of origin presently residing in the United States equal access to the naturalization process.

SPECIAL ISSUES

By the 1980's, illegal immigration had become a concern for many in the United States. The Immigration Reform and Control Act of 1986 addressed the realities of undocumented residents in the United States by providing the opportunity for undocumented immigrants to apply for naturalization provided they could prove that they had been in the United States for at least four years. Although the law was criticized by some for providing "amnesty" to people who had lived in the United States illegally, the legislation included new sanctions against American employers who knowingly hired undocumented workers.

During the 1980's and 1990's, many American couples looked to other countries to adopt children. The Child Citizenship Act of 2000 made the process of naturalization much easier for foreign adoptees. Under this law, children under the age of eighteen who were adopted by American citizens and were under their adoptive parents' custody automatically became naturalized upon their entry into the United States.

MODERN NATURALIZATION PROCESSES

During the early twenty-first century, immigrants who had attained permanent resident status and obtained green cards could apply for naturalization after five years of residence in the United States or only three years if they were married to American citizens. Applicants for naturalization had to demonstrate permanent residence in the states or districts in which they made their applications. They also had to show "good moral character," which was determined through criminal background checks, and "an attachment to the Constitution," which was demonstrated through a basic civics test. Finally, applicants also had to be able to communicate in basic English and swear an oath of allegiance to the United States.

Between the mid-1990's and the early twenty-first century, the number of immigrants who became naturalized citizens increased dramatically.

In 1996, there were approximately 6.5 million naturalized citizens in the United States. In 2005, that figure had risen to more than 11 million. By that time, almost one-half of all foreign-born immigrants who were legally residing within the United States had been naturalized. Reasons for this large increase in naturalization included several negative incentives, such as the trend to restrict certain public benefits to U.S. citizens. Another incentive to naturalize was the government's making the cost of replacing green cards comparable to the cost of applying for naturalization.

Most recently naturalized citizens live in California, New York, Texas, Florida, New Jersey, and Illinois, and most have come from European and Asian nations. However, the fastest-growing segment of the naturalized population comes from Mexico and Central America.

During the late twentieth century, the subject of dual citizenship began receiving national attention. At issue has been how immigrants can reconcile their dual citizenship with the oath they take in which they renounce their previous citizenship. Despite this apparent contradiction, there have been some high-profile cases of naturalized citizens who have retained their previous citizenship. California governor Arnold Schwarzenegger, who has retained his Austrian citizenship, is perhaps the best-known example. The U.S. State Department's policy on dual citizenship has been that the U.S. government does not recommend it but will recognize it. The government recognizes that some newly naturalized citizens may have responsibilities to fulfill to the countries of their birth. For example, naturalized U.S. citizens from Israel may still be liable for Israeli military service that does not affect their U.S. citizenship. However, the Department of Homeland Security has come under criticism for detaining naturalized U.S. citizens traveling with foreign passports.

William Carney

FURTHER READING

Aleinikoff, Thomas A., et al. *Immigration and Citizenship: Process and Policy.* 6th ed. St. Paul, Minn.: West Group, 2008. Popular legal textbook that discusses legislation and court cases relating to all aspects of immigration and naturalization.

Bray, Ilona. *Becoming a U.S. Citizen: A Guide to the Law, Exam, and Interview.* 4th ed. Berkeley, Calif.: Nolo Press, 2008. Practical and clearly written guide explaining the advantages and disadvantages of obtaining American citizenship, as well as current American rules for naturalization.

LeMay, Michael C., and Elliott Robert Barken, eds. *U.S. Immigration and Naturalization Laws and Issues: A Documentary History.* Westport, Conn.: Greenwood Press, 1999. Collection of 150 unabridged historical documents pertaining to immigration and naturalization issues.

Schreuder, Sally A. *How to Become a United States Citizen.* 5th ed. Berkeley, Calif.: Nolo Press, 1996. Concise guidebook that clearly explains the rules and procedures of the naturalization process.

Schuck, Peter. *Citizens, Strangers, and In-Betweens: Essays on Immigration and Citizenship.* Boulder, Colo.: Westview, 1998. Collection of essays on a wide variety of topics relating to citizenship and naturalization by a recognized authority on legal aspects of immigration and naturalization.

Smith, Roger M. *Civic Ideals: Conflicting Visions of Citizenship in U.S. History.* New Haven, Conn.: Yale University Press, 1999. Liberal analysis emphasizing racial and gender discrimination in naturalization laws from the colonial era to the early twentieth century.

Spiro, Peter J. *Beyond Citizenship: American Identity After Globalization.* New York: Oxford University Press, 2008. Investigation into the changing nature of American identity that touches on the changing nature of citizenship and nationality in an increasingly globalized culture.

SEE ALSO: *Boutilier v. Immigration and Naturalization Service*; Citizenship; Citizenship and Immigration Services, U.S.; Dual citizenship; Immigration and Nationality Act of 1965; Naturalization Act of 1790; *Ozawa v. United States*; Permanent resident status; Resident aliens; *United States v. Bhagat Singh Thind.*

NATURALIZATION ACT OF 1790

THE LAW: Federal legislation establishing rules and procedures for naturalization of aliens

DATE: Enacted on March 26, 1790

ALSO KNOWN AS: An Act to Establish an Uniform Rule of Naturalization

SIGNIFICANCE: This act was the first federal law to establish procedures for naturalization under the U.S. Constitution. Although it required only two years' residence prior to naturalization, less time than any succeeding law, it restricted the right of naturalization to white male immigrants.

In accordance with Article I, section 8, clause 4 of the Constitution, which grants Congress the power "to establish an uniform Rule of Naturalization," Congress passed a naturalization act, which was signed into law on March 26, 1790. The act granted foreign-born free white men the ability to naturalize after two years' residence in the United States.

When weighing the provisions and residency requirements, congressional legislators debated the relative merits of a liberal conception of citizenship, and its transferability, while also debating whether the danger of immigrants refusing to shed their antirepublican, old-world traditions outweighed their value as a source of wealth and increased population. Idealists who viewed the United States as a republican asylum allied themselves with moderates whose mercantilist outlook caused them to see new migrants, rich or poor, as an asset to the nation. Future Democratic-Republicans John Page and James Madison of Virginia and future Federalist John Lawrence were particularly active in the debates that shaped the law into its final form.

Congressmen also debated to what degree the law should supersede or defer to existing state naturalization laws. Concerns about conflicts with state laws ultimately led to another change from the original bill, which had stipulated that the rights of citizenship would be granted in steps, withholding the right to hold office until the second year of residence. Rather than entangle the law with conflicting state requirements, the final bill that was passed granted all rights of citizenship at the end of the second year. This conflict would come to the fore in U.S. courts, with federal authority over citizenship being fully confirmed in the 1817 decision *Chirac v. Chirac*. Also left unanswered was the status of foreign-born colonists who had allied themselves with the patriot cause in the American Revolution, which led to controversy over the seating of Swiss-born U.S. senator Albert Gallatin in 1793.

The act built upon earlier existing legislation and legal tradition, modeling the law on existing state naturalization laws. A precedent for citizenship at the national level already existed in article IV of the Articles of Confederation. The law differed from Articles of Confederation provisions chiefly in explicitly restricting naturalization to whites only. The 1790 act also followed trends in the legal concept of naturalization, and the existing common-law tradition of feme covert, attaching the legal identity to the implicitly male head of household, to the exclusion of his wife, dependent children, slaves, and indentured servants. Although citizenship status descended to the acknowledged free white sons, the law excepted the children of fathers who had never resided in the United States.

The act also reflected the trend of the increasing concentration of citizenship at the federal or national level of government. Through the passage of the act, it was possible to be a citizen of the United States and, owing to religious or residency restrictions, not a citizen of one's state of residence; conversely, a person could be a citizen of a state but not of the United States. The Naturalization Act of 1795 would attempt to further federalize citizenship and was aided by court cases confirming the federalization trend in evolving legal precedent.

The Naturalization Act of 1790 had a shorter residency requirement for heads of household than any succeeding federal legislation: The 1795 act lengthened the residency requirement to five years, to which it returned in 1802 after the longer, fourteen-year requirement under the Alien Friends Act of 1798.

John O'Keefe

FURTHER READING

Baseler, Marilyn C. *"Asylum for Mankind": America, 1607-1800.* Ithaca, N.Y.: Cornell University Press, 1998.

Kettner, James H. *The Development of American Citizenship, 1608-1870*. Chapel Hill: University of North Carolina Press for the Omohundro Institute of Early American History and Culture, 1978.

LeMay, Michael C., and Elliott Robert Barkin, eds. *U.S. Immigration and Naturalization Laws and Issues: A Documentary History.* Westport, Conn.: Greenwood Press, 1999.

Somerville, Siobhan B. "Notes Toward a Queer History of Naturalization." *American Quarterly* 57, no. 3 (September, 2005) 659-679, 1002.

SEE ALSO: Alien and Sedition Acts of 1798; Congress, U.S.; Constitution, U.S.; Immigration law; Naturalization.

NEBRASKA

SIGNIFICANCE: Nebraska has always been primarily an agricultural state. During the nineteenth century, its chief attraction to immigrants was its cheap farm land. By the end of the century, fully one-half of the state's farmers were foreign born. Throughout the twentieth century, the state's population growth was relatively slow, but toward the end of the century the state began receiving an influx of Latin American immigrants, primarily from Mexico.

Early European settlement of the Nebraska region was spurred by the Homestead Act of 1862, a federal land law that made public lands in the West almost free to immigrant families. It gave settlers 160-acre plots of land in return for minimal registration fees and the promise to improve the land and live on it for at least five years. The Timber Culture Act of March 3, 1873, introduced by Nebraska's Senator Phineas W. Hitchcock, added to the allure of Nebraska land. Under this law, homesteaders could get additional land by planting trees and caring for them for a period of ten years.

NINETEENTH CENTURY IMMIGRATION AND RAILROADS

Wagon trains carried the first settlers into Nebraska, but by the 1850's, railroads were becoming the primary means of transportation. The railroad companies were aggressive in campaigning and used a variety of promotional campaigns. They placed standing advertisements in East Coast papers and offered trips to editors and their wives on their lines. Pamphlets were often published in vast quantities and distributed in various foreign languages to attract more settlers. Immigration agents were sent to European countries to conduct lectures and public forums about the availability of free land on the western plains. The railroads occasionally even reduced fares for large family groups. In 1864, the federal government granted the railroad companies twenty-mile-wide blocks of land on both sides of their tracks west of the Missouri River that the railroads were entitled to sell to settlers. Settlers naturally preferred to farm as near the tracks as possible, but the railroads generally sold the land to speculators.

To attract new settlers to Nebraska, the state government aggressively promoted Nebraska's agricultural potential. Under the leadership of Governor Robert W. Furnas, the state agricultural board sent native-born plants and crops to exhibitions in the

---

PROFILE OF NEBRASKA

Region	Midwest
Entered union	1867
Largest cities	Omaha, Lincoln (capital), Bellevue, Grand Island
Modern immigrant communities	Hispanics

Population	Total	Percent of state	Percent of U.S.	U.S. rank
All state residents	1,769,000	100.0	0.59	38
All foreign-born residents	100,000	5.6	0.27	38

Source: U.S. Census Bureau, *Statistical Abstract for 2006*.
Notes: The U.S. population in 2006 was 299,399,000, of whom 37,548,000 (12.5%) were foreign born. Rankings in last column reflect total numbers, not percentages.

East to counter the belief that the regions west of the Mississippi River were unsuitable for agriculture.

Because they owned 17 percent of Nebraska's land, the railroad companies had a vested interest in attracting settlers. As the railroads extended their lines and built bridges, they also developed new towns in rural areas. Built on local agricultural economies, these towns tended to follow a common pattern: Grain elevators were erected next to railroad tracks, followed by schools, churches, post offices, and business districts within walking distances of the railroads that developed into the classic American "Main Streets." Grocery stores and post offices frequently became centers where local immigrants gathered and bonded with other members of the communities. The towns' clubs, lodges, and churches helped to cement social ties.

Large numbers of Swedish immigrants settled in Nebraska's Saunders and Polk counties, but Germans constituted the largest immigrant group. They settled primarily in the northeastern section of the state. Eventually, Nebraska became home to more Swedes, Danes, and Czechs than any other state in the region.

Twentieth Century Developments

Nebraska's population growth throughout most of the twentieth century was slow compared to that of the United States as a whole. The 1900 census recorded 1,066,910 residents of Nebraska. By the year 2004, the state had 1,711,000 residents. The Great Depression of the 1930's devastated Nebraska's economy. Many farmers went west to find agricultural work in California, Oregon, and Washington. The latter half of the century saw an influx of Hispanics, many of whom took jobs in the meatpacking and construction industries. By the early twenty-first century, illegal immigration was a major issue, and many native-born Nebraskans were complaining that undocumented workers were taking jobs away from American citizens. In 2009, Nebraska's unicameral legislature took up the subject of implementing a new system to verify the legal status of foreign-born applicants for jobs.

Gayla Koerting

Further Reading

Blouet, Brian W., and Frederick C. Luebke. *The Great Plains: Environment and Culture.* Lincoln: University of Nebraska Press, 1979.

Gjerde, Jon. *The Minds of the West: The Ethnocultural Evolution of the Rural Middle West, 1830-1917.* Chapel Hill: University of North Carolina Press, 1979.

Olson, James C., and Ronald Nagle. *The History of Nebraska.* Lincoln: University of Nebraska Press, 1997.

Wishart, David J., ed. *Encyclopedia of the Great Plains.* Lincoln: University of Nebraska Press, 2004.

See also: Czech and Slovakian immigrants; Flanagan, Edward J.; German immigrants; Iowa; Kansas; Literature; Missouri; *My Ántonia*; Westward expansion.

Nevada

SIGNIFICANCE: Long a lightly populated, arid, and undeveloped region, Nevada began its modern development during the mid-nineteenth century, after silver was discovered in its west-central area. Since that time, Nevada has always depended on immigrant labor to help develop its economy. Beginning with railroads and mining and continuing with its modern entertainment and hospitality service industries, immigrant groups have provided a large and effective workforce throughout Nevada.

Nevada became a U.S. territory in 1861 and a state in 1864, but major events in 1859 had a dramatic impact on its future development and began attracting immigrants into the region. Discovery of the famous Comstock silver lode quickly established Gold Hill and Virginia City as major mining centers, and new immigrants began pouring in, hoping to strike it rich in the booming silver mining industry. Along with American investors and miners came large numbers of foreign laborers who worked in the mines and provided essential services to the growing population. Immigrants from Ireland, Greece, Italy, Japan, Mexico, and the Balkan peninsula all came to Nevada seeking employment or fortune. These immigrants joined already established communities of Chinese laborers who had been brought in to help build railroad lines connected to the transcontinental railroad.

PROFILE OF NEVADA

Region	West
Entered union	1864
Largest cities	Las Vegas, Paradise, Reno, Henderson, Sunrise Manor
Modern immigrant communities	Hispanics, Chinese

Population	*Total*	*Percent of state*	*Percent of U.S.*	*U.S. rank*
All state residents	2,496,000	100.0	0.83	35
All foreign-born residents	476,000	19.1	1.27	17

Source: U.S. Census Bureau, *Statistical Abstract for 2006.*
Notes: The U.S. population in 2006 was 299,399,000, of whom 37,548,000 (12.5%) were foreign born. Rankings in last column reflect total numbers, not percentages.

By 1870, the state had almost 3,000 Chinese workers, who trailed only American-born residents and Irish immigrants in numbers. Ten years later, the state had more than 5,000 Chinese, who by then outnumbered the Irish immigrants. U.S. Census figures for 1880 show Nevada with the highest percentage of foreign-born residents in the union.

TWENTIETH CENTURY ARRIVALS

Although most of Nevada's immigrant communities had been brought in to provide cheap and efficient labor, many of the immigrants faced discrimination and violence throughout the nineteenth and early twentieth centuries. In 1908, Reno's city government tried to discourage more Chinese from coming by burning down the city's Chinatown for "sanitary reasons." Such actions were not, however, directed only against Asian immigrants. For example, the town of McGill tried to expel all its Greek residents in 1908. Violence was also routinely directed against Italian and Serbian immigrants as nativist fervor captivated much of Nevada during the early twentieth century.

Mexicans began immigrating into Nevada during the silver boom years but did not arrive in large numbers until the mid-twentieth century, when the state participated in the bracero guest-worker program, which was stated in 1942 to provide low-cost labor for American farmers. Most bracero workers returned to Mexico after completing their labor contracts, but some remained and estab-

lished homes in and around the main urban centers of Las Vegas and Reno. By 1950, nearly 10 percent of the residents of Las Vegas's Clark County were counted as Hispanic.

As the cities of Las Vegas and Reno established themselves as major national centers of gaming and tourism, new immigrants were drawn to the expanding employment opportunities that the cities offered. Since the late 1940's, Nevada's casinos have steadily multiplied and grown ever larger, creating an increasing need for service workers. Immigrants from both foreign countries and other parts of the United States have flooded into the state. A high percentage of the foreign immigrants have been Latin Americans, particularly Mexicans. By 1980, Clark County's Hispanic population had increased by 600 percent since 1950.

By the year 2007, Nevada was one of the fastest-growing states in the union, with a total population of approximately 2.5 million people. Nevada was also the most culturally diverse state within the Rocky Mountain region, with African Americans accounting for 7 percent of the total population and Asian Americans 6 percent. The state's Hispanic population was second only to its "white" population in numbers, with approximately 500,000 residents, who accounted for 20 percent of the total population. The state's largest cities have also developed notable ethnic enclaves. Within the major urban areas, Las Vegas, for example, has a dynamic Chinatown along the western edge of Interstate 15 and a large shopping district catering to Asians in its downtown area.

Robert D. Mitchell

FURTHER READING

BeDunnah, Gary P. *A History of the Chinese in Nevada.* San Francisco: R&E Research Associates, 1973.

Elliott, Russell R. *History of Nevada.* 2d ed. Lincoln: University of Nebraska Press, 1987.

Hulse, James W. *The Silver State: Nevada's Heritage Reinterpreted.* 3d ed. Reno: University of Nevada Press, 2004.

James, Ronald M. *Comstock Women: The Making of a Mining Community.* Reno: University of Nevada Press, 1998.

Shepperson, Wilbur S. *Restless Strangers: Nevada's Immigrants and Their Interpreters.* Reno: University of Nevada Press, 1970.

SEE ALSO: Arizona; California; Chinese immigrants; Economic opportunities; Employment; History of immigration after 1891; Irish immigrants; Italian immigrants; Labor unions; Railroads.

NEW HAMPSHIRE

SIGNIFICANCE: Because it borders Canada's Quebec province, New Hampshire has long attracted French Canadian immigrants but relatively few immigrants from other countries. During the late twentieth century, increasing numbers of Asians began coming to New Hampshire.

The earliest New Hampshire immigrants were chiefly French Canadians who had farmed in Quebec. Many of these people took up farming in New Hampshire, but others worked as lumberjacks in the state's timber industry. During the late nineteenth century, many of them worked in the state's expanding textile mills, which often employed entire families. They characteristically tended to retain their language and culture.

The history of Manchester, New Hampshire's, Amoskeag textile mill, at one time the largest fabric plant in the world, provides a window into immigrant life in the state. Its labor force was at first dominated by young descendants of early English settlers. During the 1850's and 1860's these workers were gradually replaced by the incoming Irish immigrants. By 1860, the city of Manchester's population was 27 percent foreign born, more than 70 percent of whom were Irish. Other immigrants included much smaller numbers of Germans and Swedes, many of whom were skilled craftspeople.

During the 1870's, land scarcity in Quebec impelled more French Canadians to go to New Hampshire, where many of them worked in the Amoskeag textile mill. These people were found to make docile, industrious, and stable workers. Moreover, French Canadians generally had large families and were willing to let their children work in the mill, so the company solicited more emigration from Quebec. By the turn of the twentieth century, Greek and Polish immigrants were being absorbed into the mill's workforce, which by then numbered 17,000.

Until 1922, Amoskeag had avoided the labor strikes that had begun to disrupt production in other New England textile mills. However, during that year, the company's simultaneous increase of hours and reduction of wages provoked a strike. After the strike was settled, worker confidence in both their company and their union declined. During the Great Depression of the next decade, the century-old company went out of business. However, despite the hard times they faced, relatively few of the displaced workers left Manchester.

TWENTY-FIRST CENTURY TRENDS

New Hampshire has attracted fewer immigrants than the majority of states. During the early years of the twenty-first century,

PROFILE OF NEW HAMPSHIRE

Region	New England
Entered union	1788
Largest cities	Manchester, Nashua, Concord (capital)
Modern immigrant communities	Hispanics, Asian Indians, Chinese, Koreans

Population	Total	Percent of state	Percent of U.S.	U.S. rank
All state residents	1,315,000	100.0	0.44	41
All foreign-born residents	71,000	5.4	0.19	40

Source: U.S. Census Bureau, *Statistical Abstract for 2006.*
Notes: The U.S. population in 2006 was 299,399,000, of whom 37,548,000 (12.5%) were foreign born. Rankings in last column reflect total numbers, not percentages.

only about 5 percent of its citizens were foreign-born immigrants—a percentage less than half of the national average. However, between 2000 and 2005, new immigration saw an increase of 36 percent in the state's Hispanic population and 40 percent in the Asian population. Both groups are quite diverse in New Hampshire. The Hispanics include Puerto Ricans, Mexicans, and immigrants from several Central American countries. The Asians include Indians, Chinese, and Koreans. The majority of the Asian immigrants are already well educated when they arrive and generally find high-paying jobs without difficulty. Many of the immigrants have been attracted by the high quality of life in New Hampshire, as well as its good schools and low crime rates.

New immigration has brought new concerns to New Hampshire. While many residents of the state welcome the immigrants' contributions to the workforce, others are worried about the numbers of undocumented immigrants entering the state. The state legislature has enacted laws providing penalties for employers who hire undocumented immigrants. Related to this issue is concern that illegal immigration is tied to rising crime rates. A 2007 report presented on public radio found that New Hampshire's residents were becoming less welcoming to immigrants than the residents of many other states.

Robert P. Ellis

FURTHER READING

Armstrong, John Borden. *Factory Under the Elms: A History of Harrisville, New Hampshire, 1774-1969.* Cambridge, Mass.: MIT Press, 1969.

Brault, Gerard J. *The French-Canadian Heritage in New England.* Hanover, N.H.: University Press of New England, 1986.

Hareven, Tamara K., and Randolph Langenbach. *Amoskeag: Life and Work in an American Factory-City.* New York: Pantheon Books, 1978.

Heffernan, Nancy Coffey, and Ann Page Stecker. *New Hampshire: Crosscurrents in Its Development.* 3d ed. Hanover, N.H.: University Press of New England, 2004.

SEE ALSO: British immigrants; Canada vs. United States as immigrant destinations; Canadian immigrants; French immigrants; Great Depression; Illegal immigration; Labor unions; Vermont.

NEW HARMONY

IDENTIFICATION: German immigrant utopian community later purchased by a Scottish reformer

DATE: 1814-1827

LOCATION: New Harmony, Indiana

SIGNIFICANCE: New Harmony proved to be a failed millenarian utopia for German Har-

Architect's rendering of Robert Owen's vision for New Harmony. (Library of Congress)

monists and a failed secular utopia for the Scottish-led Owenites, but it helped spread reform and socialist ideals.

In 1803, George Rapp, a German who called himself a prophet and proclaimed that the millennium was near, led hundreds of his followers to Pennsylvania. There they formed the Harmony Society, giving up everything they owned to live communally and pledging themselves to celibacy. In 1814, the society moved to Indiana, where they founded the town of New Harmony. New Harmony prospered as new immigrants increased the population, and the inhabitants were successful at farming. While they awaited the millennium, they kept their German language and customs. Trouble with surrounding towns, however, led Rapp to move his flock back to Pennsylvania, selling the town to Robert Owen.

Owen had made his fortune from textile mills in his native Scotland, but his great concern for his workers led him to favor reform. He purchased New Harmony in 1825 as a utopian experiment to prove the viability of socialism. About eight hundred reformers and educators at New Harmony shared their property communally and favored gender equality. Unlike the Harmonists' commune, Owen's was purely secular on the assumption that rationality could create a more moral society.

Owen's experiment soon failed. The town drained his finances, and the freethinking reformers turned out not to be as manageable as Scottish laborers. The utopia disbanded in 1827, but its ideas later influenced other American reform communities.

Lincoln Austin Mullen

FURTHER READING

Taylor, Anne. *Visions of Harmony: A Study in Nineteenth-Century Millenarianism.* New York: Oxford University Press, 1987.

Thompson, Brian. *Devastating Eden: The Search for Utopia in America.* New York: HarperCollins, 2004.

Wilson, William E. *The Angel and the Serpent: The Story of New Harmony.* Bloomington: Indiana University Press, 1964.

SEE ALSO: British immigrants; German immigrants; History of immigration, 1783-1891; Indiana; Rapp, George; Religion as a push-pull factor; Westward expansion.

NEW JERSEY

SIGNIFICANCE: Because of New Jersey's location next to New York Harbor, the state historically drew many immigrants entering the United States through its main port of entry. This pattern has continued into the twenty-first century, as new immigrants have arrived at Newark, New Jersey's, and nearby New York City's international airports. The state's earliest immigrants were mostly from Europe; by the end of the twentieth century, New Jersey was one of the top-ranking states in percentages of immigrants from Mexico, China, and the Philippines, and it was also welcoming significant numbers of Asian Indians.

One of Great Britain's original North American colonies, New Jersey drew its earliest immigrants from England. Many of them were Quakers and Baptists seeking religious freedom. After the United States achieved its independence, the heaviest influx of European immigrants into New Jersey began arriving during the 1840's. Later, Irish immigrants came as laborers. Possessing the advantage of already speaking English, they quickly became prominent in political life and would eventually come to dominate the governments of such major cities as Jersey City, Trenton, and Paterson. German immigrants were slower to arrive, but by 1890 there were about 120,000 foreign-born Germans settled in New Jersey. They were prominent as craftsmen and established reputations as skilled glassmakers and woodworkers. Many Italian immigrants relocated from New York City to New Jersey. Others came directly from Italy and worked as farmers in the rural southern portion of the state. Over time, however, many of these people gravitated to industrial cities such as Trenton and Newark.

MODERN TRENDS

By the turn of the twenty-first century, New Jersey had one of the richest mixtures of world cultures in the United States, with people from nearly one hundred different nations speaking more than 165 different languages. In 2009, an advisory panel on the state's immigrant policy reported that fully 20 percent of the state's 8.7 million residents

PROFILE OF NEW JERSEY

Region	Atlantic coast
Entered union	1787
Largest cities	Newark, Jersey City, Paterson, Elizabeth, Edison
Modern immigrant communities	Asian Indians, Mexicans, Chinese, Filipinos

Population	Total	Percent of state	Percent of U.S.	U.S. rank
All state residents	8,724,000	100.0	2.91	11
All foreign-born residents	1,754,000	20.1	4.67	6

Source: U.S. Census Bureau, *Statistical Abstract for 2006.*
Notes: The U.S. population in 2006 was 299,399,000, of whom 37,548,000 (12.5%) were foreign born. Rankings in last column reflect total numbers, not percentages.

were foreign born, and most of these people had entered within the previous twenty years. About 46 percent of the foreign-born residents were Latin Americans, 30 percent were Asians, 18.6 percent were Europeans, and 4.5 percent were Africans. The largest single national group among the foreign-born New Jersey residents were Asian Indians, who constituted almost 10 percent of the immigrant population. They were followed by immigrants from Mexico, China, the Philippines, and Colombia, in that order.

The advisory report also noted that New Jersey has a comparatively high rate of naturalization among its immigrant communities. In 2006, 48 percent of its foreign-born residents were naturalized citizens. Although immigrants as a whole were more likely than native-born Americans to live in poverty, naturalized immigrants were less likely to live in poverty than natives. The advisory report did not deal at length with the subject of illegal immigration but noted the U.S. Department of Homeland Security estimate of approximately 430,000 undocumented immigrants in New Jersey.

Among other findings of the advisory report on immigration was the fact that one-third of all children in New Jersey were members of families with at least one foreign-born parent. Consequently, the state needed more instruction in English as a second language and more resources for preschool children.

Several positive factors were noted in the report. Immigrants were less likely than native-born New Jersey residents to be incarcerated or on public assistance. Immigrants were also more likely to be employed, although they generally received lower wages. More than 40 percent of the state's scientists and engineers with higher degrees were foreign born, as were medical professionals. Without these foreign-born professionals New Jersey would face serious shortages.

Robert P. Ellis

FURTHER READING

Fleming, Thomas J. *New Jersey: A Bicentennial History.* New York: W. W. Norton, 1977.

Green, Howard L., ed. *Words That Make New Jersey History: A Primary Source Reader.* Piscataway, N.J.: Rutgers University Press, 2006.

Mappen, Mark. *Jerseyana: The Underside of New Jersey History.* Piscataway, N.J.: Rutgers University Press, 1992.

Montalto, N. *One of the Many: Integrating Immigrants in New Jersey.* Washington, D.C.: National Integration Forum, 2006.

SEE ALSO: Alien land laws; Brazilian immigrants; Delaware; German immigrants; Irish immigrants; New York State; Political parties; Statue of Liberty; Transportation of immigrants.

NEW MEXICO

SIGNIFICANCE: As one the last American frontier territories to be settled, New Mexico offered opportunities for better lives to a wide variety of immigrants from throughout the world during the nineteenth century. After becoming a state in 1912, New Mexico developed into an area in which immigrants have been able to integrate into the community while still preserving their cultural heritages.

During the nineteenth and twentieth centuries, immigrants from both Asia and Europe joined large numbers of immigrants from Mexico to New Mexico. New Mexico shares a long border with Mexico, which it had been part of until the United States won the Mexican War in 1848. The most numerous European groups were Germans, including significant numbers of German Jews, through both centuries; Italians came during the nineteenth century and Spaniards during the twentieth.

The first German immigrants in New Mexico were Jewish merchants and traders who had pushed west to sell their wares along the Santa Fe Trail. They opened stores in the towns that developed along the trail and soon arranged for additional family members to follow them to New Mexico. German Lutherans started immigrating during the 1880's; most of them settled in and around Albuquerque, to which they encouraged other Germans to come. The next significant wave of Germans came after World War II, when many German scientists worked at the state's White Sands Missile Range. The German immigrants readily assimilated to the life and culture of New Mexico, particularly during the war years when anti-German sentiment was strong throughout the United States.

Italian immigrants began arriving in Albuquerque at the same time as the railroad. These immigrants found success in all types of business ventures and particularly in construction trades. During the twentieth century, a small number of Spanish immigrants came to New Mexico. Many of them became affiliated with the Cervantes Institute, which promotes Spanish culture and heritage in the state.

New Mexico's Asian communities are mostly concentrated in Albuquerque. The first Asians to arrive were Chinese and Japanese laborers who came during the late nineteenth century. Many of them worked on the railroads. Not fully accepted into the life of the city, they established their own communities and built businesses that served their own people. After the Vietnam War ended in 1975, Albuquerque's Asian community was augmented by the arrival of about 3,000 Vietnamese immigrants. Like the other Asians who had preceded them, they established their own restaurants and shops.

Around the turn of the twenty-first century, New Mexico's Asian population became even more diversified as Koreans and Filipinos began settling in the state. By this time, Asians were fully integrated into the life of Albuquerque, where they found opportunities in all sectors of business and the professions. Asian professionals include engineers, physicians, university professors, and information technology specialists. The culture of the various Asian communities has also become an important part of New Mexico's lifestyle. Asian restaurants and groceries are found throughout Albuquerque. Culture centers and ethnic festivals not only maintain Asian traditions but also have made them part of the culture of New Mexico.

Despite the important contributions of European and Asian immigrants, the strongest cultural influences in New Mexico are Mexican. The state's large Mexican American community includes families who trace their ancestry back to the time when New Mexico was part of Mexico and even earlier, when the region was ruled by Spain. Other families trace their roots to nineteenth and early twentieth century Mexican immigrants, but a substantial part of the state's early twenty-first century population was made up of both docu-

PROFILE OF NEW MEXICO

Region	Southwest
Entered union	1912
Largest cities	Albuquerque, Las Cruces, Santa Fe (capital), Rio Rancho
Modern immigrant communities	Mexicans, Vietnamese, Koreans, Filipinos

Population	Total	Percent of state	Percent of U.S.	U.S. rank
All state residents	1,954,000	100.0	0.65	36
All foreign-born residents	197,000	10.1	0.52	27

Source: U.S. Census Bureau, *Statistical Abstract for 2006.*
Notes: The U.S. population in 2006 was 299,399,000, of whom 37,548,000 (12.5%) were foreign born. Rankings in last column reflect total numbers, not percentages.

mented and undocumented immigrants who were born in Mexico.

Shawncey Webb

FURTHER READING

Citola, Nicholas P. *Italians in Albuquerque.* Chicago: Arcadia Publishing, 2002.

Gutiérrez, David G. *Walls and Mirrors: Mexican Americans, Mexican Immigrants, and the Politics of Ethnicity.* Berkeley: University of California Press, 1995.

Rodriguez, Havidán, Rogelio Sáenz, and Cecilia Menjivar. *Latinas/os in the United States: Changing the Face of America.* New York: Springer, 2008.

Zolberg, Aristide. *A Nation by Design: Immigration Policy in the Fashioning of America.* Cambridge, Mass.: Harvard University Press, 2006.

SEE ALSO: Arizona; Bracero program; German immigrants; Italian immigrants; Mexican immigrants; Texas; Vietnamese immigrants; Westward expansion.

NEW YORK CITY

IDENTIFICATION: Largest city in the United States and the most important business and financial center in the nation since colonial times

SIGNIFICANCE: The most important metropolis in the United States, New York City was essentially built and populated by immigrants and their children. Its Ellis Island was the leading port of entry for immigrants from 1892 until 1954, and its Statue of Liberty was an important symbol of welcome.

The first European immigrants to New York were Dutch who settled the southern end of Manhattan Island during the early seventeenth century. Before the Dutch arrived, Manhattan was sparsely populated by the Lenape people, from whom Peter Minuit famously purchased the island for the equivalent of twenty-four dollars in 1626. The Dutch named their colony New Amsterdam and built it into a bustling, heterogeneous commercial port that attracted visitors from all over the world. The same traits would continue to characterize New York City through the next four centuries, as the city developed into the leading destination for immigrants in the United States and perhaps in the entire world.

EARLY IMMIGRANTS

After the English seized New Amsterdam from the Dutch in 1664, they renamed the city New York. Under English, and later British, sovereignty, thousands of English, Welsh, and Scots immigrated to Manhattan, and slaves were imported from Africa. The next great wave of immigration occurred during the 1830's and 1840's, with the arrival of hundreds of thousands of German immigrants fleeing the political and economic turmoil of revolutionary Europe, and Irish immigrants escaping the ravage of their homeland's great potato famine.

By 1855, more than one-half of New York City's residents were foreign born. These immigrants represented a new alignment in American history. Most were Roman Catholics and did not speak English as their first language. They settled in New York City's ethnic enclaves and looked to maintain their cultural traditions. Poorer immigrants were packed into tenements such as the notorious Five Points Slum. Anti-immigrant sentiments increased as well, as exemplified by the nativist and Americanist movements and the rise of the Know-Nothing Party. Tensions reached a peak in draft riots during the Civil War over the issue of conscription. By the 1870's, however, immigrants had become a political force within the city, their votes courted by urban political machines such as the infamous Tammany Hall of William Marcy "Boss" Tweed. Ethnic politics would remain a dominant feature of New York City history.

ELLIS ISLAND AND THE STATUE OF LIBERTY

Through the first century of American independence, immigration remained basically open and unregulated. Immigrants arrived at ports, went through state customs houses, and became American residents. In New York City, shipping companies submitted the passenger lists to the local collector of customs. However, on August 1, 1855, the state of New York began operating a processing center for arriving immigrants on the southern tip of Manhattan known as Castle Garden. It was the first such center in the United States. After the federal Immigration Act of 1882 gave jurisdiction over immigration to the U.S. Department of the Trea-

New York City

New York City's bustling Hester Street in the city's lower East Side Jewish ghetto in 1914. (Getty Images)

sury, the secretary of the Treasury contracted with New York State to continue its processing of immigrants.

The federal Immigration Act of 1891 made supervision over immigration policy an exclusively federal process, so Castle Garden was closed. On January 1, 1892, the federal government opened its own processing center on Ellis Island, off the southern tip of Manhattan, to examine newly arrived immigrants and determine whether they should be admitted to the United States. Over the next thirty-two years, more than 16 million immigrants passed through Ellis Island, accounting for 71 percent of all immigrants to the United States. Most of those immigrants passed through New York City after being processed. Many stayed in the city—some temporarily before moving on to other

places, but approximately one-third settled permanently in New York City or the surrounding area.

The Statue of Liberty, located on Liberty Island near Ellis Island in New York Harbor, was also owned and administered by the federal government. A gift from France in 1886, the statue had no formal connection to the immigration process, but as one of the first sights that greeted passengers of ships sailing into the harbor, its glowing presence was accepted as a symbol of welcome to the new nation.

A CITY OF IMMIGRANTS

By the late nineteenth century, New York stood as the most populous and commercially significant city in North America. It was also the leading immigration destination in the nation and perhaps the world. Immigrants took up multifarious forms of employment within the city and established their own ethnic neighborhoods up and down Manhattan.

During the second half of the nineteenth century, the demographics of immigration changed again. The 1880's and 1890's began an era of mass immigration from eastern and southern Europe. Consequently, New York City absorbed hundreds of thousands of Italian and Jewish immigrants, the latter primarily from Russia and Poland. Smaller but still significant numbers of new immigrants came from the Austro-Hungarian Empire, Greece, Poland, Spain, the West Indies, and China. Manhattan was becoming a bustling collection of ethnic neighborhoods: Chinatown and Little Italy in Lower Manhattan, Jewish enclaves in the lower East Side and the Grand Concourse in the Bronx, an Irish neighborhood in Hell's Kitchen, Germans and Czechs in Yorkville. The northern end of the island has an Italian Harlem, a Spanish Harlem, and an African American Harlem, the last of which would witness the famous Harlem Renaissance of the 1920's.

The term "melting pot" was coined to describe the incredible mix of groups that had become New York. The lives of the new immigrants drew both hostility and sympathy. Pressures to restrict immigration persisted. Jacob Riis's book *How the Other Half Lives* (1890) documented the miserable conditions of urban slums. The Triangle Shirtwaist Factory fire in 1911, in which 146 mostly young European-born female garment workers died, demonstrated the miserable working conditions of many immigrants.

In 1898, New York City expanded into greater New York, adding the boroughs of Brooklyn, Queens, and Staten Island to its charter. At that time, Queens and Staten Island were largely rural, but Brooklyn already had the cosmopolitan makeup that immigration had given to Manhattan and the South Bronx, with Scandinavian and Italian neighborhoods in Bay Ridge, Jewish neighborhoods in Williamsburg, Flatbush, and Brownsville, German neighborhoods in Ridgewood, and Syrians in Red Hook. New York was a teeming mixture of ethnic groups, but many Americans across the country were becoming alarmed by the numbers of immigrants flooding into the United States. Federal legislation was enacted during the 1880's and 1890's to gain control over the immigration process—with more administrative oversight, but also with an eye to shaping the country's ethnic make-up.

TWENTIETH CENTURY IMMIGRATION

During the twentieth century, immigration continued largely unabated, even though immigration to the United States as a whole was becoming more restrictive with the introduction of national origins quotas in 1921 and 1924. However, the quota system tended to affect the ethnic mixture more than the numbers of new immigrants coming into New York. Because immigration from other countries in the Western Hemisphere remained relatively unrestricted through the quota system years, much of the immigration to New York immediately after World War II was from Latin America. Residents of Puerto Rico, regarded as U.S. citizens since 1917, were unaffected by immigration quotas. During the 1950's more than 1 million Puerto Ricans came to New York City. As British subjects, residents of the British West Indies were also privileged in immigration and flocked to the city. The overall rate of immigration into the city slowed somewhat throughout the century until passage of the Immigration and Nationality Act of 1965, which repealed national quotas.

The revival of New York City from an economic slump during the 1980's saw the city's rate of immigration climb again. As native-born New Yorkers moved to suburban communities, they were replaced within the city by immigrants. In 1970, 18.2 percent of the city's population were immigrants; by 2005, that percentage had doubled. Between 1964 and 1990, the leading sources of immigrants to New York City were

- Dominican Republic (202,102 immigrants)
- China and Taiwan (145,362)
- Jamaica (101,580)
- Guyana (70,523)
- Haiti (65,287)
- Colombia (61,383)
- Soviet Union (60,110)
- Korea (55,688)

Between 1990 and 2000, about 1.25 million immigrants settled in New York City, with others settling in nearby suburbs. By 2007, it was estimated that more than 3 million immigrants were living in New York City, out of a total population of approximately 8 million. Moreover, about 60 percent of New York City's residents were either immigrants themselves or children of immigrants. By the early twenty-first century, one-third of the city's immigrants during the twenty-first century were from Latin America, with the majority from the Dominican Republic, Ecuador, Mexico, and Colombia. One-quarter of the city's immigrants were Asian; Chinese were the largest group, but there were also many Koreans, Asian Indians, and Filipinos. A large number of immigrants from Caribbean countries have transformed the city's traditionally black neighborhoods. During the early years of the twenty-first century, Dominicans, Chinese, Jamaicans, and people from the former Soviet Union made up the largest of arriving groups to New York. About 170 languages are spoken in the city.

QUEENS AS A MICROCOSM OF THE CITY

New York City is a city of neighborhoods that reflect the ethnic origins of different immigrant groups. In no part of the city, however, have the transformations wrought by immigration been more apparent than in the borough of Queens. Once an ethnically homogenous and rural suburb, Queens has become the most ethnically diverse county in the United States. During the early twenty-first century, one-half of its residents were foreign born. Most of New York City's 275,000 Asian Indians and other South Asians live in Queens. A similar pattern is true of the city's approximately 215,000 Filipino residents. Queen's Astoria neighborhood has the largest concentration of Greeks outside Athens, Greece. Flushing has one of the largest Chinatowns in the country. Arabic and Middle Eastern populations are clustered around Steinway Street. Colombians and South Asians are clustered in Jackson Heights; Bangladeshis and Brazilians on the Astoria-Long Island City border.

The history of Queens is a microcosm of New York City immigration history. Like Manhattan, it was first settled by the Dutch and English. Irish, German, and Italian immigrants settled in western Queens during the nineteenth century. The beginning of the twentieth century saw millions of immigrants arriving from southern and western Europe. Around the turn of the twenty-first century, new immigrants poured in from Latin America, the West Indies, and Asia.

Howard Bromberg

FURTHER READING

Almeida, Linda. *Irish Immigrants in New York City, 1945-1995*. Bloomington: Indiana University Press, 2001. Study of late twentieth century Irish immigration into the city. Although most Irish immigrants arrived during the mid-nineteenth century, they remained an important stream of immigrants into the following century.

Baily, Samuel. *Immigration in the Land of Promise: Italians in Buenos Aires and New York City, 1870-1914*. Ithaca, N.Y.: Cornell University Press, 2004. Comparative study of the large turn-of-the-twentieth-century waves of Italian immigration into New York City and Argentina's capital city, Buenos Aires.

Foner, Nancy. *From Ellis Island to JFK: New York's Two Great Waves of Immigration*. New Haven, Conn.: Yale University Press, 2000. Study by a leading immigration historian comparing the mass migrations of Russian Jews and Italians to New York City around 1900 to the wave of immigrants from Asia, Latin America, and the Caribbean a century later.

_____, ed. *Islands in the City: West Indian Migration to New York*. Berkeley: University of California, 2001. Collection of scholarly essays on the impact of immigration to New York from the multicultural West Indies.

_____. *New Immigrants in New York*. New York: Columbia University Press, 2001. Collection of sociological studies of New York City's recent Chinese, Dominican, Jamaican, Korean, Mexican, Soviet Jew, and West African immigrants, examining how members of these groups have interacted with the city.

Glazer, Nathan, and Daniel Moynihan. *Beyond the Melting Pot: The Negroes, Puerto Ricans, Jews, Italians, and Irish of New York City*. 2d ed. Cambridge, Mass.: MIT Press, 1970. First published in 1963, this study of the assimilation of ethnic New York immigrants into American culture is a classic of American sociology.

Kasinitz, Philip. *Caribbean New York: Black Immigrants and the Politics of Race*. Ithaca, N.Y.: Cornell University Press, 1992. Examines migratory patterns of Caribbean New Yorkers, with tables and figures documenting the highly mobile West Indian immigration patterns.

Kasinitz, Philip, John Mollenkopf, and Mary Waters, eds. *Becoming New Yorkers: Ethnographies of the*

New Second Generation. New York: Russell Sage Foundation, 2004. Collection of sociological essays examining the experiences of New Yorkers under the age of eighteen who are children of immigrants.

Kessner, Thomas. *The Golden Door: Italian and Jewish Immigrant Mobility in New York City, 1880-1915.* New York: Oxford University Press, 1977. Quantitative study of the experiences of the greatest immigration wave to the "Immigrant City," with twenty-five tables showing occupational distribution.

Smith, Robert Courtney. *Mexican New York: Transnational Lives of New Immigrants.* Berkeley: University of California, 2005. Ethnographic study of the families of transnational Mexican immigrants living in Mexico and New York. With a methodological appendix.

Waldinger, Roger. *Still the Promised City? African Americans and New Immigrants in Postindustrial New York.* Cambridge, Mass.: Harvard University Press, 1999. Study of employment, demographics, ethnicity, and race in recent immigration to New York. With appendixes on shift-share analysis and field research methods.

SEE ALSO: Ellis Island; Ethnic enclaves; Garment industry; Little Italies; Machine politics; Melting pot theory; New York State; Puerto Rican immigrants; Statue of Liberty; Tammany Hall; Triangle Shirtwaist fire.

NEW YORK STATE

SIGNIFICANCE: The history of immigration into the state of New York has been dominated by immigration into New York City, in which about 90 percent of the state immigrant population lives. The rest of the state has had a somewhat different but nonetheless significant immigration history.

In the first U.S. Census of 1790, New York ranked as the fifth-most populous of the country's eighteen states and territories with a total population of 340,120. About one-half of its residents were of English descent and one-fifth were of Dutch descent. By 1820, New York ranked as the most populous state in the union and remained so until the 1960's, when it was overtaken by California. The state's earliest Jewish immigrants were mostly Spanish and Portuguese, but German Jews began arriving during the 1830's. From then until the end of the nineteenth century, the Irish, Germans, and English furnished the largest numbers of immigrants to the state.

Through New York's history, the majority of new immigrants to the state have settled, at least initially, in New York City, which was both the largest city in the United States and the country's primary port of entry for immigrants. During a single year, 1853, about 300,000 immigrants passed through the port of New York City. Most of these people were Irish fleeing from their homeland's devastating potato famine, and most of them crowded into the tenements of New York City.

Between the 1880's and World War I (1914-1918), the numbers of Italian, Polish, Greek, and Russian immigrants entering New York increased rapidly. Most of these immigrants were laborers, but many of their children became important professional figures, politicians, and entertainers. Fiorello La Guardia, who was mayor of New York City for eleven years; Herbert H. Lehman, who was state governor for nearly ten years; and Jacob K. Javits, who represented New York in the U.S. Senate for twenty-four years, were all children of immigrants.

TWENTIETH CENTURY TRENDS

Studies of immigration into the state of New York typically focus on New York City, through which many millions of immigrants have entered the country. This is natural, as during the early years of the twenty-first century, 90 percent of the state's entire immigrant population resided in the city. However, more than 200,000 other immigrants were living in other parts of the state. Immigration patterns in upstate New York are quite different from those of the city. A study of the foreign-born population of upstate New York completed in 2007 by the Federal Reserve Bank of New York revealed some of those differences, drawing on data from the 2000 U.S. Census.

According to the 2007 report, Latin American immigrants constituted more than one-half of all foreign-born residents of New York City but only 13 percent of the populations of such major upstate cities as Buffalo, Rochester, Albany, and Syracuse. In contrast, European immigrants accounted for 43 percent of all foreign-born residents in the upstate cities but only 17 percent of New York City's foreign born. Recent immigrants from Germany and Poland were prominent among the foreign born in the upstate cities, along with newcomers from eastern Europe and the former Soviet republics. As might be expected, the percentage of Canadian immigrants is much higher upstate than in New York City, especially in Buffalo, which stands on the Canadian border. However, the proportions of Asian immigrants both upstate and in the city are roughly the same: 25 percent in the city and 30 percent upstate.

Upstate New York and Long Island also differ from New York City in having many immigrant agricultural workers. Their exact numbers are difficult to establish, because many of these immigrants are undocumented. However, of the 47,000 immigrants known to be working on fruit, vegetable, and dairy farms at the turn of the twenty-first century, 80 percent were Mexicans. As many as one-half of these people may have been undocumented. As in other states, many of them are impoverished and without heath care insurance.

The Hispanic immigrant population of upstate New York also includes many Portuguese and Brazilians. A 2006 state government report on Hispanic immigrants and their children, including Puerto Ricans, in upstate areas found that members of the younger generations still faced many of the same problems that their immigrant ancestors faced. Limited education and English language proficiency were particular problems.

Robert P. Ellis

FURTHER READING

Bogen, Elizabeth. *Immigration in New York*. New York: Praeger, 1987.

Klein, Milton M. *The Empire State: A History of New York*. Ithaca, N.Y.: Cornell University Press, 2005.

Pencak, William, et al., eds. *Immigration to New York*. Philadelphia: Balch Institute Press, 1991.

Youssef, Nadia H. *The Demographics of Immigration: A Socio-Demographic Profile of the Foreign-Born Population in New York State*. New York: Center for Migration Studies, 1991.

SEE ALSO: Asian immigrants; Canadian immigrants; Canals; Dutch immigrants; Farm and migrant workers; *Golden Venture* grounding; Jewish immigrants; New Jersey; New York City.

NEW YORK V. MILN

THE CASE: U.S. Supreme Court decision on state regulation of immigrants

DATE: February 16, 1837

SIGNIFICANCE: Ignoring congressional power under the U.S. Constitution's commerce clause, the *Miln* decision gave individual states power over arriving immigrants by allowing them to regulate passengers on ships entering their ports under the doctrine of the state police powers. In later years, however, the Court would reverse this ruling.

In an attempt to gain control over indigent aliens and others likely to become public charges, New York's state legislature enacted a law requiring ships docking in New York Harbor to pay a head tax on each passenger and to provide an accurate rec-

---

PROFILE OF NEW YORK

Region	Atlantic coast
Entered union	1788
Largest cities	New York City, Hempstead, Brookhaven, Islip, Oyster Bay, Buffalo
Modern immigrant communities	Chinese, Mexicans, Asian Indians

Population	Total	Percent of state	Percent of U.S.	U.S. rank
All state residents	19,306,000	100.0	6.45	3
All foreign-born residents	4,179,000	21.6	11.13	2

Source: U.S. Census Bureau, *Statistical Abstract for 2006*.

Notes: The U.S. population in 2006 was 299,399,000, of whom 37,548,000 (12.5%) were foreign born. Rankings in last column reflect total numbers, not percentages.

ord of all passengers. Failure to comply with the law was to result in hefty penalties. Because the transportation and ingress of persons was considered a form of commerce, the law raised the explosive issue of the U.S. Constitution's commerce clause, which gave the federal government ultimate authority to regulate all foreign and interstate commerce. When New York City fined the master of the ship *Emily* for not reporting a hundred passengers, the master argued in federal court that the New York law was unconstitutional.

After the case reached the U.S. Supreme Court, the Court upheld the New York law by a 6-1 margin. Writing for the Court, Associate Justice Philip P. Barbour ignored the explosive issue of the commerce clause, while asserting that the state's "police power" was just as applicable to "precautionary measures against the moral pestilence of paupers, vagabonds, and possible convicts, as it is to guard against the physical pestilence, which may arise from unsound and infectious articles imported." The state's right to protect the health and welfare of its citizens, moreover, was "complete, unqualified, and exclusive." Justice Joseph Story issued a strong dissent. The *Miln* decision, insofar as it related to the regulation of commerce with foreign nations, would later be overturned in the *Passenger Cases* (1848) and *Henderson v. New York* (1875).

Thomas Tandy Lewis

FURTHER READING

Legomsky, Stephen. *Immigration and the Judiciary: Law and Politics in Britain and America.* New York: Oxford University Press, 1987.

LeMay, Michael, and Elliott Robert Barkan, eds. *U.S. Immigration and Naturalization Laws and Issues: A Documentary History.* Westport, Conn.: Greenwood Press, 1999.

SEE ALSO: Congress, U.S.; Constitution, U.S.; Due process protections; History of immigration, 1783-1891; Immigration law; *Passenger Cases*; Supreme Court, U.S.

NGUYEN V. IMMIGRATION AND NATURALIZATION SERVICE

THE CASE: U.S. Supreme Court decision concerning citizenship of immigrant children
DATE: Decided on January 9, 2001

> **SIGNIFICANCE:** The *Nguyen* ruling upheld a federal law giving a gender-based preference in rights to citizenship of illegitimate children born abroad when only one parent is a U.S. citizen.

Tuan Anh Nguyen, who was born out of wedlock in Vietnam, was the son of an American father and a Vietnamese mother. At the age of five, the boy was brought to the United States and raised by his father. When he was twenty-two years old, Nguyen was found guilty of sexually abusing a young child. Under U.S. law, a child born to an unmarried American mother was automatically considered a natural-born citizen, whereas a child born to an unmarried father was not a citizen unless the father proved paternity with a blood test and formally claimed paternity before the child's eighteenth birthday. Because the father had not satisfied these requirements, the Immigration and Naturalization Service (INS) ruled that Nguyen was not a citizen and therefore deportable. Nguyen argued in federal court that the gender distinction in the law was discriminatory and therefore unconstitutional.

By a 5-4 margin, the Supreme Court held that Nguyen could be deported and that the gender distinction in the law was "consistent with the constitutional guarantee of equal protection." Writing for the majority, Justice Anthony Kennedy explained that such distinctions are permissible if they serve "important governmental objectives" and employed means that are "substantially related to the achievement of those objectives." While the majority concluded that the law satisfied the two standards because of different relationships between children with their mothers and fathers, Justice Sandra Day O'Connor and three other justices vigorously disagreed.

Thomas Tandy Lewis

FURTHER READING
O'Brien, David M. *Constitutional Law and Politics.* 7th ed. New York: W. W. Norton, 2008.

Phelan, Margaret, and James Gillespie. *Immigration Law Handbook.* 5th ed. New York: Oxford University Press, 2007.

SEE ALSO: Amerasian children; Amerasian Homecoming Act of 1987; Child immigrants; Citizenship; Congress, U.S.; Constitution, U.S.; Deportation; Supreme Court, U.S.; Vietnamese immigrants.

NICARAGUAN IMMIGRANTS

SIGNIFICANCE: Despite deep historical ties between Nicaragua and the United States, significant Nicaraguan immigration did not begin until after the start of the Sandinista revolution of the 1970's. Since then, Nicaraguans have become one of the largest groups of Central American immigrants and have made their presence especially felt in South Florida and Southern California.

Ties between the United States and Nicaragua have historically been marked by U.S. political, economic, and military intervention in the Central American nation. In 1909, for example, the U.S. government supported a revolution that replaced

PROFILE OF NICARAGUAN IMMIGRANTS

Country of origin	Nicaragua
Primary language	Spanish
Primary regions of U.S. settlement	South Florida and Southern California
Earliest significant arrivals	Late nineteenth century
Peak immigration period	1990's-2008
Twenty-first century legal residents*	53,176 (6,647 per year)

*Immigrants who obtained legal permanent resident status in the United States.
Source: Department of Homeland Security, *Yearbook of Immigration Statistics, 2008.*

a liberal military ruler with a conservative regime. Afterward, the United States maintained a military presence in the country until 1933, when it defeated an uprising by rebel leader Augusto César Sandino. With support from the United States, General Anastasio Somoza seized control of Nicaragua in 1936. His sons, Luis and Anastasio Somoza Debayle, assumed control of the country and continued the family rule through more than four decades.

EARLY IMMIGRATION

Early immigration from Nicaragua to the United States was facilitated by the country's political and economic dependency on the United States. Like other Central Americans, some of the earliest Nicaraguans who came to the United States were industrialists and workers associated with the nation's coffee industry who began going to San Francisco, California, during the late nineteenth and early twentieth centuries.

During the 1930's, Nicaragua's repressive Somoza regime drove large numbers of people to flee the country. Many of these people settled in Southern California and the state of New York. During World War II and afterward, many Nicaraguans found employment at U.S.-based shipyards and wartime industries in the U.S.-administered Panama Canal Zone, and many of them later moved to San Francisco. By the 1940's, Nicaraguans were the largest Central American community in the San Francisco Bay area and second only to Mexicans among Latin American immigrants.

According to data from the U.S. Census, some 28,620 Nicaraguans were living in the United States in 1970. Many had immigrated after passage of the federal Immigration and Nationality Act of 1965, which significantly loosened U.S. immigration rules. Interestingly, most Nicaraguan immigrants during the late 1960's were women. Most of them were domestic workers who found employment through well-established immigrant networks in San Francisco and Los Angeles.

IMPACT OF THE SANDINISTA REVOLUTION

By 1979, Nicaragua's Somoza regime had alienated most of its political base and was toppled by a leftist guerrilla organization, the Sandinista National Liberation Front (FSLN). The Sandinistas' unsteady assumption of power over the next decade triggered the largest exodus of Nicaraguans in the country's history.

The Sandinista revolution spurred three waves of Nicaraguan immigration to the United States. The first took place during the time of the revolution, when perhaps 20,000 members of wealthy families closely associated with the Somoza regime fled to Miami, Florida.

The second wave occurred during the early 1980's. It brought many non-Sandinista members of the new government coalition, along with business people and professionals whose companies had been seized by the state or who found it increasingly difficult to maintain their lifestyle within the constraints of the socialist-leaning government.

Meanwhile, because of the Sandinista government's efforts to sever Nicaragua's dependence on the United States and fears of the U.S. government that Nicaragua would boost Soviet communist influence in the region, the United States launched a multifaceted assault against the Sandinista regime. U.S. actions included a trade embargo against Nicaragua and support for a counterrevolutionary army in exile that was known as the "Contras." By 1990, Nicaragua was engulfed in a severe economic crisis and growing violence, and the Sandinistas were voted out of power. The third wave of immigration took place during this period, and brought to the United States thousands of young men of all classes dodging military conscription, along with poor families fleeing the country's harsh economic conditions and the ravages of a festering civil war.

By the time of the 1990 U.S. Census, the three recent waves of Nicaraguan immigration had brought into the United States 202,658 documented immigrants and an unknown but probably substantial number of undocumented immigrants. The bulk of these people settled in South Florida, where the total Nicaraguan population in Miami alone was estimated at 175,000 during the early 1990's. That number made Nicaraguans the second-largest Hispanic community in South Florida after Cubans.

Nicaraguans fleeing the Sandinista regime did not receive automatic refugee status or asylum privileges in the United States. Indeed, of those who applied for asylum, only about one-quarter were successful during the 1980's. In 1997, U.S. deportations of Nicaraguans who were not granted asylum were temporarily halted in 1997. However, during the following year, when the U.S. Congress froze

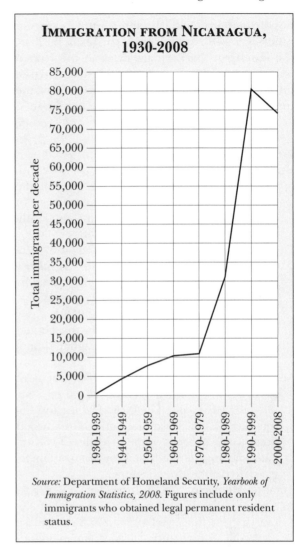

IMMIGRATION FROM NICARAGUA, 1930-2008

Source: Department of Homeland Security, *Yearbook of Immigration Statistics, 2008.* Figures include only immigrants who obtained legal permanent resident status.

military support for the Contras and Nicaraguan immigration began increasing again, the government reversed its position and began treating Nicaraguans as illegal immigrants. The 1997 federal Nicaraguan Adjustment and Central American Relief Act allowed Nicaraguans who had entered the United States before 1995 to obtain permanent residency.

The exodus from Nicaragua continued during the 1990's and into the early twenty-first century because of the country's shattered economy and social conditions. Meanwhile, Nicaraguans have become part of the flood of undocumented immigrants coming to the United States. Most have settled in the well-established Nicaraguan communities of Southern California and South Florida, but others have settled in large cities in Texas. By 2008, the number of Nicaraguans living in the United States was estimated at 300,000, but that figure must be considered conservative because of the undocumented status of many of the immigrants.

Mauricio Espinoza-Quesada

FURTHER READING

Bucuvalas, Tina. *South Florida Folklife.* Jackson: University of Mississippi Press, 1994. One of the chapters in this book provides an overview of Nicaraguan immigration to Miami and traditions maintained by this community.

Fernández-Kelly, Patricia, and Sara Curran. "Nicaraguans: Voices Lost, Voices Found." In *Ethnicities: Children of Immigrants in America,* edited by Rubén Rumbaut and Alejandro Portes. Berkeley: University of California Press, 2001. Essay detailing the impact of settling in the United States on the children of Nicaraguan immigrants.

Menjívar, Cecilia. "Salvadorans and Nicaraguans: Refugees Become Workers." In *Illegal Immigration in America,* edited by David Haines and Karen Rosenblum. Westport, Conn.: Greenwood Press, 1999. Account of the struggles of Nicaraguans fleeing the Sandinista conflict to attain legal status in the United States.

Solaún, Mauricio. *U.S. Intervention and Regime Change in Nicaragua.* Lincoln: University of Nebraska Press, 2005. Well-organized historical account of U.S intervention in Nicaraguan politics and its impact.

Walker, Thomas. *Nicaragua: Living in the Shadow of the Eagle.* Boulder, Colo.: Westview Press, 2003. History of the Nicaraguan nation and its ties with the United States.

SEE ALSO: Deportation; El Rescate; Florida; Honduran immigrants; Illegal immigration; Immigration waves; Latin American immigrants; Latinos and immigrants; Miami; Refugees; Salvadoran immigrants.

9/11 AND U.S. IMMIGRATION POLICY

THE EVENT: Reexamination of U.S. immigration laws from a security perspective following the terrorist attacks of September 11, 2001 on New York City and Washington, D.C.

SIGNIFICANCE: The fusing of immigration policy to the U.S. war on terrorism—and the resultant tightening of access to the country by foreign students, professionals, and immigrants from areas regarded as most likely to contain potential terrorists—generated a major debate over the goals of immigrant policy, and led to substantial changes in the day-to-day operation of U.S. policies toward the nationals of other countries.

The immigration policy of the United States was already in the process of being revised in 2001, when Middle Eastern operatives of the Muslim extremist organization al-Qaeda hijacked four American jet airliners for use as flying bombs against targets in New York City and Washington, D.C., on September 11 of that year. Prior to that moment, however, the main issue driving the national immigration debate had been primarily economic—the charge that the influx of illegal immigrants was driving down U.S. wages and depriving American citizens of employment. To that argument, the attacks on the World Trade Center and Pentagon building added a major national security issue to immigration reform.

The significance of that change in policy direction was quickly dramatized when the U.S. Immigration and Naturalization Service (INS) was reconstituted as the U.S. Citizenship and Immigration Services (USCIS) and placed under the aegis of the newly created Department of Homeland Security on March 1, 2003. Elsewhere, the government moved aggressively to tighten the rules governing admission to the United States, to secure its borders more tightly to prevent hostile aliens from entering the country illegally, and to identify illegal immigrants who were already inside the country.

RESTRICTING ADMISSION TO THE UNITED STATES

The most widely criticized of the government's post-9/11 actions were proposals—later abandoned—to criminalize entering the United States illegally. Nearly as controversial, however, were administrative reforms mandating special registration of certain categories of immigrants. For example, international students were to register their names and addresses with the government and regularly update that information. Even more draconian were requirements for male immigrants from twenty-four predominantly Muslim countries to be photographed, fingerprinted, and annually interviewed by government officials. The new regulations also made it easier to deport aliens for even minor criminal transgressions. Visa application and renewal procedures were expanded, along with the discretionary authority of U.S. officials stationed abroad to deny visas to applicants unable to meet the heightened security requirements for entry to the United States. Critics have argued that the net result of these moves has been to deny entry or reentry to many valued people because their points of origin happened to be in the Muslim world.

SEALING THE BORDERS AND IDENTIFYING ILLEGAL IMMIGRANTS

A collateral consequence of the 9/11 attacks was that they focused new attention on the large numbers of non-European aliens who were in the United States illegally, thereby generating new calls to bolster border security against unsanctioned immigrants. The focus of these calls was the long U.S. border with Mexico. The U.S. Congress responded

THE EVENTS OF SEPTEMBER 11, 2001

At 8:45 A.M. on September, 11, 2001, an airliner flying out of Boston crashed into the north tower of New York City's World Trade Center, ripping a hole in several upper floors and starting a fire so intense that people on higher floors could not evacuate the building. At first, the crash was believed to be an accident. However, when a second airliner struck the Trade Center's south tower eighteen minutes later, it was clear that neither crash had been accidental. Fearing that a large-scale terrorist attack was underway, government agencies shut down local airports, bridges, and tunnels. Less than one hour after the first crash, the Federal Aviation Administration ordered—for the first time in history—a stop to all flight operations throughout the United States. Only moments later, a third airliner crashed into the Pentagon Building outside Washington, D.C.

Meanwhile, the intense fires in the Trade Center towers—fed by the airliners' jet fuel—so weakened the buildings that they could no longer support their upper floors. At 10:05 A.M., the entire south tower collapsed; twenty-three minutes later, the north tower collapsed. Between those events, a fourth airliner crashed in a field outside Pittsburgh, Pennsylvania.

As was later determined, all four airliners had been hijacked by operatives of a shadowy Middle Eastern organization known as al-Qaeda that was determined to kill as many Americans and do as much damage to the United States as possible. By any measure, the scheme was a great success. The cost of the physical damage of the attacks could be measured in billions of dollars. Although the extent of human fatalities was not as great as was initially feared, about three thousand people lost their lives—a number greater than all the American fatalities during the Japanese attack on Pearl Harbor on December 7, 1941. In addition, the sense of security from outside threats that Americans had long enjoyed was shattered. The impact of the terrorist attacks on American attitudes toward immigrants would be significant.

Dust clouds enveloping Lower Manhattan after the collapse of the World Trade Center towers on September 11, 2001. (www.bigfoto.com)

in 2006 by authorizing the expansion of a secure fence along the border. Another step taken to advance border security was requiring, on a phased-in basis, U.S. citizens to carry passports when traveling to—and especially when returning from—neighboring Mexico and Canada, which were once free from that requirement.

To prevent future terrorist attacks on the United States, new and often highly controversial policies were implemented to identify and respond to the growing number of illegal immigrants already inside the country. The Patriot Act, passed less than six weeks after 9/11, expanded the Federal Bureau of Investigation's authority to monitor people living inside the United States. The National Security Entry-Exit Regulation System put into effect in 2002 required male noncitizens over the age of sixteen to register with the government. A computerized entry-exit system at ports of entry enhanced the federal government's ability to identify more easily those staying beyond the time permitted by their visas.

Meanwhile, raids were launched on the sites of companies suspected of employing illegal immigrants, especially at locations judged to be near potential terrorist targets, such as construction areas near Dulles International Airport outside Washington, D.C. In this endeavor, federal agents were often assisted by state and local enforcement agencies. In fact, the latter often carried the greater burden. Ironically, federal scrutiny of firms suspected of harboring illegal employees actually declined in the years immediately following 9/11, when the government focused more on identifying likely Arab terrorists.

To heighten national security, Congress passed the Real ID Act in 2005. This law's main purpose was to standardize procedures across the United States involving the acquisition of driving licenses by specifying the requirements that must be met for state licenses and for identity cards used for such "official purposes" as entering federal buildings and security-sensitive private facilities such as nuclear power plants, and for boarding commercial aircraft. The federal act also authorized federal magistrates to require additional proofs of identity and status of aliens already in the country who are seeking asylum.

Joseph R. Rudolph, Jr.

FURTHER READING

Alden, Edward H. *The Closing of the American Border: Terrorism, Immigration, and Security Since 9/11.* New York: Harper, 2008. Thoughtful assessment of post-9/11 immigration policy based on interviews with Bush administration officials and persons adversely affected by those policies.

Farnam, Julie. *U.S. Immigration Laws Under the Threat of Terrorism.* New York: Algora, 2005. Thorough treatment of the subject that examines the post-9/11 restrictions on immigration in the context of the restrictive immigration and asylum laws that resulted from the first World Trade Center bombing in 1993.

Kettl, Donald F. *System Under Stress: Homeland Security and American Politics.* Washington, D.C.: Congressional Quarterly Press, 2004. Excellent introductory reading for those seeking to place post-9/11 changes in immigration policy into the broader context of U.S. counterterrorism policy.

McEntire, David A. *Introduction to Homeland Security: Understanding Terrorism with an Emergency Management Perspective.* Hoboken, N.J.: John Wiley & Sons, 2009. Covers the same ground as Kettl's work but in a more extensive manner.

U.S. Senate. *War on Terrorism: Immigration Enforcement Since September 11, 2001: Hearing Before the Subcommittee on Immigration, Border Security, and Citizenship.* Washington, D.C.: Government Printing Office, 2003. For researchers with access to public documents, an outstanding source for testimonial arguments for and against the tightening of U.S. borders after 9/11.

SEE ALSO: Arab immigrants; Aviation and Transportation Security Act of 2001; Border fence; History of immigration after 1891; Homeland Security, Department of; Loyalty oaths; Muslim immigrants; Patriot Act of 2001; Supreme Court, U.S.

NISHIMURA EKIU V. UNITED STATES

THE CASE: U.S. Supreme Court decision concerning habeas corpus petitions by aliens
DATE: Decided on January 18, 1892

> **SIGNIFICANCE:** The *Nishimura Ekiu* decision recognized the constitutionality of a federal law that authorized immigration officials to refuse to admit aliens into the country, without any opportunity for habeas corpus relief. The ruling also ignored minor procedural mistakes by immigration officials acting in pursuance of the law.

Nishimura Ekiu, a female citizen of Japan, arrived at the port of San Francisco in 1891. When she was interviewed by immigration officials, she claimed that she was going to meet her husband, who was living in the United States, but did not know his address. Having only twenty-two dollars in her possession, she said that she would stay at a hotel until her husband called her. A recent federal law of 1891 required the U.S. Treasury Department to refuse admittance to several categories of persons, including persons without succifient financial resources to avoid becoming public charges. After officials refused to allow Nishimura into the country, she petitioned the district court for a writ of habeas corpus, claiming that denial of such relief would deprive her of liberty without due process of law.

The U.S. Supreme Court voted 8-1 to approve both the constitutionality of the 1891 law and the officials' refusal to allow Nishimura to land. Writing the majority opinion, Justice Horace Gray concentrated on the wording of the relevant statute, which referred to the concurrent jurisdiction of the district and circuit courts. He concluded that Congress had clearly and explicitly authorized immigration officials within the Treasury Department to make the final determination for refusing admittance of the categories of aliens enumerated in the statute.

Thomas Tandy Lewis

FURTHER READING
Galloway, Donald. *Immigration Law.* Concord, Ont.: Irwin Law, 1997.

LeMay, Michael, and Elliott Robert Barkan, eds. *U.S. Immigration and Naturalization Laws and Issues: A Documentary History.* Westport, Conn.: Greenwood Press, 1999.

SEE ALSO: Congress, U.S.; Due process protections; History of immigration, 1783-1891; *Immigration and Naturalization Service v. St. Cyr*; Japanese immigrants; *Lem Moon Sing v. United States*; Supreme Court, U.S.; *United States v. Ju Toy.*

NORTH AMERICAN FREE TRADE AGREEMENT

THE TREATY: International agreement among the United States, Canada, and Mexico creating the largest free trade zone in the world
DATE: Ratified in 1993; went into effect on January 1, 1994
ALSO KNOWN AS: NAFTA

> **SIGNIFICANCE:** This international agreement facilitated the movement of trade goods and persons among the United States, Canada, and Mexico, and had the effect of accelerating the influx of undocumented Mexican migrants into the United States.

The North American Free Trade Agreement (NAFTA) was signed in 1992 and ratified in 1993 by the governments of the United States, Canada, and Mexico and took effect on January 1, 1994. NAFTA established a free trade zone in North America by immediately lifting tariffs on the majority of goods produced by the signatory nations. It also called for the gradual elimination, over a period of fifteen years, of most remaining barriers to cross-border investments and to the movement of goods and services among the three countries.

MOBILITY OF IMMIGRANTS
Chapter 16 of NAFTA specifically concerns cross-border movement of persons within the NAFTA region. It makes four categories of travelers eligible for temporary entry from one NAFTA country into another: business visitors, traders and investors, intracompany transferees, and profes-

NAFTA initialing ceremony in October, 1992. Standing, from left to right: Mexican president Carlos Salinas de Gortari, U.S. president George H. W. Bush, and Canadian prime minister Brian Mulroney. Seated: Jaime Serra Puche, Carla Hills, and Michael Wilson. (George Bush Presidential Library and Museum)

sionals. There are more than sixty listed qualifying NAFTA Professional (TN) titles, including computer systems analysts, accountants, hotel managers, management consultants, economists, engineers, scientists, and teachers. NAFTA defines "temporary entry" as entry without the intent to establish permanent residence. For example, the United States specifies that visiting aliens must satisfy inspecting immigration officers that their proposed stays are temporary. A temporary period has a reasonable, finite end that does not equate to permanent residence. In order to establish that visits will be temporary, alien visitors must demonstrate to the satisfaction of inspecting immigration officers that their work assignments in the United States will end at predictable times and that they will promptly return home upon completion of their assignments. For each of the above four categories, spouses and dependents can enter NAFTA member countries as visitors so long as they meet

the member country's existing temporary entry immigration regulations.

Citizens of Canada and Mexico who wish to enter and work as professionals in the United States need NAFTA-based nonimmigrant TN visas. To apply for and receive such visas, applicants must provide the U.S. immigration agencies with all necessary documentation, such as passports to prove their Canadian or Mexican citizenship. They must also show proof of their professional qualifications, such as transcripts of grades, licenses, certificates, degrees, or records of previous employment, and letters verifying their employment in the United States. Application fees of fifty U.S. dollars are charged.

Canadian citizens can apply for TN visas at U.S. ports of entry; Mexican citizens must do this at U.S. embassy consular sections and submit to appointed interviews there. The maximum period of stay for TN visa holders in the United States was originally one year; this period was extended to three years in October, 2008, and U.S. Citizenship and Immigration Services (USCIS) can grant extensions in increments of one year. There is no limit on the number of years that a TN visa holder may stay in the United States. When the applicants are already in the United States, their employers may file Form I-129 (Petition for Non-immigrant Worker) with the Nebraska Service Center of the USCIS, or the applicants may reapply at a port of entry using the same application and documentation procedures above as required for the initial entry.

According to the Department of Homeland Security's *Yearbook of Immigration Statistics*, during fiscal year 2006 (October, 2005, through September, 2006), 74,098 foreign professionals (64,633 Canadians and 9,247 Mexicans) were admitted into the United States for temporary employment under NAFTA. Additionally, 17,321 of their family members (13,136 Canadians, 2,904 Mexicans, as well as a number of third-country nationals married to Canadians and Mexicans) entered the United States.

INCREASED ILLEGAL IMMIGRATION

Implementation of NAFTA accelerated the movement of undocumented immigrants from Mexico to the United States in several ways. First, the economic integration under NAFTA created increased cross-border traffic, which made illegal migration easier. Second, NAFTA functioned to expand and then contract Mexico's *maquiladora* industry, which assembled a large, mobile workforce just across the Rio Grande, leading to the unemployment of many Mexican workers. Third, the import of inexpensive American agricultural goods caused the bankruptcy of many Mexican farmers and therefore pushed large numbers of Mexican farmworkers out of work. These dislocated Mexican workers increasingly chose to seek a new life in the United States.

Before NAFTA went into effect, undocumented Mexican immigrants came mainly from four or five Mexican states and a limited number of mostly rural municipalities. Since NAFTA has been in effect, immigrants have come from all Mexican states and practically all municipalities. The counterpart of this hollowing out of the Mexican countryside is the growth of the Mexican migrant population in the United States, much of it undocumented.

American states that had only handfuls of Hispanics in 1990 counted sizable Hispanic populations by 2006. In Georgia, for example, the Latin-origin population went from 1.7 percent in 1990 to 5.3 percent in 2000, due to an inflow of 300,000 persons, overwhelmingly from Mexico. Cities such as Charlotte, North Carolina, whose Hispanics in 1990 consisted of a few wealthy Cuban and South American professionals, had more than 80,000 Hispanic residents in 2006, mostly undocumented Mexican laborers. These Mexican migrants were without any significant political voices and proved vulnerable to exploitation.

To prevent or discourage undocumented migrants from entering the United States, U.S. authorities began working to tighten border enforcement in 1993 by building new physical fortifications and virtual surveillance systems. By 2006, more than $20 billion had been spent on this project. Nevertheless, the project proved ineffective, and massive illegal Mexican migration to the United States continued. To evade apprehension by the U.S. Border Patrol and to reduce the risks posed by natural hazards, Mexican migrants have turned increasingly to people smugglers (coyotes), which in turn has enabled smugglers to charge more for their services. With clandestine border crossing an increasingly expensive and risky business, U.S. border enforcement policy has unintentionally encouraged undocumented migrants to remain in the United States for longer periods and settle permanently in the United States in much larger numbers.

Yunqiu Zhang

FURTHER READING

Ashbee, Edward, Helene Balslev Clausen, and Carl Pedersen, eds. *The Politics, Economics, and Culture of Mexican-U.S. Migration: Both Sides of the Border.* New York: Palgrave Macmillan, 2007. Collection of essays examining all aspects of Mexican immigration to the United States from both American and Mexican perspectives.

Belous, Richard S., and Jonathan Lemco, eds. *NAFTA as a Model of Development.* Washington, D.C.: National Planning Association, 1993. Collection of twenty-one conference papers presents a good variety of viewpoints, including several from the perspective of Canada and Mexico.

Cameron, Maxwell A., and Brian W. Tomlin. *The Making of NAFTA: How the Deal Was Done.* Ithaca,

N.Y.: Cornell University Press, 2000. Covers the background of the diplomatic process and offers a full account of the negotiations resulting in the NAFTA agreement.

Cornelius, Wayne A., and Jessa M. Lewis, eds. *Impacts of Border Enforcement on Mexican Migration: The View from Sending Communities.* La Jolla, Calif.: Center for Comparative Immigration Studies, 2007. Essays examining Mexican perspective on immigration to the United States.

Grayson, George W. *The North American Free Trade Agreement: Regional Community and the New World Order.* Lanham, Md.: University Press of America, 1995. Presents a narrative history of the debates and negotiations surrounding NAFTA up to the time the treaty was approved.

Kingsolver, Ann E. *NAFTA Stories: Fears and Hopes in Mexico and the United States.* Boulder, Colo.: Lynne Rienner, 2001. Presents a wide variety of viewpoints about NAFTA as revealed in stories told by people from many different backgrounds.

Weintraub, Sidney, ed. *NAFTA's Impact on North America: The First Decade.* Washington, D.C.: Center for Strategic and International Studies, 2004. Collection of essays examining the political, social, and nontrade impact of NAFTA through its first decade.

See also: Border fence; Border Patrol, U.S.; Canada vs. United States as immigrant destinations; Canadian immigrants; Economic opportunities; Homeland Security, Department of; Illegal immigration; Mexican immigrants.

North Carolina

Significance: One of the original thirteen colonies, North Carolina began its existence as an immigrant society. After the United States became independent, it received few foreign immigrants until the 1960's and 1970's, when significant economic growth brought waves of new people looking for work. By the turn of the twenty-first century, the state had one of the nation's fastest growing population of Latinos, a large but unknown number of whom were undocumented laborers.

The non-Native American population of early colonial North Carolina was necessarily a product of immigration, not all of it foreign. Many of North Carolina's earliest settlers came from other colonies, such as Virginia, Maryland, South Carolina and Pennsylvania. Indeed, the first permanent white settlers came to Albemarle Sound from Virginia during the 1650's. Mostly of English extraction, they numbered several hundred farmers and traders. North Carolina's first significant conflict with Native Americans, the Tuscarora War of 1711, was in part sparked by the settlement of Swiss and German colonists at New Bern. Its outcome, the defeat of the Indians, spurred new European immigration to North Carolina's Coastal Plain.

Colonial Society

The colony's growing population was quite diverse. In addition to settlers of English ancestry, Scottish, Irish, Welsh, French, German, and Swiss settlers were well represented. Black slaves, most of whom came from either the West Indies or directly from West Africa, arrived in increasing numbers. They were concentrated mostly in the Lower Cape Fear region, where the plantations of affluent South Carolina and Virginia immigrants produced naval stores, indigo, and rice.

North Carolina had the distinction of attracting more Scottish Highlanders in the eighteenth century than any other future state. From 1732 to 1775, between 15,000 and 30,000 Highlanders came to North Carolina's Cape Fear Valley. Among them were the poet John MacRae and the Jacobite heroine Flora MacDonald. Their communities were highly insular, and Gaelic prevailed as the majority language—even for slaves in the region—into the early nineteenth century.

Westward expansion into North Carolina's Piedmont region was similarly diverse. While the first settlers there were English colonists from the coast, they were soon joined by others—including the stream of Germans and Scotch-Irish who by the mid-eighteenth century had begun moving southward from Pennsylvania along the Great Valley of Virginia. In 1753, Pennsylvania Moravians began work on the planned community of Salem. They would also establish several other settlements in the region. Immigration into the mountain region—which, by 1830, would give western North Carolina a preponderance of the population—

followed a similar ethnic profile. Most migrants were of Scotch-Irish, English, or German ancestry. Many came directly from the Piedmont region.

NINETEENTH CENTURY TRENDS

Because of a slow-down in immigration and a significant degree of out-migration during the nineteenth and early twentieth centuries, several attempts to attract immigrants to North Carolina were concocted. These began during the post-Civil War era under the auspices of the state Department of Agriculture, Immigration, and Statistics and its subordinate organization, the North Carolina Bureau of Immigration. The bureau's successes were mostly modest; they included the settlement of sixty-nine immigrants described as "German Polanders" in Salisbury in 1881. Private citizens also attempted to attract foreign labor and capital to the state through colonization schemes. The most famous of these, Wilmington entrepreneur Hugh Mac-Rae, founded several settlements of Italian, Polish, Dutch, German, and Hungarian immigrants in the southeastern part of the state between 1905 and 1908.

TWENTIETH CENTURY DEVELOPMENTS

North Carolina had little significant immigration until the 1960's and 1970's, when economic growth and the end of racial segregation in public accommodations encouraged people from out of state and overseas to enter the state. Most of the population growth since that period has been centered in the state's major urban regions—the so-called Research Triangle that encompasses the major university towns of Raleigh, Durham and Chapel Hill; the Piedmont Triad of Winston-Salem, Greensboro, and High Point; and Asheville and Wilmington. Many immigrants from around the world have settled in these areas in search of economic opportunities and education, bringing a degree of cultural diversity unprecedented in North Carolina history.

PROFILE OF NORTH CAROLINA

Region	Atlantic coast
Entered union	1789
Largest cities	Charlotte, Raleigh (capital), Greensboro, Durham, Winston-Salem, Fayetteville
Modern immigrant communities	Mexicans, Asian Indians, Chinese, Vietnamese, Koreans

Population	Total	Percent of state	Percent of U.S.	U.S. rank
All state residents	8,856,000	100.0	2.96	10
All foreign-born residents	614,000	6.9	1.64	14

Source: U.S. Census Bureau, *Statistical Abstract for 2006.*
Notes: The U.S. population in 2006 was 299,399,000, of whom 37,548,000 (12.5%) were foreign born. Rankings in last column reflect total numbers, not percentages.

During the 1970's and 1980's many Southeast Asian immigrants entered North Carolina. A large portion of these people were refugees fleeing the aftermath of the Vietnam War, which ended in 1975. Of the 125,000 Vietnamese refugees authorized to enter the United States during President Gerald Ford's administration, about 2,400 were living in North Carolina by 1980. They were joined by another stream of Vietnamese migration during the 1980's. Many Montagnards joined this stream of post-Vietnam War refugees. By the early twenty-first century, North Carolina had the largest population of Montagnards—about 5,000—outside Vietnam. Hmong immigrants fleeing Laos's Vietnam-backed government also came in large numbers to the United States. The estimated 7,100 to 12,000 refugees who settled in North Carolina formed one of the largest Hmong communities in the United States.

The 1960's also saw the immigration of people from other parts of Asia into North Carolina. Many are involved in business, education, research and other middle-class pursuits, and most live in the Raleigh-Durham-Chapel Hill Triangle. By 2000, roughly 26,000 Asian Indians, 19,000 Chinese, 15,000 Vietnamese, 12,000 Koreans, and 9,000 Filipinos resided in the state.

The single largest-growing immigrant group in North Carolina, however, has been Latinos. Mostly of Mexican origin but also including people from South and Central America, the Latino population of North Carolina saw the highest increase in the nation (394 percent) between 1990 and 2000. This growth has been in large part due to the U.S. demand for cheap, unskilled labor, combined with the potent push factor of poverty and limited jobs in Mexico and other countries. It was sped by an economic boom experienced in the South during the 1990's that was particularly strong in Charlotte and Raleigh-Durham.

Latinos have been especially attracted to the construction industry in North Carolina, in which they made up about 29 percent of the labor force during the early twenty-first century. They have also been heavily employed in North Carolina's agricultural and agricultural processing sectors, in which they have rapidly displaced African American workers. About one-third of the nation's documented guest workers labor on farms in North Carolina. However, a large but unknown number of Latino workers are undocumented.

Jeremiah Taylor

FURTHER READING

Blethen, H. Tyler, and Curtin W. Wood, Jr. *From Ulster to Carolina: The Migration of the Scotch-Irish to Southwestern North Carolina.* Raleigh: North Carolina Department of Cultural Resources, Division of Archives and History, 1998.

Haines, David W., ed. *Refugees as Immigrants: Cambodians, Laotians, and Vietnamese in America.* Totowa, N.J.: Rowman & Littlefield, 1989.

Nazario, Sonia. *Enrique's Journey.* New York: Random House, 2006.

Sherman, Spencer. "The Hmong in America: Laotian Refugees in the Land of the Giants." *National Geographic* (October, 1988).

SEE ALSO: British immigrants; Economic opportunities; Ethnic enclaves; European immigrants; Georgia; German immigrants; Guest-worker programs; Mexican immigrants; South Carolina; Vietnamese immigrants; Westward expansion.

NORTH DAKOTA

SIGNIFICANCE: North Dakota stands apart from most U.S. states in its geographical remoteness, the small size of its population, and the small number of non-European immigrants it has attracted. As younger residents of rural counties have gravitated to the major cities of Bismarck and Fargo or left the state permanently to seek employment elsewhere, the state's traditionally strong agricultural industry has faced a growing labor shortage that has not been alleviated by significant new immigration.

Located in the upper Midwest, North Dakota has experienced its own unique pattern of ethnic group immigration. Most of the states in its region had received most of the immigrants that would come to them before 1890. During the early twentieth century, North Dakota was the only state in the region to continue receiving significant numbers of new immigrants. Most of these late arrivals were northern Europeans who settled in the western part of the state, which had a strong agricultural economy.

NINETEENTH AND TWENTIETH CENTURY TRENDS

Dakota Territory, which was created in 1861, was split in 1889, when the states of North and South Dakota entered the union. During the late nineteenth century, European immigrants settled throughout the Great Plains. The 1900 U.S. Census revealed that 30 percent of North Dakota's residents were Scandinavians, particularly Norwegians. Most of them settled in the eastern and northern areas of the state. Germans formed the second-largest immigrant group. Ethnic Germans from the Russian Empire were particularly prominent in the south-central part of the state. In North Dakota's northern counties, Canadians were the largest immigrant group.

In contrast to most other states, North Dakota did not undergo a surge in population growth or experience an infusion of non-European immigrants during the late twentieth century. In 1970, fully one-third of the state's population still spoke German at home, and one-sixth retained Norwegian and Swedish as their mother tongues. However, since the mid-twentieth century, the state has undergone a significant demographic shift, as the youngest generations of immigrant families have sought economic opportunities outside North Dakota. Between 1950 and 1970 alone, 382 of the state's towns lost 80 percent of their population. Over the ensuing decades, the use of ethnic languages faded as third-generation family members left the state for good. Nevertheless, the immigrants' core values of family, church, and community remained strong.

North Dakota's aging workforce has created a labor shortage that was approaching crisis proportions during the early twenty-first century. The traditionally strong agricultural economy has been particularly threatened. However, native-born North Dakotans have resisted proposals to invite new manufacturing industries into the state, fearing that they might attract a wave of illegal immigrants who would undermine longstanding traditions within the tight communities of northern European immigrant descendants. Declining rural population has led to farm consolidations, as well as school district consolidations, and mergers of church congregations.

Gayla Koerting

PROFILE OF NORTH DAKOTA

Region	North-central
Entered union	1889
Largest cities	Fargo, Bismarck (capital), Grand Forks
Modern immigrant communities	Germans

Population	Total	Percent of state	Percent of U.S.	U.S. rank
All state residents	635,000	100.0	0.21	48
All foreign-born residents	13,000	2.1	0.03	50

Source: U.S. Census Bureau, *Statistical Abstract for 2006.*
Notes: The U.S. population in 2006 was 299,399,000, of whom 37,548,000 (12.5%) were foreign born. Rankings in last column reflect total numbers, not percentages.

FURTHER READING

Blouet, Brian W., and Frederick C. Luebke. *The Great Plains: Environment and Culture.* Lincoln: University of Nebraska Press, 1979.

Gjerde, Jon. *The Minds of the West: The Ethnocultural Evolution of the Rural Middle West, 1830-1917.* Chapel Hill: University of North Carolina Press, 1979.

Kiely, Kathy. "Can Aging N.D. Resist Change Amid Immigration Debate?" *USA Today,* November 25, 2007.

Wilkins, Robert P., and Wynona Wilkins. *North Dakota: A Bicentennial History.* New York: W. W. Norton, 1977.

Wishart, David J., ed. *Encyclopedia of the Great Plains.* Lincoln: University of Nebraska Press, 2004.

SEE ALSO: German immigrants; Minnesota; Nebraska; Scandinavian immigrants; South Dakota; Westward expansion.

O

OHIO

SIGNIFICANCE: Although Ohio was one of the first territories in the Midwest to become a state, its history of foreign immigration began relatively late, after major conflicts with Native Americans opened the region to settlement.

Ohio's first immigrants were Native Americans of the Miami, Shawnee, Ottawa, Tuscarora, Wyandotte, Seneca, and Delaware tribes. Many of these people were relatively late arrivals who moved to the region to get away from expanding European settlements to the east and from conflicts with the Iroquois and Cherokee peoples. In 1763, during the British colonial era, white settlement in the Ohio region was banned to prevent conflicts with Native Americans. However, after the United States became independent in 1783, restrictions on settlement were lifted. A coalition of Native American forces under the Miami war chief Little Turtle fought a four-year war against U.S. occupation of the region, but the U.S. victory at the Battle of Fallen Timbers in 1794 effectively ended Native American resistance.

IMMIGRATION UNDER STATEHOOD

After the United States became independent, the future of the Ohio Territory was defined by the Northwest Ordinance of 1787. That law's banning of slavery north of the Ohio River profoundly affected the character of all the future midwestern states, especially those which the Ohio River separated from the slave states of Kentucky and Virginia. In 1788, Marietta, a Massachusetts colony on an island in the Ohio River, became Ohio's first permanent American settlement.

Although New England Yankees were making claims on Ohio territory, the first settlers who came in significant numbers were Scotch-Irish. Most of these people were children and grandchildren of immigrants from Ulster in Northern Ireland who had settled in Virginia, Kentucky, and Pennsylvania. These early immigrants spread out along the Ohio River, northward from Marietta. By 1803,

their numbers were large enough to make Ohio eligible for U.S. statehood. The federal government's liberal land sales policy attracted many more settlers to the southern part of the state. By 1810, Ohio had more than 230,000 American and foreign residents.

The first immigrants to enter Ohio directly from Europe in substantial numbers were six hundred French, who were lured to Ohio by a land scheme promoted in France. In 1790, they founded a colony called Gallipolis on the Ohio River and soon assimilated into American culture. More French immigrants came during the nineteenth and twentieth centuries. Many of them were fleeing political and economic crises in Europe. Ohio also received immigrants from French-speaking Quebec. According to the U.S. Census, in the year 2000, almost 45,000 Ohio residents reported speaking French at home—a number exceeded only by German and Spanish speakers.

GERMAN IMMIGRATION

After the War of 1812 ended, the first German-speaking immigrants arrived in eastern Ohio, where they settled along a ridge of high land nicknamed the "Backbone." However, these people did not come directly from Europe; they were mostly Pennsylvania Dutch who were already American citizens—Amish and Mennonites who lived in close-knit communities and maintained their ancestral language. Their communities, their language, and conservative style of dress have survived into the twenty-first century, in both Ohio and other parts of the Midwest. The 2000 U.S. Census recorded more than 16,000 Ohio residents who still spoke the Pennsylvania Dutch dialect of German at home.

Revolutions in 1830 and 1848 helped propel the first German immigrants who came directly to Ohio. By 1850, Germans made up 5.6 percent of the state's total population and were more numerous even than British and Irish immigrants, who collectively constituted 4.4 percent. The densest concentration of Germans was in the Cincinnati area, along the Ohio River. In 1830, Germans made up only 5 percent of that city's population, but by 1850 that figure had risen to 23 percent. Cincinnati by then was becoming known for its German breweries and opera. Similar increases in German population occurred in Chillicothe, Dayton, and Portsmouth.

The northern part of Ohio was also receiving its share of foreign immigrants. Cuyahoga County, which included Cleveland, was more than one-third foreign born by 1870. Most of its immigrants were Germans. By the turn of the twentieth century, the Germans had been joined by substantial numbers of Bohemians, Canadians, Hungarians, Poles, Austrians, and Italians.

A little-known but important aspect of Ohio's immigrant communities has been German's influence on the English spoken in the state. Many of southern Ohio's first American settlers came from Kentucky and Virginia, but traces of southern accent are mostly confined to rural areas. New England Yankees, who spoke a dialect of English that has been popularly, though mistakenly, called "general American," settled mostly in cities. There they were joined by German immigrants, many of whom learned their English from Yankee teachers. Because the Germans rarely learned English from Southerners in Ohio, they helped make southern accents less evident in the state's cities.

LATE TWENTIETH CENTURY TRENDS

The late twentieth century saw the first waves of Hispanic immigrants entering Ohio. Most of these people were Mexicans, whose immigration grew even heavier after the turn of the twenty-first century. By 2006, the state's Hispanic population reached 265,762—about 2.3 percent of Ohio's total population. Just over 50 percent of these people were Mexicans.

Although Mexicans have constituted a smaller percentage of the total population in Ohio than in some other states, their growing presence has led to a revival of nativism and racism. In October, 2004, an arson fire in Ohio's largest city, Columbus, burned ten Mexican workers to death. Similar hate

PROFILE OF OHIO

Region	Midwest
Entered union	1803
Largest cities	Columbus (capital), Cleveland, Cincinnati, Tolelo, Akron, Dayton
Modern immigrant communities	Mexicans

Population	Total	Percent of state	Percent of U.S.	U.S. rank
All state residents	11,478,000	100.0	3.83	7
All foreign-born residents	412,000	3.6	1.10	19

Source: U.S. Census Bureau, *Statistical Abstract for 2006.*
Notes: The U.S. population in 2006 was 299,399,000, of whom 37,548,000 (12.5%) were foreign born. Rankings in last column reflect total numbers, not percentages.

crimes have occurred in other cities, and the state has intensified its efforts to reduce illegal immigration.

Timothy C. Frazer

FURTHER READING

Daniels, Roger. *Coming to America: A History of Immigration and Ethnicity in American Life.* New York: HarperCollins, 1990. Thorough but readable treatment of groups of immigrants from the seventeenth century through the 1980's: why they came, where they settled.

Frazer, Timothy C., ed. *"Heartland" English: Variation and Transition in the American Midwest.* Tuscaloosa: University of Alabama Press, 1993. Collection of essays that describe the impact immigrants and settlement had on the spoken English of several midwestern states, including Ohio.

Izant, Grace Goulder. *Ohio Scenes and Citizens.* Cleveland: World Publishing Company, 1964. Sketches and case histories illustrating twentieth century life in Ohio.

Quinones, Sam. *Antonio's Gun and Delphino's Dream: True Tales of Mexican Migration.* Albuquerque: University of New Mexico Press, 2007. Narrates the causes for the economic crisis in Mexico, which led to the large Mexican immigration into the United States that began during the 1970's. Describes the experiences of eight Mexicans who arrived after 1990.

SEE ALSO: Connecticut; French immigrants; German immigrants; Irish immigrants; Iron and steel industry; Italian immigrants; Kentucky; Language issues; Pennsylvania.

OKLAHOMA

> SIGNIFICANCE: During the nineteenth century, the availability of free public land in Oklahoma played a major role in attracting immigrants to the United States from Europe. The building of railroads and the development of coal mines and oil fields brought additional waves of immigrants.

During the nineteenth century, poverty, harsh living conditions, and religious persecution caused vast numbers of Europeans to immigrate to the United States. Many settled in the major cities of the East and Midwest and in the coal mining regions of Pennsylvania and West Virginia. Others went to the agricultural areas of the Midwest and Great Plains where they successfully established farms. By the late nineteenth century, European immigrants, seeking to improve their lives, were still coming to the United States; however, they found a lack of both jobs and land in the east and the Midwest. The best land in the Great Plains had also been claimed. In April of 1889, Oklahoma, which at that time was administratively an Indian territory of the United States, was opened for white settlement, and the first great "land run" took place that same year. A large majority of the new immigrants sought land and a new life in the territory.

FARMERS AND MERCHANTS

Many of Oklahoma's first foreign immigrants were Germans from Europe's German states and from the Russian Empire. Many of them also shared a common religion, as members of either the Mennonite Church or the Lutheran Church. They set-

tled in areas of north central, northwestern, and southwestern Oklahoma. Those who had come from the Russian steppes and the eastern part of Germany were able to tolerate the dry, windy climate of Oklahoma and prospered as farmers. They tended to keep to themselves, establish their own churches, and maintain both their language and their customs. During World War I, they faced severe discrimination and personal danger as the anti-German sentiment intensified in Oklahoma. The teaching of German in school was forbidden, and German newspapers were burned. Even making German sauerkraut was condemned as subversive. In an attempt to prove their allegiance to the United States, members of the German community that had founded the town of Kiel in 1894 renamed it Loyal.

Around the same time the first German immigrants were arriving, many Jewish merchants from Bavaria and Austria were coming into Oklahoma to supply the crews building railroads. After the main railroad lines were completed, many of these merchants stayed and opened shops in the newly formed towns. In 1899, the first Jewish temple was established at Ardmore. More Jewish merchants as well as Syrian peddlers came after oil was discovered and boomtowns began arising after 1900.

During the early years of the twentieth century, peasant farmers from Bohemia arrived. Many of them were from the region known as Czechoslova-

---

PROFILE OF OKLAHOMA

Region	Midwest
Entered union	1907
Largest cities	Oklahoma City (capital), Tulsa, Norman, Lawton
Modern immigrant communities	Mexicans, Vietnamese, Asian Indians

Population	Total	Percent of state	Percent of U.S.	U.S. rank
All state residents	3,579,000	100.0	1.20	28
All foreign-born residents	176,000	4.9	0.47	30

Source: U.S. Census Bureau, Statistical Abstract for 2006.
Notes: The U.S. population in 2006 was 299,399,000, of whom 37,548,000 (12.5%) were foreign born. Rankings in last column reflect total numbers, not percentages.

kia after 1918. Most engaged in farming, but others established flour mills or became merchants selling agricultural equipment. The Bohemians generally clustered together in and around Oklahoma City and maintained the traditions of their homeland.

COAL MINING

Land was not the only attraction that drew immigrants to Oklahoma. Coal mining began in the territory in 1872, and the first commercial coal mining was started in 1873. Most of the coal was mined in eastern Oklahoma, in districts belonging to Native American tribes. However, enterprising entrepreneurs, such as James McAlester, married into the tribes or paid special taxes that permitted them to use non-Indian labor to work the coal mines. Consequently, many immigrants who had hoped to find work in the mines of Pennsylvania and West Virginia instead went to Oklahoma. Many of these people had immigrated from Ireland, Scotland, and Wales. Others came from Poland, Lithuania, Hungary, Russia, Germany, England, and Italy. Although mining wages were relatively high in Oklahoma, the work was difficult and dangerous. The miners typically worked in inadequately ventilated shafts so cramped they were unable to stand erect.

Among immigrant coal miners, Italians were most numerous. In 1910, they constituted the largest group of foreign-born residents in the three major coal-producing counties of Pittsburg, Coal, and Latimer. After 1920, the state's coal mining industry steadily declined, reducing its need for labor. Many of the immigrant coal miners from Poland, Lithuania, and Ukraine sought new jobs in the slaughterhouses and on the farms in the Oklahoma City area. Many Italian coal miners bought farms and businesses and stayed in the mining region.

MEXICAN AND ASIAN IMMIGRANTS

Mexican immigration into Oklahoma began around the turn of the twentieth century, but many of these early immigrants came only as seasonal agricultural workers and returned home. The railroad crews of that time were predominantly Mexican, and Mexican immigrants also worked in a wide variety of other jobs, from picking cotton to mining coal to working on oilfields. Eventually, some of these workers brought their families with them and established homes in Oklahoma. By 1930, approximately 7,500 Mexicans were permanent residents of Oklahoma.

After World War II, the numbers of Mexicans immigrating to Oklahoma increased, but the first truly large wave of Mexican immigration did not occur until the last two decades of the twentieth century. Mexicans spread throughout the state, working primarily as laborers on farms, in factories, in construction, and as restaurant employees. By the early twenty-first century, Mexican culture and the Spanish language played very visible and important roles in Oklahoma.

The first substantial number of Asians to enter Oklahoma were Vietnamese, who began coming in 1975, after the Vietnam War ended. They readily adapted and opened various businesses, particularly restaurants and grocery stores. During the 1980's, considerable numbers of other Asian immigrants moved to Oklahoma. These included Korean, Chinese, Japanese, and Asian Indians. The Asian immigrants, while maintaining their own culture, have been successful in adapting to life in Oklahoma.

Shawncey Webb

FURTHER READING

Bicha, Karel D. *The Czechs in Oklahoma*. Norman: University of Oklahoma Press, 1982. Excellent and thorough coverage, discussing where Czechs have settled, their culture, and their role in the state's agriculture.

Franks, Kenny Arthur, and Paul F. Lambert. *Oklahoma: The Land and Its People*. Morris Plains, N.J.: Unicorn Publishing, 1994. Good discussion of where immigrant groups have settled in Oklahoma and what their lives in the state have been like.

Luebke, Frederick C. *Germans in the New World: Essays in the History of Immigration*. Champaign: University of Illinois Press, 1990. Particularly good for language issues and prejudices faced by Germans in Oklahoma.

Portes, Alejandro, and Rubén G. Rumbaut. *Immigrant America: A Portrait*. 3d ed. Berkeley: University of California Press, 2006. Good presentation of the life of immigrants in different social and economic situations. Also treats assimilation.

Zolberg, Aristide. *A Nation by Design: Immigration Policy in the Fashioning of America*. Cambridge,

Mass.: Harvard University Press, 2006. Excellent for its objective presentation of U.S. immigration policy and its changes. Good for Mexican immigration.

SEE ALSO: Coal industry; Czech and Slovakian immigrants; German immigrants; Homestead Act of 1862; Irish immigrants; Italian immigrants; Jewish immigrants; Railroads.

OPERATION WETBACK

THE EVENT: Massive federal-state effort to remove unauthorized Mexican workers from the United States

DATE: June-September, 1954

LOCATION: U.S.-Mexican border areas

SIGNIFICANCE: Considered an extreme example of overaggressive immigration enforcement, Operation Wetback rounded up and deported nearly 300,000 Mexicans working in the United States and detained more than 1 million more Mexicans who crossed the U.S. border.

Operation Wetback was a response to mounting American sentiment against the large numbers of Mexicans who entered the United States illegally after World War II and the Mexican government's concern that its citizens working in the United States should not be employed without labor contracts. Between 1942 and 1964, almost 5 million Mexicans were admitted into the United States as bracero workers under a series of U.S.-Mexican agreements that became progressively more favorable to American farm employers over the years. Under the program, the U.S. government guaranteed the wages promised to braceros during World War II. Afterward, however, the American farmers who employed the workers were made responsible for paying both the wages of the workers and their transportation costs from the interior of Mexico to their farms.

Meanwhile, the large numbers of Mexicans who continued to enter the United States illegally saved many American employers the cost of their transportation. Known as "wetbacks" even in official documents, these workers were returned to the border when they were detected inside the United States and were then issued work permits and returned to the farms on which they had been previously employed. Between 1947 and 1949, two "wetbacks" were legalized in this way for every Mexican who was legally admitted to the United States under the bracero program.

The Migratory Labor Agreement of 1951 shifted more authority over bracero workers from the Mexican government to American farm employers. The Mexican government wanted American employers to recruit their workers within the interior of Mexico, but under the 1951 agreement, the U.S. Department of Labor opened five reception centers along the international border to which Mexicans seeking American jobs could report. Employers arranged and paid for transportation from the reception centers to their farms.

One day after he signed the Migratory Labor Agreement into law, President Harry S. Truman asked the U.S. Congress to approve legislation making it a federal crime knowingly to hire unauthorized immigrant workers. Congress refused. Two sections of the Immigration and Nationality Act of 1952 included the so-called Texas proviso, which made harboring illegal immigrants subject to a two-thousand-dollar fine and up to five years imprisonment, while exempting employment from the definition of "harboring."

Meanwhile, illegal immigration from Mexico surged, and U.S. attorney general Herbert Brownell called what he observed "shocking" during his August, 1953, visit to the Mexican border. Brownell appointed General Joseph Swing to be commissioner of the Immigration and Naturalization Service (INS), instructing him to "clean up" the border. Operation Wetback began June 17, 1954, in Arizona and California, with 750 INS agents assigned to farming areas trying to arrest 1,000 unauthorized Mexican immigrants a day.

State and local police joined the sweeps of Latino barrios as the program spread to other states, and thousands of Mexicans returned home on their own. The setting up of highway checkpoints and railroad checks resulted in the detainment of thousands of Mexicans and Mexican Americans on vagrancy charges until INS agents could verify their status. When the INS ran out of funding in mid-September, 1954, the operation was halted. By then, some 1.1 million unauthorized foreigners had been apprehended during the federal fiscal year that had ended on June 30, 1954, but only 254,000 had been apprehended during the following fiscal year. Meanwhile, the U.S. Department of Labor had made it easier for farmers to hire braceros by relaxing rules such as minimum six-week contracts and the enforcement of wage and housing regulations. Consequently, the number of braceros admitted to the United States rose from 200,000 in 1953 to 400,000 in 1955.

Operation Wetback had several long-term effects. The first was the public revulsion at the rough rounding up of families who included U.S. citizens with young babies. It seemed unlikely that the U.S. government would again attempt a similar mass repatriation. Second, easing farmers' access to bracero workers encouraged the expansion of labor-intensive agriculture without raising wages, sowing the seeds for subsequent unauthorized migration. Finally, Operation Wetback made future efforts of the United States to negotiate migration agreements with Mexico more difficult.

Philip L. Martin

FURTHER READING

Garcia, Juan Ramon. *Operation Wetback: The Mass Deportation of Mexican Undocumented Workers.* Westport, Conn.: Greenwood Press, 1980.

Garcia y Griego, Manuel. "The Importation of Mexican Contract Laborers to the United States, 1942-64." In *Between Two Worlds: Mexican Immigrants in the United States,* edited by David G. Gutierrez. Wilmington, Del.: Scholarly Resources, 1996.

Kirstein, Peter. *Anglo over Bracero. A History of the Mexican Worker in the United States from Roosevelt to Nixon.* San Francisco: R&E Associates, 1977.

SEE ALSO: Border Patrol, U.S.; Bracero program; Deportation; El Paso incident; Guest-worker programs; Mexican deportations of 1931; Mexican immigrants; Texas.

ORDERLY DEPARTURE PROGRAM

THE EVENT: U.S.-supported United Nations program designed to facilitate immigration of Vietnamese refugees

DATE: 1979-1999

LOCATION: Bangkok, Thailand, and Ho Chi Minh City (Saigon), Vietnam

SIGNIFICANCE: The Orderly Departure Program was instituted by the communist government of Vietnam in cooperation with the United Nations to ease the plight of refugees attempting to leave Southeast Asia on small boats. Through the program, about 500,000 Vietnamese immigrated to North America.

After the communist victory ended the Vietnam War in early 1975, tens of thousands of Vietnamese people wanted to escape from the newly reunited country's communist regime. In 1978, the Socialist Republic of Vietnam turned against the ethnic Chinese minority in Vietnam known as Hoa. Repressive measures drove many of these people to leave the country on small boats. The great perils that these boat people faced on the high seas aroused international attention. In the face of growing international concern, leaders of the Vietnamese government began meeting with representatives of the office of the U.N. High Commissioner of Refugees (UNHCR) and the U.S. government to find a mutually satisfactory settlement.

THE PROGRAM IN OPERATION

After intense negotiations, Vietnam and the UNHCR signed a memorandum of understanding on May 30, 1979. The agreement established the Orderly Departure Program (ODP) for Vietnamese citizens requesting to emigrate from Vietnam to Western countries. The United States agreed to accept a majority of the emigrants.

The program got off to a slow start. In January 1980, the ODP opened its offices in Bangkok, Thailand. From there, ODP missions went to Ho Chi Minh City—as Saigon had been renamed by the Vietnamese government—to interview potential immigrants and process their departures. However, immediately after U.S. president Ronald Rea-

Young Vietnamese refugees, who were relocated to the Philippines after the closure of refugee camps in Thailand, staging a demonstration at the U.S. embassy in Manila in September, 1996, urging the U.S. government to resettle them in the United States, as they believed it had promised to do. (AP/Wide World Photos)

gan took office on January 20, 1981, Vietnam suspended the program. In October, 1981, Vietnam resumed the program after resolving differences with the new U.S. administration. It was not until 1983 that the ODP was running smoothly. By then, the majority of Vietnamese refugees who went to the United States were leaving through the program's provisions rather than risking perilous ocean voyages on their own.

After U.S.-Vietnamese relations improved with the lifting of a U.S. trade embargo against Vietnam in early 1994, the two countries decided to close registration for the ODP on September 14, 1994. In 1999, the ODP office in Bangkok shut its doors and the remaining work was handled by the U.S. Refugee Resettlement Section at the U.S. consulate in Ho Chi Minh City. On November 15, 2005, the United States and Vietnam agreed to allow the last Vietnamese who had been eligible to emigrate to the United States under the program but had missed the 1994 deadline for registration to do so.

In all, about 500,000 Vietnamese immigrated to the United States under the ODP. Most of these people either had worked with Americans during the Vietnam War or were family members of people who had. Others were relatives of Vietnamese already living in the United States. While eventually reducing the numbers of desperate boat people, the ODP contributed substantially to Vietnamese immigration to America.

In American popular culture, the ODP was immortalized in the musical *Miss Saigon* (pr., pb. 1989) and the autobiography of Kien Nguyen, *The Unwanted* (2001), depicting the plight of the Vietnamese affected by its operation.

R. C. Lutz

FURTHER READING

Kumin, Julie. "Orderly Departure from Vietnam: Cold War Anomaly or Humanitarian Innovation?" *Refugee Survey Quarterly* 27, no. 1 (2008): 104-117.

Nguyen, Kien. *The Unwanted.* Boston: Back Bay Books, 2001.

U.S. General Accounting Office. *Refugee Program: The Orderly Departure Program from Vietnam.* Washington, D.C.: Government Printing Office, 1990.

SEE ALSO: Amerasian children; Amerasian Homecoming Act of 1987; Asian immigrants; Child immigrants; Refugees; Vietnam War; Vietnamese immigrants.

OREGON

SIGNIFICANCE: A destination for immigration since before it was a state, Oregon has drawn immigrants from all over the world. However, through much of its history as a state, it actively resisted the immigration of people from regions other than northern and western Europe.

White settlers, both European and Americans of European descent, poured into Oregon during the middle of the nineteenth century, seeking land for homesteading. The settlers clashed violently with Native Americans, many of whom were killed, died of disease, or sent to reservations. At the same time, the state's territorial and state governments enacted laws to reserve Oregon citizenship for white settlers. Black people were barred from Oregon in 1844, and both African Americans and Chinese were barred from voting or owning land by Oregon's state constitution. An 1866 miscegenation law prohibited white people from marrying blacks, Chinese, or Native Americans. Founded as a white, agrarian, frontier state, Oregon retained an ambivalence and even hostility toward immigration into the twentieth century.

NINETEENTH CENTURY PATTERNS

At the time Oregon became a state in 1859, only about 10 percent of its residents were foreign born. Afterward, however, foreign immigration increased, but many of the new immigrants were secondary migrants who had originally settled in the Midwest. Many were attracted to Oregon's mild climate and good farmlands.

Early on, the state of Oregon established a clear preference for German and Scandinavian immigrants, believing that these people would integrate well and achieve social and economic success. Southern and eastern European immigrants, however, were unwelcome and were described as "undesirable" in a 1912 report of the Oregon State Immigration Commission. Oregonians tended to view themselves as thrifty, independent farmers and pioneers and regarded southern and eastern Europeans as having values that were incompatible with their own.

By 1910, Scandinavian immigrants from Sweden, Denmark, Norway, and Finland made up 40 percent of Oregon's population. In addition to farming, these immigrants worked as carpenters, longshoremen, and in lumber mills. Many of the women worked as domestics or ran boardinghouses. Despite the state's bias against eastern Europeans, Jews from Germany and eastern Europe also did well in Oregon during the late nineteenth century. Taking advantage of a relatively open class structure and growing economy with few labor unions, the Jews were generally regarded as shopkeepers and small business owners and were consequently not perceived as competing with native-born laborers.

ASIAN IMMIGRATION

Members of other ethnic groups, however, were not welcome—especially immigrants from China and Japan. Chinese workers who had come to the western states to escape poverty found themselves barred from holding mining claims and land in Oregon soon after statehood. About 5 percent of Oregon's residents were Chinese in 1880, but they were finding life increasingly difficult in the face of violent nativist opposition. After the federal Chinese Exclusion Act of 1882 was passed, mobs of Oregonians drove Chinese residents out of Oregon City, Salem, and Yamhill. Attempts to drive the Chinese out of Portland failed, but the city's Chinese population afterward went down. In 1887, horse thieves murdered forty-three Chinese miners at the Snake River and were subsequently acquitted. As in California, white citizens perceived the Chinese as strange, pagan, and unwilling to assimilate, and also saw them as undercutting American wages.

Anti-Chinese violence subsided by the 1890's, but the state government continued to explore methods of reducing the Chinese population. In 1903, the state Bureau of Labor collected data on Chinese and Japanese immigrants to determine the extent to which they were in competition with white workers.

During the first four decades of the twentieth century, Japanese workers became targets of violence and negative public feelings in Oregon. Nevertheless, many Japanese immigrants achieved success as farmers, hotel owners, and business operators. They also established the Japanese Association of Oregon, which gave legal and financial aid to new arrivals. However, after Japan launched its sneak attack on the U.S. naval base at Pearl Harbor on December 7, 1941, Japanese immigrants felt the effects of a major backlash. Most of the Japanese nationals and Japanese Americans were interned throughout World War II, giving white Oregonians opportunities to take over Japanese-owned businesses. Some Oregonians hoped to drive the Japanese out of their state permanently. After the war ended in 1945, returning internees were met with suspicion. By the late 1940's, Oregon's state government had partially compensated Japanese American families for their economic losses during their internment and began lifting laws that had restricted Japanese from owning land.

After the Vietnam War ended in 1975, many Vietnamese people immigrated to Oregon. By the early twenty-first century, the Vietnamese were one of the largest immigrant communities in Oregon.

LATIN AMERICAN IMMIGRANTS

Latin American immigration into Oregon began in earnest during the 1930s, when Hispanic workers began arriving to work in the state's agricultural industry. Many Hispanics took jobs that opened up as American citizens found employment in the growing defense industry on the eve of American entry into World War II. Mexican immigration to Oregon increased sharply with the 1942 establishment of the bracero program, which was designed to import seasonal agricultural workers during the war. Braceros working in Oregon were often subjected to substandard working and living conditions, but the program continued until 1964. Meanwhile, as native-born American workers found better-paying jobs in other industries, Oregon's farmers became increasingly dependent on Mexican and other Latin American workers.

Mexican immigrants also worked in Oregon's food, construction, and manufacturing industries and began small businesses. They formed organizations to assist immigrants and advocate for workers' rights and established church- and community-based organizations to provide job training and other services for new arrivals. The long history of Hispanic immigration into Oregon has created multiple-generation households in which some members are naturalized American citizens, while others may be undocumented immigrants. This complicates integration of immigrants into society and makes their utilization of social services difficult.

REFUGEES AND IMMIGRATION REFORM

During the 1960's, efforts to admit refugees from Cuba and other countries and lift discriminatory quotas met with resistance in Oregon, as prejudice against Asian, southern and eastern European, and Latin American immigrant groups continued. How-

PROFILE OF OREGON

Region	Northwest Pacific coast
Entered union	1859
Largest cities	Portland, Eugene, Salem (capital), Gresham
Modern immigrant communities	Mexicans, Vietnamese

Population	Total	Percent of state	Percent of U.S.	U.S. rank
All state residents	3,701,000	100.0	1.24	27
All foreign-born residents	360,000	9.7	0.96	20

Source: U.S. Census Bureau, *Statistical Abstract for 2006.*

Notes: The U.S. population in 2006 was 299,399,000, of whom 37,548,000 (12.5%) were foreign born. Rankings in last column reflect total numbers, not percentages.

ever, with the passage of the federal Immigration and Nationality Act of 1965, Oregon's immigration rates increased dramatically. During the 1980's, the state became a popular destination for refugees, particularly from the Soviet Union. After the collapse of the Soviet Union in 1991, many refugees from Soviet republics were fundamentalist Christians seeking greater religious freedom—a fact that helped win them sympathy and acceptance in Oregon. By that time, the numbers of refugees from African and Southeast Asian nations were also increasing. Many of these people, like the eastern Europeans, made use of church and state assistance for refugees as well as kinship networks to ease their transition into American society. African and Asian immigrants have encountered some resistance, particularly after the terrorist attacks on the United States of September 11, 2001, but many have established businesses and strong communities.

Twenty-first Century Trends

By the turn of the twenty-first century, Oregon ranked eleventh among all states in numbers of refugees taken in, and the state could be fairly described as a major immigrant gateway. Reasons for this change in demographics have included the decline of employment opportunities in other traditional immigrant gateway states, agricultural opportunities in Oregon that have drawn new immigrants from Mexico and other Latin American countries, and the presence of strong resettlement and social service networks that serve refugees and other immigrants. The state's refugee social service organizations provide refugees with housing, employment, and other services during their first year in Oregon.

Despite Oregon's growing diversity, its history as a primarily European-descended state hostile to immigrants has made it difficult for many immigrants, especially refugees, to integrate into mainstream society. Moreover, a growing percentage of Oregon's jobs are in technology fields that require more specialized training and skills than jobs in traditional immigrant occupations, such as lumbering, farming, and fishing.

By the year 2005, 9.7 percent of the residents of Oregon were foreign born, and 60 percent of these people had arrived in the state since 1990. Most of the state's immigrants were living in the Portland metropolitan area near the state's northern border with Washington.

Melissa A. Barton

Further Reading

Do, Hien Duc. *The Vietnamese Americans.* Westport, Conn.: Greenwood Press, 1999. Brief history of Vietnamese Americans, who constituted one of Oregon's largest immigrant communities during the early twenty-first century.

Hoobler, Dorothy, and Thomas Hoobler. *The Scandinavian American Family Album.* New York: Oxford University Press, 1998. Illustrated with historic photographs, this book covers the history of Scandinavian immigration to the United States, including to Oregon.

Nokes, R. Gregory. "'A Most Daring Outrage': Murder at Chinese Massacre Cove, 1887." *Oregon Historical Quarterly* 107, no. 3 (2006): 326-353. Detailed reconstruction of the massacre of Chinese miners at Snake River.

Ross, Alexander. *Adventures of the First Settlers on the Oregon or Columbia River, 1810-1813.* Lincoln: University of Nebraska Press, 1986. Ross, one of the original clerks at Astoria, gives a colorful firsthand account of the venture.

Tolzmann, Don Heinrich. *The German-American Experience.* Amherst, N.Y.: Humanity Books, 2000. Study of German immigrants in America, including western settlement.

See also: Anti-Japanese movement; Bracero program; Farm and migrant workers; Japanese American internment; Japanese immigrants; Mexican immigrants; Snake River Massacre; *United States v. Bhagat Singh Thind*; Vietnamese immigrants; Washington State.

Oyama v. California

The Case: U.S. Supreme Court decision concerning the right of aliens to own land
Date: Decided on January 19, 1948

Significance: The influential *Oyama* decision overturned the portions of the California Alien Land Laws that discriminated against U.S. citizens on the basis of race, but the Supreme Court chose not to rule on the constitutionality of discrimination against noncitizens based on their race or ethnicity.

During the 1930's, Kajiro Oyama, a Japanese immigrant ineligible for American citizenship, purchased eight acres of land in Southern California. Because the state's Alien Land Laws of 1913 and 1920 prohibited noncitizens from owning land, he deeded the property to his minor son, Fred Oyama, who was a U.S. citizen by birth. The father then succeeded in gaining legal guardianship over his son. The local court at the time ignored a provision in the 1920 law requiring proof that land transfers in such circumstances were genuine gifts, not subterfuges to evade the restrictions on alien ownership. During World War II, when the Oyama family was displaced and residing in Utah, the state of California seized the family's eight acres in an escheat trial, based on the accusation that Kajiro Oyama had violated the 1920 law. The state's highest court upheld the action. Fred Oyama, with the support of the American Civil Liberties Union (ACLU), petitioned the Supreme Court for a writ of certiorari.

By a 6-3 vote, the U.S. Supreme Court ruled in Fred Oyama's favor and struck down relevant portions of the Alien Land Laws as inconsistent with the equal protection clause of the Fourteenth Amendment. Writing the opinion for the majority, Chief Justice Fred M. Vinson considered only the issue of discrimination against Fred Oyama and other U.S. citizens who had the difficult burden of proving that their ownership of land was not the result of an intentional effort to evade the 1920 law—a burden not required of other citizens. Vinson's opinion ignored the broader issue of the state's discrimination against Kajiro Oyama and other alien residents illegible for naturalization. In concurring opinions, three liberal members criticized the narrowness of the opinion. Four years later, however, California's Supreme Court would decide the case of *Sei Fujii v. State of California* (1952), which overturned both Alien Land Laws as incompatible with the state's constitution.

Thomas Tandy Lewis

FURTHER READING

Chuman, Frank. *The Bamboo People: The Law and Japanese Americans.* Del Mar, Calif.: Publisher's Inc., 1976.

Itō, Kazuo. *Issei: A History of Japanese Immigrants in North America.* Seattle: Japanese Community Service, 1973.

SEE ALSO: Alien land laws; California; Citizenship; Due process protections; History of immigration after 1891; *Sei Fujii v. State of California*; Supreme Court, U.S.; *Terrace v. Thompson.*

OZAWA V. UNITED STATES

THE CASE: U.S. Supreme Court decision concerning whether Asian immigrants were eligible for naturalization
DATE: Decided on November 13, 1922

SIGNIFICANCE: The *Ozawa* ruling interpreted the word "white" in U.S. naturalization law as referring exclusively to persons of European ancestry (or Caucasians), thereby holding that federal legislation disqualified all persons of Asian ancestry from becoming naturalized citizens.

U.S. naturalization laws enacted between 1790 and 1870 limited the privilege of American citizenship to "free white persons." In 1870, the privilege was extended to persons of African descent but not to immigrants from Asia. Although the Naturalization Act of 1906 was somewhat ambiguous on this point, it implicitly continued the long-standing racial restriction on eligibility for naturalization.

Takao Ozawa, a resident of Hawaii, was a person of Japanese ancestry born in Japan. In 1914, after continuously living in the United States for over twenty years, he applied for U.S. citizenship. Both he and his children had attended American schools. The family used English at home, and they attended an American Christian church. Based on these facts, combined with his relatively light skin color, Ozawa claimed that he could be classified as a "white person." He argued that the purpose of the relevant laws had been to exclude African and Native Americans. The district court, however, rejected the claim and denied his application.

Agreeing to review the case, the Supreme Court upheld the decision of the lower court. Writing for a unanimous Court, Justice George Sutherland considered two issues: first, whether the 1906 statute allowed the naturalization of a nonwhite person, and second, whether a person of Japanese ancestry might be classified as white. In an exegesis of the relevant portions of the statute, Sutherland found no evidence that the 1906 law eliminated the racial exclusion. If Congress desired to alter "a rule so well and so long established," Sutherland asserted that such a purpose would have been definitely disclosed in unambiguous language.

Discussing the term "white person" in the 1790 law, Sutherland rejected the argument that its purpose was to exclude only Africans and American Indians. A color-test definition of "white," moreover, seemed inadequate, because all racial groups had complex gradations of darkness. Anglo-Saxons were frequently of darker complexions than persons belonging to the "brown and yellow races of Asia." Deciding that the term "white person" was synonymous with the words "a person of the Caucasian race," Sutherland wrote that the applicant was "clearly of a race which is not Caucasian." Because of the dominant ideas in 1790, combined with the U.S. Constitution's explicit authorization of Congress to enact naturalization laws, he saw no need to question whether a racial exclusion might be inconsistent with the due process clause of the Fifth Amendment. The ineligibility of Japanese immigrants for naturalization would continue until passage of the Immigration and Nationality Act of 1952, which was also known as the McCarran-Walter Act of 1952.

Thomas Tandy Lewis

FURTHER READING

Chuman, Frank. *The Bamboo People: The Law and Japanese Americans.* Del Mar, Calif.: Publisher's Inc., 1976.

Hyung-chan, Kim, ed. *Asian Americans and the Supreme Court: A Documentary History.* Westport, Conn.: Greenwood Press, 1992.

SEE ALSO: Citizenship; Congress, U.S.; Constitution, U.S.; Immigration law; Japanese immigrants; Naturalization; Naturalization Act of 1790; Supreme Court, U.S.; "Undesirable aliens"; *United States v. Bhagat Singh Thind.*

P

PACIFIC ISLANDER IMMIGRANTS

SIGNIFICANCE: Although Pacific Islander immigrants have probably received less attention than most other immigrant communities, more Pacific Islanders reside in the United States—including the Pacific Island state Hawaii—than remain in many of their island homelands. Coming from many separate islands with many very different cultures and languages, Islander immigrants are almost impossible to identify in early U.S. censuses, in which they were typically counted under the category of "others" or lumped with Asians.

Pacific Islander immigration to the United States is best understood by recognizing that Pacific Oceanic peoples have a long history of long-distance ocean voyages. Prehistoric inhabitants of South Pacific islands—especially the widespread archipelagoes of Melanesia and Polynesia—constructed sturdy canoes and developed surprisingly advanced navigation systems to find their way around the distantly separated islands. Their island-based regional interactions resulted in marriages, trade contacts, and political relationships, including warfare. During the sixteenth century, the Islanders' regional dynamics were disrupted by the arrival of European explorers, who brought novel technologies, new diseases, and very different cultural concepts to the region.

THE AMERICAN PRESENCE IN THE PACIFIC

Over the ensuing centuries, the Pacific Islands and their inhabitants came increasingly under the domination of Euro-American political rule, economic expansion, and religious beliefs. With increasing contacts came increased population movements, including European settlements on many islands. Many indigenous inhabitants moved away from the islands; some relocated within the Pacific region, others went as far as Europe and the Americas. Most of these population movements were sporadic, small scale, and poorly documented.

By the mid-nineteenth century, American whaling ships were operating regularly in the Pacific Ocean, and Samoans and Hawaiians began to work in the whaling industry. Ultimately, some of these people ended up far from their island homes. Oceanic people were further incorporated into American spheres by the sudden U.S. colonial expansion into the Philippines, Guam, Samoa, and Hawaii between 1898 and 1900, when the United States annexed the Hawaiian islands and occupied Spain's Pacific Island possessions after winning the Spanish-American War.

Extensive military, missionary, and trading links between the United States and its Pacific Island possessions helped prompt large numbers of Islanders to immigrate to the mainland United States. During World War II (1941-1945), the presence of American military bases on many of the region's islands brought the U.S. war with Japan directly into the homelands of Pacific Islanders. The result was tremendous carnage and destruction that would contribute to postwar migration.

PUSH-PULL FACTORS

Pacific Islander immigration can be understood broadly as the product of several push factors that operated across the islands, and also several pull factors that made the United States a compelling migration destination. Push factors have included local political conditions, such as Tonga's monarchy, which many commoners find oppressive. Environmental disasters have also been important, especially hurricanes, which often create havoc on small islands. Other push factors have included economic conditions, especially low wages on many islands; limited higher educational facilities; health services that are inadequate for treating some ailments; and limited opportunities for skilled and professional workers.

The most important pull factors that have drawn Islanders to the United States have been relief from all the Islanders' push factors: nonoppressive government, greater safety from natural disasters, higher wages, and almost unlimited educational and professional opportunities. Moreover, established Pacific Islander communities within the United States provide kin networks that ease adjustments to immigration by giving newcomers places to stay on their arrival and strong support groups. Local contacts also assist new immigrants with health, educational, and work opportunities.

POPULATION DATA

The hundreds of populated islands spread across the Pacific Ocean, particularly in the South Pacific, are made of independent nations, European dependencies, and American possessions. A sizable number of Pacific Islanders live on territories that were incorporated into the United States during the late nineteenth century. Some sporadic Pacific Islander immigration to the mainland United States probably occurred before that time, but large numbers of Islanders did not begin com-

ing to the United States until the 1950's and 1960's and particularly during the 1970's.

At the time of the 1990 U.S. Census, 365,000 Pacific Islanders lived in the United States. This figure compares with about 30,000 Islanders living in Australia and 531,000 in New Zealand. Only ten years later, the U.S. Pacific Islander population had jumped to 874,000. However, a variety of changes in the methods used in the 2000 U.S. Census mean that the 2000 data are not directly comparable to earlier census information. For example, the 2000 figure for total Islanders includes some people who also reported some non-Pacific Islander ancestry.

Approximately 58 percent of the 2000 U.S. Census group counted as "Native Hawaiian and Other Pacific Islander" were living in Hawaii and California, with sizeable populations also found in Wash-

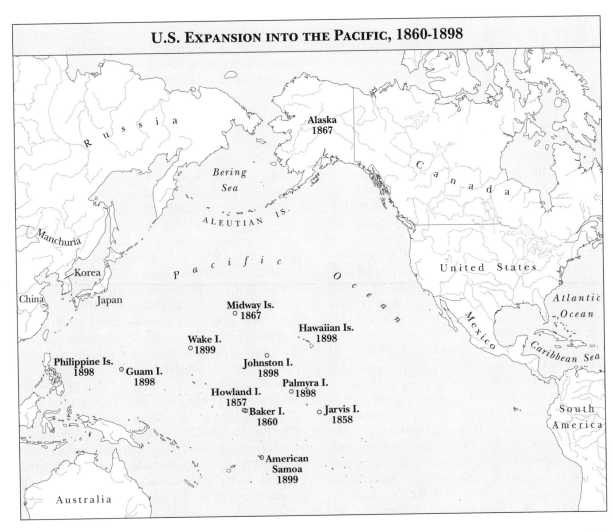

U.S. EXPANSION INTO THE PACIFIC, 1860-1898

PROFILE OF PACIFIC ISLANDER IMMIGRANTS

Countries of origin	American Samoa, Fiji, Guam, French Polynesia, Kiribati, Marshall Islands, Micronesia, Palau, Samoa, Tonga, Solomon Islands
Primary languages	English, Polynesian languages
Primary regions of U.S. settlement	Hawaii, California, Utah, and Washington
Earliest significant arrivals	Late nineteenth century
Peak immigration period	Mid- to late twentieth century
Twenty-first century legal residents*	16,925 (2,116 per year)

*Immigrants who obtained legal permanent resident status in the United States. Figures do not include Hawaiians.

Source: Department of Homeland Security, Yearbook of Immigration Statistics, 2008.

ington, Oregon, Texas, Utah, Nevada, Arizona, New York State, and Florida. Pacific Islanders, including Native Hawaiians, made up more than 22 percent of the population of Honolulu.

In the mainland United States, significant proportions of Pacific Islanders lived in urban locations, with major concentrations in California (especially Hayward, Vallejo, Oceanside, Long Beach, Sacramento, and Daly City), Utah (West Valley City, Salt Lake City), and Washington (Tacoma). Much of this population concentration has occurred as the result of chain migration, with important founding families often identifiable in many of these locations.

In Utah, religion plays a special role. Many of the early Hawaiian and Tongan immigrants to the state were members of the Church of Jesus Christ of Latter-day Saints, which is better known as the Mormon Church. The church has long sent missionaries to the islands and has had particular success in Tonga, and Mormon links have been strong throughout Utah, Hawaii, and Tonga, which explains ongoing shifts in population. There are also

strong connections between the Mormon tertiary education facility, Brigham Young University (BYU), which was founded in Provo, Utah, in 1875, and BYU-Hawaii, which was founded in 1955. The Mormon Church assisted many Pacific Islander church members to immigrate to the mainland United States, especially to California and Utah. These connections are ongoing, and continue to facilitate immigration of Pacific Islanders.

The 2000 U.S. Census also reported that the largest Pacific Islander group in the United States was Native Hawaiians (401,162 people), followed by Samoans (133,281), and Guamanians or Chamorros (92,611). Approximately 70 percent of the Pacific Islander population in the United States fit into these three ethnic categories. Additional groups represented in the census included Tongans (36,840), Fijians (13,581), Marshallese (6,650), Palauans (3,469), and Tahitians (3,313).

Census data have also shown that members of these immigrant groups are young, on average. They include large numbers of individuals in their child-bearing years, and children. Because Oceanic peoples favor large families, it seemed that the U.S. Pacific Islander population would continue to grow rapidly through natural increase, along with ongoing immigration from the islands. Another projected trend was a growth in the number of Pacific Islanders who identify with more than one ethnic group. There are already high levels of intermarriage among different island communities, and also with non-Pacific Islander people. Although this generalization holds less with Tongan and Fijian populations, it suggests that Pacific Islander communities in the United States are increasing in their internal diversity. Older Islanders tend to worry that marriage with outsiders will weaken communal cohesion and eventually cause the loss of languages and cultural traditions, but members of the younger generation typically do not share these concerns.

Intermarriage and other intercultural links are also facilitated by participation in church activities. Many Christian congregations offer services in Pacific Islander languages, and some have Pacific Islander ministers in areas with high numbers of Oceanic people. Pacific Islanders living in the United States tend to identify socially through their memberships in specific church congregations, much as people living on the islands identify themselves as originating from specific villages on specific islands.

PACIFIC ISLANDER AMERICAN CULTURE

Although Pacific Islander groups originate from different island archipelagoes, and their members possess different cultural practices, and speak different languages, certain broad cultural norms prevail across the islands that have been imported to the United States in varying degrees. For example, in contrast to the American cultural emphasis on individualistic traits, Oceanic peoples place greater value on collectivism, which encourages them to subordinate their personal interests to those of the family or wider kinship network. This trait may often be described by members of the Pacific Islander community as the respect owed by young people to their elders, and there are many cultural ideals about how it should be expressed, including lack of questioning of the older generation by youngsters, and the lowering of one's eyes and body height before elders. Differences between American and Islander styles of socialization sometimes result in conflicts between generational groups. Elder immigrants believe in greater levels of communal involvement and decision-making power by family networks, while their American-born children tend to focus more on their individual needs and desires and personal decision-making.

Divisions between the younger and older generations also may be exacerbated by language differences. Older immigrants typically find it more challenging to learn new languages than their children do, which often means that the children have greater skills in English than their parents or grandparents. Pacific Islander children who grow up the United States also tend not to learn the languages of their parents or to learn to speak them only at rudimentary levels. Community elders may consequently feel disappointment when young members of their communities do not speak their home languages well enough to participate in traditional orations at culturally important events, such as weddings and funerals.

At the same time, non-English-speaking family members may find their employment opportunities are limited and also have difficulty communicating with mainstream cultural brokers, such as teachers, community leaders, and government of-ficials. Outsiders often do not realize the extent of these language problems when they interact with Pacific Islanders, whose cultural norms encourage politeness that may be expressed through head nods, or other body language that seems to indicate agreement or understanding to Americans.

Accustomed to a communal way of life, Pacific Islanders often cook and eat together and live in close proximity to one another. This sometimes translates to situations in which members of extended families share American houses designed for small nuclear families. Their non-Islander neighbors and local social workers and health authorities may find it difficult to understand why so many people would wish to live together. Pacific Islanders also tend to view kinship ties in a more expansive manner than non-Islander Americans. For example, they are more likely to include all their extended family members in their conception of "family," not merely members of their nuclear families, as Americans are more likely to think of "family."

These broader conceptions of family may also include adopted siblings. In the Pacific, people often practice formal and informal adoption. For example, if a woman has no biological children, her brother may give her one or two of his own children, whom she will then raise as her own. The adoptions may never be formalized, and this arrangement is considered to be an expression of love from a brother for his sister, and does not devalue the adopted child or children according to local norms. Children may also live for considerable periods of time with relatives in order to attend schools or for other reasons. Many of these informal adoptions are never documented officially. For this reason, often Pacific people may describe households with fluctuating numbers of children and acknowledge as "sisters" and "brothers" individuals who may not even be biologically or legally related to them. These practices can cause problems to families wishing to immigrate to the United States together, or who are in the United States and wish to obtain health care and educational benefits.

Pacific Islanders typically settled in towns in the United States that already have sizeable Pacific Islander populations. This allows them to replicate much of their island lifestyles if they so desire. Older immigrants especially wish to retain impor-

Members of the Brigham Young University football team performing a Polynesian war dance under the leadership of one of the team's many Polynesian American players before a 2006 game. For many young Pacific Islanders, football has provided a ticket to college education in the United States, and some of them have achieved prominence in professional football. (WireImage/Getty Images)

tant aspects of their home cultures. For example, Samoans practice their *Fa'a-Samoa* belief system, the "Samoan way," and Tongans their *Anga Fakatonga* belief system, or "Tongan way." At times, however, maintaining cultural norms may simply mean eating the same kinds of food that is typically consumed in the islands.

U.S.-Pacific Island Links

Many Pacific Islanders living in the United States during the early twenty-first century believed that they would one day return to their island homelands. This belief would be more typical of the older first-generation immigrants than younger American-born family members. Reverse migration does occur, but less frequently than immigrants typically imagine when they first arrive in the United States. The initial dream of immigrants is to make a lot of money and then retire to the islands and live out their lives in style. In reality, by the time many elderly members of the Pacific Islander community are ready to retire, they find little in the islands to which to return. Many of their

family members are in the United States, and many of their old friends and networks are spread across the United States, Australia, New Zealand, and other islands. Elderly Islanders may also have health needs that are best treated in the United States. Some people do, however, maintain strong connections to their island homelands that draw them back.

More immigrants return to the islands for temporary visits than ever return permanently. There is much prestige in visiting, and providing gifts for those who remain. Moreover, maintaining links to the homelands and their people are important for community well-being and self-identity.

In addition to taking gifts with them on visits home, people in the United States often send remittances, in the form of money or goods, back to the islands. Island homelands benefit immensely from these cash infusions into their local economies. Some immigrants load large shipping containers with goods to send home. Like other traditions, this one means more to older members of the immigrant communities than to their offspring.

Although many young people oppose the idea of sending remittances and gifts, they sometimes become involved in this exchange network. There is a tradition in both the United States, and other diaspora communities of sending misbehaving youngsters back to their homelands for socialization into appropriate cultural norms. After miscreant children have spent a year in the islands looked after by extended family members, they may be deemed sufficiently well behaved to be returned to their U.S. homes.

An issue for all ethnic community members living in the United States is the prevalence of stereotypes and ongoing discrimination. Pacific Islanders may be easy targets because they are often identifiable based on their appearance, which means that American-born members of the community may be equally vulnerable. Members of Pacific Islander communities often are active in service organizations and educational initiatives to counteract the local effects of these stereotypes. Communities may also harshly sanction Pacific Islanders who act according to the stereotypes, such as those who join gangs, or are violent to their families since this behavior affects the entire group in a negative manner. Communities also celebrate the achievements of Pacific Islanders and strive to make mainstream Americans aware of these success stories and the history of their ethnic group in the United States.

Susan J. Wurtzburg

FURTHER READING

Duranti, Alessandro, Elinor Ochs, and Elia K. Ta'ase. "Change and Tradition in Literacy Instruction in a Samoan American Community." In *Many Pathways to Literacy: Young Children Learning with Siblings, Grandparents, Peers, and Communities*, edited by Eve Gregory, Susi Long, and Dinah Volk. New York: RoutledgeFalmer, 2004. Study of Samoan methods of instruction and how these may be incorporated into American educational institutions.

Halualani, Rona Tamiko. "Connecting Hawaiians: The Politics of Authenticity in the Hawaiian Diaspora." In *Intercultural Alliances: Critical Transformation*, edited by Mary Jane Collier. Thousand Oaks, Calif.: Sage Publications, 2003. Discussion of cultural authenticity, or what it means to be Hawaiian for people living outside Hawaii—a study that has implications for all Pacific Islanders.

Lee, Helen Morton. *Tongans Overseas: Between Two Shores*. Honolulu: University of Hawaii Press, 2003. Anthropological study of the lives of Tongan community members living in Melbourne, Australia that provides insights into the challenges that Pacific Islanders face when they immigrate to the United States.

McGrath, Barbara Burns. "Seattle Fa'a Samoa." *The Contemporary Pacific* 14, no. 2 (2002): 307-340. Discussion of how Samoan immigrants living in Seattle, Washington, have structured their lives to maintain Samoan culture while adapting to the United States.

Small, Cathy A. *Voyages: From Tongan Villages to American Suburbs*. Ithaca, N.Y.: Cornell University Press, 1997. Anthropological study of twenty-five years of migration from Tonga to Northern California viewed from the perspectives of both the immigrants to the United States and people who remained in Tonga.

Spickard, Paul R., Joanne L. Rondilla, and Debbie Hippolite Wright, eds. *Pacific Diaspora: Island Peoples in the United States and Across the Pacific*. Honolulu: University of Hawaii Press, 2002. Broad history of Pacific Islander migrations across the Pacific Ocean with an emphasis on their contemporary incursions into the United States.

Wurtzburg, Susan J. "Households and Families: Micronesia and Polynesia." In *Routledge International Encyclopedia of Women's Studies: Global Women's Issues and Knowledge*, edited by C. Kramarae and D. Spender. Vol. 1. New York: Routledge, 2000. Brief outline of commonalities in family structures and social organization across the Pacific Islands that is applicable to understanding the challenges that Pacific Islander families face in the United States.

SEE ALSO: Asian Pacific American Labor Alliance; Australian and New Zealander immigrants; California; Chain migration; Families; Hawaii; Mormon immigrants; Remittances of earnings; Stereotyping; Utah.

PACIFIC MAIL STEAMSHIP COMPANY

IDENTIFICATION: Shipping company that carried mail and passengers between Asia and the United States

DATE: Established on April 12, 1848

SIGNIFICANCE: Formed to carry mail from Central America to California, the Pacific Mail Steamship Company also carried many immigrants up the Pacific coast. During the early decades of Asian immigration to the United States, the Pacific Mail Steamship Company was the primary shipping line that carried Chinese and Japanese immigrants to the West Coast.

Between the time gold was discovered in California in 1848, and 1869, when the first transcontinental railroad was completed, a large portion of the people going from the East Coast to the West Coast of the United States traveled primarily by ship, usually crossing Central America by overland routes along the way. During this same period, increasing numbers of Asians—particularly Chinese—were coming to California to work in the mines and railroads. For a large number of these travelers, ships of the Pacific Mail Steamship Company provided not only oceanic transportation but also the mail service to communicate with families left behind.

The Pacific Mail Steamship Company was chartered in New York in April, 1848, by William Aspinwall. In October, the company was granted a contract by the U.S. government to carry mail from the Isthmus of Panama to San Francisco, in the recently acquired territory of California. The company went into service with three new paddlewheel steamers. In addition to carrying the U.S. mail, the company's ships carried immigrants, businessmen, and gold seekers on the twelve- to fourteen-day voyage up the Pacific Coast. In 1855, completion of a railroad line across Panama made the overland part of travelers' journeys quicker, safer, and more comfortable. However, completion of the transcontinental railroad across the United States in 1869 would eventually doom the company's Panama to California service. However, between 1848 and 1869, the company's ships carried 19,000 passengers per year to California.

Meanwhile, the company's immediate future was assured in 1865, when it was granted a contract to carry U.S. mail between the West Coast of the United States and East Asia. After collecting mail in San Francisco, company ships sailed to Yokohama, Japan, and Hong Kong, China. By this period, large numbers of Asians, mostly Chinese, were coming to the United States and Canada to work. As Pacific Mail expanded its fleet, it carried tens of thousands of Asians to the United States, typically charging the immigrants forty dollars to make the passage in steerage class. By 1873, Pacific Mail was running forty ships on various routes. A large majority of them worked the Asian routes. The company also had smaller vessels running routes among U.S. and Canadian ports along the West Coast.

Federal restrictions on Asian immigration that began with the Chinese Exclusion Act of 1882 gradually cut into the Pacific Mail's Asian passenger trade, but the shipping company opened new routes to other regions, including Australia. However, over time, the company failed to keep up with competing lines. In 1893, it was purchased by the Southern Pacific Railroad Company, which resold it to another shipping company in 1916. In 1938, its ownership passed to the American President Lines, but by then the company existed only on paper. It was formally dissolved eleven years later.

Robert J. Stewart

FURTHER READING

Barde, Robert Eric. *Immigration at the Golden Gate: Passenger Ships, Exclusion, and Angel Island.* Westport, Conn.: Praeger, 2008.

Chandler, Robert J., and Stephen J. Potash. *Gold, Silk, Pioneers and Mail: The Story of the Pacific Mail Steamship Company.* San Francisco: Friends of the San Francisco Maritime Museum Library, 2007.

Page, Thomas W. "The Transportation of Immigrants and Reception Arrangements in the Nineteenth Century." *Journal of Political Economy* 19, no. 9 (1911): 732-749.

SEE ALSO: California; California gold rush; Chinese immigrants; Hamburg-Amerika Line; Japanese immigrants; Korean immigrants; Railroads; San Francisco; Transportation of immigrants.

PAGE LAW OF 1875

THE LAW: Federal legislation prohibited entry of Chinese contract workers and prostitutes into the United States

DATE: Enacted on March 3, 1875

ALSO KNOWN AS: Act Supplementary to the Acts in Relation to Immigration

> **SIGNIFICANCE:** Originally designed to prohibit Chinese contract workers and prostitutes from entering the United States, this federal law eventually excluded Asian women in general.

On February 10, 1875, California congressman Horace F. Page introduced federal legislation designed to prohibit the immigration of Asian female prostitutes into the United States. Officially titled An Act Supplementary to the Acts in Relation to Immigration, the Page Law evolved into a restriction of vast numbers of Chinese immigrating into the country regardless of whether they were prostitutes. Any person convicted of importing Chinese prostitutes was subject to a maximum prison term of five years and a fine of not more than five thousand dollars.

An amendment to the law prohibited individuals from engaging in the "coolie trade," the importation of illegal Chinese contract laborers. Punishment for this type of violation, however, was less severe and much more difficult to effect, given the large numbers of Asian male immigrants arriving at the time. Consequently, the law was applied in a gender-specific manner, effectively deterring immigration of Asian females into the United States. Within seven years following the implementation of the law, the average number of Chinese female immigrants dropped to one-third of its previous level.

An elaborate bureaucratic network established to carry out the Page Law's gender-specific exclusions was a cata-lyst for the decline in Chinese immigration rates. American consulate officials supported by American, Chinese, and British commercial, political, and medical services made up the law's implementation structure. Through intelligence gathering, interrogation, and physical examinations of applicants, the consulate hierarchy ferreted out undesirable applicants for immigration and those suspected of engaging in illegal human trafficking.

This investigative procedure was complicated. Any characteristic or activity that could be linked, even in the most remote sense, to prostitution became grounds for denial of the right to immigrate. Most applications to immigrate came from women from the lower economic strata of Chinese society; low economic status was linked to prostitution and therefore became a reason for immigration exclusion. Navigating language barriers through official

Chinese woman with her children and brother-in-law awaiting a streetcar in San Francisco around 1904. The sedate black outfit worn by the woman is typical of the dress worn by married Chinese women who wanted to distinguish themselves from prostitutes. (Library of Congress)

interviews aimed at evaluating personal character often produced an atmosphere of rigid interrogation, bringing subsequent denial of the right to immigrate. In addition, passing stringent physical examinations performed by biased health care officials was often impossible.

Because Hong Kong was the main point of departure for Chinese immigrating to the United States, all required examinations were performed there with a hierarchy of American consulate officials determining immigrant eligibility. The consular general had such authority in implementing the Page Law that there was a wide opportunity for abuse of power. In 1878, Hong Kong consul general John S. Mosby accused his predecessors, David Bailey and H. Sheldon Loring, of having amassed thousands of dollars in extra income by charging additional examination fees regardless of whether an examination was performed and by falsifying test results to deny immigration permission to otherwise legal immigrants. Federal investigations of Bailey and Loring produced no official indictments; instead, they revealed the simple fact of overly aggressive officials who made preventing the immigration of Chinese women to the United States a top priority of their respective tenures, rather than an opportunity for profit.

Regardless of the personalities of the consulate officials in charge of implementing the Page Law, the results were the same: The number of Chinese who immigrated to the United States decreased dramatically between the 1875 enactment of the law and the enactment of its successor, the Chinese Exclusion Act of 1882.

Cynthia Gwynne Yaudes

EXTRACTS FROM THE PAGE LAW

Be it enacted by the Senate and House of Representatives of the United States of America in Congress-assembled, That in determining whether the immigration of any subject of China, Japan, or any Oriental country, to the United States, is free and voluntary, as provided by section two thousand one hundred and sixty two of the Revised Code, title "Immigration," it shall be the duty of the consul-3-general or consul of the United States residing at the port from which it is proposed to convey such subjects, in any vessels enrolled or licensed in the United States, or any port within the same, before delivering to the masters of any such vessels the permit or certificate provided for in such section, to ascertain for a term of service within the United States, for lewd and immoral purposes; and if there be such contract or agreement, the said consul-general or consul shall not deliver the required permit or certificate. . . .

SEC. 3. That the importation into the United States of women for the purposes of prostitution is hereby forbidden; and all contracts and agreements in relation thereto, made in advance or in pursuance of illegal importation and purposes, are hereby declared void; and whoever shall knowingly and willfully hold, or attempt to hold, any woman to such purposes, in pursuance of such illegal importation and contract or agreement, shall be deemed guilty of a felony, and, on conviction thereof, shall be imprisoned not exceeding five years and pay a fine not exceeding five thousand dollars.

SEC. 5. That it shall be unlawful for aliens of the following classes to immigrate into the United States, namely, persons who are undergoing sentence for conviction in their own country of felonious crimes other than political or growing out of or the result of such political offenses, and women "imported for the purposes of prostitution." Every vessel arriving in the United States may be inspected under the direction of the collector of the port at which it arrives . . .

FURTHER READING

Foner, Philip, and Daniel Rosenberg. *Racism, Dissent, and Asian Americans from 1850 to the Present.* Westport, Conn.: Greenwood Press, 1993.

Peffer, George Anthony. "Forbidden Families: Emigration Experiences of Chinese Women Under the Page Law, 1875-1882." *Journal of American Ethnic History* 6 (Fall, 1986): 28-46.

SEE ALSO: Bayard-Zhang Treaty of 1888; Chinese Exclusion Act of 1882; *Chinese Exclusion Cases*; Chinese immigrants; Citizens Committee to Repeal Chinese Exclusion; Coolies; History of immigration, 1783-1891; Marriage; Women immigrants.

PAKISTANI IMMIGRANTS

SIGNIFICANCE: Pakistani immigration only became a distinctive part of South Asian immigration during the 1960's. The United States has never been a primary destination for Pakistani immigrants, but they have formed distinctive subgroups in certain areas of settlement. After the September 11, 2001, terrorist attacks on the United States, their Muslim identity became problematic.

Pakistan did not exist as a distinct nation until 1947, when both it and India were formed from British India. The reason for the split was primarily religious. Though it had a secular government, India became a Hindu-majority state, while Pakistan became a primarily Muslim state.

In terms of U.S. government statistics, no separate statistics of Pakistani immigration were kept until after 1981. Before that year, Pakistanis were grouped under "Other South Asians." Of the South Asians, only Indian immigrants had their own separate category. Statistics are further confused by the emergence of Bangladesh as a separate country in 1971 out of what was previously known as East Pakistan, the eastern wing of the two-part country formed in 1947. Bangladeshis and Pakistanis were grouped together until 1973, though probably very few Bangladeshis did immigrate at that time. In 1973, fewer than two hundred Bangladeshis were counted in the United States.

Before 1947, Pakistani immigration would have been counted as Indian. At the beginning of the twentieth century, there had been a small-scale immigration of farmers and farm laborers to Southern California, mainly to work in the newly developed rice farms of the Sacramento Valley, but no other significant influx.

FIRST GROWTH

After independence, most Pakistani emigrants went to the United Kingdom. British law at that time allowed previous colonials unfettered entry into Great Britain. Other Commonwealth countries, especially Canada and Australia, also had generous provisions for other Commonwealth immigrants. By contrast, U.S. immigration policy allowed little possibility for Pakistani entry.

This policy began to change after 1965, when passage of the Immigration and Nationality Act of 1965 allowed professionals and other people with needed skills entry. A slow trickle of Pakistani professionals began to take advantage of the liberalized immigration policy, aided by tightening restrictions in the United Kingdom and lack of job opportunities in their native country. The tendency of Pakistan to drift into undemocratic military regimes also alienated a number of professionals and skilled workers.

The main professions of these immigrants were in medicine and engineering. In 1971, just over two thousand immigrants joined the five thousand or so Pakistanis already in the United States, mainly in the larger population centers of New York, Chicago, Los Angeles, and San Francisco. Numbers edged up during the 1970's and 1980's but never reached more than six thousand per year. Some also came as students or tourists and then changed their status while in the United States.

At first, the trend was for single men to come, establish themselves, then sponsor spouses to join them, or return to Pakistan, marry, and bring their spouses back with them. Those who failed to qualify as doctors or pharmacists in the United States reinvented themselves as small businessmen, often running convenience stores or gas stations. Taxi driving was a favored occupation among those who came with less education.

SUBSEQUENT DEVELOPMENT

The turning point in numbers came in 1991, when the annual immigration suddenly jumped to 20,355. The lottery system allowed a number of unskilled Pakistanis to immigrate. Meanwhile, provisions for wider family sponsorship allowed a number of brothers, sisters, and parents to enter. Pakistani society is very family-oriented, with the extended family being the norm. During the 1990's, some 124,500 Pakistanis were admitted, making the Pakistani community the ninth-largest of all Asian communities.

Certain stresses began to manifest themselves as a second generation grew up in the United States. The arranged marriage system was still enforced where possible to maintain cultural identity, but spouses from Pakistan found it difficult to adjust to new gender roles within American culture. Divisions between religious groups, especially Sunnis

PROFILE OF PAKISTANI IMMIGRANTS

Country of origin	Pakistan
Primary languages	Urdu, English, others
Primary regions of U.S. settlement	California, New York, and Chicago
Earliest significant arrivals	1950's
Peak immigration period	1990's
Twenty-first century legal residents*	117,143 (14,643 per year)

*Immigrants who obtained legal permanent resident status in the United States.
Source: Department of Homeland Security, Yearbook of Immigration Statistics, 2008.

and Shias, kept communities divided. Though Pakistanis mixed easily with other South Asian Muslims, they found it difficult to mix with Muslims from the Middle East or of African origin. The desire for fair-skinned spouses was especially troublesome, fed as it was by the Bollywood movie culture.

The September 11, 2001, terrorist attacks in New York City and Washington, D.C., and the subsequent involvement of Pakistan on the American political stage were especially problematic for both the existing community and new immigrants. Numbers of immigrants actually declined, with 51,600 entering between 2001 and 2004 and 14,900 in 2005. Persian Gulf states absorbed a growing number of Pakistani migrant workers, who were much more at home there in a Muslim culture. Also, immigration to the Commonwealth countries continued at quite high levels. Movement among the worldwide Pakistani diaspora was also a significant feature.

David Barratt

FURTHER READING

Aswad, Barbara C., and Barbara Bilgé, eds. *Family and Gender Among American Muslims: Issues Facing Middle Eastern Immigrants and Their Descendants.* Philadelphia: Temple University Press, 1996. Sociological study with a chapter devoted to the problems of South Asians, especially in terms of family ties, marriage, and education.

Leonard, Karen. *The South Asian Americans: The New Americans.* Westport, Conn.: Greenwood Press, 1997. Studies the impact South Asian immigrants have made on American culture.

McCloud, Aminah Beverly. *Transnational Muslims in American Society.* Gainesville: University Press of Florida, 2006. Places Pakistani immigration in the wider context of Muslim South Asians and distinguishes the various religious subgroups.

Narayan, Anjana, and Bandana Purkayastha. *Living Religions: Hindu and Muslim South Asian-American Women Narrate Their Experiences.* Sterling, Va.: Kumarian Press, 2009. Written in light of the September 11, 2001, terrorist attacks, individual women narrate their experiences as South Asian immigrants and how they challenge borders and stereotypes.

Prashad, Vijay. *The Karma of Brown Folk.* Minneapolis: University of Minnesota Press, 2000. Interviews and analyses of South Asians, piecing together how their image as a successful immigrant group has been constructed.

U.S. Census Bureau. *Statistical Abstract of the United States: 2007.* Washington, D.C.: Author, 2006. Includes separate figures for Pakistani immigrants from 1981.

Waters, Mary C., and Reed Ueda, eds. *The New Americans: A Guide to Immigration Since 1965.* Cambridge, Mass.: Harvard University Press, 2007. The chapter on South Asia, by Nazli Kibria, sufficiently discusses Pakistani immigrants.

Williams, Raymond B. *Religions of Immigrants from India and Pakistan: New Threads in the American Tapestry.* New York: Cambridge University Press, 1988. Studies various religions and how they have adapted to and influenced American culture.

SEE ALSO: Asian immigrants; Asian Indian immigrants; Canada vs. United States as immigrant destinations; History of immigration after 1891; Immigration and Nationality Act of 1965; Muslim immigrants; Religions of immigrants; Sidhwa, Bapsi.